# Frantz Fanon

*Also by David Macey*

Lacan in Contexts
The Lives of Michel Foucault
The Penguin Dictionary of Critical Theory

# Frantz Fanon

## *A Biography*

### DAVID MACEY

Picador USA
New York

www.picadorusa.com

Picador® is a U.S. registered trademark and is used by St. Martin's Press under license from Pan Books Limited.

For information on Picador USA Reading Group Guides, as well as ordering, please contact the Trade Marketing department at St. Martin's Press.
Phone: 1-800-221-7945 extension 763
Fax: 212-677-7456
E-mail: trademarketing@stmartins.com

Library of Congress Cataloging-in-Publication Data

Macey, David, 1949–
    Frantz Fanon : a biography / David Macey.
        p. cm.
    Includes bibliographical references and index.
    ISBN 0-312-27550-1 (hc)
    ISBN 0-312-30042-5 (pbk)
    1. Fanon, Frantz, 1925–1961. 2. Intellectuals—Algeria—Biography.
3. Revolutionaries—Algeria—Biography. 4. Psychiatrists—Algeria—Biography.
5. Algeria—Biography.  I. Title.

CT2628.F35 M34  2001
965'.046'092—dc21
[B]                                                              2001021807

First published in Great Britain by Granta Books

First Picador USA Paperback Edition: June 2002

10 9 8 7 6 5 4 3 2 1

*For Aaron, John and Chantelle, and all your brothers and sisters in Martinique and Algeria.*

# Contents

# Acknowledgements

This study could not have been written without the generous help of many individuals and institutions. My thanks are due to the following: Margaret Atack (as always), Jacques Azoulay, Neil Belton, Robert Berthellier, Bibliothèque Médicale Henri Ey (Paris), Bibliothèque Nationale de France, Bibliothèque Populaire Frantz Fanon (Rivère-Pilote, Martinique), Bibliothèque Publique d'Information (Centre Georges Pompidou, Paris), Brotherton Library (University of Leeds), Centre Culturel Algérien (Paris), Charles Cézette, Alice Cherki, Patrick Chamoiseau, Fanny Colonna, Olivier Corpet, Basil Davidon, Assia Djebar, Jean-Marie Domenach, Edouard Fanon, Joby Fanon, Olivier Fanon, Odette Fresel, Charles Geronimi, Nicole Guillet, Institut Mémoires de l'Edition Contemporaine (Paris), Marie-Hélène Léotin, André Mandouze, Marcel Manville, Mireille Fanon Mendès France, Jacques Postel, Service Historique de l'Armé de Terre (Château de Vincennes).

# Abbreviations

| | |
|---|---|
| AJAS | Association de la Jeunesse Algérienne pour l'Action Sociale |
| ALN | Armée de la Libération Nationale |
| BMA | Bataillon de Marche (Antilles) |
| CEE | Comité de Coordination et d'Exécution |
| CNRA | Conseil National de la Révolution Algérienne |
| CRS | Compagnies Républicaines de Sécurité |
| CRUA | Comité Révolutionnaire pour l'Unité et l'Action |
| CSP | Comité de Salut Public |
| DCI | Division Coloniale d'Infanterie |
| DOM | Département d'Outre-Mer |
| DOP | Dispositif Opérationnel de Protection |
| DST | Direction de la Surveillance du Territoire |
| DUP | Détachement Urbain de Protection |
| FAF | Front de l'Algérie Française |
| FIS | Front Islamique de Salut |
| FLN | Front de Libération National |
| FLQ | Front de Libération Québecoise |
| FRELIMO | Frente de Liberaçao de Moçambique |
| GPRA | Gouvernement Provisoire de la République Algérienne |

| MDRM | Mouvement Démocratique de la Rénovation Malgache |
| MIM | Mouvement Indépendantiste Martiniquais |
| MNA | Mouvement Nationaliste Algérien |
| MPLA | Moviment Popular de Liberaçao de Angola |
| MTLD | Mouvement pour le Triomphe des Libértés Démocratiques |
| NAACP | National Association for the Advancement of Coloured People |
| OAS | Organisation Armée Secrète |
| OJAM | Organisation de la Jeunesse Anti-colonialiste Martiniquaise de la Martinique |
| OS | Organisation Spéciale |
| PCA | Parti Communiste Algérien |
| PCF | Parti Communiste Français |
| PCM | Parti Communiste Martiniquais |
| POLISARIO | Popular Front for the Liberation of Saquia, al Hamra and Riu de Oro |
| PPA | Parti Populaire Algérien |
| PPM | Parti Progressiste Martiniquais |
| RCP | Régiment de Chasseurs Parachutistes |
| REP | Régiment Etranger Parachutiste |
| RPC | Régiment Parachutiste Coloniale |
| RTS | Régiment de Tirailleurs Sénégalais |
| SAS | Sections Administratives Spécialés |
| SDECE | Service de Documentation Extérieure et de Contre-Espionnage |
| TAT | Thematic Apperception Test |
| TOM | Territoire d'Outre-Mer |
| UNITA | Uniao para la Independencia Total de Angola |
| UPA | Uniao das Populaçoes de Angola |
| UPC | Union du Peuple Camerounais |

# The Lesser Antilles

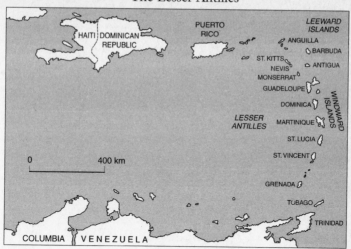

LEEWARD ISLANDS

HAITI DOMINICAN REPUBLIC

PUERTO RICO

ANGUILLA
BARBUDA
ST. KITTS
NEVIS
ANTIGUA
MONSERRAT
GUADELOUPE
DOMINICA

WINDWARD ISLANDS

LESSER ANTILLES

MARTINIQUE
ST. LUCIA
ST. VINCENT
GRENADA
TOBAGO
TRINIDAD

0        400 km

COLUMBIA   VENEZUELA

# Martinique

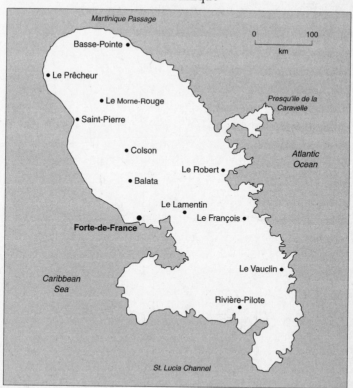

Martinique Passage

0       100
km

Basse-Pointe

Le Prêcheur

Le Morne-Rouge

Saint-Pierre

Presqu'île de la Caravelle

Colson

Le Robert

Atlantic Ocean

Balata

Le Lamentin

Forte-de-France

Le François

Le Vauclin

Caribbean Sea

Rivière-Pilote

St. Lucia Channel

xi

# Fort-de-France

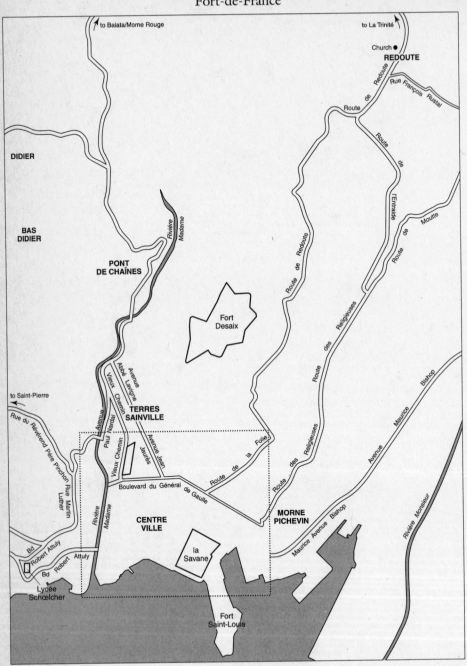

# Central Fort-de-France

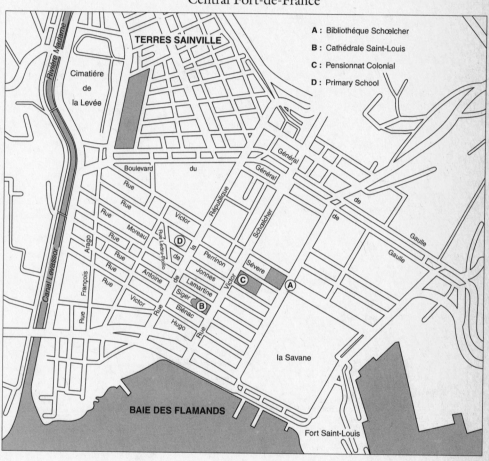

A : Bibliothéque Schœlcher
B : Cathédrale Saint-Louis
C : Pensionnat Colonial
D : Primary School

# Battle of the River Doubs

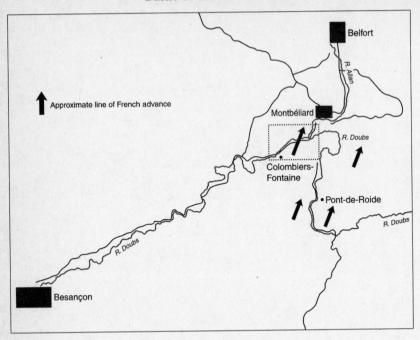

# Battle of the River Doubs (detail)

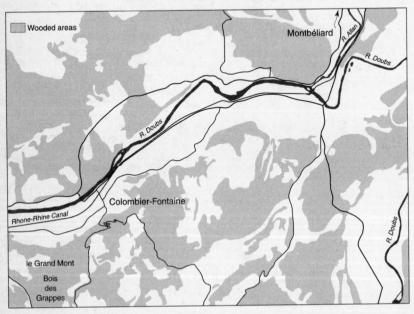

## The Maghreb

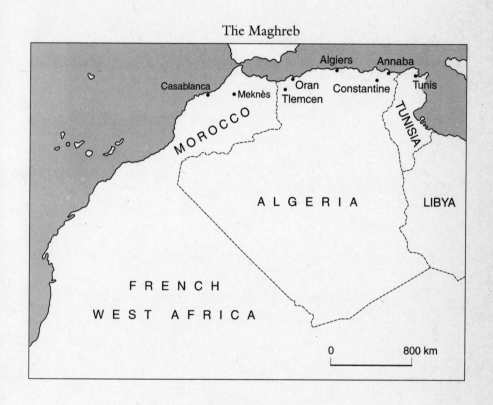

# The expedition across Mali

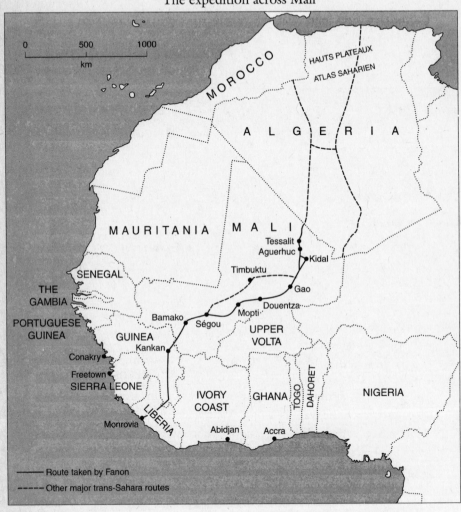

# 1

# Forgetting Fanon, Remembering Fanon

EARLY IN MAY 1962, a French journalist working for the daily *Le Monde* arrived in Ghardimao, a small Tunisian town only a few kilometres from the border with Algeria. Once a French military base, Ghardimao was now the headquarters of the Algerian Armée de Libération Nationale (ALN) (National Liberation Army) and the situation there was tense. Two photographs decorated the otherwise bleak walls of the political commissariat. They were of Fidel Castro and Frantz Fanon.[1] In the last week of June, *Paris-Presse*'s Jean-François Khan also travelled to Ghardimao to report on the situation there. He too saw a photograph on the wall. It was of Frantz Fanon, 'the pamphleteer from Martinique'. Algeria's long war of independence was virtually at an end; the Evian agreements had been signed by the French government and the Gouvernement Provisoire de la République Algérienne (GPRA) (Provisional Government of the Algerian Republic) on 18 March and a ceasefire had come into effect the following day. Relations between Algeria's 'forces of the interior' and the 'frontier army' penned behind the Morice Line of electrified wire entanglements, floodlights and mine-fields, had long been strained and were now almost at breaking point. Tensions between the GPRA, headed by Ahmed Ben Bella, and Colonel Houari Boumédienne's ALN were also dangerously high. Khan was

1

convinced that a coup led by Boumédienne was in the offing. He was both right and wrong; Boumédienne's Armée Nationale Populaire entered Algiers in triumph on 9 September 1962, but the coup against Ben Bella did not occur until 1965. Boumédienne remained in power until his death in December 1978; Ben Bella remained in detention until 30 October 1980. He then spent ten years in exile, returning to Algeria only in September 1990.

The *djounoud* (soldiers; the singular is *djoundi*) Khan met in their stark concrete barracks were dressed in Chinese-style uniforms and wore neither decorations nor insignia of rank. They did not salute their officers, and addressed them in French with the familiar *tu*. Khan asked a young officer what would happen if 'certain leaders' attempted to put a brake on their revolution. The officer was young – perhaps in his thirties – handsome and romantic-looking, but his tone was harsh and his answer brooked no argument: 'We would eliminate them.' The journalist concluded: 'If one had to find an ideological name for the mystical faith that inspires these men, it would have to be "Fanonist".'[2]

Khan's 'Fanonists' did indeed eliminate their enemies. As Boumédienne's tanks swept into Algiers, they left corpses in their wake; an embittered Ferhat Abbas, who was the GPRA's first president, later remarked that this was the only war ever fought by Boumédienne and his *djounoud*.[3] Khan's spontaneous association of Fanon with 'mystical' violence sets the tone for much of the subsequent discussion of the man and his work. Fanon came to be seen as the apostle of violence, the prophet of a violent Third World revolution that posed an even greater threat to the West than communism. He was the horseman of a new apocalypse, the preacher of the gospel of the wretched of the earth, who were at last rising up against their oppressors. Although this image of Fanon is by no means inaccurate, it is very partial. The Fanon who advocated the use of violence in his *Les Damnés de la terre*, which was published as he lay dying far from Algeria, was the product of the most bloody of France's wars of decolonization. There were other Frantz Fanons.

Frantz Fanon had been dead for six months when Khan visited Ghardimao, and it is possible that some of the *djounoud* he met there had been part of the honour guard that saluted Fanon's body as it lay in ceremony in the field hospital. Fanon did not die, as might reasonably have been expected, in combat or at the hands of an assassin, although he did survive at least one assassination attempt. He died of leukaemia in an American hospital, and his body was flown back to Tunis in a Lockheed Electra II for burial on Algerian soil. At 14.30 on 12 December 1961, a small column crossed the border into Algeria. For the first and only time in the war of independence they had been waging since November 1954, the FLN and ALN were able to bury one of their own with full honours:

> On the Algerian border. Two ALN platoons present arms as the coffin enters national territory. The coffin is placed on a stretcher made of branches, raised and carried up the slope by fifteen *djounoud*. An astonishing march through the forest begins, while two columns of ALN soldiers stand guard on the hillside and in the valley floor to protect the path the column is following. The forest is majestic, the sky dazzling; the column moves along silently and in absolute calm, with the bearers taking it in turn to carry the coffin.
>
> Gunfire can be heard in the valley, further to the north. Very high in the sky, two aircraft fly over. The war is there, very close at hand, and at the same time, things are calm here. A procession of brothers has come to grant one of their own his last wish.
>
> In a martyrs' cemetery. Once the site of an engagement, now in liberated territory. The grave is there, carefully prepared. Speaking in Arabic, an ALN *commandant* pronounces a final farewell to Frantz Fanon, who was known to everyone present: 'Our late lamented brother Fanon was a sincere militant who rebelled against colonialism and racism; as early as 1952, he was taking an active role in the activities of liberal movements while he was pursuing his studies in France. At the very beginning of the Revolution, he joined the ranks of the Front de Libération Nationale and was a living model of discipline and respect for its principles during all the time that he had to carry out the tasks with which he was entrusted by the Algerian Revolution. During one of the missions he carried out in Morocco, he was the victim of an accident which probably brought on the illness that has just carried him away. He continued to work unrelentingly and redoubled his efforts, despite the illness that was gradually gnawing away at him.

3

Realizing that his health was obviously deteriorating, the higher authorities advised him on several occasions to cease his activities and to devote himself to treating his illness. He answer was always the same: "I will not cease my activites while Algeria still continues the struggle and I will go on with my task until my dying day." And that indeed is what he did."[4]

It was then the turn of the GPRA's Vice-President Belkacem Krim to bid Fanon farewell:

In the name of the Provisional Government of the Algerian Republic, in the name of the Algerian people, in the name of all your brothers in struggle and in my personal capacity, I bid you farewell.

Although you are dead, your memory will live on and will always be evoked by the noblest figures of our Revolution.

Born into a large family, you experienced at a very early age the privations and humiliations which colonialists and racists inflict upon oppressed peoples. Despite these difficulties, you succeeded in becoming a brilliant student and then began an equally brilliant career as a doctor, especially at the psychiatric hospital in Blida. But even while you were at University, your desire to be a serious student did not prevent you from taking part in the anti-colonialist struggle; the heavy obligations you faced as a conscientious doctor did not interfere with your militant activities on behalf of your oppressed brothers. Indeed, it was through your professional activities that you arrived at a better understanding of the realities of colonialist oppression and became aware of the meaning of your commitment to the struggle against that oppression. Even before our Revolution was launched, you took a sustained interest in our liberation movement. After 1 November 1954, you flung yourself into clandestine action with all your characteristic fervour, and did not hesitate to expose yourself to danger. More specifically, and despite the dangers you could have encountered, you helped to ensure the safety of many patriots and party officials, and thus helped them to accomplish their missions.

Responding to the call of your responsibilities, you then joined the FLN's foreign delegation.

*Résistance algérienne* and then *El Moudjahid* then benefited from your precious help, characterized by your vigorous and accurate analyses.

Various international conferences, and especially those in Accra, Monravia, Tunis, Conakry, Addis-Ababa and Léopoldville provided you with an opportunity to make known the true face of our revolution and to explain the realities of our struggle. The many messages of sympathy that have been sent to the Provisional Government of the Algerian Republic since the announcement of your death bear testimony to the profound influence you exercised as you performed your duty.

Because of the brilliant qualities you displayed in all these activities, the Algerian Government designated you as its representative in Accra in February 1960.

Frantz Fanon!

You devoted your life to the cause of freedom, dignity, justice and good.

Your loss causes us great pain.

In the name of the Provisional Government of Algeria, I offer your family our most sincere and most fraternal condolences.

I also offer our thanks to the representatives of those friendly and fraternal countries who, by being present at our side, have expressed their wish to join us in our mourning.

Frantz Fanon!

You will always be a living example. Rest in peace. Algeria will not forget you.[5]

The speeches made at Fanon's funeral provide an accurate picture of how he was viewed by his Algerian comrades at the time of his death. Both Krim and the unnamed commandant (the rank is equivalent to that of a major in the British army) were speaking in all sincerity, but they had known Fanon in only one context. They never knew the child who was born in Martinique in 1925, and who was always marked by the experience of being born in that place and that time. They knew the dedicated revolutionary, but not the equally dedicated psychiatrist. They were familiar with a polemicist, but not with the young man who once wanted to write plays. Fanon was always reluctant to talk about himself, and it is by no means certain that he told his Algerian brothers that he had fought with the French army during the Second World War and had been decorated for bravery.

Granting Fanon his last wish – to be buried on Algerian soil – had not been an easy task. It had involved some delicate negotiations with the Tunisian government, with the US State Department and even the CIA, whose agent Ollie Iselin was present at the funeral. The border crossing itself was made with the help of local people, without whom it would have been impossible for the funeral party to evade French patrols. Three days after the burial, ALN intelligence officers learned that most of the French officers responsible for the sector had been relieved of their functions: 'Fanon had won his last victory.'[6] For those who knew Fanon, the revenge must have been sweet; on the very day that the news of his death had reached Paris, the publisher's stock of *Les Damnés de la terre* had been seized by the police on the grounds that it was a threat to national security.[7] This did not prevent it from becoming an international bestseller and making Fanon the most famous spokesman of a Third Worldism which held that the future of socialism – or even of the world – was no longer in the hands of the proletariat of the industrialized countries, but in those of the dispossessed wretched of the earth.

Fanon was buried a mere 600 metres inside Algerian territory because French static defences made it impossible to take his coffin further into his adopted country. On 25 June 1965, his remains were exhumed and reinterred in the martyrs' cemetery in the hamlet of Ain Kerma, where a tombstone was at last erected.[8] His family's requests to have Fanon's body returned to his native Martinique have always met with a negative response from the Algerian government. After the suicide of his mother on 13 July 1989,[9] Fanon's son Olivier requested permission to have his father's remains interred with hers in Algiers, where she was buried as 'Nadia', the name she used when she and Fanon were living in semi-clandestinity; she could not be buried in a Muslim cemetery under her Christian name Josie. This time, the refusal came from the people and local authorities of Ain Kerma; in their view, Fanon is *their* martyr and his grave is inviolable. Fanon's body still lies in the far east of Algeria.

There is a memorial to Fanon in the town where he was born. The white-walled Cimetière de la Levée in the Martinican capital of Fort-de-France is the resting place of many of the town's notables, and is known locally as the 'cemetery of the rich' – the poor are buried in the Cimetière du Trabaud on the hill on the other side of the Canal Lavassoir. French cemeteries are urbanized cities of the dead, and have none of the verdant charm of the traditional English graveyard. The Fanon family grave stands at the intersection of two asphalted paths and contains the remains of his parents, his brother Félix and his sister Gabrielle. Their photographs appear on the memorial plaques on the plinth inside the white marble construction. Frantz Fanon's memorial is in the form of an open marble book. The left-hand page bears a photograph and the inscription: 'To our brother Frantz Fanon, born 20 July 1925 in Fort-de-France, died 6 December 1961 in Washington (USA)'. The facing page is inscribed with the final words of his first book: 'My final prayer: make me always a man who asks questions.'[10] The grave is well tended, but it has not become a place of pilgrimage.

Over seventy years after his death, Fanon remains a surprisingly enigmatic and elusive figure. Whether he should be regarded as 'Martinican', 'Algerian' 'French' or simply 'Black' is not a question that can be decided easily. It is also a long-standing question. Just four years after his death and a year after Boumédienne's coup, a Swiss commentator could write with some justification that

> The men who run Algeria today would have little use for Fanon's exhortations; and the Algerian 'masses' would make a Martinican negro feel foreign in ways he would never have experienced in Paris. The prophet of Algeria's national revolution would have found himself an exile from his chosen homeland, in search of another revolutionary war with which to identify himself.[11]

Despite Krim's assurance that Algeria would never forget him, Fanon has never really become part of the pantheon of Algerian nationalism, even though he was posthumously awarded the Prix National des Lettres Algériennes in 1963, and even though copies of *Les Damnés de la terre* were given as school prizes in 1964.[12] The standard history books studied by Algerian schoolchildren contain photographs and short biographies of the heroes of the FLN's revolution, but Fanon is not counted amongst their number.[13] In 1965, a group of Algerian students complained that it was impossible to find *Peau noire, masques blancs* in any bookshop in Algiers.[14] The hospital where Fanon worked in Blida bears his name, and an Avenue du Dr Frantz Fanon (formerly the Avenue du Maréchal de Lattre de Tassigny) was inaugurated in Algiers in March 1963. There is a Lyceé Frantz Fanon on the edge of the city's Bab El Oued district, and yet in 1982 a group of teachers at the University of Algiers could complain that it was still necessary to ask 'Who is Fanon?' because there had been nothing on either the radio or the television to mark the twentieth anniversary of his death.[15] For the youth of Algeria, 'Fanon' was no more than a name inscribed in capital letters on public buildings or street signs.[16] The names of streets and institutions do not necessarily indicate that the memory of their eponyms is still alive. Even when Fanon is remembered in Algeria, the memory can be clouded by partial amnesia and ignorance. Fanny Colonna, who taught at the University of Tizi-Ouzo until she was forced by the rising tide of violence and xenophobia to leave for France in the early 1990s, recalls meeting school students who had read Fanon in their French class but did not know that he was black.[17]

The reasons for Fanon's partial eclipse in Algeria are political and ideological. The insistence that, as the old slogan put it, the revolution had 'only one hero: the people', is designed to play down the role of specific individuals, as well as to mask internal divisions behind a façade of unity. The Algerian historiography of the war was for a long time designed to legitimize the one-party rule of the supposedly monolithic FLN, and the appearance of revisionist studies that began to show that it was a murderously divided party that killed some of those it officially venerated as heroes, is a recent phenomenon.[18] The nature of Algerian nationalism itself is an obstacle to a serious re-evaluation of Fanon's role. Ever since its birth in the 1930s, modern Algerian nationalism has been defined as 'Arab-Islamic', and it is very difficult to absorb a black agnostic into that nationalism. Within two years of independence, it could be argued by certain Algerians that 'Fanonism' was an alien ideology which was foreign to Islam, and therefore to the Algerian nation, and that Fanon could not be Algerian because he was not a Muslim.[19] In the 1970s, similar points were being made by Mohammed El Milli, a graduate of Cairo's Al-Azhar University and Director of Information for the Algerian Ministry of Information and Culture. El Milli once worked with Fanon on the FLN's newspaper *El Moudjahid*, but he was at pains to stress that Fanon owed much more to the Algerian revolution than it owed to him.[20] Attempts to turn Fanon into 'a key figure in the Algerian FLN'[21] or 'one of the chief theoreticians of the Algerian struggle'[22] are simply not consonant with Algerian perceptions or Algerian realities. Nor are they consonant with either contemporary or historical accounts of the Algerian revolution, none of which gives Fanon a leading role.[23]

In his autopsy of the war of independence, Ferhat Abbas, who was the GPRA's first president and was for a while quite close to 'this psychiatrist-doctor', does not accord him any great importance in either organizational or political terms.[24] Even as a roving ambassador for the Provisional Government of the Republic of Algeria, Fanon had little power. Ambassadors for self-proclaimed provisional governments have little or no internationally recognized authority; Fanon did not have a diplomatic passport and travelled on short-term tourist visas. He was never a member of the FLN's ruling body, the Comité de coordination et d'exécution, or of the Provisional Government established in September 1958. A colleague who worked with him in both Algeria and Tunisia recalls one of the inevitable discussions in Tunis in which Algerian exiles speculated about what they would do 'after independence'. Someone half jokingly told Fanon that he would become Minister for Health. He was certainly better qualified than most in the FLN and even the GPRA to hold that position, but a touchy Fanon snapped that he did not want to be a minister. He was a psychiatrist, and he wanted to go on being a psychiatrist in an independent Algeria.[25] Fanon himself certainly did not see himself as the Algerian Revolution's chief theoretician and he has been cast in that role by default. The Algerian Revolution did not produce a Lenin, a Mao or a Ho Chi Minh. There was 'only one hero' and in a sense, this was a revolution without a face. For many outside Algeria, Fanon became its face or perhaps its mask. The mask of 'chief theoretician' conceals as much as it reveals about both Fanon and Algeria.

In Martinique, Fort-de-France has its Avenue Frantz Fanon, as does the neighbouring town of Le Lamentin. There is a Centre Culturel Frantz Fanon in the suburbs of the capital, and a dilapidated Forum

Frantz Fanon on the Savanne once hosted open-air events and meetings. The town of La Trinité has a Lycée Frantz Fanon. Yet, here too, it was possible to complain in 1991 that 'For a very long time, Fanon has been marginalized by everyone, including the Martinique Communist Party.' Here too, it could be said that even the generation of 1968 completely eclipsed Fanon, so great was the enthusiasm for revolutions that had taken place elsewhere in China and Albania.[26] Fanon is an uncomfortable presence in Martinique, and particularly in Fort-de-France. It is difficult to reconcile the existence of an 'Avenue Frantz Fanon' and the inevitable evocation of the wretched of the earth, with the street names that invoke a republican and abolitionist tradition (rue de la Liberté, rue Lamartine, rue Victor Hugo, rue Marat . . .) in such a way as to suggest that the history of Martinique began with the final abolition of slavery in 1848. A slightly different note is struck by the name of a street in the Terres-Sainville area, just outside the centre. Here, the rue de la Pétition des ouvriers de Paris recalls that, in 1844, the Parisian working class petitioned for the abolition of slavery in the French colonies, but it still suggests that Martinique's history centres on Paris. The statue in front of the Palais de Justice or court house depicts Victor Schoelcher (1804–1893), the parliamentary architect of abolition: 'the liberator frozen in a liberation of whitened stone'.[27] In a paternalistic gesture, his right arm is draped around the shoulder of a black child; his left hand points the way to freedom. This is 'white France caressing the frizzy hair of this fine negro whose chains have just been broken'.[28] Only the graffiti on Schoelcher's plinth suggest that his statue might not tell the whole story: 'Death to the colonists'.

A further hint that the urban landscape of Fort-de-France might not tell the whole truth about its history can be seen on the Savanne, the large grassy square where a young Fanon played football on Sundays. The Savanne's most famous monument is the statue of Joséphine. Marie-Josephe Tascher de la Pagerie (1763–1814) was a white Creole born in Les Trois Ilets across the bay from Fort-de-France, and wife to Napoleon from 1794 to 1809, when he repudiated her because she could not give him an heir. The cult of Joséphine is alive and well in Martinique and there are still those who, like the Mayotte Capécia Fanon despised so much, can say that 'The fact that a woman from Martinique could become Empress of the French, of the whole French

Empire, filled us all with pride. We venerated her and, like every little girl in Martinique, I often dreamed of that unparalleled destiny.'[29] Others do not take that view. 'Josephine, Empress of the French, dreaming very high above the nigger mob [*la négraille*]',[30] is widely believed to have been responsible for the reintroduction of slavery, which was first abolished in 1794, in the Napoleonic period. In the early 1990s, Josephine's head was removed by some unknown supporters of independence for Martinique, and it has never been replaced. The plinth of her statue has been daubed in red with Creole slogans demanding 'Respect for Martinique'. Precisely how the head of a marble statue standing within earshot of a police station could be removed at night without anyone seeing or hearing anything is one of Martinique's mysteries.

The streets of the little southern town of Rivière-Pilote tell a different story to those of Fort-de-France. A plaque in the rue du Marronage records the history of the runaway slaves or *marrons* who launched armed attacks on the white plantations.[31] It explains: 'In the Caribbean, some slaves fled to the hills and woods in order to rebel against slavery and to prepare for insurrection. This was *marronage*. The marron-blacks [*les nègs-marrons*] formed communities and organized themselves into small armies under the command of one leader in order to launch attacks on the plantation of the white masters so as to liberate their brothers and their country. Their heroic leaders included: Makandal, Boukman, Palmarès, Pagamé, Moncouchi, Simao, Secho . . .'

Nearby, a plaque in the rue des Insurrections antiesclavagistes records the history of two centuries of slave rebellions. The French text reads: 'Brought by force from Guinea, Senegal, Dahomey, Angola, etc. by French slavers, our Ancestors waged a fierce struggle for freedom from the very first days of their deportation and throughout the two hundred years of slavery: 1639, 1748, 1776. 1801: revolt in Le Carbet, led by Jean Kira, who raised the black and red flag. 1817: insurrection in St.-Pierre, organized by Molière. 1822: rising in Le Carbet. 1831: insurrection in St.-Pierre. 1833: Revolt in Le Lorrain (formerly known as Grande Anse). May 1848: the slaves are victorious.' It ends with an inscription in Creole: '*Nég pété chenn*' ('The black man broke his chains'). Slavery was abolished in the French colonies on 27 April 1848, but before the official decree reached Martinique, one final insurrection forced the governor to make a premature declaration of its abolition.[32] That Fanon never mentions this insurrection, and believed that France simply granted her colonial slaves their freedom without a struggle,[33] is a telling indictment of the history he was taught at school.

It is very unusual to see Creole inscribed in a public space, other than in the form of a graffitied '*Wançais dewo*' ('French out'). Since 1946, Fort-de-France has been the fief of Aimé Césaire, mayor, *député* poet of negritude, former Communist and founder, in 1956, of the Parti Populaire Martiniquais; Rivière-Pilote is the stronghold of Alfred Marie-Jeanne, former teacher, mayor and founder, in 1972, of the small Mouvement Indépendentiste Martiniquais (MIM).[34] In the general election of June 1997, Marie-Jeanne won the parliamentary seat of Le François and Le Robert with 64.07 per cent of the votes cast.[35] It is probable that the vote reflected the popularity of an energetic mayor rather than active support for independence for Martinique, but Marie-Jeanne has been described by a political opponent as 'the marron who slumbers in all of us'; he himself claims to be 'one of those negroes that France despises so much' and as ' a great rebel before the Lord'.[36] Two years later, Marie-Jeanne was elected president of the Regional Council, which made him one of the most powerful men in Martinique.[37] For the MIM, Martinique is a colony, 'politically domi-nated, economically exploited, culturally impoverished and militarily occupied'.[38] It is Rivière-Pilote and not Fort-de-France that is home to the Bibliothèque Populaire Frantz Fanon, which houses a good collec-tion of Fanon material. The guiding spirit behind the library project was of course Alfred Marie-Jeanne. The library and the small gallery associ-ated with it are on the second floor of a building housing a number of community associations. The façade is decorated with a mural of an open book. The text is from *Peau noire, masques blancs*: 'I do not want to sing the past at the expense of my present and my future. I want only one thing: an end to the enslavement of man by man, that is to my enslavement by the other. May it be granted to me to discover and to will man wherever he may be.'[39]

Fanon seems quite at home in Rivière-Pilote but his memory remains rather marginal to Martinique as a whole. There is no 'Fanonist' party. The connection between Fanon and the supporters of independence is somewhat tenuous and *Peau noire* is not a pro-independence manifesto.

His association with Martinican nationalism was at its strongest in the early 1960s when, inspired by the Algerian Revolution and Fanon's interpretation of it, a group of young students founded the Organisation de la Jeunesse Anticolonialiste de la Martinique (OJAM) and called on their fellows to join the struggle for the liberation of the island.[40] OJAM's leading members were arrested for 'plotting against the State' and put on trial in France. They were finally acquitted on appeal in April 1964.[41]

Neither the tiny Communist Party of Martinique nor Césaire's much more powerful party can take full responsibility for Fanon's Martinican eclipse, but it is true that neither has done a great deal to preserve his memory. In 1982, a 'Mémorial International' to honour Fanon was organized in Fort-de-France, but no political party supported or financed it. The members of the small 'Cercle Frantz Fanon' founded by Fanon's childhood friend Marcel Manville had to rely upon public donations from the people of Martinique to finance it.[42] A total of 200,000 francs was raised and the organizing committee brought speakers from twenty-five countries to Fort-de-France.[43] Aimé Césaire did not attend the celebrations, but he did at least make municipal facilities available to the organizers.[44] According to a somewhat optimistic commentator on nationalism in Martinique and Guadeloupe, the *Mémorial* marked the return to their people of the first heroes of a pantheon: the *marron* and Frantz Fanon.[45] Not everyone agreed. In the course of a televised debate, members of the audience asked why so much publicity was being given to someone who had betrayed France and taken the side of the terrorists of the FLN in Algeria.[46]

The underlying reason for the – at best – ambivalence towards Fanon is captured by a rare Martinican review of *Les Damnés de la terre*:

> The fact is that Fanon denounces with extreme rigour all the ugliness of old Europe's policy of colonization, without ever taking into account what the France of the Rights of Man and the Citizen, republican and secular France, has done for the country he came from: the French West Indies, for Fanon is Martinican. It was a result of his noble freedom as a free and independent Frenchman that he felt himself obliged to side with the FLN and to place his science and conscience at its service.[47]

13

There are still those in this Département d'Outre-Mer who regard Fanon as a traitor to the republican and secular France of which it has been an integral part since 1946, when the former 'old colony' acquired the same constitutional status as Charente-Maritime or Seine-et-Marne. One of his nieces has remarked that it is 'not easy' to be a Fanon in Martinique,[48] though it has to be said that the family is prosperous enough. When he visited Martinique for the first and last time, Olivier Fanon discovered that many Martinicans regarded his father as a pariah. When he produced his passport – he is by choice an Algerian national – he sensed a certain hostility even within his own family, and had the impression that he was in the same position as the son of a *harki* – an Algerian who fought on the French side in the war of independence – who had returned to Algeria.[49] Others interested in Fanon have experienced more overt hostility. When his first biographer told his hotelier what he was working on, he was unceremoniously asked to find alternative accommodation. He discovered that none of Fanon's works were on sale in Fort-de-France, and that booksellers refused to order them.[50] Such hostility is now a thing of the past, and mention of an interest in Fanon provokes little more than polite indifference. Fanon's books, or at least *Peau noire, masques blancs* and *Les Damnés de la terre* – the only two titles in print in French at the time of writing – are on sale in Fort-de-France's few bookshops, where they are somewhat incongruously shelved alongside the 'Creolist' works of Raphaël Confiant and Patrick Chamoiseau in the 'local interest' section. There is no hint outside Rivière-Pilote that Fanon might possibly be regarded as a national hero.

The novelist and poet Edouard Glissant, who knew Fanon, describes the delighted reactions of the black American students who realized that he came from the same island as their hero, and then adds that years can go by without the author of *Les Damnés de la terre* being mentioned in even left-wing newspapers published in Martinique. He explains: 'It is difficult for a West Indian to be Fanon's brother or friend, or simply his comrade or "compatriot". Because, of all the French-speaking West Indian intellectuals, he was the only one who really matched action to words by espousing the Algerian cause.'[51] The Algerian novelist Assia Djebar recalls with some amusement how her casual remark that she had known Fanon immediately raised her status in the eyes of black Americans.[52] She would not have got the same reaction in his native Martinique. Speaking for a younger generation of Martinicans, Patrick Chamoiseau compares the memory of Fanon to that of the *marrons*. There were in fact relatively few *marrons* in Martinique, mainly because there are very few places to run to on an island with a surface area of only 1,080 square kilometres, but that does not diminish their importance for the collective memory of Martinique, as they are proof that the wretched of the earth can rise up. For Chamoiseau, who first read Fanon in his teens and at a time when he was influenced by the American black power movement, Fanon plays a similar role.[53]

There is no 'Avenue Frantz Fanon' in metropolitan France. Even though some psychiatrists who work with immigrants acknowledge, like Robert Berthellier, that Fanon's clinical writings provide at least a starting point for reflections on transcultural psychiatry, no psychiatric institution bears his name.[54] When Jacques Postel, who knew Fanon at medical school in Lyon, suggested that the journal *Information psychiatrique* should devote a special issue to reprinting a selection of Fanon's papers, a number of his colleagues objected and muttered about the need to respect the memory of 'our boys who died in Algeria'. It should be noted that *Information psychiatrique* has always been the most liberal of French psychiatric journals, and that Fanon published some important articles in it. And when Postel distributed a questionnaire to his psychiatry students at the Censier faculty in Paris, he discovered that whilst 95 per cent of them had heard of Fanon, only 5 per cent knew that he was a psychiatrist.[55]

It is not difficult to understand why Fanon has been largely forgotten in France, where there is now little interest in his work. Almost ten years after Fanon's death, a critic noted that Fanon had been forgotten because France wanted to forget something else, namely a war in Algeria that lasted for eight years. France wanted to forget 'one million dead, two million men, women and children in camps, police raids and torture in Paris itself and, at the same time, apart from rare fits of indignation, the passivity of the masses and the spinelessness of the entire Left'.[56] It is of course difficult to remember something that never happened, and France has been slow to recognize that there was indeed an Algerian war. From 1954 onwards, peace was maintained in Algeria, police operations were undertaken, and rebels, terrorists and bandits were hunted down, but there was no war. Algeria consisted of three French départements, and a nation-state cannot declare war on part of its own territory. It was only in 1999 that France finally accepted that the Algerian war did indeed take place and that references in legislative documents to 'peace keeping operations' should be replaced by references to 'the Algerian war'.[57] The war, or 'the war without a name', has never been truly forgotten.[58] There is an abundant literature on the subject, with new histories appearing at regular intervals. There is, however, no definitive 'History' and no public consensus as to the meaning of France's actions in Algeria between 1954 and 1962. The issues of torture, of the fate of the *harkis*, of the tens of thousands of *pieds noirs* or Algerian-born Europeans who were 'repatriated' to a France in which many of them had never set foot before 1962, and of just how many died when the police opened fire on Algerian demonstrators in Paris in October 1961, all remain bitterly controversial.[59]

The memory of Algeria is still an uneasy one. A stamp issued on 10 May 1997 commemorates the 'French combatants' who served in North Africa between 1952 and 1962, and thus blurs the Algerian war and the lesser conflicts that took place in Morocco and Tunisia. Even before it was issued, François Fillon, Minister for Posts, Telecommunications and Space, was at pains to stress that it did not commemorate the ceasefire of 19 March 1962.[60] The names of the streets of Paris and other French cities provide a laconic account of important dates and names in French history. There is no 'rue du 19 mars 1962' in Paris, but there are streets and squares of that name in, for instance, a number of small towns in the Breton department of Finistère. Such street names are testimony to the efforts of veterans' associations anxious to ensure that their members do not become part of a forgotten generation. They have fought a long and difficult battle: it was only in 1974 that they were officially recognized as veterans and granted the appropriate pension rights.[61] Whether or not French war memorials commemorate the memory of young men who died in Algeria depends upon the decisions – and the political complexion – of local councils, though they were informed as early as July 1959 that the names of France's Algerian dead could join those of the victims of the two world wars and Indochina.[62] Gillo Pontecorvo's film *The Battle of*

*Algiers* was made in 1966, and won the Venice International Film Festival's Grand Prix. It was a popular success in Algeria, but it was not until 1970 that it was granted a certificate for exhibition in France. Protests and threats of violence from veterans' associations and groups representing the *pied noir* community forced the distributors to cancel the planned screening,[63] and it was only October 1971 that the film was finally shown in Paris. The memory of Frantz Fanon is therefore not a comfortable one. It is the memory of a black Frenchman from one of the old colonies who eventually spoke the defiant performative: 'We Algerians'.[64] Aimé Césaire puts it very simply: 'He chose. He became Algerian. Lived, fought and died Algerian.'[65] Such a man is not easy to remember in France.

Given his posthumous fame as a Third World revolutionary to be discussed alongside Amilcar Cabral, Che Guevara or Vo Nguyen Giap it is somewhat paradoxical to recall that Fanon was not particularly well known in his own lifetime. Editions du Seuil's file on his first book, *Peau noire, masques blancs,* contains pitifully few reviews and not many of them are flattering. At the time of its author's death, *Peau noire* had been out of print for years, and it was not reprinted until 1965. The articles Fanon wrote for the FLN's paper *El Moudjahid* in Tunis between 1957 and 1960 were published unsigned, and few of their readers could have identified them as being by Khan's pamphleteer from Martinique. It was only when they were reprinted together with other materials in 1964 that they were identified as being by Fanon.[66] In response to Ernest Gellner's sneering comment that Fanon had no influence in Algeria and was 'for export only', Eqbal Ahmad, the Indian political scientist who once worked with Fanon and who tends to overstate his impact upon Algerian politics, rightly points out that he was 'barely known in "international literary-intellectual circles" until after his death at thirty-six'.[67] The first French edition of *Les Damnés de la terre* which by 1985 had sold 155,000 copies and had been translated into nineteen languages, sold only 3,300 copies in France – poor sales figures for what has come to be known as one of the classics of decolonization.[68] It was the publication in 1965 of the American translation which turned it into a bestseller that was reprinted twice before it reached the bookstores and went through five paperback reprints within the space of a year.[69]

Jean-Paul Sartre's notorious preface to *Les Damnés de la terre* introduced an inflammatory text, and attracted more hostility than Fanon's essay itself but did little to present its author, who remained an almost anonymous 'African, man of the Third World and former colonial subject' who happened to be a doctor.[70] An obituary tribute to Fanon published in the Tunisian press adds to the air of mystery. It is by Maurice Maschino, one of the few young Frenchmen to have refused to serve with the French army in Algeria and to have chosen exile in Tunis, and the classic personification of the so-called 'Algerian generation'.[71] In some ways, the almost anonymous image of Fanon provides the basis for later identifications with and appropriations of Fanon, precisely because it is at once so ill-defined and so stereotypical. For Maschino:

> Fanon is essentially a militant; more so than anyone else, he was what he did and existed in terms of his commitment – and the rest is of no consequence. Given that his existence merges into the fight he fought, the best tribute we can pay to our departed friend – or brother – is to evoke the continual struggle he waged, even as a young man, for freedom.
>
> But how can we fail to see that the best way to kill Fanon is, precisely, to treat him as though he were dead. And that, what is more, we betray him – this man who never said 'I', who existed only through and for the revolution – if we make a front-page splash of elements of a biography which seem to turn this Algerian resistance fighter into a particular case (not everyone is a psychiatrist and not everyone was born in Martinique).[72]

Revolutionaries, it would seem, are destined for heroic anonymity. It is true that Fanon never gave a personal interview, but it is also true that in *Peau noire*, by far the most personal of his works, Fanon does say 'I' or, rather, that a variety of 'I's speak there. The anonymous integrity Maschino ascribes to Fanon easily becomes a source of confusion as to who and what he was. The militant was also a husband and a father, as well as a Martinican who enjoyed both the local rum and the *béguine* music of Alexandre Stellio, but he readily becomes an all-purpose revolutionary icon who can be transported anywhere and invoked in the name of any cause. Fanon's complexity becomes obscured, and it is easily forgotten that the revolutionary psychiatrist – and it must be stressed from the outset that he was *not* a psychoanalyst – was also a clinician who worked well within the parameters of normal science and who, even as he was on the point of resigning his post and leaving Algeria, was conducting drug trials in time-honoured fashion.[73]

Maschino is a member of a generation who, faced with the prospect of a lengthy and potentially dangerous period of military service in a war they could not assume as their own, could find a new relevance in the opening words of Paul Nizan's *Aden-Arabie*, first published in 1931 and republished in the spring of 1960: 'I was twenty. I will never let anyone say that those are the best years of your life. Everything threatens a young man with ruin . . .'[74] Nizan left the Parti Communiste Français (PCF) in protest at the signing of the Soviet–German non-aggression pact of 1939 and was killed in May 1940 as the British unit with which he was serving as a liaison officer retreated towards Dunkirk. He was promptly denounced by his former comrades as a traitor who had always been a police spy. When *Aden-Arabie* was republished in 1960 with an angry preface by Sartre, Nizan became an important icon for those who, like Maschino, both supported the FLN and savagely criticised the French left, and especially the PCF, for its failure to lend any real support to the cause of Algerian independence.[75] *Aden-Arabie* and *Les Chiens de garde*, which is its more philosophical companion volume, were calls to arms and critiques of the official philosophers whose very 'humanism' was a betrayal of a suffering and oppressed humanity: 'Today's philosophers still blush when they admit to having betrayed men for the bourgeoisie. When we betray the bourgeoisie for men, let's not blush when we admit to being traitors.'[76] For Sartre, Nizan was 'the man who said "no" to the very end'; in 1960, it was no bad thing 'to begin with this naked revolt: everything begins with a refusal'.[77]

'Refusal' [*refus*] was the title of Maschino's autobiographical account of his desertion. Another deserter was quick to identify with Nizan, and explains why one of the tiny groups that actively supported the FLN by channelling its funds across the Swiss border took the name 'The Nizan Group': Nizan was 'the name of Sartre's friend, who had just been republished by Maspero. He said there was only one solution: betray the traitors.'[78] Fanon never read Nizan's words, but there is an almost uncanny similarity between Nizan's call for the betrayal of the traitors and Fanon's insistence in *Les Damnés de la terre* that the 'national bourgeoisie' must betray its own interests to remain true to the revolution. Nizan and Fanon briefly fused into a composite icon of total revolt.[79] Significantly, both were published by François Maspero, whose young publishing house was, like the older Editions de Minuit, becoming a focus for opposition to the war. Maspero explains his decision to publish them as stemming from his early conviction that the colonial wars in Indochina and then North Africa were intolerable, and from his disillusionment with the orthodox left: 'Nizan's radical critique was directed against both the bourgeoisie (the same bourgeoisie that was sending us to fight in an unjust war) and what communism had become.'[80]

In France, the composite figure of Fanon-Nizan came to signify total revolt against French society and the PCF. For a tiny minority, Fanon also inspired a positive commitment to Algeria. Few young French people actually went to Algeria after the war, but Fanon was their inspiration. They read Fanon's *L'An V de la révolution algérienne* and *Les Damnés de la terre* and were inspired to go along with the young Algerian republic as it took its first steps into what they thought was the socialist future.[81] Juliette Minces, who went to Algiers to work on the Third Worldist journal *Révolution africaine*, describes in the preface to a collection of reprinted articles from that journal how a reading of Fanon inspired the conviction that Algeria's long struggle for independence would inevitably produce a socialism that would work to the advantage of the wretched of the earth, and especially women and the poor peasantry. She also has to admit that this 'lyrical enthusiasm' was short-lived,[82] as Algeria rapidly became mired in corruption and bureaucracy. As Maschino and his Algerian wife put it, their revolution had been confiscated.[83] The promised liberation of the women of Algeria had not come about.[84] On their return to France, these young people were dubbed '*pieds rouges*' – a cruel pun on *pieds noirs*, the term used to designate the French population of Algeria, and particularly the defenders of French Algeria who finally fled when the prospect of independence offered them a grim choice between the suitcase or the coffin.

The period of what Minces calls 'revolutionary Algeria' represents the high tide of French Third Worldism, and Fanon helped to create that Third Worldism. A generation's disillusionment with the orthodox left, and particularly with the Communist Party coincided with the rise of nationalism in the Third World and gave birth to the belief that the emergence of new states there would create a new humanism or even a new socialism. Algeria, like Cuba, seemed to have a leading role in this process of rebirth.[85] Disillusionment with Algeria, which soon came to look more like a sclerotic one-party despotism rather a beacon of hope, and the ebb of Third Worldism, have brought about a decline in the French reputation of Frantz Fanon in France. When he is read, the readings are negative. In an essay which turns the 'white man's burden' (*le fardeau de l'homme blanc*) into the 'white man's sob' (*le sanglot de l'homme blanc*) and argues that there is no viable alternative to white European civilization, Pascal Bruckner claims that Sartre's support for Fanon was no more than masochism, and argues that Fanon's writings are based upon an analogy between the thesis that maturity is a form of decadence that has not lived up to its early promise, and the adulation of the south, seen as the north's only future.[86] In 1982, former Maoist turned New Philosopher and anti-Marxist André Glucksmann could claim that Fanon was responsible for celebrating the 'second wave' of 'planetary terrorism' that came to Paris when a bomb exploded in the rue Mabeuf.[87]

As Third Worldism declined, former leftists found themselves in agreement with the author of *The Closing of the American Mind*, who, speaking at Harvard in 1988, described Fanon as 'an ephemeral writer once promoted by Sartre because of his murderous hatred of Europeans and his espousal of terrorism'.[88] By 1990, it had become possible to argue in the French press that 'the recurrent theme of the noble savage who has been perverted by Western modernity and alienated by three-piece suits' is a masochism that is 'cultivated by the heirs of Frantz Fanon'.[89] In 1962, these themes, and the underlying revisionism that suggests that colonialism was not so harmful, were those of the French right. So incensed by *Les Damnés de la terre* was one commentator that he reviewed it twice in different journals. With remarkable bad taste, he wrote: 'In December, a mulatto from Martinique died of cancer in an American hospital, despite the efforts his doctors made to save him. Why did he ask the West he hated so much to prolong his life? His choice seems just as disturbing as his hatred, to judge by the written testimony he has left.' In a second article, Comte opined that Fanon's 'brutal frankness and the pitiless hostility that screams in the mad darkness' was reminiscent of Hitler's *Mein Kampf*.[90] Three decades later, alarmingly similar views were being expressed by the liberal left. Alain Finkielkraut, for example, accused Fanon of reviving a 'European' and *völkisch* nationalism,[91] even though the most striking feature of Fanon's Algerian nationalism is that it does not define 'the nation' in ethnic or *völkisch* terms.

In 1990–1, a French sociologist was involved in a study of a deeply unpleasant but frighteningly articulate group of skinheads in Paris. Their racism was predictable, as was their apologia for violence. They were convinced that violence was the motor of history, and that 'it is because we live in a degenerate society that people reject violence'. Their violence was, they claimed, a creative force, and it would help to create or recreate a nation. On hearing this, the sociologist was reminded of Sorel's *Reflections on Violence*, and then of Fanon.[92]

In Algeria, Fanon's fate has been still stranger. His writings on revolutionary violence can now be evoked by the fundamentalist Front Islamique de Salut (FIS) (Islamic Salvation Front) in its journal *El-Mounquid* to justify the wave of appalling violence that has been visited on that country since the elections of 1992 were annulled after it won a majority in the first round. The FIS's war is, it is argued, a continuation of the war against France, and the same redeeming violence has to be used to win it.[93]

One of the striking features of many of the tributes to Fanon that were published immediately after his death is the stress placed upon his fundamental humanism. The negative emphasis on the theme of violence is probably a reflection of the American reception and of the way in which Fanon is read by Hannah Arendt in her book *On Violence*. She looks at Fanon's influence on the violence that affected American university campuses in the 1960s, but fails to make any mention of Algeria.[94] The small group that worked on *Partisans*, the classic Third Worldist journal published by Maspero, read him in a different way: 'On reading his work, it was clearly obvious to those who help to edit *Partisans* that Frantz Fanon has given a new meaning to their thinking, their political actions and even their lives. For us, it is very simple: anyone who has in recent years read those pages that blaze with lucidity,

22

inevitably finds born in them a new vision of men and a burning desire to take the dimensions of this vision into the future.'[95]

Outside France, the most familiar image of Fanon was for a long time that created in the United States, where Grove Press advertised Constance Farrington's flawed translation of *Les Damnés de la terre* as 'The handbook for a Negro Revolution that is changing the shape of the white world':

> Here, at last, is Frantz Fanon's fiery manifesto – which in its orig-inal French edition served as a revolutionary bible for dozens of emerging African and Asian nations. Its startling advocacy of vio-lence as an instrument for historical change has influenced events everywhere from Angola to Algeria, from the Congo to Vietnam – and is finding a growing audience among America's civil rights workers.[96]

The book was reviewed very widely in the American press, usually in terms of warnings about James Baldwin's 'The Fire Next Time' syn-drome. A reviewer writing for the *Durham Morning Herald*, and identified only as 'C.B.', compared Fanon's book to Truman Capote's *In Cold Blood* on the grounds that both described the same hatred and despair, and turned them loose amongst the population at large. He or she went on to state that the wretched of the earth 'are not commu-nists. They are quite simply at the extremity of deprivation and despair, but surrounded by affluence. And there is a moral. If you have what it takes to be interested in the Feature Section of the *Durham Morning Herald*, chances are you've got what they want. If not a pile of milo, then a pile of something. Don't knock the poverty programme; the life it saves may be your own.'[97] Nat Hentoff put forward a similar argu-ment in the *New Yorker*:

> His arguments for violence are the most acute in current revolu-tionary theory . . . they are spreading amongst the young Negroes in American slums and on American lecture plaforms. Those who are engaged in rebutting these precepts of violence (which includes arming for self-defence) ought to find his book a funda-mental challenge, and for this reason, if for no other, Fanon

should be read by the non-violent activists, and by people who are simply opposed to violence.[98]

William V. Shannon for the *New York Times* wrote, 'The statements of H. Rapp Brown and other young radical Negro leaders are in accord with Fanon's exalting of violence for therapeutic reasons.'[99] At the opposite extreme of the political spectrum, a spokesman for the 'counter-culture' could claim that: 'The important literature now is the underground press, the speeches of Malcom [i.e. Malcolm X], the work of Fanon, the songs of the Rolling Stones and Aretha Franklin.'[100] Fanon was one of Stokely Carmichael's 'patron saints',[101] and Eldridge Cleaver could claim that 'every brother on a roof top' could quote Fanon.[102] Unlike the French Third Worldists, most of Fanon's American readers appeared not to have noticed that *Les Damnés de la terre* is, at least in part, a book about Algeria and not America. Carmichael seems not to have realized that his patron saint was simply not a black nationalist.

Further afield, similar images of Fanon as global theorist of revolution proliferated. It was argued that the war of liberation waged by FRELIMO in the Portuguese colony of Mozambique 'verified' Fanon's theses about the cleansing and unifying function of violence.[103] Visiting the office of a Palestinian organization in Amman in 1968, a journalist noticed a pile of books in the corner: Fanon's *Les Damnés de la terre*, *Quotations from Chairman Mao Tse-Tung* and Régis Debray's Guevarist handbook on guerrilla warfare.[104] In Cuba, a 'Movimento Black Power' flourished briefly at the end of the 1960s, and its members, who adopted 'Afro' hairstyles, met to discuss Fanon and other black writers. Most were arrested in 1971.[105] In the Canadian province of Quebec, militants of the separatist Front de Libération Québecoise (FLQ) defined themselves as the 'white niggers of North America'. One of the FLQ's spokesmen wrote of himself that he was a 'Québecois proletarian, one of America's white niggers, one of the "wretched of the earth"'.[106] Interestingly, he, like Maschino, invokes the composite Nizan-Fanon icon. Another spokesman for the FLQ argued that the Québecois's use of the French language was the mark of his blackness, and that to speak French in front of an 'Anglo coloniser' was an act of self-decolonization to be described in Fanonian terms.[107] It was, that is, assumed that an analysis made of the Algeria of 1959 could be transposed directly to the Québec of 1968: 'Prior to 1954, speaking Arabic and rejecting French as both a language and a modality of cultural oppression was a privileged and day to day form of singularization, of national existence.'[108]

Two related processes are at work here. On the one hand, Fanon is being given an abstractly heroic status worthy of Maschino's anonymous revolutionary. It is being forgotten that he was also 'a particular case'. After all, Fanon *was* a psychiatrist and he *was* born in Martinique. On the other hand, the self-identification of civil rights workers, black power activists and Québequois separatists with Fanon's wretched of the earth necessarily involves the misrecognition of exaggeration. In the United States, civil rights workers did encounter terrible violence and the protests of the Black Panthers did meet with armed repression. But they were not faced with General Jacques Massu's Tenth Parachute Division and the mercenaries of the Foreign Legion. When Fanon speaks of 'violence', he is speaking of the French army's destruction of whole villages and of the FLN's bombing of cafés, or in other words of total war and not of limited low-level conflict. The extreme violence of the Algerian war was, fortunately, not reproduced in the United States or Canada. In some cases, the desire to be the wretched of the earth borders on the ludicrous as members of the Parti National Occitan and Basque separatists claim Fanon as their patron saint,[109] or when Breton Nationalists equate the black's creation of negritude with the Breton's construction of a 'Breton personality' and conveniently overlook Fanon's comment that, whilst it is true that the Breton language was suppressed by a centralizing French state, its suppression was not the result of a black/white divide or of a white civilizing mission in a non-white country.[110]

For a short period after his death, Fanon was viewed as 'the most original and articulate spokesman for a theoretical tendency which represents an important strand in the thinking of the Third World'.[111] Some twenty years later, *Les Damnés de la terre* could be dismissed in France as 'A dated work, a book of witness . . . Mao Tse-tung, Guevara, Fanon: three voices for a Tricontinental, fostering the illusions of a western youth that had been won over by a new Third-Worldist myth'.[112] With the decline of Third Worldism, attention has shifted away from *Les Damnés de la terre* and back to *Peau noire, masques blancs*, which is more widely read now (at least in Britain and the United States) than at any time since its publication in 1952.[113] The paradox is that, whilst *Peau noire, masques blancs* is read more and more intensely, fewer and fewer of Fanon's other works are read at all.

The new interest in Fanon's first book is a product of the emergence of post-colonial studies as a distinct, if at times alarmingly ill-defined, discipline. A canonical text defines the post-colonial field as comprising 'all the culture affected by the imperial process from the moment of colonization to the present day'.[114] Despite the inclusive 'all', 'culture' effectively means 'literature' and the focus is inevitably on the English-speaking (or, more accurately, English-writing) world. Post-colonial theory developed in and around university Departments of English and it is difficult not to see it as a continuation of English Literature by other means. A 'cultural studies' approach to literature and an attempt to expand and challenge the canon reinforces, that is, the academic hegemony of 'Eng. Lit'. Fanon is one of the very few non-Anglophones to be admitted to the post-colonial canon, and alarmingly few of the theorists involved realize – or admit – that they read him in very poor translations. The most obvious example of the problems posed by the translations is the title of the fifth chapter of *Peau noire, masques blancs*. Fanon's 'L'Expérience vécue de l'homme noir' ('The Lived Experience of the Black Man') becomes 'The Fact of Blackness'. The mistranslation obliterates Fanon's philosophical frame of reference, which is supplied by a phenomenological theory of experience, but it also perverts his whole argument; for Fanon, there is no 'fact of blackness'. The world is, in his view, experienced in particular ways by 'the black man' (*sic*), but that experience is defined in situational terms and not by some trans-historical 'fact'. In 1995, London's ICA – obviously quite oblivious to translation problems – hosted a season of exhibitions, screenings and events inspired by Fanon's writings; a year later, the related conference proceedings were published as *The Fact of Blackness*.[115]

The danger is that Fanon will be absorbed into accounts of 'the colonial experience' that are so generalized as to obscure both the specific features of his work and the trajectory of his life. Edward Said can cite Fanon and W.B. Yeats in a single paragraph.[116] And whilst it is difficult to disagree with Homi K. Bhabha's comment that the force of Fanon's vision 'comes . . . from the tradition of the oppressed, the language of a revolutionary awareness that, as Walter Benjamin suggests, "the state of emergency in which we live is not the exception but the rule"',[117] it is startling to find that he makes no mention of Martinique. The argument that 'one of the original and disturbing qualities of *Black Skin, White Masks* [is] that it rarely historicizes the colonial experience. There is no master narrative that provides a background of social and historical facts against which emerge the problems of the individual or collective psyche'[118] is no less jarring, though it is less alarming than a Fanon *Critical Reader* which tells the reader that 'In Fanon's seventeenth year, Martinique was under occupation by the Nazis'.[119] It was not. Growing up in Martinique was a very specific, even peculiar, 'colonial experience' and, whether or not one believes in the relevance of master narratives, *Peau noire* does provide an autobiographical background of social and historical facts. Fanon himself prefaces *Peau noire, masques blancs* by restricting the validity of his observations and conclusions to the French West Indies.[120] Given that he never visited Guadeloupe, this can only mean that, whatever post-colonial theorists may say, Fanon himself thought he was writing about Martinique. There are times when it is advisable to ignore the proclamation of the 'death of the author' and to take authorial statements very seriously indeed.

The recent crop of books and articles – and one film [121] – on Fanon contains very little that is of relevance to a biographer, not least because they construct a Fanon who exists outside time and space and in a purely textual dimension.[122] Little will be said about them here. Although there are obvious exceptions – notably Françoise Vergès, whose essays on Fanon and psychiatry are very valuable[123] – few of the authors concerned stray far away from the most familiar of his texts and appear to have consulted nothing produced by the FLN. Post-colonial theorists' enthusiasm for Derrida and Lacan tends to blind them to Fanon's debts to Sartre and Merleau-Ponty, not to mention the similarities between his work and that of his contemporaries Albert Memmi and Jean Amrouche. In a way, the very sophistication of the post-colonial readings of Fanon is the source of their weakness. Such sophistication can co-exist with the crude empirical errors that put Martinique under 'Nazi occupation'. Psychoanalytic readings of Fanon may or may not be valid in their own terms but it is futile to try to turn

Fanon into the psychoanalyst he was not or, like Bhabha, to read him as a black Lacan in the making. He was a psychiatrist working in a very specific and important tradition and in purely quantitative terms his papers on psychiatry greatly outweigh his scattered (and often muddled) allusions to psychoanalysis. Bhabha's claim that there is no 'master narrative' in *Peau noire* has surely to be countered by the argument that there is most definitely a master narrative at work in *L'An V de la révolution algérienne* and *Les Damnés de la terre*. It is the narrative of the Algerian Revolution. It may be difficult to believe in it at the beginning of a new millennium, but Fanon did believe in it and died for it.

The 'post-colonial' Fanon is in many ways an inverted image of the 'revolutionary Fanon' of the 1960s. 'Third Worldist' readings largely ignored the Fanon of *Peau noire, masques blancs*; post-colonial readings concentrate almost exclusively on that text and studiously avoid the question of violence. The Third Worldist Fanon was an apocalyptic creature; the post-colonial Fanon worries about identity politics, and often about his own sexual identity, but he is no longer angry. And yet, if there is a truly Fanonian emotion, it is anger. His anger was a response to his experience of a black man in a world defined as white, but not to the 'fact' of his blackness. It was a response to the condition and situation of those he called the wretched of the earth. The wretched of the earth are still there, but not in the seminar rooms where the talk is of post-colonial theory. They came out on to the streets of Algiers in 1988, and the Algerian army shot them dead. They have subsequently been killed in their thousands by authoritarian Algerian governments and so-called Islamic fundamentalists. Had he lived, Fanon would still be angry. His readers should be angry too.

Despite the inversion, there are constants in the presentations of Fanon, and not least a tendency towards hyperbole. The editors of Blackwell's *Critical Reader* opine that Fanon was 'one of the most influential figures in Third World revolutionary thought – equalled in influence only, perhaps, by Karl Marx'.[124] Faced with such inflated claims, one can only wonder what became of Fidel Castro, Amilcar Cabral, Mao Tse-tung, Ho Chi Minh, General Giap and so many others. Hyperbole such as this does Fanon no favours and does not do him justice. It is exaggerations of this kind that prompted one of Fanon's Algerian comrades, Mohammed Lebjouai, to remark: 'Fanon is one of the greatest revolutionaries that Africa has ever known, and yet almost none of his theories proved to be accurate.'[125] Lebjouai exaggerates too, but it is quite true that Fanon was often wrong – disastrously so when it came to analysing developments in Angola. Recognizing that Fanon could be – and often was – wrong is part of what Henry Louis Gates has called 'the challenge of rehistoricizing Fanon'.[126] Resisting the temptations of hagiography, to which Fanon's first biography certainly surrendered, is part of the same process.[127] A biography of Fanon must begin with the reconstruction of a dimension that has been erased from almost all accounts of his life.

The eradication of the specifically French and Martinican dimension of Fanon's colonial experience has been a gradual process, and it began with Charles Lam Markmann's seriously flawed translation of *Peau noire*. Fanon refers at three points to an image of a grinning *Tirailleur sénégalais* (a black colonial infantryman) who is eating something from a billy can. He is saying '*Y a bon Banania*', which is an advertising copy-writer's idea of how an African says '*C'est bon, Banania*'. In the English translation, this becomes 'Sho' good' and then 'Sho good eating'.[128] The *tirailleur* has become the caricatured black of the Deep South, and he is supposedly eating 'some chocolate confection'.[129] In the original, he is actually eating something very specific, and with specific connotations. Banania is a 'breakfast food' made from banana flour, cocoa and sugar that was first marketed in 1917. Posters of the *tirailleur* and his dish of Banania were still a familiar sight in the France of the 1940s and 1950s; the Senegalese poet and politician Léopold Sédar Senghor wanted to rip them down from all the walls of France.[130] Such posters helped to convince the Fanon who went to study in France that he was not, as he had been taught to believe, a French citizen from Martinique who was like any other French citizen, but a *nègre* who was no better than a colonial black. The Americanization of Fanon wrought by the translation thus erases a very specific dimension of his text. It also creates the categories of 'the almost white, the mulatto and the black'; Fanon himself speaks of '*la békaille, le mûlatraille et la négraille*'.[131] There were white colonialists in France's black African colonies and in North Africa, but there were no *békés* there. The *béké*, the island-born white Creole descended from the original French planters, is unique to the French West Indies. Fanon's Americanization can also take the

grotesque form of the projection on to Europe of 'racial' categories specific to the United States, as when Lewis R. Gordon observes that
'Arabs and North Africans are defined in the racial constructions that
dominate the European world as Caucasian'.[132] 'Caucasian' is simply
not used in its American sense (i.e. 'white') in France; the *Petit Robert*
dictionary defines *caucasien* as 'from the Caucasus, family of language
from the Caucasus region, including Georgian'. Arabs and North
Africans are called many things in French – most of them appallingly
insulting – but they are never called 'Georgians' or 'Caucasians'.

The 'Banania' example relates to an aspect of colonialism that is
specifically French and that can be incorporated into a broader colonial
experience only at the cost of a serious loss of focus. A Senegalese like
Senghor could react to the Banania poster with the same anger as a
Martinican like Fanon. But *Peau noire* also contains phrases that no
Senegalese could have written. Martinican mothers did not, as the
translation would have it, 'ridicule' their children for speaking Créole;
they called them '*tibandes*' to remind them that they were 'better' than
the little gangs (*[pe]tites bandes'*) of children who worked in the sugar-
cane fields, and should behave accordingly.[133] At one point, Fanon uses
the adverb '*souventefois*',[134] which looks to a French reader like either a
misprint or a strange combination of *souvent* and *maintes fois*; it is
simply the Creole version of *souvent* or 'often'. The Anglo-
Americanized Fanon asserts 'And to declare in the tone of "it's all my
fault" that what matters is the salvation of the soul is not worth the
effort'; the Martinican Fanon states that it is pointless to adopt 'a
"*crabe-ma-faute*" attitude'.[135] In fairness to Markmann, it has to be said
that the expression is almost untranslatable. Its literal meaning is 'a
my-fault-crab', but in English the beast is known as a fiddler crab.
Martinique's fauna includes an extraordinary variety of crabs, and the
*crabe-ma-faute* is a denizen of the mangrove swamps and other wet
places that resembles a miniature armoured vehicle. One of its claws is
much larger than the other, and the creature appears to be beating its
chest and saying a *mea culpa*. Only a Martinican, or possibly a
Guadeloupean, would use this expression. Fanon 'lived, fought and
died Algerian', but he was also a product of French culture and French
colonialism. He was also born a native son of Martinique.

# 2

# Native Son

MARTINIQUE IS NOT, remarks its finest contemporary poet and novelist, 'an island in Polynesia'.[1] Whilst this statement may appear to be so self-evident as to be redundant, anyone who has encountered the density of Glissant's poetry and prose will be aware that he is not a man given to stating the obvious. The questions 'Where is Martinique?' and even 'What is Martinique?' are not idle ones, and they are far from irrelevant to any understanding of Frantz Fanon. Fanon became Algerian or, to be more accurate, recreated and defined himself as Algerian, but he could eradicate neither the influence of the time and place of his birth nor the circumstances in which he grew up. His relationship with the island where he was born was complex and tormented but he was born on and of that island. In some respects, Fanon remained Martinican to his death.

For official purposes, Martinique is in France and its capital is Paris. In French atlases, especially those used in schools, the sheet depicting France often features three insets showing small islands that appear to float in either the western Mediterranean or the Western Approaches to the English Channel. Certain maps, including some on display in classrooms, adopt the same convention.[2] Perhaps it was one such atlas or map which, in the 1970s, inspired a Martinican schoolchild to write in an essay that the island on which she lived was surrounded by 'the Ocean, the North Sea and the English Channel'. Or perhaps it was the geography lesson in which she learned about the nature of promontories and peninsulas by studying the example of Quibéron, which is in Brittany, and not that of the spectacular Caravelle peninsula, which was clearly visible from the window of her classroom in La Trinité.[3]

The small islands depicted in the insets are, respectively, Martinique, Guadeloupe and Réunion. Martinique and Guadeloupe are in the Caribbean; Réunion in the Indian Ocean. Since 1946, all three have been Départements d'Outre-Mer or 'Overseas Departments' of the French Republic and they have, at least in theory, exactly the same status as the *départements* of Loire-Atlantique or Seine-et-Marne. The fourth DOM is Guyane which, being part of the Latin-American land mass and lying between Belize and Brazil, cannot easily be depicted in this manner and tends literally to be off the map. Unlike Martinique, Guadeloupe or Réunion, it is not a popular holiday destination and very rarely impinges upon the metropolitan consciousness, except insofar as it is remembered as the home of Cayenne pepper, as the launch site for the Ariane rocket or as a training base for the Foreign Legion. It is probably best known for its offshore islands. These include Devil's Island, once home to the hellish penal colony where Alfred Dreyfus spent the years 1895–9 after having been unjustly found guilty of treason, and from which 'Papillon' (Henri Charrière) escaped; first published in 1969, his account of his escape was one of the bestselling popular adventure stories of the 1970s.[4] None of the DOMs is in Polynesia, but French Polynesia is a Territoire d'Outre-Mer (Overseas Territory) with a slightly different legal status.[5]

School atlases and geography lessons are not the only sources of the confusion as to just where Martinique lies. The covers of the brochures for exotic holidays on display in French travel agents are often illustrated with photographs of a palm-fringed beach and over-printed 'Martinique, Guadeloupe, Réunion, Tahiti'. The beach and the palm tree could be in any of these places, and the casual browser could be forgiven for believing that Martinique is in Polynesia. If it does describe Martinique or Guadeloupe in any detail, the brochure may speak of emerald conical peaks, a sapphire ocean and rivers of crystal, of pink and white villas and picturesque bamboo huts. It will certainly describe the humming birds shimmering amongst the magnolia flowers. All these clichés are borrowed from an exoticist novel of the 1930s;[6] but they still figure in today's enticing descriptions of exotic holidays.

The very fact that France has DOMs is, according to official discourse, proof that the existence of a nation implies neither territorial continuity nor ethnic uniformity; their 'assimilation' into France in 1946 marked 'an important stage in the formation of the French nation', and allowed France to 'reassert its rejection of the racist theories that had recently cost humanity so dear'.[7] Assimilation or 'departmentalization', was viewed as an alternative to colonization, or even an alternative form of decolonization.[8] The DOMs have long been French, but they have not always been part of France. Martinique, Guadeloupe and Guyane are the last remnants of the transatlantic Empire that was established by the France of the *ancien régime* and then lost to Britain in the eighteenth century. These were the 'Old Colonies'. Under the terms of the Franco-British peace treaty of 1763, France ceded Canada to Britain, and most of Louisiana to Spain, and withdrew from her Indian possessions. Guadeloupe and Martinique were briefly under British control in 1762, but then reverted to France. Apart from a brief British occupation in 1794–1802, Martinique has been a French possession ever since. The concessions that were made elsewhere by France are an indication of the importance of her Caribbean possessions. They were a source of valuable commodities, especially sugar; Canada, in contrast, consisted of 'a few acres of snow', as Voltaire so famously wrote in *Candide*.

Insofar as it figures at all in the official record, Martinique tends to be subsumed into the general category of Départements d'Outre-Mer/Territoires d'Outre-Mer. It does not merit a separate entry in the annual survey of world events published by *Le Monde* and Editions Gallimard. To find a trace of anything that occurred in Martinique means searching through all the entries for the DOM-TOMs. The search is all too often fruitless. One could read *Le Monde* or any other French newspaper for a long time without realizing that Martinique is in France. Inclusion goes hand in hand with exclusion. Bookshops classify works by Martinican authors in a category of not-quite-Frenchness that shelves them next to the 'North African literature', even though the authors in question are, unlike Algeria's Rachid Boudjedra or

Rachid Mimouni, French citizens. The Centre Georges Pompidou's Bibliothèque Publique d'Information in Paris follows the same convention: West Indian literature is, like writing from Québec, North Africa and the former colonies in sub-Saharan Africa, regarded as a subset of the literature of Francophonie, a generic term applied to French-speaking communities around the world. Patrick Chamoiseau's *Texaco* won the Prix Goncourt in 1992 but it is not shelved in the same section of the library as the novels of metropolitan Goncourt winners.[9]

Even as it is insisted that Martinique is French, it is hinted that it is not quite in France. This is not a purely literary question. There is abundant sociological evidence that citizens from Martinique and the other DOMs are widely regarded as 'immigrants' and 'foreigners' when they visit what is supposed to be their own country.[10] It is not uncommon for the Martinican who arrives in Paris and asks a policeman for directions to be asked to produce his residence permit. On stammering that he is a French citizen from a DOM and therefore the holder of a French passport, he will be told: 'You should have said you were a West Indian. How am I supposed to know? OK, on your way.' The policeman has just noticed an Arab who is a shade too dark to be honest and loses interest in the Martinican.[11] This was Fanon's experience too: 'We [Martinicans] have often been stopped by police officers who have mistaken us for Arabs, and when they find out where we are from, they quickly apologize: "We know very well that a Martinican is not the same as an Arab".'[12]

Even the armchair traveller who never leaves Paris quickly senses that there is something particular about this integral part of France. The Institut Géographique National map (sheet 3615 of the *Editions spéciales de l'IGN*) he or she has bought from the specialist Le Vieux Campeur bookshop in the rue du Sommerard features a symbol that is not to be found on a map of any metropolitan *département*. It is a stylized cock, and signals the site of a 'Gallodrome', known in Martinique as a *pitt* (from the English 'cock pit'). Cock-fighting is a popular entertainment, and the birds are sometimes also pitted against poisonous snakes. The bets are high and large sums of money change hands. This would be illegal in metropolitan France. Guidebooks also give the impression that Martinique is a rather strange part of France. No Parisian visiting Brittany or the south coast of France needs to be reminded that it is inadvisable to use the familiar pronoun *tu* – which is usually reserved for children, relatives and close friends – when addressing a waiter or barman. Guidebooks to Martinique do have to warn visitors from *la métropole* against infantilizing its black French citizens with an over-familiar *tu*. The guidebooks do not point out the other uses to which *tu* can be put; when the policeman asks the 'Martinican who looks like an Arab' for his papers, he addresses him as '*tu*'. When Fanon was completing his medical studies in Lyon, he was a decorated and wounded war veteran. He was also black. The examiner presiding over his oral examination initially addressed him as '*tu*', and patronizingly asked him what topic he would like to be examined on. No white student would have been addressed in this fashion. Fanon chose a subject at random, and was awarded five marks out of ten instead of the nine he thought he deserved. He later told Simone de Beauvoir: 'But he called me *vous*.'[13]

Martinique is one of the Windward Islands and part of the Lesser Antilles chain of islands stretching from Grenada to St Kitts. It is surrounded by the Atlantic Ocean to the east, and by the Caribbean Sea to the west. With a surface area of only 1,000 square kilometres, Martinique is so small that nowhere is more than sixty kilometres from the capital, Fort-de-France. This does not make for easy communications. The transport network centres on Fort-de-France and the easiest way to go from Le Robert on the Atlantic coast to Le Carbet on the opposite side of the island is to make a detour via the capital. When Fanon lived in Martinique, transport was poor and roads, especially in the north, were often blocked by landslips and mud slides. Despite its small size, the island's terrain is very varied, and its flora rich and diverse. Its mammalian fauna is relatively poor, largely because of the predatory talents of the mongoose which was introduced in a vain attempt to control the snake population. The mongoose quickly learned that there were many easier things to kill than snakes and the highly venomous fer de lance viper (*Bothrops atrox.*) reproduces with impunity in the damp forests despite the financial rewards on offer for bringing in a dead specimen. There is no truth in the story that the snakes, which are an endemic species, were introduced to dissuade slaves from running away from the plantations but, although rarely glimpsed, they are greatly feared, so much so that the fer de lance is not spoken of as such: it is '*la bête longue*' ('the long animal').

In the north of Martinique, the rainfall is heavy and the slopes of the precipitous mountains are clad in the vestigial remnants of a rain forest; the west and particularly the south are much drier and water is in short supply. Most of the terrain is hilly and the rolling volcanic *mornes* are its most distinctive feature. The island is dominated by the peak of Montagne Pelée (1,250 metres). The volcano is dormant, but far from extinct. Although a child in La Trinité can still be asked to produce essays on 'My Village in Autumn' or 'Christmas in the Snow',[14] Martinique has only two seasons: the dry and warm *Carême* (literally Lent) from December to June, and then a hotter season (*hivernage*) with heavy rain and occasional cyclones. Fanon does not describe his lessons in meteorology, but he does describe what happens when ten-to fourteen-year-olds in Martinique are asked to describe what summer holidays mean to them: 'They reply like proper little Parisians: "I like holidays because I can run through the fields, breathe fresh air and come back with *rosy* cheeks".'[15]

French representations of Martinique defy physical geography, and the syllabus taught in Martinique can ignore elementary climatology. The educational system treats history in cavalier fashion too. Unless a particularly committed teacher introduces an option in 'local' history, the history taught in schools is that of metropolitan France and its succession of revolutions and republics, and not that of Martinique itself.[16] In ideological terms, this history has been described as serving mainly to legitimize the position of the tiny white minority by stressing the importance of their metropolitan origins, no matter how tenuous the links may actually be, whilst implying that the black majority has no history worth recording.[17] Even locally produced histories tend to rely upon a Francocentric chronology.[18] Fanon's comments on history in colonial societies in *Les Damnés de la terre* refer to the Third World in general, but they echo the lessons he learned as a child in Martinique. It is the colonist who makes history and 'The history he writes is not the history of the country he is stripping, but the history of his own nation as it plunders, rapes and starves.'[19] An alternative history is being created in Martinique, but it is the creation of novelists and poets rather than professional or academic historians. Edouard Glissant proposes a chronology divided into seven periods: the slave trade; the world of slavery; the plantation system; the emergence of the elite and of towns:

sugar-beet's victory over cane-sugar; assimilation; possible annihilation.[20] Patrick Chamoiseau divides the history of Martinique into five ages: the age of *ajoupas* (shelters) and longhouses; the age of straw; the age of crate wood; the age of asbestos, and the age of concrete.[21] Raphaël Confiant retells the story of Martinique during the Second World War in distinctly unofficial terms, and that of the serious riots that broke out in 1959 after an apparently trivial incident in which a white incomer's car collided with the Vespa scooter owned by a black docker; the latter story is also told by Vincent Placoly.[22] These were the riots that inspired Fanon's final article on Martinique.[23]

Martinique was 'discovered', as the Eurocentric tradition has it, by Columbus in the fifteenth century, but it was only in 1635 that it was claimed for France by Pierre Belain d'Esnambuc, the conquistador whose heroic statue – erected in 1935 to mark the tricentenary of the French presence and not a masterpiece of public statuary – looks out to sea from Fort-de-France's waterfront. The original European colonizers had shown little interest in Martinique as it soon proved to have no reserves of precious metals. They were also wary of the inhabitants. The Caribs, who knew the island as Madinina,[24] were not the aboriginal people of Martinique. They had migrated from Latin America and decimated the earlier population of Arawaks. The Caribs had a reputation for being good warriors, and were also said to be cannibals. 'Cannibal' is derived from 'Carib', as is the name of Shakespeare's Caliban. Although the flesh-eating Carib figures prominently in literary accounts of the region, no one ever met one. As Marina Warner, a specialist in cultural mythologies, remarked in her 1994 Reith Lectures: 'Like the gold which he [Columbus] was certain was always around the next headland, it was always the tribe over the next ridge who were feasting on human flesh. Columbus left the myth of cannibalism thriving, but no account of the practice.'[25] Carib resistance was overcome by European weaponry, and according to legend many committed suicide by jumping from cliffs rather than be enslaved by the French. The cliff between St Pierre and Le Prêcheur on the Caribbean coast is still known by the alternative names of 'The Coffers of Death' or 'Tomb of the Caribs'. Little trace or memory of the pre-colonial culture of Martinique remains. There are only some artefacts in museums, a few place names, and mysterious carved rocks in certain of the forests.

Under the colonial system that developed from the seventeenth century onwards, the role of the West Indian colonies of Martinique, Guadeloupe and Saint Domingue (now divided into Haiti and the Dominican Republic) was defined with brutal clarity. Their sole *raison d'être* was to supply the metropolis with tropical produce. They were not expected to develop an economy of their own or to accumulate wealth in their own right. Trade with countries other than France was forbidden by law. The initial work of colonization was undertaken mainly by *engagés* or endentured labourers recruited from France's Atlantic seaboard who worked in conditions of near-slavery; it is no semantic accident that *engagé* can also refer to someone who has signed a pact with the devil and exchanges temporary wealth or material advantage for eternal torment. The economy based upon cotton, tobacco, indigo and coffee was not a success. Sugar, introduced in the late seventeenth century, was to prove the source of the wealth of Martinique's planters, and the success of the island's dependent economy was driven by the rising European demand for a luxury that was increasingly becoming part of everyday life. Like the British ports of Bristol and Liverpool, French cities such as Bordeaux and above all Nantes grew wealthy on the Atlantic trade and the traffic in slaves that supported it. Until the beginning of the twentieth century, Martinique's economy was based almost exclusively on sugar, but the industry began to decline in the fifth of Glissant's ages, when it was faced with competition from the sugar-beet that was and is intensively farmed on the plains of northern France. Rum replaced sugar as the island's prime export. Although it is still grown, sugar is now of minimal importance to the economy of Martinique, whose only real export crop is now the banana. Martinique's plantations are relatively small and the island's banana growers find it difficult to compete with the giant American-owned plantations in Latin America. The future looks grim.

Tobacco could easily be produced by independent small-holders, but the production of sugar required both a high level of initial capital investment and a large labour force. The labour force came from West Africa. In 1664, it was estimated that Martinique had a white population of 2,904, and a black population of 3,158; by the middle of the next century, the total population was over 56,000.[26] It was not the white population that grew at this pace. In the eighteenth century alone, merchants from Nantes, Bordeaux, La Rochelle, Le Havre and St Malo fitted out a total of 2,800 ships for the triangular trade that took European trade goods to Africa, slaves to the Caribbean, and sugar back to their home ports.[27] During that century, over one million black Africans were transported to the sugar islands. The casualty rate was high: a death rate of 5 to 15 per cent was regarded as commercially acceptable and calculations of profit were made accordingly. Malaria, yellow fever, poor food and bad water could take an appalling toll on the hundreds of slaves forced into the between-decks of a ship with a length of sixty-five feet and a beam of nineteen feet.[28] The memory of the slave trade has not faded. Writing of it in 1955, Glissant puts it thus: 'They nailed a people to rated ships, sold, rented and bartered flesh. Old people for small change, men for the sugar harvests, women for the price of their children. There is no more mystery and no more daring: the Indies are a market in death; the wind proclaims it, blowing full on the prow.'[29] The plantation system required continual imports of new slaves as the mortality rate in the French colonies was always higher than the birth rate; working conditions were so harsh, and nutrition so poor, that the slave population did not reproduce itself. A form of resistance may also have had an impact on demographic rates on the plantations, and folk memory recalls that some women would rather use abortifacents than give birth to children destined for slavery.

The slave economy was tightly regulated by the so-called 'Code noir' which was adopted in 1685 and revised in 1724; it remained in force until 1848.[30] The code was harsh and governed every aspect of daily life. The punishment for striking a master or a member of his family, assault on free men and the theft of livestock was death. A slave who ran away had his ears cropped and was branded with a fleur de lis on one shoulder; if he made another attempt to escape, his hamstrings were cut and he was branded on the other shoulder. The punishment for a third escape attempt was death and no appeal against the sentence was possible. Slaves were commodities and did not enjoy property rights. The Code noir also gave slave-owners certain obligations. Under the terms of Article 22, every adult slave had to be given food rations including 'two pounds of salt beef, three pounds of fish or its equivalent'. Relatively little land could be spared for stock-breeding and Martinique's inshore fishing grounds were not rich. The island therefore began to import food. The staple of the slave's diet was salt cod imported from Canada and New England. It was a good source of both protein and salt. The trade provided a new outlet for Martinique's rum and molasses; fishermen in the far north were happy to accept rum in exchange for their lowest-quality cod, which they could never have sold in Europe. That this was technically illegal – the British Molasses Act of 1733 imposed heavy duties on molasses from the non-British islands- – did little to prevent the flourishing trade.[31] Supplemented by locally grown fruit and vegetables, this restricted diet was just enough to sustain life on the plantations. Salt cod – the 'saltfish' of the English-speaking Caribbean – is still an important ingredient in the Creole cuisine of Martinique and Guadeloupe.

Sugar production was not a difficult process. Pieces of stalks from mature canes were placed in shallow holes, covered in earth and left to germinate in the rich volcanic soil. Within fifteen months, the new crop was ready for harvesting. The harvest involved everyone. The cane was cut by teams of men wielding machetes (the local name is *coutelas*, meaning cutlass, and this instrument of daily labour became a deadly weapon in times of revolt) and tied into bundles by women known as *amarreuses* (from the verb *amarrer*: 'to tie down', 'to make fast'). Gangs of young children – the *tibandes* – cleared up anything that was left. The bundled cane was then taken to the mill to be crushed. The mills were driven by either animals, water or wind-power, and the cane was fed into rollers to extract the sweet juice. The juice was boiled a number of times to remove impurities and then left to crystallize; the final process of refining rarely took place in Martinique itself. The syrup was also distilled locally to produce an aromatic, and very strong, rum. A much cruder variety of white rum known as *tafia* was distributed to the slaves who produced it. All this is still part of Martinique's collective memory and it was part of Fanon's memory too.

For the planter, the beauty of the system was its simplicity and economy: the crushed stalks could be burned to fire the boilers, and the waste products could be fed to the animals that powered the mills. Although animals were gradually replaced by other forms of motive power, the actual production process has changed little. Small vans equipped with miniature mills (either operated manually or driven by portable generators) to crush cane and extract the sweet juice are still a common sight at the points where minibuses that serve as collective taxis (*taxi-pays*) congregate to wait for passengers. It is a refreshing drink and a popular one. The production of sugar posed no great technical problems, but the work in the fields was brutally hard, especially at harvest time. The fires lit to clear the undergrowth and to drive off snakes created a suffocatingly hot and dusty atmosphere. Some cane is still cut by hand. Unlike their ancestors, who worked barefoot, the modern cutters wear rubber boots, gloves and face-masks. As the shade temperature regularly reaches 30°C in Fort-de-France, it is difficult to imagine what the temperature must be in a cane field that is exposed to the sun but sheltered from the wind, and where a fire is burning. It was the slave societies of the Caribbean that gave birth to the myth of the zombie or of the soulless corpse that is revived by witchcraft and set to work in the cane fields. It is a fitting myth: working in the fields was a form of living death.

Slavery was abolished by the French Convention in 1794 (at which date Martinique was in British hands) but was re-established by Napoleon in 1802. Abolition finally came in 1848. The abolition of slavery was commemorated in somewhat muted fashion in April 1998. Philately provides a curious index of just how quiet the celebrations were. A single stamp was issued to mark the 150th anniversary of abolition; a whole set was issued to mark the World Cup that was hosted by France that summer. President Chirac described abolition as a form of 'integration' and went on to state that the 'open and generous attitude' it implied had allowed France to 'welcome and integrate into the national community successive generations of men and women who have chosen to settle in our land. In return, those men and women, who have a rich culture, a rich history and rich traditions, have given new blood.'[32] There was no mention of the equally 'rich history' of slave revolts, and abolition was represented as France's gift to her old colonies. It was forgotten that slavery had already been abolished in 1794. Towards the end of *Peau noire, masques blancs*, Fanon defiantly states: 'I am not the slave of the slavery that dehumanized my ancestors.'[33] In 1998, his words were invoked by the French Ministry of Culture,[34] which presented 1848 as a radical break with a racist past. The posters on the walls of French cities depicted a 'rainbow coalition' of children and young people and the legend 'All born in 1848'.[35] The whole point of Fanon's book is that racism was not abolished in 1848. When he refused to be defined as the slave of the slavery that dehumanized his forefathers, he was not asking the white world to feel guilty about 'the past of my race',[36] but he was refusing to be defined by that past. *Peau noire, masques blancs* does not end with a plea for racial equality but with a Sartrean bid for total freedom as a radicalized consciousness leaps into a future that escapes all ethnic determinations.

The commemoration also marked another anniversary that could scarcely be celebrated. It was in 1848 that Algeria was officially declared to be an integral part of France. Victor Schoelcher was the architect of the decree that abolished slavery in the name of the republican principle of assimilation; he justified the annexation of Algeria by referring to the very same principle.[37] Colonization does not depend solely upon slavery; there are other ways of dehumanizing men and women. Nothing of this was mentioned – or could be mentioned – in April 1998.

The plantation system outlived the abolition of slavery, which was not accompanied by any land reform. Writing in 1843, the great liberal Aléxis de Toqueville had argued that: 'Whilst the Negroes have the right to become free, it is undeniable that the colonials have the right not to be ruined by the Negroes' freedom.'[38] The colonials' 'right not to be ruined' ensured that they were compensated for the loss of their property, and that the plantations remained intact. Whilst some freed slaves acquired land of their own – usually on higher and less fertile ground – and some drifted into the expanding towns, many were obliged to become rural wage-earners working on the plantations. Martinique began to develop a dual and lopsided economy. The white-owned plantations produced sugar for export, while freed black slaves engaged in food production on a scale that made individual families self-sufficient but could not feed the whole population. Martinique continued to import food. From 1858 onwards, the labour of the black plantation workers was supplemented by that of bonded labourers brought in from France's enclaves in India, most of them Tamils from Pondicherry.[39] Known as *coulis*, they and their descendants became the most despised sector of the population.

Born in 1928, Edouard Glissant is the son of a *géreur* (a ganger who organized the workers who cut the cane) and often accompanied his father to the plantations. Writing in 1958, he described the system he saw as a boy, and which still existed:

> The agricultural workers are the prisoners of a system developed over a period of three hundred years. Each *habitation* is a social unit and is independent. The shacks belong to the owner, and he also owns a shop which has all the products anyone wants. The money that is given to the workers is immediately spent in the shop. The economy is a closed circuit. If a worker refuses to accept these working conditions, he is black-listed and cannot find work anywhere else.[40]

The cyclical nature of sugar production means that it cannot provide employment throughout the year, and the regular periods of enforced semi-idleness encouraged reliance on credit and a neverending cycle of debt. A form of unofficial debt-bondage replaced institutionalized slavery. Even when work was available, the plantation worker of the 1950s had to work for up to four days to cover his most basic needs.[41]

The abolition of slavery made the freed slaves French citizens and gave them the right to vote, but not necessarily the ability to exercise that right. Many were indifferent to politics and economic insecurity made them all vulnerable to pressure. Those who rented land were in a particularly difficult position. Many families in Martinique have stories about the great-uncle or grandparent who was driven from his shack and kitchen garden because he had offended a planter by disobeying an order or voting the wrong way in a local election. The memory of the *béké* on horseback and with a whip in his hand is a powerful and intimidating figure in the Martinican imagination. And that memory is part of the Fanon family's collective memory too. Fanon's brother Joby still speaks bitterly of a grandfather who was driven off his patch of rented land by just such a figure.[42]

A *béké* is a white Creole born in the Caribbean, or a descendant of one of the original settler-planters. 'Creole' derives from the Spanish *criollo* and was originally used to describe anyone born in Latin America or the Caribbean islands, regardless of their race. The origins of the word *béké* are obscure, but it is usually held to derive from an Ibo word meaning both 'white' and 'foreigner'. The *békés* have been a small

43

minority ever since slave times, and have never numbered more than 2,000. Writing in 1937, Victor Curidon, a minor poet and songwriter from Martinique, described their power, which was quite disproportionate to their numbers:

> The whites of Martinique . . . own eight tenths of the land and all that it produces. In their deliberately closed and clenched hands, they in fact control every aspect of production and manufacture. Basically, they have their hands on all the control levers. The levers that control the economy: factories and shops, banks, bazars and distilleries; the levers that control politics: parliamentarians and others, elected politicians, powerful men at the bottom and powerful men at the top; the levers that control society: the churches, charitable works and mutual aid organizations.[43]

When he briefly visited Martinique in 1941, the surrealist poet André Breton met a *béké* named Aubéry: 'the master of the biggest rum distillery in Martinique . . . the supreme expression of the feudal system that anachronistically prevails in Martinique: all the plantations, factories and shops are in the hands of a few families who have been there since the conquest; they make up a real de facto dynasty and jealously ensure that their prerogatives and privileges are preserved'.[44] The name Aubéry is still one to be reckoned with in Martinique.

In 1950, the anthropologist Michel Leiris estimated that some four-fifths of the land was owned by 'big white landowners with a feudal mentality',[45] and in a major study of contacts between civilizations in Martinique and Guadeloupe commissioned by UNESCO, he describes them as living in a closed, endogamous society, and as being both parochial-minded and clannish.[46] Their refusal to invite into their homes in the rich quarter of Didier, which is in the hills above Fort-de-France, the blacks with whom they worked quite happily during the day was legendary; marriage between a black and a *béké* was unthinkable.[47] A Martinican politician quotes a *béké* as saying that 'If a mulatto married an English princess, we would be very happy for both him and the country; but we would be very upset if he married one of our girls. That really would be the end of an era.'[48] Needless to say, this did not prevent male *békés* from having sexual relations with black or mulatto women. According to Fanon, it was rumoured that the head of the Aubéry clan had had almost fifty children by such women.[49] Ownership of most of the best land was not the only key to continued *béké* dominance; the foundation of the privately owned Crédit Martiniquais bank in 1922 gave the ethno-class a stranglehold on credit and finance too. Like most of the sugar industry, it was – and is – controlled by a handful of families who intermarried over the generations to produce a tightly knit oligarchy.

The ideological self-perception of the *béké* is well expressed in two novels that appeared in 1989 and 1991. Marie-Jeanne de Jaham is herself a Martinican-born *békée*, and her *La Grande Békée* and its sequel *Le Maître-Savane* tell the story of a woman's struggle to recreate and preserve a plantation destroyed by the eruption of Montagne Pelée in 1902. They combine elements of family saga, romance, exoticism and popular history. The first volume is dedicated to 'All the great *békés*: those who have existed, and those who still exist.' In the second volume, Fleur Mase de la Joucquerie, who is the eponymous *grande békée*, tells her French-born grandson: 'Remember that the blood of your pioneer ancestors runs in your veins. They did not hesitate to leave their peaceful lands in Poitou three hundred years ago, and to come here to build a new world. We *békés* are like that, capable of dropping everything to go somewhere else to build something.'[50] As in so many myths of empire, the master – or in this case the mistress – simply forgets that it was the slave who laboured in the cane-fields. Fanon was to encounter the same mythology in Algeria: 'The colon makes history. His life is an epic, an odyssey. He is the absolute beginning: "This land is a land that we have made".'[51]

Jaham's proud reference to blood and landed estates in France points to a major theme in *béké* mythology, but it is unlikely to be grounded in reality. Martinicans take a malicious glee in pointing out that the ancestors of the white minority are more likely to have been whores and vagabonds from the slums of the Atlantic ports than aristocrats.[52] The existence of some *békés-goyaves* (guava-*békés*, or poor whites) also tends to undermine aristocratic pretensions, whilst the insistence on the metropolitan origins of the *békés* masks some odd contradictions. Pride in being French goes hand in hand with a resentment of metropolitan dominance and metropolitan institutions. The expression *béké-France*, as applied to metropolitans living in or visiting Martinique, is not a flat-tering one. Hostility to the ban on free trade with countries other than France during the early colonial period found expression in periodic planter revolts, and the *békés* have not always been averse to greater independence from France. They were not supporters of assimilation in 1946, and their enthusiasm for the wartime Vichy regime established on the island might be described as a final planter revolt intended to seize back the political power that had gradually been acquired by the black-mulatto middle class. The power of the *béké* has in fact always depended upon the existence of the French market, and sometimes on more direct intervention. In the mid-1990s, the Crédit Martiniquais found itself in serious difficulties as it was faced with a steep rise in bad debts. State intervention was necessary to save the private institution, which survived at the expense of French tax-payers.[53]

The main effect of the *békés*' concern with the supposed purity of their blood line has been on the non-white population. In the eigh-teenth century, Moreau de St.-Méry, a white planter with philosophical leanings, elaborated a taxonomic table that distinguished between no fewer than 128 categories of 'mixed blood'.[54] The heritage of such tax-onomies is the extraordinary 'shadism' that is part of everyday life, and the problems with identity that are so central to Fanon's *Peau noire, masques blancs*. Complex distinctions made on the basis of degrees of pigmentation are still commonplace: a *chabin* has reddish hair, and sometimes blue eyes; a *câpresse* is a woman with long wavy hair and a cinnamon-coloured skin. A mulatto woman has long silky hair, whilst an 'African' has crinkly hair and will, if he is particularly dark-skinned, be said to be 'blue'. A sociometric study of the racial attitudes of school-children carried out at the beginning of the 1970s showed that there was a close correlation between skin colour and perceived social status. Children who assumed that one of their fellows was of higher social standing regularly described him or her as lighter-skinned.[55] The chil-dren's perception of skin colour was found by this study to intersect with a sharp sense of socio-economic differentiation which can distort the stereotyping; as proverbial wisdom has it, a rich negro is a mulatto, but a poor mulatto is a negro.[56] This 'shadism' was originally overde-termined by economics and property relations: wealthy mulattos owned black slaves and treated them no better than the *béké*. In 1998, both *Le*

*Monde* and *Libération* sent journalists to Martinique to investigate the 'heritage' of slavery. The eighteen- and nineteen-year-olds they interviewed told stories that could have been told by Fanon. A young woman identified as 'Jeanne' said that it was commonplace for parents to warn their daughters against going out with black boys because their 'babies would have crinkly hair'. The twenty-year-old Jean-Philippe, who described himself as a *métis* ('half-caste'), complained that he often had the impression that the girls who went out with him did so only because they could not find a white boy.[57]

The Martinique described by Fanon in *Peau noire* is obviously not today's Martinique, but some things have not changed. Even though the rate of unemployment runs at about 30 per cent (and reaches 60 per cent in some areas), subsidies from France ensure a level of prosperity that is higher than that of the other islands of the Eastern Caribbean. Yet underlying attitudes seem surprisingly constant. Just like the heroines of Mayotte Capécia's novels, the adolescent girls interviewed by Michel Giraud still dreamed of marrying white husbands, and saw such a marriage as a form of social promotion. In that sense, they were still negrophobic.[58] The use made of the terminology of shadism is complex and even confusing. Terms like *nègre* can be used both as a compliment and as an insult, depending on who is speaking, and to whom. To complicate matters, the Creole equivalent (*Nèg*) can be used to mean simply 'man' or even 'friend', as in *awa nèg* ('Don't count on me, man') or '*Sé nèg-an-mwen*'('He's my pal'). The vocabulary of shadism can also be imbued with humour: the attractive little town of Morne-Rouge has a dry-cleaners' (*un pressing*) called '*Pressing la belle câpresse*'.

It is by no means easy to trace the genealogy of a black or mulatto family from Martinique.[59] Family trees that can be traced as far back as the abolition of slavery in 1848 disappear into the relative anonymity of servitude and then into the lost African past that preceded it. Names and dates become confused. Documents in the possession of Fanon's uncle and research carried out by his brother Joby make it possible to trace an outline family history back to the 1840s, but no further. The origins of the very name 'Fanon' are obscure, but it can be reasonably assumed that it was given by a master to an African slave brought to Martinique at some forgotten date. This would not have been unusual.

Fanon's friend Marcel Manville was convinced, rightly or wrongly, that his surname derived from 'Mandeville', which is the name of both a village in Normandy and a family from that region.[60] The Atlantic ports of Bordeaux, Le Havre, Nantes and La Rochelle were the main centres for the slave trade, and many Martinican names do appear to originate in Normandy and Brittany. There does not, however, appear to be any great concentration of Fanons there. The family history therefore begins in Martinique in the 1840s.

Fanon's great grandfather was the son of a slave of African origins and was said in 1842 to be a *nègre à talent*, or in other words 'a negro with a trade'. He owned some land in the area around Le Robert on the Atlantic coast, where he grew cocoa, and must therefore have been a free man. In 1848, his wife stated to the authorities that she was a 'free negress', and she was therefore either the daughter of manumitted slaves or had herself been granted her freedom prior to abolition. Their son Jacques-Bernardin was born in La Trinité, another small settlement on the Atlantic coast, and married Françoise Vindil, born in 1857. They too were small farmers, and had six children. Born in 1891, Félix Casimir married Eléanore Médélice, who came from Le Vauclin, some thirty kilometres to the south of La Trinité. Eléanore's origins were, according to the Fanon family's collective memory, more exotic than her husband's. She was, it is said, an illegitimate child of mixed race, and her white ancestors came from Strasbourg, the capital of Alsace, having been forced to leave their native Austria as a result of religious persecution. The name 'Frantz' is believed by members of the family to allude to the distant Alsatian strand in his ancestry. Like many of their generation, Casimir and Eléanore drifted away from the land. After working at a number of different trades, he entered the customs service as an inspector in Fort-de-France; she opened a shop selling hardware and drapery. This was not unusual; civil servants had regular salaries, but were not well paid and the small retail sector was largely a female province.[61] The upward social mobility of Frantz's parents was parallelled by that of his two uncles: Edouard became a schoolteacher, whilst Albert worked for the Office des Eaux et Forêts, which is France's equivalent of the Forestry Commission.

If there is a dominant image of a childhood spent in pre-war Martinique, it is probably that enshrined in Joseph Zobel's popular novel *La Rue des cases-nègres*, (*Black-Shack Alley*; the US title is *Sugar-Cane Alley*), first published in 1955 and long banned because of its brutal portrayal of rural Martinique. Often described as a classic of Francophone literature, the novel gained a new popularity – and an international audience – thanks to Euzhan Palcy's cinematic adaptation, which won both a French 'César' and four prizes including Best First Film and Best Actress at the 1983 Venice Film Festival. The novel and film tell the story of José, a young boy born on a sugar plantation who succeeds against the odds in acquiring the education that will spare him a brutally harsh life in the cane fields and the 'black shacks' of the title, thanks largely to the self-sacrificing efforts of the grandmother who brings him up. The portrayal of rural poverty is eloquent; that of the relationship between José and '*m'man Tine'* or 'Grandma Tine', touching (in the film adaptation, M'man Tine is played by the wonderful Darling Legitimus who, as a young woman, once danced in Paris with Josephine Baker's troupe).

*La Rue des cases-nègres* is in many ways a classic novel of education, but it describes an education that is also an alienation. An unresolved dilemma faces José: if he obtains a grant, he may be able to study in France like the 'sons of modest civil servants or small shopkeepers' who obtained grants 'because their fathers were used as front men by *députés*'.[62] Those boys will be able to enter a higher social class, but they will be forced to deny their origins. José's only real alternative is to enter the competitive examination that will give him a modest position in the local civil service. José's years at school confirm his intuitive realization that 'the inhabitants of this country really are divided into three categories: Negroes, Mulattos and Whites (not to mention the sub-divisions), that the former – by far the most numerous – are belittled, like tasty wild fruits that need no attention; the second might be regarded as varieties that have been produced by grafting; and the rest are the rare, precious variety, even though most of them are ignorant and uneducated'.[63] As a result, many black Martinicans suffer from an 'inferiority complex' that inspires a forlorn desire to 'whiten their race'.[64] Zobel's analysis and even his vocabulary here are obviously similar to those of Fanon's *Peau noire, masques blancs*. It is not that Zobel was influenced by Fanon: both are writing of the same reality, and writing within a specific tradition going back to at least the 1930s, when René Ménil, who taught at the Lycée Schoelcher in Fort-de-France, wrote of the 'tragic history of a man who cannot be himself, who is ashamed and afraid of what he is'.[65]

Fanon's early experience was not that of Zobel's fictional José. He was one of the sons of modest civil servants and small shopkeepers, though there has never been any suggestion that his father was anyone's 'front man', and rural poverty was at least a generation away. Unlike José, Fanon was the descendant of the 'free men of colour' who, by the end of the eighteenth century, were equal in numbers to the white population.[66] Their descendants developed into a Martinican middle class as the 'Old Colony' was gradually 'assimilated' into France during the nineteenth century and particularly under the Third Republic (1871–1940). By the time Fanon was born, Martinique's institutions – schools, courts and the civil service – were all modelled on their French equivalents. Martinique had an appointed Governor with far-reaching powers, but also an elected 'Conseil régional' responsible for running its day-to-day affairs. It was democratically represented in both the Assemblée Nationale and the Senate. The existence of a black and mulatto middle class was no threat to the *békés*, who clung to their economic power and subtle political power: 'Being in the numerical minority, that landed aristocracy does not provide Parliament with representatives. It buys them ready-made. The representatives are chosen mainly from the coloured bourgeoisie.'[67] It was this combination of a black middle class and a seemingly quiescent plantocracy that led a normally perceptive British travel writer to conclude in the 1950s that there was little evidence in Martinique of a colour bar or of racial discrimination.[68] Both existed but they were not written on the streets of Fort-de-France.

On 20 July 1925, Frantz Fanon was born into a relatively prosperous middle-class family living in the capital of Martinique. The Fort-de-France where he was born was effectively a new town.[69] In 1890 the town's wooden buildings had been largely destroyed when a fire broke out after a child upset a cooking stove in the rue Blenac. Rebuilding had scarcely got underway when, a year later, a cyclone swept through the town and destroyed the remaining buildings. Fort-de-France was rebuilt to its original pattern of a grid of narrow streets flanked by two- and three-storey houses with wrought-iron balconies. Despite the risk of fire, most houses were rebuilt in wood; Fort-de-France stands on swampy ground and the unstable subsoil made it difficult to build in stone. A third natural disaster now accelerated the growth of the town. Originally known as Fort Royal (the name was condensed to 'Foyal'; its inhabitants are still known as 'Foyalais'), Fort-de-France has always been Martinique's administrative capital, but was not its first social or cultural capital. For much of its history Fort-de-France's importance was eclipsed by that of St Pierre. Built entirely of stone, the so-called Athens of the Antilles stood on a bay on the Caribbean coast, and at the foot of Montagne Pelée. Even though the lack of port facilities meant that ships had to ride at anchor in the bay and be loaded and unloaded by lighters, St Pierre was a more important port than Fort-de-France at the turn of the century. Sugar and rum were its principal exports. The population was more mixed than that of the administrative capital and the influence of the rich *békés* was much more noticeable. Unlike Fort-de-France, St Pierre had a vibrant cultural life and was home to Martinique's first theatre – a scaled-down replica of that in Bordeaux.[70] At eight in the morning on 8 May 1902, Montagne Pelée erupted and a *nuée ardente* (a burning cloud) of gas and volcanic dust engulfed the town, leaving an estimated 30,000 dead in little over ten minutes. The sea itself burned as the rum and sugar in the holds of the ships at anchor were ignited. The eruption shifted the ethnic balance of Martinique's population: the majority of the dead were *békés*. St Pierre never recovered its ascendancy, even though it was rebuilt. The ruins of the theatre and other buildings now make it a popular, if somewhat melancholy, tourist attraction.

The destruction of St Pierre worked to the advantage of its old rival, which now expanded rapidly. In 1902, Fort-de-France had a population of 14,000; by the mid-1930s, 43,000 people lived there, many of them seeking an alternative to the harsh conditions of the *habitations*, others driven there by the agricultural downturn as sugar became less and less profitable. Although the port and its associated facilities – the dry dock, the ship-repair facilities, the major coaling depot and the naval base- – employed a large workforce, the capital never became a manufacturing centre. Its only sugar mill was burned down in 1890 and was never rebuilt. The centre of Fort-de-France was home to a population of shopkeepers, minor officials and members of the liberal professions, most of them living in the narrow streets between the Canal Levassoir to the west, the park known as the Savanne to the east, the boulevard de la Levée (now the boulevard du Général de Gaulle) to the north and the sea to the south. The town centre was flat – it is in fact one of the very few flat places in Martinique – and hemmed in by an amphitheatre of steep hills. It was also small and covered an area of little more than forty-two hectares. Central Fort-de-France was a predominantly black and mulatto town. White officials and *békes* tended to live in the spacious colonial-style villas of Didier, an exclusive district in the hills above the town. A declining number of planters still lived on their self-sufficient *habitations* and rarely visited Fort-de-France.[71] The poorer black population was largely confined to the Terres-Sainville area beyond the boulevard de la Levée, which followed the course of the old drainage canal that once marked the town's boundary. From the 1920s onwards, little wooden houses were constructed here on small plots, many of them without running water or electricity.

Although Fort-de-France was a new town in 1925, it was not a modern town. It was 'a little town in the Caribbean, with no châteaux and no seigneureries, no ruins and no monuments'.[72] It had few public buildings of any note, and still fewer cultural amenities. Sanitation was not good, and the open drains – home to thriving populations of rats and land crabs- – were not a pretty sight, whilst the Canal Levassoir served as an open sewer as well as an anchorage for fishing boats. Fort-de-France is at sea level, and a rising tide would drive sewage back up the drains into the town. It was only in 1951 that Fort-de-France began to build a proper sewage system; until then, 'organic waste' was simply dumped in the open drains and rivers. The same year saw the beginning of a serious campaign, co-ordinated by Aimé Césaire, against typhoid.[73] Sheltered from sea breezes by the headlands of the Pointe des Nègres to the west (once the site of the slave market) and the Pointe des Carrières to the south-east, Martinique's capital could be stiflingly hot as well as dusty. Aimé Césaire described it in unflattering terms:

An old life with a lying smile, its lips open with disaffected anxieties; an old poverty rotting silently in the sun, an old silence dying of warm pustules . . . This flat town – sprawling, tripped from its right direction, inert, breathless under the geometric burden of a cross that is constantly being reborn, rebellious against its destiny, frustrated in every way, incapable of growing along with the sap of this soil, ill at ease, clipped, diminished, at odds with its fauna and flora.[74]

Fanon found this description 'magnanimous'.[75] Both Césaire and Fanon described Martinique as disease-ridden, and it was. For Césaire, the Antilles were 'pitted with smallpox', and Fort-de-France was an inert town with 'leprosies, consumption and famines'.[76] He goes on to describe 'the parade of risible and scrophulous buboes, a fattening ground for very strange microbes, poisons for which there is no known alexiteric, pus from very old wounds, the unpredictable fermentations of putrescible species'.[77] These are no metaphors. Diseases like elephantiasis were still endemic during Fanon's childhood. Tuberculosis and even leprosy were still being fought in the 1950s. It was only then that malaria was eradicated as the swamps around Le Lamentin were drained and cleared to allow the construction of Martinique's airport.[78] A visitor from the metropolis describes his feelings on landing in Martinique in 1952, the year in which *Peau noire* was published:

When I landed at Fort-de-France, I was ashamed. Ashamed of the wretched airport. Ashamed of the sloppy policemen and customs officers in their tattered uniforms. Ashamed of what I saw on the road from the airport: shacks of rusty corrugated iron, barefoot children dressed in brownish rags, worn-out adults dragging their deformed legs in the dust: I could see the ulcers through the holes in their shirts and trousers.[79]

Extreme rural poverty was far from unknown during Fanon's childhood. It was common for agricultural labourers to wear roughly cut garments made from guano sacks and known as 'Aubéry khaki'.[80] In 1937, Victor Curidon wrote of the 'termite hills of thatch' that had grown up around the colonial mansions of Martinique's lords and masters and of the ignorant, misbegotten children who still worked in the cane fields 'sunburned, burned and cooked by the murderous sun, bent over at their thankless, interminable task from morning to night' and wore loincloths of jute and skirts of straw. Their legs were deformed and their faces were lined with premature wrinkles.[81] This was what lay behind the exotic façade of 'the isle of eternal sun, with its sweet-smelling tuberoses, its giant ferns, picturesque gorges and smiling creeks, and its intoxicating women, who really are like living flowers'.[82]

Both Césaire and Fanon were relatively insulated from the grimmest aspects of Martinican reality, though they were clearly aware of their existence. Fanon did not, however, live in a shack built from rusty corrugated iron. The Fanon family home and Eléanore's shop were in the rue de la République, which ran from the waterfront to the boulevard de la Levée. The house no longer exists, and the site – 33 rue de la République – is now occupied by a branch of Tati, a chain store specializing in cheap clothing and household goods. There is nothing to indicate that Frantz Fanon once lived here. Just a few doors down, on the corner with the rue Lamartine, stands what is claimed to be Martinique's oldest bookshop – the Librairie Papet, founded in 1910. The central location was convenient: Fanon's father lived a few minutes' walk away from the customs office where he worked. The state primary school attended by Fanon and his brothers in the rue Périnnon was even nearer. Its proximity was actually a disadvantage in the eyes of the Fanon brothers: their mother could hear the school bell and expected her sons home minutes after it rang. They therefore had to forgo the pleasures of football on the dusty little playground – now a baseball court – outside the school. On getting home, the rule was that they had to kiss their mother and then go to their bedroom to do their homework. The school has now been demolished to make way for another of the car parks that appear to do nothing to control Fort-de-France's interminable traffic jams.

The Fanons' dual income made them relatively prosperous, prosperous enough to afford servants and music lessons for the girls. In January 1945, Frantz Fanon wrote to his mother to tell her what he wanted when he got home from a war with which he was increasingly disillusioned: 'A big meal. Menu: punch (in the plural), *blaffe*, rice, chicken, red beans. Mangoes.'[83] This was not the diet of a poor family, and not many Martinicans ate chicken on a regular basis. As a student in Lyon in 1947, Fanon would nostalgically recall Sunday mornings at home, the sound of his father's slippered footsteps on the stairs, his mother scolding the servant who had just announced that lunch would be late, and the piano recitals given by his sisters Marie-Flore and Marie-Rose. The ability to hire servants was a prized symbol of social status and the family were acutely aware of their status as recent recruits to the urban middle class. The Fanons were careful to avoid the trap that snared so many middle-class families: debts occasioned by conspicuous consumption and the acquisition of the outward signs of relative prosperity. They treated their country cousins with amused if slight condescension and, being self-consciously new recruits to their class, were very punctilious about observing the social conventions. Church-going was something to be taken seriously, and so were the unwritten rules that prevented the sons of customs officials from playing with the sons of lawyers or doctors. The girls attended the private Pensionnat Colonial (now the Collège Ernest Renan) on the grounds that fee-paying schools were better than state schools at inculcating the social graces. Such considerations were important to respectable families whose rural past was long behind them and who would have been insulted to have been reminded that they were only two generations removed from slavery.

Thanks to the income generated by Eléanore's shop – and her acute business sense – the family was able to build a second house, which was originally used for weekends and holidays. Redoute is now a middle-class suburb of Fort-de-France but it was a separate community in the 1930s. The solidity of the houses – and the presence of the best pâtisserie in Martinique – testify to its contemporary prosperity, as do the well-kept graves in the cemetery behind the church of Notre Dame du Rosaire, a peaceful place with spectacular views of the conical Pitons du Carbet to the north. A number of Fanons are buried there, including Albert, the generous uncle who always had small change and sweets in his pockets for his nieces and nephews. Fanon's uncle Edouard, who was born in 1907, calmly informs interested – and suddenly disconcerted – visitors that he will soon join his brother in the family grave. Like most of Fort-de-France's outer suburbs, Redoute is built on a steep ridge and straggles along the main road leading north to St Joseph. The Fanon house was off the main road on an unpaved lane (now the rue François Rustal) that plunged steeply down towards the Madame river. The plot of land faced north and stood on a slope above one of the river's minor tributaries. If the purchase of the plot was testimony to Eléanore's business acumen, its development was testimony to her tenacity. Bringing in water and electricity meant crossing a neighbour's property and caused quarrels; in order to provide vehicular access, the boys had to pave the lane as best they could with local stones and gravel. The house itself was a single-storeyed wooden construction built in a traditional style designed to provide shade and to keep out the heat. For the children, the large garden was a greater attraction than the house itself. There were no gardens in the rue de la République, and this was a paradise with a profusion of breadfruit trees, mangoes and coconut palms and views across the bay to the Lamentin plain. This was a place to watch the darting humming birds, the spectacled thrushes and the enormous butterflies. Each child had their own mango tree, where they could read or doze, perched in the branches. Left in the care of servants while their parents were at work, they experienced a wild freedom in the garden that they could never have in Fort-de-France itself. Like so many traces of Fanon's childhood, the house has disappeared. After Eléanore's death in 1982, it was sold to speculators and demolished to make way for two small blocks of flats built in the ugly concrete that covers so much of modern Martinique. Fanon never speaks of this side of his childhood.

Whilst it was a status symbol, domestic help was also something of a necessity: Frantz was the fifth of eight children: Mireille (who was also his godmother), Félix, Gabrielle, Joby, Marie-Flore, Marie-Rose and Willy. There were often twelve to fifteen members of the extended family present for meals in the rue de la République. Eléanore was the central authority figure and has been described by Manville as a 'strong-minded intellectual woman' whose malicious irony masked an enormous generosity,[84] and by her son Joby as *une maîtresse-femme*, meaning a competent woman with a firm belief in her own authority, and not one to be trifled with. There appears, on the other hand, to be no basis for the suggestion made in Irene Gendzier's *Critical Study* of Fanon that she was 'of rather difficult temperament', 'not overly affectionate' and 'favoured her daughters'.[85] She was ambitious for her children and anxious to see them succeed. No child of hers was going to go back to rural poverty. Family loyalty was, in her view, the cardinal virtue and she liked to tell her children that: 'Unity is the one thing that saves the family, and every one of us. So long as you are friends, you are strong. What belongs to one of us belongs to all of us, and that way we are all rich.' So strong was the sense of loyalty and unity that the family effectively excluded anyone who was not a blood relative. Marrying into the Fanon clan was conditional upon a demonstration of worthiness and a promise of loyalty.

Casimir Fanon was not an active participant in the day-to-day activities of his family and appears to have taken little interest in his children. He worked long hours, and then kept his distance. To that extent, he was, recalls Joby, a typical father in a matrifocal society. The domestic authority wielded by Eléanore was as typical as Casimir's non-involvement. Significantly, there are very few positive father-figures in Martinican fiction, but there is an abundance of devoted mothers and grandmothers. Whilst Joby Fanon shrugs off his father's passivity as an effect of Martinican society, Frantz seems to have resented it bitterly, as is evident from the harsh letter he wrote in 1944:

Papa, you really have sometimes failed to perform your duty as a father. I allow myself to judge you in this way because I am no longer of this earth. These are the reproaches of someone living in life's beyond. Sometimes Maman has been unhappy because of you. We made her unhappy enough. In future, you will try to return to her one hundredfold all she has done for the equilibrium of the family. The word now has a meaning that was previously unknown. If we, the eight children, have become something, Maman alone should take all the glory. She was the spirit. You were the arm. That is all. I can see the face you will pull when you read these lines, but it's the truth. Look at yourself. Look back at the years that have passed, lay your soul bare and have the courage to say: 'I deserted'. And then, repentant parishioner, you will be able to return to the altar.

The apocalyptic tone, and Fanon's claim that he was no longer of this earth, reflect his conviction that he was about to die in a war he no longer perceived as his own, but the sense of bitterness must have gone further back than that.

Alliances were formed within the tightly knit family. Frantz was closer to Gabrielle (born in 1922) than to his other sisters, and closer still to

Joby, his elder by two years. They shared a bed, played the same sports and had the same friends. Their strong mutual affection remained unspoken: overt displays of affection were to be avoided at all cost. One of their shared passions was football. This was not unusual: Martinique had many teams, and the 1930s have been described as the golden age of Martinican football.[86] While they were at primary school, the Fanon brothers were too young to play league games, but they took an active role in the informal matches that were played on the Savanne on Sunday mornings. There were no pitches marked out on the Savanne so these were impromptu affairs, but Fanon, an outgoing personality with an easy ascendancy over others of his age, created 'his' club, which he called 'Les Joyeux Compagnons'. It was on the football field that Fanon first met long-standing friends like Pierre Marie-Claire Mosole, Marcel Manville and Charles Cézette, the son of a grocer living in the rue Périnnon. All three would fight alongside him in the Second World War.

In *Peau noire, masques blancs*, Fanon describes the Savanne in jaundiced terms: 'Imagine a space two hundred metres long and forty metres wide, with its sides bounded by worm-eaten tamarind trees, with the immense war memorial, the fatherland's gratitude to its children at one end, and the Central-Hôtel at the other; an unevenly paved and tortured space, with pebbles that roll under your feet.'[87] There are strategic reasons why Fanon describes the Savanne – and the rest of Fort-de-France- – in such negative terms,[88] but for the boy who played football there it was a space of freedom and offered a welcome escape from the choking grid of narrow streets. The negative description is intended to counter the 'exoticist' descriptions given in books like *Sonson de la Martinique*, a very poor novel published in 1932:

Who hasn't heard of Fort-de-France's Savanne? It must be as famous as the Cannebière and the place des Quinconces. Well, Martinicans think so at least. They say that it is so famous because sailors from all over the world have always been in the habit of mentioning it when they get home: its welcomingly tree-lined walks, cooled by the breeze that comes from the far horizon, the Pitons du Carbet whose sharp teeth stand out against the blue of the sky, its huge sandalwood trees and its shady little wood which shelters children accompanied by their *das* by day and, by night, homeless vagabonds and lovers.[89]

Other pastimes were rather less innocent than football. When they could escape their mother's supervision, Joby and Frantz were also members of a juvenile gang known as '*la bande raide*', whose territory extended from the abattoir on the banks of the canal Levassoir to the Pont de chaines in the Terres-Sainville. For reasons that no one can now explain, Frantz – as always, the dominant figure and organizer – was known as 'Kabère', whilst Joby was 'Pipo'. Although they were from time to time involved in scuffles with rival gangs like the Terreur de la Grosse Roche, the boys' activities were usually confined to minor mischief. Writing to his mother in 1947, Fanon recalled with some amusement how a teacher called Madame Philoctète had had to write to his father to complain about the 'infamies' committed by 'his rascal of a son'. The boys stole marbles from shops, and found their mother's shop an irresistible target. When they could, they sneaked into cinemas and sporting events without paying. Such activities did not pass unnoticed in the closely knit society of Fort-de-France and were quickly reported to the boys' parents, who were convinced that they would end up in prison. The high point of their criminal career was, however, a piece of childish devilry which caused annoyance and scandal but no real harm. Using stolen safety-pins they fastened together the best dresses of a group of ladies in church, and then watched the chaos that ensued when they tried to stand up to take communion. Imbued with the prim values of the Pensionnat Colonial rather than those of the street, the Fanon sisters were as scandalized as their parents.

Fanon's talent for mischief and football went hand in hand with a remarkable degree of self-possession. One incident, which reportedly occurred when he was eight, was potentially serious. The fourteen-year-old Félix had a friend called Kléber Gamess, and one day he 'borrowed' his father's revolver to impress the Fanon boys. Félix was out on an errand, and Kléber went to wait for him in Frantz's room. Slipping off the safety catch, he began to clean the gun, not realizing that it was loaded. Accidental pressure on the trigger realized a shot that could have killed Frantz, but the only injury was to Kléber's finger. Shouting down to his mother that the noise had been caused by a toy car backfiring, Frantz bandaged the boy's finger with a torn sheet and then took him to hospital, telling Eléanore that they were just going out for a walk. Forty years later, Félix commented: 'It was in his nature to be like that. Playing soccer, it was the same thing. He never got excited; he was always very efficient.'[90]

As he reached his teens, the footballer and apprentice juvenile delinquent began to spend less time on the Savanne and the street, and took to reading in the Bibliothèque Schoelcher. The library is Fort-de-France's strangest public building. Built of cast-iron and glass, designed to resemble a pagoda, decorated with coloured mosaics and surmounted by a glass dome, it was first erected in the Tuileries gardens in Paris in 1887 and then dismantled and shipped in pieces to Martinique, where it was re-erected on a swampy patch of ground adjacent to the Savanne in 1893. The entrance lobby is emblazoned with the name of the philosophers of the age of enlightenment: Rousseau, Diderot, Montesquieu and Voltaire. The library originally held the estimated 10,000 volumes from the personal library of Victor Schoelcher. Most of the Schoelcher bequest was destroyed by the disastrous fire of 1902, and the library acquired a rather sinister reputation. In the late 1940s, an English visitor was warned by a local lady not to touch any of the books because they were all 'infected with leprosy germs'.[91] Neither the comparative poverty of the library's holdings nor talk of leprosy germs deterred Fanon from spending hours in this polychrome building, where he read as widely as possible, concentrating on the classical French literature and philosophy of the seventeenth and eighteenth centuries. Outside the library, books were not easy to come by and one of the reasons why *Peau noire* is so replete with quotations and references is simply that its author spent his youth in a book-poor town, and then found himself in the book-rich culture of a major French university. He had been let loose in a large library, and he took advantage of it.

This adolescent initiation into French classicism was the culmination of a process which had begun long ago. At primary school, Fanon had made good progress but he had done so at a price. Like any other child, he was discouraged from speaking the Creole that is in effect the first language of any Martinican. Creole is a rich mixture of French, African survivals and fragments of the many European languages spoken in the eastern Caribbean by planters, traders, slavers and merchants. It developed out of the lingua franca that allowed white masters to communicate with black slaves on the plantations, and is spoken by *békés* and blacks alike. The use of Creole can at times create a feeling of Martinican identity that transcends the usual divisions. It is said that when violent riots hit Fort-de-France in 1959 some local *békés* escaped physical assault or worse by addressing the rioters in Creole; metropolitans who could speak only French were not so lucky. Fanon's own attitude towards Creole was ambivalent and even contradictory. In 1952, he agreed with Michel Leiris that it would gradually die out or be reduced to residual status by the spread of (French) education;[92] six years later, he argued that Creole was an 'expression of the Antillean consciousness' and that it might even provide the linguistic basis for a West Indian Federation to which Martinique could belong.[93]

Syntactically, Martinican Creole resembles a simplified form of French, but its vocabulary is a rich gumbo of many things. Fanon had been taught that it was not a language, but a patois that was midway between *petit-nègre* (literally 'little-negro', this is the French equivalent to pidgin English) and French. Lessons learned at school were reinforced at home, where children who lapsed into Creole were told by their mothers that they were *tibandes* or no better than the children who worked in the cane fields.[94] The shift from Creole to French is an important aspect of the donning of the white mask that covers the black face, and it is one of the major themes of Fanon's first book: 'The black West Indian will become all the whiter, or in other words come closer to being a true man, to the extent that he makes the French language his own.'[95] Fanon does not speak of his schooldays in very specific terms, but education in Martinique was – and is – an induction into linguistic and cultural schizophrenia. The novelist Patrick Chamoiseau was born in 1953, but his account of a Creole childhood has a lot in common with Fanon's allusions to his education.[96] Part of the problem arises from the centralizing and Jacobin tradition within the French educational system, which has never been tolerant of diversity or particularisms. Within metropolitan France, schoolchildren were, within living memory, forbidden to speak Breton and were punished if they did so.[97] In Martinique, the ban on speaking Creole resulted in a conflation of linguistic and racial problems. The middle classes of

Fort-de-France did not want to be reminded of the slave time that produced Creole: 'In its desire to be equal with the Whites, the mulatto class did everything to erase its negro origins, and using Creole seemed to be the ignominious stigma of those origins. It even forbade its children to speak it; even the *békés* did not go to such extremes.'[98] To remind a child of its negro origins was a harsh reproach; a child who was misbehaving would be told: *Ja nègre* ('you're already becoming a negro').[99] A senior politician describes Martinican Creole as a 'rich and subtle' instrument for the expression of 'our states of mind and daily needs', but insists that the claim that it is a national language is either pure snobbery or militant illiteracy: 'It was the French language that brought Martinicans out of the darkness of obscurity and into the light of a universal culture.'[100] This was the lesson learned by Fanon, who spoke Creole with Martinican friends but wrote in standard French.

The lessons of school and home were reinforced by other media. When Fanon and his gang crept into cinemas without paying, they were not going to watch the art-house classics of the golden age of French cinema. Fanon's mother used to sing him French songs which never mentioned negroes,[101] but he watched films in which he could see them. They were Johnny Weismuller's *Tarzan* films, and he identified with the white lord of the jungle, not with his black inferiors.[102] Films like this served to teach children what *nègres* really were, and to instil in them the idea that they were not *nègres*. French West Indians did not even think of themselves as black; they were simply West Indians, and everyone knew that blacks lived in Africa.[103] Fanon had encountered *nègres*. In either 1938 or 1939, a group of *tirailleurs sénégalais* stationed in Guyane briefly visited Martinique.[104] Fanon and his friends had heard of these famous colonial troops and their colourful uniforms, and went looking for them in the streets. He knew what he had been told about them by veterans of the First World War: 'They attack with the bayonet and, when that does not work, they charge through the bursts of machine-gun fire, machete in hand. They cut off heads and collect ears.'[105] The *tirailleurs* also had a reputation for looting, brutality and especially rape. To Fanon's delight, his father brought two of them home, providing concrete confirmation that he and his family were not *nègres*, but Martinicans. Ironically, and quite spontaneously, the Fanon family behaved in just the way that a white family in

France might have done: they charitably entertained the troops from the black African colonies.[106]

Fanon sums up his situation as follows: 'I am a negro – but I naturally do not know that, because that is what I am.'[107] It would take a brutal encounter with a white 'other' to destroy the unthinking naturalness of Fanon's perception of himself. It came in the form of a brush with a child in France who said: 'Look a negro . . . Mum, look at the negro, I'm frightened.'[108] Fanon himself dates his first experiences of overt racism in Fort-de-France to the Second World War, when the sailors of the French navy revealed themselves to be authentic racists and when the *békés* began to take back the political power that had been largely lost to the black-mulatto ethno-class. He does not describe pre-war Martinique as a non-racist society, but nor does he describe it as overtly or aggressively racist. Although there was a family – and collective – memory of the *béké* on horseback with a whip in his hand, the 2,000 Europeans in pre-war Martinique were, he thought, 'integrated into social life, involved in the economy of the country'.[109] As a teenager, Fanon had minimal contact with the minority white population. He would obviously see white officials, white soldiers and white policemen in their colonial uniform of shorts and knee-length socks, but had few real dealings with them; there was no reason for a boy, black or otherwise, to come into direct contact with, say, the white owners of the Crédit Martiniquais. Still less did he have any reason to meet the white plantocracy. The young Edouard Glissant had a much more direct knowledge of the plantations than Fanon, but he had no direct contact with the *békés* himself.[110] What he did experience was the depersonalization born of what colonial France had been saying to Martinicans for hundreds of years: 'No, no. You're like us. You're French, completely European.'[111]

The outbreak of the Second World War put an end to both Fanon's delinquency and his studies in the Bibliothèque Schoelcher. He was now attending the Lycée Schoelcher. This too was an indication of the family's status and relative prosperity: fees ensured that poor blacks did not attend the lycée. The same system ensured that few working-class children in France attended lycée either. One of the stranger myths that circulates through the extensive literature on Fanon is the story that he attended 'a segregated black lycée which had a religious atmosphere'.[112]

It would be difficult to miss the point more widely. Like any other school in the French system, the Lycée Schoelcher was militantly secular, and displays of any religious belief were forbidden by law. A 'lycée with a religious atmosphere' is simply a contradiction in terms. If any of the Fanon children received religious education at school, it must have been the girls at their private school. And whilst colonial Martinique was certainly a racist society, its racism did not take the form of apartheid. The *békés* sent – and still send – their children to religious schools like the Collège Saint-Joseph-de-Cluny, but this does not mean that the lycée was officially segregated. 'Separate development' was not the policy of the old colonies. On the contrary, the difficulties experienced by the lycée's pupils stemmed from the fact that it took no account of ethnic differences and taught them that they were Europeans. That Fanon's teachers and fellow pupils were from the mulatto ethno-class is a reflection of economic realities rather than institutionalized segregation.

The lycée, built in the late 1930s on the site of the old Governor's Residence, was one of Fort-de-France's first reinforced concrete buildings. It still squats heavily and somewhat ominously on the steep hill across the Canal Levassoir, and seems to echo the forbidding military architecture of the Fort Saint-Louis which dominates the eastern side of the Savanne. A few months into the war, it was empty and deserted. The declaration of war had caused panic in Martinique. Trenches were dug on the Savanne in anticipation of some improbable invasion from the sea. Fort-de-France's schools were closed in preparation for air raids that never came. The trenches were never used, and quickly became stinking open latrines. Abandoned to their own devices, Frantz and Joby were running wild. In desperation, their mother dressed them in their sisters' dresses to try to keep them at home. In November 1939, she took the extreme measure of exiling Joby to Le François. Edouard Fanon taught there, and the school was still open. Returning from work to find that his son was missing, Casimir Fanon turned on his wife in anger, demanding that she bring Joby home and pointing out that she had no right to send his children away without his express permission. In legal and even constitutional terms, he was perfectly right and his paternal authority was absolute, but he was no match for his wife. Eléanore announced before the whole family that Joby was not coming back and, what was more, Frantz was going to join him. She was tired of him returning home only for meals and then disappearing again. She won the argument and Frantz and Joby spent the next year in Le François. Accustomed to eating with a large family, they now found themselves living in the little town's one hotel and taking lonely meals with their bachelor uncle. Eléanore's one piece of advice to them as they left was typical: 'Be irreproachable.'

Only twenty-four kilometres from Fort-de-France, Le François was a small town dominated by the sugar industry and surrounded by fields of cane. It had a sugar mill which has now been demolished. There was also some fishing, though the town is slightly inland and cut off from the sea by a dusty plain, the fishing boats anchored in a tidal canal. Eduard Fanon was quite a prominent citizen with connections on the Conseil Général that could later be exploited to his nephew's advantage. The school where he taught did not have the prestige of the lycée in Fort-de-France, but he was an able and committed teacher. He was also the founder of a literary, cultural and sporting society known as Le Club franciscain – the football team still exists and, to its founder's great satisfaction, still performs well in the island's junior league. Fanon played occasionally, but was too young to become a regular member of the team. Edouard Fanon was strict with his nephews, kept them to a tight timetable and insisted on disciplined schoolwork. They responded well to the regime he imposed and their work improved greatly, perhaps because they knew that any misbehaviour would be immediately reported to their formidable mother. Joby Fanon recalls that Edouard had a good influence on him and his brother and, at least for a while, he acted as their true father. It must have helped that there were few distractions in Le François. There were very few shops to steal from, and no cinema to sneak into without paying. Frantz's behaviour did not occasion much cause for reproach, but there was one untoward incident. One day in late 1939, he failed to return to school after lunch. Eventually, he did reappear, but looked distinctly ill. At first, Edouard thought he was drunk, and he almost struck him in anger. It was not until years later that he found out what had happened. Frantz had slipped out of school, behind the church and into the mairie, a pleasant colonial style building whose upper storey is constructed in wood. Somehow, he had heard that a post-mortem was going to be performed on the victim of a drowning and he was determined to be present.

Creeping unobserved into the room where the autopsy was to take place, he watched the dissection from beginning to end, and then staggered back to school feeling nauseous. As a medical student in Lyon, Fanon would never be good at dissection.

The only other notable incident known to have occurred in Le François came when Edouard took his class of twenty-three boys on an educational visit to the 'château' near Monnerot, a few kilometres to the north. The 'château' was in fact a typical plantation house, and the trip was an exercise in local history. The topic for the next day's work was, predictably enough, 'our day out'. Frantz handed in a carefully written essay centred on the story told to the class by the guide who had shown them around. It was one of the Caribbean's many tales of buried treasure, but also a reminder of the violence of slave-time: long ago, the *béké* who owned the château buried his gold in the cellar with the help of a slave. He then murdered his slave and buried him beside the gold to ensure that his ghost would protect the treasure from would-be robbers. Edouard Fanon was impressed with his nephew's work, and began to think that he might have some literary talent.

After almost two years in Le François, the brothers returned to Fort-de-France, which had not been invaded after all, and to the reopened lycée. A very self-confident Frantz had decided that it was time to sit his *baccalauréat* a year earlier than he had been expected to. He was successful in the written papers that made up the first part of the examination at this time. Events ensured that it would be some time before he sat the oral and was awarded the qualification that would allow him to go to university in France. The examination scripts were marked by teachers from Guadeloupe, and their visit provides another example of the young Fanon's sense of self and perception of others. One of the teachers, a philosophy specialist identified by Fanon only as 'Monsieur B.', was reputed to be 'excessively black', or 'blue' in local parlance, and Fanon and friends pursued him to his hotel to see just how black he was.[113] Their curiosity was no doubt stimulated by the common belief, which Fanon admitted to being unable to explain, that Martinicans were superior to, and 'less black' than Guadeloupeans. Guadeloupe had traditionally been less prosperous than Martinique, and its white population smaller. The historical explanation is that, whilst the British occupation of 1794–1802 meant that the

Convention's abolition of slavery in 1794, which proved to be temporary, did not apply in Martinique, it also spared the island the Terror instituted in Guadeloupe by Victor Hugues, the Jacobin commissioner. Unlike its sister island, Guadeloupe was quickly retaken by the French and 865 people were guillotined for having collaborated with the British. Many of the heads that fell belonged to white planters; a lot more whites fled the island, leaving Guadeloupe with a much 'blacker' population than Martinique.[114] Fanon's curiosity about a 'blue' philosopher from Guadeloupe, and the assumption of Martinican superiority that was its sub-text, was deeply rooted in colonial history.

It was on his return to Fort-de-France that Fanon first came into contact with Aimé Césaire.[115] Césaire was not yet the politician who was to become the most important man in Martinique for almost fifty years. And he was not yet the most famous poet to be associated with negritude. The first version of his great *Cahier d'un retour au pays natal* had appeared in the Parisian journal *Volontés* in August 1939 – not the most auspicious moment to publish that scream of rage – but it cannot have been widely read even in France let alone Martinique. It was the second edition of 1947 that was to make him famous. In October 1939, Césaire was a twenty-six-year-old teacher who had failed to pass his *agrégation* after three years at the Lycée Louis-le-Grand and four years at the Ecole Normale Supérieure in Paris. Césaire was born in 1913 in Basse-Pointe, a small settlement on the north Atlantic coast. The name means 'low point' and the village is on a low promontory that breaks the high cliffs of that dangerous coast. It was not a beautiful spot. The Corbière river flowed through it and across the volcanic beach – 'the sand is black, funereal, you've never seen such black sand' –[116] where dead cats and dogs were washed up from the sea: 'heaps of garbage rotting away, furtive rumps relieving themselves'. Basse-Pointe was at the heart of the plantation system of the north. With a surface area of up to 200 hectares, the plantations here were bigger than those in the south and they produced sugar on a large scale (with the decline in the sugar industry, the plantations have now diversified into the production of bananas and pineapples). During Césaire's childhood, the traditional plantation system was still largely intact and the sugar was cultivated by descendants of the Indian bonded labourers who replaced the old slaves from 1858 onwards. Basse-Pointe was (and is) home to Martinique's largest concentration of Indians or 'coulis'. Césaire's father was économe (steward) on the Eyma planta-tion, which was within walking distance of Basse-Pointe itself, and the future poet's early childhood was spent there. A line from the *Cahier* is presumably a memory of walking to school in Basse-Pointe: 'Me on a road as a child, chewing a sugar-cane root'.[117]

The *Cahier* gives a poetically overstated account of a childhood spent in rural poverty, but the degree of personal exaggeration does not make it an unrealistic account of other Martinican lives:

> At the end of the early morning, another little house that smells very bad in a very narrow street, a minuscule house which shelters in its entrails of rotten wood tens of rats and the turbulence of my six brothers and sisters, a cruel little house . . . and my mother whose tireless legs pedal, pedal day and night for our insatiable hunger, even at night I am woken up by those tireless legs ped-alling by night and the bitter biting into the soft flesh of the night of a Singer that my mother pedals, pedals for our hunger day and night.[118]

Césaire's mother did take in sewing, but the family was not especially poor. When he was twelve, Césaire won a scholarship to the Lycée Schoelcher and the entire family moved to Fort-de-France, where they lived in the rue Antoine Siger. The boy, whose father had now studied to gain a post in the tax service, made excellent progress at school; in 1934 he won a scholarship that took him to Louis-le-Grand, one of Paris's most prestigious schools, and then on to ENS.

Césaire may not have passed the agrégation that might have given him a university career, but he was a good teacher. The post at the Lycée Schoelcher was his first and he taught there for only four years before going into politics, but his own immodest account of what he achieved as a teacher is not an inaccurate one: 'I was a teacher. I gave courses on literature to *une classe de première* [equivalent to an English sixth form] . . . I had some disciples. That was very important. I trained a lot of young people – they're men now – and some became friends, others enemies, not that that matters much. They all came out of me, out of my teaching. I was a teacher, and quite an effective one it seems, and I undoubtedly influenced a whole generation.'[119] Many of his pupils, who included Edouard Glissant as well as Fanon, would have endorsed this self-appraisal. Marcel Manville speaks of Césaire's 'flamboyant' teaching, and of the impact of his introduction to Lautréamont, the surrealists, Malraux and Rimbaud. This was, he recalls, 'a literature charged with powder and contestation'.[120]

In 1958, Glissant paid tribute to his old teacher: 'For my generation, he was an exemplary pedagogue, a man who awakened consciences and taught us everything that was not normally taught in lycées: Lautréamont, Rimbaud, Malraux.' Glissant also recalled that he and his classmates would copy out Césaire's lessons, and then recopy them in their best writing into expensive notebooks. The hand-copied texts circulated through the lycée like clandestine documents.[121] Césaire could begin a class by entering the room and saying: 'Rimbaud: the power of revolt', and would declaim classical verse as he stood perched on a chair. His pupils dubbed him 'the green lizard' because he wore a green checked suit. This was a sign of affection; the green anoli lizard (*anolis carolinensis*) is a popular little creature.

Césaire has said little about his former pupil. The tribute to him that he published in *Présence Africaine* celebrates Fanon's revolutionary virtues in an almost florid rhetoric, but gives little sense of any personal affection, or indeed of any great personal acquaintance with its subject.[122] Césaire's one contribution to the 1982 Mémorial International held to honour Fanon, which his Parti Populaire Martiniquais did nothing to support, was a poem published in the PPM's paper *Le Progressiste*, but not included in the collected *Poésie*. It ends

> *par quelques-uns des mots obsédant une torpeur*
> *et l'accueil et l'éveil de chacun de nos maux*
> *je t'énonce*
> *FANON*
> *Tu rayes le fer*
> *Tu rayes le barreau des prisons*
> *Tu rayes le regard des bourreaux*
> *guerrier-silex*
> *vomi*
> *par la gueule du serpent de la mangrove*[123]

*(I speak your name*
*FANON*
*with some words that obsess a torpor*
*the welcome and awakening of all of our ills*
*You lash the iron*
*You lash the prison bars*
*You lash the gaze of the torturers*
*Silex-warrior*
*spat*
*from the mouth of the snake in the mangrove swamp)*

Although he would always be able to cite from memory long passages from the *Cahier d'un retour au pays natal* and Césaire's other poems, Fanon's attitude towards Césaire and the negritude with which he is associated was complex and ambivalent, and would change considerably between their first encounters and the publication of *Peau noire* in 1952. For the moment, the astonishing thing about Césaire was that: 'For the first time, we saw a lycée teacher, and therefore an apparently respectable man, saying to Antillean society that it is fine and good to be a *nègre*.'[124] It was a rare voice that dared to say this in late 1939, and attempts would soon be made to still it through censorship. The atmosphere in Fort-de-France had changed during Frantz and Joby's stay in Le François. The stinking trenches were still there on the Savanne, but the feverish panic of 1939 had given way to a sullen mood of depression. Martinique was now living '*An Tan Robè*', as the saying went in Creole. It was living 'in Robert time'.

It had, on the whole, been an unexceptional boyhood, typical of a child of the Martinican middle classes. Fanon was at times unruly and a worry to his parents, but he could also work hard and he did well at school. He enjoyed the usual pleasures of sport and going to the cinema. He had experienced no major traumas and, like any other child, perceived his own existence as perfectly normal. He was French and identified with the French culture in which he had been brought up and educated. There was nothing in his background to suggest that he would become a major icon of revolutionary Third Worldism. Although his father is said to have been a freemason – which, in French terms, made him a supporter of the secular left – his family had no history of political activism, or even of any interest in politics. When Fanon returned to Fort-de-France from Le François, the major traumas were still ahead of them. Life in *Tan Robè* would bring his first serious encounter with racism and would teach him a lesson that would be reinforced in the army and then again by life in metropolitan France: whilst he thought he was French like any other French person, many of his fellow French nationals saw him as simply one more *nègre*.

# 3

# *An Tan Robè*

ON 25 MARCH 1941, the Compagnie des Transports Maritimes' steamer *Capitaine Paul Lemerle* left Marseille, bound for Fort-de-France. The passenger manifest made for interesting reading. The 350 passengers on board included Victor Serge and his family, the novelist Anna Seghers, the Cuban painter Wilfredo Lam, the anthropologist Claude Lévi-Strauss, the painter André Masson, and André Breton, the magus of surrealism, who paced the few empty spaces on the crowded deck, dressed in a thick overcoat and looking 'like a blue bear'.[1] Their departure from Marseille was the first stage on a circuitous journey that would eventually take them all to the USA. Together with an Austrian metal-dealer and a Tunisian with a Degas canvas in his suitcase who claimed, somewhat improbably in the circumstances, to be going to New York for 'only a few days', Breton and Lévi-Strauss soon found that they had boarded a ship with only two passenger cabins and a total of seven proper bunks. Most of the passengers spent an uncomfortable voyage sleeping on the straw-mattressed bunk beds that had rapidly been constructed in the hold. All had good reasons for leaving France. In May 1940, the German army's rapid advance through the supposedly impenetrable Ardennes had routed the French. On 14 June, the Wehrmacht entered Paris unopposed.

The Third Republic which had changed Martinique so much no longer existed. On 16 June, Marshal Philippe Pétain, the eighty-year-old hero who had defended Verdun in 1916 and was now head of the newly established Etat français ('French State'), concluded that further resistance was impossible. On 22 June he signed a humiliating armistice with Germany that divided France into an occupied northern zone and a southern 'free' zone under the control of a 'Vichy regime' eager to collaborate with Germany.[2] Pétain's actions were perfectly constitutional, as he derived his powers from the last government of the Third Republic. Communists, Jews and surrealist subversives were, however, well aware that, whatever the constitutional status of the Etat français may have been, any life they could lead under Vichy would be an uncomfortable one. Leaving Vichy France was not easy. Exit visas had to be obtained. Affidavits from sponsors in the intended host countries had to be provided to support the application for a visa. Those who, like Breton, hoped to go to America, had to obtain appropriate papers from an uncooperative American Embassy. It took Breton months to complete all the formalities and to find a ship.

Life on the *Capitaine Paul Lemerle* was not easy either. The ship limped across the Mediterranean to Oran, west to the Straits of Gibraltar and on to Casablanca and then Dakar before heading out into the Atlantic. So much time was spent avoiding British patrols and hugging the coastline that Lévi-Strauss was convinced that she was carrying some clandestine cargo. After a month at sea, the ill-assorted company reached Martinique, where they had an unfriendly reception. For the military interrogators who boarded the ship, the non-French passengers were enemies, whilst their French companions were traitors who had deserted their country in its hour of need.[3] Lévi-Strauss was accused of being 'a Jewish freemason in the pay of the Americans'.[4] Denied the baths they were longing for, all but three of the passengers – a rich *béké*, the mysterious Tunisian and Lévi-Strauss himself – were interned under armed guard in the Lazaret camp on the south side of Fort-de-France's great natural harbour. As its name suggests, Le Lazaret was once a leper hospital; the site it occupied on the Pointe-du-Bout peninsula is now a concrete hotel complex.

The internees were finally released, not because of humanitarian concerns on the part of the authorities, but because local tradesmen in

Fort-de-France argued that their continued detention was depriving the town of a potential source of income.[5] As it happened, there was little for them to spend their money on. Lévi-Strauss was not impressed by what he saw on landing in Fort-de-France for the first time:

> At two o'clock in the afternoon, Fort-de-France was a dead town: it was impossible to believe that anyone lived in the ramshackle buildings which bordered the long market-place planted with palm trees and overrun with weeds, and which was more like a stretch of waste-ground with, in its middle, an apparently forgotten statue, green with neglect, of Joséphine Tascher de la Pagerie, later known as Joséphine de Beauharnais.[6]

Breton's experience of Martinique was equally depressing. The local students he met in a bar and who so kindly offered to show him around proved to be working for the police. The shops were virtually empty and all sold the same cheap and nasty goods, and the few bookshops offered for sale only a score of books so tattered as to be unreadable. Cheap white rum distracted the most disinherited of the local population from the bitter thoughts that might otherwise have come to their minds. In the spring of 1941, Martinique was, Breton concluded, a poor advertisement for three centuries of French colonialism.[7] All the European visitors he spoke to were struck by the destitution and delapidation they saw in Martinique. Breton was, however, more impressed than Lévi-Strauss by the 'blue-tinted statue of Joséphine' with her breasts spilling out of her high-waisted Empire dress. He thought that it placed the town under 'a tender, feminine sign'.[8]

As he wandered through the forlorn streets of Fort-de-France, Breton did at last find something to read. He was looking for a ribbon to give to his daughter Aube but the draper's shop in which he found it also had something else on display. It was a little magazine, which Breton bought for twelve francs. Having seen something of the intellectual poverty of Robert's Martinique, he expected to be disappointed:

> I couldn't believe my eyes: but what was being said there was what had to be said, not only as well as it could be said but as loudly as it could be said! All the grimacing shadows were torn

apart and dispelled; all the lies and all the derision turned to rags: the voice of a man which had not been broken or drowned out stood up like a sword of light. Aimé Césaire was the name of the man speaking.[9]

Breton had stumbled across the first issue of *Tropiques*, which was published in April 1941.[10] Césaire's short 'introduction' was in itself stunning:

A silent, sterile land. It's our land I am talking about. By the Caribbean Sea, my ear takes stock of the terrifying silence of Man. Europe, Africa, Asia. I can hear the steel screaming, the tomtoms in the bush, the temple praying among the banyans. And I know that it is man who is speaking. And I still listen, keep listening. But here, the monstrous atrophy of the voice, the centuries-long despondency, the prodigious dumbness. No town. No art. No poetry . . . A death worse than death, where the living wander. Elsewhere, the sciences progress, philosophies renew themselves and aesthetics succeed one another. And on this land, our hand sows seeds in vain. No town. No art. No poetry. Not a seed. Not a shoot. Or only the hideous leprosy of imitations. In truth, a sterile, silent land . . . Wherever we look, the darkness is gaining ground. The lights go out one after another. The circle of darkness closes in, amidst the screams of men and the howling of wild animals. And yet we are some of those who say *no* to the darkness. We know that the salvation of the world depends on us too. That the world needs its sons, no matter who they are. The humblest . . .[11]

The shop in which Breton bought *Tropiques* belonged to the sister of René Ménil who, along with Césaire and his wife Suzanne, was the main inspiration behind the journal. All three were teachers at the Lycée Schoelcher. Their paths were to diverge, with Césaire becoming Martinique's best-known poet-politician, whilst Ménil became the Martinican Communist Party's chief spokesman on cultural affairs,[12] but for the moment they formed the nucleus of a highly innovative undertaking. Given the small scale of Foyalais society, it was not difficult for Breton to arrange to meet both men. The final product of the meeting was Breton's essay 'A Great Black Poet', which was printed as the preface to the bilingual edition of *Cahier d'un retour au pays natal/Memorandum on my Martinique* published in New York by Brentano's in 1947. Here, Breton remarks of Césaire: 'This is a black man who handles the French language better than any white man can handle it today.'[13] Césaire did not take exception to this, and Breton's essay was first published in the May 1944 issue of *Tropiques*. Although it now sounds patronizing, the remark was well-meaning; André Breton has been accused of many things but casual racism is not one of them. Fanon, though, took the view that there was no reason for this to be said.[14] No one would describe Breton as 'a great white poet', and Césaire was not writing in a foreign language.

Eleven issues of *Tropiques* were published between 1941 and 1945. Exploiting elements of surrealism, psychoanalysis and anthropology, it began to take a new look at Martinican realities and to dig beneath the veneer of universal French culture. To that extent, it anticipates the negritude with which Césaire was so closely associated in the post-war years, and which both attracted and repelled Fanon. Writing in the April 1942 issue, Suzanne Césaire, who appears to have quite disappeared from public life after 1945, made an astonishing analysis of the 'discontents' of Martinican civilization. The desire to imitate French culture that was originally a defence against an oppressive society, was now unconscious:

> No 'evolved' Martinican is willing to admit that he is no more than an imitation, because his current situation appears to him to be natural, spontaneous and born of his most legitimate aspirations. To that extent, he is being sincere. He really does not KNOW that he is an imitation. He is *ignorant* of his own nature, but it exists all the same . . . The hysteric is unaware of the fact that he is merely *imitating* a disease . . . Similarly, analysis shows us that the attempt to adapt to a foreign style that is made of the Martinican, has the effect of creating a state of pseudo-civilization which we can describe as abnormal or teratoid.[15]

There is no indication in his published work that Frantz Fanon ever read Suzanne Césaire's essay, and whether or not he ever read *Tropiques* must remain a matter for conjecture. It is, on the other hand, almost inconceivable that he did not know something about it. The little journal was produced by teachers at the lycée he attended and, whilst he was not taught by Ménil, he was in contact with Césaire. René Ménil is mentioned only once in *Peau noire, masques blancs*. A single quotation is borrowed by Fanon from Leiris's 'Martinique, Guadeloupe, Haiti', and it comes from Ménil's 'Situation de la poésie aux Antilles', published in *Tropiques* in May 1944. Ménil is describing his 'analytic and historical examination of the Antillean mentality'. It reveals that:

The contemporary *super-ego* of the Antillean people, which was shaped, let us not forget, in the not-so-far-off good old days of slavery, is the result of an operation in three parts. First, the traumatic repression of the way of life of the negro slaves (African totemism): this explains the centuries-old charge of anxiety which . . . drowns the collective consciousness in the Antilles. Secondly, the replacement, within the consciousness of the slaves, of the repressed spirit by an agency representing the master, an agency established within the depths of the collectivity, and which keeps it under guard in the way that a garrison keeps guard over a conquered town: this explains the Antillean people's inferiority complex. Thirdly, the negro turns his aggressivity against himself. As it can find so little expression in a society founded upon exceptional cruelty, that aggressivity is turned against him and strangles him within his own consciousness: this explains the existence of a certain masochism amongst the Antillean people.[16]

Like Leiris, Fanon mentions only the second of Ménil's three stages.[17] This strongly suggests that he had not read Ménil's article itself; had he done so, he would surely have picked up the reference to aggressivity. He clearly recognized his own concerns in the passage he found in Leiris, and those concerns have to be recognized as being profoundly Martinican.

*Tropiques* was a rare beacon of hope in an otherwise bleak Fort-de-France and it was soon extinguished, if only temporarily. All those who arrived on the *Capitaine Paul Lemerle* found their enforced stay in Martinique frustrating. Rumours about boats that were about to leave inevitably proved to be unfounded, and obtaining visas from the Dominican consulate was a slow process. On 16 May, Breton at last boarded the *Presidente Trujillo,* which took him to Guadeloupe and then the Dominican Republic, from whence he finally reached New York. Lévi-Strauss spent more time in Martinique. He had time to witness Martinican justice at work when he attended the trial of a peasant who had bitten off part of the ear of an opponent during a fight. It took five minutes for the three judges to sentence him to eight years' imprisonment. Writing about the incident in 1955, Lévi-Strauss commented: 'Even today, no dream, however fantastic, can inspire me with such a feeling of incredulity.'[18] Had he spent more time in Martinique, his credulity would have been very strained. Although the atmosphere was sinister, with the police spinning webs of deceit around everyone, the anthropologist enjoyed what he saw of the countryside and especially the 'huge, soft, feathery fronds of the tree-ferns, rising above the living fossils of their trunks'.[19] He finally negotiated a passage on a Swedish banana boat bound for Puerto Rico and was eventually allowed to enter the United States. The *Capitaine Paul Lemerle*'s erstwhile passengers had the luck – and the requisite papers – to get away from Martinique. The local population was not so fortunate.

Lévi-Strauss and Breton had escaped Vichy France only to land in a very strange time and place. They had briefly encountered the Martinique of '*Tan Robè*' or 'Robert Time'. *Tan Robè* and its aftermath had an incalculable effect on the young Fanon, who now began to learn precisely what it meant to be a black Martinican wearing a white French mask. 'Robè' was the Creolized name given by the locals to Admiral Georges Robert, High Commissioner for the French West Indies and Commander-in-Chief of the West Atlantic Fleet. Born in 1875, and a former commander of the Mediterranean squadron, Robert had reached retirement age in 1937 but volunteered for active service in August 1939. Awarded the rank of a Five-Star Admiral by Georges Mendel, the Minister for the Colonies, he sailed from Brest on the cruiser *Jeanne d'Arc* on 1 September 1939 and reached his new and important post a fortnight later. His appointment was in keeping with a pre-war plan to create a Western Atlantic theatre of operations centred on Fort-de-France.[20] Shortly after the armistice of June 1940, the forces at Robert's disposal – the *Jeanne d'Arc*, three auxiliary cruisers and one submarine – were reinforced by the arrival of the aircraft carrier *Béarn*, carrying one hundred planes purchased from the American government, and then the cruiser *Emile Bertin* with 300 tons of gold from the Bank of France. Protecting the gold, and not establishing a theatre of operations, was to be the main task of Robert's men.

Under the terms of the armistice, France retained full sovereignty over her colonies and the forces stationed in them. When General Charles de Gaulle rejected the armistice on 18 June 1940 and called for continued resistance in a speech that was in legal terms a call for sedition, the colonies therefore took on a new importance. As Fanon's childhood friend Charles Cézette likes to recall with an ironic smile, the first 'Free French' were France's colonial subjects.[21] In his appeal to the nation de Gaulle stressed that 'France is not alone. She has an immense Empire behind her.'[22] France's Indian and Pacific territories rallied to his side almost immediately. In August, the colonial authorities in Chad declared their support for de Gaulle, and Cameroon, the Congo and Ubangi-Shari (the modern Central African Republic) followed the example set by Governor Félix Eboué, a black civil servant from Guyane who had spent his entire career as an administrator in Equatorial Africa before becoming Governor of first Guadeloupe and then Chad in 1938. He was the first black to reach this elevated rank. Fanon had little patience with West Indians who became colonial administrators in Africa, but admired Eboué who addressed the Africans he met at the Brazzaville Conference of 1944 as 'My dear brothers'. Fanon comments: 'This fraternity was not evangelical, it was based on colour.'[23]

News of the armistice and of de Gaulle's defiance reached Martinique on 24 June, just over a month after Fanon's fifteenth birthday. The immediate reaction of the island's mayors and the Conseil Général was to pledge Martinique's 'continuation of the struggle alongside the Allies with the French overseas Empire' and a telegram was drafted to that effect.[24] The text begins: 'Meeting in Fort-de-France on 24 June 1940, the Mayors and members of the Conseil Général proclaim in the name of the island's population Martinique's unfailing loyalty to France, her readiness to consent to the ultimate sacrifices in order to achieve the final victory by continuing the struggle alongside the Allies and the French Overseas Empire.'[25] The text faithfully captured the patriotic fervour of the moment but its signatories were to be frustrated. Robert flatly refused to send the message on the grounds that, whilst doing so might have flattered its signatories, it was both 'inoperative and inopportune'. On 26 June, he issued a proclamation of his own:

> The armistice is about to come into force. Metropolitan France finds it impossible to continue the struggle, and although it was defended inch by inch with the most admirable heroism, her ancient land is strewn with dead bodies, ruins and immense pain.
>
> Such is the situation. As a result, we wish more than ever to be French. We wish to be French and we will remain French in order to support the mother-land in her terrible ordeal, and in order to put all our forces at her disposal so that she may be delivered and may rise again.[26]

In practice, this meant support for Pétain and the collaborationist Vichy government. One of the effects of the French presence in Martinique has long been the construction in the tropics of a miniaturized France. The theatre whose ruins can be seen in St Pierre was a small version of the theatre in Bordeaux. One of the more improbable sights to be seen from the centre of Fort-de-France is the gleaming white building in the green hills to the north. This is Balata's 'Eglise de Montmartre', a scaled-down replica of Paris's Sacré-Coeur built in 1935 to honour the memory of the Martinican soldiers who died in the First World War. In 1940, Robert began the formation of a miniature Vichy regime, with himself cast in the role of Pétain in a white tropical uniform.

In international terms, Robert's position was not a strong one and he was forced to negotiate with the Allies, who viewed him as a potential enemy. His relationship with the Royal Navy soured when the British bombed and sank the French fleet in the Algerian port of Mers-el-Kéber in July 1940 to forestall the possibility of its coming under German control, and he feared that his own ships might face a similar fate. He was aware that the US press was calling for the occupation of Martinique, but probably did not know of the existence of an Allied plan – codenamed 'Asterisk' – to provoke an uprising on the island if he refused to negotiate a neutral settlement.[27] In August 1940, Robert entered into negotiations with Admiral Greenslade of the US navy. The initial negotiations ended in failure and Martinique was blockaded by the US cruisers that Breton and Lévi-Strauss saw as the *Capitaine Paul Lemerle* sailed into Fort-de-France. Operation Asterisk was quietly shelved when the attempt to land Free French forces in Senegal ended in a disastrous fiasco.[28] The stalemate in Martinique lasted until the Japanese attack on Pearl Harbor on 7 December 1941 brought the US into the war, and tensions increased even further as the Vichy government in France collaborated more and more closely with the Germans.

In May 1942, the Allies finally recognized Robert's internal authority in exchange for his assurance that the ships in Fort-de-France's harbour would be immobilized under US supervision, and that the planes on the *Bearn* remained grounded and were made incapable of flying. The famous gold bullion was to be placed in Fort Dessaix, which was just outside Fort-de-France, for the duration. One clause of the agreement had immediate repercussions for the local population: all naval personnel were to be based permanently on shore. The population of the capital increased dramatically and its ethnic balance shifted. In his retrospective account of wartime Martinique, Fanon speaks of the island being 'submerged' by 10,000 men, but in his memoirs, Robert speaks of 2,500 sailors and a similar number of colonial infantry.[29] The latter figure is the more accurate (and is confirmed by other sources[30]), but Fanon's inflated statistics are an accurate reflection of what he thought he saw when he returned from his exile in Le François to a town that was suddenly crowded with unusually high numbers of sailors. He had simply never seen so many white people and quite understandably overestimated their numbers.

Robert's internal authority was quickly established and that of Martinique's Governor overruled. A grandiosely named Légion des combattants et des volontaires de la Révolution Nationale was established to promote Vichy values,[31] and it became a regular participant in the parades and military displays so beloved by the Etat français. Robert's attitude towards his new subjects was dismissively paternalistic – like all 'native populations', Martinicans were basically 'good and simple', but they were also 'infantile, superstitious and easily led astray'[32] – and he had no qualms about removing their elected representatives from the Conseil

Général. They were replaced by appointees chosen from lists drawn up by the new mayors, who were themselves appointed and not elected. All the appointees were from very specific socio-economic categories: landowners, industrialists, artisans, reserve officers and veterans, mothers and fathers involved in charitable works.[33] All were white. In the eyes of the majority of the population, the *békés* were taking their revenge on the black and mulatto population with the full backing of the civil authorities and the church.

The nomination of councillors such as this was a faithful reflection of Vichy's corporatism, which was designed to overcome the divisions that were supposedly introduced by class loyalties and political parties. As in France itself, the Republican motto of 'Freedom, Equality, Fraternity' was replaced by Vichy's 'Fatherland, Family, Labour'. In 1940, the absurdity of appointing a ship's captain to represent the interest of the workers of Fort-de-France was tragic rather than comic but other aspects of *tan Robè* did border on the farcical. While the trenches were being dug on the Savanne, a blackout was imposed in anticipation of air raids, even though it was far from clear where the Luftwaffe's fighters would actually take off from. Panic spread when German submarines were seen in Martinican waters. The anticipated invasion never came and the only Germans to set foot on the island during the war were the two wounded sailors who were landed from a submarine in February 1942. Their story figures prominently in Martinican novels about *tan Robè*.[34]

The new newspaper, *La Petite Patrie*, quickly began to promote a personality cult: Admiral Robert was 'our Pétain transposed. Let us never speak of him other than with admiration and respect. For us, he is the *guide*, and he is pure and beyond reproach; the resolute and paternal chief; the worthy representative of the France that loves and understands us.'[35] Photographs and portraits of Robert were soon on sale in the shops and markets, and in many homes they hung alongside pictures of Pétain himself. Vichy's ideology placed enormous emphasis on the family – hence the appointment to office of 'mothers and fathers of families' – and Robert himself became Martinique's symbolic father when he agreed to become the godfather of a local child. As a British historian of Martinique notes, it was certainly no accident that the child was from Schoelcher, a *commune* on the outskirts of Fort-de-France that is named after the 'liberator' who freed the slaves.[36] Robert became both a symbolic father and the liberator who would dispel the dark mood of 1940. That mood was captured in a poem published in a newspaper:

> *Peuples noirs, c'en est fait; le malheur est sur nous;*
> *Celle qui se penchait sur notre triste sort,*
> *Qui guidait notre marche et nous montrait la voie,*
> *Celle qui tendrement préparait notre essor,*
> *La France, en butte aux trahisons, succombe et ploie*
>
> *Celle qui sur nos fronts faisait luire l'espoir*
> *La grande nation puissante et généreuse*
> *Qui, seule dans le monde, aimait vraiment le Noir,*
> *Doit subir du Germain l'odieuse tutelle.*[37]
>
> *(Black peoples, it is over; misfortune has befallen us;*
> *The France who watched over our sad fate,*
> *Who guided our steps and showed us the way,*
> *Who was tenderly preparing us for our rise,*
> *Has been exposed to treason, bends her knee and succumbs.*
>
> *The France who made our faces shine with hope,*
> *The great nation, powerful and generous,*
> *The only nation in the world to truly love the black man,*
> *Must submit to the odious sway of the German.)*

As in metropolitan France, paternalism went hand in hand with repression. Freemasonry was made illegal. The small Communist Party was proscribed. Vichy's 'Jewish Statute' was introduced and enforced, even though Martinique's Jewish population was so tiny as to be statistically insignificant. The Statute excluded Jews from senior positions in the civil service, the officer corps, the ranks of non-commissioned officers and all professions that might influence public opinion. A quota system was devised to limit the number of Jews in the liberal professions.[38] By August 1942, a total of sixteen Jews in Fort-de-France had registered, as required, with the police.[39] It was forbidden to listen in public or in private to BBC radio, whose broadcasts were relayed from Dominica to the north and St Lucia to the south. A law adopted in July 1940 imposed the death penalty on anyone convicted of entering the service of a foreign power, and the same penalty was later extended to those who, like Fanon, joined the Free French forces outside Martinique. The student-policemen encountered by Breton were part of an island-wide network of agents and spies who encouraged the denunciation of subversives.[40] *Tropiques* was, like all journals and newspapers, subject to pre-publication vetting by a heavy-handed Information Service and when, in May 1943, Suzanne Césaire requested a paper ration to print a new issue, she was refused it on the grounds that it was 'revolutionary, racial and sectarian'.[41] *Tropiques* was banned. Publication began once more when *tan Robè* was over.

The attempt to establish a local version of the Vichy regime was not popular with the majority black population of Martinique. The countless portraits of Pétain that André Breton saw on the walls of Fort-de-France in 1941 were regularly slashed with knives, and he quickly became convinced that the vast majority of the working population were hoping for an Allied victory. He was probably right. Many black Martinicans would have agreed with the basic argument of Curidon's *Mon Pays, Mon Pays*: the best defence against the white plantocracy was the extension of republican institutions, and it was the power of those very institutions that was being eroded by Robert. The black population was not, according to Breton, taken in by the patronizing use of Creole to promote the image of '*Li bon papa Pétain*' ('good father Pétain').[42] Martinique was both hungry and unhappy. The prudence dictated by the repressive atmosphere meant, however, that there were as yet few acts of defiance.

One of the reasons for the sullen discontent was the rise of overt racism. Food rationing had been introduced, and the queues in the half-empty shops were segregated, as they never had been in pre-war Martinique. In normal years, the crews of visiting naval ships had only a week's shore leave, but now they were permanently on shore with little to do. They could now take off their masks and behave as 'authentic racists'.[43] What Lévi-Strauss described as the 'excessive drinking of punch',[44] the increase in prostitution, and the rise in sexual tensions as local girls like Mayotte Capécia's heroine consorted with white and relatively rich officers, all contributed to the increasingly ugly mood. The strong naval presence caused a housing shortage, and property prices soared. Food shortages and the rise of the black market fuelled discontent, both in the capital and the countryside. The monoculture of sugar co-existed with small-scale agriculture geared towards self-sufficiency, but the economy could not really cope with the influx of non-productive sailors. A character in Glissant's novel *Le Quatrième Siècle* describes a typical foraging party arriving in trucks at a small *habitation* and taking away all the yams, breadfruit and bananas they could carry. 'A whip was being wielded against the blacks.'[45]

The dominant memory of the war years is that of hunger, and it has become part of a collective memory that can be shared even by those who are too young to have lived through the war. In his semi-autobiographical *Ravines du devant-jour*, Raphaël Confiant, who was born in 1951, recalls that when he refused to eat his soup as a child, his grandmother would tell him that if there was ever a return to 'tan Robè', he would eat it because he would understand what hunger really meant.[46] The blockade had disastrous effects, which are described by Chamoiseau in his novel *Texaco*: 'We had to do without oil, salt, dried vegetables, salted meat, soap, garlic, shoes. The poor could no longer find wood, corrugated tin or nails. Coal was becoming scarce, and more and more expensive. Those who lit a fire no longer had matches and did all that was possible to keep it glowing ad aeternam.'[47] In 1939, 76 per cent of all foodstuffs had been imported, and those imports had now ceased. Even if there had been no blockade, things would have been difficult. Most of Martinique's food imports came from France, and France's agricultural produce was now being diverted to Germany. Between 1940 and the end of the war, retail prices in Fort-de-France rose by 600 per cent, and in 1943, the kilo of cod that had cost 3.8 francs in 1939 had risen in price to 32 francs.[48] By 1943, near-famine conditions were being reported in the countryside. And yet Glissant, adopting a famous phrase from Sartre, claims that the people of Martinique had never been so free as they were during the 'Occupation'.[49] Isolation meant that the island had to make a bid for self-sufficiency for the first time since 1635. Some of the land that had been left derelict by the decline in sugar production was brought back into food production. A more or less satisfactory substitute for cooking oil was made from coconuts. Shoes and sandals were made from old tyres. After three hundred years of colonialism, it was finally realized that Martinique was surrounded by salt water and that its climate was such that salt water could easily be evaporated to produce salt. Salt did not have to be imported from France.[50]

By 1942, a traditional sign of revolt had reappeared. The cane fields were being set ablaze at harvest time. This form of primitive rebellion was made a capital offence.[51] It was at roughly this time that Fanon saw something so strange that he could scarcely believe his eyes: a crowd of Martinicans refusing to bare their heads as the 'Marseillaise' was played, and armed sailors forcing them to stand to attention in silence.[52] He concluded that his fellow islanders had 'assimilated the France of the sailors to the bad France, and the "Marseillaise" those men respected was not their "Marseillaise"'. Scuffles between local youths and Robert's sailors became increasingly common, and Fanon is reported to have been involved in some of them. Manville has described how, as they were going home after playing football one morning, he, Fanon and Mosole encountered two sailors kicking a youth they had knocked to the ground on the Savanne. Fanon immediately ran to help him. Less impulsive than their friend, Manville and Mosole intervened to ask what was going on. The sailors said that the boy had tried to rob them, and then walked off. The three friends took the boy to the police for first aid, but never got a real explanation for the incident.[53] Intervening in a fight like this was obviously dangerous. Had there been more sailors about, the schoolboys might well have taken a bad beating themselves. Fanon and his family also took risks by breaking the law to listen to the BBC in secret. Like many a boy around the world, Frantz plotted the movements of the Allied armies on a map. He almost provoked a quarrel with a friend whose father was Italian by rejoicing at the British victory at Benghazi and making disparaging remarks about Italians, yet either he was badly informed at the time or his memory failed him when he wrote *Peau noire, masques blancs*: it was Wavell and not Montgomery who took Benghazi from the Italians on 7 February 1940.[54]

On 3 March 1943, Governor Nicol issued a circular to the mayors of Martinique, noting that a number of boats had recently been stolen. It was, he suggested, advisable that all boats should be beached at points where they could be kept under watch at night, and that it was unwise for boat-owners to leave oars, sails or other tackle on the beach after dark.[55] It was not only boats that were disappearing. Queries about young men who had not been seen for a while were becoming increasingly common, and the standard answer to them was: '*Sill pay neyè, i Ouchingtone*' ('If he hasn't drowned, he's in Washington'). A new form of *marronage* had emerged, and young dissidents were leaving Martinique by clandestine means. Their choice of destination was restricted to St Lucia or Dominica, where they could join the Free French. St Lucia and Dominica are, respectively, only twenty-seven and thirty-five kilometres away from Martinique, but the journey was dangerous. The dissidents (*dissidence* is the Martinican equivalent to *résistance*) travelled in open boats propelled by oars or sails. The boats were the locally built craft normally used for in-shore fishing. Brightly painted and with high prows, they still bore a distinct resemblance to the dug-out canoes they had replaced long ago. The seas around Martinique are home to populations of sharks, and both the St Lucia Channel to the south and the Martinique Passage to the north are treacherously dangerous stretches of water where powerful Atlantic currents converge in narrow straits. In purely maritime terms, it would have been safer to leave from Fort-de-France itself, but the strong possibility of detection there meant that most of the clandestine departures were from Sainte-Anne and Le Diamant in the south, or Saint-Pierre and Le Prêcheur on the northern Caribbean coast. Some of the *passeurs* or smugglers who carried the dissidents on their boats were acting out of patriotism, and some were themselves dissidents, but others were less altruistic and charged high prices for their services. There were rumours that some would-be *dissidents* had been thrown overboard by unscrupulous *passeurs* and left to drown or to deal with the sharks as best they could. An estimated 4,500 Martinicans made the dangerous voyage and they were joined by some 500 metropolitan Frenchmen, most of whom had deserted from their ships in Fort-de-France.[56]

Fanon left no written account of his departure from Martinique in early 1943, and seems to have been as reluctant to speak of it as he was to talk of his subsequent wartime experiences in France. After the event, a disillusioned Fanon would tell his parents that he had left Fort-de-France because he still believed in the 'obsolete ideal' of French patriotism,[57] but in 1943 he clearly still believed that the cause of France was his cause. His place was not, he thought, on the sidelines, but 'in the heart of the problem', or in other words, in the war.[58] Charles Cézette, who did not go to Dominica but did fight with the Free French, puts it with heartbreaking simplicity: 'We were twenty, and we believed in France.'[59] Fanon ignored the warnings of Joseph Henri, who had taught him at the Lycée Schoelcher and who once studied in Paris with Alain, the anti-militarist who converted so many young men to radical pacifism. He also ignored the warnings of his brother Joby, who can still cite Henri's words from memory: 'Fire burns and war kills. The wives of dead heroes marry men who are alive and well. What is happening in Europe is no concern of ours. When white men kill each other, it is a blessing for blacks.' According to his brother, Fanon was outraged by this and called his teacher a 'bastard'. At seventeen, he was still convinced that 'freedom is indivisible'. He would, however, recall a further piece of advice from the same teacher: 'When you hear people speaking ill of the Jews, keep your ears pricked; they're talking about you.'[60] The decision to leave for Dominica was an early indication of both a character trait and a pattern of behaviour. The decision was taken suddenly, with little consultation and little foreknowledge of its consequences. It was also irrevocable.

Fanon's convictions may have been sound, but his finances were not. He was still at school and had no source of income, and whilst finding a *passeur* was not difficult, finding the means to pay him was. The solution was a temporary return to delinquency. Fanon's father had slowly accumulated sufficient clothing coupons to buy a bolt of cloth and was looking forward to wearing the suit he would have made from it. Fanon appropriated the cloth, and sold it to pay for his clandestine passage to Dominica. For the rest of his life, Casimir Fanon (who died in 1947) would complain to his wife about how 'her son' had stolen his suit. To make matters worse, Frantz's departure was planned for the day of his brother Félix's wedding in Morne-Rouge. A great deal of money and a great many precious food coupons had been spent to celebrate the occasion. A bullock, two sheep and a pig had been slaughtered, and between 150 and 200 guests were expected. Joby tried to argue with him, but Fanon was adamant and made his way to Le Prêcheur. Bitterly disappointed, his mother mourned the loss of two sons on the same day: one to a wife, and one to de Gaulle's Free French.[61] Precisely how Fanon made his way from Morne-Rouge, a pleasant town on the southeastern slopes of Montagne Pelée, to the beach where he met his *passeur* after dark that night is not on record but, although short, it cannot have been an easy journey as he must have had to make his way on foot across the lower slopes of the volcano and through steep ravines choked with dense tropical vegetation.

The absence of any first-hand account makes it difficult to trace Fanon's movements after his secretive and illegal departure from Martinique. He reached Dominica safely and was, like any other clandestine arrival, interrogated about his reasons for trying to join the Free French. He underwent very basic military training. He did not, however, follow the other dissidents south to St Lucia, on to Trinidad and finally the United States, from whence they shipped out for the battlefields of Europe. At seventeen, he may have been considered too young for active service. More significantly, events had overtaken his plans, and Martinique was no longer an outpost of the Vichy regime. *Tan Robè* was at last over. Fanon's adventure ended in bathos. After a few weeks, he was repatriated to Martinique and went back to school.

In the spring of 1943, pro-Gaullist slogans could be seen scrawled on the walls of Fort-de-France and in June leaflets were calling on the population to join in illegal demonstrations to be held in both the capital and St Pierre. A Comité Martiniquais de Libération came into being. The colonial infantry units based at Balata, just outside Fort-de-France, were becoming restive and their commanding officer Henri Tourtet was rumoured to have pro-Gaullist sympathies. Tourtet was a career officer with a deep sense of loyalty to his superiors and therefore a very reluctant rebel, but his decision to move against Robert's sailors was the decisive factor in Martinique's 'June Days'. Robert's position was increasingly untenable, and his actions increasingly irrational. He had on three occasions refused to obey Vichy's orders to scuttle the ships under his command, and was still convinced that he might have to use them to defend Martinique from an American invasion.[62] Faced with popular unrest in the streets and a growing mutiny in Balata, he was forced to negotiate a 'change of regime' at the end of June. In order to avoid bloodshed, he now agreed to surrender his authority to a French plenipotentiary.[63]

On 14 July, the destroyer *Terrible* docked in Fort-de-France and Henri Hoppenot, representing the Free French, announced to the delirious crowd on the Savanne: 'I bring you back France and the Republic.' Speaking on behalf of the Comité de Libération, Dr Emmanuel Véry went on:

> Henri Hoppenot has come to deliver us from the yoke of the men of Vichy, who are Hitler's lackeys. For us, he is the France that made the Revolution of 1789, the France that flung in the face of the world the immortal principles of the Rights of Man and the Citizen, the generous France of 1848, the France which, after the defeats of 1940, and faithful to her past and traditions, took up the fight once more alongside the Allies, the France which we can never divorce from the Republic, because we cannot forget that it was the Republic that made us men and citizens.[64]

In September 1944, Admiral Georges Robert was sentenced by the courts of the Provisional French Government to ten years' hard labour for hampering the French war effort. In October 1946, he was released on bail after suffering a brain haemorrhage and eighteen months later his sentence was quashed because of irregularities during the original trial.[65] In 1950, he published his own self-serving account of the last days of *tan Robè*:

> This was a time when the idea spread throughout the island that General de Gaulle was a black general who, just like Toussaint L'Ouverture, wanted to liberate people of colour from the yoke of the white land-owners. To complement this fable, *dissidence* was either the General's wife – and, like him, coloured – or a neighbouring island under his control. And so people left *en dissidence*, in the way that one went to Guadeloupe for a change of air and to find better conditions of existence than those prevailing in Martinique, which was subject to the rigours of the American blockade. And this later came to be known as the Resistance.[66]

The story of those who believed that *dissidence* was de Gaulle's wife has become part of the collective memory of *tan Robè*, but its meaning shifts considerably depending on whether it is told by the ever-patronizing Robert, or by a self-aware Martinican with a critical perspective on his or her history.

A fortnight after the arrival of Hoppenot, the decision was taken to raise a local unit of volunteers to fight alongside the Free French and the Allies. It was a light infantry battalion known as the 5ème Bataillon de Marche des Antilles (5BMA) but, although recruitment began almost immediately, its actual formation was delayed by a shortage of weapons and trained men.[67] It was not ready to leave Martinique until the following March. Young men volunteered for all the reasons that lead young men to volunteer for war. Some wanted adventure, others glory. Some no doubt saw the war as a means of fulfilling the classic Martinican dream of leaving the island, which really had come to resemble a prison. Fanon's own motives were grounded in the conviction that his own freedom, that of Martinique and that of France were inextricably bound up together. His decision to enlist meant that he once more had to go against his family's wishes and the advice of his elder brother. He again ignored Henri's warnings about the fire that burns and the wars that kill. Manville recalled that Fanon told his teacher that, when freedom was at stake, 'we are all involved, white, black or yellow'.[68] He was not alone in believing this. His fellow volunteers included Charles Cézette, Marcel Manville and Pierre Marie-Claire Mosole, who had also made the dangerous voyage to Dominica.[69] As they prepared to board ship, Manville promised a tearful Eléanore Fanon: 'Yes, yes, Madame Fanon, I will look after Frantz for you', but he was only too aware that his size – and Manville was a big man – could offer no one any protection in a modern battle.[70] This must have been the one occasion in his life in which the voluble Marcel Manville was almost lost for words.

At 14.00 hours on 12 March 1944, the *Oregon*, a cargo boat converted into a makeshift troop ship, slipped out of Fort-de-France with a lone Dutch torpedo boat as an escort. The 1,000 men on board were under the command of Tourtet and, with the exception of the officers and some of the NCOs, all were black. The *békés'* attempt to create a local version of the Vichy regime had ended in failure, and they were not about to fight for de Gaulle's Free French. No *béké* volunteered. Fanon, who at eighteen was the youngest man on the *Oregon*, muttered to Manville that they should be flying the black flag. As they sailed out of the harbour, the elated volunteers sang in Creole: '*Hitler, nous ké roule en bas morne-là*' ('Hitler, we're going to knock you off your hilltop').[71] The elation masked fear. Manville recalls that he and Fanon were afraid that they were going to a watery grave rather than to the glory of battle. Such fears were not entirely unfounded. The *Oregon* carried only the light weaponry of a transport, and her tiny escort could have provided little protection against a submarine attack. Most of the men on board were violently seasick as the ship hit the rough waters of the Martinique Passage. Fanon had entered a military world of confusion and secrecy, and had no idea of where he was going on the ship that was taking him away from the Caribbean for the first time. Some of his comrades thought they were going to Italy, while others were convinced that their destination was the Far Eastern theatre. The *Oregon* was in fact steaming north-west towards Bermuda, and reached it within four days. After a night in port to take on supplies and fresh water, she joined a convoy of 120 ships and sailed east into the Atlantic. After fourteen days at sea, she reached the Moroccan port of Casablanca on 30 March, and Fanon's battalion was immediately transferred to the El Hajeb camp near Meknes. They remained there for two months of very basic training as officer cadets.

The anonymous soldier who meticulously kept 5BMA's daily log or *journal de marche* noted that his unit received a very poor reception and wrote that their living conditions were deplorable. He gives no explanation for his remarks, but a later entry in the log suggests that inter-ethnic tensions were high. The camp was crowded with Algerians, Moroccans and troops from the African colonies, and on 22 May, a new Mobile Field Brothel – that most curious item of French *matériel de guerre* – was brought in for the exclusive use of the Martinican contingent. Whether this was because certain of the prostitutes were reluctant to service Martinicans, or whether the latter were reluctant to share 'their' women, is not made clear by the *journal de marche*, which provides a terse and sometimes incomplete record of events, but no analysis. It is, on the other hand, quite clear from 5BMA's records that, on other occasions, the sexual rivalry between the West Indians and the Africans led to physical violence, as there were serious outbreaks of brawling when some *Tirailleurs sénégalais* attacked those West Indians they found in the company of white women in Nantes in August 1944.

Fanon and Manville's knowledge of Morocco was restricted to the little that they had learned at school: 'From a geographical point of view, it was a beautiful country where the sun was cold; from a historical point of view, it was a country conquered by Marshal Lyautey, who declared that in a colony you have to show your strength so as not to have to use it.' They now found that the French protectorate was also a divided country in which there co-existed a privileged world of European conquerors, and a devalorized world in which an Islamic people lived in squalor.[72] The camp at El Hajeb was another divided world. The Martinicans and the volunteers from Guadeloupe were not billeted in the same barracks as the African troops. They did not eat the same food, much to the annoyance of Manville, who would much rather have eaten spicy African stews than 'the food served to those who came from the great cold'.[73] And they did not wear the same uniforms. The West Indians were from the 'old colonies', were treated as semi-Europeans, and wore the same uniform as their metropolitan counterparts. The Africans of the *Tirailleurs sénégalais* wore the traditional *chechia* or fez, red flannel belts and jerkins with rounded collars. Not all of them were happy with this convention, and unsuccessfully demanded the right to wear standard-issue French uniform.[74] It was becoming clear that the heteroclite army which Fanon and Manville had hoped would free Europe and the world from fascism and racism was in fact structured around an ethnic hierarchy, with white Europeans at the top and North Africans at the bottom. Black colonial troops were seen as superior to Arabs, and the position of West Indians was ambiguous in the extreme.

At the beginning of July, Fanon's unit entrained and went east to Algeria, which was the springboard for the landings in southern France. Fanon knew no more about Algeria than he knew about Morocco, and what little he did know derived from what he had learned at school. Algeria became part of the school history syllabus in 1928.[75] Every schoolchild knew that France invaded Algeria in 1830 to avenge the insult suffered by the French Consul in April 1827, when the Bey of Algiers struck him with a fly whisk. Everyone knew that France wanted to rid the Mediterranean of pirates, that Algiers lived by kidnapping and ransoming foreigners and that those unfortunate enough not to be ransomed became galley slaves. Piracy had certainly been an Algerian industry, but it was also practised throughout the Mediterranean and was by no means a specifically Algerian practice.[76] It was also very much in decline by 1830. It was also claimed by French schoolbooks that the Algerian expedition was intended to free Algeria from the Ottoman Turks who were its nominal rulers. Everyone knew that Algeria had been an integral part of France since 1848, and that France had a civilizing mission there. The reality was much more prosaic. The incident between the Bey and the Consul related to unpaid bills for grain supplied to French forces during the Napoleonic era. The imperial gesture of dispatching a fleet to Algiers was an attempt to boost the popularity of a failing regime in Paris. No one was taught at school that most of Algeria's ten million 'natives' were colonial subjects and not citizens with full voting rights, that only a tiny élite belonged to a second 'junior' electoral college that returned members to the Assemblée algérienne, or that Arabic and the various Berber tongues were officially regarded as 'foreign languages'. Until 1944, the daily lives of Algeria's 'natives' were governed by the *code de l'indigénat*, based on a list of thirty-three infractions that were not illegal under French common law but were illegal when committed by Muslims. Defaming the French Republic, travelling without a permit, refusing to fight forest fires and plagues of grasshoppers, begging outside one's home commune and firing weapons into the air during celebrations were all offences under the *code de l'indigénat*. Refusing to pay taxes was an offence under both the code and the common law.[77] The abolition of the code did not greatly change anyone's life. There was no reason for Fanon to have known any of this when he first set foot on Algerian soil. Nor was there any reason for him to have known that all attempts to introduce reforms had been frustrated by the representatives of a European population which was 'French' only because it had been naturalized from the 1870s onwards.

Under the terms of the 1940 armistice, France retained its sovereignty over Algeria and, although there was initially considerable local enthusiasm for continuing the war, the colony soon rallied to Pétain.[78] Most of the *pied noir* population became enthusiastic supporters of Pétain's National Revolution, and particularly of its anti-Semitic laws, which deprived the substantial Jewish population of their rights as naturalized French citizens and removed them from public office.[79] The

Arab-Berber population was divided, with many of the notables being attracted to the paternalism of the new regime, whilst more nationalistic elements were more likely to take a pro-German stance on the traditional grounds that my enemy's enemy is my friend. Still others hoped that an American invasion would free them from French colonialism. The Atlantic Charter signed by Churchill and Roosevelt in 1941 had spoken of the right of all peoples to choose their own form of government and some saw this as a promise of at least self-determination.

In December 1942, Ferhat-Abbas and a delegation of twenty-four Algerian notables drafted a 'Manifesto of the Algerian People' and presented it to the French authorities. It called for the condemnation and abolition of colonization, recognition of the right of all peoples to self-determination and the establishment of a constitution for Algeria. The latter should guarantee the absolute freedom and equality of all without distinction as to race or religion, the abolition of feudal property, the recognition of Arabic as an official language, freedom of the press and association, free compulsory education for children of both sexes, freedom of religion and the effective participation of Algerian Muslims in their own government.[80] The document's significance is almost incalculable. It was produced by *évolués* who were, in French terms, the finest products of the colonial system. These were men who had rejected the populism of most forms of Algerian nationalism, typified by Messali Hadj's Parti Populaire Algérien, in favour of integration or assimilation into France. Many had, like Abbas, one of the rare Algerians to have studied at the University of Algiers where he qualified as a pharmacist, been members of the 'Young Algerian' movement, a classic *évolué* movement;[81] those who had seen their salvation in assimilation were now thinking of independence within the framework of a new commonwealth. Although the Governor General accepted the Manifesto as a basis for further reforms, it was made clear that decolonization was not on the agenda. Reforms were indeed introduced in 1944. The *code de l'indigéna*t was abolished. It could now be claimed that all the inhabitants of the country were subject to the same laws, and that the 'natives' administered their own affairs with French assistance and in accordance with their own conceptions and the rules of democracy. Where Europeans were in the majority, the basic administrative unit was the *commune de plein exercise* where officials were elected, as in France. Most natives lived in *communes mixtes*, where French officials were appointed from above and ruled with the help of nominated Muslim judges and bureaucrats known to all as *beni-oui-oui* or yes-men. France was a secular republic in which the separation of Church and State was strictly observed; in Algeria, mosques were under the control of the State.

For the first three years of the war, Algiers was a city of plots and conspiracies where factions manoeuvred for power and influence, but one in which the future of Algeria itself was definitely a secondary issue. This was a world in which double and even triple agents fought secret wars of their own. Pétainistes and Gaullistes struggled for power. The Gaullist secret service, officially known as the Bureau Central de Renseignements et d'Action, recruited agents with contacts in Algiers' extensive criminal underworld. Assassinations took place, and the corpses of suspected Vichy agents floated in the Bay of Algiers. The sinister atmosphere of the early 1940s is well captured in Emmanuel Roblès's novel *Les Hauteurs de la ville*, which deals with an Arab's assassination of a French businessman who is recruiting Algerians to work for the Todt organization, which built fortifications in France for the German army.[82] In November 1942, Allied troops landed in Algeria and Morocco and effectively made the two countries American protectorates in which the old Vichy supporters remained in power. Although successful in North Africa, Operation Torch was the trigger for a full German occupation of France. It did not free Algeria from French rule.

De Gaulle arrived in Algiers on 30 May 1943,[83] and the establishment of the Comité français de libération nationale made Algiers his capital. It also became the logistical base for Operation Anvil (later codenamed Dragoon), which was planned for August 1944. It was a controversial operation. Churchill was reluctant to support it and was convinced that the main thrust should be through Italy and then into Austria. In his view, landings in the south of France would merely divert resources away from the main task. De Gaulle's argument in favour of Anvil was highly politicized. It had long been clear that the landings in Normandy – Operation Overlord – would be mainly an Anglo-American operation and, if the whole of France were liberated by non-French forces, there was a distinct possibility that the country would come under an Allied military government. Anvil was planned as a Franco–American operation designed both to assert de Gaulle's own authority and to establish French sovereignty. In military terms, landings in the south would provide the anvil on which the hammer blows of Overlord would pound the Germans. After a lot of political manoeuvring, de Gaulle got his way.[84]

On 14 July 1944, de Gaulle took the salute at the Bastille Day parade, and watched 5BMA as it marched past him. Fanon's unit was in fact merely passing through Algiers on its way to a new camp near Orléansville (now known as Chlef) to await embarcation for France. Conditions were little better than they had been in El Hajeb, and the welcome that awaited the Martinicans was not a friendly one. They reached camp at four in the morning, and then had to erect their own tents on an exposed hillside. There were few distractions, apart from the occasional afternoon of leave that allowed Fanon and his friends to visit a local cinema. Manville still recalls how Fanon tricked him into wasting time on a 'terrible film' by telling him that he had just been to see a 'wonderful American musical'.[85] The troops were isolated from the local population and the minimal contacts that he did make led Fanon to the depressing discovery that 'the North Africans loathed men of colour. It was quite impossible to make contact with the natives . . . The French do not like Jews, who do not like Arabs, who do not like negroes.'[86]

After their arrival in Oran, 5BMA enjoyed a period of relative inactivity. It was near Oran that Fanon watched soldiers throwing pieces of bread to starving Arab children who fought savagely over the scraps of food.[87] He would never forget the sight. Since 1939, many areas and notably Kabylia were famine zones. Albert Camus published damning articles on the famine in *Alger républican* in June of that year, describing how he had seen ragged children fighting with dogs over the contents of a dustbin in the Kabyle capital of Tizi-Ouzou. He learned that, in the villages, poor people had been reduced to supplementing the small amount of grain they could obtain by eating the roots and stalks of thistles and nettles.[88] Wartime rationing made matters much worse. 'Europeans' and 'natives' had ration cards of different colours entitling them to different rations. There were 'native' and 'European' distribution centres in the countryside. In some areas, rations were limited to four kilos of barley per person per month. In some cases even the barley had been replaced by what the locals called 'American flour'; the maize flour caused food poisoning and other digestive disorders because the recipients did not know how to cook it properly.[89] The children Fanon saw near Oran were the lucky ones; bread was a luxury for many of their fellows. Disease was taking its toll too; in 1941 alone, typhus killed 16,000 people in Algeria.[90]

Fanon did not have much time to observe the harsh realities of wartime North Africa. On 10 September, he was crossing the Mediterranean on an American-flagged transport. 5 BMA's training had not been particularly thorough, and it was not particularly well armed, its main weapons being First World War vintage Lebel rifles, the 1915-model Chuchat light machine gun, and Hotchkiss machine guns.[91] The crossing took two days, and Fanon's first sight of France was an invasion beach near St Tropez and the shattered town of Toulon. His unit was not part of the spearhead. Operation Anvil got underway early on the morning of 15 August, when 10,000 men of the US First Airborne Task Force jumped to a drop zone a few miles inland from Fréjus and St Tropez. French and American commandos were landed and took very heavy casualties. At eight, three US infantry divisions hit the beaches of the south coast, which had been heavily bombarded from both the air and the sea. By mid-morning Allied troops had reached the centre of St Tropez, where American paratroops and the French Forces of the Interior were already besieging the German garrison. A bridgehead had been established and the French divisions of de Lattre's 'B Army' landed the next day. The German infantry regiment stationed to the east of St Tropez was in retreat and the other German forces – seven infantry divisions and one Panzer tank division – were so thinly deployed that they could not be regrouped to offer much resistance. The Allied objective was now the road and rail corridor leading to Toulon, and then the Rhône valley.

After heavy street-fighting, Toulon was taken on 19 August by the sixth regiment of *Tirailleurs sénégalais* (6RTS), which was part of the Ninth Division of Colonial Infantry. Formed in June 1943, 9DCI was made up of a Moroccan infantry regiment, the Fourth, Sixth and Thirteenth Regiments of *Tirailleurs senégalais* and an artillery division from Morocco. The 6RTS had already seen combat in Corsica and Elba, where it took heavy casualties. These were tough troops who were particularly good at fighting at close quarters, and the Germans were afraid of them. So much so that, according to Cézette, they took no black prisoners. On 20 August, Général de Brigade Pierre Magnan issued an order of the day, congratulating his men on their victory:

> You defeated the enemy in a three-day battle that took you from the Cuers region to the gates of Toulon. And then, taking responsibility for the conquest of the town, you wrested this old colonial city, which is the cradle of your army, from the enemy inch by inch. The high number of prisoners in your hands, and the quantity of munitions and *matériel* you have captured, are testimony to the valour of your efforts and the greatness of your victory.[92]

Magnan was apparently quite oblivious to the irony of his words. Toulon was the cradle of the colonial army in more than one sense: it was the main port of embarcation for the invasion of Algeria in 1830.

Magnan had unwittingly touched upon the vital question of what happens when the colonized liberate their colonizers, and then realize that they themselves are still colonized. Similar questions had begun to be asked during the Italian campaign. When New Year parcels from America arrived for the mixed colonial and French units, a French officer decided that they should be distributed on the basis of one parcel for each Frenchman, and one parcel to be shared between three Moroccans. When an Algerian sergeant protested, he was told that he was an agitator and did not deserve the *médaille militaire* for which he had been recommended. The sergeant was Ahmed Ben Bella, the future first president of independent Algeria, and his feelings about the war he was fighting were becoming dangerously ambiguous: 'I was fighting for a just cause, and I believe that I was happy. Or at least I would have been happy, if the thought of unhappy Algeria had ever left me for a moment.'[93] Fanon was probably not worrying about the unhappy Algeria of which he had seen so little, but his doubts as to just what he was doing would soon grow.

On landing in France, where it was immediately involved in mopping up operations, 5BMA was split up as part of the seemingly endless and confusing reorganization of France's fighting forces.[94] Most of its men were transferred to the Atlantic coast, where they fought bravely in the battle to retake the Royan 'pocket' at the mouth of the Girone estuary – which had been bypassed by the Allies after their breakout from the Normandy bridgeheads – and lost their commanding officer in doing so. The remainder, including Fanon, Manville, Cézette and Mosole, were incorporated into 9DIC's Sixth regiment of *Tirailleurs sénégalais*. Astonishingly, the friends remained together, although Cézette became a semi-detached member of the little group when he became a driver attached to a liaison officer and acquired what he calls 'my own jeep'. As the Division took Aix-en-Provence and then moved north along the Rhône valley towards Grenoble, Fanon was forced to wonder who he was: 'on the one hand, the Europeans, either native or from the old colonies; on the other, the *tirailleurs*'. He no longer knew whether he was a black 'native' or an honorary white *toubab* (European), but he did have the impression that the black troops were taking the brunt of the fighting and casualties and were being sent into action first.[95]

As the division headed north, the weather was becoming colder, and the High Command decided on 27 October that the three regiments of *Tirailleurs sénégalais* could not be expected to fight in winter conditions to which they were not acclimatized and should be pulled back to more temperate areas. Some of the beneficiaries of the decision were ungrateful enough to see it as a ploy designed to deny them the military glory of crossing the Rhine into Germany.[96] The official documents described this as the 'whitening'(*blanchiment*) of the division, which was now officially a European unit. Not all its 'European' soldiers were European in any real sense and they were definitely not white: some, like Fanon, came into the strange category of neither 'native' nor '*toubab*'. Fanon had never seen snow and, having been brought up on an island where the temperature rarely falls below the high twenties, he had never been cold. He had no more experience of the harsh winters of Eastern France than his Senegalese comrades, but he had to fight on in increasingly difficult conditions as the temperature fell to well below zero. Whether or not the decision to send the small group of Martinicans and Guadeloupeans north into the snow was deliberate or an instance of military incompetence is not clear. Charles Cézette is still tempted to think that they were simply 'forgotten about'. He also suggests that there may have been other factors behind the decision to whiten the Division. He hints, that is, that the Senegalese may have been pulled back in order to intimidate the local *French* population and to forestall possible outbreaks of 'people's justice', a murderous purge of collaborators or even an attempted Communist insurrection. There is no proof that this was the case, but such fears were real enough in 1944 and the explanation is therefore not to be rejected out of hand.

In early September, the Germans were retreating north from Lyon, which was liberated on the first of the month, under heavy rearguard cover, and their resistance stiffened as they moved north-eastwards towards Belfort. The French supply lines were now becoming dangerously extended. The initial advance had been rapid, and Cézette recalls that his unit, advancing on foot, was often far ahead of the American-built GMC trucks carrying its supplies. It was now obvious to all that the French objective was Alsace and then the Rhine. By the middle of the month, French intelligence reported that two or three infantry battalions with artillery support were reinforcing their positions inside the great loop made by the Doubs river near the industrial town of Montbéliard, which guarded the approaches to Belfort. The French advance slowed, and the two armies became engaged in two months of almost static warfare, characterized mainly by sporadic exchanges of machine-gun and mortar fire.

The weather deteriorated steadily, and by November the keeper of the *journal de marche* was complaining of intense cold and heavy snow. As he drove north from Lyon, Cézette had been unsure as to precisely what was landing on the windscreen of his jeep, and it took him some time to realize that this was the snow he had heard so much about in Martinique. He soon became all too familiar with it. To make matters worse, the snow was alternating with freezing rain that thawed the ground just enough to bog down both vehicles and men in mud. Fanon and his comrades were sleeping in two-man tents that were barely a metre high, and often had to dig themselves out. The poor atmospheric conditions hampered radio communications, and the dank pine forests had been both mined and booby-trapped. It was in these conditions that a general French advance under the command of Commandant Bourgoin began in November. In the meantime, the US Seventh army and units of the First French army were attacking from the east. To the north, German forces were regrouping in Alsace. Individual soldiers on the ground rarely have any sense of the broader picture and Fanon cannot have known that he was taking part in the gradual build-up to the Battle of Alsace.[97] Cézette, Manville and Mosole all fought with distinction in that battle. Mosole was awarded the Croix de Guerre and silver star for his distinguished conduct. During a skirmish in a cemetery in Wittenheim, which fell to the French on 30 January 1945, Manville succeeded in knocking out a tank by firing a rifle bullet into its canon and detonating the shell in the breech. Whilst this was clearly a matter of good luck rather than good marksmanship, it won him the rank of corporal and the Croix de Guerre.

The terrain to the south-east of Montbéliard favoured the attacking forces, but the advance was still not an easy one. To the north of the French positions, the Doubs and the Rhine–Rhône canal ran in parallel across a sodden plain. Above it, rolling hills rose to an altitude of 400 metres. This was not easy ground: the hills were covered in pines, and cut by minor rivers and streams flowing into the Doubs. Intelligence-gathering was a matter of listening rather than of visual observation, and the sound of ongoing building work had been detected in the Bois de Grappes, which covered the steepish slopes of a hill known as Le Grand Mont, where it appeared that a German unit was digging in. On 25 November, Private Frantz Fanon was serving an 81-millimetre mortar in the wood under enemy fire and was hit by shrapnel from an incoming mortar round. Badly wounded in the chest, he was cited in a Brigade dispatch for his 'distinguished conduct', and awarded the Croix de Guerre with a bronze star. The citation was signed by the Sixth RTS's commanding officer, Colonel Raoul Salan, who would later be one of the staunchest defenders of French Algeria and a leading figure in the April 1961 putsch against de Gaulle.[98] Ironically, France had already decorated another of its future enemies; Ben Bella was mentioned in dispatches on four occasions and was finally awarded the *médaille militaire* for the bravery he showed while retrieving three abandoned machine guns under fire. Shortly after the capture of Rome, he was awarded his medal by de Gaulle in person.[99]

Fanon was evacuated and hospitalized in Nantua, a small lakeside town in the Jura mountains some ninety kilometres to the north of Lyon. He made a quick recovery from his wounds and was soon playing football for a local team as part of his convalescence. According to his brother Joby, he made good friends in the region and was particularly fond of his *marraine de guerre*, or 'godmother', who remained in touch with him when he left Nantua for a brief stay in Paris before going back to his unit in January. The regiment was now officially being 'rested', but its rest-period took the uncomfortable form of night patrols on the banks of the Rhine. Fanon did, however, have time to write to his brother. On 16 January 1945, he wrote:

My Dear Joby,

We don't have the luxury of having pens here, so you will have to try to decipher my letter . . . You must have heard by now that I was wounded. I have rejoined my unit and I am on the banks of the Rhine. When I get the chance during our night patrols, I wash my face in the Rhine . . . Listen to me, I've grown a lot older than you. *Man la prend fé tant pis pou moins, mais pas vini en France avant la fin la què va* (I've been deceived, and I am paying for my mistakes, but I won't be back in France before the end of the war.) I'm sick of it all. Don't worry: Pierre Mosole and Marcel Manville were still alive a week ago. You asked me if I got the cross. Yes, with bars and medals, and all the rest of it. I wanted to tell you we are still alive, but we don't want to talk about the war. I could tell you certain things, but I'm a soldier and you won't know them until later. You'll have to be satisfied with knowing that I've had enough. But it's still rough twenty-four hours a day. And we have to stay in holes because the Boches are on the other side, and they don't miss. Roll on the end of the war, and my return.

Fanon had learned that freedom was not indivisible. He was a black soldier in a white man's army. Writing to his mother that same month, Fanon tried to hide his true feelings, and spoke longingly of the punch and *blaff* he was looking forward to when he got back to Martinique, but another letter written to both his parents on 12 April 1945 tells a different story:

Today, 12 April. It is a year since I left Fort-de-France. Why? To defend an obsolete ideal. I don't think I'll make it this time.

During all the scraps I've been in, I've been anxious to get back to you, and I've been lucky. But today, I'm wondering whether I might not soon have to face the ordeal. I've lost confidence in everything, even myself.

If I don't come back, and if one day you should learn that I died facing the enemy, console each other, but never say: he died for the good cause. Say: God called him back to him. This false ideology that shields the secularists and the idiot politicians must not delude us any longer. *I was wrong!*

Nothing here, nothing justifies my sudden decision to defend the interests of farmers who don't give a damn.

They are hiding a lot of things from us. But you will hear them through Manville or Mosole. The three of us are in the same regiment. We've been separated, but we write to each other, and even if two of us die, the third will tell you some dreadful truths.

I've volunteered for a dangerous mission, and I leave tomorrow. I know I won't be coming back.[100]

The nature of Fanon's 'dangerous mission' is not known. Perhaps he simply did not have time to go on it: just over three weeks after this letter was written, Germany capitulated.

Fanon and Manville were back in Toulon for the festivities that marked the liberation of France, and were reunited with those members of 5BMA who had fought in the Royan pocket. The port was crowded with soldiers and sailors, and there was a strong American military presence. Whilst the GIs appeared to lack for nothing, the French and Martinican troops were, according to Manville, living in bad conditions and felt that they were being treated as second-class citizens rather than as liberating heroes. That the local girls preferred American dancing partners who could give them chewing gum and nylons to black Martinicans who had nothing, added to a growing sense of disillusionment. In *Peau noire, masques blancs*, Fanon describes with considerable bitterness how white French girls backed away in fear when black French soldiers asked them to dance.[101] Fanon and his comrades wanted only one thing: to get back to the West Indies and to tell everyone how the French, for whom they had given and suffered so much, had abandoned them.[102] Martinique was very much on Fanon's mind, and he kept in touch with developments there as best he could. On 5 August 1945, he wrote to a correspondent in Martinique who has been identified only as 'Mme. L.C.' and remarked that the fact that Aimé Césaire had been elected as Mayor of Fort-de-France 'proved that our compatriots are not as blind as they would have us believe'. Now that the 'fine hours' of action were over, he was leading a static life that did not appeal to him. The calm of peace was 'flat, morbid and stagnant', and the material power of money was becoming the dominant force in France. The only solution to his boredom was a return to Martinique.[103] Cézette paints a similar picture, but it is less gloomy than the one described by Manville and Fanon. Boredom was, he recalls, a growing problem, as the main task of the day was now getting out of bed in the morning. His primary duty now was to drive off in 'his' jeep to collect the day's ration of wine and bring it back to their billets outside the town; his main complaint was that he and his comrades were not allowed to go into Toulon on their own. Had he been on his own, he thought, he might have had more success with the local girls.

If Fanon and his friends had expected to be repatriated directly from Toulon, they were to be very disappointed. With an inscrutable logic of its own, the army now transported them from a port in the Mediterranean to one on the Seine estuary. Their port of embarcation should have been Le Havre at the mouth of the river's estuary, but the port facilities had been badly damaged by Allied bombing and they were therefore now taken to Rouen, which was ninety kilometres upstream from Le Havre. Rouen is a beautiful city with fine Gothic architecture and medieval streets, but in August 1945 it was in a sorry state. During the previous summer, the bridges across the Seine had been a major target for the US air force. They were at the time the last bridges before the sea and they had to be bombed to prevent the Germans bringing reinforcements into Normandy from the south-west. The bridges were destroyed and so too was everything between the river and the cathedral, which was itself badly damaged. Much of medieval Rouen disappeared during the raids before the city was liberated on 1 September 1944.

The men of 5BMA had expected to be in Rouen for a week, but they were there for a month. This time it was not military bureaucracy that caused the delay. There were still German mines in the Seine and its estuary, and they had to be cleared before any ship could leave in safety. In the meantime, Fanon and his comrades were billeted in what Manville called a 'disused château'. This was the Château du chapitre, an abandoned country house in the richly wooded hills to the north-east of Rouen. It was badly dilapidated but, for soldiers accustomed to sleeping in two-men tents, being under any kind of roof felt like luxury. The house no longer exists and the Bois-Guillaume area is now covered with handsome and expensive suburban housing. There were few houses in 1945 and there was little for bored soldiers to do. They had been granted free use of public transport but the privilege did not mean a great deal in practice. The only link between Bois-Guillaume and central Rouen was a light railway with an infrequent passenger service. It was more convenient to use an army truck when one was available. The only alternative was a long walk. Some thought that the walk was worth the effort. Marcel Manville found Rouen 'bourgeois, puritanical, reserved and austere'[104] but Cézette, who still lives there, thought otherwise. Although in ruins, the city was in festive mood as it prepared to celebrate the anniversary of its liberation and open-air dances were held. Cézette met his future wife at a dance in the place du Marché during his enforced stay in Rouen.

The boredom of Bois-Guillaume was relieved when the unit commander was invited by a local councillor to come to dinner on Sunday 2 September with fifteen of his men. Marcel Lemonnier was a prosperous businessman who sold stationery and supplies for artists and architects. He had also been a member of the local Resistance. The invitation was readily accepted. The guests now had to be selected. The unit commander was anxious to make a good impression and was slightly worried when he learned that Marcel Lemonnier had three teenaged daughters. He wanted men who could be trusted to be on their best behaviour and therefore selected fifteen soldiers who came from good families and who had reached a relatively high standard of education. Fanon, Cézette and Manville all passed muster. As they approached the Lemonnier home, Manville thought he was going to a real château. The large thatched house standing in an extensive garden was originally part of the farm buildings belonging to the Château du chapitre. Marcel Lemonnier bought it in the late 1920s and gradually converted it into a large and very comfortable family residence. The house still stands, with its low thatched roof and thick whitewashed walls, and is the only *chaumière* of its vintage in the area to have survived. It is no longer in the possession of the Lemonnier family.

The dinner was a great success. For the first time in a very long time, Fanon and his friends dined off white linen tablecloths and ate good home-cooking. The talk was not of the war but of plans for the future. The young Martinicans talked excitedly of what they wanted to be. Manville was going to be a lawyer, and so was Fanon. The law was a good choice for Manville. In colloquial French, a lawyer is '*un bavard*' or a chatter-box, and Manville was very rarely silent for long. Mosole was going be a pharmacist, but eventually became a dentist. The young black soldiers proved to pose absolutely no threat to the Lemonnier girls. Given Fanon's subsequent traumatic encounter with the white gaze ('Look, maman, a negro'), it is ironic that it was he and Manville who gazed at the children and could not take their eyes off them. They had never seen a girl with truly red hair, or such a blond boy, and they were fascinated. There was one slightly embarrassing moment, however. When Monsieur Lemonnier learned how his guests had been chosen, he protested that surely not everyone in 5BMA was a middle-class young man with good educational qualifications and insisted on meeting some of the others. A second and larger meal was arranged for the next Sunday, and it was just as successful and enjoyable.

In the east of France, Fanon had met peasants who had been reluctant to fight on their own behalf and who seemed to show no gratitude to their liberators. The hospitality of the Lemonnier family showed him that France could and did have a very different face. Odette Fresel (née Lemonnier) still speaks with great emotion of the young black troops 'who left their beautiful Martinique to liberate us'. Inviting two groups of soldiers into his house was an act of great generosity on Marcel Lemonnier's part; Rouen may well have been in festive mood, but food was still in short supply and it was expensive. The generosity was typical of the man: he simply liked inviting people into his home. After the war, he would take an indirect route home from work in the hope that he might meet foreign cyclists or hitchhikers he could take home for dinner. As his daughter admits, this did make for a rather eventful and unpredictable home life as the house was often full of unexpected guests. Her mother's visitors' book contained expressions of thanks from numerous servicemen, cyclists, hitchhikers and walkers – many of them English. It also contained several pages headed 'In memory of a good evening, hoping that we meet again' and dated '9 September 1945'. Two of the inscriptions read as follows: 'With thanks for the pleasant evenings spent under the sign of the great friendship shown by the welcoming Lemonnier family to some sons of the far-off Martinique' and 'I beg the Lemonnier family to believe that our West Indian gratitude will think for a long time to come, despite the distance and the passage of time, of these evenings when the family was unstintingly kind and generous to these spiritual sons of the immortal France. We will continue to love our motherland and her children, who were so hospitable.' They are signed, respectively, 'Charles Cézette, 36 rue Perinnon, Fort-de-France, Martinique' and 'Marcel Manville, 72 rue Victor Hugo, Fort-de-France, Martinique'. A third and shorter message is signed 'F. Fanon, 33 rue République F de F': 'With thanks for the generous hospitality and homely quality of the evenings spent with the Lemonnier family.'[105] Whether or not Fanon remained in contact with the family is unclear. Odette Fresel was no longer living at home at the time, but thinks that both he and his sister Gabrielle visited her family when the latter was studying pharmacy in Rouen after the war. She remained in touch with both Manville and Cézette, and that evening in 1945 provided the basis for lasting friendships.

The return journey to Martinique began in October, and it was not a comfortable one. The *San Mateo* was a cargo boat normally used for transporting cattle and provided poor accommodation for the 700 Martinicans, Guadaloupeans and Guyanese who were shipped out of Rouen. The food was worse. The hard biscuits came from the supplies issued to the army that was defeated in 1940. The meat was corned beef, which was so loathed by the French troops who first encountered it in the trenches of the First World War that they called it *singe* ('monkey'). Manville shared their opinion.[106]

On his return to Martinique, Fanon found himself in a curious position. At the age of twenty, he was a decorated war veteran but he had yet to complete his secondary education. He had successfully taken the first part of his *baccalauréat* before his departure for Dominica, but now had to return to the Lycée Schoelcher to prepare for the orals. He passed and was awarded the *baccalauréat* that gave him the right to go to university. Fanon was aware that government grants were available for demobilized soldiers who were returning to education, but was not entirely sure how to obtain one. The funds were controlled by the Conseil Général, which had been re-established after the 'June Days', and Fanon decided to approach one of its members. He called at the home of Georges Gratiant, a prominent Communist councillor, in the rue Victor Hugo, and was immediately shown the door by Madame Gratiant. He had breached convention by attempting to approach an official at home rather than in his office. Disappointed and angry, Fanon turned to his uncle Edouard for advice. The school teacher refused to act on his behalf, but advised him to speak to a councillor of his acquaintance from Le François. The response was disappointing. Fanon was told to apply in writing and to attend a council meeting. The general opinion of Martinique's elected representatives was that it was not their role to train *bourgeois* by sending them to elite lycées; they were there to produce farmers. It was only after a stormy meeting that Fanon was accorded the rights – and the money – that were his according to the French government.[107]

As Fanon approached the end of his secondary education, he was still unsure of what he wanted to do or be. Career guidance was not one of the French education system's strong points at this time and school-leavers were largely on their own when it came to choosing their direction. Martinique offered few possibilities. There were no higher education facilities apart from a teacher-training college and a law school, and few opportunities for graduates who returned from university in France. Some found employment in the local state sector, and others became one of Martinique's stranger exports by joining the colonial administration in France's African colonies. Despite his real admiration for Félix Eboué, the comments Fanon makes in *Peau noire, masques blancs* on René Maran, who did work in the African administration, show that he did not regard this as either a viable or a desirable possibility.

Fanon's education had been primarily a literary one, and he had talked in Rouen of studying law, but he now made the surprising decision to become a dentist. The decision may have been influenced by Mosole or simply by the belief that a career in dentistry would give him a solid social position and a higher income than that earned in the customs service by his father. Becoming a dentist would have been quite in keeping with the family's history of upward social mobility, and would have satisfied Eléanore Fanon's ambitions for her children. Student grants were available for veterans. Years of study at the Paris Dental School seemed a logical step. In the meantime, Fanon lived with his family, attended the lycée and played football. Football was now a more serious matter for Fanon than it had ever been. Joby was teaching in St Pierre while he was preparing for the competitive examination that would lead to a career in the Customs Service, and was playing regularly for the local team. Both Frantz and Willy joined him, and the three played almost as a team within the team. At 1.65 metres, Frantz was not particularly tall, but he was wiry and strong and made an effective centre-forward. His brothers played outside him as inside-forwards and they played in a triangular formation, passing the ball backwards and forwards on Frantz's shouted command. Whilst this must have been very frustrating for their flanking wingers, the three brothers made a powerfully effective attacking unit. St Pierre was a successful team.

Fanon was also aware that Martinique was going through a decisive period. In October 1945, Aimé Césaire ran for parliament as a member of the Communist Party, and Fanon was present at the meeting at which a woman fainted, so powerful was the poet-politician's oratory.[108] Césaire was one of three Communist députés returned by Martinique. In 1956, he resigned from the Communist Party to found his own Parti Populaire Martiniquais, but he held his parliamentary seat until 1993.[109] Writing in 1955, Fanon would describe the liberation of Martinique in 1943 as the island's first metaphysical experience and as the first awakening of a distinctively Martinican political consciousness.[110] The election of Communist députés was a logical development of that consciousness, but it was still an ambiguous consciousness in that Martinique had relied on 'the France of the Liberation to struggle against the economic and political power of the sugar plantocracy'.[111] Fanon's experience of racism in the French army and of the racism of sections of the French population had sown serious doubts in his mind as to what 'the France of the Liberation' really meant. Perhaps more significantly still, Martinicans were discovering that the Césaire of the *Cahier* was right: they were black, and not Europeans.

Fanon rarely spoke of his wartime experience, even when he was with friends, but on a number of occasions he did cite a very bitter passage from Césaire's 'discourse on colonialism' of 1951. Here, Césaire speaks of the need to explain to 'the very distinguished, very humanistic and very Christian bourgeois of the twentieth century' that a Hitler slumbers within him and that what he cannot forgive Hitler for is not his crimes in the abstract, but 'the crime against the white man, the humiliation of the white man, the fact that he applied to Europe the colonial practices that had previously been applied only to the Arabs of Algeria, the coolies of India and the negroes of Africa'.[112] It is unlikely that Fanon reached this conclusion in 1945, and his obvious conviction that the angry Césaire was right was influenced by his experiences in Algeria from 1953 onwards. It is, on the other hand, clear that the disillusionment he had felt had opened up a festering wound that would not heal.

# 4

# Dr Frantz Fanon

It was a familiar scenario. He had watched them leaving Fort-de-France. He had seen the families accompanying the young men to the foot of the ship's gangway, and had glimpsed the coming mutation and the power in the eyes of the exile-to-be as he ironically hummed or sang 'Adieu foulard, adieu madra'.[1] This is the sad song in which a girl from Martinique laments the loss of her white sweetheart or *doudou*:[2]

> *Adieu foulard, adieu madras,*
> *Adieu graine d'or, adieu collier chou,*
> *Hélas, hélas, c'est pou toujours*
> *Doudou à moi, lui parti*
> *Hélas, hélas, c'est pou toujours*
>
> *('Farewell foulard, farewell madras,*
> *Farewell graine d'or, farewell collier chou,*
> *Alas, alas, it is for ever,*
> *My sweetheart has gone.*
> *Alas, alas, gone for ever)*

Fanon turns the lament into a farewell to a certain Martinique and to the image of Martinique conveyed by the clothes and jewellery worn by the girl in the song. That image figured on the banknotes and stamps that were issued when Martinique was still a colony and not a *département*; it still appears on the labels on bottles of rum. A *madras* is a skirt or dress of checked cotton, and a *foulard* a headscarf twisted into a turban; a *graine d'or* and a *collier chou* are highly prized and expensive items of gold jewellery. Fanon's version of the song can also be read as a farewell to the *doudouiste* literature typified by the dedication to a Creole poem by Gilbert Gratiant, the brother of the councillor he had approached in his unsuccesful attempt to obtain his student grant:

> *Aux jeunes filles créoles:*
> *Câpresses, droites et provocantes,*
> *Békées de lys et de langueur altière,*
> *Chabines, enjouées marquées de soleil,*
> *Coulies si fragile aux purs traits d'Indiens*
> *Bel ti-négresses fermes et saines,*
> *Mulatresses aux grand yeux, souples reines de tout le féminin*
>   *possible*
>
> (*'To the Creole girls:*
> *Straightbacked and provocative câpresses,*
> *Lily-like békées in their haughty langour,*
> *Coolies, so fragile with their pure Indian features,*
> *Beautiful little negresses, firm bodied and healthy,*
> *Mulatresses with big eyes, supple queens who could not be more*
>   *feminine).*[3]

He had seen them leaving, and he had also seen them returning. The Martinican who had been to the metropolis was, like the 'been-to' of Anglophone Africa who is so proud of having been to London,[4] a demi-god but he could also be a pathetic figure. Anyone who had been to France and had not succeeded in seeing a mounted policeman there was the object of mockery.[5] Those who came back so convinced of their superiority that they refused to speak Creole were soon put in their place, and Fanon knew the story of the been-to who could not recognize a familiar piece of agricultural equipment . . . until his peasant father dropped it on his foot.[6] He also knew that the Martinican who landed in France could be a comic figure, especially if he hypercorrected his natural tendency to 'swallow' his 'r's' by addressing a waiter in Le Havre as '*garrrçon*', and then giving the game away by ordering '*un vè de biè*' and not '*un verre de bière*'.[7] He knew that a magic circle surrounded the young man who was leaving, and that the words 'Paris, Marseille, La Sorbonne, Pigalle' were its keystone.[8] The erotic promise of Paris was the stuff of adolescent male folklore and he could recall how, as he finally approached a delayed puberty, a friend had told him of how he had held a young *Parisienne* in his arms.[9] Curiously, he appears to have been unaware before he left that many Martinican men were so eager to sleep with a white woman that their first port of call was a brothel in Le Havre; in *Peau noire* he remarks with what sounds like genuine surprise that this was a recent piece of information.[10] Many of the fantasies and hopes about Paris mentioned – and no doubt entertained – by Fanon could of course have been shared by any provincial youth dreaming of the capital, but they are overdetermined by the racial question. The dream of sleeping with a white woman in France was all the more alluring in that it was virtually impossible for a young black man to do so in Martinique. The opening sections of *Peau noire, masques blancs* paint a composite picture of the lived experience of the young Martinican in France – and it is a specifically male experience. Fanon's sister Gabrielle, who also left for France in 1946, would have had a different tale to tell.

Writing of his childhood in the black-mulatto society of Fort-de-France, Fanon remarks: 'I am a *nègre*, but naturally I don't know that because that is what I am.'[11] His experiences in the army and in liberated France had begun to teach him what he was in the eyes of most French people. The lesson was now to be reinforced. And it is a lesson that is still being learned by students from the 'French' West Indies: 'The West Indian who comes to France is steeped in what he believes to be French culture; he is sometimes "more French than the French" and believes that he will find a milieu into which he will be accepted, into which he can merge immediately. Despite his (legal) Frenchness, he finds that he is a foreigner living amongst whites and other foreigners. Because of his colour, he is rejected by a world whose culture he had, he thought, absorbed.'[12]

Sitting on a train on an unspecified date, Fanon heard a Frenchman who stank of cheap red wine rambling on about the need for a National Union to defend French values against foreigners. Looking towards the corner where Fanon was sitting, he then added 'Whoever they are.'[13] Fanon knew that Europeans had a definite idea of what a black man should be. He knew that he would probably be asked how long he had been in France, and be complemented on his 'good French'.[14] He realized that he would suffer the humiliating experience of being addressed in *petit-nègre*, or the French equivalent to pidgin English, by white people who called him '*tu*' because they spoke to blacks in the way that an adult speaks to a child;[15] Cézette can still recall how it felt. In 1946, Fanon had probably seen neither the image of the grinning *Tirailleur sénégalais* on the posters advertising Banania nor the images of Bamboulinette, the black maid from Martinique whose broad smile was used to sell shoe-polish. At home in Martinique, he had no reason to know that for many of his fellow French citizens, he *was* that soldier and that his sister *was* that maid.

Nothing could prepare him for the most devastating experience of all. It occurred on a cold day in Lyon when Fanon encountered a child and its mother. This is possibly the most famous passage in *Peau noire, masques blancs*. The child said to its mother: 'Look, a negro' and then 'Mum, look at the negro. I'm frightened! Frightened! Frightened!'[16] Fanon's own analysis of this traumatic encounter is discussed in detail in the next chapter. In the meantime, it is useful to ask how and why the child *knew* that Fanon was a negro. Part of the answer may come from a geography textbook for use in schools that was published in 1903:

Paul is usually a very punctual pupil, but one day, he is late for school. 'I'm sorry, sir', he says, 'I didn't realize what time it was. I was watching a *nègre* on the Grand' Place.' 'Was he a real *nègre*?' 'Yes! Yes sir. A real *nègre* with all black skin and teeth as white as milk. They say he comes from Africa. Are there lots of *nègres* in that country?' 'Yes, my friend.'[17]

A more complete explanation comes from the extraordinary childhood correspondence of the nine-year-old Françoise Marrette who, as Françoise Dolto (1908--88), became a psychoanalytic grandmother to the nation. During the First World War, she met a black family on the beach at the fashionable Normandy resort of Deauville; her nanny laughed at the sight. Another significant encounter came when she met a wounded *Tirailleur sénégalais* who was being cared for by her mother. The soldier kissed the little girl because she reminded him of his own daughter. Her nanny washed her vigorously. There follows an exchange of letters with relatives. Her uncle warns here not to play with any black troops she might meet on the beach: they are handsome, but not as good as 'our' mountain troops. From London, her father sends her a comic postcard of 'four little *nègres*' who look as though they were a group of street minstrels. Young Françoise describes a school composition she has written about a bayonet charge. It features a *Tirailleur* she calls Sid Vava Ben Abdallah, whom she describes as having a black face, white teeth, a flat nose and a red turban – she clearly identifies with him as 'Vava' was her family nickname. Finally, her mother sends her a postcard of a *Tirailleur* smoking a cigarette. On the back, she has written: 'Here is Bou'ji ma's portrait. Are you frightened of him?'[18] After this, there are no more images of black people in Dolto's juvenilia. French children of her generation were, in other words, taught both to recognize a *nègre* when they saw one, to laugh at him, and then to be afraid of him.

In late 1946, Fanon was twenty-one. He was a decorated war veteran and had passed his *baccalauréat*. His *bac* gave him the right to go to university, and legislation introduced on 4 August 1945 gave veterans free tuition and the right to small maintenance grants. He was free to study any subject he liked at the university of his choice. He had good reason to be somewhat apprehensive about leaving Martinique, but he was not reluctant to do so. On the contrary, like many young Martinicans he felt he was 'a prisoner on his island, lost in an atmosphere from which there was no way out' and the appeal of France was irresistible.[19] Fanon and his siblings were the first members of their family to attend university, and their entry into higher education was a further advance in the family's upward mobility. This could be described in class terms as a move from the petty bourgeoisie to the liberal professions, but Fanon does not speak in class terms and was not the classic *boursier* or 'grammar school boy'. The Martinican conflation of class with race meant that going to university was a further stage in becoming French, or in other words becoming white: 'The West Indian who comes to France sees his journey as the last stage in his personality. We can say quite literally and without any fear of being mistaken that the West Indian who goes to France in order to convince himself of his whiteness will find his true face there.'[20] And yet Fanon was in one sense a *boursier* rather than 'an inheritor' whose family and extracurricular activities equipped him with the symbolic capital that allowed him to negotiate the system and to profit from it.[21] Some of the decisions he would make about his education were to be strange, even perverse, and one explanation for them is quite simply that he made them alone and had no one and no training to guide him through the system.

His destination was Paris. The Atlantic crossing took twelve days, with the weather growing colder as he went north. Fanon's port of entry was Le Havre, which he had seen from the decks of the *San Mateo* just over a year earlier. Like so many Martinicans, he landed in a port that had once fitted out slave ships for the triangular trade that took their distant ancestors from Africa to the Caribbean. Fanon's first sight of France had been the invasion beaches of the south and the shattered city of Toulon. His second introduction to *la métropole* was another city in ruins. Le Havre – Bouville in Sartre's *La Nausée* – had been badly damaged by Allied bombs and German resistance in the last months of the war. The docks the *San Mateo* had been unable to use in 1945 were now functioning, but the town itself was still a bomb-site. It was not an auspicious time to go to France. The economy was in as bad a condition as Le Havre. The Fourth Republic, which had been in existence for only two years, was already revealing its chronic instability and weakness. The transport system was still in chaos, and fuel supplies were poor. It was to be a cold, harsh winter. Food rationing was still in force, and by May 1947 the daily bread ration had been reduced to 250 grammes. In September, riots broke out when it was further reduced to 200 grammes per day – 75 grammes less than in the bleakest years of the Occupation.[22] By the end of the year, or just as Fanon was settling down to his studies, a wave of strikes was in progress throughout the country. When the miners of northern France also struck in November, the government sent in troops and the mining areas were under virtual military occupation.[23]

For Fanon, Le Havre was no more than a staging post and he continued his journey by rail to Paris. He planned to enrol at the School of

Dentistry there and, in the absence of any pre-entry selection or pre-enrolment, this was quite literally a matter of queuing up at the relevant office. The decision to study dentistry must have been taken suddenly; in September 1945, Fanon had spoken of becoming a lawyer. There are minor but unresolved discrepancies in accounts of Fanon's experience at the dental school. According to his first biographer, he lasted three weeks before walking out, complaining that he had never met 'so many idiots in his life'.[24] According to his uncle, he did not even complete the enrolment formalities, and suddenly decided that he did not want to study dentistry and that he did not wish to be in Paris. All sources agree that he left Paris quickly. There were, he told both his brother Joby and his friend Marcel Manville, 'too many negroes [*nègres*]' in Paris.[25] There were fewer of them in Lyon, and that was where he was going . . . to study medicine and not dentistry. The reported comment on the number of *nègres* in Paris was obviously a joke, but it is not easy to interpret. According to Manville, Fanon wanted to 'lactify' or whiten himself, 'as though the man who had committed himself to France during the war was at once regretting and rediscovering his merits and qualities as a Frenchman'.[26] His brother takes the view that Frantz wanted to get away from Paris's resident Martinican community – a community at once cemented together and isolated by its ritual loyalty to a culture founded on rum, the beguine and accras – deep-fried fritters of cod or prawn. That was one of the possibilities open to the Martinican student in Paris: rejecting Europe, using Creole and 'settling very comfortably into what we can call the Martinican *Umwelt*'.[27] Fanon himself remarks that he disliked the Martinican students' tendency to deflate anyone who attempted to initiate a serious discussion by accusing him of being self-important and cutting him down to size by reverting to Creole.[28] The other possibility was to identify with and become part of the white host community: 'I am French. I am interested in French culture, in French civilization.'[29] Whilst he may have been reluctant to join in the classic expatriate culture of the Martinican community in Paris, when he did spend time there while visiting his brother during vacations, he spent it with that very community. He did, after all, enjoy rum, accras and the beguine. Edouard Glissant, who met him briefly in Paris in 1946, describes Fanon as being deeply concerned with developments in Martinique, which was now beginning the process of departmentalization. He was, according to Glissant, 'extremely sensitive'. Fanon was *un écorché vif,* which literally means someone who has been flayed alive and whose every raw nerve has been exposed.[30] Fanon's attitude towards his fellow Martinicans was based upon a profound ambivalence and a deeply troubled sense of his own identity, but it was the characteristic combination of impulsiveness and determination that took him to Lyon, just as it had taken the teenage dissident to Dominica in 1943.

Fanon's decision to read medicine may, according to his brother Joby, have been prompted by the mistaken belief that it required a shorter course of study than dentistry, but that does not explain the decision to leave Paris. Lyon was not the obvious place to study, though the fact that the cost of living was lower than in Paris may have been part of the attraction. Although the Lyon medical faculty was perfectly respectable, it did not have the prestige enjoyed by Paris's Ecole de médecine. A brass plate on a surgery door saying that Dr Fanon had studied in Paris and had worked in a Parisian hospital would have made a much better impression on Martinican patients than one describing him as a graduate of a provincial Faculté Mixte de Médecine et de Pharmacie. Joby Fanon suggests that his brother chose to go to Lyon because he had made friends in Nantua during his wartime convalescence, and had kept in touch with them.[31] Lyon was close enough to Nantua to maintain the connection. Even so, he had no direct contacts in Lyon itself. In Paris, Fanon could have remained in close contact with friends and family. Mosole was studying dentistry in Paris and Joby was studying there in preparation for a career in the customs service that would take him much higher than his father. Manville was completing the final year of his law degree and would be called to the bar in October 1947.[32] It would also have been much easier to remain in touch with Gabrielle. She was studying pharmacy in Rouen, which is a short train journey away from the capital. He did visit her when he could and may have had some further contact with the hospitable Lemonnier family, but travelling between Lyon and Rouen was far from easy.

Fanon had, probably without realizing it, chosen to live and study in a city which was – and is – notoriously unfriendly to strangers. Lyon was neither more nor less racist than any French city, but even white fellow students like Robert Berthellier, who was born in Royan, felt themselves unwelcome there. Berthellier's outsider status, together with his love of jazz – he played piano – meant that he felt more at home with Fanon and the handful of black students at the university than with the native *lyonnais* students.[33] Living in Lyon accentuated Fanon's sense of isolation and estrangement. He was already familiar with the town–country relationship that existed between little settlements like Basse-Pointe and 'the imposing Fort-de-France'; he could now detect a similar dialectic between Paris and Lyon. 'Take a Lyonnais in Paris; he will boast of how peaceful his city is, of the intoxicating beauty of the banks of the Rhône, the splendour of the plane trees and all the other things that are praised by people who have nothing to do. If you meet him when he comes back to Paris, and especially if you do not know the capital, he won't stop singing its praises: Paris-city-of-light, the Seine, the open-air cafés, see Paris and die . . .'[34] Fanon could play all the parts in the scenario of exile and alienation.

Like the rest of France, Lyon suffered a severe housing crisis after the war. In Paris, the crisis was so acute that, according to urban myth, anyone who saw a potential suicide poised to leap into the Seine would run up to him – not to offer help, but to ask if he was leaving an apartment free. Matters were not quite so bad in Lyon, but the accommodation crisis does explain why Fanon found himself living in a former brothel requisitioned by the Ministry of Education and converted into rudimentary student housing.[35] It was one of the famous *maisons closes* or state-regulated brothels which were closed in 1946 when the Assemblée Nationale adopted a bill pushed through by a zealous Communist Party member. Although Fanon's accommodation was rather unusual, this was a convenient solution, as a lone black student with no contacts and little money would not have found it easy to obtain rented accommodation in the private sector.

There were indeed fewer *nègres* in Lyon than in Paris, but France's second city stands at the junction of major trade routes and has absorbed wave after wave of immigrants. Italians, Greeks and Armenians flooded there before and during the First World War. In the 1920s and 1930s, the deteriorating economy of Algeria forced many peasants – the majority of them from Kabylia – to migrate and find work in Lyon's factories. Others had simply stayed on after being demobilized during the First World War. In the early 1930s, the Algerian community in Lyon was estimated to be 2,200. Most were single men, living ten or twelve to a room in the slums of the rue Moncey and the Guillotière quarter, only a few hundred yards away from the city's historic centre on the east bank of the Rhône.[36] An Algerian who migrated to the city in 1950 describes his living conditions thus: 'I was living in a rooming house [*un garni*] in the rue Garibaldi. There were a lot of us in that *garni*, twenty or thirty people. It's true. We paid 1,000 old francs a month; at the time I was earning 13,000 . . . We were overrun with rats in that *garni*. It was a scandal, yes, yes . . . pitiful, yes . . . and a scandal.'[37] The *garni* and the café – a poor imitation of the Moorish cafés of Algeria, but always a major centre of political activity – were the social poles of the urban immigrant's world. Conditions had changed little since the 1930s, when a local Communist paper described the rooming houses in the Molière area:

In order to get an idea of the social wound known as a slum you have to have gone down those narrow corridors, climbed the wooden staircases with their uneven or missing stairs, breathed the revolting smells from the gutters, cesspools and courtyards of certain houses. Let's not talk about the flats. Let's not talk about the garrets they call rooms, as their low ceilings and sweating walls defy description. And yet miserable wretches live in them, and at a horribly high price they are sold the right to sleep under a roof, despite the rancid smell and the inadequate air-space.[38]

Compared to this, a cubicle in a former brothel was luxury indeed.

It was in Lyon that Fanon first came into contact with the North Africans he had been unable to meet during his brief stay in Algeria in 1944. Although Lyon was, even in the harsh climate of the post-war years, a relatively prosperous city, the home visits he made to the rue Moncey as a young doctor taught him that the wretched of the earth were not far away. The Algerian community had rapidly acquired the reputation for criminality and violence that still clings to North African immigrants. According to a 1923 police report, the rue Moncey was a nest of filth, a centre of anti-hygiene, a threat to public order and a social danger.[39] Such views were – and are – not uncommon; the image

of the Algerian with a knife is deeply rooted in a certain French imaginary[40] which, since at least the 1930s, has seen the 'Sidi' as a barbarian
who is invading the white citadel.[41] Given their living conditions, it is
not surprising that the Algerian immigrants provided Lyon's hospitals
and psychiatric centres with large numbers of patients, and it was in that
context that Fanon first came to know 'all these men who are hungry,
all these men who are cold, all these men who are afraid . . . All these
men who make us afraid.'[42]

Fanon's sense of isolation was increased by the news that reached
him in the first week of February 1947. Félix Casimir Fanon had died
unexpectedly on 30 January at the age of only fifty-six. A telegram was
dispatched to Lyon and, on receiving it, Fanon left immediately to talk
to Gabrielle in Rouen. It was a long and uncomfortable overnight journey. Rouen is 600 kilometres from Lyon and the journey involved a
change of train and station in Paris. Fanon spent a sleepless night trying
his best not to think about the telegram. Despite the gestures of sympathy that had been made by friends, he could not believe that he had
been orphaned, so difficult was it to imagine the death of his father. In
1945, he had written in very harsh terms to him, but was now anxious
to know if his father had spoken of him before he died. He wanted to
know what his father thought of him, because a paternal opinion would
help him to 'reform his norms' and to work harder at his daily tasks. He
was also afraid that his mother would lapse into despair or even die of
grief, and begged her not to leave her children: 'What would we be
without you?'[43] His fears were not realized: Eléanore Fanon lived on in
her cool, dark house in Redoute until July 1981. In Rouen, Gabrielle
was also in tears. Well aware that her father's death was a blow to the
stability – and finances – of the family, she was talking of abandoning
her studies and returning to Fort-de-France to find work. It took Frantz
a night of persuasion to convince her that this was the wrong course.
After what her brother called 'a good talking to', she capitulated and
agreed to go on with her university course. When she did return to
Martinique, it was as a qualified pharmacist. Fanon himself could offer
little help in the impending financial crisis, as his grant was proving
almost inadequate for his own needs. Joby was able to help a little. He
was playing semi-professional football on a part-time basis and was able
to send his younger brother a little money occasionally.[44]

Fanon's geographical-racial isolation was compounded by the need to study a new and unfamiliar subject. His lycée education had left him able to cite Kant on the sublime[45] (not that this implied any great acquaintance with critical philosophy), but had given him little scientific knowledge. As a preliminary to his five years of medical studies, he therefore had to take a year-long foundation course in biology, physics and chemistry. *Peau noire* tells us little about Fanon's medical studies, though it is informative about his initiation into psychiatry. It does, however, tell us that he was bored by the 'objectivity' of anatomists who could describe the tibia, but reacted with astonishment when he asked them how many pre-peroneal depressions *they* had. It rapidly became clear that he was not destined to be a surgeon. As he should have foreseen after his reaction to watching the autopsy in Le François, even basic dissection made him feel nauseous and a more hardened student's advice to regard the cadaver as though it were a mere cat did not help.[46]

Fanon had some difficulty in integrating himself into the academic community, and often remained both aloof and isolated. There were few other black students, and it would have been more usual to find a young West Indian washing the floor of the dissecting room than cutting up cadavers in it. Fanon was older than most of his fellow students and, unlike them, had fought a war that had left him bitter and angry, and with his supposedly 'French' identity largely in tatters. Yet he rarely talked about either his experiences in Dominica or during the war in France; a close acquaintance like Nicole Guillet, who is now a psychoanalyst in Paris, had no idea that he had been a soldier and had been decorated. Some younger students such as Jacques Postel found him slightly intimidating. He was not always easy to approach, and was sharp-tongued and ferocious when involved in arguments, as he constantly attempted to defeat people on their own ground, to make them admit defeat. He could be cuttingly aggressive, but also often appeared to be under great stress. Guillet suggests, with hindsight, that the displays of aggression were a defence against an underlying sense of self-doubt or insecurity.[47]

Yet the same Fanon could also be boisterously outgoing, and was given to declaiming from memory – and in a very loud voice – long passages from Aimé Césaire's *Cahier d'un retour au pays natal*. He enjoyed dancing and listening to his Stellio records. This was a very Martinican taste. Alexandre Stellio (1885–1939) was the leader of the most famous of the Creole orchestras that took France by storm just before the Second World War. He was an accomplished clarinettist, and his *beguine* music was a pleasantly syncopated dance music with hints of New Orleans jazz. By 1946, the *beguine* was no longer particularly fashionable in France; Fanon was quite simply listening to the music of his childhood. He had no great liking for classical music but claimed to have an interest in jazz, although a friend who worked with him in Algeria and then Tunisia believes that he was less interested in the music itself than in the sociological phenomenon of black music in the racist white society of the United States.[48] The parody of the 'negritude' vision of Louis Armstrong's music in *Peau noire* suggests that this was indeed the case: 'I am black, I bring about a total fusion with the world, a sympathetic understanding of the earth and lose my ego in the heart of the cosmos; no matter how intelligent he may be, the white man cannot understand Armstrong.'[49] In 1959, he discussed the reactions of white jazz fans to the development of new styles such as be-bop, which he saw as a reflection of the new-world view of a black community that had glimpsed a new hope for the future. For the white fans, this was a betrayal: jazz had to be 'the broken and despairing nostalgia of an old negro trapped between five whiskies, the curse upon him and the racist hatred of whites'.[50] The sociology of jazz and the blues does appear to have interested him more than the music itself.

Fanon is reported to have been close to the student branch of the Parti Communiste Français but he did not become a member, even though he was active in student politics and took part in anti-colonialist demonstrations. Some of the demonstrations concerned the case of Paul Vergès, the leader of the Communist Party of Réunion, who was arrested on a murder charge in May 1946. Convinced that he could not hope to have a fair trial in Réunion, anti-colonialist groups there succeeded in having the hearings transferred to metropolitan France. Between April and August 1947, when he was acquitted, Vergès was held in prison in Lyon.[51] In the course of a demonstration organized to demand the release of Paul Vergès, Fanon was clubbed and trampled underfoot by the police, and he did not forget the experience.[52] The tone of *Peau noire, masques blancs* and his other early texts indicates that Fanon's political views were at this time a product of his own anger and a spontaneous sympathy with the 'wretched of the earth' rather than of any interest in party politics.

The outgoing side to his personality that had made him the dominant figure in games of football in Martinique now made Fanon an imposing participant in the Association lyonnaise des étudiants de la France d'Outre-mer, or Overseas Students' Association. Sadly, there appear to be no extant records of that small organization's activities. Fanon's forceful personality also made him very attractive to the women he encountered in the caféteria and meeting rooms of the Association générale des étudiants, or Students' Union. It probably helped that Fanon, who could be seductively charming when he wanted to be, always dressed very smartly and conservatively, as Martinicans of his generation tended to do (the habitually dishevelled Manville was, even in later life, a conspicuous exception to the rule). His contacts were not restricted to his contemporaries. He was in touch with the Martinican Louis-Thomas-Eugène Achille, who taught English at the prestigious Lycée du Parc – still regarded as Lyon's best school. Born in 1909, a prolific writer of articles on black issues and an authority on negro spirituals (he had recorded with the 'Park Glee Club de Lyon'),[53] Achille, whose brother taught at the Lycée Schoelcher in Fort-de-France, was a Catholic and of a different generation to Fanon. But they had experiences in common, and Fanon could recognize himself in Achille's anecdote about going on a Catholic pilgrimage in June 1950. Seeing a 'tanned' man in his flock, the priest in charge approached him with the words 'You done left big Savanne, why come long us?' The impeccable French of Achille's courteous reply meant that it was the priest who was left embarrassed by the exchange.[54] His good French did not, however, make it any easier to find a hotel in Paris; the hotels refused to take in the black pilgrims 'simply because the Anglo-Saxon guests (who, as everyone knows are rich and negrophobic) might have moved out'.[55] Although novelists like Richard Wright, who lived in France from 1947 onwards, and musicians like Bud Powell, found Paris less hostile than the United States, the city was by no means free of racism. Like Achille, the American novelist Chester Himes recalled being turned away from the cheap hotels frequented by young white Americans: 'They said they couldn't rent to *noirs*; their clients wouldn't like it.'[56] An Algerian would have found it even more difficult to find a room.

At the beginning of his second year in Lyon, Fanon wrote to his mother to tell her that the days when his teachers had had to complain to her about his bad behaviour were long gone, that he was working very hard, and that he was anxious to bring her the joy she had always taken in her children's academic success. He was, he said, making up for lost time, and outlined an ambitious programme: a second diploma in February, his second medical exams in June and then, at an unspecified date, a non-resident post in a Lyon hospital.[57] He did not in fact keep to this programme, and made another change of direction as his studies progressed, but he was working hard and not only at his medicine. The footnotes to *Peau noire* indicate that he was reading very widely, and that his reading was by no means restricted to medical textbooks. The plethora of notes and quotations is an indication of a major change that had occurred when he moved from Fort-de-France to Lyon: he had moved from a book-poor to a book-rich culture, from the limited resources of the Bibliothèque Schoelcher to the bookshops and libraries of a large university town, and he was taking advantage of the facilities on offer. He was reading journals like *Esprit*, the voice of the Catholic left, Sartre's *Les Temps modernes* and *Présence africaine*, which began publication in 1947. He read quite extensively in philosophy, showing a particular interest in the Hegelian-existentialist strand that was so important in the immediate post-war years, and attended lectures by Merleau-Ponty, but later told Simone de Beauvoir that he found the philosopher 'distant' and never tried to speak to him.[58] The opening words of the first chapter of *Peau noire* come directly from his study of phenomenology: 'I attach a fundamental importance to the phenomenon of language. Hence, I believe, the necessity of this study, which should provide us with one element that will help us to understand the *for-others [pour autrui]* dimension of the man of colour.'[59] The appeal of phenomenology was that, as will be argued in Chapter 5 below, of all the philosophical discourses available to him in the late 1940s, this was the philosophy that could be best adapted to an analysis of his own 'lived experience'. The classics of French phenomenology – Merleau-Ponty's *Phénoménologie de la perception* and Sartre's *L'Etre et le néant* – are obviously not treatises on racism and anti-racism, but they provided tools that were much better suited to the analysis of 'the lived experience of the black man' than either Marxism or psychoanalysis.

In *Peau noire, masques blancs*, Fanon's vocabulary is that of the modernism of the 1940s. And it is the modernity of his non-medical reading that is so striking: most of the books cited in *Peau noire* were published in the period 1947–50, which makes it likely that its final composition dates from 1950–51. Richard Wright's *Native Son* and Chester Himes's *If He Hollers Let Him Go* (which appeared in translation in 1947 and 1948 respectively) were of obvious interest to someone intent on analysing the lived experience of the black man, but it is also significant that they were part of the new 'committed' culture so actively promoted by *Les Temps modernes* in particular and provided a contemporary counterbalance to *Présence africaine*'s more traditionalist approach to African culture. The novels were also his main – if not sole – source of information about race relations in the United States. When he contrasts the surprise expressed by Americans in Paris on seeing so many racially mixed couples with Simone de Beauvoir's experience of hostility from an old lady when walking through New York with Wright, he is, although he gives no reference, alluding to a book published in 1948.[60] Whilst Fanon's reading was wide, it was also very selective and tightly focused. He was reading philosophy and psychology in order to find the theoretical tools to analyse his lived experience, and fiction, poetry and drama to illustrate it. He read Beauvoir's account of her travels in America and of her friendship with Wright, but there is no direct evidence that he knew her *Le Deuxième Sexe*.[61] Feminism was not on Fanon's agenda. He refers to and cites Sartre's play *La Putain respectueuse*, which was inspired by the Scottsboro (Alabama) affair of 1931, in which nine young black men were sentenced to the electric chair for the alleged rape of two white prostitutes and served long terms of imprisonment (the last of the Scottsboro boys was finally freed in 1951), but not the novels of his *Les Chemins de la liberté* ('Roads to Freedom') trilogy, which do not deal with the race question.[62] His knowledge of the personalist philosopher Emmanuel Mounier was restricted to a reading of his account of a journey through France's West African colonies.[63]

Fanon was now beginning to write, but nothing has survived from this period. He used a roneo machine in the Students' Union to produce a small magazine entitled *Tam-tam* (*Tom-tom*), and appears to have been its sole contributor as well as its editor. Whilst nothing is known of its content, the title has a very Césairean ring to it – the word *tam-tam* appears in the title of three of the poems included in Césaire's first collection[64] – and suggests that Fanon was experimenting with some variant of negritude. Although sections of *Peau noire, masques blancs* reveal a certain gift for narrative, he does not appear to have tried his hand at prose fiction but he was very interested in the theatre and frequented the Théâtre de la Comédie, where he saw early stage productions of Roger Planchon, who was director there from 1952 to 1957.[65] The interest in drama explains some features of *Peau noire*, in which Fanon makes use of an almost theatrical delivery and writes fragments of dialogue that are most effective when read aloud. By 1949–50, he had written three plays. They remained unpublished and were never performed, even though a very optimistic Fanon sent at least one of them to the actor-director Jean-Louis Barrault, who never replied. One friend recalls having seen them in manuscript and, whilst she has no real memory of their content, does remember that they were 'not very good'.[66] According to Fanon's widow, the manuscripts were lost during one of the many moves that took them from Lyon to Algeria, from Algeria to Tunis and then to Accra. In a rare interview, she recalled only that they dealt with 'philosophical themes' and above all with that of 'action'.[67] This, together with the titles – *Les Mains parallèles* ('Parallel Hands'), *L'Oeil se noye* ('The Eye Drowns' or 'The Drowning Eye') and *La Conspiration* ('The Conspiracy') – suggests that they were variants on the themes of Sartre's plays of the 1940s. In the late 1940s, Sartre was a very major figure in the French theatre and he had created a philosophical style of drama centred on the themes of 'action' and responsibility, notably with *Les Mains sales* (1948), and Fanon was an assiduous reader of his work.

According to his own account, it was soon after his arrival in Lyon that Fanon began work on what was to become his first book. He writes that *Peau noire, masques blancs* was the conclusion of 'seven years of experiments and observations', but also that it was 'three or four years' before its publication that he began to experiment with the free association tests whose findings he incorporates into his text.[68] The book was published in 1952 and, allowing for submission and production, this indicates that the project dates back to either 1945, which is improbable in the extreme, or to about 1947–8. Although Fanon attempted to submit it as his degree dissertation, it is unlikely that *Peau noire* began life as a thesis. There was no indication in 1947 that he was going to study psychiatry, and it is a very odd first-year student who begins to prepare – or even think of – a final-year project in his first year at medical school. There is the further possibility that the idea for it was sparked by the study of 'the genesis of the myth of the negro' launched in the second issue of *Présence africaine*. Fanon administered what he calls his 'free association tests' to some three to four hundred individuals from the white race, inserting the word 'negro' into a random series of twenty or so other words. Almost 60 per cent of the tests produced the associations: biological, penis, sport, sportsman, powerful, boxer, Joe Louis, Jess (sic) Owen, *Tirailleurs sénégalais*, savage, animal, devil, sin. A white prostitute told him that the idea of going to bed with a black man brought her to orgasm. Subsequent experience taught that they were 'no more extraordinary' than her white clients: 'I was thinking (imagining) about everything they could do to me: that was what was fantastic.'[69] Fanon does not say whether he approached her in the interests of research, or as a client. Technically, Fanon was not using free association but a Jungian word association test in which the subject's immediate response to the stimulus word is interpreted as revealing a thought process, personality characteristic or emotional state.[70] The terminological slip that allows Fanon to describe this as 'free association' (in which a patient lying on an analytic couch describes everything that comes into his mind and in which the analyst listens with suspended attention, and without supplying any stimulus) implies a surprisingly slight acquaintance with Freudian practice. Here, Fanon is not exploring the unconscious of an individual but the stereotypical associations of a culture.

*Peau noire, masques blancs* supplies a few indications as to the nature of Fanon's extra-curricular activities in Lyon, and his difficult situation there. He was both respected by his colleagues and the object of their casual and unthinking racism. He recalls, for instance, that 'just over a year ago (i.e. 1949–50) I gave a lecture in which I traced a parallel between black poetry and European poetry'. After it, a metropolitan friend congratulated him warmly but unthinkingly said: 'Basically, you're white'.[71] Assuming that Fanon's dates are correct, it seems reasonable to assume that the lecture was a discussion of one of the first anthologies of Black and Malagasy poetry to be published in French.[72] He was also asked by the Association lyonnaise des Etudiants de la France d'Outre-mer to respond to an article that had described jazz as an irruption of cannibalism into European purity. In his angry reply, he told the 'defender of European purity' that there was nothing cultural about his 'spasm'.[73] Neither Fanon's talk, the article about jazz nor his response to it have survived, but one extant document provides a useful insight into the cultural concerns of his circle.

Nicole Guillet believes that the unsigned 56-page typescript entitled *Le Surréalisme* dating from her student days in Lyon and still in her possession is Fanon's work, but the internal evidence suggests otherwise. A reference on the sixth sheet to the lecture 'Your brother Frantz' gave on the 'solar poetry' of Negro art makes it improbable that Frantz Fanon wrote it ('Frantz' is not a common name, and the likelihood of there being two black students called 'Frantz' in Lyon at the same time is almost absurdly slight), but it could be an allusion to the talk on Black and European poetry. It does, however, indicate that the typescript originated from within the circles in which Fanon was active. Given that the author mentions having seen an exhibition of Central African masks and 'idols' in Brussels and comments that it had inspired in him a feeling of 'sacred horror' that he had never experienced while looking at 'art from your countries', it would appear that he was a black student speaking to a mixed audience. Although the text is undated, it refers to Julien Gracq's essay 'Lautréamont toujours', which was originally published in 1947, and it therefore cannot have been written before that date. A frustratingly vague reference to Glissant also points to a date after 1947 – the year in which he published his poem 'Terre à Terre', followed by 'Laves' in 1948 – as does the author's ability to cite in its entirety André Breton's 'Sur la route de San Romano', written in 1948.[74] It is, then, more than probable that this is the text of a talk given to a group of students in Lyon in about 1949 or 1950, and that it is representative of cultural concerns shared by Fanon.

Whoever did write 'Le Surréalisme' clearly had a very good knowledge of the subject, and a passion for it. It must have taken the better part of two hours to read the lecture, which deals in some detail with the origins and development of surrealism, looking at its beginnings in the 'Cubist' poetry of Apollinaire and in the manifestos of Breton, at the techniques of automatic writing, and even at the parallels between Salvador Dali's notion of critical paranoia and Lacan's early theory of the origins of psychosis. Obviously addressed to an audience with no more than a passing knowledge of surrealism, this is a paper by a young enthusiast anxious to share his passion for the topic rather than an academic intent upon analysing it. The general characterization of surrealism as a 'new poetic activity characterized by mysticism and the spirit of revolt' is unexceptional but not inaccurate, and it is the concluding remarks that are of most interest. Summing up, the anonymous author describes Rimbaud as one of surrealism's most important forebears, and then refers to him as the first link in a new poetic chain which, through its 'absolute and brutal aspirations', links surrealism to the black poetry of Césaire, Senghor, Glissant 'and so many other contemporary black poets'.

Reviewing *Peau noire* in 1952, the Martinican novelist Léonard Sainville remarked that it reminded him of *Légitime Défense*, a little magazine published in 1932. *Légitime Défense* was one of the first attempts to create a specifically Martinican literary-political culture, and the precursor of *Tropiques*. René Ménil worked on both journals. *Légitime Défense* was an angry little magazine, and its brutal denunciations of social conditions in Martinique led to its being banned as subversive. Only one issue was published. The title is borrowed from that of the 1926 pamphlet in which André Breton both declares himself in solidarity with the coming Communist revolution and denounces the PCF daily *L'Humanité* for its intellectual 'cretinism' and its failure to play its self-appointed role as an organ of proletarian education.[75] The young collective that produced *Légitime Défense* was not so critical of the PCF, but one of its contributors – the twenty-five-year-old Ménil – outlined a programme that was scarcely in line with the orthodox Marxism of 1932:

The coloured West Indian expresses the feelings of an Other because the powers of his passions and imagination are not recognized. The black West Indian should therefore begin by recognizing his own passions, express only himself and, going against utility, take the path of dreams and poetry. In the course of his effort, he would encounter the fantastic images of which

African and Oceanic statuettes are one expression, poems and stories, the jazz of black Americans and French works which by going
beyond industry and by using the powers of passion and dreams,
have conquered the freshness of Africa.[76]

A footnote points out that the 'French works' in question are those of
Lautréamont, Rimbaud, Apollinaire, Jarry, Reverdy, the Dadaists and
the surrealists, or in other words the very authors discussed by the
author of 'Le Surréalisme'. These were also the authors to whom
Césaire introduced his students at the Lycée Schoelcher.

Sainville added that it seemed to him that Fanon knew nothing of his
predecessors, and that his *prise de conscience* began with Césaire.[77] When
Sainville remarks that *Peau noire* 'reminded' him of *Légitime Défense*, he
is in effect saying that there is nothing new in it. It might be fairer to say
that, without realizing it, a small group of students in Lyon had
returned to the starting-point for a distinctively Francophone tradition
that goes back to the publication by an earlier group of students of
*Légitime Défense*, or in other words to the Caribbean version of surrealism that so influenced Aimé Césaire and the poets of negritude.[78] In
Martinique itself, the tradition of *Legitime Défense* was of course continued by *Tropiques*. The circle in which Fanon was moving in Lyon
thus reproduces the cultural programme of the forefathers of the negritude of the 1940s and 1950s. It would in fact have been extremely
difficult for them to have known the work of their predecessors in any
detail. It is improbable that *Légitime Défense* circulated widely outside
Paris, or even outside the Latin Quarter, and the war and occupation
must have destroyed any continuity between 1932 and 1949. Jazz,
surrealism, existentialism and the poetry of negritude were all part of a
young, modern culture and whilst Lyon was not the bohemian Paris
where Miles Davis was pursuing an affair with Juliette Greco in 1949[79]
and whilst the Students' Union building was no *cave* in St-Germain des
prés, Fanon was nevertheless deeply involved with the modernism of his
day. He enjoyed discussing surrealism, and it is apparent from his degree
dissertation that he was familiar with Henri Ey's article on psychiatry
and surrealism.[80] As will be argued later, the cultural politics of *Peau
noire* can be read in terms of his ambivalent relationship with both
negritude and existentialism.

The student circles in which Fanon was moving were racially mixed, but the racial mix was not reflected in the sexual mix: there were few or no black women. Whilst mixed race couples were far from uncommon in Paris, Lyon was a deeply conservative town and Fanon's first relationship with a younger white woman cannot have been an easy one. Michelle B. was a fellow medical student and a daughter of the middle classes – her father was an engineer who had worked on the Rhine's dams – though not of the formidable bourgeoisie of Lyon. The relationship was not long-lasting, but it was one-sided and her commitment was much greater than Fanon's. It ended in disaster for the young woman. In 1948, Michelle B. gave birth to Fanon's daughter. The scandal was devastating. Pre-marital sex was bad enough, but having a black baby was worse still. Abortion was of course both illegal and unacceptable. Fanon was unwilling to marry her, having fallen for someone else, and had probably never taken the relationship as seriously as her. After some considerable persuasion from friends and family, and although he was under no legal obligation to do so, Fanon did recognize the child as his own, which allowed her to use the name Fanon in later life. Although there is a striking family resemblance, Mireille Fanon never knew her father and it was only as a young adult, and on Joby Fanon's initiative, that she became part of the extended Fanon family. Inevitably, the brief affair with Fanon put an end to Michelle B.'s hopes of a medical career; she failed her exams and never qualified as a doctor. She did, however, marry a psychiatrist and eventually pursued a successful administrative career in that sector.[81]

Fanon had refused to marry the mother of his first child because he was now involved with Marie-Josephe Dublé (known to all as Josie), whom he met in 1949 when she was still at her lycée. She was a strikingly good-looking eighteen-year-old classicist, slim, dark-haired and with a contralto voice and the eyes of a gypsy: according to family memory, she was of mixed Corsican-gypsy descent, and had the temperament – and the temper – to match. Her family was from the Lyon region, and her parents were trade unionists working in the postal service. Their leftist politics ensured that there was no parental disapproval of the relationship and no opposition to the marriage that followed.[82] Josie Fanon, who committed suicide in Algiers in 1989, was always very reluctant to talk about her private life, and especially her life with

Fanon, and their relationship has never really been described. The couple married in 1952 and it is clear that she played an important role in the composition of *Peau noire*. Fanon never learned to use a typewriter and dictated his text to Josie as he strode up and down the room like an actor declaiming his lines. Traces of the oral origins of the text are visible in the sudden breaks and changes of direction, as Fanon suddenly recalls or thinks of something. If there is an element of free association here, it is Fanon and not his informants who is free associating. When he writes, or rather says, 'When my ubiquitary [*ubiquitaire*] hands caress these white breasts, I am making white civilization and dignity mine,'[83] he is speaking to the young woman he will marry. Commenting on the mythical size of the black man's genitals, he adds: 'One can easily imagine what such descriptions could provoke in a young Lyonnaise', but then hesitates: 'Horror? Desire? Not indifference, in any case.'[84] But he does not ask the young *Lyonnaise* who is with him and taking down his words.

As he pursued his studies, Fanon began to turn away from general medicine and to develop an interest in psychiatry. The reasons for this new change of direction were probably subjective. It is not unusual for psychiatrists in the making to take up the specialism in an attempt to understand their own behaviour, even their own problems. *Peau noire* is many things, and it can be read as a self-exploration or even as a wild self-analysis; to the extent that it is a socio-diagnostic or an analysis of the social origins of psychological phenomena,[85] Fanon is his own case-material: the *écorché vif* encountered by Glissant and others. The overlap between psychiatry, psychology and philosophy also allows Fanon to pursue his interests in ways that would not have been possible in other areas of medicine. He has no difficulty in introducing elements of Sartrean phenomenology into his socio-diagnostics, but would have found it difficult indeed to produce a Sartrean theory of dentistry. He had found his subject. Although Fanon is often described as a 'psychoanalyst', he was not and his relationship with psychoanalysis was always fraught.[86] His references to psychoanalysis are grafted on to his phenomenology and his knowledge of psychiatry.

Psychiatry was not a prestigious specialism at the time, and the training was not particularly rigorous. Nor was it particularly well developed. Only the universities of Paris, Strasbourg and Algiers had chairs in psychiatry. The discipline was marginalized in medical schools in general and Lyon in particular was a 'psychiatric desert', according to one who traversed it at much the same time as Fanon.[87] The city's Vinatier psychiatric hospital would have provided a better training but, being both unsure of his career direction and ill-informed as to the possibilities open to him, Fanon followed only one year of a basic course there and opted to study at the University's medical school. The teaching of psychiatry there was dominated by Professor Dechaume, who was interested solely in psychosurgery, neuropsychiatry and neurology. The fact that Dechaume had lost an arm in the First World War, and therefore could not operate himself, did nothing to deter him: every morning he could be seen in theatre, directing his surgical assistant by prodding him with his stump.[88] He presided over a large psychosurgical ward and the basement of his clinic housed an impressive ECG unit, but the child psychiatry unit was crammed into a room with a total surface area of forty square metres. Witnesses like Guillet, Berthellier and Postel do not recall that patients received particularly progressive treatment, or that they were given anything to do other than lie in their beds all day. The Lyon faculty was dominated by an organicist and neuropsychiatric approach to both diagnosis and treatment: patients suffering from anxiety were treated with ECT, which is more normally used to treat depression.[89] Social psychology was unknown, and so was psychoanalysis. There were no psychoanalysts in Lyon at this time, and therefore no means of having any practical training in analysis. An enthusiastic novice could have gone to Paris or Geneva to hear lectures, but Fanon could obviously not have gone into a personal analysis requiring daily sessions of an hour, and still less a subsequent training analysis. The references to psychoanalysis in *Peau noire* are evidence of Fanon's wide reading, and not of his official studies. His knowledge of the subject – and it is far less sophisticated than some recent readings would suggest – was textually based, and it was only from 1952 onwards that he began to acquire some rudimentary analysis-based clinical experience.

As his initial clinical training was coming to an end in 1951, Fanon took a temporary post as a houseman in the Saint-Ylié hospital in Dôle, a small town in the Jura 150 kilometres north of Lyon, but with a rail connection that allowed him to go back for Saturday ward rounds with

Dechaume. He may now have regretted his decision not to study in Paris; the salaries of junior doctors working in the psychiatric hospitals of the Seine *département* were 20 per cent higher than those of their provincial colleagues.[90] Financial considerations aside, Fanon's stay in Dôle was not a happy one. Twenty-two years after the event, his consultant, Dr Madeleine Humbert, replied to Jacques Postel's enquiries about Fanon's early career: 'I have no memory of Fanon deigning to note down any observations. He left the most unpleasant memory possible of his stay, and treated the nurses . . . like a colonialist. It has to be said that, at the time, he was the only intern for five hundred patients.'[91] The claim that Fanon acted 'like a colonialist' is clearly grounded in a retrospective vision filtered though a negative perception of Fanon as theorist of colonization, but Humbert's memory is faulty. The final section of *Peau noire, masques blancs* shows quite definitely that Fanon did note down observations at Saint-Ylié, and that he made good use of them.

The case he discusses was brought to Fanon's notice by the doctor in charge of the female ward – presumably Humbert herself – and involved a nineteen-year-old who was suffering from obesity, as well as a variety of tics and other nervous problems. The symptoms had first appeared when she was ten and had worsened at puberty. Now that she was living and working away from home, she was also suffering from depression and experiencing panic attacks. During an interview with the consultant psychiatrist, it emerged that she was experiencing hallucinations, and she described them in a waking-dream state: 'Deep, concentric circles that expand and contract to the rhythm of a negro tom-tom. This tom-tom brings to mind the danger of losing her parents, and especially her mother.'[92] When she glanced towards the drum, it was surrounded by half-naked men and women performing a terrifying dance. Told not to be afraid of joining the dance, she does join in. The appearance of the dancers changes immediately; they are now guests at a splendid party. Further sessions revealed more hallucinations of a group of negroes dancing around a cooking pot, and preparing to burn a white man in his fifties.

Having read his colleague's case notes and having held 'many conversations' with the patient, Fanon concluded that the young woman's fear of negroes dated from the age of ten and was associated with a memory of her father, who had served in the colonial army, listening to radio broadcasts of 'negro music'. As she lay in bed, the house throbbed to the sound of a tom-tom. She could see negroes dancing and hid from them under the blankets. Circles would then appear and 'sco-tomize' the negroes or make them disappear; they were a defence against the hallucinations. At a later stage, the circles appeared without the negroes; the defence mechanism was now coming into play in the absence of its determinant, and the circles alone were enough to trigger the facial tics. Fanon argues in conclusion that her condition was the result of a fear of negroes and that its emergence had been triggered by 'determinate circumstances'.

The Saint-Ylié case was of obvious interest to someone working on the psychology of negrophobia: 'It shows that, in extreme cases, the myth of the negro, the idea of the negro, can determine an authentic alienation.'[93] But it also provides an insight into the clinical methods and techniques with which Fanon had become familiar in Lyon. He is clearly more interested in the effects of the 'myth of the negro' than in how a neurosis originates in the individual unconscious of the patient, and does not trace it back to unconscious sexual fantasies. He explicitly refuses to elaborate on 'the infrastructure of this psycho-neurosis', but it is surely of more significance that he devotes so little of his discussion to the figure of the patient's father – not something that any Freudian psychoanalyst would overlook. He refers to the use of the 'waking dream' technique without comment or question, indicating that it was something with which he was so familiar as to find it unremarkable. The technique was originally developed in the 1920s in connection with research into mental imagery, but R. Desoille's *Le Rêve éveillé dirigé* (1945), which was presumably the source of Fanon's knowledge, gave it wider currency. Although the technique has something in common with Freud's free association technique – the patient lies on a couch and describes the 'affects' or emotions associated with the images that come into his or her head – it is more closely related to Pavlov's research into the higher nervous system than to psychoanalysis. The material thrown up during the daydream allows the therapist to provoke new situations so as to observe the subject's affective reactions and gradually to reduce the level of anxiety by releasing tension at both the psychological and physiological level. There is no attempt to establish transference, or the relationship that allows the patient to actualize unconscious wishes by projecting them on to the figure of the analyst. Infantile prototypes and memories re-emerge and are experienced with a very powerful sense of immediacy.[94]

Fanon has no criticisms to make of waking dream therapy. Yet one word indicates that he was also interested in going beyond the parameters of the psychotherapy in which he had been trained. He writes: 'Then increasingly small circles appear and scotomize the negroes.'[95] *Scotomiser* is a very rare word, and it has a very peculiar history in French psychoanalysis.[96] It derives from the Latin *scotoma,* and originally meant an obscuration of part of the field of vision due to a lesion on the retina. Tentatively introduced into psychoanalysis by René Laforgue to describe a process of psychic depreciation by means of which the individual attempts to deny everything which conflicts with his ego, it was rejected by Freud. It was then used by Lacan in his 1938 article on the family to describe the mechanism that triggers a psychosis (Lacan later ceases to use the term and replaces it with 'foreclosure').[97] The discussion of the Saint-Ylié case indicates that there was already a tension between the tradition in which Fanon had been trained, and a Freudian–Lacanian discourse which he knew only from his personal reading. The same tension structures his medical dissertation of 1951. Although Fanon's dissertation is often referred to as his 'thesis', it was part of a first degree and not a submission for a postgraduate qualification. Its purpose was to demonstrate his competence within his field and not to make any original contribution to it.

Fanon remarks that he had intended to submit *Peau noire, masques blancs* as the dissertation he was required to write in order to qualify as a doctor of medicine, and then adds somewhat mysteriously 'And then the dialectic forced me to take a much firmer stance'.[98] His failure to submit it had in fact nothing to do with any 'dialectic', and it is wounded pride that prevents him from admitting that the planned thesis was angrily rejected before he was able to submit it by an outraged Professor Dechaume on the predictable grounds that it defied all known academic and scientific conventions. A medical thesis is not the place for such an experimental exploration of the author's subjectivity or for such lengthy quotations from Aimé Césaire. Fanon had to begin again with a more conventional topic, and rapidly produced a seventy-

five-page typescript (typed by an unknown hand) with the cumber-
some descriptive title of 'Altérations mentales, modifications
caractérielles, troubles psychiques et déficit intellectuel dans l'hérédo-
dégénération spino-cérébelleuse. Un cas de maladie de Friedrich avec
délire de possession' ('Mental disturbances, changes in character, psychic disturbances and intellectual deficiency in spinal-cerebral
degeneracy. A case of Friedrich's disease with delusions of possession').
Defended before a board of examiners on 29 November 1951, it deals
mainly with the mental symptoms associated with a case of Friedrich's
ataxia, which is a recessive hereditary disease of the central nervous
system. As is the convention with a thesis, the first section summarizes
the literature on the condition whilst the second summarizes Fanon's
observations of the female patient in question. In the concluding section, Fanon moves into a discussion of the respective roles and nature
of neurology and psychiatry.[99]

Fanon never again mentioned his thesis, and made no attempt to
publish it. He was, on the other hand, sufficiently proud of it to dedi-
cate a copy to his brother Félix with a rather wordy inscription:

> To my brother Félix,
> I offer this work.
> The greatness of a man is to be found not in his acts but in
> his style. Existence does not resemble a steadily rising curve, but
> a slow, and sometimes sad, series of ups and downs.
> I have a horror of weaknesses – I understand them, but I do
> not like them.
> I do not agree with those who think it possible to live life at
> an easy pace. I don't want this. I don't think you do either.[100]

Although Fanon did follow the academic conventions this time, even
to the extent of citing Dechaume (of whom he had a very poor private
opinion), the dissertation still reflects the main concerns of Fanon's earliest writings as it looks at the issue of the causality of mental illness. The
academic context means, however, that he does not introduce the
socio-genetic theory of 'Le Syndrôme nord-africain' outlined in his
first published article, and that the discussion concentrates on organo-
genesis and psycho-genesis or, in other words, the relative roles played

in the triggering of mental illness by organic-somatic and purely mental factors.

There is a significant indication of just how rapidly Fanon wrote his thesis. The section dealing with Lacan refers to the latter's thesis of 1932, and to his 1938 article on the family, but primarily to a text that he claims is entitled *La Causalité essentielle de la folie*. There is no such text by Lacan: the title given by Fanon is the sub-title of the second part of the paper 'Propos sur la causalité psychique';[101] to make matters worse, Fanon gives no page references, and most of his quotations prove to be from the third section, which is sub-titled 'Les effets psychiques du monde imaginaire'. These are easy mistakes to make when working at speed and under pressure, but the fact that Fanon's examiners apparently failed to pick them up during the two-hour viva voce examination he took up says little for the academic standards in force at Lyon's Faculté mixte de médecine et de pharmacie in 1951. More significantly, it may indicate just how unknown a quantity Lacan was for Fanon's examiners.

That Fanon should have had an adequate knowledge of Henri Ey's organo-dynamic psychiatry is scarcely surprising; Ey (1900–97) was a very senior figure in the psychiatric establishment, the general editor of the journal *Evolution psychiatrique* and the organizing secretary of the First International Congress of Psychiatry in 1950. His lectures at the Sainte-Anne hospital in Paris were so famous that it would have been almost inconceivable for any medical student beginning to specialize in psychiatry not to have had some acquaintance with his work. Lacan was a different matter altogether. Fanon's acquaintance with Lacan is more surprising. Lacan was by no means the notorious figure he was to become from the mid-1950s onwards. 'Propos' would have been available to Fanon in a collective volume published in 1950,[102] though it has to be said that it is an unusual final-year student who can cite such recently published literature. Its interest is, of course, that it is a critique of Ey's organo-dynamism.The 1938 study of the family was published in the *Encyclopédie française* and was readily available for consultation in any major library. Lacan's thesis on paranoia was a much rarer item in 1951. It was published in a small edition in 1932, and Lacan was always reluctant to have it reprinted.[103] In 1967, a would-be purchaser was told by a bookseller in the Le François bookshop in Paris that Lacan had at some point 'swept into the shop and bought up all the copies that were still unsold'.[104] So great was Lacan's fear of being criticized or persecuted, and so great his anxiety that his ideas might be stolen, that he can scarcely have been pleased to learn from a letter he received during the war informing him that 'homemade copies' of his thesis were circulating at the Saint-Alban hospital, a remote institution high in the mountains of the Lozère département.[105] There were links between Saint-Alban and Lyon. Its former director, Paul Balvet, was now working and teaching in the city.

Lacan's mystery correspondent was François Tosquelles, who had first read the thesis in Catalonia before the war and who was one of the most significant influences on the young Fanon. It is improbable that they had actually met as early as 1951, but all the evidence suggests that Fanon had had sight of one of the 'homemade copies', and was therefore already in touch with the Saint-Alban community, at least indirectly. It also seems that the anonymous author of 'Le Surréalisme' had seen one too. The go-between was a young woman to whom he had been introduced by Michelle B. Nicole Guillet was born in 1930 and her father had been bursar at Saint-Alban since 1934. During her medical studies in Lyon, which she began in 1948–9, she lived in the home of her father's friend Paul Balvet. Fanon was a frequent dinner guest there, and enjoyed discussing both psychiatry and surrealism with Balvet. In other words, while Fanon was still living and studying in the psychiatric desert, he already had some contact with and knowledge of the most progressive current within French psychiatry.

For the moment he was trying to navigate a path between Ey and Lacan, and their very different conceptions of mental illness. Ey's 'organodynamic psychiatry' draws heavily upon the work of the British neurologist John Hughlings Jackson (1835–1911) whose first studies dealt with aphasia and epilepsy. Jackson developed a dynamic neurology which stresses the physiological rather than the anatomical, and the functional rather than the organic. He argues that the nervous system is a product of human evolution and that those centres that developed at later stages are more susceptible to damage than the older centres. When they are damaged, the older centres become more active. The delusions and hallucinations characteristic of mental illness are, according to the dynamic view, caused by a deterioration of the intellectual faculties and a concomitant reactivation of vestigial psychic activities and processes.[106] Ey, for his part, makes a distinction between the elementary sensor-motor functions that are the object of neurology, and the higher psychic functions (memory, judgement) studied and, when appropriate, treated by psychiatry. He denies the possibility of a specifically psychic causality and argues that a condition such as psychosis always has an organic dynamic stemming from an endocrinal disorder.[107] Ey classifies mental illnesses by describing the degree to which mental functions are 'dissolved' by the disintegration of functional hierarchies, and describes madness as a loss of 'freedom of being' or loss of 'freedom to be oneself'. His theory is an attempt to synthesize a psychodynamic model, which sees mental illness purely as a product of mental conflict, the sociogenetics which reduces it to a reflection of social conflict, and an organico-mechanistic model which relates mental symptoms to organic lesions.

Fanon is respectful of Ey, but is clearly more sympathetic here to the 'psychogenetic determinism' he detects in Lacan, and describes it as pointing to a 'science of personality' based upon a genetic study of intentional functions that are integrated into human relations of a social order. The coherent development of the psychotic's delusions are, that is, consistent with both the lived history of the subject, and its conscious and unconscious manifestations , and it is determined by the psychic tensions specific to social relations. It is in this context that Fanon first uses the term *Erlebnis* – the 'lived experience' of *Peau noire*.[108]

The dissertation of 1951 contains Fanon's first references to Lacan, and those references are of course expanded in *Peau noire*. It would, however, be dangerous to make too much of them or to turn Fanon into an apprentice Lacanian, particularly as the reference to Lacan's logic and value of madness is glossed in a footnote by an allusion to 'a Lyonnais psychiatrist, M. Balvet' who represents a rather different tradition. The allusion is to the latter's article on the human value of madness.[109] Here, Balvet argues that, if a comprehensive view is taken of mental illness, 'the madman gradually ceases to look like a monster; whilst he is certainly still ill, one does not have to live with him for very long to feel that he can bear witness in the same overwhelming way that the poet or the mystic bears witness. That is what places him over and above strictly scientific preoccupations. Bears witness to what? To our depths, to ourselves.'[110]

Although Fanon's dissertation was written both reluctantly and hastily, the underlying issue of causality in mental illness was highly relevant to a phenomenon he often encountered during his earliest clinical experience in Lyon. This experience predates his psychiatric training. As a young doctor, he would be called out early in the morning to attend an emergency in the Algerian quarter around the rue Moncey. He would find a patient writhing on a dirty bed in a sordid room, with his friends and relatives crying and screaming. Death seemed imminent, but a hasty examination revealed nothing significant. Eventually, the doctor would make the provisional diagnosis 'acute abdomen' and admit the patient to a clinic for further tests. Three days later, the patient would reappear, smiling and completely cured. Like all North Africans, he had been suffering from a purely imaginary illness. Fanon had had similar experiences. When he asked his patient where the pain was, the patient answered 'In my stomach', and pointed to his liver. He would then rub his hand over the entire abdominal area: 'It all hurts'. As Fanon well knew, there were several organs in that 'all', each with its own pathology. The correct diagnosis was 'North African syndrome'.[111] This curiously asymptomatic syndrome defied the medical law that stated 'where there is a symptom, there is a lesion'. Medical personnel had discovered a new syndrome, not experimentally, but thanks to an oral tradition.[112] And when he came across that syndrome in Lyon, Fanon encountered something he would combat both in some of his most effective polemical writing and in his clinical practice as a psychiatrist, namely the theories associated with the 'Algiers school'. He also encountered a more personal difficulty. It was the norm for doctors to address their North African patients as *tu* and to speak to them in *petit nègre*. Although Fanon was very sensitive about being addressed as *tu* by whites, he did find himself 'slipping' into that very way of addressing North Africans.[113] His spontaneous use of *tu* stemmed not only from his medical superiority, but also from his internalization of the hierarchy that made Martinicans superior to Arabs: they were *indigènes*, but *he* was an honourary *toubab*.

The Algerian patients Fanon encountered in the slums of the rue

Moncey presented an asymptomatic syndrome. Fanon contended that, whilst their symptoms seemed unclassifiable, their sufferings were real:

> Threatened in his affectivity,
> Threatened in his social activity,
> Threatened in his membership of the *polis,*
> The North African brings together all the conditions that create a sick man.
> With no family, no love, no human relations, no communion with the collectivity, his first encounter with himself will take place in a neurotic mode, in a pathological mode, he will feel empty, lifeless, fighting bodily against death, a death that comes before death, death that exists in life. What could be more pathetic than this man with strong muscles who tells us in a truly broken voice: 'Doctor, I'm going to die?'[114]

Fanon was coming to realize that his North African patients were suffering not from hallucinations or imaginary illnesses but from psychosomatic complaints. His introduction to psychosomatic medicine did not come from a lecture at medical school, but from his reading of an article by a Doctor Stern in the professional journal *Psyché*. He cites Stern in his article on the 'North-African Syndrome', and describes him as having outlined 'a magnificent plan'.[115] According to Stern, psychosomatic medicine does not regard an illness as an 'isolated fact' that is unrelated to the life of the individual patient: 'On the contrary, it tries to see it in relation to the whole life of the patient, to understand what it means in terms of the whole of that life. It asks why the illness takes up its abode in the individual at a given moment.'[116] Reading Stern's article provided the inellectual basis for an encounter with something still more important: the institutional psychotherapy associated with François Tosquelles.

The psychiatry Fanon studied in Lyon was neither rigorous nor satisfactory, but his stay in that city brought him into contact with Nicole Guillet and Paul Balvet, and it was through them that he first heard of Tosquelles and of the Saint-Alban psychiatric hospital. That hospital has a legendary place in the history of mental health care in France, and Tosquelles is scarcely less of a legendary figure. Sadly, there is as yet no full biography of him, and he would not have appreciated one being written. After his death in 1994, one of Tosquelles's former students imagined him in heaven, dancing a Catalan *sardana* as the celestial pipe and drum band played, and chuckling as his surviving disciples struggled to turn memories into hagiographic biographies. He saw Tosquelles lighting yet another cigarette and grumbling, with the pronounced Catalan accent he never even tried to lose, 'It's just a way of putting me away in a drawer.'[117]

In Tosquelles, Fanon at last found his true mentor. Tosquelles' description of the training Fanon had received so far would probably have met with his approval. The style is typical of the man:

Fanon came from Lyon, from the Faculty of Medicine in Lyon. A caricature, if one is needed, of analytic Cartesianism applied to the pathological event, the flagship of its efficacy on the anatomico-physio-pathological object that founds medicine in general and then crumbles into endless and boundless specializations. Lyon had produced . . . two volumes devoted to psychiatry and the professional training of psychiatrists. One chapter per illness. The well known sequence: diagnosis, prognosis, treatment. Diagnosis, okay. Unsurprised amazement at the many clinical forms that are described, at the dozens – even hundreds – of pages. Then the outcome and pragmatic justification of such praiseworthy work: treatment. It's clear and precise. And the treatment can be summed up in a line. What am I saying? Not a line. One word will do. No possible error in the prescription. No nuances, and no generous doses of lamentable errors. Here it is in capitals: TREATMENT: COMMITAL. Nothing more, nothing less.[118]

François Tosquelles was born in the Catalan city of Reus in August 1902. The son of petty bourgeois shopkeepers with, as he himself put it, 'cultural pretensions',[119] he developed a very early interest in both psychiatry and left-wing politics, and was encouraged to do so by his uncle, an enlightened and philanthropic doctor who had founded a psychiatric institute in Reus. Tosquelles read Marx at a very early age and rapidly became an enthusiastic supporter of Catalan nationalism. After qualifying as a doctor of medicine in 1927, he trained as a psychiatrist in Reus with Emile Mira i Lopez, a phenomenologist and psychoanalyst who established Spain's first chair in psychiatry at the Autonomous University of Barcelona.

By 1931, Catalonia had become a place of refuge for Jews fleeing from Austria and Germany. One of the refugees was a certain Sandor Eiminder, a Jewish paediatrician and psychoanalyst who had worked with August Aichorn, a member of Freud's circle in Vienna. Eiminder claimed to be a cousin of Freud's, and Tosquelles never did discover whether he meant this literally or metaphorically, even though he was in analysis with him from late 1931 to 1935.[120] During the first year of his analysis, Tosquelles organized an evening seminar on the relationship between Marx and Freud; more surprisingly, he was also a member of a study group in Reus that was reading Lacan's thesis.[121] Tosquelles never explains how copies came to be available in Catalonia, but they must have been rare items.

By 1934, Tosquelles was becoming aware of how difficult it was to use the classic analytic technique of placing the patient on a couch in an institutional setting, and of the problems inherent in using it with children, psychotics or psychopaths. The next year, one of his female patients suddenly refused to go on talking on the couch. A puzzled Tosquelles turned for advice to his supervisor and was told what everyone else knew: his patient had been in contact with another patient who was both deaf and blind, and had 'adopted' her afflictions. An Austrian colleague then began to explore the idea that the hospital itself was a *Gestalt*, or a set of elements and 'articulated spaces' with a life of its own, and explained that it was impossible to separate out the individuals who inhabited those spaces and acted on one another within them. In retrospect, Tosquelles described this discovery as the starting point for his notion of institutional psychotherapy.[122]

Franco's military rebellion and the outbreak of the Spanish Civil War put an abrupt end to the progressive experiments going on in Reus and Catalonia. An active member of the semi-Trotskyist Partido Obrero de Unifación Marxista, Tosquelles served on the Aragon front, where he helped to organize a psychiatric service and was responsible for the selection of troops for tank and machine-gun units. Early in 1938, he was appointed head of the Republican Army's psychiatric services and held that post until 1 April 1939, by which time it was obvious to all that the Republic's fate was sealed.[123] One of his experiences at the front would stay with him, and he often talked about it as he insisted on the need for psychiatrists to make physical examinations of their patients before doing anything else. He had, he would recall, encountered a soldier crawling on all fours and barking like a dog. Convinced that this was an obvious case of malingering, the army doctors did not trouble to examine him properly. The soldier died of a brain tumour. For Tosquelles, the lesson was obvious and he liked to spell out with typical bluntness that psychotherapy had its limitations: 'No point in psychotherapy for a dead man: too late. No point in interpreting the orality of someone who is hungry, or the castration complex of a man with a wooden leg.'[124]

On 1 September 1939, Tosquelles crossed the Pyrenees on foot. He had been forced to leave his wife and children behind to join him later, but his light luggage included his prized copy of Lacan's thesis.[125] Confident that his recent experience would be useful in what he now saw as the inevitable war between France and Germany, Tosquelles approached a gendarme in Louchon to offer his services, only to receive the standard advice given to able-bodied refugees: he could return to Spain, join the Foreign Legion, find work, or be interned. Bristling with anger, he told the understandably bewildered gendarme: 'If you want to lose the war, you can lose it on your own; I am not a foreigner.'[126] France was prepared for the influx of refugees. A decree adopted in November 1938 had provided for the establishment of 'special centres' to house prisoners whose criminal past or dangerous activities meant that they posed too great a threat to state security to be held under house arrest. The press was less euphemistic: on 3 February 1939, the daily *Le Matin* calmly announced that France had opened its first concentration camp.[127]

One of the camps was at Sept-Fonds to the north of Toulouse and it was here that, at the request of the commanding officer, Tosquelles set up a rudimentary psychiatric unit to help those of his compatriots who were suffering the psychological consequences of their traumatic defeat and enforced exile. At the beginning of 1940, he joined them inside the camp as an internee,[128] but was released after only a few days by an extraordinary telegram. It was from Paul Balvet and offered him a position at Saint-Alban, a psychiatric hospital near the small provincial centre of Mende. According to Tosquelles, the Prefect of the Lozère *département* had originally wanted to recruit 'reds' from Sept-Fonds for rebuilding work at Saint-Alban, but its director Balvet refused to have anything to do with the plan. He was, on the other hand, willing to employ an interned psychiatrist in a professional capacity, and had heard of Tosquelles's case from a mutual acquaintance.[129] Two years and eight months after the Catalan's release, Sept-Fonds and the other French camps found their true vocation. With France under a full German occupation after the Allied landings in North Africa, they now housed Jews – many of whom had actually been deported from the Reich – who were subsequently taken by train to the Drancy camp north of Paris, and then north and east into the night and fog of the death camps.[130]

Tosquelles was now free and could arrange for his family to be smuggled across the Pyrenees to join him, but his position was still precarious. His degrees and diplomas were not recognized by the French Ministry of Health, and he could not be employed as a psychiatrist. Nor could he be paid. Initially, he was paid a modest 'salary' by representatives of the government of Mexico, which was the only country not to grant diplomatic recognition to Franco's Spain, but an improvised solution was eventually found: the psychiatrist was employed as a nurse, and paid on that basis.[131] In order to regain his true professional status, Tosquelles had to retrain. In 1948, he successfully submitted his thesis on the meaning of lived experience in psychopathology,[132] and in July 1952 he finally passed the competitive examination that meant he could officially be appointed *chef de service* at Saint-Alban.[133]

Like many psychiatric hospitals in the provinces, Saint-Alban was originally a religious foundation and in 1940 it was still staffed by nuns wearing full habits and answering to their superior, Sister Théophile.[134] Balvet, the hospital's director since 1936, was a practising Catholic and appeared to Tosquelles to be a genuine supporter of the Vichy regime. Balvet's initial Pétainist sympathies – which were by no means unusual in 1940 – soon faded as the persecution of Jews began,[135] and Saint-Alban became a haven for fleeing resistance fighters and racial undesirables alike. Part of the legend of Saint-Alban is based upon the role it played as a centre for the Resistance. Communist poets like Paul

Eluard found temporary refuge here. Wounded fighters were treated on the wards, some of them by Georges Canguilhem, the great historian of the sciences who worked here under the name 'Lafont' in the summer of 1943.[136] It is not inconceivable that it was one of his Saint-Alban connections who inspired Fanon to read Canguilhem's thesis on the normal and the pathological;[137] he is unlikely to have come across it at the recommendation of any of his official teachers in Lyon.

Between 1940 and 1944, an estimated 40,000 patients died of cold and malnutrition in France's psychiatric hospitals; in some hospitals, the death rate was 60 per cent.[138] Some 2,000 died in Lyon's Vinatier hospital alone. At Saint-Alban, the death rate did not rise significantly during the war and Occupation. Patients worked under supervision on local farms in exchange for food, and everyone – nuns, patients and doctors – took part in extensive foraging expeditions. It was the wartime experience of this survivalist form of occupational therapy that helped to transform the hospital into a therapeutic community: 'During the Occupation, the French underwent the individual and collective experience of a "great confinement". The word "liberation" therefore had a very profound resonance, and its echoes shook the walls of the asylum (to use a heroic metaphor, the liberation of the asylum was an extension of the liberation of the country).'[139] The struggle against the concentration-camp world of Nazism was continued by a struggle against the carceral world in which the insane were confined. Chance conversations with Nicole Guillet and, presumably, Paul Balvet, had brought Fanon to the heart of a psychiatric revolution that began with the Resistance. It was here that he would acquire some of the weapons to be used in his battle against the North African syndrome.

Entering the citadel of Saint-Alban was no easier than marrying into the Fanon clan in Martinique, however. There were no longer any walls but Fanon first had to convince Tosquelles that he was a suitable houseman. Guillet introduced the two, but was not present at their first real meeting. She did, on the other hand, overhear the loud and at times angry exchange of views that took place in her mother's salon and imagined Fanon and Tosquelles charging at each other like bulls. The metaphor is eloquent: both men were aggressive and noisy and did not like to give ground to an antagonist. Whatever was said, it proved to supply the basis for a good working relationship that lasted for almost two years. Fanon was Tosquelles' houseman, and he learned a great deal from his teacher.

Although she was sent to boarding school in Mende, which is the nearest town of any size to the village of Saint-Alban sur Limagnole, Nicole Guillet spent a lot of her childhood and adolescence in the psychiatric hospital; it was the norm for the staff to live in. She recalls it as having a warm atmosphere not unlike that of a large family, though that impression is obviously reinforced by her own situation as one of six children. There were no perimeter walls around the hospital, but its isolated location and the harsh countryside around it did a lot to discourage potential absconders. Winters in Lozère are harsh and the roads are snowbound for months. Even in summer, the distances involved in getting anywhere are such that few would try to run away.

Saint-Alban was the laboratory for the first experiments in what has come to be known in France as institutional psychotherapy.[140] Its general principles are well described by Félix Guattari, who was in some ways a product of the school: 'Its main characteristic is a determination never to isolate the study of mental illness from its social and institutional context, and, by the same token, to analyse institutions on the basis of interpreting the real, symbolic and imaginary effects of society upon individuals.'[141] The basic ambition of Tosquelles and the Saint-Alban group was to humanize their institution by recognizing and promoting what Balvet called the human value of its inmates. A variety of therapeutic techniques ranging from drug therapy and ECT to psychoanalytically influenced psychotherapy and encounter groups were used, but the central emphasis was on group work. The theories involved were also varied, almost to the point of eclecticism. Living together inevitably meant working together, and that implied breaking down the rigid hierarchies that divided doctors from nurses, and patients from staff. The key element was the therapeutic club, to which all patients belonged as of right. A general assembly elected delegates to a bureau and to the commissions responsible for the secretariat, the library, the film club and the all-important newspaper. The underlying thesis was that psychotherapy dealt with individuals who were *aliénés*, meaning 'alienated' in both the clinical and the social sense. Their flight into psychosis or schizophrenia had led them to break the social contract, to become outsiders who were excluded from social life. Although the causes of their alienation were biopathological, and therefore to be treated as such, the club's existence was founded upon a gamble: the possibility of transfusing a social life into its patient-members, of reintegrating them into some form of symbolic exchange (it is this that provides the important link with Lacanian psychoanalysis). The gamble could be seen to have paid off when, for example, the schizophrenic took it into his head that he would like to drink a coffee in the canteen. In order to do so, he had to obtain money and in order to obtain money, he had to work. With the money he had earned, he could go to the canteen, where he had to speak to whoever was serving. He then had to pay for his coffee, wait to be given his change and thank the canteen lady. The goal of all the preceding therapy was to bring the patient to the point where he could begin to enter a process of social exchange and intercourse by deciding that he wanted a coffee and starting the chain of events.

Fanon soon settled into this isolated but supportive community. According to Nicole Guillet, the warm atmosphere reminded him of that of his own large family, and he was now sufficiently relaxed to begin to talk more about home, and especially his mother. He was a very active participant in the club, and helped to organize film shows and musical evenings. The latter became the occasion, or perhaps the excuse, for the elaborate ritual of borrowing the piano from the bursar's wife. The instrument had to be physically moved from one room to another by a group of patients assisted by Fanon, who turned the process into a comic performance by ceremoniously donning a pair of white gloves.[142] Tosquelles was impressed by the way Fanon's physical presence occupied the space around him, as well as by his gift for polemic, and appreciated his occasional lack of the 'so-called virtue of patience' – a virtue that he himself did not possess in any great quantity. In 1975, Tosquelles would recall an evening in Mende in Fanon's company. The context was a meeting for patients and their families and for anyone else 'concerned with culture and therefore, to some extent, with madness'. The discussion turned to the topic of space and spaces, and Fanon digressed into an analysis of the space of tragedy, using examples taken from classical plays to explore the question of the limits of the psychiatrist's field of professional action.[143]

Fanon learned a great deal at Saint-Alban. For the first time, he was involved in a clinical situation that allowed patients to contribute to their own recovery. He learned to listen with a sympathetic clinical ear to their pain and suffering. In a wonderful display of the mixed metaphors he was so good at spinning, Tosquelles describes the distance Fanon had covered by going from Lyon to Saint-Alban:

> Like so many others, Fanon walked the same path, the same distance, made the same detours and settled into the same valleys, the same forests and the same gap between:
>
> *on the one hand*, a very particularly analytic, descriptive and Cartesian clinical medicine, with its doctrines and application, to say nothing of the way it is put into practice (*son passage à l'acte*[144]) – for I would not want anyone to dream of denying its efficacy, not even in psychiatry.
>
> *and on the other hand*, clinical psychiatry, in which the previous style of isolating the subject proves ineffective simply because we are dealing here with a suffering subject. The breakdown, if we want to talk mechanics, is the process of the presentification, even the production, of the ill patient. Let me make it clear that we are not talking about the 'social and negotiable production' produced by an individual – a socially determined individual – but of the subject's self-production. It is the subject that is produced. And it is his production that has broken down.[145]

At Saint-Alban, Fanon straddled two disciplines or even two clinical worlds. He was also in a transitional space in another sense. Although he was a qualified doctor of medicine and had acquired valuable experience in clinical psychiatry, he had yet to take the examination that would finally qualify him to hold a permanent and more senior position in a psychiatric hospital. He also had to resolve the question of his relationship with, and attitude to, Martinique.

Accompanied by Joby, Fanon returned to Fort-de-France in February 1952, partly because he wanted a break before he started to prepare for his final postgraduate examinations, and partly because he wanted to test the water there. He had little money and decided to finance his stay by working on a temporary basis as a general practitioner. This was also a good solution for a man who did not like taking 'proper' holidays, which he regarded as a waste of time – there are in fact no records of his ever taking a real holiday. Although he had relatively little practical experience in general medicine and had no intention of becoming a general practitioner, he was perfectly qualified to practise. He also needed money. However, he had no surgery and no real contacts with local doctors. Family connections soon overcame that problem, as a friend of his mother's was willing to let him use her house in Le Vauclin. Fanon's very brief experience of medicine in Martinique was disappointing. The fact that Martinique was now officially part of France had done little to change its basic structures or to remedy its basic problems. Nor did the fact that its leading political figure – Aimé Césaire – was a Communist. The doctors Fanon met were cynical and corrupt. They abused the system and were much more interested in accumulating fees than in curing patients. By mid-March, he had seen enough and left for Lyon, telling his uncle that Martinique was not the place to do what he wanted to do. In some respects, it had been a pleasant few weeks, as he had had time to see his family and his old friends, to play some football and to go swimming and dancing. In professional terms, it convinced him that he would find it very difficult if not impossible to work in Martinique.[146] He returned to Lyon's Faculty of Medicine. He had seen his birthplace for the last time.

# 5

# 'Black Skin, White Masks'

FANON'S LITERARY CAREER began quietly with the appearance of his essay on 'the lived experience of the black man' in the May 1951 issue of the journal *Esprit*, which took as its theme 'the lament of the black man'. There was no indication that it was a chapter from a forthcoming book. The second of Fanon's contributions to the journal came in February 1952, when his article on the 'North-African Syndrome' appeared as part of a dossier on 'The North-African Proletariat in France'. It was complemented by M'Hamed Ferid Ghazi's statistically based article on the growing immigrant population, which argued that the Algerian community was 'the most proletarian' and most under-privileged of all the foreign communities – Italian, Spanish and Polish – that co-existed within the 'French' proletariat.[1]

Founded in 1932 by the philosopher Emmanuel Mounier, the monthly *Esprit* had been relaunched in 1944 as the main platform for the Catholic left and was widely regarded as one of the great expressions of the spirit of the wartime Resistance.[2] Rather like Sartre's journal *Les Temps modernes*,[3] it provided a non-aligned or 'new left' alternative to the Communist press. Although Mounier and his deputy editor Jean-Marie Domenach were both devout Catholics, their religious beliefs did not take a dogmatic form and there was always room on *Esprit*'s editorial board for sympathetic Protestants, Jews, agnostics and atheists. The journal enjoyed complete financial and editorial independence but had close connections with Editions du Seuil, which had been in existence since 1937. Now one of France's major publishing houses, Seuil was in the early 1950s a small and none too prosperous company. Its biggest success to date had been the French translation of *The Little World of Don Camillo*, which ensured the firm's financial survival by selling over a million copies.[4] In the summer of 1952, it published Fanon's first book.

Fanon's association with *Esprit* and his decision to publish with Seuil are intriguing and even somewhat mysterious. *Esprit*'s archives contain no information on how or when his manuscripts reached the warren of offices it shared with Editions du Seuil in the rue Jacob. Domenach, who died at the age of seventy-five in July 1997, recalled only that he saw the manuscript of *Peau noire, masques blancs* before passing it on to Francis Jeanson, his co-editor on the 'Esprit' series of books.[5] Fanon's choice of publisher was in fact very limited, as was his knowledge of the publishing world. The relative isolation of Lyon did not make it easy to establish contacts within a tightly knit intellectual world centred almost exclusively on Paris, though it is true that Balvet and Achille – both known to Fanon – had made minor contributions to *Esprit* and could have provided a link. *Peau noire* had been rejected as an academic dissertation and it was not an easy book to publish. The psychiatric and psychoanalytic content that puzzled so many of Fanon's early readers would have made it unacceptable to more literary publishers such as Gallimard, and its politics would have made it anathema to any house close to the Parti Communiste Français. Academic medical publishers would have reacted to Fanon's juxtaposition of clinical data, literary allusions and personal reflections in precisely the same manner as Professor Dechaume in Lyon.

In retrospect, it is perhaps surprising that Fanon appears not to have approached Présence africaine, which was France's first black publishing house. The journal *Présence africaine* was founded in 1947 to establish an 'African presence' within French culture and rapidly became the main support for negritude, with which Fanon always had an ambiguous relationship. In 1949, the journal's founders established a publishing house of the same name.[6] Fanon read *Présence africaine* regularly and was to be a major speaker at the international conferences it organized in 1956 and 1959, but he made no contributions to the journal itself and appears not to have considered it as a potential publisher for *Peau noire*. He had, of course, decided to study in Lyon because there were 'too many negroes' in Paris. He described himself as being reluctant to live in a purely Martinican environment in France (even though he did frequent precisely that milieu when he was in Paris) and must have been equally reluctant to associate himself too closely with the main journal of negritude. As he puts it towards the end of *Peau noire*: 'In no way must I derive my original vocation from the past of peoples of colour. In no way must I devote myself to resurrecting a negro civilization that has been unfairly misrecognized.'[7]

The first book published by Présence africaine in 1947 was Placide Tempels's *La Philosophie bantoue* and its content explains why Fanon was reluctant to be closely associated with the company.[8] Tempels, who was a missionary in the Belgian Congo, contended that the Bantu peoples of Africa had elaborated a complex belief system founded upon an 'ontology' that described a chain of being linking vital forces, dead ancestors, the living community and the inanimate world into a cosmic harmony. Tempels's argument was a reaction to the widespread notion of an African 'primitive mentality' and sought to promote the idea of an innate African philosophy that was expressive of an African spirit or genius. In his introduction to the book, *Présence africaine*'s founder Alioune Diop wrote that 'the very notion of culture, seen as a revolutionary will, is contrary to our genius, as is the very notion of progress. Progress would have haunted our consciousness only if we had some grievance against life.'[9] The vision of an almost immobile, timeless and tranquil Africa became an important strand within certain versions of negritude. Other thinkers associated with negritude were highly critical of Tempels. Writing in 1951, Césaire pointed out that talk of ontology, life forces and the kernel of truth contained in traditional thought did nothing to alter the fact that colonialism in the Congo was based upon forced labour, torture and ferocious exploitation.[10] Fanon himself was even more dismissive and contended that it was pointless to discover 'Being in Bantu thought, when the existence of the Bantu is situated at the level of non-being . . . There is nothing ontological about segregation.

Enough of this scandal.'[11] *Peau noire, masques blancs* would have looked very out of place in Présence africaine's catalogue.

By accident or design, Fanon found the right publisher in Editions du Seuil. Seuil and *Esprit* had long been critical of French colonial policy, but the journal also took an interest in the psychiatry that was Fanon's first love. The December 1952 issue on 'the poverty of psychiatry' was, for instance, a devastating critique of the situation in France's mental-health institutions and included an article by Tosquelles on the psychiatric patient's experience of society.[12] Seuil, for its part, was beginning to emerge as the main publisher of fiction from North Africa and its 'Méditerranée' collection, edited by the French-Algerian novelist Emmanuel Roblès from 1952 onwards, was giving a totally new meaning to the expression 'Algerian literature'.[13]

An unsigned editorial note to *Esprit*'s dossier on the North-African proletariat ends with the rhetorical question: 'If the scandalous way North Africans are treated in France does not provoke a scream of anger, why were we given the ability to scream?'[14] *Esprit* had long been amplifying screams from what would soon become known as the 'Third World' – the expression was coined in 1952 but had yet to pass into general usage. Mounier's *L'Eveil de l'Afrique noire* of 1947 is a liberal-humanist critique of colonialism in the tradition of André Gide's *Voyage au Congo* and *Retour du Tchad*.[15] *Esprit* had already published articles critical of French policy in Algeria and its April and July 1947 issues had appeared under the title: 'Preventing War in North Africa'.[16] The most significant contributor to those numbers was the classicist André Mandouze, whom Fanon would come to know in Algeria. The journal did not really make a case for the independence of Algeria, but did argue that if reforms were not introduced, there was a real danger that France would eventually lose Algeria and that lives would be lost too. *Esprit* had published material critical of French policy in Indochina and in Madagascar;[17] after 1954, it became, together with *Les Temps modernes*, one of the most important outlets for criticisms of the war in Algeria and especially of the French army's use of torture.

Fanon's editor at Seuil was the twenty-nine-year-old Francis Jeanson, who was also the editorial director of *Les Temps modernes*. Although recurrent bouts of tuberculosis had prevented him from taking the philosophy *agrégation,* he had published a well-received study of Sartre at the age of twenty-four.[18] His interest in Algeria was long-standing; like Fanon, he had first visited the country in 1943 as a volunteer in the African Army, and he had travelled widely there in 1948–9.[19] When he first met Fanon, he had recently published a long two-part article that began by questioning the very idea that the country had been either 'conquered' or 'pacified' by France and went on to give a scathing account of attempts to 'reform' the colonial system.[20] As he pointed out, the reforms introduced by the Organic Statute of Algeria of 1947 had established a system under which one million Europeans and nine million 'Arabs' elected the same number of *députés* to the Assemblée algérienne: the Algerian people could accede to the theoretical equality it had been offered only by acknowledging its own de facto inferiority.[21]

The first meeting between Fanon and Jeanson took place in Seuil's offices at 27 rue Jacob and it was not a happy one. Jeanson had been given Fanon's manuscript by Domenach, and found it 'exceptionally interesting'. When he met the author, he told him so, but something in his tone made Fanon think that what he really meant was 'Not too bad, for a negro' and he reacted accordingly. As he was about to show his author the door, Jeanson replied in 'the sharpest terms' to Fanon's suggestion that he was being patronized and Fanon 'had the good sense to take it positively'.[22] The editor should have been forewarned. It is very obvious from the text that Fanon was, like most Martinicans, extremely sensitive to being complimented on his 'good French', and the scene with Jeanson is an almost literal re-enactment of the passage in *Peau noire* where Fanon attacks Breton for saying that Césaire was 'a great black poet': 'Don't accuse me of affective anaphylaxis; what I mean is that there is no reason why M. Breton should say of Césaire: "And he is a black man who handles the French language better than any white can handle it today".'[23] Fanon may not have used precisely these words in his exchange with Jeanson, but they involve a typically Fanonian use of medical terminology without any regard for either context or interlocutor; 'anaphylaxis' means an allergic reaction to an antigen or foreign substance, but Fanon makes it synonymous with 'hypersensitivity'.

The two men never became real friends, and they were to have major political differences, but this frank exchange at least allowed them to work together. Like Glissant, Jeanson thought that Fanon was *un écorché vif*, but, like Tosquelles, he was also struck by the man's sheer physical presence or the 'bodily aspect of his intellectual approach'.[24] Once he had calmed down and was convinced that he was not being patronized, Fanon proved to be a surprisingly cooperative author and when Jeanson asked him to clarify a particularly obscure passage, he explained it at some length and then added a very rare personal comment: 'I cannot explain this sentence. When I write things like that, I am trying to touch my reader affectively, or in other words irrationally, almost sensually. For me, words have a charge. I find myself incapable of escaping the bite of a word, the vertigo of a question mark.' He went on to say that, like Césaire, he wanted 'to sink beneath the stupefying lava of words that have the colour of quivering flesh'.[25]

Francis Jeanson contributed a substantial preface of twenty-three pages to Fanon's book. It illustrates why he found it 'exceptionally interesting' and anticipates many of the positive responses to Fanon's work on the part of the 'Third Worldist' generation. For Jeanson, the book was a hymn to human freedom, but a very concrete one:

The man who has to be saved is not that timeless abstraction whose destiny can so easily be entrusted to the workings of an ill-defined dialectic: it is this negro who has been snatched away from his village, treated like a convict, beaten and humiliated; it is this young black gynaecologist who cannot practise his profession because, one day in the hospital he was wounded in his very flesh by a white patient who exclaimed: 'If he touches me, I'll slap him. You never know with his kind . . .',[26] it is this *tirailleur séné-galais* who has been forced to fight in Vietnam in a war that has nothing to do with him; it is this political prisoner in Madagascar; it is all these existences that are at stake *now*, and each one of which is unique, irreplaceable and lived as something from which there is no hope of turning back. Fanon is speaking for these people, for all his real brothers and all his living sisters – just as he is speaking for all those who, because they fail to recognize them and challenge their membership of the human race, therefore fail to recognize themselves and exclude themselves from the human race.[27]

The 'exceptional interest' of *Peau noire, masques blancs* did not make it a publishing success. There were few reviews and they were largely uncomprehending. None of the major newspapers – *Le Monde*, *Le Figaro*, the Communist *L'Humanité* – reviewed it, and nor did *Les Temps modernes* or the weeklies of the new left. Some of the brief reviews that did appear were in rather obscure Christian journals – a reflection, no doubt, of Seuil's largely Catholic constituency. The consensus that emerged was that, whilst this was an important indictment of European racism, it was very opaque and relied too heavily on psychoanalysis to make for comfortable reading.[28] A longer and more sympathetic review appeared in *Esprit* itself, where Maxime Chastaing, a Protestant from Bordeaux and an old associate of Mounier's, described what Fanon was doing in his first book as follows:

> Diagnosing the inhumanity of a society whose pathological culture creates both alienated (*mystified*) blacks and equally alienated (*mystified and mystificatory*) whites, and allows the flourishing of the dual narcissism of the black man who is black and the white man who is white; determining the genesis, origins and causes of these morbid manifestations and making us conscious of them; making it possible to understand those who suffer because of them and to establish an understanding relationship between negroes and Europeans.[29]

Although his comments in *Les Lettres françaises* bordered on the condescending and suggested that Fanon was saying nothing new, Léonard Sainville was the only critic to sense that the book in fact belonged to an identifiable tradition going back to *Légitime Défense*. Few of Fanon's readers can have known of its existence. The study of Francophone literature, or literature from the colonies and other French-speaking countries, is very much a post-war phenomenon and the literature itself was still in its infancy in 1952.[30] Fanon's book could not therefore easily be fitted into a broader body of work or judged within a wider context.

There are obvious circumstantial reasons why the book went virtually unnoticed. Never a major concern for metropolitan France, Martinique was quite simply not on anyone's agenda in the summer of 1952. The

Old Colony had been quietly 'departmentalized' and did not seem to pose any problems. In international terms, the Cold War and the hot wars in Indochina and Korea were the main concerns of the day. The Communist left – and many outside it – was preoccupied by the aftermath of the demonstrations held on 28 May to protest at the presence in France of General Matthew B. Ridgway, who had been accused of using bacteriological weapons in Korea and was being described as 'Plague Ridgway'. There had been one death and over 700 arrests, the most celebrated victim being PCF Secretary-General Jacques Duclos. He had been arrested and imprisoned on charges of threatening state security when two pigeons, a radio transmitter and a gun were found in the boot of his car. The legal basis for Duclos's arrest was the law, dating back to the First World War, requiring carrier pigeons to be registered with the Defence Ministry and the Ministery of the Interior. It was repealed in 1994.[31] The gun was proved to belong to Duclos's driver, who had a permit for it. The 'transmitter' was a receiver. The birds which the police had claimed were to be used for communicating with a foreign power were quite incapable of communicating with anyone, being dead and destined for the dinner plate. For its part, the non-Communist left was being torn apart by the rather more parochial Sartre–Camus quarrel, which broke out when Jeanson reviewed Camus's *L'Homme révolté* in extremely negative terms and scathingly described him as 'a soul in revolt' whose claims to be a true 'rebel' were unfounded.[32]

In the circumstances, it must have been easy to overlook a book by an unknown author such as Fanon, but the real reason for its neglect was quite simply that it was so difficult to read: most reviewers spoke of the difficulty and indigestibility of Fanon's psychoanalytical and philosophical references, and were not, unlike Sainville, able to situate the book in any tradition or context. *Peau noire* was and is an elusive book, not least because it is so difficult to categorize in terms of genre. It is difficult to think of any precedent for it, and it did not establish any new genre or tradition. It had no sequel. Fanon did not write the study of 'Language and aggressivity' which was, he claimed, in preparation,[33] and the style of his later writings is very different. Although written largely in the first person and although a rich biographical source, *Peau noire, masques blancs* is not a pure autobiography: the 'I' that speaks in it is often a persona. The text contains, for instance, no hint that Fanon had enjoyed a comfortable middle-class childhood. It is in part an account of colonialism in Martinique but it is a very partial one: there is little or no description of the economy, and no references to theories of colonialism. It contains no description of the island's political institutions, though it does vividly capture the place's profound alienation. It does not offer any real political solution to Martinique's problems, and is by no means a pro-independence manifesto.

The opacity of the language, and the constant shifts of register as Fanon moves from medical discourse to poetry and back again, often make the text uncomfortably difficult to read. When, for instance, at the beginning of his first chapter Fanon remarks that 'The black man has two dimensions. One with his congeneric, the other with the White man', he goes on to describe this duality as 'scissiparity'. Although it does convey a general sense of 'splitting' or 'double consciousness', this is the technical biological term for 'reproduction by fission'[34] and it is being used in a very idiosyncratic way. As a doctor, Fanon often used medical terminology quite spontaneously (and without much concern for the non-medical reader) but this would appear to be an instance of difficulties with self-expression rather than of diagnostic sophistication. Describing the 'white gaze' that transfixes him, he uses a metaphor drawn from the microscopy techniques he had learned in Lyon and from the instrument used for cutting specimens into thin sections: 'Having adjusted their microtome, they objectively make sections of my reality.'[35] To make things more difficult still, Fanon has a disturbing habit of coining neologisms, often forming verbs from nouns in a disconcerting manner, whilst the occasional use of typically Martinican turns of phrase provides a further obstacle for the average metropolitan reader.

The best way to approach *Peau noire, masques blancs* is to regard it as an extended exercise in *bricolage*, the term Lévi-Strauss used to describe how myths are assembled from the materials that are to hand: the word literally means 'do it yourself'.[36] *Bricolage* is a good way of describing just what Fanon was doing as he plundered the libraries and bookshops of Lyon and then strode up and down, dictating his text to Josie. The main materials to hand were the phenomenology of Sartre and Merleau-Ponty, the cultural discourse or tradition of negritude, the psychiatry in which Fanon had just trained, and the fragments of psychoanalytic theory he had absorbed from books. His relationship with his raw materials was never easy – the relationships with negritude and psychoanalysis were particularly fraught – and their synthesis was far from being a smooth one. To describe *Peau noire* as the product of *bricolage* is not to disparage either Fanon or his book. The term quite simply describes what he was doing: using elements of a then modernist philosophy and psychoanalysis to explore and analyse his own situation and experience, even though he had no real academic training as a philosopher and no extensive knowledge of psychoanalysis.

In philosophical terms, it is obvious from the outset that it is the existentialist phenomenology of the 1940s that supplies Fanon with a framework for his analysis of the lived experience (*l'expérience vécue*) of the black man. Neither Sartre's *L'Etre et le néant* nor Merleau-Ponty's *Phénoménologie de la perception* is a treatise on racism and anti-racism, though Sartre was also the author of an essay on anti-Semitism that would prove useful to Fanon, who describes it as 'magisterial'.[37] Yet of all the theories available to him, phenomenology was the most useful and the most concrete. Although the final section of *Peau noire* is prefaced by one of Fanon's rare quotations from Marx,[38] the crudely dogmatic Marxism of the 1950s was of little help to anyone intent upon analysing the black lived experience and, as Fanon had seen for himself in early 1952, the election of Communist députés had not brought about any far-reaching changes in Martinique. The Hegelianism that was, thanks to Alexandre Kojève and Jean Hyppolite,[39] so popular and so influential in the France of the late 1940s and the 1950s, was also ill-suited to Fanon's purposes. For both Kojève and Hyppolite, the key moment in Hegel's phenomenology of mind was the dialectic between the master and the slave, with both parties seeking a recognition of their humanity in the eyes of the other. In the colonial context, remarks Fanon, the master sought not recognition but work from the slave, whilst the slave wanted to be like the master.[40]

Sartre, in particular, provided a description of 'bad faith' and the 'alienated consciousness', but it could not be mechanically applied to the alienated consciousness of the black man because, in the colonial context, 'the White man is not simply the Other, but the master, real or imaginary'.[41] The attraction of Sartre's philosophy was its immediacy and its concentration on the category of experience. It was also a philosophy of freedom, but it still had to be adapted to the experience of a black Martinican.

The central term in Fanon's analysis is 'lived experience'. The French *expérience vécue* is the normal translation of *Erlebnis*, the technical term used by Husserl and Heidegger and then popularized by Merleau-Ponty in particular. Whilst Fanon had not read Husserl and Heidegger, he does cite Merleau-Ponty, and the notion of *Erlebnis* was current in the psychiatric circles in which he moved in Lyon. Balvet, for instance, identifies 'the essence of madness' with 'the schizophrenic *Erlebnis*, or in other words the specific frame of mind that disturbs the personality'.[42] *Erlebnis* is not simply synonymous with 'experience' in its everyday sense, and its analysis is by no means simply a matter of 'telling it like it is'. As Heidegger's English translators comment, 'An *Erlebnis* is not just *any* experience [*Erfahrung*], but one which we feel deeply and "live through".'[43] Merleau-Ponty himself defines *Erlebnisse* (in the plural) as 'acts of consciousness'.[44] Such acts are not the actions of a subject who stands outside the world and appropriates it as a neutral object; they are a mode of being through which the subject encounters a pre-existing world, and attempts to mould it to a project: 'To be a consciousness or rather an experience is to be in internal communication with the world, the body and other, to be with them rather than alongside them.'[45]

Fanon's central concern is with a 'frame of mind' and the 'living through of a situation or a being-in-the-world'. The phenomenological framework is immediately perceptible in the opening words of the first chapter on 'The Black Man and Language', where Fanon speaks of the need to understand the man of colour 'in the dimension of his being-for-others [*pour-autrui*]'.[46] This dimension situates his man of colour in a world in which he never exists in-himself as a monad, but always in a conflict-ridden relationship with others, or the other. He exists to the extent that he is seen and heard by others, to the extent that he *is* for others. So too the white man. Hence the concluding argument that the negro 'is' not (does not exist), and nor 'is' the white man.[47] Trapped in their respective 'whiteness' and 'blackness', they 'are' only insofar as they create one another, though this does not imply any reciprocity.[48] Fanon was not the only black writer of his generation to reach this conclusion and to sense that phenomenology could be adapted to give an analysis of the situation of the black man. Speaking on the same platform as Fanon at Présence africaine's 1956 Congress of Black Writers and Artists, the Barbadan Georges Lamming argued in very Sartrean terms that: 'The Negro writer is a writer who, through a process of social and historical accidents, encounters himself, so to speak, in a category of men called Negro . . . The Negro is a man whom the Other regards as a Negro.'[49] Colour and race are not essences, but the product of an existence and a situation. Lamming also describes 'the Negro becoming conscious of his presence, as a result of the regard of the Other . . . he is not simply *there*. He is there in a certain way. The eye which catches and cages him, has seen him as a man, but a man *in spite of*. . . As a result, he encounters himself in a state of surprise and embarrassment. He is a little ashamed, not in the crude sense of not wanting to be this or that, but in the more resonant sense of shame, the shame that touches every consciousness which feels that it has been *seen*.'[50]

Being the object of the gaze is the classic instance of being for others. The gaze of the child and its words objectify Fanon, denying his possible freedom in the alienation of 'being looked at'.[51] 'I arrived in the world, anxious to extract a meaning from things, my soul full of the desire to be at the origin of the world, and here I find myself an object in the midst of other objects.'[52] He had constructed a 'corporeal schema' on top of a 'historico-racial schema', building it – in another example of *bricolage* – from 'residues of sensations and perceptions'. The reference to a 'corporeal schema' is glossed by a footnote reference to Jean Lhermitte's *L'Image de notre corps*, which is the primary source for Merleau-Ponty's account of the 'synthesis' of the body in *La Phénoménologie de la perception*.[53]

Lhermitte, a doctor who had also written on the mechanisms of the brain and on the biological foundations of psychology but who also borrowed from Gestalt psychology, insists that the acquisition of an image of the body – 'the image of our body, the image of the self, the complex but strong feeling of our physical personality that is always present on the edge of consciousness'[54] – is a necessary precondition for action on and in the world. How, he asks, 'could we act on the external world if we were not in possession of a schema of our attitudes and of our situation in space, if we did not have in our minds the *idea* of our body?'[55] The construction of the image of the body is a gradual process in the course of which exteroceptive and proprioceptive sensations (or perceptions of the outside world and of oneself, respectively), memories of kinetic activity and barely conscious visual representations, are slowly synthesized into a mental perception of the physical self.[56] Merleau-Ponty puts it rather more succinctly: a corporeal schema is 'a resumé of our bodily experience' and 'a way of expressing the fact that my body is in the world'.[57]

Fanon's corporeal schema had helped him to 'construct a physiological ego, to balance space and to localise sensations', but something else —a 'supplement' – was now being demanded of him:

> 'Look, a negro!' It was an external stimulus that flicked me in passing.[58] I smiled slightly.
>
> 'Look, a negro!' It was true. I laughed.
>
> 'Look, a negro!' The circle was gradually getting smaller. I laughed openly.
>
> 'Mum, look at the negro, I'm frightened!' Frightened! Frightened! Now they were beginning to be frightened of me. I wanted to laugh till I burst, but that had become impossible.
>
> . . .
>
> Having come under attack at several points, the corporeal schema collapsed, giving way to an epidermal racial schema.[59]

The being-in-the-world that he had established for himself collapses into a being-for-others. Under the gaze of the child and its mother, Fanon now becomes 'responsible for my body, responsible for my race, for my ancestors. I cast an objective gaze at myself, discovered my blackness, my ethnic characteristics – and my eardrums were bursting with cannibalism, mental retardation, fetishism, racial taints, slave-traders and above all, above all, "*Y a bon banania*".'[60] He feels nauseous. Nausea is, in Sartrean terms, an expression of shame: 'Being ashamed of oneself is a recognition that I am indeed the object the other is looking at. I can only be ashamed of my freedom to the extent that it escapes me in order to become a given object.'[61] Shame is a form of consciousness, 'a shameful apprehension *of* something and that something is *me*. I am ashamed of what I *am*.'[62] In the eyes of a white child who, like the young Françoise Dolto, had been brought up to recognize a *nègre* when she saw one, Fanon *was* the grinning black soldier in the Banania poster and he now had to recognize himself as such. In a colonized society, remarks Fanon, the role of the black man is no longer to be black, but to be black in the eyes of the white man, and his revolt must therefore be based upon an assumption of his blackness.[63] The imaginary or recollected scene continues: '"Look, he's handsome, that nigger." The handsome nigger retorts: "Bugger you, Madame"' . . . Given that it was impossible for me to start out from *an innate complex,* I resolved to assert myself as BLACK. Given that the other was reluctant to recognize me [*me connaître*], there was only one solution left: to make myself known [*me faire connaître*].'[64]

Fanon was by no means alone in being caught up in the 'look, a negro' scenario. Lamming was clearly familiar with it. Léopold Sédar Senghor, the future president of Senegal, had precisely the same experience while walking in the Luxembourg Gardens in Paris but shrugged it off.[65] A character in one of the first novels about the lives of West Indian immigrants in London experiences it too: '"Mummy, look at that black man!" A little child, holding on to the mother hand, look up at Sir Galahad. "You mustn't say that, dear!" The mother chide the child.'[66] From 'the veil of invisibility' of Du Bois's *Souls of Black Folk* to bell hooks's *Wounds of Passion,* the trope of visibility/invisibility has consistently been used to trace the line of 'difference' that helps to construct the scenario.[67] The theme of the white gaze can also take on a more specifically Martinican dimension. In his reworking of *The Tempest,* Aimé Césaire has Caliban say to Prospero: 'You have finally imposed upon me an image of myself. An underdeveloped man, as you put it, an under-capable man. That is how you have made me see myself.'[68] The gaze of the white man creates the black slave and forces him to recognize that he is a slave. Fanon remarks in *Peau noire* that 'the negro is afraid of blue eyes' and, speaking of his encounter with the child and his mother, he writes: 'All this whiteness burns me to ashes.'[69] This is not simply an extreme reaction on the part of an *écorché vif* suffering from 'affective anaphylaxis'. Fanon's references to the Martinican's fear of blue eyes and to his own sensation of being burned to ashes contain a allusion to, or a memory of, the Creole saying '*Zié békés brilé zié nèg*' ('The eyes of the *béké* burned the eyes of the negro').[70] The entry for '*béké*' in Raphaël Confiant's 'Creole Lexicon' begins thus: 'The blue of his eyes burned the eyes of the negro in slave-time'.[71] For the Martinican Fanon, the experience of coming under the white gaze reproduces the primal experience of his island's history: slavery and a colonization so brutal as to be a form of trauma or even annihilation.

'Making myself known' is not an unreasonable description of what Fanon is about in his first book, but that project also implies the acquisition of self-knowledge and self-understanding. In terms of the phenomenology that is so important to Fanon's analysis or socio-diagnosis, *Peau noire, masques blancs* might well be described as an analysis of the author's situation or being-in-the-world, and as a bid for black authenticity in a white world. Much of the text is therefore an exercise in negativity in which Fanon works through a number of instances or examples of inauthenticity. Some instances are the effect of the being-for-others that is thrust upon him, not least by the white gaze and Banania posters; others are exemplified by texts in which others portray what Fanon clearly regards as inauthenticity. A lot of Fanon's evidence is drawn from fictional or semi-fictional texts – Mayotte Capécia's *Je suis Martiniquaise* and *La Négresse blanche*, Abdoulaye Sadji's novel *Nini*, and René Maran's *Un Homme pareil aux autres* – rather as though fiction is credited with having an immediacy and emotional veracity that sociological statistics, had they been available and had Fanon been a sociologist, might lack. It is also important that they are contemporary works, all published between 1947 and 1950, and deal in their own way with a modern lived experience.

As a teenager in Martinique, Fanon had been warned by his philosophy teacher that 'When they are talking about Jews, they are talking about you' and he took the lesson to heart: 'Anti-Semitism touches me right in the flesh and upsets me. A terrible contention anaemicizes me [*m'anèmie*], I am denied the possibility of being a man. I cannot dissociate myself from the fate that awaits my brother. Each of my acts commits the man. Each of my reticences, each of my acts of cowardice, manifests the man.'[72] The profession of faith is backed up by a reference to Jaspers on Germany's post-war metaphysical guilt and, in a sense, this is the fundamental political message of Fanon's first book, which advocates a humanism of solidarity and not some form of black nationalism. Sartre's short essay on the 'Jewish question' is not one of his most subtle texts, but its central proposition did have an immediate resonance for Fanon: 'The Jew is a man whom other men regard as a Jew: that is the simple truth we have to start out from . . . It is the anti-Semite who creates the Jew . . . It is not the Jewish character that provokes anti-Semitism; on the contrary, it is anti-Semitism that creates the Jew.'[73] At times Sartre implies that his analysis of anti-Semitism supplies a model for the analysis of other forms of racism, and notes that Richard Wright's remark that the United States had a white problem and not a black problem can be taken to imply that 'anti-Semitism is not a Jewish problem; it is *our* problem'.[74] Fanon, however, is quick to point out that whilst Sartre's Jew does exemplify a mode of being for others, that mode is not 'epidermally' determined: 'The Jew is a white man and, apart from a few debatable features, he can sometimes pass unnoticed . . . I am not the slave of the idea others have of me, but of my appearance.'[75]

Her 'appearance' is Mayotte Capécia's main problem, and the manner in which she attempts to deal with it supplies Fanon with an exemplary instance of the inauthenticity he is trying to combat in himself. Until very recently, little was known of Mayotte Capécia, except that she was born in Martinique in 1916, was living in Paris when she published her two novels, and died there in about 1955.[76] Recent research has demonstrated that 'Mayotte Capécia' was the pseudonym of Lucie (or 'Lucette') Combette (*née* Céranus), who was indeed born in Le Carbet in 1916 and did die in Paris in 1955.[77] *Je suis Martiniquaise* (1948) and *La Négresse blanche* (1950), both of which are strongly autobiographical, are her only publications; neither has ever been reprinted in France, though they have been translated in the United States.[78] Were it not for Fanon's very harsh criticisms of her work, it is, paradoxically, unlikely that the microfiche copies in the Bibliothèque Nationale de France would find many contemporary readers.

The first-person narrator of *Je suis Martiniquaise* is living in Paris, where her marriage plans have fallen through. Her ancestors were slaves and, ever since her girlhood, she has been determined to be independent. Her childhood was spent in rural Martinique, but a visit to

Fort-de-France inspired a deep admiration for the statue of Joséphine: 'The fact that a woman from Martinique could become Empress of the French, of the whole French Empire, that she could have become the wife of the greatest sovereign in the world, filled us all with pride. We venerated her and, like every little girl in Martinique, I often dreamed of that unparallelled destiny.'[79] Mayotte also has another dream: having discovered that her grandmother was a white French Canadian, she 'resolved that I would only love a white man, a blond with blue eyes, a Frenchman'.[80] A blond-haired, blue-eyed priest encountered in her childhood is her first love-object and she is intent upon finding an equivalent to him. Mayotte's infatuation with her white priest even influences her vision of the afterlife. She dreams of becoming an angel and flying up to heaven, 'all pink and white'. She has seen the film *Green Pastures* but cannot identify with it. Based on a successful Broadway play, the 1936 film depicts biblical characters and the heavenly host as southern blacks and represents heaven as 'a perpetual Negro holiday, one ever lasting weekend fish fry'.[81] Mayotte finds it shocking: it is impossible for her to imagine a God with black features.[82]

Most of the action of the novel takes place *an tan Robè*. Mayotte is now working in Fort-de-France as a laundress. The French term is much more loaded than the English equivalent suggests. Mayotte is *une blanchisseuse*, or a woman who literally turns things white. And she is trying to whiten her own life by pursuing an affair with a white officer. The outcome is inevitable: he goes back to France and marries a white woman. Mayotte also leaves for France, where she sadly concludes: 'I wanted to get married, but I wanted to marry a white man. The trouble is that a woman of colour is never quite respectable in the eyes of a white man. Even if he loves her, and I knew that.'[83] Her dilemma has always been the same: 'I no longer wanted to touch those men of colour who cannot stop themselves running after every woman they see, and I knew that white men do not marry black women.'[84] But they do have children by them: Mayotte is left with her lover André's child, and some very firm instructions: 'You will bring him up. You will tell him about me, and say "He was a superior man. You must work at being worthy of him".'[85]

Its sexual-racial politics aside, the novel is remarkable for its astonishing snobbery. According to Mayotte, the blacks who join '*la dissidence*' in 1943 are 'niggers of the lowest category' and, after the war, the black population of Martinique is said by her to be becoming 'arrogant'.[86] She shares her lover's Vichyist sympathies, and his admiration for Admiral Robert. *La Négresse blanche* is similar in tone and explores many of the same themes. It is the story of Isaure Thérésia, a mulatto woman (the white negress of the title) who keeps a bar in Fort-de-France during the war years. Her bar is a meeting place for sailors from the *Emile Bertin*, and they are sympathetically portrayed as the victims of the hostility of the *békés*, the mulattoes and especially the blacks, 'who were becoming incredibly insolent. They were openly talking of revolution.'[87] And it is the death of her husband at the hands of a mob of black 'dissidents' that finally forces Isaure to leave for Paris with her young son. Like Mayotte, Isaure has a white grandmother, and a French officer tells her that she herself is almost white: 'In a few years' time, when you have made millions from your bar, you will have a house built on the Plateau Didier and you will pass for a [white] creole.'[88] At the end of the novel, she realizes just how illusory this vision of the future was and almost despairs of finding a country where she can 'escape the curse of being neither black nor white'.[89] Both Capécia's novels portray a woman of mixed race who identifies with whites – to the extent that Isaure describes the sexuality of her black servant Lucia as 'animal'[90] – but who is inevitably used and then rejected by them. At the same time, she is threatened by what she perceives as a black revolt or even a revolution with Gaullist backing. Living in wartime Martinique, she shares or identifies with the values of the *békés* who are supporting Robert's regime.

*Le Monde*'s book reviewer found Capécia's style 'lively' and her *La Négresse blanche* 'entertaining'.[91] Edmond Buchet, who was Capécia's editor at Corréa, somewhat inaccurately told a writer on *Présence africaine* that *Je suis Martiniquaise* was the first novel by 'a French woman of colour', and that it was essential reading for anyone who wished to understand 'the character of West Indian women'.[92] Not everyone acquainted with Martinique agreed. Although she was pleased to see that one of her compatriots was sufficiently 'emancipated' to have written a novel that had an impact in metropolitan France and hoped to find in it an answer to 'the many problems posed by the problem of our *métissage*', the Martinican Jenny Alpha was disappointed to find that the novel did not capture 'the soul of Martinique: that rainbow of races'.[93] Although she comments favourably on Capécia's depiction of her girlhood, Alpha is disappointed that the attempt to capture Martinican French is the insertion of a few creolisms and the tired device of omitting intervocalic 'r's' in a clichéd transliteration of a Martinican accent. On the whole, the novel reminds her of the timeworn conventions of the colonial novel at its dullest.[94] Finally, she attacks Capécia's realism, remarking that a naval officer did not need to discover that his mistress was of mixed blood before he spurned her: any excuse would have done. Alpha also notes that the title is misleading. *Je suis Martiniquaise* means, of course, 'I am Martinican', but in the absolute sense of 'I am Martinican Woman'; it should, she thought, be changed to *Je suis une martiniquaise* or 'I am *a* Martinican woman'. 'Capécia' does reproduce many of the clichés of the regionalist or exoticist image of Martinique, but neither the text nor the clichés are of her own making. As it has long been rumoured, the manuscript she took to Paris in 1947 was in fact the work of the 'André' character and was dedicated 'To Mayotte, in memory of our divine love'.[95] The original script sent to her was supplemented by Capécia's own memories of her childhood in Martinique, edited and 'reworked' by a series of copy-editors from Editions Corréa. Much of *La Négresse blanche*, which also draws on Capécia's own life, proves to have been concocted in collaboration with another lover and to have undergone some very creative editing.

Both Capécia's novels are *doudouiste* tales of Martinican women abandoned by white lovers, and it has been suggested that *Je suis Martiniquaise* can be read as a historical-political allegory:

In the face of the phallic colonial government, the entire coloured population was reduced to sighing, just as Mayotte Capécia sighs to her French officer: 'I am a Martinican woman: take me'. Mayotte is Martinique, and Martinique is Mayotte. The officer's departure to rejoin his legitimate wife and children represents France's refusal, prior to 1946, to take fully into the bosom of the family the Antilles . . . the Antilles that people so liked to call 'the daughters of France'.[96]

Such an interpretation may be a little forced, but it is a reminder that Capécia's novels have to be read in context. It is important to recall that they are about wartime Martinique, and that they are about a specific category of Martinican women and not about a general category of 'black women'. As the journalistic accounts of the 'heritage' of slavery and of 'castes' in contemporary Martinique cited in Chapter 2 above indicate, it is very difficult to apply any such general category to a society that is still so marked by its colonial heritage of shadism. Indeed, Capécia's problem is precisely that she does not consider herself to be – and does not wish to be – 'a black woman'.

The latter point is particularly important in view of how Fanon's comments on Capécia have been interpreted by some feminist critics. It is futile to deny that, by contemporary standards, Fanon is a very masculinist writer and that he largely ignores the issue of what has come to be called 'gender'.[97] It is true that, whilst he criticizes Mayotte for her desire to marry a white man, his own marriage to a white woman does not seem to him to represent an 'abdication' of his personality.[98] It cannot, on the other hand, be argued in Mayotte's defence that she is 'a working-class black woman' and that her economic situation is such that prostitution is her only alternative to becoming a laundress.[99] Mayotte is not a poor woman working barefoot in the cane fields, and nor is she a poor washer-woman scrubbing clothes on a stone in the Rivière Madame (as women did within living memory; they were one of the more 'picturesque' details in the Martinican landscape). She does not heave sacks of coal on the docks, as did a small number of women.[100] She charges her clients high prices and is proud of the fact;[101] Isaure owns a bar. It would be difficult indeed to turn Fanon into a feminist or even a pro-feminist by the standards of the 1990s, but it is equally difficult to see Capécia's heroines as feminist icons of exploited womanhood and, by Martinican standards, she is not 'working-class'. It has rightly been said of readings such as those made by Bergner and other American feminists that it is dangerous to 'romanticize *Je suis Martiniquaise* as simply a black feminist manifesto on gender and class'.[102] Although the quality of Christiane Makward's research on 'Mayotte Capécia' cannot be disputed, her sardonic sub-title 'Alienation according to Fanon' indicates that something else is at stake. The book opens with a parodic 'trial scene' which provides a crude summary of the argument:

Counsel for the prosecution: Frantz Fanon (27, Doctor of medicine and psychiatrist).
Accused: Mayotte Capécia (32, 'novelist', mother of three children).
Charge: wanting to marry a blond Frenchman with blue eyes.
Verdict: guilty of expressing the Antillean lactification complex.
Sentence: forbidden to be read.[103]

Fanon's 'attack' on Capécia is said to be determined 'more by the sex of the authors in question than by any objective consideration'.[104] His criticisms of her are said to be informed by 'the racial Manicheanism that underpins the vision of this angry young mulatto'.[105] Such comments merely reproduce the offensive stereotyping of which Fanon stands accused.

Fanon is indeed highly critical of *Je suis Martiniquaise* and he had many reasons to dislike it. Disillusioned as he may have been by the war, neither he nor any other 'dissident' or veteran of the Cinquième Bataillon de Marche could have had much sympathy with a novel that describes him and his comrades as belonging to the 'lowest category of *nègres*'. He calls it a third-rate work that recommends 'unhealthy behaviour'.[106] It is 'unhealthy', but it is also symptomatic: 'Mayotte is striving for lactification. Because, after all, the race has to be whitened and saved; all Martinican women know it, say and repeat it.'[107] As a child, Mayotte tried to 'blacken' her schoolfriends by pouring ink over them; she is now a *blanchisseuse* who whitens things: 'now that she can no longer blacken or negrify the world, she will attempt, in her body and her soul, to whiten it'.[108] She is caught up in a 'bodily struggle with her blackness or with whiteness, totally caught up in a narcissistic drama'.[109] And she is, for Fanon, a symptom of all that is unhealthy about the Martinican psyche: 'It is customary in Martinique to dream of a form of salvation that consists of being magically whitened.'[110] The fantasy of 'being whitened' or of lactification has been described by two of the modern 'Creolist' writers as 'the mulatto ideology . . . save the race by marrying someone whiter than you, the logical outcome of the process being the extinction of any non-white trace, either cultural or racial, from the social body'.[111]

What is really at stake in Fanon's reading of *Je suis Martiniquaise*

174

emerges more clearly from a comparison of the comments made by the author of one of the other 'mulatto problem' novels discussed in *Peau noire*. Often overlooked in discussions of Fanon's text, Abdoulaye Sadji's *Nini, mulâtresse du Sénégal* first appeared in instalments in *Présence africaine* in 1948. Sadji (1910–61) was a Senegalese schoolteacher, who produced a number of essays and articles on Senegalese culture, but only one other novel. *Maimouma* (1951) is a fairly minor work, and deals with the corrupting effects of city life on a young woman. There is a biography of Sadji by his son but, whilst it is informative about his career in education, it has regrettably little to say about the origins, themes and reception of his fiction.[112] Like *Je suis Martiniquaise*, *Nini* is the story of a mulatto woman who loves and is abandoned by a white Frenchman who returns to France to marry a white woman, but whereas Capécia paints a tragically lachrymose picture of her heroines, Sadji claims to be offering a diagnosis of Nini's profound negrophobia. In an undated preface that did not appear in the serialized version, he makes his intentions quite plain:

> Nini is the eternal moral portrait of the mulatress, be she from Senegal, the West Indies or the two Americas. She is the portrait of a physically and morally hybrid being who, in the thoughtlessness of her most spontaneous reactions, always tries to rise above the condition that is hers, or in other words above a humanity she regards as inferior but to which her destiny inexorably links her.[113]

The same point is made in the body of Sadji's heavily didactic novel:

> All mulatto women, the Ninis, the Nanas and the Nénettes live outside the natural conditions of their country. The great dream that haunts them is that of being married by a White from Europe. One might say that their every effort is devoted to this goal, which is almost never attained. Their need to gesticulate, their love of ridiculous display, their calculated, theatrical and nauseating attitudes are so many effects of their mania for grandeur. They need a white man, a proper white man, and nothing but a white man.[114]

Their very existence is a lie, and is contrasted with the genuine authentic existence of the blacks with their toms-toms.[115] The criticisms of the ideology of the mulatto merge into a vision of negritude as pastoral. The narrative is not complex: in pursuit of her dream, Nini angrily rejects a proposal of marriage from a young black man, and even refers to him as a *bougnole* - an extremely pejorative term from French's rich repertoire of derogatory racial epithets.[116] After the departure of her white lover, Nini resigns from her secretarial post in the civil service on learning that she was appointed at the recommendation of a black and, just as Capécia's heroines leave Martinique, leaves Senegal for Paris and, presumably, further disappointments.

Fanon takes a few pages from Sadji's novel in an attempt to 'get an immediate picture of the woman of colour's reaction to the European man'.[117] He then refers to the long passage describing a successful mixed-race engagement as 'an excipient'.[118] His choice of terminology is strange: in pharmacology, an excipient is the neutral substance that serves as a medium for a drug; in art, it is the material or surface that receives the pigment. Given that Fanon had no technical or practical knowledge of painting, he must be using the term in its scientific sense, and may be extending the metaphor used by Sadji when he remarks that mulatresses like Nini have been 'poisoned by their status as hybrids who do not belong to any normal society'.[119] Nini's essential 'abnormality' or 'non-belonging' is signalled by her name; it is a diminutive form of 'Virginie' but can easily be read as '*ni . . . ni*' ('neither . . . nor').

Although Fanon does not challenge Sadji's own analysis of Nini in so many words, a brief comment in his discussion of Capécia indicates that he does in fact depart from it considerably. Discussing the incident in which Mayotte is taken to a party in Didier and finds that she is snubbed, he comments: 'Her facticity was the starting point for her resentment.'[120] He adds, 'rather than discovering herself to be black in an absolute sense, she will accidentalize [*accidentaliser*] that fact'.[121] '*Accidentaliser*' is Fanon's own – and clumsy – neologism, but 'facticity' is pure Sartre. Facticity refers to the objective factors that define a situation and my being-in-myself: 'my birth, my class, my nationality, my physiological structure, my body . . . my race, to the extent that it is indicated by the attitude of Others'.[122] 'Black' and 'white' do not, that is, exist as essential categories; they are situational categories defined by the encounter with others.

If Sadji is describing an 'eternal moral portrait', Fanon is describing a situation or a mode of being in the world in the Sartrean sense. In 'accidentalizing' her blackness and in resenting her facticity, Mayotte is living in bad faith and lapsing into inauthenticity. Bad faith is, in Sartrean terms, a form of self-deception, a denial of human freedom and an abdication of responsibility towards oneself and others. The repeated 'I know [that is impossible]' that Mayotte appends to her wish to marry a white man is the index of her bad faith and of her inability to be what Heidegger would call 'resolute' or what Sartre calls 'authentic': 'Authenticity . . . consists in a lucid and truthful consciousness of the situation, and in assuming the risks and possibilities inherent in that situation, in claiming responsibility for it, in pride or in humiliation, sometimes in horror and hatred.'[123] For Sartre, freedom means 'the apprehension of my facticity'.[124] Apprehending her facticity is precisely what Mayotte cannot and will not do. The inauthenticity of a Mayotte or a Nini is, according to Fanon, the key to their psychopathology: 'It is because the negress feels herself to be inferior that she aspires to being admitted to the white world. And in her attempt to do so, she will be helped by a phenomenon that we will call *affective eretheism*.'[125] Unlike Sadji, he does not suggest that it is a false essence to be counterposed against a genuine African essence. In terms of the philosophical framework of Fanon's analysis, Mayotte's bad faith is more important than her gender. But as the chapter of *L'Etre et le néant* devoted to the topic demonstrates at some length, it is always dangerous to accuse someone of being in bad faith without lapsing into it oneself. And Fanon does precisely that when he 'accidentalizes' his own marriage.

The discovery of being black 'in an absolute sense' and accepting one facticity might be one way of describing the negritude that is a major influence on the 'rebel' aspects of *Peau noire*.[126] It so happens that it is one of the more militantly defiant assertions of negritude that provides Fanon with the title of his most famous book: *Les Damnés de la terre* or *The Wretched of the Earth*. The obvious allusion to the '*Internationale*' ('*Debout, les damnés de la terre*' / 'Arise, ye wretched of the earth') is mediated through an allusion to something less obvious. Written in either 1938 or 1939 by Jacques Roumain, who was the founder of the Communist Party of Haiti, 'Sales nègres' ('Dirty Niggers') is first cited by Fanon in 1958, but another poem by him is quoted in *Peau noire*.[127] 'Sales nègres' begins thus:

> *Right then*
> *It's simple*
> *It's over*
> *We*
> *The nègres*
> *The niggers*
> *The dirty niggers*
> *Will no longer accept*
> *Being your nègres*
> *Your niggers*
> *Your dirty niggers*
> *In Africa*
> *In America*.

And it ends thus:

> *It will be too late*
> *To stop*
> *The harvest of vengeance*
> *Of the* nègres
> *Of the niggers*
> *Of the dirty niggers*
> *It will be too late I tell you*
> *For even the tom-toms will have learned the language*
> *of the* Internationale
> *For we will have picked our day*
> *The day of the dirty niggers*
> *Of the dirty Indians*
> *Of the dirty Arabs*
> *Of the dirty Malays*
> *Of the dirty Jews*
> *Of the dirty proletarians*

*And up we rise*
*All the wretched of the earth*
*All the dispensers of justice*
*Marching to attack your barracks*
*And your banks*
*Like a forest of funeral torches*
*To put an end*
*Once*
    *and*
        *for*
            *all*
*To this world*
*Of* nègres
*Of niggers*
*Of dirty niggers.*[128]

It is a commonplace to describe Aimé Césaire, Léopold Sédar Senghor and the lesser known Léon-Gontran Damas as the fathers of negritude, but that movement also has a forgotten mother. Fanon forgets her too (if, that is, he ever knew of her) when he remarks that 'It was only when Aimé Césaire appeared that one could see someone taking responsibility for and assuming their negritude.'[129] Even less is known about Suzanne Lacascade than was until now known about Capécia, except that she was born in Guadeloupe and her only novel caused such a scandal there that she was forced into exile in Paris.[130] Presumably autobiographical and set in Paris before and during the First World War, *Claire-Solange: âme africaine* ('Claire-Solange, African Soul'), is the story of the daughter of a black Martinican woman and a white civil servant who has worked in France's African colonies (and thus adds a nice twist to the 'mulatto problem' novel). Martinique is described as a 'land where men are governed by prejudice' where Claire-Solange's father was criticized for marrying a black woman,[131] but it was the heroine's profession of faith that was truly scandalous in 1924. She declares that her one passion in life is 'to defend and glorify the black race . . . I am African . . . atavistically African, despite my paternal heritage. African, like the first of my foremothers who was brought as a slave to the West Indies, and whose savage name is unknown.' She asks: 'What are we doing in this civilized society? Nostalgia and an immense bitterness are welling up inside me. I would like to scream and go off into the wildness of nature. Everything here seems artificial to me . . . like the gas lamps, drowning in the mist. Everything here seems dark to me: your dusty days, your lustreless stars, and your black clothes.'[132] *Claire-Solange* is not distinguished by its literary qualities but, as the Guadeloupean novelist Maryse Condé has remarked, the fact that Lacascade apparently lacked 'any particular gift for writing' does not in itself explain why a novel that anticipates so many of the themes of negritude has been so totally forgotten: negritude is a very masculinist discourse and does not celebrate its mothers.[133] Yet the forgotten Lacascade's rejection of Europe and her hymns to a largely mythical Africa do outline the themes dealt with by a later generation of writers.

Neither Lacascade nor the contributors to *Légitime Défense* use the term 'negritude', but, as is apparent from the anonymous 'Le Surréalisme', it was very familiar to Fanon and his friends in Lyon. Until approximately 1936, Senghor himself uses the phrase '*nègre nouveau*' (which is a direct translation of 'new negro' – the title of the American anthology edited by Alan Locke in 1925[134]), and the word 'negritude' first appears in a poem written in 1936, when he was teaching in Tours:

> *The European spring*
> *Makes advances to me*
> *Offering me the virgin scent of its fields*
> *The smile of façades in the sun*
> *And the soft grey of the roofs*
> *In gentle Touraine.*
> *It has yet to know*
> *the demands of my imperious negritude.*[135]

Born in Joal, Senegal, on 6 October 1906, Léopold Sédar Senghor was educated locally and then at the Lycée Louis le Grand in Paris, where his friends included future president Georges Pompidou, and at the Sorbonne.[136] As a student, his circle of acquaintances included René Maran, Louis T. Achille, Césaire and Damas. He was the first black

African to pass the *agrégation*, which is the highest competitive examination in the French system, and taught in French schools and at the Ecole Nationale de la France d'Outre-mer. He subsequently enjoyed a long and successful political career, being first elected to the Assemblée nationale in the same year as Aimé Césaire. In 1960, he was elected President of the newly independent Republic of Senegal and remained in office until 1980. Four years later, he was elected to the Académie française. A Catholic who once dreamed of becoming a priest, Senghor was strongly influenced by Teilhard de Chardin and the nationalism of Maurice Barrès, who defined the French national identity in terms of its fidelity to the land and its dead. His broadest definition of negritude describes it as the totality of the civilizing values of the African world or the common denominator between all black Africans.[137]

In a paper read to a conference on the African influence on West Indian literature held in Cuba in 1968, Léon-Gontras Damas (1912–78), a Guyanese-born poet who is now less well known than either Senghor or Césaire but whose work was appreciated by Fanon,[138] describes why the term was coined: 'The word "negritude" . . . had a very precise meaning in the years 1934-35, namely the fact that the black man was seeking to know himself, that he wanted to become a historical actor and a cultural actor, and not just an object of domination or a consumer of culture . . . The word "negritude" was coined in the most racist moment of history, and we accepted the word *nègre* as a challenge.'[139] Or as Fanon put it in 1959: 'It is the white man who creates the negro. But it is the negro who creates negritude.'[140]

Negritude obviously derives from *nègre*, and its coinage involves some sophisticated political semantics. *Nègre* can, depending on the context and the speaker, mean both 'negro' and 'nigger'; used as an adjective it had been popularized and given a certain respectability by expressions such as *art nègre* and *La Revue nègre*. The pejorative connotations of the noun, on the other hand, were so strong by the 1930s that it began to be replaced by the periphrastic *homme de couleur* or *noir*. One of the main creators of negritude was Césaire, with his *Cahier d'un retour au pays natal*, and one of his great achievements in his epic poem is to reappropriate a negative term and to give it a positive sense. As Fanon puts it, 'For the first time, we saw a lycée teacher, and therefore an apparently worthy man, simply tell

181

West Indian society that it is "good and well to be a *nègre*". Of course it was a scandal.'[141]

First published in 1938 but better known – and known to Fanon – in the revised edition published in 1947, the *Cahier* describes a return to Martinique and a defiant acceptance of its reality: 'my original geography; the map of the world made for my use, dyed not with the arbitrary colours of the scientists, but with the geometry of my spilt blood . . . and the determination of my biology . . . and the nigger every day more debased, more cowardly, more spread out of himself, more estranged from himself, more cunning with himself, less immediate with himself, I accept, I accept all this.'[142] This is no passive acceptance of colonial reality, but also a defiant challenge: 'Accommodate me. I am not accommodating you!'[143] Although he does not signal the fact, Fanon cites Césaire's 'accommodate me' in an imaginary dialogue with 'the white man' who denies that Africa has made any contribution to world history.[144]

Césaire's first use of the word 'negritude' occurs in a reference to Haiti, 'where negritude stood up for the first time', and it is followed by the obvious historical allusion to Toussaint L'Ouverture's rebellion of 1794–1801:

> *A man alone, imprisoned by whiteness*
> *A man alone who defies the white scream of a white death*
> *(TOUSSAINT, TOUSSAINT L'OUVERTURE)*[145]

In the poem's most famous lines, which combine phallic imagery with memories of the eruption of Montagne Pelée, the narrator becomes the heir to Toussaint and the rebels of 1791:

> *my negritude is not a stone, its deafness hurled against the*
> *    clamour of the day*
> *my negritude is not an opaque spot of dead water on the dead eye*
> *    of the earth*
> *my negritude is neither a tower nor a cathedral*
>
> *it plunges into the red flesh of the soil*
> *it plunges into the blazing flesh of the sky*
> *it pierces opaque prostration with its straight patience*[146]

The long poem is also a reappropriation and celebration of an African heritage, though it is largely an imaginary one as Césaire had no direct knowledge of Africa at this time. Although powerfully expressed, Césaire's brief images of a timeless Africa come close to reproducing European stereotypes of a continent that has produced nothing:

> *those who invented neither powder nor the compass*
> *those who have never been able to tame steam or electricity*
> *those who have explored neither the seas nor the sky*
>
> *Eia for those who have never invented anything*
> *for those who have never explored anything*
> *for those who have never tamed anything*[147]

Negritude is not a particularly stable body of thought and it does not of itself lead to any specific politics. Indeed, it can lead in very different political directions. To take two antithetical examples from the founding fathers. Writing in 1938, Senghor salutes the African dead of the First World War thus:

> *Tirailleurs sénégalais*
> *WHO DIED FOR THE REPUBLIC ,*
> [MORTS POUR LA REPUBLIQUE]
> *Your black comrades salute you.*[148]

*Morts pour la République* and the *morts pour la France* of the title are commonplace inscriptions on French war memorials. Writing at much the same time, Damas strikes a very different note:

> I ask
> The Senegalese old soldiers
> The future Senegalese soldiers
>
> To start by invading Senegal
> I ask them
> To leave the 'Boches' in peace.[149]

Predictably, his book was banned because it was deemed to pose a threat to national security; no book by Senghor has ever been banned by a French government.

The political contrast between the two poems is indicative of the fault line running through negritude. On the one hand, there is in Senghor's prolific writings a celebration and endorsement of specifically black-African culture and values; on the other, there is the cry of revolt voiced by the wretched of the earth. Both assert or affirm a black presence – hence the journal title *Présence africaine* – but they do so in very different terms, and with different implications. Fanon takes a dim view of the Senghorian strand and of the celebration of traditional African values that provides the ideological underpinnings for the vision of negritude as pastoral in Sadji's novels. Although he took a passing interest in Cheikh Anta Diop's research into African languages, which anticipates by forty years Martin Bernal's attempts to demonstrate that the Ancient Egyptians were black and that the Afro-Asiatic roots of classical Greek culture were obscured by the West's construction of an 'Aryan' foundation myth,[150] he became very critical of it by 1959 and was always sceptical about Senghor. In his *Ce que l'homme noir apporte*, the latter writes that the black man's contribution to world civilization is an innate sense of rhythm. 'Listen to Senghor, our bard', writes Fanon before going on to quote a passage in which Senghor speaks of the pure primitive rhythms of African sculpture, of the rhythm that allows the black man to penetrate into that sculpture's spirituality. This is Fanon's response to that view: 'In no way must I strive to bring back to life a negro civilization that has been unfairly misrecognized. I will not make myself the man of any past. I do not want to sing the past at the expense of my present and my future . . . My black skin is not the repository of specific values.'[151] Speculation as to links between African philosophers and Plato, or as to the existence of an ancient Negro architecture or literature, are all very well but, like Tempels's Bantu ontology, their existence will do nothing to alter the situation of an eight-year-old boy working in the cane fields of Martinique or Guadeloupe.[152]

Fanon could have mentioned other contradictions inherent in Senghor's negritude: his Catholicism, his frequent use of verse forms derived from Paul Claudel, and a form of nationalism that has much in common with Maurice's Barrès's celebration of the land and the dead. For Senghor, negritude defines 'the collective negro-african personality', and that personality is characterized by its sense of rhythm and its capacity to be emotionally moved.[153] The extent to which this description reproduces European and Eurocentric stereotypes can be gauged by a modern summary of the positivist philosopher Auguste Comte's views on these matters:

> Comte posits the existence of three great human facilities, intelligence, action and feeling, and he declares that each of the three great 'races', white, yellow and black, has uncontested superiority in one of these faculties. Whites are most intelligent, yellows work hardest, blacks are the champions of feeling.[154]

It is a long way from Senghor's celebration of an African essence to Fanon's phenomenology of the '*Erlebnis*' of the black man, and to the scream of revolt uttered by Roumain, Césaire and Fanon, and echoed by the Guadeloupean Guy Tirolien in a poem that suggests why negritude could take a specific form in the French West Indies:

> *We will no longer sing the outdated lovesongs*
> *That the honeyed doudous once whispered*
> *As they unfurled their foulards on our beaches of sugar*
> *To salute the departure of winged schooners*
>
> . . .
>
> *We will no longer repeat those facile poems*
> *Extolling the beauty of the fortunate islands*
> *Odalisques lying on carpets of azur*
> *And caressed by the breath of the sweet trade winds*
>
> *We will unite our voices in a bouquet of cries*
> *And shatter the eardrums of our sleeping brothers*
> *And the flame of our anger*
> *Will burn in anger in the braziers*
> *On the blazing prow of our islands.*[155]

The final pages of *Peau noire*, entitled 'By Way of Conclusion', are a hymn to freedom in which Fanon rejects in very Sartrean terms all determinism, insists that his freedom is both absolute and self-founding to the extent that it transcends history. 'Superiority? Inferiority? Why not quite simply try to touch the other, feel the other, reveal the other to me? Wasn't my freedom given to me to build the world of the *You?*'[156] And yet the way in which he reacts to Sartre's essay on the poetry of negritude points to the constraints on his freedom and to his need to cling to an identity. 'Orphée noir' is Sartre's preface to Senghor's 1948 anthology of negritude poetry, and in it he describes negritude both as a mode of black being-in-the-world and as an anti-racist racism. Negritude is, according to Sartre, the weak moment in a dialectical process. The theoretical and practical assertion of the white man is the thesis, and the positing of negritude as an authentic value, the moment of negativity or anti-thesis. It will in its turn be transcended by the synthesis or realization of the human 'in a society without races'. A similar schema is at work in the *Refléxions sur la question juive* and in Beauvoir's *Le Deuxième Sexe*: all look to a classless-raceless society in which neither the Jewish question, the 'woman question' nor the black question will have any meaning.

Fanon's reaction on reading these lines was to realize that his last chance had been taken from him: 'I declared to my friends: "The generation of young black poets has received a blow they will not recover from". We appealed to a friend of peoples of colour, and that friend found nothing better to do than demonstrate the relativity of their action. For once, this Hegelian forgot that consciousness has to lose itself in the night of the absolute, which is the sole precondition for arriving at a self-consciousness. Arguing against rationalism, he recalled the negative side, but forgot that this negativity derives its value from an almost substantial absoluity [*absoluité*].'[157] Although Fanon would soon reject negritude on the grounds that it was no more than a 'black mirage' that was replacing 'the great white mistake', in 1952 he could still say: 'I needed to lose myself in negritude in an absolute sense',[158] and that is what Mayotte Capécia could not do. In general terms, *Peau noire* advocates a politics of solidarity that speaks on behalf of all the wretched of the earth, but there are moments when Fanon has to speak as the essential black man. The white woman whose gaze burns him to ashes has to be told 'Bugger you, Madame'.

In describing negritude as a temporary 'racist anti-racism' that will be transcended by the dialectic of history, Sartre falls into a trap of his own making, and he describes that very trap in his *Refléxions* when he speaks of the 'democrat's' inability to recognize the Jew in the assertion of his Jewishness and his insistence on the need to recognize him as a universal (and 'democrat' was not a positive term for the Sartre of the late 1940s, who used it to mean 'woolly liberal'). Both Jewishness and negritude must be transcended by the entry into universalism. Whilst the trap can be described in purely Sartrean terms, it also relates to other questions. On the one hand, Hegel's elision or eviction of Africa from history in his quintessentially Eurocentric history of Spirit's journey from East to West;[159] on the other, the universalism of a French Republicanism that recognizes – or calls into existence – abstract subjects who are French, but neither black nor white, Jewish or gentile, male or female.

Neither negritude nor phenomenology provide an adequate description of Fanon's *Erlebnis*. Nor does psychoanalysis. Fanon had little or no practical experience of psychoanalysis, and his knowledge of that discipline is, despite his close contacts with a practitioner like Tosquelles, primarily textually based. It is also highly eclectic: Adler is cited alongside Anna Freud, references to Lacan occur alongside largely forgotten figures. Although *Peau noire* begins with the assertion – and it is an assertion rather than an argument – that 'I think that only a psychoanalytic interpretation of the black problem can reveal the affective anomalies that are responsible for the complex-structure',[160] Fanon does not, ultimately, produce that interpretation. Psychoanalysis does allow him to describe the transference of white fantasies on to the black man – but even here there is some uncertainty; strictly speaking, this is projection or the externalization of aspects of an inner psychical reality, and not transference. From the outset, Fanon stresses that psychoanalysis may not in fact provide a full explanation and insists that a theory of phylogeny and ontogeny must be complemented by one of sociogeny: the black man's alienation is not an individual question, and its causes are socially determined.[161] Neither phylogenesis, or the history of the human species, not ontogenesis (the history of the individual) can, that is, explain a socio-political phenomenon.

The application of psychoanalysis to the 'black problem' is also highly problematic in other respects. Classical psychoanalysis implicitly relies upon a universalist model of the psyche that takes no account of ethnic differences ('Neither Freud, nor Adler nor even the cosmic Jung gave a thought to blacks in the course of their research'[162]), but it is also underpinned by a theory of social evolution that moves from 'primitive' to 'archaic' and it looks to supposedly primitive or archaic societies to provide analogies with the workings of the unconscious and the drives. Freud's anthropology is, to say the least, dubious by contemporary standards. The sub-title of *Totem and Taboo* is symptomatic: 'Some Points of Agreement between the Mental Lives of Savages and Neurotics'. That white European society represents a higher – or even the highest – stage of civilization goes without saying. Modern psychoanalytic culture tends simply to ignore the issue of ethnic difference. There is, for instance, no hint in Elizabeth Roudinesco's compendious and in many ways excellent history of psychoanalysis in France that France is a multicultural and multiracial society.

The problems of 'applying' psychoanalysis in this area are inadvertently illustrated by the one analyst with whom Fanon engages at any length in *Peau noire*. Octave Mannoni (1899–1989) had spent twenty years in Madagascar as an ethnologist and director-general of the information service before he began analysis with Lacan in 1947, and then broke it off almost immediately. 'After an interruption I began again in 1952 . . . Lacan didn't prevent me from undergoing psychoanalysis, but I wasn't interested in it since, in Madagascar, I had cured myself of an obsessional neurosis . . . dislocation can do the job of analysis. Being a white man among the blacks is like being an analyst among the whites.'[163] It was during this strange psychoanalytic apprenticeship that he wrote the articles that caught Fanon's eye. Fanon thought of writing to Mannoni to ask him to describe to him the conclusions he had reached, but the appearance of *Psychologie de la colonisation* spared him the need to do so.[164]

Mannoni's self-analysis and the writing of his psychology of colonization coincided with the rebellion of 1947, and it is that event that provides the context for Fanon's critique of it.[165] Madagascar was occupied by France in 1895, but it took a further eight years for it to be sufficiently 'pacified' for serious colonization to get underway. The colonial presence was never large in numerical terms; at most there were 3,700 *colons* compared with an indigenous population of 4,150,000. French colonial policy was based upon a classic divide and rule strategy that left the twenty or so ethnic groups under the day-to-day administration of their traditional rulers, and exploited rivalries between them very effectively. The uprising of 1947 is generally viewed as being a product of the Second World War. In 1942, British and Commonwealth forces occupied the island and demonstrated beyond doubt that the French colonial army was not invincible. The withdrawal of British troops in 1946 seemed to herald a new stage in France's relationship with the colonies. On 23 March, the Minister for Overseas France told the Constituent Assembly that a decisive moment had been reached: France could either recognize that the colonies had a legitimate desire to become equals within a loose union or commonwealth, or reconcile herself to their eventual loss: 'A nation – and especially our nation – can retain its influence in its overseas territories only with the freely given consent of the populations that inhabit them.'[166]

Such words were very acceptable to the Mouvement Démocratique de la Rénovation Malgache (MDRM), legally established in Paris in 1946 and seemingly recognized by the French government as a potential interlocutor. Three MDRM députés represented the colony in the Assemblée Nationale and argued that Madagascar should be a free state within the Union Française. Whether or not the MDRM was actually responsible for the uprising that broke out in March 1947 is still a matter for controversy; much of the organization of the rebellion appears to have been the work of secret societies which combined a basic nationalism with a millenarian vision of a holy war against colonialism. Their organized forces numbered at most 15,000 to 20,000 poorly armed fighters, and the response to the uprising in which 350 French soldiers and 200 civilians were killed, was overwhelming. The French brought in a total of 18,000 troops, some rerouted whilst on their way to Indochina, where France was fighting another colonial war. They included a battalion of Foreign Legion Infantry and two battalions of *Tirailleurs sénégalais*, as well as Moroccan and Algerian units. The Legion and the *Tirailleurs*, in particular, lived up to their well-deserved reputation for brutal efficiency. Torture, summary executions, the punitive burning of villages, rape and the mutilation of the dead were all commonplace. An official report claimed that some 11,000 died during the repression of the uprising; a confidential Army report spoke of 89,000 dead and the figure of 100,000 has also been suggested. In May 1948, the MDRM was banned as a subversive organization and its leaders were put on trial. Although they argued that they had in fact appealed for calm and restraint when the rising broke out, they were sentenced to death or long terms of forced labour. Political pressure exerted by the PCF and the parties of the left led to them being amnestied in 1954. One of the arrested leaders was Jacques Rabemanjara, a former civil servant in the *Direction des Finances*, a friend of Senghor and Alioune Diop, and a distinguished poet whose work was included in Senghor's anthology.[167] In 1956, Fanon would share a public platform with him in Paris.

It was against this background that Mannoni elaborated his psychology of colonization, which was viewed by Fanon as an 'honest' but 'dangerous' piece of work.[168] Mannoni's working hypothesis was that modern psychology made it possible to understand a 'colonial situation' without having to borrow from 'Ethics, Law or History'.[169] His analysis of the colonial situation centred on the notion of an inferiority complex that is instilled when skin colour becomes a mark of inferiority or disadvantage, but also on the notion of a dependency complex. As an administrator, Mannoni had noted that making a gift – of, say, a pair of cast-off tennis shoes – to a Malagasy created the expectation of other gifts: 'The gifts that the Malagasy first receives passively, and which he then asks for – and which in fairly rare cases he eventually demands – are none other than the visible sign of [a] reassuring relationship of dependency.'[170] The dependency complex is rooted in a religious cult of dead ancestors and protective supernatural powers, but can easily accommodate the figure of the *vazaha* ('honourable foreigner') as a symbolic father figure. The colonial situation is, thus, characterized by a psychological relationship in which the Malagasy transfers on to the colonizer the feelings of dependency characteristic of the relationship between father and son.[171]

Mannoni's conclusion is as inescapable as it is astonishing: 'In my view, there is no doubt that colonization has always been based upon the existence of need and dependency. Not all people are suitable for being colonized; only those who feel this need are suitable. In almost all cases where Europeans have founded colonies of the type that is now "in question", we can say that they were expected, and even desired in the unconscious of their subjects.'[172] Even the rebellion itself proves the existence of the dependency complex; threatened with being abandoned by traditional colonialism, the rebels are looking for new protectors and find them in the MDRM:

> Abandoned to their own devices, the vast majority of the Malagasy would indeed try to reconstruct a feudal society, spontaneously and without even realizing it. They might call it a Republic or a Democracy, but their dependency complex would lead them gradually but quite inevitably, to organize client groups around suitable patrons. They would not have the courage to face up to the torments of their real personal liberation.[173]

As one critic remarks, colonies are defined as being essentially amenable to colonization, and their history is one that can be deduced from essences; by the same logic, it can always be proved that the rape-victim was essentially consenting.[174]

By his own standards, Mannoni was a liberal and a proponent of a universalist psychology. Even though his book is objectively an apologia for colonization, it would be absurd to describe Mannoni as a racist in the normal sense of the word, and he appears to have taken a sympathetic view of the Malagasy, though his sympathies are those of the 'old African hand' and not those of a 'Third Worldist'.[175] Unlike the psychiatrists of the Algiers school who elaborated the 'North-African syndrome' and whose work is examined in the next chapter, he does not argue that the behaviour and psychology of the Malagasy is so different from those of Europeans as to be almost incomprehensible. On the contrary, he believes that there is 'no watertight barrier between the psychology of the colonized and that of the European' and that modes of thought to be observed in 'primitive' peoples have been 'attributed to an obscure mentality that cannot be assimilated to our logic, and into which we *cannot* enter because we *refuse* to enter into it. We have scotomized the thought of backward groups by using the very mechanism we use to repress part of our own thought. Psychoanalytic methods alone can free the researcher from this repression, and allow him to apprehend a foreign thought which is *only too similar* to his own.'[176] The existence of a universal psychical structure means that 'If we examine a black man, we may perceive our own unconscious . . . The Negro is the white man's fear of himself.'[177]

Analysing a series of dreams recounted by seven Malagasy, Mannoni notes the recurrence of black bulls, black men and Senegalese soldiers, and duly interprets them as real and ancestral father figures: a gun is a transparent phallic symbol. Fanon's objection is the obvious one: 'The *Tirailleur sénégalais*'s rifle is not a penis; it really is a 1916-model Lebel rifle.'[178] Mannoni's disastrous psychologization of the colonial situation is, he notes, akin to the medicalizing discourse that explains the appearance of varicose veins in terms of the constitutional fragility of the walls of the vein, and forgets that the sufferer had to spend ten hours a day on his or her feet; we must not, he concludes, 'lose sight of the real'.[179] Not losing sight of the real also provides the basis for Fanon's lapidary but decisive critical comment to the effect that, whatever Hegel may say, the Martinican master was not interested in obtaining his slave's recognition of him as a man, but in extracting labour from him.

The need not to 'lose sight of the real' may explain the strangest aspect of Fanon's attempt to use psychoanalysis. There are only two direct quotations from Freud in *Peau noire, masques blancs* and Fanon does not identify their provenance. He cites Freud to further his contention that neuroses originate in a determinate *Erlebnis*, but fails to situate his quotations in terms of the development of psychoanalysis. The quotations are from the first and second of the five lectures on psychoanalysis delivered by Freud at Clark University in September 1909. Freud is describing his early collaboration with Breuer and the elaboration of his early aetiology of neurosis, or, in other words, the so-called seduction theory which traces neurosis back to a primal trauma such as sexual abuse in childhood.[180] When he appeals to Freud, Fanon is in fact appealing to a text in which Freud is distancing himself from the theory he elaborated with Breuer. One of the crucial – and controversial – moments in the history of psychoanalysis is the curtailing of the search for a 'first trauma' and the adoption of the thesis that neurosis stems, not from a real trauma, but from incestuous fantasies linked to the Oedipus complex. Fanon explicitly rejects that thesis. It is, he argues, the encounter with the white world that creates the black man's neurosis: 'a normal black child who has grown up in the bosom of a normal family will be made abnormal by the slightest contact with the white world'.[181] In psychoanalytic terms, the argument is quite untenable but it is consistent with the primal experience of the burning gaze of the *béké* and the absolute wound inflicted on Martinique by colonialism. It is also consistent with both a dream of a 'natural' pre-colonial Martinique and the natural being of a black boy who grew up there without knowing he was black because no one had told him he was.

The white gaze creates the black as a phobogenic and anxiogenic object. The black man becomes both the focus of irrational fears and a source of anxiety.[182] The phobic object then becomes the screen on to which white fantasies, fear and guilt can be projected in the form of perverted desires. Desire for the black man becomes fear of the black man, who represents in fantasy a 'genital potency that transcends moralities and prohibitions'.[183] The female negrophobe is a putative sexual partner; her male equivalent is a repressed homosexual – and in the 'natural' Martinique, there are, according to Fanon, no homosexuals.[184] In America, Fanon remarks in a footnote, the usual response to the demand for black emancipation is to say: 'They're just looking for an opportunity to jump on our women. As the white man behaves towards the black man in an insulting fashion, he realizes that, were he in the black man's position, he would have no pity for his oppressors.'[185] Fanon's knowledge of America derived primarily from literary sources and he uses Chester Himes's novel *If He Hollers Let Him Go* to illustrate the thesis that the white woman's fear of rape is in fact a desire to be raped: 'The big blonde feels faint every time the negro comes near her. And yet she has nothing to fear, as the factory is full of whites. In the end, they go to bed together' and 'the big blonde who is always getting in his way, fainting, sensual, offering herself, open, fearing (desiring) rape, finally becomes his mistress'.[186]

Published in 1945, Himes's first novel is a violent depiction of racism in the shipyards of wartime California and it does deal with a relationship of attraction–repulsion between a black man from Cleveland, Ohio and a white woman from Texas, but this is not how it ends. Madge Perkins refuses to work with Bob Jones :'"I ain't gonna work with no nigger!" "Screw you then, you cracker bitch".'[187] He is immediately demoted from his supervisory position. He wants to kill her, but also thinks of raping her in revenge. Bob Jones persuades Madge to let him into her hotel room and a violent encounter follows: '" All right, rape me then, nigger." Her voice was excited, thick, with threads in her throat.'[188] He flees in panic. A second encounter takes place in a cabin on the ship they are both working on. As Madge attempts to kiss Bob, they both realize that they cannot be found together and she cries rape: 'Help! Help! My God, help me! Some white man, help me! I'm being raped.'[189] As he is being dragged away by a mob of white workers, her last words are, 'I'm gonna get you lynched, you nigger bastard.'[190] She in fact drops the rape charge and the judge before whom Bob Jones is brought 'allows' him to join the armed forces. Bob Jones is drafted into the army, the implication being that he will die in the Pacific war. Fanon's own analytic schema, and perhaps at some level his own desires, almost forces him to misread the novel.

The crucial part of Fanon's argument with Freud and Lacan is the claim that: 'It would be relatively easy for me to demonstrate that in the French West Indies, 97 per cent of families are incapable of giving birth to an Oedipal neurosis. And we can congratulate ourselves highly over that incapacity.'[191] Hence the reluctance to accept Lacan's claims that the ills of modern society stem from the decline of the paternal imago. The footnote which adds that 'psychoanalysts will be reluctant to share my opinion on this point' is redundant; Fanon is questioning one of the cornerstones of their doctrine. As in the discussion of the 'North-African syndrome', sociogenesis takes precedence over psychogenesis: in Martinique, mental illness is the result of a cultural situation determined by the existence of colonialism. In his attempt not to lose sight of the real, Fanon may well be misrecognizing an aspect of psychoanalysis, but he is also insisting that psychoanalysis itself may be projecting European cultural values. Fanon does not pursue his criticisms to their logical conclusion, but his theses imply a critique of both Mannoni's psychoanalytic universalism and the psychiatric differentialism he had encountered in Lyon, and which he would have to combat in Algeria. The diagnosis and treatment of mental illness in the colonial situation must begin, not with metapsychology, but with a situation and the lived experience it induces. Whereas psychoanalysis speaks of fantasy, Fanon consistently speaks of trauma and explains mental illness as a form of social alienation.

Fanon's most extensive borrowings from psychoanalysis are not from Freud, but from the little-known Swiss analyst Germaine Guex whose *La Névrose d'abandon* appeared in 1950. According to René Henry, who prefaced a new edition in 1973, the book was a commercial success but Guex remains a minor figure and the notion of an 'abandonment neurosis' has not really become a part of psychoanalysis's conceptual discourse.[192] Guex's book describes 'a pre-Oedipal neurosis dominated by the abandonment syndrome' which is rooted in a real or imagined lack of maternal care and affection in very early childhood. That lack of care reflects a family environment that is incapable of preparing the subject for the frustrations of normal life. Guex uses the neologism *abandonnique* to describe a type of neurotic whose life is governed by an anxious fear that he or she will be abandoned:

> The abandonment syndrome is manifested in the various affective reactions that mark the subject's character and behaviour from a very early age, but which are characterized by a particular violence whenever the circumstances of his life reactivate the feeling of frustration and abandonment. Whilst they do vary from one individual to another, its manifestations always have two characteristics in common – anxiety and aggressivity – and are all related to an initial psychological state characterized by the absence of any true sense of the ego or of one's own value. The symptomatology of this form of neurosis is based upon the tripod of the *anxiety* aroused by any abandonment, the *aggressivity* to which it gives rise, and a resultant *non-valorization* of the self.[193]

The *abandonnique* is trapped at a very primitive stage of development in which all instinctive and affective forces are channelled into the need to ensure that he is loved, and therefore safe. The underlying fantasy is one of a fusion with the mother (or a 'maternalized' paternal imago). Guex recommends that the analysis of such patients should focus on the ego and on past and present lived experience because the symptoms are presented at the level of the ego and not the unconscious; the emergence of Oedipal feelings is a sign that a cure is beginning to be effected.[194] In the absence of this ego-reinforcement, the *abandonnique* remains trapped: 'Non-valorized by an anxiety-ridden childhood, and then devalorized by the errors and failures of his chaotic life, the *abandonnique* generally has a vague and incoherent notion of himself, and it is always a false notion. Like any inferiorized being, he oscillates between self-doubt and excessive ambition, and moves from one extreme to the other.'[195] The attraction of Guex is that she offers a theory of neurosis which does not depend upon the existence of the Oedipus complex which, according to Fanon, could not be observed in Martinique.

Fanon finds in René Maran a classic *abandonnique* and his discussion of his novel *Un Homme pareil aux autres* takes him back to the problem of inter-ethnic sexuality, though the focus is now on a black man and not a mulatto woman. It is noticeable that Fanon is much less harshly critical of Maran than of Mayotte Capécia; this is probably because the former's character does not express the vehement negrophobia of Capécia's heroines. Maran was born in Fort-de-France in 1887 to parents of Guyanese extraction who moved to Bordeaux after the volcanic eruption that destroyed Saint-Pierre in 1902.[196] Like his hero Jean Veneuse, Maran attended a 'large, sad lycée in France' from the age of seven.[197] His subsequent career as a colonial administrator in Tchad and French Equatorial Africa is a reminder that Martinique's strangest exports were the citizens of the old colonies who ruled the subjects of the new. Maran began to write and publish poetry at a very early age, and in 1921 he became the first non-white writer to win the prestigious Prix Goncourt[198] with his novel *Batoula*. It was the preface, with its harsh criticisms of French colonialism, rather than the novel itself that caused the scandal, and Maran continues in the same vein in the later novel discussed by Fanon: 'A colonial official . . . It could have been such a beautiful, generous and noble job! Alas! Colonization is a harsh and cruel goddess who does not just talk hot air and who feeds on blood. She is too practical to be sensitive, and nothing distracts her from her projects. Colonization is based upon injustice and arbitrary rule . . . Might is stronger than right, murder is celebrated and honoured. That is what colonization is; that is what civilization is.'[199]

Perhaps surprisingly, Fanon is less interested in Maran's denunciations of colonialism than in his *abandonnique* symptoms, but he is right to surmise that *Un Homme pareil aux autres* is autobiographical and that Maran shared Jean Veneuse's problem: 'Jean Veneuse is a negro. Of

West Indian origins, he has lived in Bordeaux for a long time; therefore he is a European. But he is black; therefore he is a negro. That is his drama. He does not understand his race, and the Whites do not understand him.'[200] Veneuse's departure for the African colonies is a flight from disappointment and frustration; racial prejudice and the social conventions of Bordeaux, as conservative a city as Lyon, have prevented him from marrying the white woman he loves. And it is in the colonies that he finally learns what he is for others: 'I now know that neither education nor learning can prevail against race prejudices. I know that most of my superiors have always insisted on seeing me simply as a negro, a "dirty nigger" who has to be kept out of the way, a "dirty nigger" who is not worthy of the slightest promotion or, despite his conduct or perhaps because of it, of the slightest consideration.'[201] He also learns what he is for himself: 'All I know is this: the negro is a man like any other [*un homme pareil aux autres*], and that his heart, which seems simple only to the ignorant, is as complicated as that of the most complicated of Europeans.'[202]

Given that the abandonment neurosis is said by Guex to be pre-Oedipal, it allows Fanon to construct a scenario in which it is the relationship with France and white French people, and not the actual parent–child relationship, that is crucial. It is because of Jean Veneuse's feeling of betrayal that Fanon describes him as an *abandonnique*: 'I'm beginning to wonder *if I haven't been betrayed by everything around me*, as the white people do not recognize me as one of their own, and with the black people virtually rejecting me. That is the precise situation I am in.'[203] So quick is Fanon to see Veneuse as an *abandonnique* that he in fact confuses the story with the analysis, and attributes quotations from Maran's novel to Guex's treatise on the abandonment neurosis. Whether or not that textual confusion is indicative of anything more than carelessness on Fanon's part is a matter for pure speculation, but it is difficult to avoid the conclusion that he does identify to some degree with Maran's character. The wartime experiences of the Fanon whom both Jeanson and Glissant described as *un écorché vif* left him feeling that he had been deceived and convinced that he had been wrong. Fighting with the Free French forces was no more 'beautiful, noble and generous' than being a despised member of the colonial administration. The wound inflicted during the war was still festering.

There was no sequel to *Peau noire, masques blancs*. Fanon's later frame of reference moves away from negritude and even psychoanalysis (even though he attempted to use psychoanalytic methods with his patients in Algeria, Freudian theory was no longer a major point of reference), but not from Sartre. There are no further references to Guex or Mannoni. In a sense, the whole project and indeed the achievement of Fanon's first book are summarized by two sentences in, respectively, the introduction and the conclusion: 'I do not come armed with decisive truths . . . My final prayer: Oh, my body, always make me a man who asks questions.'[204]

# 6

# In Algeria's Capital of Madness

JUST OVER A year after his return from Martinique and the publication of his first book, Fanon sat the *médicat des hôpitaux psychiatriques* on 2 June 1953. This was the competitive examination that qualified successful candidates to hold the position of *médecin-chef* and to use the prestigious title *médecin des hôpitaux psychiatriques* – an important piece of cultural capital for the many doctors who moved into the private sector after working for some years in public hospitals. The examination was not particularly demanding and consisted of four papers, one each on hospital administration, mental pathology, internal pathology or clinical hygiene, and anatomy and physiology. In June 1953, the topics were 'calculation of the daily cost of treatment', 'obsessional neuroses', 'abcessses of the lung' and 'the occipital lobe'. Fanon had no difficulty with them and duly qualified as a psychiatrist. Fifty-four candidates took the written and oral examinations and twenty-three of them passed; Fanon was ranked thirteenth.[1]

He now had reasonable, if not brilliant, career prospects in both medical and literary terms. It is, however, an exaggeration to say that the publication of *Peau noire, masques blancs* had marked 'his entry into the Parisian intelligentsia'.[2] The book had attracted little attention and Fanon had not spent enough time in Paris to exploit the few contacts it might have made him. He had made no attempt to establish a lasting relationship with either the influential Jeanson or with *Esprit*. Pursuing a career in psychiatry was more important to him than breaking into Parisian intellectual life. He was ambitious and was making good progress. In the same month that he qualified, three papers co-authored with Tosquelles and two written in collaboration with colleagues from Saint-Alban were presented to the Pau Congress of France's most important college of psychiatrists, and such papers were significant milestones in a medical career.[3]

Two of the papers dealt with indications for the Blini method of convulsive therapy and describe cases in which it was used. Their interest is primarily technical, but the third gives a more concrete account of the methods used by Tosquelles and Fanon. It was not a complete case history on the lines of 'illness–treatment–recovery', as the patient was still in hospital at the time of writing. It concerned a woman who, at the age of twenty-eight, had been committed to the Vinatier clinic in Lyon after being found in a confused state in the city's Perrache railway station in the summer of 1942. She had seen both her parents die in a bombing raid, but laughed when she mentioned their death. The original diagnostic statement read 'Melancholic state, suicidal thoughts and suicide attempts. Long-term epilepsy. To be kept in hospital.'[4] Eight years later, she was still in the Vinatier and was diagnosed as suffering from epilepsy, serious behavioural problems, outbursts of rage and periods of depression, suicide attempts and dangerous reactions. She could, in the opinion of Dr Christy, be transferred to a closed institution but she was probably beyond psychotherapy. At the insistence of Fanon's colleague Maurice Despinoy, she was transferred to Saint-Alban, where it was hoped that social therapy would have a beneficial effect. After numerous suicide attempts, the patient had spent years in a straitjacket. In Saint-Alban's admissions ward, she initially refused to eat or to take the drugs she had been prescribed; the staff did not intervene. The woman was disoriented and subject to unpredictable mood swings, but did begin to respond to drug therapy and to the friendly atmosphere of a ward with only sixteen patients. Even so, she was disruptive, making a noise at night and occasionally breaking windows. She cut her wrists and went on hunger strike. No attempt was made to restrain her, but her behaviour was discussed in the occupational therapy sessions and she was encouraged to write for the ward newspaper. Within three weeks, she could be trusted with scissors for sewing. Two months later, her fellow patients elected her to be their ward representative and she was moving freely around the hospital. Yet her appearance on the ward had had a seriously disruptive effect: relations between patients and nurses, patients and patients and even nurses and nurses had all deteriorated. The level of tension was very high. The patient herself alternated between sulking and outbursts of aggression. After being moved to an open ward, she was given convulsive therapy on twenty-five occasions. She was taken off the anti-convulsants and sedatives she had been taking and began to sleep properly for the first time in years. Rorschach tests suggested that her behavioural problems were related to her epilepsy. The patient's behaviour was improving and her anxiety level had fallen, but she could still be difficult and disruptive.

This short and incomplete account is not exactly a success story, but it gives some indications of how Saint-Alban worked. Drug therapy and shock treatment were obviously important, but so were the effects of occupational therapy, participation in group discussions and involvement in the collective life of the institution. Allowing patients a degree of freedom within the hospital also had a beneficial effect. It is almost as though, rather than being cared for by individual doctors and nurses, the woman was being treated by an environment that functioned as a whole or a Gestalt and had a collective life of its own. It is also clear from Tosquelles and Fanon's account that institutional psychotherapy was risky: this patient was allowed to disrupt and even endanger an entire ward before her condition began to improve. Saint-Alban was a pioneering institution, but it had no easy solutions to offer.

Fanon had gained valuable clinical experience at Saint-Alban and he was in contact with the most progressive elements in French psychiatry, but in terms of the medical establishment they were also marginal elements. His personal life was now more settled. The brief relationship with Michelle B. long over, he was happily married to Josie. Her academic career was also progressing well. On the day that Fanon sat his paper in social psychology, she successfully took her examination in Latin philology at the University of Lyon.[5] Fanon's immediate problem was that he had yet to find a clinical post, and he was aware that his ranking in the *médicat* meant that obtaining one might not be altogether easy. Psychiatry was still an underdeveloped specialism and there was not an infinite number of career openings. Not all the successful candidates who had taken the *médicat* were in search of hospital positions, but eight of those who were had been ranked higher than Fanon and had the right of first refusal on available positions. The reputation he had gained in Saint-Ylié did little to improve his chances, and nor did the minor scandal he had caused in Lyon by attempting to submit *Peau noire, masques blancs* as a dissertation. In the small and tightly structured psychiatric community, reputations and patronage were all-important, and Fanon's track record to date had done little to enhance his reputation or to win him patronage from the establishment. His publication record was promising, but Fanon was clearly not an easy person to have on a hospital's staff.

In the centralized French system, applications for clinical posts were handled not by individual hospitals but by the Ministry of Health in the rue de Tilsit in Paris. A list of vacant positions was regularly published in the *Journal officiel* or government gazette. It was from its pages that Fanon learned that posts were available in Aurillac, Aix-en-Provence, Auch and Rennes, but the idea of working in those provincial towns did not appeal to him. There was also a post in the Algerian town of Blida, but Fanon expressed no special interest in going to Algeria in the letter he wrote to a colleague from Saint-Alban shortly after taking the *médicat*. He had applied, he said, for a position in Guadeloupe (which would not become vacant until December), adding without further explanation that 'Martinique was out of the question'. Even though he had already established a track record with the papers presented at Pau, he complained that he was falling behind with his work.[6] Although Fanon does not expand on why Martinique was 'out of the question', his disgust with the doctors he had encountered when working in Le Vauclin had obviously been enough to convince him that the Département d'Outre-Mer was no place for a young doctor with his humanist convictions.

His sister Gabrielle had fared no better in Martinique. After qualifying as a pharmacist and marrying a dentist called Marcel Richer, she had opened a pharmacy in Le Lorrain, a pleasant town on the North Atlantic coast, forty-seven kilometres from Fort-de-France. Her arrival threatened to upset the comfortable arrangement that existed between the local doctor and the established pharmacist; in a small town the relationship between doctor and pharmacist was a delicate one, but also a potentially profitable one. A pharmacist who did not charge fees for an informal consultation was often the first port of call for anyone seeking medical advice, and could thus influence their decision to go to a doctor and pay fees for an official visit. A doctor's prescribing habits could, conversely, have a direct influence on a pharmacist's income by determining which drugs the patient bought. Having indignantly refused a bribe to go elsewhere, Gabrielle was told in brutal terms by the doctor that she should not count on him for help. Very few of his patients were referred to her and as the few that did come had prescriptions for only the cheapest drugs, she did not find it easy to make a living.[7]

The final decision was taken as suddenly as those that had taken Fanon to Dominica in 1943 and to Lyon in 1946. In an undated letter, he unexpectedly told his brother Joby: 'I'm going to Algeria. You understand: the French have enough psychiatrists to take care of their madmen. I'd rather go to a country where they need me.'[8] Philippe Lucas, a sociologist who knew Fanon in Algeria, reports a conversation with Josie Fanon in which she told him that whilst Fanon settled on Blida after a process of elimination, or in other words because no other post appealed to him, he also had an 'obvious' preference for working in the colonies rather than in the metropolis.[9] Once taken, the decision was, as always, irrevocable.

Fanon had little knowledge of Algeria but he had worked with North African patients in Lyon and he remembered the starving children he had seen in Oran when he was in the army. He may not have been particularly well informed about the country, but he had a very definite idea of what had to be done in Algeria. His contacts with the North African population of Lyon had taught him that: 'There are houses to be built, towns to be made to rise from the earth, men, women and children to be wreathed in smiles.' He added that there are 'tears to be dried throughout the whole French territory (the metropolis and the French union)'.[10] There is no hint that Fanon believed in 1953 that Algeria should be an independent nation. Although he had every sympathy with the people of Algeria, he had no real vision of their future. At this point, his politics consisted of the 'humanist solidarity' that informs *Peau noire, masques blancs* and he was not a member of any political organization or party. Still less did he have any direct contact with or knowledge of the complex world of Algerian nationalism. And he certainly had no idea that he was soon going to be working in a war zone. Ironically, his decision to apply for the post in Blida put him in the traditional position of the black citizen from an 'old colony' with a civilizing mission to perform amongst the North African or black African subjects of a 'new colony'.

Fanon did not go to Algeria armed with any decisive truths or revolutionary doctrines. He did not go there as the apocalyptic prophet of the Third Worldism of *Les Damnés de la terre*. Nothing in his early work anticipates the theses on the cleansing and liberating effects of revolutionary violence with which he would become so closely associated. The Fanon of *Les Damnés de la terre* was a product of Algeria and its war of independence. He was not a clairvoyant. In mid-1953, there were few grounds for Fanon or anyone else to suspect that November 1954 would bring the beginning of France's most brutal war of decolonization, and still fewer grounds for knowing that, according to some Algerians, it had already begun. For the moment, Algeria was 'quiet'. There were reasons for the quiet in Algeria. One of them is still inscribed on the rock walls of a mountain gorge near the village of Kherrata in the Constantinois *département*: '*Légion étrangère: 1945*'.[11] This is the only monument to the untold number of Algerians who were killed in those mountains during a dress rehearsal for what was to come in Madagascar in 1947 and throughout Algeria from 1954 onwards. An Algerian novelist describes the significance of May 1945 thus: '8 May means two different things. In France, it means the jubilation of the Liberation. In Algeria, it means the horror of repression. Between 25,000 and 40,000 victims in three days, in three small towns in the east of Algeria. With the charming and exotic names of Sétif, Guelma, Kherrata. Just one example. That was the day the Algerian war began. Not in 1954.'[12] In May 1945, Fanon and his comrades in 5BMA were half-heartedly celebrating victory in Europe and fretting over their delayed repatriation to Martinique. Many of the Algerian soldiers who had served in the same colonial divisions were just as anxious to return home, but when they did so they found that their families and villages had been decimated in the first days of a new war.

The prelude came on 1 May, when Algeria celebrated Labour Day.

For the first time, Algerian trade unionists and youth organizations did not march alongside their European counterparts. Placards calling for independence were carried, and homemade Algerian flags were unfurled in a number of towns. In Algiers, two died in scuffles with the police. In Sétif, a market town on a treeless plain some 130 kilometres to the west of Constantine, 5,000 took part in a march that ended without incident, even though banners reading 'Long live free Algeria' were openly carried. The demonstrations had been organized by Ferhat Abbas's Amis du Manifeste et de la Liberté, which was a broad coalition supporting the demands of the 1943 Manifesto rather than a true political party, and the proscribed Parti Populaire Algérien. There were also some ominous signs of future divisions. In a joint leaflet dated 3 May, the Parti Communiste Français and the Parti Communiste Algérien denounced the organizers of the demonstrations as 'Hitlerite provocateurs', arguing that the slogan of 'independence for Algeria' was merely a way of sowing 'hatred among Algerians'.[13] By this, they meant between 'European Algerians' and 'the natives'.

On 8 May, Algeria celebrated Victory in Europe and another demonstration took place in Sétif. It was Tuesday – market day – and the town was crowded. British, French, American and Russian flags were carried by the demonstrators, who marched behind a delegation of 200 uniformed scouts. An Algerian flag and pro-independence banners suddenly appeared and when the police ordered their removal, fighting broke out. The police reportedly fired into the air with a machine gun. Axes and knives were produced, and the demonstrators began to attack Europeans at random. Within an hour, the police were firing at will. As the situation deteriorated, the army was brought in and the troops opened fire without waiting for orders. The crowd retaliated with further murderous assaults on any Europeans they could find. Twenty-two Europeans were killed, and forty-eight wounded; there are no figures for Algerian casualties.[14]

Events in the neigbouring town of Guelma followed a similar pattern, and news of what was going on soon reached Kherrata, fifty kilometres away, where the town crier suddenly announced: 'Our brothers have risen against France in Sétif. France has killed a lot of them.'[15] Arms had been distributed to the European population, who took refuge in a fort. By dawn, the little town was besieged by up to

205

10,000 men. Only 110 Europeans died, but the violence inflicted on them was terrible. Dead and dying men were castrated, and women were raped before having their throats cut. Armoured cars were brought in and opened fire with canon and machine guns; turning her big guns inland, the cruiser *Duguay-Trouin* shelled the mountains from the Bay of Bougie. Civilian militias were organized and armed. In normal times, Fanon later remarked, there is always something of the cowboy and the pioneer about the colonist; in times of crisis, 'the cowboy draws his gun and his instruments of torture'.[16] Very little of what happened in Sétif was known in France. Simone de Beauvoir knew only what she had read in *L'Humanité*: fascist provocateurs had opened fire on Muslims taking part in a victory parade, and they had retaliated. The army had restored order and there had been perhaps a hundred deaths.[17] Her ignorance was excusable. No French newspaper had thought it necessary to send a special correspondent to the area.[18]

On the evening of 9 May, a Foreign Legion unit moved into the now deserted village of Kherrata, and then into the mountain gorges. Forty years after the event, a local newspaper published an account of what happened based on the stories of survivors:

> The people were massacred without warning and without pity . . .
> The Kherrata gorges filled up with corpses. People were thrown,
> dead or alive, into deep crevasses . . . Thousands of people were
> killed in this way. The smell of native blood had reawakened colo-
> nialism's bloodthirsty instincts. For several months, Kherrata lived
> in a state of siege, the inhabitants were subjected to all kinds of
> tortures, and villages and the harvests were burned.[19]

Five days later, the rebellion was officially over and, according to the local authorities, the 'rebels' were begging forgiveness but reprisals by European militias continued. Italian prisoners of war were released and encouraged to take part in the 'Arab hunt'. Military operations continued until well into June and the manhunts went on. Accurate statistics are impossible to obtain. The FLN has always maintained that 40,000 Algerians died; official French sources put the death toll at 1,500.[20] In Kabylia and some other areas, those who escaped the repression fled into the hills and began to organize themselves into guerrilla bands.[21] They were joined in the mountains by embittered veterans who had fought in the European compaign. For these men, a new war had begun. There were many 'tears to be dried' in the 'quiet' Algeria of 1953.

On 22 October 1953, the *Journal officiel* announced that 'Monsieur le Docteur Fanon' had been placed at the disposal of the Government-General of Algeria and would be posted to a psychiatric hospital there'.[22] This is a reminder that psychiatrists in Algeria answered not to the Ministry of Health in Paris, but to Gouvernement Général in Algiers, the local Préfecture and the civil authority. At the time of this announcement, Fanon was working as a temporary locum in Pontorson, a small town in the Manche *département* and on the border between Brittany and Normandy. A few miles from the sea and with commanding views across the flat sands and salt marshes of the bay where Mont-Saint-Michel appears to hover in the air, Pontorson would have been a paradise for an ornithologist with a special interest in waders and shore birds; for anyone else, it was a cold and forlorn place to be in the autumn. The hospital itself was an old private religious establishment which, under the terms of the 1838 law, contracted its services to the *département*. It functioned as a closed and self-contained community, with all services being provided by the 600 patients who worked under the orders of a Mother Superior. As was the norm, the clinical staff lived in the hospital.

Fanon arrived in the little town on 21 September. He had not announced his arrival and, having never before seen a black psychiatrist, the bursar at first refused to believe he was who he claimed to be. It took a phone call to the local préfecture to confirm the newcomer's identity. Fanon then displayed a disconcerting lack of etiquette by failing to ask to have his quarters redecorated in accordance with the prerogatives of a new resident. In later years, Fanon took a grim satisfaction in recounting the story – no doubt embellished in the telling – of how he had been appointed to replace a consultant who was suffering from psychotic problems and delusions of persecution, and of how he had been greeted by a colleague who cowered behind a barricade of books and his desk, and who refused to come out from behind his defences to show the newcomer around.[23]

Fanon remained in Pontorson until late September and was not to be fondly remembered. When he was doing research for the *Information psychiatrique*'s special issue on 'Fanon at Fifty', Jacques Postel spoke to staff who had heard sinister tales of a West Indian doctor who used to lock his patients in darkened rooms and leave them there.[24] His informants clearly had little grasp of the history of psychiatry. Fanon was using narcotherapy, which was often indicated for the treatment of anxiety, post-traumatic disorders and sometimes psychoses, as well as drug addiction. From a neurophysiological point of view, the main benefit came from the relaxation of the higher nervous system induced by the use of psychotropic sedatives and the isolation; in psychiatric terms, the induced sleep was beneficial in that, rather like hypnosis, it encouraged dreaming and abreaction, or the cathartic discharge of the emotions attached to a memory of a traumatic event. Publications by Soviet doctors had led to a revival of interest in a therapeutic technique that had almost fallen into disuse after the introduction of insulin or convulsive therapy. Fanon had learned to use narcotherapy at Saint-Alban, and had described its use in a co-authored paper presented at the Pau Congress. In it, he and his colleagues described using an electric metronome and sedatives to trigger a conditioned sleep-reflex that allowed their patients to sleep for up to six hours at a stretch, and demonstrated that it had a good effect in cases of acute psychosis, the main difficulties being the development of the appropriate conditioned reflex, and the prevention of spontaneous awakening.[25]

However, Postel found more than memories of sinister darkened rooms in Pontorson. The archives proved to contain a chit dated '13 October 1953' and signed by Fanon. It authorized twenty-nine patients, accompanied by nurses, to go to the local market to make various purchases. Monsieur Jarriges, who was the director of the hospital, refused to countersign Fanon's chit or to back his decision. His refusal sparked a strike. What happened the next morning is described in the formal note M. Jarriges received from the bursar the next day:

Monsieur le Directeur,

I have the honour of informing you that at about nine o'clock this morning, 14 October 1953, I was told by Madame Superior that no male patient was at work in the general services department, the kitchen or the laundry.

In my attempts to find an explanation for the disturbances caused in the workshops by the absence of the work force, I encountered the doctor in charge of the men's ward [*Monsieur le Médecin-chef du service des hommes*], who told me that the patients 'had gone on strike', but that he had just got them back to work.

The patients were indeed back to work in all the general services by 9.45.[26]

Having instigated or at least supported the strike, Fanon had been forced to back down and to persuade his patients to go back to work. After this unsuccessful attempt at psychiatry 'outside the walls', relations between Fanon and his superiors deteriorated rapidly but the life of the hospital went on as normal. Just how dreary its normal life could be is apparent from the annual report for 1953: 'The rotting crosses have been removed from the hospital cemetery. Eight hundred new crosses have been erected, and 1,200 graves have been tidied up.'[27]

Fanon was not sorry to leave Pontorson but there were also other reasons for his discontent. When his uncle Edouard visited him in the course of a trip to France, Fanon grumbled bitterly about the work he was being forced to do: many of the patients committed to the hospital were suffering from the effects of alcoholism, and he had not become a psychiatrist in order to treat alcoholics. The production of Calvados was a major local industry in the area around Pontorson and its consumption was a popular local pastime, but Fanon's real loathing was directed at the *bouilleurs de cru* or 'home distillers'. These were legally defined as individuals who derived their main income from agriculture, and they had the hereditary right to distil spirits for their own consumption. They were exempt from paying the duty levied on commercial distillers.[28] There was inevitably an illicit trade in this tax-free alcohol, which could be lethally powerful. In Fanon's view, those who made and sold it were poisoners who expected him to cure their victims.[29] Fanon was no teetotaller but his views may have been influenced by what he knew of the ravages of rum in Martinique, where it was quite normal for workers to begin the day with a *décollage* (literally a 'take-off' in the aeronautical sense of the term), consisting of a large measure of neat white rum. For once in his life, Fanon was in agreement with a senior French politician. Prime Minister Pierre Mendès France, who represented a Normandy constituency and was only too aware of the problems posed by the *bouilleurs de cru*, was actively campaigning against the over-consumption of alcohol and had been the object of ridicule when he ostentatiously drank milk in the Assemblée Nationale. The opposition of the *bouilleurs de cru*, who formed a powerful lobby, helped to bring down his government in February 1955.[30]

Fanon's brief stay in Normandy reveals a characteristic and in some ways contradictory pattern. His very obvious commitment to his patients and his frustration with the almost carceral institution in which he worked, together with his headstrong political impulses, led rapidly to conflict with the authorities. He had effectively provoked a strike, and then persuaded the strikers to go back to work. He tried to humanize the hospital and to introduce new techniques, but remained within the parameters of psychiatry and did not challenge the existence of the institution itself. The radical – and soon to become revolutionary – psychiatrist remained in some ways a very conventional one, as can be seen from a reported conversation. Shortly before he went to work in Pontorson, Fanon had one of his very few encounters with the Parisian intelligentsia when he dined with the anthropologists Michel Leiris and Alfred Métraux at Leiris's home on the Quai des Grands Augustins. Precisely how they met is not on record, but Leiris and Fanon had interests in common; Leiris had visited Martinique and the account of his stay there published in *Les Temps modernes* is cited favourably by Fanon in *Peau noire*. Commissioned by UNESCO, Leiris's classic account of contacts between civilizations in Martinique and Guadeloupe confirms in general terms the accuracy of Fanon's description of Martinique.[31]

Discussion over dinner did not, however, focus on Martinique but on the topic of possession – a subject dear to Métraux, whose major work was a study of Haitian voodoo.[32] In his diaries, Métraux describes Fanon, whom he mistakenly believed to be from French Guyana, as 'likeable, polite and slightly semitic-looking'. He also found that he had 'an unfortunate passion for literature', and actively disapproved of the young doctor's belief in the 'magical virtues of electro-shocks'. Fanon had told him that he had shocked one woman patient 'ten times a day' and that her condition improved dramatically within ten days. Discussion then turned to possession as Fanon described the TB patient who seemed to have become possessed by demons once the

administration of antibiotics and streptomycin had stabilized his physical condition. When he fell into a trance, he would accuse himself of
'having brought on the war' and of other crimes. It finally transpired
that, according to Fanon, he was suffering from an internalized sense
of guilt: his three brothers had all died of TB. Fanon argued that possession was always the result of a feeling of guilt.[33] The readiness to use
ECT so extensively and the belief in its virtues were less shocking in
1953 than they would be now. It was still a relatively novel form of
therapy, and its public image had yet to be tarnished by anti-psychiatry
and the association with torture that influenced the way it is described
in popular novels and films such as Ken Kesey's *One Flew over the
Cuckoo's Nest*. Fanon was simply using the techniques and technology
of the day, but remained well within the parameters of conventional
psychiatry. He did not really believe that ECT had 'magical virtues'.
He and Tosquelles had, as good pragmatists, come to the conclusion
that shock therapies were legitimate 'solely because they are effective'.[34]

Ironically, a post did become vacant at Martinique's Colson psychiatric hospital six months after Fanon arrived in Algeria, and Maurice
Despinoy was appointed to it. As Fanon must have known, and ministerial advertisements notwithstanding, the Colson hospital existed in
name only and mental-health provision in Martinique was appallingly
poor. There had once been an asylum in Saint-Pierre but it was
destroyed along with the rest of the town by the volcanic eruption of
1902. As a temporary solution, patients were housed in wretched conditions in a disused wing of Fort-de-France's prison. In the late 1930s,
the establishment still held an average of thirty-eight patients under the
care of a prison doctor whose specialism was ophthalmology and who
had no technical knowledge of psychiatry. They were periodically transferred by cargo-boat to Guadeloupe, where they were treated at the
chronically over-crowded Saint-Claude hospital. Plans had been drawn
up to build a new hospital at Sainte-Marie on the North Atlantic
coast,[35] but psychiatry was not a priority for the Robert regime and, in
1953, a dilapidated prison wing was still the best Martinique could
offer its mentally ill. In that year, the Conseil Général finally voted to
convert a former Navy sanatorium at Colson into a psychiatric hospital.
It was 14 kilometres to the north of Fort-de-France and huddled in a

wooded valley at an altitude of 600 metres. Above it towered the Pitons du Carbet, four conical peaks rising to over 1,000 metres and clad in dense tropical vegetation. Colson itself was below the spectacular Route de la Tracée, once used by Jesuit missionaries travelling to the north. While the buildings were being converted, Despinoy began to build a real psychiatric service, his first achievement being to ensure that patients were no longer treated by prison doctors.[36] Colson was so remote and difficult of access that in the 1980s a young doctor from the metropolis who finally got there to take up his post had the impression that he had reached the end of the world and had entered a nature reserve for the mad.[37]

Having presented his credentials to the authorities in Algiers at the beginning of November, Fanon travelled the fifty kilometres that separated Blida from the capital on a road much better than the one that led to Colson. He found himself, not in a nature reserve, but in Algeria's 'capital of madness'.[38] Throughout Algeria, 'Blida' was synonymous with 'madness', and telling someone that he should be 'in Blida with the madmen' had become a conventional way of ending an argument.[39] The town was just to the south of the Mitidja plain and at the foot of the mountains of the Blidean Atlas, a few kilometres away from the popular resort of Chréa, which was a place for picnics amongst the cedar trees in summer and for skiing in winter.[40] The Mitidja was colonial Algeria's show-piece. It was originally a swampy region that had been drained and then properly irrigated to create extremely fertile farmland producing grain, fruit, tobacco and grapes. Neatly laid out along the main road, the little towns resembled those of southern France with their avenues of cyprus and chestnut trees, their churches and the war memorials and the bandstands where military music was played in the warm evenings. Bougainvillaea grew everywhere.[41] Larger than the towns of the Mitidja itself and effectively a distant suburb of Algiers, Blida was surrounded by groves of lemon trees and was a pleasant place to live. Its European population was particularly proud of the bandstand on the tree-lined Place d'Armes, where French Algerians could enjoy drinking sweet anisette in the cafés and have their shoes polished by little Arab boys in exchange for a few coins. The Arab population, for whom military music did not have the same meaning that it had for the French, did not drink anisette; for them Blida's main attraction was the domed white tomb (*koubba*) that stood in an ancient olive grove outside the town itself.[42] For the Arab population the grove was known as *zenboudj sidi Yakoub* (*zenboudj* means 'wild olives'), and they believed that the *koubba* contained the remains of a marabout or saint known as Sidi Yakoub Ech-Cherif; Europeans knew it as the 'Mount of Olives' or simply the 'sacred wood'. It was something of an attraction for European travellers in search of the exotic. Eugène Fromentin painted it in 1846 and Charles Marville photographed it in 1851.[43]

Within little more than a year of Fanon's arrival in Blida, a new entertainment became available; it was possible to sit in the Place d'Armes and watch the puffs of smoke over the mountains where French warplanes were harassing the guerrilla fighters of the FLN. Like other towns in Algeria, Blida had a dual identity: a well-laid out European town, and a jumble of an Arab town referred to, as were all Arab quarters, as 'nigger town'. In Algiers, the spacious villas on the heights overlooked one of the most spectacular bays in the world; only a short distance away, the labyrinth of the Casbah was one of the most densely populated places on earth, with 100,000 people packed into an area of one square kilometre. Fanon had entered the Manichaean world he describes at the beginning of *Les Damnés de la terre*:

> The town of the *colon* is a gorged, lazy town and its stomach is full of good things on a permanent basis. The town of the *colon* is a town of whites, of foreigners. The town of the colonized, or at least the native town, the nigger village, the medina or the reservation, is an infamous place, populated by infamous men. There, people are born anywhere, and anyhow. They die anyhow, of anything.[44]

Blida was similarly divided. The European part of town resembled those of southern France. In the old Arab quarter all the houses looked the same, with their rough-cast whitewashed walls: 'every home is at the end of a cul de sac where you come to a halt after getting lost in a labyrinth of alleys and silence'.[45] As a liberal *pied noir* put it, 'Between the European town and the native town, there is the interstellar distance of colonialism.'[46]

Until the 1930s, Algeria had no real psychiatric institutions of its own, though some minimal facilities were provided by the Army's medical corps. In 1845, an agreement was reached with asylums in the south of France and patients committed under the terms of the 1838 law were taken there for treatment, usually at the Montperrin asylum in Aix-en-Provence. A former director of that establishment once described with horror how 'men and women, *colons* and natives alike' were transferred there in lamentable conditions that reminded him of how convicts had once been marched to prison in chains. The mortality rate was high, and it was estimated that almost half those transferred died from tuberculosis. Bodies that were not claimed by relatives in Algeria and taken back there for burial were sold to the University of Montpellier's Faculty of Medicine, where they were dissected by apprentice surgeons.[47]

Legislation adopted in 1838 required every French *département* to have a state institution providing care for the mentally ill, or to buy in the services of a private institution like that in Pontorson. This provided the legal basis for a system that was to remain intact for the next 150 years; the 1838 law remained in force until 1990. In 1878, the legislation was in theory extended to the three Algerian *départements* but the absence of specialized hospitals meant that it could not really be implemented. The one specialist unit that did exist was the Pinel Ward in Algiers's Mustapha Hospital, though the fact that it had only twenty beds meant that its efficacy was very limited. In 1873, three years after its opening, it was described by a Dr Voisin as being 'a cellular prison rather than a ward for patients'.[48] When the process of institutional reform began in the 1930s, some 1,400 patients from Algeria were still interned in the South of France.

The reforms of the 1930s were largely the work of Antoine Porot, the prime mover behind the so-called 'Algiers school' of psychiatry, and the descendant of a medico-psychiatric dynasty who had established North Africa's first open psychiatric unit in Tunis in 1912. In 1916, Porot became head of the Nineteenth Military Region's neurological centre in Algiers, and he stubbornly advocated the need to create appropriate institutional structures to treat the mentally ill in Algeria.[49] In 1934, the regulations were altered to allow psychiatrists to be recruited from metropolitan France and reform got under way in the three *départements*. 'Front-line' units were established in Algiers, Oran and Constantine, and they were backed up by second and third-line institutions. The 'front-line' units were triage centres which also treated patients with acute psychoses; second-line units had closed wards, and third-line units consisted of 'annexes' for long-term patients who were deemed to be incurable or beyond redemption.[50] One such patient was the mother of the novelist and playwright Kateb Yacine, who was committed to the Blida annexe after suffering a breakdown when her son was interned in a camp after the Sétif uprising.

The Blida-Joinville hospital was a second-line unit and, although it was not officially opened until 1938, it had begun to admit patients in 1933. With a total official capacity of 700 beds, it was housing 1,500 patients by December 1938. Sixty-five per cent of them were Algerian.[51] They were under the care of four doctors, all Europeans working under Porot, who had struggled hard to get his hospital; an early plan drawn up just after the First World War to build a 700-bed institution had been rejected in 1924, even though Blida's municipal council was willing to make available a seven-hectare site. According to a somewhat rhapsodic report published in 1939, the hospital that was finally built stood on what had once been a desolate plain. The landscape had been transformed by planting flowers, shrubs and trees. The well-designed wards were housed in pavilions laid out to look like a pretty village. The construction of Blida-Joinville was one of the great achievements of French colonialism, and both the colony and its government could be proud of their new hospital.[52]

In the autumn of 1953, Fanon took up his post in a modern and well-equipped hospital that was a great improvement on Pontorson. Accommodation for the young doctor and his wife was provided within the hospital grounds, where they had a pretty house with flowers around the door. It was designed as a family home, and their only son would be born there in 1955. Like most institutions of its kind – Saint-Alban was very much the exception – the hospital was surrounded by a high perimeter wall and looked sinister from the outside. Visitors who went through the supervised gate in fact found themselves in the pleasant environment of a large park with sports facilities and gardens where tree-lined avenues and paths linked the two-storey buildings. In accordance with French custom and, as at the great Sainte-Anne hospital in

Paris, the individual wards were named after important figures from the history of psychiatry: the Clérambault Ward was home to the female patients, and the medical-surgical ward was named after Charcot. Blida-Joinville proved to be a good environment to bring up a child who, from a very early age, learned to be tolerant of the behaviour of his more eccentric neighbours.[53] It was a comfortable home, and Josie Fanon later recalled that they had been happy there, and that Fanon did his best to keep his private and professional lives separate; their son Olivier, whose memories are understandably hazy, dimly recalls the professional demands on his father's time were so great that the family had little private life.[54] Before long, dangerous political commitments would also make encroachments on it. For the moment, though, Blida did provide the family with a high degree of material comfort. As its practitioners liked to grumble, psychiatry was not a particularly well-paid specialism, but with a monthly starting salary of 63,000 francs, Fanon was earning considerable more than the average 'French' Algerian on an annual income of 600,000.[55]

Fanon was one of four *médécins-chefs*. Dr Ramée was a student of Porot's, but Lacaton, Micucci and Dequeber were 'metropolitans' and more sympathetic to Fanon's outlook. The four had four interns or housemen working under them: Sliman Asselah, Georges Counillon (who had already met Fanon in Lyon), Titchine and Jacques Azoulay.[56] Azoulay, who worked closely with Fanon on a number of projects, had not originally wanted to be doctor. He had wanted to study philosophy, but bowed to family pressures and accepted the argument that, in both financial and social terms, medicine was a better prospect than an academic career in philosophy. He settled down reluctantly to his studies in the Algiers Faculty of Medicine, where most of his fellow students talked of nothing but money and women. Psychiatry seemed to provide a possible way of reconciling his family's demands for a career with his own more philosophical leanings. His successful application for a junior post at Blida led to the encounter with Fanon, and with a form of psychiatry that provided an escape from the 'pretentious, ignorant and racist' psychiatrists he had met in Algiers.[57]

In early 1956, the little group was joined by Charles Geronimi. Algerian-born and of Corsican stock, he had first heard Fanon's name in early 1954 while he was working in the neuropsychiatric ward at the

Mustapha hospital in Algiers. A doctor from Blida who visited the ward had told him of a new doctor who was boring everyone stiff with his talk of revolutionary methods and institutional psychotherapy. The new doctor had, he went on, just scraped through the *médicat*, and the fact that he was black did not give him the right to stir things up. Geronimi actually met Fanon very briefly a few months later and was struck by how young he looked. Having learned from third parties about Fanon's political leanings, he asked Azoulay to arrange a meeting. After an afternoon spent discussing psychiatric matters in late February or early March 1956, Fanon invited Azoulay and Geromini to a meal in a restaurant, where he displayed an unexpected taste for good cuisine and fine wines. Geronimi passed what he soon realized was a sort of informal examination, and found a houseman's position in Fanon's ward. He became a close collaborator. Geronimi was also one of the few *pieds noirs* to take the side of the FLN and, eventually, to follow Fanon into exile in Tunisia.[58]

Fanon had first-hand experience of the venality of the medical profession in Martinique, but the situation in Algeria was worse. Medicine was an integral part of an oppressive system; a local doctor could also be the owner of a mill, a vineyard or an orange grove, and behaved accordingly.[59] Travelling around the country in a professional capacity, Fanon once visited Rabelais (now Ain Merane) in the Orléansville (Chleff) region. Here, he met a European doctor who boasted that he could make 30,000 francs – half Fanon's monthly salary – on a market-day. He would show patients three syringes of different sizes, and explained that their respective cost was 500, 1,000 or 1,500 francs. The patients inevitably chose the largest. It, like the others, was filled with saline – a harmless salt-water solution. The annual salaries paid to Algerians in 1954 ranged from 150,000 to a maximum of 200,000 francs.[60] In rural areas, doctors would give their patients injections of distilled water, claiming that it was either penicillin or vitamin B; others placed their patients behind a sheet for an X-ray and left them there for fifteen minutes, well aware that they owned no X-ray equipment. Some regarded their patients as little better than animals, and described themselves as practising veterinary medicine. Some of Fanon's colleagues in Blida also had lucrative private practices, and did not view their work in the hospital as a full-time commitment. For other doctors working in

Algiers, the Blida hospital was no more than a convenient dumping ground for patients whose conditions were such that they could not be effectively – or profitably – treated in the private sector. Fanon accepted that there were decent and humane European doctors working in Algeria, but added 'It is said of them that "They are not like the others".'[61]

Fanon was well aware that working as a psychiatrist in Algeria would never be easy. The endemic corruption was only one aspect of the problem. In the letter of resignation he finally sent to the Resident Minister at the end of 1956, he admitted that he had always known that to attempt to practise psychiatry in French North Africa was to fly in the face of common sense, but he also insisted that, in 1953, he had still been convinced that it was possible to reform a system 'whose doctrinal basis' was a permanent obstacle to the development of 'an authentic human perspective'.[62] Utimately, it was the Algerian war that put an end to Fanon's planned reforms but his first battles were with the 'doctrinal basis' of the Algiers school of psychiatry, whose effects he had first observed in Lyon when he encountered the 'North African syndrome'. In order to understand the battles he fought and those sections of *Les Damnés de la terre* that deal with psychiatry, it is therefore necessary to digress and to look at the history of the Algiers school.

France conquered Algeria with a gun in one hand and quinine in the other. The expeditionary force that landed at Sidi-Ferruch, which is to the east of Algiers, in 1830 included 167 surgeons and doctors. They were to play an important role. There was a high incidence of disease among both the military and the early settlers who followed them into the interior, where strange illnesses were spread by unfamiliar vectors. As towns fell to the French, hospitals staffed by military doctors were established and by 1876, even the most remote tribal areas had resident military physicians.[63] The role of the medical corps was not simply one of prevention and cure; it was also a cognitive role and doctors took 'the initial steps in institutionalizing the view of humanity from a racial standpoint'.[64] The accounts of their epidemiological studies that they sent back to France in the form of *mémoires* made an important contribution to France's understanding of her new colonial subjects. The model for their *mémoires* was supplied by the mass of documentation sent back to France by the scholars and scientists who accompanied

Napoleon's army on the Egyptian expedition of 1793. The doctors played their own role in the creation of what Edward Said terms 'orientalism', or a set of representations that allows the West to dominate the Orient by understanding it.[65] That understanding was inevitably framed by a race 'science' that viewed ethnic groups almost as though they were different biological species, each with a distinct language and genius. Disconcertingly, Algeria proved to be home to two 'races': an Arab majority and a minority of tribes speaking a variety of Berber languages, the most important being the Kabyles who lived in the harsh mountains to the east of Algiers. Although it is not really relevant to Fanon – who would define 'Algerian' in very broad terms that subordinated ethnicity to a nationalism of the will – French colonial discourse did attempt to construct a 'bad Arab/good Kabyle' dichotomy and a crude divide-and-rule policy was at times pursued on that basis.[66] The 'good Kabyle' pole of the opposition impinges on the discourse of the Algiers school to only a minimal degree, and its real focus of attention is 'the Arab'.

From the earliest stages of the conquest of Algeria, theories of heredity were invoked to explain the 'Arab mentality' in terms of supposedly innate racial character traits. Anthropology had its own contribution to make with observations such as: 'The climate is excellent, the soil is admirable and all that is lacking here is civilization. And it really is lacking. These Bedouin are terrible people, and it is difficult to imagine the ferocious pleasure with which they will cut off a head.'[67] The interaction between medical and anthropological discourse means that the work of the Algiers school is characterized by 'a primordial slippage from the study of mental pathology to an ethnic psychology'.[68] The slippage is not simply an expression of racial prejudice, though it is also that; the work of the first doctors and anthropologists, and then the psychiatrists of the Algiers school, involved the actual construction of racial types and groups. It is grounded in a desire to know, but that desire is in fact frustrated by its own stereotyping. As Philippe Lucas and Jean-Claude Vatin put it in the introduction to an important anthology of anthropological writings on Algeria: 'What mattered was not so much the native in himself, but what would be said about him. The Algerian disappeared behind his appearance, behind the image of him that the colonial majority wanted to give of him.'[69]

In 1845, a civilian doctor called Eugène Bodichon published a volume of *Considérations sur l'Algerie*. Patricia Lorcin summarizes his findings in her major study of racial stereotyping in colonial Algeria:

The Arabs were a pure race whose moral and intellectual traits had altered little down the ages. The present-day Arabs, more than any other branch of the Caucasian family having reached the same degree of civilization, were pillagers and thieves. A lack of cross-breeding with other races meant that their love of thieving and raping, traits which had characterized their ancestors, had developed and had been passed down the generations. They were now the dominant passions of their race . . . The Arab propensity to theft was underscored by indolence, cupidity and fanaticism. Bodichon saddled the Arabs with two other 'major' hereditary characteristics: over-excitability and unreliability.[70]

The manner in which anthropology and a crude psychology combine to produce the dominant image of 'the Arab' is illustrated by a 'psychological study of Islam' published in 1908 by an army doctor serving with the locally recruited Third Zouave Regiment. Boigey's study is based upon both an evolutionary schema and a psychological typology. The European race has, that is, constantly evolved within the orbit of civilization, has produced more than any other race, and corresponds to the active type. Muslims correspond to the inactive type, and can only live in exceptionally fertile and hot regions where subsistence requires only minimal manual labour.[71] This is a good example of how theories can override empirical observation. Much of Algeria is not exceptionally fertile, and the cultivation of barley, figs and olives in the mountains of Kabylia is very labour-intensive. And, as many a French conscript huddled on a mountainside at night would discover to his extreme discomfort after 1954, parts of Algeria can be very cold.

The major characteristic of the Muslim personality is, according to Boigey, the stunting of natural instincts whose natural expansion has been halted by 'the work of a brilliant imposter known as Mahomet'.[72] European hostility towards (and ignorance of) Islam is a phenomenon with a long history. Dante, for instance, argues that Mahomet is a Christian schismatic and condemns him, with the other *seminatori di discordia* ('sowers of discord'), to the eighth circle of Hell in Canto XXVIII of the *Inferno*. The great innovation of the forerunners of the Algiers school was the transformation of one of the three great monotheistic religions into a symptom or even a pathogenic agent: 'The dogma of Islam was to spread with the speed of a contagious epidemic. Its progress had less to do with theology than with mental pathology . . . In a sense, the Koranic hordes spread a real epidemic madness, arms in hand.'[73] Boigey goes on to describe the symptomatology of Islam's 'neuropathic state'. Its symptoms include fatalism, an obsession with words (the repeated 'Allah, Allah'), delusional sadness, the perversion of the sexual instinct (masturbation and pederasty), and auditory hallucinations that provoke sudden outbursts of violence. The only cure is the eradication of Islam because 'Islam does not bring with it any justification for its existence, because it is *destructive*. It neither creates nor produces anything, and therefore could not survive at all if it could not live parasitically on human groups that do work.'[74]

Whilst it would be absurd to suggest that every French psychiatrist working in Algeria shared completely the views that are expressed so crudely by Boigey, similar assumptions do inform the thinking of the Algiers school. The paradox is that a tendency within psychiatry that reproduced a reductive racial stereotyping originated in a reformist project: Antoine Porot and his son Maurice are remembered in North Africa as great reformers.[75] In 1912, the Congrès des médecins aliénistes et neurologues de France et des pays de langue française adopted a lengthy report on mental-health provision in the French colonies and contrasted in very unfavourable terms the situation prevailing there with that in the British and Dutch colonies. The report expresses a real sense of shame at France's failures in this domain and, whilst it is easy to dismiss talk of a 'civilizing mission' as hypocritical, many of the doctors – and even military men – who spoke in such terms were sincere. The report concluded that the deplorable situation in Algeria in particular could be remedied only by training a medical corps capable of understanding Arabic and, more important, the 'normal mentality' of the Arab, his customs and mores, as well as his 'pathological mentality'. The colonial doctor had to be a 'civilizing agent', but could carry out his civilizing mission only if he understood those he was civilizing.[76]

The 'understanding' recommended by the report was of course predicated upon the knowledge garnered by the first doctors and anthropologists who worked in Algeria. A further parameter was introduced by the political-legal discourse that defined the status of the colony and its inhabitants. Although they lived in Algeria, the latter were not Algerians – that term originally applied to the Algerian-born French – but merely 'natives', 'Arabs' or 'Muslims' who in later decades mutated into 'French Muslims of North African origin'. This crude classification both created and masked a number of problems, some of which border on the comic, as when Kabyle Berbers who had long ago converted to Christianity were officially referred to as 'Christian Muslims'. For the majority of the anthropologists who studied Algeria, Islam was defined as a culture rather than as a religion, and as the 'dark' side of the West rather than as a monotheism that might be compared with both Judaism and Christianity. What is more, the 'real' North Africa was defined in terms of its Graeco-Roman heritage, whilst Islam was constructed as alien, artificial and incomprehensible.[77] Significantly, a volume of archaeological studies published in 1937 to mark the centenary of the capture of Constantine exhaustively lists the city's Graeco-Roman remains, but not its mosques and Islamic monuments.[78] The 'Latin heritage' became a major theme for the writers of the so-called 'Algerian school'. The *locus classicus* is Louis Bertrand's preface of 1939 to his novel *Le Sang des races*, first published in 1920: 'Behind the modern Mediterranean, I can see the eternal Latin. For me, Latin Africa shows through the *trompe l'oeil* of the modern Islamic decor . . . The Africa of the triumphal arches and the basilicas rises before me: the Africa of Apuleius and St Augustine. That is the real Africa.'[79] The same mythology informs Albert Camus's lyrical descriptions of the Roman ruins at Tipasa.[80]

The attempt to understand the Arab mentality was based upon a theory that defined Islamic culture as unreal and virtually unknowable. The Algerian population reacted to this religious-cultural stereotyping with stereotypes of its own, referring to the French as 'Christians' and *Roumi*, a word derived from *Roumain* ('Roman'), and not used with friendly intent. Geographical terminology testifies to the mutual incomprehension inherent in the attempt to understand Algeria. For France, Algeria, Tunisia and Morocco were part of an 'Orient' that also included the Holy Land. North African restaurants in France served 'Oriental' cuisine. In Arabic, the three countries are collectively known as the Maghreb, meaning the lands to the west of the Nile.

Writing in 1918, Antoine Porot speaks of the Muslim native's remarkable propensity for the passive life, his habitual insouciance about the future, and his childlike credulity and stubbornness (adding that the well-known tendency of *European* children to ask endless questions reveals an embryonic scientific mind; Arabs, it would seem, are not even real children).[81] Establishing even a rudimentary psychology of the Muslim native was, admits Porot, very difficult because 'there is so much mobility, and so many contradictions in a mentality that has developed on such a different level to our own, and which is governed both by the most rudimentary instincts and a sort of religious and fatalistic metaphysics'.[82]

Porot and his colleague Arrii paint a similar picture in their clinical study of forty cases of 'criminal impulsiveness' amongst native Algerians, a study dismissed in very harsh terms by Fanon in *Les Damnés de la terre*.[83] The forensic role of the doctors involved in these cases, most of which involved murder, was to establish the degree of criminal responsibility. Under the terms of the law of 1838, no crime or misdemeanour had been committed if it could be demonstrated that the accused had acted in a state of diminished responsibility because of his mental condition; offenders suffering from diminished responsibility were committed to psychiatric hospitals. Porot and Arrii describe the native Algerian in terms that are familiar from the earlier literature. The Algerian is credulous and suggestible (witness the prevailing belief in djinns, the spirits of air and fire described both by the Koran and Arabic literature; the genie in Aladdin's lamp was originally a djinn in the *Arabian Nights*),[84] prone to outbursts of homicidal rage, fanatical, possessively jealous and fatalistic. As usual, Islam has a pathogenic role in the clinical picture. Islam induces credulity and superstition, but it can also encourage a religious fanaticism and a xenophobia that can lead to murder.

To illustrate the point, the authors remark with the cynical wisdom of old colonial hands: 'The oldest among us have not forgotten the bloody events that took place in Marguerrite some thirty years ago.'[85] The Marguerrite rebellion began in April 1901, when a group of a hundred men attacked and killed a forest ranger and a French-appointed *caïd* (a local government appointee, and not to be confused with a *cadi* or Muslim judge). They then seized the settlement of Marguerrite (now Ain Torki), where they killed five people who refused to recite the *shahada* or Muslim profession of faith. The rebellion was quickly suppressed, but it shook the colony's confidence. This was not, however, a spontaneous outburst of Islamic fanaticism. Over a period of thirty years, land acquisition by settlers and the forestry service had reduced the arable acreage available to the local population and had virtually blocked all access to the scrub areas where their animals traditionally grazed.: 'By the turn of the century, this particular native group was living off 1.2 hectares per capita compared to 5.6 hectares per capita thirty-two years previously. They were farming only 2,343 hectares; their herd of cattle had shrunk from 2,000 in 1896 to 1,122, and their flock of sheep from 10,943 to 1,537.'[86] What Porot and Arrii describe as an instance of innate Arab fanaticism might more properly be described as a classic case of primitive rebellion. Islam had, of course, long been seen as the occult force behind all resistance to colonialism; a government document published in 1844 argued that the Koran would be 'the epicentre for the potential administrative difficulties of the French'.[87] Over one hundred years later, an official booklet on 'understanding Algeria', produced by the Army's Psychological Service for the benefit of officers, put forward the same argument in almost identical terms and argued that Islam was a 'determinant psychological factor':

One might find it surprising that the occupation of Algeria was not followed by a psychological conquest, and some regard the fact that the Muslim masses remain impermeable to our civilization and our customs as an argument against our methods. We should not, however, forget the enormous economic and social backwardness of a human mass that is constantly increasing, or that the diffusion of ideas is slow and often has little lasting effect; despite the efforts that have been made by our teachers, primary schools can have a liberalizing effect only if their influence is not resisted by sectarianism and fanaticism in the home. The West's complex and abstract notions, and its spirit of tolerance are opposed by the simple and concrete imperatives of Islam.[88]

The obvious methodological flaw in Porot and Arrii's study is its extrapolation of the findings of a study of a criminal sample to the population at large. No comparisons are made with a control group, and as a result the entire Algerian population is psychopathologized. The lack of social relativism is startling. Belief in djinns is seen as the effect of a pathological credulity, yet the belief in witches that prevailed in many areas of rural France is not mentioned. Vendettas in Kabylia had psychopathological causes; it would have been a brave psychiatrist who argued that this was also the case with Corsican vendettas. As Lorcin puts it, the prevailing wisdom was that 'A European who stole committed a calculated act which contradicted an innate instinct of honesty; an Arab who stole indulged an innate instinct.'[89]

The discourse of the Algiers school takes on its final and complete form when it incorporates the anthropological notion of a primitive or pre-logical mentality, as described by Lucien Lévy-Bruhl.[90] Working with a primitive-civilized dichotomy, Lévy-Bruhl posits the existence of a primitive mentality which is mystical in that it is based on a belief in supernatural forces, and pre-logical in that it takes no account of the logical principle of identity. It is concrete, does not foster abstraction or generalization, makes individuals more sensitive to qualitative rather than quantitative relations, and promotes an identification with the collective. In fairness, it should be added that Lévy-Bruhl revises his views in his posthumously published *Cahiers* and argues that what he once saw as a 'primitive mentality' is no more than a more pronounced form of a mystical mentality that exists, in varying degrees, in all human beings.[91] There is a close fit between the primitive mentality described by Lévy-Bruhl and the 'Algerian personality' constructed by the Algiers school. In 1939, Porot and his junior colleague Sutter establish a direct correlation between the two. The North African is not, they admit, a true primitive; to discover true primitivism, the psychoanthropologist would have to look to black sub-Saharan Africa. They do, however, demonstrate to their own satisfaction that North African psychiatry will provide important clinical material for the study of primitivism because 'the Algerian, Tunisian or Moroccan native represents an intermediary type, midway between the primitive and the evolved Westerner; the native cannot be judged on the same scale as the two extremes'.[92]

The most surprising thing about the Algiers school of psychiatry is not that it existed, but that its theses were reiterated for so long. In 1961, it was still possible for one of their successors to congratulate Porot and Sutter on their description of a 'mental syndrome' in which a magical and mystical notion of causality was associated with a subjective notion of time, a lack of precision and abstraction, and an empirical notion of ethics.[93] The third edition of Antoine Porot's dictionary of psychiatry, published by France's leading academic publishing house in 1975, still contained entries by Henri Aubin on 'North African Natives (psychopathology of)', 'Blacks (psychopathology of)' and 'Primitivism'.[94] The former begins: 'The primitive mentality must be evoked here, particularly as we are speaking of a less highly evolved ethnic group . . .' It need scarcely be added that the same dictionary contains no entry on 'White Europeans (psychopathology of)'. No one attempted to explain the massacres at Sétif and Kherrata in terms of the innate psychological traits of white settlers.

The work of the Algiers school supplied the 'doctrinal basis' for the practice of psychiatry in Blida and the other hospitals of the colony. The attitude of doctors and nurses alike was, as Fanon puts it, based on a priori attitudes. As in Lyon, an Algerian who entered the hospital did so bearing what Fanon called 'the dead weight of all his compatriots' and was quite spontaneously inserted into a pre-existing framework constructed by Europeans.[95] Although Fanon refers to the work of the Algiers school in his article on the North African Syndrome, and returns to it in even harsher terms in sections of *Les Damnés de la terre,* the clinical papers based on his experience in Blida are not polemics against Porot and his colleagues. He could, no doubt, have published such polemics in *Esprit* or *Les Temps modernes,* but they would not have been accepted by professional journals. Porot, now professor of psychology at the University of Algiers, was a powerful figure and the collective psychiatric *esprit de corps* was a force to be reckoned with. The papers Fanon did publish consist largely of descriptions of his work at Blida and of the reforms he attempted to institute there. Polemic would have done little to improve things. The slow process of imaginative reform could and did so.

Interviewed by an Algerian journalist in 1987, a surviving witness who once worked in Blida as a ward orderly recalled that, before Fanon's arrival, doctors would make ward rounds at set times but were more interested in checking that the beds had been properly made than in actually treating their patients, who were left largely to their own devices. Post-admission follow-ups were a matter of surveillance rather than therapy. Fanon, in contrast, would visit the wards at any hour of the day or night to ensure that the nursing staff had carried out his instructions.[96] He began work early and was always on the ward before his interns. He was an impressive and even intimidating figure: 'immaculate shirts with cuff links chosen in the best shops in Algiers, carefully knotted ties which he made an effort to change morning and afternoon, big monogrammed handkerchiefs which he used to wipe his face . . . He wore made-to-measure white coats with broad lapels and no buttons, and fastened them with a belt.'[97]

Fanon's reforming role has become the stuff of legend, but not all the stories that are told are necessarily true. It has often been claimed that Fanon literally unchained his patients. Irene Gendzier, for one, describes how Fanon 'walked through the hospital wards unchaining men and women',[98] but some of those who, like Jacques Azoulay, worked with him deny that anyone was ever held in chains in Blida. Fanon himself does not speak of unchaining patients. The major tranquillizers used today had yet to be developed, and straitjackets and other physical restraints were certainly used, as they were in other psychiatric institutions like the Vinatier in Lyon, but in their accounts of their attempts to elaborate a transcultural psychiatry adapted to Algerian conditions, the doctors of the Algiers school speak of chained or shackled patients as part of the shameful past they had eradicated. As Françoise Vergès argues, the literal veracity of the stories about chains and shackles is probably less important than its symbolic content.[99] In such representations, Fanon's reforms appear to have been overlaid by the classic image of psychiatric radicalism: the picture that hangs in Sainte-Anne of Philippe Pinel releasing patients from chains in Paris's Bicêtre hospital in 1793.[100]

The wards at Blida-Joinville were segregated along ethnic lines, and Fanon had almost 200 patients under his care: 165 European women and 22 male Muslim patients. Some were self-referred but the majority had been committed to the institution by either their families or the authorities. Fanon also had a number of private patients.[101] In his optimistic view, the numbers were small enough to allow him to introduce

the methods he had learned at Saint-Alban. He initiated the first experiment in social therapy or institutional psychotherapy to have been
attempted in North Africa, and it was watched with a mixture of hostility and amusement by a staff accustomed to thinking in terms of the
'Algiers school' paradigm. No attempt was made to stop Fanon. As a
*médecin-chef*, he enjoyed a considerable degree of autonomy and he
answered to the Government General and not to a professor of psychology at the University of Algiers. High-ranking civil servants in
Algiers had little interest in what went on behind the walls of a hospital in Blida. That would change after November 1954 and what went
on then would become of great interest to the police and the army, but
for the moment Fanon was left in peace. Groups of students studying
under Porot in Algiers were free to visit Fanon's wards, but his case load
meant that they did not always get the friendly reception they might
have hoped for: Josie Fanon was much more welcoming and outgoing
than her husband.[102]

Fanon and his junior colleague Azoulay described the results of the
experiment in a long article published in the most liberal of France's
psychiatric journals, and they were decidedly mixed.[103] The experiment
began on the ward for European women patients. As at Saint-Alban,
meetings were organized twice a week to discuss the affairs of the therapeutic community in the making, and plans were drawn up for the
production of a weekly newspaper. Within a month, the meetings had
become an integral part of hospital life. They were attended by both
doctors and patients, and the nursing staff were also invited and encouraged to take part in the discussions of day-to-day life on the ward. The
meetings were social events in the most banal sense but they were also
an element in an organized social architecture designed to involve previously isolated patients in a collective enterprise. The first major event
to be organized was the celebration of Christmas 1953. A tree was
brought into the ward, and communal carol singing took place around
the carefully decorated nativity crib. Two days after Christmas, a ward
meeting discussed the proposal that parties should be held twice a
month. It was accepted with enthusiasm. After some initial teething
problems – it proved very difficult to involve senile and catatonic
patients in the most basic social activities – the parties were a success.
The patients themselves took responsibility for issuing invitations and

organizing the musical entertainment, with some help from one or two nurses. Fanon was soon able to attend as a guest-spectator, leaving the organizational details to his patients. In the account he co-authored with Azoulay, he gives the reader a rare glimpse of his sense of humour as he describes the growing sense of responsibility and autonomy of the paranoiac who organized a musical evening called 'Sombreros and Mantillas': her catatonic friend tended, not surprisingly, to lose the thread of what was going on, but the paranoiac kept a careful eye on her, pinching her when her attention wandered.

The social fabric of the ward was reinforced by the establishment of committees to organize film shows and musical events, and efforts were made to ensure that they did not degenerate into passive entertainments. A special column was included in the newspaper to make the discussion of the films an ongoing activity. Patients were encouraged not simply to consume the films passively but were expected to participate in active discussions of what they had seen. The more general function of the newspaper was to explain policy decisions, and to impress upon patients and staff alike that the hospital had a collective life, and that they and no one else were responsible for nurturing it. The earliest contributions from patients consisted of little more than comments such as 'I would like to thank the Doctor for the good treatment he is giving me' or 'I would like to go home', but the newspaper soon began to publish longer letters about the films they had seen and the excursions that they had enjoyed outside the hospital.

Great importance was placed upon occupational therapy, and knitting, embroidery and dress-making were strongly encouraged. For women who had worn nothing but drab hospital gowns for five or six years, owning a bright flowered dress was an attractive prospect. Even trying on a semi-finished dress for a fitting could have a therapeutic effect. When concentrating on standing still and putting herself in the hands of a dress-maker, a patient could not, according to Azoulay and Fanon, retreat into madness and had to take note of her social environment while collaborating with someone else. Occupational therapy was used by Fanon in combination with drugs, psychotherapy and ECT. As the collective life of the ward become richer and more fulfilling, the rate of discharges began to rise. The therapeutic community was succeeding.

Fanon is also reported as having experimented with psychoanalytic techniques at Blida. Psychoanalysis is notoriously difficult to practise in an institutional context. Psychiatric wards are noisy places that offer little privacy, and it is therefore hard even to commence a 'talking cure' based upon one-to-one contact. Even if that contact can be established, the patient in analysis may become the object of others' envy whilst a transference relationship between the analyst and a single patient can have detrimental effects on the rest. And it was Fanon's failure – a failure stemming from both institutional conditions and his own lack of experience – to establish transference that ended this experiment. Apparently, the staff reading group that studied Freud's five case histories was more successful, but Fanon never speaks of it in his published accounts of his work at Blida.[104]

As Fanon suspected from the outset, the techniques he had learned in Saint-Alban would be more difficult to apply to male Algerian patients than to European women. Not the least of his difficulties was that he spoke neither Arabic nor any of the Berber languages spoken in Algeria, and therefore had to work through interpreters. Although the Algiers school took its inspiration from a report that stressed the need to understand Arabic, very few of its members actually spoke the language, and there was no official interpreting service. In 1956, Fanon did begin to study Arabic by taking daily fifteen-minute lessons from a local musician,[105] but he still had to rely on whoever was at hand to translate for him. The interpreter was at best a nurse or orderly; at worst, another patient had to be pressed into service.

Undeterred, Fanon went ahead. An initial meeting was organized with great care. A large table was set up in the refectory, draped with a cloth and decorated with a vase of flowers. For over an hour, Fanon, Azoulay and some of the nurses tried to explain what they hoped to do. They had difficulty in obtaining silence: one patient continued a hallucinatory dialogue with an invisible partner, and two others pursued a noisy personal quarrel. The only person willing to pay attention was a paranoiac suffering from delusions of persecution, and one of the very few to speak French with any fluency. Far from trying to involve his fellows in a group discussion, he was, however, intent upon distancing himself from them. The meeting had to be abandoned. Over the next weeks, shorter meetings were held with no greater success. It soon became apparent that they were futile, and one of institutional psychotherapy's main tools had to be laid aside. Attempts to persuade groups of ten patients to play hide-and-seek or other games also ended in frustration and failure. They complained that they were too tired to play games, though some were eventually persuaded to play cards and dominoes. By February, it was increasingly apparent that methods that had worked with European women would not work with Algerian men. The disillusioned nursing staff were increasingly reluctant to go on with what looked like a failed experiment.

Occupational therapy for Algerian men also proved to be a failure. The hospital had a workshop producing woven straw mats, baskets and hats but it was difficult to get the men to work seriously. Once they had produced enough to buy a cake or a few cigarettes, they stopped work, complaining of stomach pains and aching legs. Sporadic outbreaks of violence on the ward itself meant that it could scarcely be used for occupational therapy. Fanon's attempts to change the punitive culture of the hospital were frustrated by the hostility of his staff. If a patient became involved in a scuffle, the nurses would ask: 'Should we restrain him or let him get on with it?' When Fanon turned to his hierarchical superiors for advice, he received the predictable reply: 'You've not been in Algeria for long. You don't understand them. When you've been here for fifteen years like me, you will understand.'[106] It would have been pointless for Fanon to have embarked on theoretical arguments about the North African syndrome. In a sense, the old colonial hands were quite right. Fanon was forced to admit in print that he had failed because he had, for once, lost sight of the real: 'We were attempting to create certain institutions, but we forgot that any attempt to do so has to be preceded by a tenacious, concrete and real investigation into the organic bases of the native society.'[107] He had spontaneously endorsed the ideology of assimilation by expecting his patients to make the effort to adapt to a Western culture. He now realized that he had to make the transition to cultural relativism rather than assuming the superiority of French culture.

A group of Algerian women patients gave Fanon an insight in what had to be done. For some months, they had been attending the musical evenings in the women's ward and had politely applauded in the European manner. One day, a group of local musicians visited the hospital. To the astonishment of the medical staff, the Algerian women responded enthusiastically with traditional *you-yous* (ululations), which were rather crudely described by Fanon as 'short, high-pitched and repeated modulations'. Before long, the shrill sound of women's *you-yous* would strike terror into French conscripts trying to control crowds in Algiers, but in this context it was a joyous noise: They were reacting in the manner demanded by the tradition that had created the music itself. For three months, Fanon worked with a musician called Abderahamane Aziz in an attempt to pursue and develop this musical therapy.[108] It was becoming obvious to Fanon that 'we had to find ways of facilitating reactions which were already inscribed in a fully elaborated personality. Social therapy would be possible only to the extent that we took into account social morphology and forms of sociability.'[109] Part of Fanon's argument here does overlap with that of the Algiers school to the extent that both posit the existence of an Algerian 'personality' and assume that psychotherapy must in some way adapt to it. The crucial difference is that, in proposing a sociological and phenomenological understanding of it, Fanon does not construct it as an unknowable object. It is therefore not entirely accurate to claim that Fanon 'arrives at his theory of the colonial personality through a conscious appropriation and inversion of the findings of ethnopsychiatry'.[110]

As Fanon began to look seriously at the forms of sociability that governed his patients' behaviour, it became apparent that the difficulties he had experienced when trying to work through interpreters were not caused by bad faith or evasiveness on the part of his patients. Outside the hospital, they encountered interpreters only when they had to deal with the French administration or when they were brought before a court of law. The very presence of an interpreter therefore provoked a distrust that made any form of communication difficult: to speak would be to admit guilt, not to enter into a therapeutic relationship. Similarly, the lack of interest in concerts and parties was not the expression of an innate reluctance to socialize; it was simply that for an Algerian Muslim, a festival that was not connected to a family or religious occasion was so abstract as to be quite devoid of meaning or purpose. The film shows had failed to interest Fanon's Algerian patients simply because they could not comprehend the psychological codes involved. 'Action' films like John Ford's classic western *Rio Grande* (1950) sparked some interest, but not the poetic psychology of Cocteau's *Noces de sable*.[111]

The gradual process of cultural change began with the creation of that essential feature of male social life in North Africa – a Moorish café where patients could play dominoes or simply talk while sipping mint tea in a room decorated with their own paintings and furnished with both European chairs and tables and the traditional floor mats and low tables. Traditional festivals began to be celebrated and the local Mufti was invited to come to the hospital twice a month to lead Friday prayers. Inviting traditional story-tellers was a successful recognition of the fact that the local culture was predominantly oral, but it was also a potentially dangerous move on Fanon's part. The colonial authorities had no love of wandering story-tellers who transmitted rumours as well as folk-tales, and such itinerants became objects of great suspicion when the war started. Itinerants carried news and spread rumours; stories could be an incitement to rebellion. Other innovations took Fanon closer still to a major rupture with the hospital authorities. He had discovered that men who could not be persuaded to weave baskets because that was 'women's work' could be persuaded to work in the grounds and to grow vegetables: 'Giving them a spade or a mattock is enough to make them start digging and hoeing.'[112] It was also enough to terrify his European staff: these were the traditional weapons of peasant revolt and they had been used to deadly effect at Sétif; they would be used again to massacre European civilians in the Constantinois in the summer of 1955. A locally recruited paramedic later recalled that the ancillary staff refused to help the patients and that Fanon was left to supervise their work himself. To general surprise, there were no incidents.[113] Before long, Fanon's gardeners were involved in the more ambitious project of clearing a football field and, to the horror of a senior administrator, were issued with spades and picks. Convinced that Fanon, whom he regarded as 'madder than the madmen', was going to be cut to pieces, he phoned the gendarmerie for help. In Fanon's absence, a fence of barbed wire was quickly erected around the pitch. A furious Fanon stormed into the administrator's office, shouting that he should finish the job by supplying sub-machine guns and building a watchtower. The care of his patients was *his* concern, and the administrator's responsibilities ended with ensuring that they were fed. The fence was taken down.[114] Not for the first time – and certainly not for the last time – Fanon got what he wanted thanks to a calculated display of anger.

In 1955, Fanon could report quite positively on the progress that had been made in the Blida-Joinville hospital.[115] The initial failure to create a therapeutic community was, however, paralleled at other clinical levels. Techniques that worked in Europe did not necessarily work in Algeria. At Saint-Alban, Fanon had been trained to administer Thematic Apperception Tests (TATs) and he now tried to use them in a very different environment. TATs are based on a theory of projection and assume that the contents of the unconscious can be projected into conscious verbal expressions. The patient is shown a set of cards showing one or more human figures involved in an ambiguous scene, and is asked to make up a story to explain it. Interpretation of the form and content of the narrative allows the therapist to identify defence mechanisms and areas of conflict within the patient's psyche. In the longer term, the tests strengthen the patient's ideal-ego (the psychoanalytic term for a narcissisic image of the self or the self-model to which the subject seeks to conform; the term 'ego-ideal' is often used in a similar sense) by allowing fantasy elements to enrich it without overpowering it. Fanon now attempted to use the TATs with a group of women patients (three Kabyles and nine Arabs) with an average age of twenty-three. Most were suffering from mild hypochondria; others were described as 'maladjusted' or 'mentally disturbed', and one was recovering from a youthful attack of mania. All were illiterate. On looking at one card, a patient told Fanon through an interpreter: 'I don't know if it's a boy or a girl. I don't know what she's doing. I don't know what to say. I don't understand. Perhaps he's ill. He has headache ("I am tired". Sighs).'[116] Fanon's impression was that his patients had somehow transformed the test into a painful intellectual examination, and that they were trying to identify as many as possible of the objects shown on the cards. They could not or would not tell stories, and at best produced dry lists of the objects they could see. Rather than constructing narratives, the women told Fanon what was in the picture, and they often got that wrong too, claiming that a picture of crosses in a cemetery was of toothbrushes or even dog kennels.

It would have been easy to explain the inadequate responses in terms of the patients' inability to think abstractly or symbolically, and thus to confirm the theses of the Algiers school, but Fanon argued that the problem was that the TATs were culture-bound. There are no crosses in a Muslim cemetery. The women's attitude was, he concluded, 'the result of the situations we put patients in. When we ask them to describe or act out a scene designed by Westerners for Westerners, we plunge them into a world that is different, foreign and heterogeneous, a world they cannot appropriate.'[117] Nor was the patients' failure to make up stories when they were asked 'What do you think will happen next?' a reflection of some mental primitivism. One of the patients explained: 'I cannot tell lies, because it is a sin. Only God knows what will happen next.'[118] Rather than dismissing her explanation as further evidence of the passivity induced by a pathogenic Islam, Fanon noted that his patients could and did invent stories when confronted with a blank card. He therefore argued that it was necessary to explore the logic of imaginary life in an Islamic country, and went on to add in very phenomenological terms: 'The imaginary life cannot be isolated from real life; the concrete and the objective world constantly feed, permit, legitimate and found the imaginary. The imaginary consciousness is obviously unreal, but it feeds on the concrete world. The imagination and the imaginary are possible only to the extent that the real world belongs to us.'[119] The solution to the problems Fanon had encountered with his women patients was therefore to develop TATs appropriate to the cultural world in which they lived. At the end of the paper Fanon and Geronimi published in 1956, they announced that they were beginning the appropriate research.[120] The war ensured that they did not have time to complete it.

Fanon left no detailed account of the research on TATs that he alludes to here, but Azoulay has stated that he made at least two field trips into the mountains of Kabylia to study traditional attitudes towards insanity.[121] Two of Fanon's younger colleagues began theses on related topics, with him acting as their supervisor, but their research material has been lost. According to Charles Geronimi, the young Dr Ziza began a research project on the role played by djinns in the social psychopathology of Algeria, whilst his colleague Dr Assehal began research on dreams. The former somehow survived the wave of repression that hit the Blida hospital early in 1957; the latter did not survive the treatment he received at the hands of his interrogators. According to Philippe Lucas, Fanon himself actually wrote a study entitled 'Le Marabout de Si Slimana' but the manuscript, like so many others, has not survived.[122] This was presumably a study of the cult of local saints, living and dead, in which popular forms of Islam fuse with pre-Islamic animism, with ritual dances being used to induce a trance-like state that could produce a cathartic effect. It may also have had political overtones, and the visits to Kabylia in search of marabouts were almost certainly a cover for making contact with the FLN or even fighting units of the ALN. The only surviving publications to reflect the evolution of Fanon's thinking are sections of *Sociologie d'une révolution* and *Les Damnés de la terre* and a short paper, co-authored with François Sanchez, on traditional Muslim attitudes to the insane. The Western belief that the Arab population respected or even venerated the mad because they were in communication with djinns was not, they argued, entirely accurate, though they did note that a few of Blida's inmates had been committed in the face of opposition from their families, who regarded them as saints. The comment that one family wanted a patient – supposedly a living saint – to be discharged so that they could profit financially from the pious faithful suggests that the author's genuine and even sympathetic interest in traditional medicine went hand in hand with a healthy scepticism about the real meaning of the cult of living saints.[123]

Western and Maghrebian perceptions of insanity differ, argued Fanon and Sanches, in that they imply very different conceptions of the relationship between the mad and 'their' madness. Speaking from experience on the wards, they noted that French-trained doctors and nurses alike tended to think that their patients were to some extent responsible for their actions. The blow struck by an aggressive patient was not purely pathological or involuntary; the intent to cause injury was real and semi-conscious, and the staff's readiness to apply physical restraints was motivated by a corresponding desire to inflict punishment. Painting a somewhat idyllic picture of traditional North African society, Fanon and Sanchez claim that the standard view was that the madman was in no way responsible for his actions, which were the responsibility of the *jinni* that possessed them. Mental illness was therefore an 'accidental' or 'contingent' condition that had no effect on the true or underlying personality of its individual victims. Treatment normally took the form of pilgrimages to the shrines of powerful marabouts, such as the one in Blida's 'sacred wood', where attempts to drive out the *jinni* were made and where magical amulets could be purchased. A patient who recovered was accepted back into the social group, and was not viewed with any distrust or ambivalence. This was 'a harmonious articulation of beliefs', imbued with a 'profoundly holistic spirit that preserves intact the image of the normal man despite the existence of the illness'.[124] Traditional society both respected the insane because they were still human beings, and treated them because they were the victims of hostile spirits. Profoundly rooted in a cultural system, the North African model had, wrote Fanon and Sanchez, 'great value' in human terms, and it was not unrelated to Western attitudes to somatic illness. Caring for a tubercular patient does not imply any veneration of tuberculosis; in most cases, the Maghrebian attitude towards the insane did not imply any veneration of insanity and mental illness.

An unpublished paper by Azoulay, Sanchez and Fanon provides further indications as to how they attempted to study the cultural world in which their patients lived.[125] It is a study of sexual dysfunctionality and concentrates mainly on male impotence. The basic premise is that, in order to understand dysfunctionality and its psychical effects, it was necessary to understand the 'knots of belief' that structured the communities in which they occurred. Although impotence was surprisingly common amongst North African men, they rarely consulted doctors and especially not European doctors. They tended to go to a marabout or *taleb*,[126] because they were convinced that their problems did not have an organic cause and had been inflicted upon them by magic. Fanon and his colleagues therefore went to consult a *taleb* who lived near Algiers in Castiglioni (now known as Bou Ismail) and who was famed for his ability to cure impotence. His knowledge of the subject derived, it transpired, from a medieval treatise on medicine by El Soyouti which Fanon and his colleagues succeeded in finding. According to Soyouti and the *taleb*, impotence could be attributed to one of three causes: malformation of the genitals, the breath of demons and magic. Traditional medicine could do little for a patient with malformed genitals, though the ingestion of the penis of a wild ass (removed from the animal while it was still alive) and certain spices might have a beneficial effect. Premature ejaculation, which was regarded as a form of impotence, was caused by coming into contact with the breath of demons, the 'demons' being djinns that had been offended by some aspect of an individual's behaviour. The affliction could be cured by making certain invocations or acquiring amulets inscribed with magical formulae and wearing them next to the skin. Further problems with the highly sensitive djinns could be avoided by making propitiatory gestures and being careful not to break certain taboos, such as treading in the blood of a sheep that had been slaughtered for the feast of Mouloud: it belonged to earth spirits, and they could easily be offended.

Most cases of impotence in the true sense of the inability to have or sustain an erection were caused by witchcraft or magic. In such cases, the man was said to have been 'bound' or 'tied' either by his wife or by a wise woman acting on her behalf and in exchange for payment. A distinction was made between two forms of binding. A woman who temporarily bound her husband because he had been unfaithful was, according to the collective's ethics, justified in doing so. Making a man totally and permanently impotent was not justifiable; such actions were carried out under the influence of 'Chitan' (Satan). The spell could be cast in a number of different ways, ranging from tricking a man into stepping over an open knife or a new mirror, to inscribing a goat's horn with magical formulae and throwing it into a cemetery. The afflicted man's potency could be restored by the use of incantations, amulets or counter-spells, and the *taleb* was very well versed in the appropriate lore.[127] The paper ends with a brief description of how different forms of magical binding could be used to preserve a girl's virginity, to ensure that a repudiated wife would remain celibate, or to prevent a woman from committing adultery. The use of magic to protect virginity was seen as legitimate; using it to take revenge on a woman was viewed as an evil deed.

The paper on sexual dysfunctionality appears to have been a draft for a more extensive study that was never completed. It is short and consists mainly of note-like observations that would have to have been expanded to make it suitable for publication in a professional journal. What makes it significant is the fact that the authors take the practices they are describing so seriously and that they obviously listened to their *taleb* with great respect. The word 'superstition' is never used. The *taleb* and El Soyouti's treatise are clearly regarded as being in possession of a coherent body of knowledge and a diagnostic system that makes sense in its own terms. Understanding that knowledge and that system was a way of coming to terms with problems the authors encountered in their psychiatric practice, because it enabled them to grasp their patients' own understanding of their sexual problems. All this is far removed from Porot's superior references to 'primitivism' and 'the primitive mentality'.[128]

Not all Fanon's work at Blida was characterized by the radical politics of the attempt to recreate the institutional psychotherapy of Saint-Alban in a very different setting. Like any working psychiatrist, he prescribed drugs and saw to it that they were taken. He was also involved in pharmacological research that remained well within the paradigms of what Kuhn calls 'normal science'.[129] From 1955 onwards, he worked in collaboration with a pharmacologist called Sourdoire on the use of lithium citrate, which was used both as a treatment for acute mania and as a prophylactic against recurrent affective disorders. Having read all the literature on the subject that had appeared since 1949, Fanon and Sourdoire concentrated on studying the rate at which the lithium citrate, administered along with sodium potassiate to a group of seven patients, was absorbed into the body tissues and then eliminated in urine.[130] The equipment and techniques available to them are a testament to Blida's modernity: a spectrophotometer to trace the movement of the iods in the blood plasma, and complexometric titration to record the concentration of lithium in their patients' urine. Although technically complex, this was not particularly advanced research, but it is a clear indication of Fanon's dedication to even the more mundane aspects of his chosen profession.

Life in Blida was not at first unpleasant, but the worsening of the war (to be discussed in the next chapter), and Fanon's involvement in it, soon made it impossible for him to lead anything resembling a normal life. The Algerian war changed Fanon completely, turning him into a true revolutionary activist but also exposing him to immense danger and risks. It did not, however, put an end to his psychiatric career, which he was able to pursue elsewhere. In Blida, he had tried to keep his political and professional activities separate from his private life, but soon he would have no private life. And it was in Blida that he experienced the extremes of emotion. The year 1955 should, in personal terms, have been a happy one, in which Josie and Fanon had their only son, but it was also a year marked by a great personal loss. The telegram from Martinique arrived at the beginning of February, and the news was confirmed by a letter from Joby in Paris: Gabrielle was dead. She had been in the seventh month of her second pregnancy when she stooped to pick up her baby, went into premature labour, and died of the ensuing complications before medical help could be brought. Almost fifty years after the event, her uncle still hints that the doctor she had crossed in Le Lorrain could have done more to save her. Gabrielle Richer was only thirty-three when she died.[131]

On 4 February, Fanon wrote to his mother and family in Martinique, pouring out his grief in a letter that is a hymn to his sister.[132] He had already tried unsuccessfully to telephone Martinique. Her death was 'unthinkable', not only because any death was 'absurd, illogical, grotesque and inexplicable' but because it made a nonsense of the way she had lived her life. Gabrielle was one of the few people in whom Fanon had never detected the slightest sign of despair. Strong and quietly self-confident, she had never been hateful or mean to others, and she had always been able to overcome her few moments of doubt or fear. 'Gabrielle dead, what could be more grotesque?' Fanon now recalled how much they had enjoyed their occasional reunions when she was studying in Rouen, how she had come to him for advice when she received Marcel Richer's marriage proposal and added, in a strangely introspective tone that in losing Gabrielle he had lost one of the few women who had trusted him. To lose Gabrielle was to lose a 'simple, tender heart with not a petty or devious thought in her mind'. The letter ends: 'And the worst impertinence, the monstrous error would be to think that she was dead. Because, you'll see, Gabrielle won't agree to leave the level of life. "She loved too much".' Neither psychiatry nor politics, nor even his own family life, provided any real defence against this loss.

# 7

# The Explosion

'T HE EXPLOSION WILL not happen today,' wrote Fanon in the opening lines of *Peau noire, masques blancs*: 'It is too early . . . or too
late.'[1] Neither too early nor too late, the explosions that went off on the
warm night of 31 October/1 November 1954 were carefully timed to
shatter Algeria's uneasy peace. Between midnight and three in the
morning, bombs exploded outside the radio station in Algiers, the city's
gas works and an oil-storage depot in the docks. The crude homemade
devices – soldered metal cylinders packed with potassium chlorate,
manufactured and planted by as-yet inexperienced terrorists – caused
some physical damage but no loss of life. Elsewhere in the country,
attacks, most of them unsuccessful or only partly successful, were made
on police stations and isolated farms. Telegraph poles were cut down
and telephone lines were cut. Fewer than a dozen people, including two
French conscripts, were killed in the whole of Algeria. The most notorious incident occurred when a bus was stopped by an armed band in
the spectacular Tighanimine Gorges on the southern flank of the Aurès
mountains. As the passengers were ordered out, a *caïd* (a French-
appointed local government official) called M'Chounèche Hadji
Ben-Saddock attempted to draw a revolver and a nervous member of
the protection group covering the roadblock opened fire with a sten

gun. The *caïd* died immediately. The burst of fire also caused the Algerian war's first civilian casualties, even though the gunmen were in theory under orders not to harm European civilians. The twenty-three-year-old Guy Monnerot was killed outright and his wife was badly injured. The couple were teachers who had been married for only three weeks. They had been travelling around the country on their honeymoon before taking up their first teaching posts in the village of Tiffelfel, only a few miles from the site of the ambush. The fighter responsible for the death of Guy Monnerot was reportedly later put on trial by an ALN tribunal and executed for disobeying orders.[2] Before long, French civilians would be regarded as legitimate targets.

There were also minor incidents in Blida and the surrounding area but these were not the work of local insurgents. The nationalist movement in the area was badly divided. The plan had been for five groups of between five and nine fighters to attack selected targets but, with the nationalist forces in total ideological disarray and poor morale, it had to be called off. A group of twenty-one Kabyles was sent in by the organizers of the insurrection, and a small assault team led by Rabah Bitat[3] made an unsuccessful attack on the Bizot barracks in Blida; three were killed and others were wounded before the survivors retreated into the mountains above Chréa, which would soon become home to guerrilla fighters rather than the picnickers and skiers who frequented them in more peaceful times. Attempts were made to sabotage bridges on the main road to Algiers, and a bomb set fire to a warehouse belonging to a citrus-fruit cooperative in Boufarik.[4] This did not look like the beginning of the bloodiest of France's wars of decolonization.

The Blida area remained relatively quiet until the spring of 1956, when the French authorities finally had to admit that some 2,000 guerrillas were operating in the quadrilateral of rugged mountains between Palestro (now Lakdaria), Aumale (Medroussa), Blida and Médéa. In the first winter of the war, things were very different. Bitat was arrested almost immediately and remained in prison until 1962. Omar Ouamrame, who took over from him, was in command of no more than one hundred men, less than half of them properly armed. A former sergeant in the French army who fought in the Alsace campaign, Ouamrame had been in the mountains since Sétif. One of those under his command in early 1955 was Azzedine (or Rabah Zerrari, to give him his real name), a twenty-one-year-old arc-welder formerly employed at the Caterpillar plant in Algiers who rose to the rank of commandant. He took to the mountains armed with an ancient two-barrelled pistol and six damp cartridges. In his memoirs, Azzedine describes life in the Blidean Atlas, where his group huddled by day in a mountain refuge, surviving on a diet of dry biscuits made from barley, onions and figs: 'We only went out at night, taking a thousand precautions. We urinated into a can. For our other needs, we waited until dusk. One by one, we could put on a *burnous* and squat down behind a cactus hedge.' The experience was not, he adds, 'exhilarating'.[5] Prior to his recruitment into the FLN, Rabah Zerrari had never taken any interest in politics. The French army soon came to know Azzedine as one of their most dangerous enemies.[6]

In its early stages, the insurgency was a low-level conflict. Between November 1954 and the end of January 1956, there were eleven attacks on French patrols in the Blida area, and eighty-four minor acts of sabotage. Farms and private vehicles were attacked on 323 occasions, but there were only three major clashes between the French army and its mysterious enemy.[7] Official government statements spoke of scattered attacks by small groups of terrorists and stated that all measures necessary would be taken to restore order, omitting to mention that large areas of the Aurès mountains – the storm centre of the Algerian revolution – were in a state of insurrection. Rumours abounded: the rebels were armed and organized by Nasser's Egypt, and foreign agents were at work. Radio Cairo added to the confusion – and to the impression that the invisible hand pulling the strings was Nasser's – by citing Algerian sources in Egypt who reported planned operations as though they had actually taken place. A week after the first explosions, Interior Minister François Mitterrand announced on the radio that Algeria was French and that only French authority would be recognized on French soil. For its part, the French Communist Party argued that these acts of 'individual terrorism' would play into the hands of the *colons*, and even hinted that they had been fomented by them.[8]

The novelist Mouloud Feraoun spoke for many, both French and Algerian, when he wrote in his diary on 6 November 1955: 'When the revolt broke out, we refused to see its full importance. It was not really important.'[9] It was so unimportant that the glossy weekly *Paris-Match* announced on its front page that 'The Terrorist Wave has Crossed the Algerian Frontier', but only in an inset dwarfed by a picture of a pouting Gina Lollobrigida.[10] The issue of *Le Monde* dated 2 November 1954 carried the news that 'several people' had been killed in Algeria, but devoted considerably more space to a report on the forthcoming American elections. On the same day, the Communist daily *L'Humanité* briefly mentioned the news from Algeria on its front page and referred interested readers to an inside page for further details. Its lead story was devoted to the news that 'twelve of Hitler's generals' had been appointed to command the Wehrmacht and to dark talk of 'German revanchism'. There was little or no reason to suspect in November 1954 that a war of national liberation had begun in Algeria, that it would bring down the Fourth French Republic, return de Gaulle to power in 1958 and bring with it the threat of a military coup in France itself. There was no reason to suspect that over one million French troops, the majority of them very young conscripts, would serve in Algeria or that over 27,000 of them would die there in the war with no name. Statistics for the number of Algerians killed are still a matter for controversy. Official French estimates speak of 141,000 fighters killed; successive Algerian governments have always insisted that one million martyrs died for the revolutionary cause, and the figure tends to rise when Franco-Algerian relations are tense.[11]

Fanon had come to Algeria in 1953 armed with elements of a critique of colonial psychiatry or ethnopsychiatry but with relatively little knowledge of Algerian politics. He had, on the other hand, worked with Algerian patients in Lyon and must have learned a great deal from journals like *Esprit*. Fanon had not found 'his' war in France in 1944–5. His disillusionment with the war he had fought radicalized him and alienated him from the France that claimed to be his country. He would find his own war – and a new country – in Algeria, but he did not go there to look for it and had no way of knowing that it would occur. He went to Blida as a psychiatrist, not as a potential revolutionary. He had gone to Algeria to dry tears and Algeria transformed him into an advocate of violent revolution. There is no record of how Fanon reacted when the explosion finally came in Algeria, and one can only surmise that he was as surprised as anyone else.

None of France's other wars of decolonization lasted so long as that in Algeria, and none produced such high casualty figures. By 1960, France's other African territories – Cameroon, Togo, Mali, Madagascar, Dahomey, Niger, the Ivory Coast, Upper Volta, Tchad, Senegal, Mauritania and the Central African Republic – had all become independent states as the map of Africa changed beyond recognition. Their decolonization had been a peaceful and relatively speedy process.[12] In Algeria, the war went on. In June 1955, Tunisia was granted internal autonomy and that country gained full independence in 1956, the same year that Morocco became an independent monarchy. There was armed conflict in both countries, but never on the Algerian scale.[13] The transition to independence in Tunisia and Morocco was facilitated by their constitutional status; both were protectorates where traditional power structures had remained relatively intact. Unlike Algeria, they were not settler colonies and they had not been declared part of France in 1848.

When François Mitterrand reiterated that Algeria was French, he was restating a truism. The Mediterranean did not separate France from Algeria; it flowed through a Greater France stretching from Dunkirk to Tamanrasset in the same way that the Seine flows through Paris. Algeria was home to over a million Europeans who were French by nationality if not birth. The initial conquest of Algeria had been a haphazard affair with no real sense of purpose or strategy. It was only in 1841 that a total war or conquest began and it was only in 1871 that the country was finally 'pacified' and that a civilian administration could be established. A small number of colonists followed the army to Algeria in 1830, and their numbers were swelled when revolutionaries and subversives were deported from France in 1848, 1851 and 1871. Immigrants also came to Algeria from all over the Mediterranean basin. In 1865, they were granted the right to become naturalized French citizens on demand. Five years later, the Jews of Algeria became French citizens. In 1889, citizenship was extended to all those European settlers who did not reject it. The 'native' population did not enjoy the same rights and privileges. The laws of 1865 defined them as French subjects but not citizens. Their daily lives were governed by Muslim law and, in order to become French citizens, they had to renounce their Islamic civil status. Few took up that option. Despite the reforms of 1944 and 1947, the 'natives' remained an inferior race. Algeria's European citizens saw themselves not as transplanted French men and women, but as a 'new race' which was creating a new Algeria and they were not going to be dispossessed. Only a tiny minority of them identified themselves as 'Algerian' in the modern sense or looked forward to being citizens of an Algerian republic. Whilst they were defiantly French, the so-called *pieds noirs* also defined themselves in opposition to the metropolitan *Francaoui. They* were generous, open-minded, virile and hedonistic; the typical *Francaoui* was mean, emotionally cold, effeminate and over-intellectual. For the average *pied noir*, the 'native' of Algeria was less than human. Not the least of the many human tragedies of the war was the eventual fate of these *pieds noirs* who, faced in 1962 with the stark choice between 'the suitcase and the coffin',[14] took the obvious option and left for a metropolitan France which few of them had ever seen and which proved reluctant to take them in.[15]

One of the reasons for the war's continuation was the French military's determination not to suffer another humiliating defeat. In 1954, seven months before the explosions in Algiers, Dien Bien Phu in Vietnam fell to General Giap's Viet Minh forces and it became obvious that French colonialism in Indochina was doomed. Garrisoned with twelve battalions, Dien Bien Phu was supposedly impregnable. The giant base close to the border with Laos was a 'hedgehog' complex of five strong-points clustered around the airstrip that provided its only lifeline. Three hundred kilometres from Hanoi, it was at the extreme range of the planes that supplied it. The hills that surrounded the base did not, according to the planners, pose any threat: Giap could deploy only 75 mm guns and would have to position them so high above Dien Bien Phu that they would be ineffective. The planners were proved wrong. Heavier guns could be dismantled, carried into the hills on bicycles or even on foot and dug in to provide withering fire. Attacking in wave formations, the Viet Minh then overran the outlying strongpoints and the base was slowly strangled. On 7 May, 'Isabelle', the last French out-post, was overrun. The entire garrison of 15,000 men was lost, with 3,000 dead and the remainder taken prisoner. Viet Minh casualties have been estimated at 8,000 dead and 15,000 wounded.[16] France's defeat at Dien Bien Phu coincided with the ninth anniversary of the massacres in Sétif. In Sétif, France had given a brutal demonstration of its power; at Dien Bien Phu, it revealed its military weakness. The lesson was not lost on Algeria's young nationalists. On 9 October,

French forces withdrew from Hanoi and the last troops pulled out of South Vietnam six months later. Many of the captives who were eventually released under the terms of the Geneva Agreements of 21 July 1954 were soon fighting France's last war of decolonization.

For the first time, a major Western power had been defeated by a Third World guerrilla force and the French military were determined that it would not happen again in Algeria. Some of those who had been defeated by Giap, and the commanders and officers of the Parachute Regiments and the Foreign Legion in particular, had learned a hard lesson from the Vietnamese concepts of 'people's war' and psychological warfare, and what they had learned would be applied in Algeria. Roger Trinquier, who created the First Battalion of Colonial Parachutists (the 'red berets'), had spent much of his war in action behind Viet Minh lines; Marcel Bigeard had been parachuted into Dien Bien Phu and led one of the most successful counter-attacks in an attempt to recapture one of the outposts. When the base fell, he spent three months as a Viet Minh captive.[17] Yves Godard commanded the 11th Shock Battalion – a 'dirty tricks' unit created by the paras and the intelligence services – in Indochina and had attempted to relieve Dien Bien Phu from inside Laos.[18] These men were to be amongst France's most important and effective commanders in Algeria, and defeat at the hands of rebels was not on their agenda.

As Fanon continued to treat his patients and to experiment with lithium citrate in Blida, and as metropolitan France settled into an uneasy phoney war, conditions in Algeria deteriorated. More perspicacious than many observers, the Catholic novelist François Mauriac, who was enjoying a second career as a columnist on *L'Express*, wrote in his diary on Tuesday 2 November that 'The Algerian war has begun' and added: 'The horror of what is about to be unleashed must be immediately tempered by a concerted offensive against low wages, unemployment, ignorance and poverty, and by the structural reforms the Algerian people are calling for. And, at all cost, we must prevent the police from using torture.' When this diary entry appeared in *L'Express* on 13 November, the reference to a 'war' had been deleted.[19] There was to be no war in Algeria. The French army was dealing with rebels, bandits, outlaws and *fellaghas* ('those who cut roads' – often abbreviated to *fells* or transformed into *fellouzes*). It was involved in a police operation and not a war. It was only in April 1955 that a full state of emergency was declared and the army was granted extensive powers.[20] A year later, Prime Minister Guy Mollet's Front Républicain government, with the support of the French Communist Party, voted through special powers that effectively created a state of martial law in Algeria. Prior to the introduction of the state of emergency, the army was hampered by the fact that when acting in support of the civil authorities, its soldiers did not have full powers of arrest. Given that they were not fighting a war, French soldiers killed in combat were deemed to have been murdered and were subjected to autopsies. In some cases, examining magistrates even thought fit to reconstruct the events that led to the 'murders'. General Spillmann, the senior officer in the Constantine region, had to make personal representations to the Minister for Justice to put a halt to that affront to military honour. It helped that the two had been at school together.[21] The state of non-war had rather more serious implications for Algerians. The conflict was an internal French affair and Algerian 'rebels' therefore did not enjoy the protection of the Geneva Convention. Even when captured in uniform, they were treated as common-law criminals. The execution by guillotine of two rebels in June 1956 would accelerate the spiral of violence. To the fury of the military, the state of non-war also meant that rebels could be tried before courts and could be represented by lawyers. Fanon's friend and comrade in arms, Marcel Manville, was one of the few lawyers who was prepared to accept such briefs, and he often visited Algiers, Constantine and Bône between 1955 and 1961 to defend his clients.[22]

Mauriac's fears about torture and the horrors that were about to be unleashed were more than justified. On the evening of 1 November, Ghedefi Ben Ali was arrested at his home in Blida and transferred to Algiers after having been held in a local police station for twenty-four hours. In an Algiers commissariat his hands and feet were bound with wet rags, and he was suspended from a pole inserted between them. He was then lowered into a bathtub filled with dirty water, with a policeman pushing his head under. When he was on the point of drowning, he was lifted out and beaten. For four days, he received the same treatment twice an evening.[23] Ben Ali was released after a fortnight. He was a man of no particular importance. Although he did have a political past, he had played no part in the insurrection and therefore had nothing to confess to in November 1954. There was nothing unusual about the treatment of Ghedefi Ben Ali. Torture had long been the rule in the premises of the Police des Renseignements Généraux (the 'security' branch of the police). Some years before the November events, Pierre Braun, a member of the Paris bar, was called to defend a client in Blida. The examining magistrate, who eventually revealed where the unnamed man was being held, asked the lawyer: 'Know what we're doing to your client? Making him sit on a bottle. Seems he enjoys it.'[24] A young Algerian described 'the bottle treatment' to the novelist Meloud Feraoun in March 1956: 'an ordinary bottle, preferably one broken at the neck. The prisoner is made to sit on it and the policemen press down on the wretch's shoulders with all their strength. The painful effects of this form of torture can last for months and months.'[25] If the intestine was perforated, it could also result in death.

In February 1999, the French army finally began to declassify its secret archives for the period March 1946 to December 1954. They contain a number of circulars issued by Governor General Marcel-Edmond Naegelen pointing out that torture was illegal and warning against the use of 'unjustified violence' against prisoners and suspects.[26] The circulars were ignored in peacetime, and torture became merely one more weapon – used by both sides – in a very dirty war. The methods came from the standard repertoire: beatings, rape, immersion in water, suspension by the wrists and the ankles, the application of electrodes to sensitive parts of the body and the insertion of bottles or sticks into the anus or the vagina. In the field, the term '*gégène*' (from '*générateur*') became a standard piece of military jargon as the generators and magnetos designed to power field telephones were put to more sinister use.

The summary execution of torture victims and of prisoners 'shot while trying to escape' was so commonplace that it became known as 'the wood-fatigue' (*la corvée de bois*). Writing anonymously to a Christian 'Spiritual Resistance Committee' in January 1957, a reservist who had been recalled (*rappelé*) for service in Algeria described some everyday events:

There was no doubt as to the ultimate fate of people who had been tortured . . . It was what we called the *corvée de bois*. At night, the police jeep would come into the barracks courtyard. The man on guard would go and find the prisoners who had been picked out and made them get into a vehicle. The executions took place a few minutes later, on a well-known cliff by the sea. It is very difficult to estimate, even approximately, how many people were sent for the *corvée de bois* each week: five or six, perhaps many more.

The fate of *fellaghas* in uniform who were captured in battle was no better. I can cite one example of the line of conduct that was usually followed. Seven *fellaghas* were taken prisoner on 31 October. Once they had been paraded through the town under heavy escort, they were handed back to the battalion that had taken them prisoner; the battalion was responsible for putting them through the *corvée de bois*.

(Note: one of the first *fellaghas* we captured in uniform was left tied up in the back of his cell for half a day. The door was open and anyone could go in and beat him up when they felt like it. There was no shortage of visitors.)[27]

Four months later, Robert Bonnaud described what had happened to a wounded prisoner brought in by a 'Rural Protection Mobile Group' made up of 'European Algerians' and commanded by metropolitan regulars. He was kicked mercilessly and the kicks were aimed at his wounds. The troops laughed, took his photograph and told him to 'watch the birdie'. A kitchen knife was then produced and slowly sharpened on a stone as the captive watched. The prisoner's throat was hacked at slowly and clumsily, with great care being taken to avoid the carotid artery. He was finally shot in the face at point-blank range and transformed into 'something filthy that has no name in the language of horror'.[28]

Even Father Louis Dounard, the priest who served as almoner to the Foreign Legion, could justify the use of torture on the grounds that it was the lesser of two evils; the intelligence gathered by torture could save innocent French lives.[29] Torture became a mundane matter of policy. In February 1959, General Jacques Massu, who commanded French forces during the Battle of Algiers, issued a directive on subversive warfare in which he remarked in coded euphemisms that

'Psychological action is completely based on the creation of conditioned reflexes. In a Muslim country, the most powerful reflex is respect for strength.'[30] Had he wanted scientific backing for his theory, the psychiatrists of Algiers could have provided it. As the use of torture became commonplace, treating its psychological effects on victims and perpetrators alike became part of Fanon's everyday clinical practice.

Ben Ali was one of the first victims of Operation Bitter Orange, in which the Police des Renseignements Généraux rounded up those it suspected of involvement in the insurrection. Six hundred and fifty arrests were made in November and on 26 November the Prefect of Police stated that 318 of those held had 'probably' been linked to the insurrection.[31] By the end of the year, some 2,000 people had been taken into custody.[32] Most belonged to the Mouvement pour le Triomphe des Libertés Démocratiques (MTLD), which had been declared a proscribed organization on 1 November. The MTLD was not, however, responsible for the insurrection. It had been planned and executed by a new force: the Front de Libération Nationale, of which the French intelligence services knew nothing. The existence of a mysterious Comité Révolutionnaire pour l'Unité et l'Action had been reported by the Service des Liaisons Nord-Africains, which reported to the Gouvernement Général in Algiers, but the intelligence services of the Tenth Military Region, which covered the three Algerian *départements*, appear to have underestimated its importance and did not link it to the FLN, which announced its existence only as the bombs went off. According to documents released in 1999, it took the French authorities another forty days to realize that they were dealing with 'Algerian revolutionaries' and not 'bandits'.[33] The police had in fact simply rounded up the usual suspects or, as Assia Djebar nicely puts it in a novel about a later stage of the war, 'those suspected of being suspects'.[34]

A Roneoed proclamation issued on 31 October 1954 and addressed to the 'Algerian people and the militants of the national cause' spelled out the new organization's political programme:

Goal: National independence through
    1. The re-establishment of the sovereign, democratic and social Algerian State within the framework of Islamic principle.

2. Respect for all basic freedoms without distinction as to race or religion.

Internal objectives:

1. Political purification by returning the revolutionary national movement to the true path and eradicating all traces of the corruption and reformism which have caused the present regression;

2. The unification and organization of all the healthy energies of the Algerian people in order to liquidate the colonial system.

External objectives:

1. Internationalization of the Algerian struggle;

2. Realization of North-African unity with its natural Arab-Muslim context;

3. The assertion, within the framework of the UN Charter, of our support for all nations that support our liberation action.

Means of struggle: in accordance with revolutionary principles and given the internal and external situation, continuation of the struggle by every means until we have achieved our goal.

Discussions with the French authorities were proposed on the basis of:

1. the opening of negotiations with the authorized spokesmen of the Algerian people, and based upon the recognition that Algerian sovereignty is one and indivisible;

2. the creation of a climate of trust through the release of all political prisoners, an official statement abolishing all emergency legislation and an end to legal proceedings against our fighting forces;

3. the recognition of Algerian nationality thanks to an official statement abolishing all edicts, decrees and laws that make Algeria a French territory by denying the history, geography, language, religion and customs of the Algerian people.

In return:

1. Honestly acquired French cultural and economic interests will be respected, as will individuals and families;

2. All French citizens wishing to remain in Algeria may choose to retain their original nationality, and will therefore be regarded as foreigners in the eyes of the prevailing laws, or may opt for

Algerian nationality, in which case they will be regarded as having Algerian rights and duties;

3. Links between France and Algeria will be defined and will be the object of an accord between the two powers based upon mutual equality and respect.[35]

The document was signed 'The Secretariat' and had been drafted by two men: Mohammed Boudiaf and Mourade Didouche.[36] Although released to the press, the original text did not circulate widely outside Kabylia, where it was written and produced;[37] the FLN leaflets that began to circulate in France's Algerian community in December were posted from Cairo.[38] The Proclamation was a major document intended to make the FLN's claims known to the world at large. A shorter statement addressed to 'the people of Algeria' was issued by its military wing, the Armée de Libération Nationale:

> Think of your humiliating position as colonized men. Under colonialism, justice, democracy and equality are nothing more than deceptions and tricks. To add to all your misfortunes, there is the bankruptcy of all the parties that claim to be representing you . . . Side by side with our brothers in the East and the West, we call upon you to reconquer your freedom by shedding your blood.
>
> Organize your actions alongside the forces of liberation, to which you must give aid, succour and protection. Not to involve yourself in the struggle is a crime . . . To hinder our actions is treason.
>
> God is with those who fight for just causes, and no force can stop them now except for a glorious death or national liberation.
> Long live the Liberation Army!
> Long live independent Algeria![39]

The 1954 proclamation clearly defines the FLN's immediate goals but says remarkably little about its vision of the future. No political structures for the post-colonial period are defined and no social goals, other than independence, are mentioned. This was a manifesto for a war rather than a blueprint for the peace that would follow it. Even the Soummam Conference of August 1956, held in secrecy in a region that had supposedly been pacified by the French Army, did little to clarify the FLN's ultimate aims and was devoted mainly to military and organizational questions.[40] The Soummam 'platform' provides a good description of the ALN's organization and even of the insignia of rank worn by its fighters. In political terms, the most important points contained in the document are the insistence that 'the political takes priority over the military' and that 'the forces of the interior take priority over the forces of the exterior'. Decisions were to be taken on a collegial basis and were collectively binding. The goal of the struggle was defined as the rebirth of an Algerian state in the form of a 'democratic social republic', but apart from references to 'people's assemblies', agrarian reform and 'giving the land to those who work it', no detailed vision of the future emerged from this lengthy document. It was only at the Tripoli conference of June 1962 that Algerian leaders began to talk of socialism, collectivization and a state-planned economy.

Paris's response to the November proclamation was eminently predictable. Interior Minister François Mitterrand is often said to have stated that war was the only form of negotiation that would take place in Algeria. Those words are apocryphal but their tone is an accurate reflection of what he did tell the Assemblée Nationale on 12 November: there would be no compromise and no negotiations with sedition. The internal peace of the nation and the integrity of the nation would be defended. Algeria's secession from the metropolis was inconceivable. That, he added, should be clear to everyone. Heavy police reinforcements were dispatched to Algeria, together with six battalions from the Twenty-Fifth Airborne Division to reinforce the standing garrison of 65,000 men, most of whom were involved in training and administrative duties and few of whom were combat-ready.[41] The 'war without a name' had begun. It was to be very different to the dirty war in Indochina, which had been fought by a combination of regulars, mercenaries and the Foreign Legion, and it was fought largely by conscripts doing their national service. In May 1955, troops were brought in from Germany and Tunisia to bring the strength of the French forces to 100,000. In August, those who had completed their service in April were recalled, and in April 1956 the 200,000 men of the classes of 1951 to 1954 learned that their military service would take them to Algeria. The length of military service was extended from eighteen to thirty months. FLN fighters committed themselves for life or the duration of the war.

The availability of huge numbers of conscripts from 1956 onwards allowed the French army to adopt the highly successful strategy of *quadrillage*. The literal meaning of the word is a pattern of checks or squares; in the Algerian context, it meant the stationing of small and static defensive units throughout the country, which was quite literally 'covered' by the military. The function of the static units was to defend villages and installations from attack and to frustrate FLN attempts at infiltration. *Quadrillage* was successful, but it was also a risky policy which left small units of relatively inexperienced conscripts in isolated positions for long periods of time. The use of national servicemen and *rappelés* in Algeria was always controversial and, when the first reservists were killed in May 1956, public opinion reacted very badly. The battalion of reservists raised in Paris formed part of the Ninth Regiment of Colonial Infantry and had disembarked in Algiers on 4 May. Fourteen days later, one of its platoons was on patrol in the Palestro area under the command of a young second lieutenant. As they approached an isolated settlement, they ran into a well-prepared ALN ambush. All but six of the twenty-one died in the initial hail of fire from point-blank range; the survivors were dragged away by the rebels. Only one survived. The troops who were sent out in search of the missing patrol eventually found mutilated bodies in the mountains. They had been disembowelled and their testicles had been removed. Three of the missing were never found.[42] It was incidents like this, together with the revulsion caused by the consistent reports of torture and fears that France was facing the possibility of civil war or even of fascism, that eventually turned public opinion against the war with no name. The army itself exploited such incidents by publicizing them in its newspaper *Le Bled* ('The Interior'; the term is derived from an Arabic word meaning 'land' or 'terrain'). This both instilled into its readers a fear of the dangers that faced them and a conviction that their enemies were sub-human sadists who were to be treated as such.

Whilst the FLN/ALN was a new and unknown force in the last months of 1954, it had not emerged from a political void and was the final product of the long history of Algerian nationalism.[43] Ever since 1830 the history of Algeria had been punctuated by unrest and periodic insurrections, but the rebellions of the past had always been regionally or tribally based. There had never been a countryside insurrection. After the repression of 1945, small groups of fighters like Ouamrame had taken to the mountains of Kabylia and the Aurès, where traditions of banditry were strong. The remote mountain regions – some of which had rarely seen a French official, much less a French settler – were home to the so-called 'bandits of honour' whose traditional codes of honour and vendetta had brought them into conflict with the authorities. Tolerated and even supported by the local population, they had never posed a serious threat to colonial rule but can be seen as typical 'primitive rebels'.[44] After November some of these groups became the nuclei of the ALN's guerrilla forces.

The FLN itself both grew out of and broke with the earlier tradition of nationalism. The father-figure of Algerian nationalism was Messali Hadj, who was born in Tlemcen in 1898.[45] As a young emigrant working in France, he joined the newly founded and Communist-dominated Etoile nord-africaine ('North-African Star') in 1928. The Etoile was declared a proscribed organization in 1929, but resurfaced again and again in different guises. Messali himself was always a dominant figure, but soon moved away from any kind of communism or class analysis and began to redefine Algerian nationalism in terms of an Arab-Islamic identity. In March 1937, he founded the Parti Populaire Algérien (PPA) or Algerian People's Party, which called for the complete emancipation of Algeria and demanded internal autonomy in political, economic and administrative terms, but also stressed that an emancipated Algeria would be part of a French system of collective security.[46] The PPA was promptly proscribed, and Messali spent years either in prison or under house arrest. In 1946, his followers established a new organization known as the Mouvement pour le Triomphe des Libertés Démocratiques (MTLD), which was actually the PPA under another name. Its political style was characterized by an angry populism or workerism that was more in keeping with Algerian realities than Ferhat Abbas's reformism, and five of its candidates were elected to the Assemblée algérienne in 1948. A different current now began to emerge.

After the Sétif massacres, a minority within the nationalist movement began to argue that armed struggle was the only means of achieving independence and formed a clandestine 'special organization' under the command of Ben Bella, who gives his own account of its history in a series of interviews with the novelist Robert Merle.[47] After an acrimonious emergency congress held in 1949, the MTLD voted to make most of its funds available to the Organisation Spéciale. In a further attempt to raise funds for the purchase of arms, the OS decided to raid the Oran post office. The raid itself was successful, but netted much less money than had been hoped. Poor organization, lack of experience and sheer bad luck on the OS's part meant, however, that it was quickly rolled up by the police. Ben Bella, who had planned the raid but did not actually take part in it, was arrested in 1950 but escaped two years later. Those members of the OS who escaped the attentions of the police went underground and eventually became the nucleus of Comité Révolutionnaire pour l'Unité et l'Action (CRUA).

By 1953, the MTLD was again badly divided and in a state of open crisis. The Central Committee was engaged in a bitter conflict with Messali and his supporters, who were accused of being authoritarian and of fostering a personality cult. The issue of political versus revolutionary means of struggle created further divisions, but the widening split also reflected geopolitical differences as Messali's power base had always been in the immigrant community in France rather than in Algeria itself. Messali himself had been released from prison in 1946 but was living under virtual house arrest and had effectively lost contact with the nationalist movement he had helped to found.

In the summer of 1954, a new clandestine organization was founded in an attempt to find a 'third way'. This was the mysterious CRUA which had come to the notice of police spies. Within weeks of its foundation, the CRUA had concluded that the political path was leading nowhere and had begun to prepare for November. The CRUA consisted of a twenty-two-strong Comité de Coordination et d'Exécution, which elected an executive of six and nominated three other exiled members. The six were Mohamed Boudiaf, Moustapha Ben Bouliad,[48] Mourad Didouche, Belkacem Krim,[49] Rabah Bihat and Larbi Ben M'Hidi;[50] the three exiles living in Cairo were Ahmed Ben Bella – the only member already known to the police – Hocine Ait Ahmed[51] and Mohammed Khider.[52] They are collectively known to Algerians as the nine *chefs historiques* of the FLN and its revolution.

The FLN was a 'front' and not a political party. All Algerians were invited to join its ranks, irrespective of their class background or individual beliefs, but they were required to do so on an individual basis. Insistent that it was the sole representative of the Algerian people and determined to be the sole 'valid interlocutor' in any negotiations with France, the FLN was not prepared to enter into alliance or pacts with other organizations. Individual members of Ferhat Abbas's moderate Union Démocratique du Manifeste Algérien and of the Parti Communiste Algérien (PCA) (most of whom were Algerian-born Europeans) were encouraged to rally to the FLN but it would not tolerate organizational rivals and was quite prepared to eliminate them. In July 1955, the PCA decided to throw itself into the rebellion, but on its own terms. It established its own military wing – the Combattants de la Libération – but this was soon eliminated by the French army. Shortly afterwards, the PCA announced its own dissolution and integration into the FLN. Abbas finally joined the FLN early in 1956 and was elected to the leadership in August of the same year. Messali refused to support the November insurrection and his response to the rise of the FLN was to establish a Mouvement National Algérien, which had its own military apparatus. A civil war began to be fought within the war of national liberation. For the FLN, Messali was simply a traitor, but the internal civil war was a naked power struggle rather than a conflict born of ideological or political differences. The FLN – and Fanon – took a *tabula rasa* view of both history and its own struggle: 1954 was the year zero in which a new period of history began. According to the platform of the Soummam Conference, Messali was an irrelevance. Algerian nationalism was a product of the natural evolution of a people that had finally shaken off its lethargy, and Messali's claim to be its founder was illegitimate. The rising of the sun was not brought about by the crowing of the cock, and Messali could take no credit for the inevitable victory of the Algerian revolution.[53] He was simply written out of history. After independence Messali Hadj lived in France, but was grudgingly granted Algerian citizenship at his own request in 1965. He was not, however, allowed to return to Algeria and died in France in June 1974.

On arriving in Blida in late 1953, Fanon had no local contacts and little or no local knowledge. He did not speak Arabic or any of the

Berber languages. In that respect at least, he did have something in common with the resident French population. It was perfectly possible to live and work in Algeria for a long time with a linguistic ability that was restricted to giving orders to a 'Fatma' or a 'Mohammed'; the underlying assumption was that, as all Algerians belonged to 'the same species' they needed 'only one forename'.[54] Living inside the walls of a hospital, Fanon was relatively isolated from the local population and encountered its representatives in a clinical and not a social context. Hostile to – and distrusted by – clinicians associated with the Algiers school, he was closer to the few 'liberals' recruited from the metropolis who worked alongside him. When Fanny Colonna visited Blida as a psychology student interested in learning something of the institutional psychotherapy she had heard was being practised there, she gained the intuitive impression that Fanon was trying, like her, to establish contact with the 'Centralists' of the MTLD, but there are no documentary records to either prove or disprove this. Fanon certainly could not have predicted the sudden emergence of the FLN at the end of October 1954, and it is generally accepted that his first real contacts with that organization were made in early 1955.[55] Clandestine organizations are, by their very nature, difficult to contact but they themselves have little difficulty in contacting those they wish to meet. Given Fanon's notorious insistence in *Les Damnés de la terre* that the only revolutionary forces in Algeria were the landless peasantry and the dispossessed wretched of the earth who had crowded into the shanty towns around the cities, it is ironic that his original links with the FLN were established in a very different milieu.

Like Charles Geronimi, Pierre Chaulet and his wife Claudine were amongst the few Algerian-born French people to sympathize with the FLN from the outset and to regard themselves as Algerian in the sense that their roots and future lay in Algeria. Pierre Chaulet was a young Catholic doctor whose father had a long history of involvement with the Christian trade-union movement. He himself had been active in a series of small groups that tried to bridge the gulf between the Arab and European communities.[56] It was through these groups that he came into contact with Salah Louanchi, a member of the Central Committee who became the fiancé of his sister Anne-Marie (the couple were married in Fresnes prison while Louanchi was being held there). Both young men had been active in the scout movement,[57] in student politics and, most significantly, the Association de la Jeunesse Algérienne pour l'Action Sociale (AJAS – Algerian Youth Association for Social Action). AJAS was essentially a small discussion group based at the University of Algiers. Chaulet describes how difficult it was for a 'mixed' group to function in the early 1950s: 'In those days, it was pornographic to say that there were *bidonvilles* in Algeria. It was more respectable for a bourgeois to have three mistresses than to mix with Arabs.'[58] A *bidon* is a metal jerrycan, and a *bidonville* is a town built from cans that have been flattened and used as building material. In 1954, there were one hundred and forty *bidonvilles* in Algiers and its suburbs, and they housed 35,000 people or almost one in four of the Muslim population.[59] Young men like Leounachi knew all about the *bidonvilles*; their European comrades now discovered their existence for themselves. They also discovered what 'a wage' meant in Algeria: 'Four walls of dried mud, a sheepskin on an earthen floor, the bread and the figs that provide the calories needed for physical survival and a ten-hour working day. Shanty towns, people living in caves, malnutrition, filth, illiteracy.'[60] In France, the sight of a five-year-old sleeping on the streets would have caused a scandal; in Algeria, it was so commonplace that no one noticed. One member of the AJAS circle described the depersonalization of the Algerian population in terms very close to those of the analysis Fanon was to make in *Les Damnés de la terre*: 'It is the Arab who is "other" . . . He is other than man. And that is why the underlying feeling that provides the basis for colonial racism is a feeling of exclusion or negation. No one hates Arabs. They know nothing about them. No one wants to know. Every detail of colonial life in Algeria is marked by this exclusion.'[61] Francis Jeanson had made the same point in 1950: 'The existence of individual Arabs is replaced by the essence of Arab . . . the native, the Other, absolutely other, inescapably different.'[62]

The prime mover behind AJAS was André Mandouze, born in Paris in 1916 and, from 1946 onwards, lecturer in classics at the University of Algiers where Josie Fanon attended some of his courses. A devout Catholic and an expert on St Augustine, Mandouze was an unusual academic. Adopting a practice he had introduced at the beginning of his career in Lyon, he would take small groups of students on what might be called 'reading parties'. In the summer, they would spend a fortnight by the sea, combining the study of the classics with swimming, dancing and experiments in self-catering that came as a total surprise to young European women who had never had to cook for themselves. In the winter, they went skiing in the mountains near Blida. Elements of scouting, intensive study and leisure activities were combined in an attempt to bring students and teachers together, and to extend their horizons beyond a narrowly defined academic world. Although Mandouze's pedagogical experiments were approved and even partly financed by the educational authorities, they would have been most unusual in any university in metropolitan France; in Algiers they bordered on the revolutionary.[63]

It was from this milieu and these activities that AJAS emerged. Mandouze was one of the few Europeans who found it more than respectable to mix with Arabs. In a bitterly ironic article written after spending a year and a half in Algiers, he described the apprenticeship in day-to-day racism that any 'Francaoui' (and any Martinican doctor) was expected to undergo:

I've been living in Algeria for a year and a half. What could I know about it? I've yet to understand that, in Algeria, day to day racism, the racism of the tram and the market, is not a right but a duty. I've yet to begin calling all the natives I need to satisfy my every whim 'Mohammed'. I've yet to understand that a pregnant Moorish woman finds it less tiring to stand in a trolley-bus than a European woman in the same condition. I've yet to succeed in understanding that, for Arabs, filth is a hygienic necessity. I'm still not scandalized that someone has seen fit to give Muslim children the same milk as European children. I've not been wise enough to let them convince me that including native workers in the Social Security plan would be a disaster for all of us, and for them in particular. I still don't believe that the only characteristics of Arabs are that they are lazy, degenerate and thieves. I still believe that Arabs are men and, fool that I am, rather than seeing them just as *pinsons* or *ratons,* I still find it hard to call them *tu.* Corollary: since I've been in Algeria, I've not forgotten that, for four years, we fought anti-Semitism.[64]

'Fighting anti-Semitism' might be thought an over-generous description of Allied goals during the Second World War, but Mandouze was one of the founders of *Témoignage chrétien* ('Christian Witness'). This was the major organ of the Christian resistance movement, and groups involved in its networks had indeed saved Jewish children from deportation and death.[65] The first volume of his memoirs is entitled *From One Resistance to Another*, and Mandouze still regards his commitment to the Algerian cause as a logical continuation of his Resistance activities.

Between 1950 and 1951, Mandouze and AJAS published a Roneotyped journal entitled *Consciences algériennes* which folded after three issues 'for lack of subscribers';[66] in 1954 it was succeeded by *Consciences maghrébines*, which somehow survived until the summer of 1956. Both journals are now very difficult to obtain – the only full runs are probably those in Mandouze's own possession – and appear not to have been studied in any detail, but the titles of the dossiers published in the *Consciences maghrébines* certainly indicate that AJAS was raising potentially dangerous issues: 'Unemployment in Algeria'; 'The French of North Africa and Public Health in Algeria'; 'The Muslims of North Africa and Algerian Workers in France'; 'Young People in Algeria'.[67] Issue 6–7 (December 1955) was entitled 'Our Fight' and abandoned the earlier thematic approach: 'The documents we are publishing today are neither statistics about standards of living nor analyses of milieus. The main goal of our "dossiers" is to explain what is going on. And what is going on in Algeria is a WAR.'[68] The documents in question were reprints of FLN statements and leaflets.

Fanon's sole contribution to *Consciences maghrébines* was a very short piece on ethnopsychiatry published in the Summer 1955 issue.[69] Apparently written in some haste and unsigned, it draws on the theses of 'Le Syndrôme nord-africain' of 1952, makes damning use of quotations from Porot and other members of the Algiers school and can, in retrospect, be seen as an early version of the chapter of *Les Damnés de la terre* devoted to 'Colonial War and Mental Illness'. It is accompanied or introduced by a note from an unidentified 'Parisian lawyer' who may well have been Marcel Manville. It provides an accurate summary of Fanon's argument:

This racism, which people living in the Maghreb know well either because they are its victims, silent witnesses to it or because they are involved in it, even affects supposedly 'scientific minds'.

Simply putting together texts or medical publications on the psychiatry of North Africans provides an adequate picture of a racism with scientific pretensions.

In this connection, we should take note of a few facts that make one think about psychiatric practices in the Maghreb.

1. There is no autochthonous psychiatry.

2. Psychiatry's essential weapon is psychotherapy, or in other words a dialogue between mental patient and doctor. In Algeria, many psychiatrists do not speak the language.

3. The psychological tests used are tests used in European countries, and they take no account of the culture, sociology or living conditions of the Algerian masses.

Fanon's own article is very short – it does not even run to two full pages of A4 – and whilst its content includes nothing that he had not said in 1952, it is a significant document. No other journal in Algeria would have published this sharp attack on the psychiatrists of the Algiers school, and it provides concrete evidence that Fanon was close to the AJAS group and Mandouze at this time. It is a clear marker of the path that brought him into contact with the FLN.

It has been claimed that one of Fanon's first actions in Algeria was to give a public lecture on racism at the University.[70] Mandouze thinks this most unlikely, and suggests that Fanon may have given a talk to an AJAS study group but has no specific memory of his doing so.[71] Alice Cherki, who worked as an intern at Blida in 1956–7 and who is now a psychoanalyst in Paris, does recall Fanon speaking to a 'Muslim scout organization' on the topic of anxiety. This was, she thinks, early in 1955. Fanon displayed a good academic knowledge of his subject, but Cherki sensed that his talk was also based on personal experience. She further recalls that Fanon himself made a great impression on an audience of young people in search of a personal and collective identity, and bored with talk of both the class struggle and Camusian gloom.[72] Whatever the truth of the matter, no trace of the lecture or talk has survived. To have attempted to lecture on racism at the University of Algiers in 1955 would have been highly dangerous, and whilst Fanon could be brave to the point of recklessness, he did not deliberately court disaster. Of the 5,146 students enrolled at the University in 1954, 4,548 were Europeans,[73] and they would not have taken kindly to being lectured on racism by a black doctor from Martinique.

The explosions of November 1954 posed a serious dilemma for the young Europeans involved in AJAS, and the issue was no longer one of fraternity across the ethnic divide. They had already been told by their Algerian comrades: 'If it does come to taking up arms, you Europeans will take them up together with us.'[74] Neither Mandouze nor Chaulet picked up a gun. Mandouze became an outspoken supporter of the Algerian Revolution and eventually published an anthology of FLN documents which gave a certain French left its first real insights into that organization's thinking.[75] His extensive political contacts on both sides of the Mediterranean also allowed him to become an informal go-between between the FLN and the French government. Chaulet picked up his car keys and his medical bag. He and his wife had reportedly paid for the Roneo machine used by the FLN to print its first leaflets, and their 2CV was now pressed into service to transport weapons, drugs and FLN militants. Their home became a safe house. One of the first beneficiaries of their solidarity was Azzedine, who had been badly wounded in the knee during an attack on a village defended by Muslim auxiliaries. Chaulet treated him, provided false papers so that he could be admitted to a private clinic for further care and then arranged for his escape into the mountains above Blida.[76]

According to an unpublished account written by Charles Geronimi, Fanon's first contacts with the FLN came via a humanitarian association known as 'Amitiés algériennes' ('Algerian Friendships') which grew out of the AJAS milieu in the early stages of the war.[77] Its ostensible purpose was to provide material and financial aid to the families of political prisoners, but it was actually controlled by nationalists who 'were in contact' with the FLN itself. Amitiés algériennes's activities were originally restricted to Algiers itself and, when it attempted to establish itself in Blida too, Fanon's name was put forward as a possible contact. He had not signed his article in *Consciences maghrébines*, but it must have been obvious to anyone with a knowledge of psychiatry or medicine in Algeria that he was the author. It had also become known that he had taken an openly anti-colonialist stance during debates at the hospital's ciné-club. Fanon's name was already known to Chaulet, who had reportedly read *Peau noire, masques blancs* and passed it on to Louanchi. When Chaulet received a message from the *maquis* saying that some fighters were having 'mental problems' and required what would now be called counselling, Fanon was the obvious and willing candidate to supply it. His growing commitment to the nationalist movement took the classic pattern of an initial contact, the rendering of minor 'favours' and the establishment of both trust and deeper involvement. The main intermediary between Fanon and the FLN was Mustapha Bencherchali, the son of a rich tobacco grower from Blida,[78] and the proud owner of a large American convertible which he drove through army roadblocks, fully and rightly confident that no one would stop such an obvious member of the local bourgeoisie. He maintained regular contact with Fanon, using the pretext of undergoing a course in psychotherapy to visit the hospital quite openly. Through Bencherchali, Fanon now came into contact with the FLN's local commanders Sadek (whose real name was Slimane Deilès) and Azzedine. A number of accounts suggest that FLN representatives, including Louanchi, were first welcomed into the Blida hospital when they attended a meeting in Fanon's quarters there in February 1955.[79]

Fanon did apparently contemplate taking up the gun and going into the mountains as early as January/February 1955,[80] but never did so. He was a trained soldier who had shown great bravery under fire, and would have made a good fighter. It was certainly not fear that prevented him from taking up arms. His son Olivier recalls his father's friends recounting how he would repeatedly challenge roadblocks by driving fast at them in his Simca, stopping only at the last moment in a calculated and highly dangerous gesture of insolence. Marcel Manville liked to tell similar stories. Fanon's recklessness could easily have had fatal consequences, as the French conscripts who manned the roadblocks were nervous and apt to fire first and ask questions later.

Fanon was more useful to the FLN in Blida than he would have been in the hills. A walled psychiatric hospital is, for most of its inmates, a place of incarceration, but it can also be a place of safety and sanctuary. The introduction of a day clinic with an open-door policy meant that anonymous Algerians could come and go with relative ease, and that wounded fighters could be smuggled into the wards. The hospital also had a small operating theatre where minor surgery could be carried out. Lacaton and Geronimi had no scruples about turning a blind eye to, or even assisting in this clandestine work, and the locally recruited nursing staff were sympathetic. One of the FLN's recurrent problems was that of procuring even rudimentary medical supplies for the field hospitals like the one established in the Koranic school in the hills between Blida and Médéa.[81] Pharmacists could no longer supply Algerian customers with penicillin, streptomycin or even cotton wool unless they could produce a prescription, and they were 'strongly advised' to inform the police of the identity of the purchaser and the address of the patient. Despite vigorous protests from the Ordre des médecins in Paris, doctors were required to inform the authorities if they were approached by Algerians with 'suspicious wounds'.[82] Given that virtually all doctors in Algeria belonged to the *pied noir* community, the vast majority of them happily complied with the new regulations. Drugs and other supplies found their way from Blida to the FLN's primitive field hospital; in exile in Tunis, Fanon sometimes spoke of having made up morphine capsules for it with the help of the hospital pharmacist.

Outside the hospital, the war that no one had expected continued. After the initial Bitter Orange, which was a police operation, the main French operations were those codenamed Véronique and Violette and were described as exercises in *ratissage* or 'combing'. These were broad sweeps through Kabylia and the Aurès mountains. Designed to eradicate or comb out an elusive enemy, they proved to be frustrating and the later policy of *quadrillage* proved much more effective. Pitched battles were rare. Influenced by the example set by Giap in Vietnam, the ALN fought in small units (*katiba* or companies with a nominal strength of one hundred fighters) which avoided contact with the French except when they could ambush patrols and then vanish into the hills. They made no attempt to build and hold liberated areas, and moved mainly by night and on foot. They were not well armed and rarely had the opportunity to eat hot food. Their weapons were either taken from the French dead or looted during attacks on farms and small garrisons. The fighters were, on the other hand, extraordinarily tough; units under the command of the skeletal Aït Hamouda, who was better known as Amirouche, were reputedly capable of covering seventy kilometres in a day across very difficult mountainous terrain.[83]

The French could use armour and trucks to control the main roads but had little hold on the rural areas where horses and mules were of more use than vehicles. Main-battle tanks were of no help in the mountains, but lighter armoured cars and half-tracks could be deployed to good effect. Airborne napalm strikes were used to destroy ALN positions, even though this was technically illegal. Rather than eradicating the ALN, *ratissage* forced young men into its ranks. The adoption of the principle of 'collective responsibility' had a similar effect: when telegraph poles were cut down, the nearest village was held collectively responsible for paying for their replacement, and all males were 'removed' or herded into internment camps. The killing of a French soldier could lead to the destruction of an entire village. More and more Algerian men of fighting age began to take to the mountains. At this stage, the FLN/ALN was less interested in holding territory than in establishing its political presence. An article published in *El Moudjahid* in 1958 to mark the fourth anniversary of November explained that the goal of the insurrection was not to provoke decisive clashes with the enemy, but to establish the FLN's structures: the strategic imperative was 'the organization of the people and the dissemination of patriotic slogans'.[84] It only in the summer of 1955 that a major insurrection was launched in the east of Algeria.

The insurrection was launched on 20 August 1955, and the violence reached appalling levels on both sides. The FLN's response to collective repression was to take collective reprisals on the European civilian population. The worst atrocities occurred in Ain-Abid, to the east of Constantine, where a woman was disembowelled, her small baby hacked to death and placed in her reopened womb, and at El Halia, a pyrite mining centre near Philippeville (now Skida). Here, Algerians armed with axes, agricultural implements and knives massacred Europeans they had known for years. In Philippeville itself, grenades were thrown into cafés and motorists were slashed to death after having been dragged from their cars.[85] Seventy-one died. A ten-year-old who survived the El Halia massacre later described it in a harrowing autobiographical novel:

Possessed by a furious madness, the assailants were running around, calling to one another, killing, coming and going, cutting throats, raping women, breaking things, burning, destroying things. Axes broke down doors, knives cut and let the red blood flow into the sand . . . The death of El Halia was murder in the pure tradition of the blood that the sand has drunk here throughout the night of time. And the weapons – like the axes and the knives – are the symbol of death on the cheap.[86]

In the reprisals that followed, the troops of the 18th Régiment de chasseurs parachutistes did not trouble to take prisoners and made no distinction between 'civilians' and *fellaghas*. A participant describes what happened when the French army caught up with a mixed group of *fellaghas* and fleeing Arab civilians:

We opened fire into the thick of them, at random. Then as we moved on, our company commander finally gave us the order to shoot down every Arab we met . . . For two hours all we heard was automatic rifles spitting fire into the crowd. Apart from a few dozen *fellagha* stragglers, weapons in hand, whom we shot down, there were at least a hundred and fifty *boukaka*. At midday, fresh orders: take prisoners. That complicated everything. It was easy when it was merely a matter of killing.[87]

In Philippeville, young Arabs were herded into the football stadium, where an unknown number of them were machine-gunned to death. At least 2,000 Algerians were killed in the next fortnight, many of them by armed civilian militias.

Philippeville marked a turning point. It was now apparent that the FLN and the ALN were actively present in at least half of Algeria. In military parlance, an area in which they were active was said to be 'rotten' (*pourri*), and the rot – the metaphor of smallpox was also used – was now spreading dangerously. More worrying still, it was also apparent that the FLN enjoyed the tacit support of the government of Tunisia, which gained its internal autonomy on 3 June 1955 and which was due to become fully independent in March 1956. Tunisia was aiding the ALN by allowing it to establish bases on its territory and to use it as a safe haven. Cross-border raids were becoming more frequent. Arms were also moving across the border to supply the ALN forces in the Aurès and the northern Constantinois. To anyone familiar with the history of the Indochina campaign, the situation looked sinister: a rebel army was establishing deep political roots and cross-border safe havens were allowing a build-up of more substantial forces with much better weaponry than that available to most FLN fighters inside Algeria, who rarely had anything heavier than machine guns and mortars. The classic scenario seemed to be emerging: a build-up of forces in safe havens, an escalation of the scale of the fighting and a transition to mobile warfare followed, eventually, by a new Dien Bien Phu. French strategists were quite familiar with the scenario, and were determined that it would not be realized. The eventual solution would be to seal the borders with Tunisia and Morocco; for the moment, *quadrillage* was used to stop the rot from spreading and the state of emergency was extended to cover the whole of Algeria.

The FLN's Military-Political Organization consisted of six-man cells, which gradually infiltrated every aspect of life in the countryside, and they were difficult to dislodge. Recruitment was by word of mouth, but acceptance into the ALN was conditional upon killing an enemy. Killing was a proof of commitment, and it meant that there was no going back. The social structure of the clans and extended families of rural Algeria meant that the actions of one individual compromised all members of his or her family, but it also bound together the fighters and the wider community. Terror was also used to demonstrate the ALN's growing power. *Caïds* and local officials were regularly assassinated, often with horrific cruelty. The slitting of throats became a speciality – French troops saw so many bodies with their throats cut that they began to refer to a slit throat as 'the Kabyle smile'. Internal discipline was strict and was enforced by brutal methods. The ALN's soldiers were forbidden to smoke or drink,[88] and breaches of discipline were, particularly in 1955–6, punished by the slitting of noses and the excision of the lips. Whatever the psychiatrists of the Algiers school may have had to say about such practices, they were not instances of an innate sadism. They were in part symbolic practices. The cutting of a throat dehumanized the victim – this is how a sheep or goat is slaughtered, and not how a man dies – and the nose is, according to Kabyle tradition, the seat of a man's honour (*nif*) and pride. The mutilated individual was indelibly marked with the sign of his disgrace, but also with the sign of a primitive, if summary, sense of justice.[89]

In an attempt to combat the growing strength of the FLN's Military-Political Organization, the French began to establish a parallel system of Sections Administratives Spéciales (SAS) from 1956 onwards. Commanded by young lieutenants or captains who reported to the civil authorities, these small units were officially designed to improve living conditions in rural villages by providing medical care, building or repairing schools and thereby winning the local population over to France. The creation of the SAS was part of an attempt to introduce at least some social reforms in Algeria, but the 600 units were also designed to help in the general task of 'pacification' by winning hearts and minds. The SAS was the brainchild of Jacques Soustelle, who was appointed Governor General by Prime Minister Mendès France in February 1955. Soustelle was an anthropologist, a recognized expert on Aztec and Mayan civilization and a liberal Gaullist. He had also been the head of the Free French secret service and de Gaulle's Minister for Information. He was convinced that the solution to the 'Algerian problem' was integration into France: Algeria had to become more French, and France had to be more liberal towards Algeria. The schools and clinics built by the SAS were designed to foster that integration and to promote that liberalism.[90] Soustelle's liberalism was soon eroded by the horrors of the war. Speaking at the funeral of a murdered civilian administrator in May 1955, the Governor General actually spoke of taking revenge.[91] The Philippeville massacres completed his conversion to the *pied noir* cause.

Many SAS officers were idealists who still believed in France's civilizing mission; others used tortured bodies in a vain attempt to win hearts and minds. The SAS also had to coexist alongside the Dispositif-Opérationnel de Protection. It was responsible for intelligence-gathering, and the DOP's mode of gathering intelligence was to use torture systematically. The diaries of Mouloud Ferraoun, who was by no means sympathetic to the FLN, contain an anecdote that illustrates the contradictory effects of these policies. A young girl had fallen from the top of a dome covering the communal fountain in his village in Kabylia, injured her head and lapsed into a coma. Her father was also in a coma because he had been tortured by the DOP and would eventually die from his injuries. On hearing of the accident, the child's mother gave birth to a premature baby and then lost consciousness. The army decided to save the girl and called in a helicopter. She was placed in the arms of a soldier who was ordered not to move a muscle until she reached hospital. Her life was saved but she lost the power of speech and could only smile at her mother when she was returned to the village. Feraoun commented that, if she did recover the power of speech, the first thing she would do would be to ask for her father. And the second would be to curse those who had saved her while he was dying. The soldiers involved were fully aware that the innocent they had saved was the daughter of the man who had been killed.[92] It is not difficult to understand why it was so hard for the SAS to eradicate the FLN's structures.

Despite his growing involvement with the FLN, Fanon was still working hard as a practising psychiatrist intent upon creating a psychiatry appropriate to Algerian conditions. Not surprisingly, there was little time for family life, even after the birth of Olivier but, given Fanon's conviction that bringing up children was a mother's concern, work and other commitments probably made little difference in that respect. He was not as 'semi-detached' from family life as his own father had been, but he did take a traditional (and very Martinican) view of the division of labour within the family, though he also argued that mothers should be granted very long periods of paid maternity leave. The experiments with lithium citrate went on. The papers describing what had already been achieved in Blida would be presented at the Bordeaux meeting of the Congrès des médecins aliénistes et neurologues at the end of August 1956; Fanon would become a full member of that organization in July of the same year, when his application was sponsored by doctors Daumézon (Sainte-Anne) and Lambert (Bassens-par-Chambéry).

There was as yet no indication that Fanon would soon take a decision that would put an end to any possibility of a career in French psychiatry. Although he wrote little on non-clinical topics during his time in Algeria, his article on 'Antillais et Africains' had appeared in the February 1955 issue of *Esprit*. The date of composition is not known, but Martinique was not his main preoccupation in the first year of the Algerian war. His true concerns emerge from some fragmentary correspondence. In November 1955, Fanon was unexpectedly contacted by Daniel Guérin, a tireless activist on the far left fringes of the Socialist

Party, a veteran of many an anti-colonial campaign and an early expo-
nent of a variety of gay liberation.[93] Guérin was about to publish a
book on the West Indies and wanted Fanon, whom he described as a
'great Martinican writer', to address a meeting he was organizing in
Paris on 27 November to discuss colonialism in the Caribbean. Fanon
declined the invitation, explaining to Guérin that 'he was sorry he could
not be with us that night, firstly because "Algeria was a long way off"
and secondly because, the next day, he was due to speak in a debate
about "fear in Algeria".' He added: 'Very much a matter of the
moment, that problem' and expressed the wish that Guérin's meeting
would be a good one. This may be a reference to the lecture on anxiety
mentioned by Alice Cherki and others, and fear was certainly on the
agenda. Three months later, Fanon wrote once more to Guérin to
describe his fears for the coming months. His tone was now apocalyptic, and it was to remain so:

> Every passing hour is an indication of the gravity and imminence
> of the catastrophe . . . For the European civilians, there is obvi-
> ously only one solution: transforming themselves into soldiers.
> They have sworn that, once they are mobilized and armed, they
> will teach Paris what energy means. If the general mobilization in
> Algeria demanded by the Comité de coordination is decreed,
> Algerian territory will run with blood. Armed with their knowl-
> edge of the natives, the Europeans are planning to punish suspects
> and sympathizers at once . . . We are receiving information about
> summary executions from many regions. The days to come will be
> terrible days for this country. European civilians and Muslim civil-
> ians are really going to take up the gun. And the bloodbath no
> one wants to see will spread across Algeria.[94]

Fanon hoped that his letter would be published in *France-Observateur*,
but insisted that his name must not appear in print. Guérin's influence
was not, in the event, great enough to have the letter published, but he
did tell Fanon that he had forwarded extracts to figures such as Mauriac
and Sartre.[95] Neither man is known to have commented on it. If, as
seems to be the case, this was an attempt on Fanon's part to sway left-
liberal opinion in France, it was to be the last.

The tone of the letter to Guérin is similar to that of the undated and posthumously published letter to an anonymous friend; whether or not it was actually intended to be sent to a friend, or whether Fanon was writing a note to himself, is unclear but the tone is not:

> When you told me that you wanted to leave Algeria, my friendship suddenly fell silent. Certain of the tenacious and decisive images that arose were on the entry of my memory. I watched you, and your wife by your side . . . You told me the atmosphere is changing for the worse. I have to leave . . . The roads are no longer safe. The cornfields are ablaze. The Arabs are turning nasty. There are rumours. There are rumours. Women are going to be raped. Testicles are going to be cut off and stuffed between men's teeth. Remember Sétif! Do you want another Sétif? They'll get one. Not us. You laughed as you said all this to me. But your wife wasn't laughing. And I could see through your laughter. I could see that basically you know nothing about what goes on in this country.

Fanon's explanation of what was going on in Algeria is harsh and couched in staccato phrases in which one can both hear the voice of the man who could declaim passages from Césaire's *Cahier* to such effect and that of the author of *Peau noire*: 'I want my voice to be brutal, I do not want it to be beautiful, I do not want it to be pure. I want it to be completely strangled. I do not want my voice to enjoy this, for I am speaking of man and his rejection, of the day to day putrefaction of man, and of his appalling abdication.' He describes the European schoolteacher who, in a country where only one in three Algerians could write their own names, complained about having to admit 'more little Arabs' to her school. He describes the children who shined shoes and carried parcels for a few coins and the treatment of agricultural workers: 'Millions of *fellahs* (peasants) being exploited, deceived and robbed. Picked up at four in the morning, abandoned at eight in the evening. From dawn to dusk. *Fellahs* swollen with water, swollen with leaves, swollen with a stale galette that has to last them the whole month' (here, Fanon inadvertently betrays his lack of Arabic by using a Gallicized plural; the Arabic plural is *fellahin*). He recalls the Europeans

273

who said that, if they left the country, the *mitidja* would revert to marshland in no time at all. And, like AJAS's Jean Cohen and Francis Jeanson before him, he speaks of 'Arabs ignored, Arabs pushed aside, Arabs rejected without effort. Arabs confined. The native town crushed', and of the Europeans 'who have never shaken the hand of an Arab. Never drunk a coffee with an Arab. Never discussed the weather with an Arab.' Algeria was, he wrote, 'one immense wound, a land immersed in mud, immersed in leprosy'.[96] These were the words of a man who would not be able to go on living in 'French' Algeria for much longer.

Fanon was right about the gravity of the situation in early 1956. It was to become more grave and infinitely more complicated. At the beginning of February 1956, André Mandouze returned to Algiers from Paris, where he had been discussing what he calls 'pre-negotiation proposals' drawn up by senior FLN figures with Pierre Mendès France, then a Minister without Portfolio in the Mollet government, and where he had also addressed one of the first big public meetings of protest against the war. The FLN leaders in question were, according to Mandouze himself, Abane Ramdane and Ben Youssef Ben Kedda.[97] Guy Mollet's Front Républicain government had taken power on 2 February and many hoped that it would be able to reach a negotiated settlement to end the Algerian crisis. In his election campaign Mollet had even spoken of 'an imbecilic war to which there seemed to be no end in sight'.[98] Mandouze was not convinced that Mollet was the man for the job and still insists that Mendès France would have been more successful. Events in Algiers now put an end to any hopes of negotiations or even pre-negotiations. The insurrection of November 1954 had led to total war.

On his return to the Algerian capital, Mandouze received an urgent phone call from Fanon. A woman patient he was treating on a private basis had, in the course of a session, let slip that her husband was organizing an armed commando and was plotting a very violent reception for Mollet, who was due to visit Algiers. The plan was to use 'criminal elements' recruited from the Casbah to carry out a series of assassinations which would be blamed on the FLN and followed by yet more violent repression, and to make resistance look like criminality. Mandouze does not name the individual concerned in his memoirs, but has stated in conversation that he was André Achiary; this is confirmed by Charles Geronimi. Achiary was a dangerous man, and one with a murky past. He had been a member of the Bureau Central de Renseignements et d'Action, which was de Gaulle's wartime secret service. Not a few of the corpses that found their way into the Bay of Algiers had been dispatched by Achiary's group.[99] As a reward for the services he had rendered, Achiary was appointed *sous-préfet* in Guelma and it was in that capacity that he helped to organize the civilian militias that rampaged through the area after the Sétif demonstrations of 1945.

Mandouze promptly returned to Paris to inform Mendès France of what he had learned from Fanon. Some old Free French networks from the 1940s in Algeria were reactivated, and Achiary's plot was foiled.[100] Mollet certainly received a harsh reception in Algiers from a European community which was convinced that he was about to sell out their interests by negotiating with the FLN, but the violence was contained. Mollet was greeted by a silent city in which virtually all European shops were closed. The volley of tomatoes flung at him by the mob as he tried to lay a wreath on the war memorial in central Algiers became part of *pied noir* folk history, but Mandouze's account suggests that they could easily have been replaced by more deadly missiles. Mollet's visit to Algiers was a serious humiliation. He backed down in the face of popular opposition from European Algerians by sacking the man he had appointed Resident Minister: General Catoux was deemed too liberal in Algiers, and he was replaced by the more robust Robert Lacoste. The crowd that had taunted Mollet represented a new and dangerous force, and it seriously destabilized the situation. Algiers had forced Paris to back down. The power of a mob stirred up by populist agitators could influence a newly elected government. A number of individuals in Algiers began to sense their power and were coming to the conclusion that the answer to any attempt on Mollet's part to negotiate with the FLN or to 'sell out' *Algérie française* might be a coup d'état backed by their many sympathizers in the army. One of the more dangerous advocates of the 'power of the street' was Pierre Lagaillarde, a vociferous student leader who would become a key figure in May 1958. Lagaillarde did his military service with a parachute unit and, although he had no right to do so, subsequently took to appearing in public in 'leopard' battledress. This was not to the liking of serving regulars, but it did symbolize the growing sympathy between the paras and the *pied-noir* population. For Jean-Marie Domenach, the February demonstrations indicated that the passions of the 'most aggressive' sections of the *pied noir* population now concealed the real nature of what was going on in Algeria: a war of independence which should be settled by negotiation.[101] On 12 March, the Assemblée Nationale voted 'special powers' to a government that had seemed ready to negotiate a settlement. That government was now a hostage of the Algiers mob. There was now no way out of the continuing war.

The new force in Algerian politics that emerged on 6 February was organized by men like the thirty-nine-year-old Jo Ortiz, who is said to have supplied the tomatoes that greeted Mollet.[102] He was the owner of a bar called Le Forum in Bab El Oued and was to become a major figure in the many plots and conspiracies that were hatched during the painful death of French Algeria. From now on, the centre of Algiers became the main theatre for demonstrations of support for *Algérie française*. The war memorial stood at the top of the boulevard de Laferrière, which ran down to the plateau des Glières, and at the foot of the monumental stairs leading up to the place du Gouvernement. This was the vast square outside the Gouvernement-Général's buildings. It came to be known as the Forum.

The realization that the war was going to go on, that the *pied noir* position was hardening and the repercussions of the Philippeville massacres led the FLN to take stock of the situation once more. There were internal differences to be sorted out, and general principles to be defined. Although the ALN had enjoyed considerable military success of late, its overall command structure was weak and there was a danger that it would lapse into what came to be known as *'fellaghaism'*, or reliance on peasant uprisings with no long-term strategy or sense of direction. All this was to be discussed at the Soummam Conference of August 1956. It is widely recognized that the political brain behind the conference was that of Abane Ramdane.[103] Born in 1920 in the Kabyle village of Azouza, Abane had attended the lycée in Blida and took his baccalauréat there. He did not attend university but was, by the Algerian standards of the day, a highly educated man. There were few employment opportunities for men like this and, after a brief period of military service, Abane worked as a secretary in a *commune mixte* in the

Constantinois. This was his only legitimate job; after 1947, Abane worked clandestinely for the PPA until his arrest in the spring of 1950. He was a difficult prisoner, often on hunger strike and more often still in solitary confinement. He was also very self-reliant, almost secretive, and spent a lot of his time in prison reading. Released from prison in 1955, he was almost immediately contacted by Krim Belkacem and became the FLN's main organizer in Algiers.

The conference was held in a forester's hut in the Soummam valley in Kabylia and began on 20 August. It was attended by sixteen delegates, all from the forces of the interior. Messages had been sent to Ben Bella and the other external delegates, telling them that they would be taken from Italy to Tripoli and then into Algeria. When they finally reached the Libyan capital, they learned that the conference was already over. Abane had engineered their non-attendance and ensured his own domination of the conference. After almost three weeks of debate, the Soummam 'platform' was adopted. The forces of the interior took priority over those of the exterior. The need for alliances with the Jewish minority, women's organizations, peasants, trade unions and youth groups was spelled out in some detail. The war could not, the conference concluded, be won in the countryside and had to be taken to the cities and above all Algiers. This implied the use of terrorism against civilians. The war would also have to be taken to metropolitan France. Major offensives on the diplomatic front were required to internationalize the Algerian question. The terms laid down for peace negotiations were starkly uncompromising and bore the hallmark of Abane's stubborn personality and politics: there could be no ceasefire until Algeria's full independence had been recognized. Algeria was defined as encompassing the whole of the national territory, including the Sahara. The FLN was laying claim to the major oil and natural gas reserves that had recently been discovered there.

At Abane's insistence, the conference reorganized the ALN on strictly hierarchical lines, with a definite chain of command and ranks from private to colonel; there were to be no 'generals' around whom a personality cult could crystallize. For administrative and military purposes, the country was divided into regions or *wilayas* – each under the command of a colonel with subalterns responsible for political affairs, logistics, and liaison and intelligence. Each of the *wilayas* –

Aurès-Mementchas, North Constantinois, Algérois, Oranie and Sahara (South) – was divided into smaller territorial units, each with the same command structure. Algiers itself was designated an autonomous zone. The conference also resulted in the reorganization of the FLN itself. A seventeen-member body known as the Conseil National de la Révolution Algérienne (CNRA) was created and effectively functioned as a provisional government. A five-member committee was also created to act as an executive. This was the Comité de coordination et d'exécution (CEE). The Soummam Conference thus gave the FLN and its military wing an organizational structure that was much more robust and stable than their earlier and largely improvised incarnations.

The conference represented a personal triumph for Abane Ramdane and appeared to establish him as the leading figure within the FLN. The clause stating that all decisions had to be made collectively was probably a sop to those who still believed in the principles of the Declaration of 1954, and some took the view that Abane was in fact making a bid for personal power. In the long term, the Soummam document would lead to serious divisions that resulted in Abane's death but for the moment it made him the leader of a 'hard-line' faction within a newly invigorated FLN. Most of the statements made by Fanon – and especially those on the conditions for independence and peace negotiations – when he became an FLN spokesman, can be traced back to the decisions of the Soummam Conference.

Despite his involvement with the FLN in Blida, Fanon had, for obvious reasons, yet to make any public statements on the war in Algeria. He would not do so until he was safely in Tunis after his expulsion from Algeria at the end of 1956, and it was only with the publication of *L'An V de la Révolution algérienne* in 1959 that he began to be widely perceived as a spokesman for the Algerian Revolution. His first and last appearance at a public meeting in Paris could easily have led to his identification with something rather different. Although he had been critical of the 'black mirage' of negritude in 'Antillais et Africains', he had accepted an invitation from Alioune Diop, with whom he had been in indirect contact since at least early 1953, to speak at a major international congress organized by *Présence africaine*. For this, he would receive a fee of just over 8,000 francs,[104] which was only enough to purchase eight copies of the conference proceedings.

An anonymous reporter working for the conservative *Le Figaro* noticed and commented on the African drum lying on a table in the Sorbonne's foyer, and remarked on the 'dazzling smiles' and colourful madras headscarves to be seen there,[105] but the Sorbonne was not hosting a colonial exhibition. An estimated 600 people had crowded into the Descartes lecture theatre on the morning of Wednesday 19 September 1956 for the opening sesssion of the First World Congress of Black Writers and Artists.[106] This was a long-awaited event, so important that it was widely described as the cultural equivalent to the Conference of Afro-Asian Nations held the previous year in the Indonesian city of Bandung to inaugurate the non-aligned movement. It was a warm morning and the temperature inside the theatre soon became uncomfortable. To make matters worse, many of those present chose to ignore the 'No Smoking' sign chalked on the blackboard.

The conference had taken a long time to organize and had a complex structure. Sixty-three delegates from twenty-four countries had been invited, and twenty-seven of them were scheduled to speak over the next three days. Most came from Francophone Africa and the Caribbean, the eight-strong delegations from Senegal and Haiti being the largest. The USA was represented by a six-man team made up of H. M. Bond, Mercer Cook, J. A. Davis, F. Fontane, J. Ivy and Richard Wright ((who was resident in France); the rest of the English-speaking world by small delegations from Nigeria, Barbados, Jamaica, India and Sierra Leone. Despite the large American contingent, the make-up of the Congress was a good reflection of *Présence africaine*'s constituency, as its geocultural politics have always been structured around the Paris–Dakar–Caribbean triangle. The fact that there were no women on the platform was an unfortunately accurate index of the journal's sexual politics, but went unnoticed except by Wright, who complained that 'there have been no women functioning vitally and responsibly upon this platform to mould and mobilize our thoughts' and expressed the hope that any future conference would make 'an effective utilization of Negro womanhood'.[107] The Maghreb countries were not represented. Fanon was in an odd and rather uncomfortable position. Although he was working in Algeria, had not been back to Martinique since 1952 and had recently refused an invitation to speak on the Caribbean, he was part of the Martinican delegation, together with Louis T. Achille, Edouard Glissant and Aimé Césaire.[108] All three were known to him. He had met Achille in Lyon, knew Glissant from Martinique and had been taught by Césaire, but now had little in common with them. Wright's novels are an important point of reference in *Peau noire*, and Fanon had tried to contact the author of *Native Son*, writing to him from Saint-Alban in January 1953, describing himself as the author of a study of the 'systematic misunderstanding between whites and blacks' and as working on a new study of the 'human breadth' of Wright's novels. He owned, he explained, copies of most of Wright's books, and added: 'I'd greatly appreciate your letting me know of the titles of those works I might be ignorant of.'[109] Wright does not appear to have replied, and no trace has been found of Fanon's projected essay.

The conference began late. Delays in setting up the microphone meant that it was ten o'clock before Alioune Diop, a tall man who reminded James Baldwin of 'an old-time Baptist minister',[110] could introduce Dr Jean Price-Mars, Rector of the University of Haiti and chairman of the Congress. Price-Mars spoke very briefly to declare the Congress open 'under the sign of human fraternity and solidarity'. The tacit consensus governing the Congress was spelled out in an editorial published in *Présence africaine* in December: '1. No peoples without culture; no culture without ancestors; 2 no authentic cultural liberation without a prior political liberation.' Its goal was 'To indicate, by means of a solemn demonstration, the black world's will fully to accept all its responsibilities, to play its own role and resolutely to occupy its place on the great stage of history.'[111] Césaire's negritude notwithstanding, it is difficult to apply such theses to Martinique, where, as the Fanon family history demonstrates, it is not easy to trace anyone's ancestors. And Fanon himself was far from convinced of the existence of a 'black people', acknowledging in 'Antillais et Africains', rather, the existence of an 'African people' or a 'West Indian people' and then amending 'people' to 'world'.[112]

It soon became apparent that the proceedings were to be punctuated by a number of silences signifying unspoken differences of opinion. After Price-Mars's brief introductory remarks, messages of solidarity and support from around the world were read out. The loudest applause was for the telegram from W. E. B. Du Bois:

> I am not present at your meeting today because the United States government will not grant me a passport for travel abroad. Any Negro-American who travels abroad today must either not discuss race conditions in the United States or say the sort of thing which our State Department wishes the world to hear. The government especially objects to me because I am a socialist and because I believe in peace with Communist states like the Soviet Union and their right to exist in security. Especially do I believe in socialism in Africa. The basic social history of the peoples of Africa is social-istic. They should build toward modern socialism as exemplified by the Soviet Union, Czechoslovakia of (sic) the China . . . I trust the black writers of the world will understand this and will set themselves to lead Africa towards the light and not backward toward a new colonialism where hand in hand with Britain, France and the United States, black capital enslaves black labor.[113]

The statement represented something of a snub to the American dele-gates, as it suggested that their very presence in the Sorbonne demonstrated a willingness to toe the State Department's line. No doubt they were quite justifiably worried about losing their passports, and some are said to have had other worries too.[114] Not even James W. Ivy's short paper on 'The NAACP as an Instrument of Social Change' made any further reference to Du Bois's enforced absence.

One message had a particular resonance for Fanon. Signed by Jean Sénac, Henri Krea, and written on behalf of a group of Algerian writers, including the novelists Mouloud Mammeri and Malek Haddad, and the historian Mostefa Lacheraf, it read:

> At a time when oppressed men on all continents are uniting in the same liberation struggle, this meeting becomes a symbol of their legitimate demands . . . This Congress is testimony to the vitality of cultures which, strengthened by the will of the people, are now shaking off the yoke of their exploiters, and a reminder that, with-out our cultural heritage, our freedom will be no more than

illusory. And so, in the midst of the painful events that are going on and from the heart of an atrocious war whose cost is being paid by our people, we Algerian writers assure our brother black writers and artists of our friendship and our hopes.

The appended poem by Sénac, an unusual supporter of Algerian independence in that he was a homosexual *pied-noir*,[115] was more outspoken:

> *We Algerian writers*
> *Greet the First World Congress*
> *Of Black Writers and Artists*
> *With the cry of our guns,*
> *The pain of our women*
> *And this crime:*
> *The bitterness of our children.*
> *Greet them with all the blood*
> *Of our people in our sentences.*
>
> *With the hopes of our dead and our living,*
> *With smiling misery*
> *With patient dignity,*
> *With the rage of the prisons,*
> *Greet them with the steadfast flower*
> *That springs from machine-gunned bodies.*
> *From our trepanned students,*
> *From our bombed villages*
>
> *If our poems too cannot be weapons of justice*
> *In the hands of our people,*
> *Let us remain silent.*[116]

And the Congress did remain silent about Algeria; after this appeal had been read out, nothing more was said about it. Even Fanon made only veiled allusions to Algeria. Whilst it must have been frustrating to keep silent, this was an elementary precaution. Fanon had travelled to Paris on his own papers, under his own name and with the travel permit that was now required by anyone travelling from 'French' Algeria to the metropolis, but is difficult to believe that he was not under some quiet surveillance. The US State Department was not the only governmental organization to take an interest in what was being said at the Sorbonne, and a declaration of support for the FLN could easily have led to Fanon's arrest. Besides, *Présence africaine* was simply not a revolutionary political journal and it was not about to provide a platform for declarations of solidarity with the Algerian revolution. One of the first speakers was Jacques Rabemananjana, a veteran of both the Madagascan rising of 1947 and of French prisons. He assured the audience that: 'This is not a gathering of politicians. Many reports are going to be presented on the most varied of subjects. Not one of them will deal with the truly political aspect of the problem. That decision was made by the organizing committee.'[117] The political discussions took place away from the public platform. It was at this conference that Fanon first met Mario de Andrade, who was to be one of the most important figures in Angola's long war to win independence from Portuguese colonialism. For the moment, Andrade was in exile and scraping a living as an editor and critic on *Présence africaine*.[118]

In his opening address, Alioune Diop noted that the common past linking all black writers and artists was one of slavery and then colonialism. Slavery had had a profound effect on both the lives of black people and the culture of the West. The Bandung conference had broken the centuries-old monologue of the West, and this Congress marked the intellectual epiphany of the black world. The decision to meet in Paris and to use the Sorbonne as a venue was a deliberate one. Paris was the great Mecca of Western thought and Western art; the Sorbonne, a symbol of reason and freedom. It was fitting that black writers and artists whose work was inscribed under the sign of freedom should meet there. Speaking in English on West African Nationalist Movements, Horace Mann Bond laid claim to the Enlightenment heritage and remarked: 'Here in the city of light, I find myself on sacred ground.'[119] Seen from Blida and Algiers, Paris did not look like the City of Light or the capital of the Enlightenment. In Algerian villages, many of the schools established in the course of France's civilizing mission had been taken over by the military – the school was often the largest building in a rural village – and were being used as torture centres. The fears that Fanon had expressed when he wrote to Guérin in February were being realized.

In the summer of 1956, the war had begun to move into the cities and its nature changed once more. Algiers, which had originally been part of *wilaya* IV, was now an 'Autonomous Zone' with its own military command structure headed by Abane Ramdane. The decision to direct urban terrorism against civilian targets was about to be implemented, and Saadi Yacef, originally a baker from the Casbah, was organizing the units of *fidayine* and *fidayate* that would fight the so-called Battle of Algiers the following year.[120] They included Ali La Pointe, a product of the Casbah, a pimp and a card sharp who had been recruited to the nationalist cause during a spell in prison. He was to become one of Yacef's most faithful followers and a very effective terrorist. The situation was exacerbated still further by French repression. On 19 June, the first two FLN prisoners were executed by guillotine in Algiers's Barberosse prison (now known as Serkadji), which looms over the edge of the Casbah; a further 110 fighters were to die there by the end of 1957. The first executions were a reaction to the public outrage at the Palestro massacre in May, but their effect was to worsen the infernal spiral of violence. In his last letter to his parents, the thirty-year-old Zabana Hamida wrote: 'I am writing you this letter; I do not know if it will be the last. Only God knows that. Whatever happens to me, you must not believe that it is all over because dying for God means eternal life. And dying for my fatherland is no more than my duty. Your duty is to have sacrificed the one who is dearest to you. You must not weep; on the contrary, you must be proud of me.'[121] As Zabana mounted the scaffold, his fellow prisoners swore that they would follow in his footsteps and that, with them or without them, Algeria would be free.

The FLN's response to the first executions was swift and deadly. Leaflets promised revenge and two French soldiers being held prisoner by the FLN were executed. In Algiers, Yacef unleashed his *fidayine* on to the streets of Bab el Oued, the quintessential 'poor white' quarter of the city. Any European male between the ages of eighteen and fifty-four was considered a legitimate target; no women or children were to be killed. Forty-nine civilians were killed or wounded in the space of three days in late June. The European population of Algiers was now in a state of panic: *any* Arab swathed in a burnous could be a potential assassin. The spiral of violence and counter-violence now accelerated. FLN acts of terrorism were inevitably followed by rat hunts – *raton-nades* – in which enraged European civilians took their revenge on any Arabs they could find. Those they killed were almost inevitably innocent, as Yacef's *fidayine* were pulled off the street once their work had been done. The courting of violent repression was deliberate and designed to ensure that all possible links between the Algerian and European populations were severed. The Casbah was now the FLN's urban stronghold. The drug dealers and prostitutes had either been driven out or had rallied to the FLN, and the remaining Messalites and Communists had either gone over to its ranks or had been physically eliminated. A French army attempt to bring the district under control in May had failed. On the night of 10 August, a group of European terrorists, which reportedly included off-duty members of the police, took matters into their own hands and planted a bomb outside a suspected FLN safe house in the rue de Thèbes, which was the only street in the Casbah wide enough to accommodate their get-away car. The explosion brought down the house and neighbouring buildings, killing seventy people (or seventeen, according to French sources).[122] A half-hearted police investigation did not result in any arrests. As *Présence africaine*'s Congress went ahead in Paris, Saadi Yacef was perfecting the organization of his *réseau bombes* ('bomb network'). Everything was in place for the Battle of Algiers to begin.

None of this was discussed in the Sorbonne, and the Algerian question therefore did not lead to any schisms. Those schisms that did appear were predictable, although not disastrous, and pertained to the very nature and relevance of Présence africaine's vision of the Black African heritage. Although the Congress was attended by delegates from twenty-four countries, a sympathetic report published in *Les Temps modernes* rightly noted that its emotional heartland was an appeal to the traditions of Black Africa.[123] To be more specific, it lay in what was still known as French West Africa, or in Senegal, the French Sudan (modern Mali) and Dahomey (modern Benin). Speakers like the Senegalese Senghor and the Sudanese Bâ devoted their papers to making inventories of their countries' respective cultural traditions. Senghor's contribution was a restatement of his version of negritude; Bâ's, a detailed and affectionate culture of the semi-nomadic Fulah people of the Senegal–Sudan region.[124] Both operated with an implicit – and sometimes quite explicit – dichotomy between Western or European rationality and African intuition. No mention was made of the fact that both the Sudan and Senegal were still French colonies. After listening to Senghor on 'The Spirit of Civilization, or The Laws of Negro-African Culture' and to E. L. Lasebikan's paper on 'The Tonal Structure of Yoruba Poetry', Richard Wright was forced to ask the inevitable question:

> This is not hostility; this is not criticism. I am asking a question of *brothers*. I wonder where do *I*, an American negro, conditioned by the harsh industrial, abstract force of the Western world that has used stern political prejudice against the society which Senghor has so brilliantly elucidated – where do *I* stand in relation to that culture.

His conclusion was as inevitable as his question: 'There is a schism in our friendship, not political but profoundly human.'[125] Senghor's vision of African unity was not at the forefront of Fanon's mind in September 1956 but, given his doubts about the existence of an undifferentiated 'black people', he must have had some sympathy for Wright.

Fanon was the fourth and last speaker to address the morning session held on Thursday 20 September. Whilst he was no stranger to public speaking and had spoken at major psychiatric conferences, this was the first time he had addressed a cultural gathering of this kind. It was also the last time he would speak in public in France. Fanon's topic was 'Racism and Culture' and, without troubling to make any preliminary remarks about the significance of the Congress or trying to gain his audience's good will, he began very abruptly and in typically non-com-promising style:

> A reflection on the unilaterally-declared normative value of certain cultures merits our attention. One of the paradoxes we rapidly encounter is the backlash of egocentric and sociocentric definitions.
>
> First, the assertion of the existence of human groups with no culture; then that of hierarchical cultures, and finally the notion of cultural relativity.

From general negation to singular and specific recognition. It is precisely this fragmented and bloody history that we have to outline at the level of cultural anthropology.[126]

As the published stenographic transcript is all that has survived, it is not possible to say with any certainty whether Fanon was reading a fully pre-pared paper, or whether he was improvising to some degree. He spoke in short sentences – some of them with no main verb – assembled into brief paragraphs, and the general impression is that of a man speaking with barely contained rage. Fanon did not use the first person pronoun, and did not employ any of the Martinican idioms characteristic of *Peau noire, masques blancs*. He was no longer concerned with the semi-auto-biographical account of the 'problem of the black man in the white world', and the implicit model of colonization and racism is supplied by Algeria rather than Martinique. Overt references to Algeria were few, but they were also highly significant. The argument that primitive or 'biological' racism is giving way to a cultural racism exemplified by calls to defend 'Western values' is illustrated with examples already used in the 1952 article on 'Le Syndrôme nord-africain', and they are culled from the work of the psychiatrists of the Algiers school. Talk of 'intel-lectual primitivism' was, he argued, typical of the initial phase of colonial exploitation; as the era of liberation begins, colonialism speaks of its subjects' 'medieval or even prehistoric fanaticism'.[127] When he turns to colonialism's creation of structures which are modelled on tra-ditional structures but placed under colonial supervision, he is referring to Kabylia and remarks: 'The Kabyle *djemmas* appointed by the French authorities are not recognized by the natives. They are shadowed by other, democratically elected *djemmas*. And the latter naturally dictate how the former behave most of the time.'[128] Whether or not his audi-ence realized it, Fanon was referring quite transparently to the SAS's frustrated attempts to win Algerian hearts and minds and to eradicate the FLN's organizational and political apparatus. The most blatant allu-sion to the ongoing Algerian war appears in Fanon's description of the subjugation of the indigenous population. Its 'systems of reference must be destroyed. The expropriation, the plundering, the *razzias* and the objective murders are replicated in the destruction of cultural schemas or at least a preconstruction for their destruction.'[129]

*Razzia* was a word with very powerful connotations. Borrowed from the demotic Arabic of North Africa, it means 'raid' or 'surprise attack' and originally referred to the traditional military tactics of the region's nomadic peoples. In the second stage of the conquest of Algeria, it acquired a somewhat different meaning when French flying columns began to make razzias of their own from 1841 onwards. These were designed to destroy or seize livestock and produce, partly to defeat the army of Abd el Kedar's embryonic Algerian state, and partly to feed a colonial army with poor and insecure supply lines. The classic description of the 'razzia' tactic is given by its main architect, Marshal Thomas Bugeaud:

> Crossing the mountains and beating these montagnards once or twice does not mean very much; in order to defeat them, one must destroy their interests . . . One must so arrange matters that one has enough victuals to remain there for as long as it takes to destroy the villages, cut down the fruit trees, empty the grain silos, search the ravines, rocks and caves and seize the women, the children and the old people, the flocks and the furniture: that is the only way one can make these proud people capitulate.[130]

Military history was now repeating itself in Algeria. A *rappelé* describes what he saw on 5 June 1956:

> 5 June–9 June. A major operation in Djebel S. The battalion can record at least fifteen Arabs killed to its credit. And yet we didn't see a single *fellagha*, and not a single shot was fired at us.
>
> An example from the first day. The villages we had to go through had been systematically machine-gunned and bombed, so the entire population had taken refuge in the caves and ravines. Some lads in the company found some people in a cave. One man came out with his hands in the air. A burst of fire, and he fell. The rest refused to come out. A comrade went into the cave and machine-gunned everyone in it (seven people). We dragged the corpses into a wadi to get rid of them.
>
> About fifty metres further on, the same lad came across a wounded man who was trying to escape. He finished him off with a burst of fire.[131]

As in *Peau noire, masques blancs,* Fanon went on to argue that racism is not a matter of degrees: a country was either racist or it was not.[132] Racism was not a wound that had been inflicted on humanity, but part of a wider phenomenon: 'the systematic oppression of a people . . . the destruction of its cultural values, of its modalities of existence, its language, its mode of dress . . .'[133] Racism had its own flawless logic: 'A country which lives by and draws its substance from the exploitation of different peoples, inferiorizes those peoples. The racist treatment of those peoples is normal. Racism is therefore not a constant feature of the human mind', but exploitation, razzia, collective liquidations and rational oppression 'literally turn the native into an object in the hands of the occupying nations'.[134]

Although Fanon does not mention that country by name, his concluding words make transparent allusion to Algerian realities:

A people that undertakes a liberation struggle rarely legitimizes racism. Even in acute periods of armed struggle, biological justifications are never used. The struggle of those who have been inferiorized takes place at a more obviously human level. Its perspectives are radically new. Here we have the now classic opposition between struggles for conquest and liberation struggles.

In the course of this struggle, the dominant nation tries to repeat its racist arguments, but the elaboration of racism proves less and less effective. There is talk of fanaticism and of primitive attitudes in the face of death but, once again, the mechanism has broken down and no longer serves its purpose. Those who were once immobile, the congenital cowards, those lazy beings who have always been inferiorized, brace themselves and emerge bristling.

The occupier no longer understands.

The end of racism begins with this sudden failure to understand.

The rigid, spasmic culture of the occupier is liberated, and opens up to the culture of a people that has become truly fraternal. The two cultures can confront one another, enrich one another.

To conclude; universality lies in this decision to take responsibility for the reciprocal relativism of different cultures once colonial status has been ruled out.[135]

It was now 12.20. Fanon fell silent, and the session was pronounced closed.

The discussion of the day's papers continued late into the night but Fanon's paper is not mentioned in *Présence africaine*'s transcripts of those debates. Press coverage of the Congress was extensive and on the whole sympathetic,[136] at least on the left-liberal edge of the political spectrum, but Fanon's speech was not widely discussed. The Communist Party's daily *L'Humanité* mentioned it in passing, but did not summarize its content, whilst *Le Monde* gave a brief account of the speech without naming the speaker.[137] A rather different note was struck by Jacqueline Delange in *Les Temps modernes* in 1957. She described Fanon's intervention as 'valuable' and as condensing all those aspects of the 'black problem' that were scattered throughout all the other contributions:

Fanon retraces the process of 'the liquidation of the native's systems of reference and cultural schemas'. Convinced that he is in the wrong pan of the scales, he has no choice and 'pounces on the culture that has been forced upon him'. Even when – and at what cost – the native achieves the status of equivalence or even technical and intellectual superiority, he finds no rest. He is rejected or discriminated against, and all that he can do is to cultivate his own culture. This painful schema would be incomplete if it remained purely psychological, and no one would feel concerned (again!) But Fanon makes accusations: 'The reality is that a colonial country is a racist country.' He carefully follows the successive faces of racism, which are bound up with the evolution of technologies and the progress of industrialization. We move from the shameless racism of the period of the establishment of the dominant society which breaks humanity into two – the good and the bad – to the 'exoticism' of the period of substitution, and then to the period when colonial society retreats under the pressure of new forces. Racism then has to collapse, and fraternity becomes possible.

Fanon's message is valuable. It brings together all those aspects of the black problem that are dispersed throughout the other messages. He draws up colonialism's moral balance sheet and announces a harmonious order. What is more important, he stops time, isolates the meaning of the Congress, qualifies it, evaluates it and makes all commentary superfluous: 'The native's bodily struggle (*corps à corps*) with his culture is such a solemn, abrupt operation that no faults in it can be tolerated'.[138]

Delange's reading is of interest in that it anticipates many of the early reviews of *L'An V de la Révolution algérienne* and *Les Damnés de la terre* by emphasizing the generous notion of fraternity and solidarity that underlies them. The references in the Paris speech to fraternity and a post-colonial future in which cultures will enrich one another also recall the politics of solidarity of *Peau noire, masques blancs*: the black man has to be liberated from his inferiority complex, and the white man from his superiority complex.

Despite the muted reception he had received in the Sorbonne, and despite his serious reservations about the politics and culture of negritude, Fanon was elected on to the executive committee of *Présence africaine*'s institutional offshoot, the Société Africaine de Culture. The executive committee's immediate task was to prepare for the second Congress of Black Writers and Artists, which was to be held in Rome in 1959. Fanon did speak in Rome, but cannot have played any great part in its organization; he was certainly not present at the major planning meeting held in London in July 1957.[139] Within months of his return to Algeria, his life would change drastically and *Présence africaine*'s discussions of negritude would not be relevant to it.

On his return to Blida, Fanon found that the situation was worsening by the day and that his own position was becoming more dangerous. On the evening of Sunday 30 September, the FLN exploded its first bombs in central Algiers. The targets were carefully chosen: the Milk Bar in the place Bugeaud, the caféteria in the rue Michelet and the Air France terminal. At the end of the afternoon, they would be crowded with young people returning from the beach. Planting the bombs had been difficult. The Casbah was now ringed with barbed wire, and no

Algerian man could have carried a bomb through the checkpoints. Yacef's bombers were young women who could pass for Europeans, and they were at first reluctant to carry out their mission. Yacef convinced them by describing in detail what he had seen in the rue de Thèbes in August.[140] The bomb at the air terminal failed to explode. Over sixty people, most of them young, were injured by the blast in the Milk Bar and the caféteria. Even Pierre Chaulet was appalled by the choice of targets, but Abane argued that there was no difference between a girl who planted a bomb in a café and an airman who bombed a defenceless village.[141] A week after the bombings, Abane published a statement in the FLN's newspaper: the struggle had now reached the stage of 'general insecurity', and the bombs were a prelude to a full-scale insurrection.[142]

Fanon did not see the bombs go off, but he did see the effects of the reprisals. In mid-October, he drove to Maison Blanche airport twenty kilometres outside Algiers to pick up Manville, who was in Algeria on legal business. On the morning of 16 October, the lawyer was abruptly woken up by a Fanon who was trembling with anger and barely able to speak coherently. Eventually, he managed to stammer: 'This is what the French do – common practice these days. And to think that some of my intellectual friends, who claim to be humanists, criticize me for being totally involved in this struggle.' Manville had no real idea what Fanon was talking about but got into the car without complaint. Fanon drove to a small hamlet called Cazouna, explaining what had happened as they went. During the night, a Unité térritoriale or locally recruited militia unit made up of twenty local European youths and acting on its own initiative, had descended on the village, taking away twenty men. They lined them up in the bed of a dry wadi and shot them dead in cold blood. There was only one survivor. He was a male nurse from the Blida hospital who had flung himself to the ground and had been left for dead. When he entered the village itself with Fanon, Manville noticed that, in the houses of the dead, all the mirrors had been covered up with towels or sheets, just as they would have been in Martinique. Fanon explained to the mourning villagers that Manville was a lawyer from France and that he was willing to act on behalf of the victims' families if they wished to lay complaints. No one was willing to do that. If they did so, the killers would return and take away other people from the same families. Always headstrong, but on this occasion also somewhat naive, Manville insisted on going to the town hall in Blida to complain. Fanon tried to dissuade him, warning him that he could easily be killed on one of his daily drives into Algiers. Manville took no heed, and went to the *état civil* office to obtain at least the relevant death certificates. The civil servant in charge politely refused his request on the grounds that this department held no statistics about Arabs.[143]

The repression and the violence were coming nearer and nearer to the hospital, which was now widely regarded by the authorities as a nest of *fellaghas*. Police raids were becoming more frequent, and seizure of any of the clandestine FLN propaganda material that circulated inside the walls would have led to arrests, and to all that being arrested in Algeria now meant. In the summer of 1956, Fanon's colleague Lacaton had been arrested on suspicion of collaborating with the insurgents. He was questioned at length and badly beaten before the police finally, and rightly, concluded that he was not directly involved in FLN activity. Badly injured, Lacaton was driven to a farm where he was flung into a pigsty and left there in the hope that the pigs would finish him off. He somehow survived, recovered and left Algeria at the end of the year.[144] Other staff members who had supported a strike called by the FLN in July had been subject to official sanctions. Certain of the more progressive members of Fanon's staff had followed a Communist colleague into the mountains; others had been interned by the police. Sackings and resignations were on the increase.[145]

The war had also entered the hospital in another sense. Fanon was now seeing more and more patients with psychosomatic complaints such as stomach ulcers, disturbed menstrual cycles, hypersomnia and muscular stiffness. Such complaints were both symptoms and partial 'cures', as the bodies of his patients tried to adapt to the extreme conditions in which they were living so as to avoid complete breakdowns. The hysterics and catatonics were being replaced by patients suffering from the reactive or situational psychoses triggered by the experience of violence or of torture – either as victims or as perpetrators. Despite his obvious political sympathy with the victims rather than the perpetrators, Fanon treated them all and published some of his case notes on them in the final chapter of *Les Damnés de la terre*. They were all victims of 'the bloody, pitiless atmosphere, the generalization of inhuman practices, of people's lasting impression that they are witnessing a veritable apocalypse'.[146]

Two of Fanon's patients did not present psychotic symptoms but rather a blank and almost depersonalized indifference to what they had recently done. Two young Algerian boys aged thirteen and fourteen had been brought into the hospital for a forensic interview, presumably with a view to establishing their degree of criminal responsibility in a murder case. They had killed a French boy of their own age after taking him up the hill behind their village where they used to go every Thursday to hunt birds with a sling-shot. They killed him with a knife they had taken from home. One of the boys held him while the other stabbed him. Asked why they had done this, they replied that they were not old enough to kill an adult. They had killed the boy because he was their age, and because he was their friend; no other child would have dared to go with them. Although Fanon reports having long conversations with the two, he does not go into any detail, merely records their explanations for the murder and makes no comment. Part of the dialogue between Fanon and the fourteen-year-old reads as follows:

– Tell me why you killed this boy who was your pal.
– I'll explain, Have you heard about the Rivet business?
– Yes.
– Two of my relations were killed that day. At home, they say that the French had sworn to kill us all, one after the other. Has any Frenchman been arrested for all the Algerians that were killed?
– I don't know.
– Well, no one has been arrested. I wanted to go to the *djebel* but I'm too young. So, we said with X . . . that we should kill a European.
– Why?
– What do you think we should have done?
– I don't know. But you're a child, and the things that are going on are for grown-ups.
– But they kill children too.
– But that's no reason for killing your pal.
– Well, I did kill him. Now you can do what you like.
– Did this pal do anything to you?

– No. He didn't do anything to me.

– Well?

– That's all there is to it.[147]

Fanon does not use the case of the two boys to illustrate the notorious thesis on the therapeutic value of violence that he puts forward in the body of *Les Damnés de la terre*, where he contends that: 'At the level of individuals, violence is a cleansing force. It rids the colonized of his inferiority complex, of his contemplative or despairing attitudes. It makes him intrepid, rehabilitates him in his own eyes.'[148] There is no precedent for this thesis, which became almost synonymous with the name 'Fanon', in any of his clinical writings. In his consulting room in the Blida-Joinville Hospital, Fanon was dealing as a psychiatrist with two lost boys, not with junior heroes of the Algerian revolution who have overcome an inferiority complex. And in dealing with French torturers, the doctor who could so easily have become their victim related to them as damaged individuals and not as enemies.

The most grotesque case concerned a thirty-year-old European policeman who referred himself to Fanon because he was worried about his growing propensity to violence. He had begun to smoke very heavily, kept having nightmares and was prone to outbursts of violent rage. He had violently assaulted his children, including his twenty-month-old son. When his wife protested, he tied her to a chair and beat her too. Finally, he decided that he had to consult what he called a 'nerve specialist' and came to see Fanon. In his own view, his problems stemmed from the difficulties he was experiencing at work, and his work consisted in torturing FLN suspects. As he had no intention of ceasing to be a torturer (which would have meant resigning from the police), he asked Fanon, 'without beating about the bush', to 'help him torture Algerian patriots, without having a guilty conscience, without any behavioural problems, in serenity'. Fanon does not state what became of his patient, merely commenting that his case revealed the existence of 'a coherent system which leaves nothing intact. The torturer who loves birds or enjoys a symphony or a sonata in peace is simply one stage. Beyond that stage, there is indeed an existence that is inscribed on the register of radical and absolute sadism.'[149]

One of the cases Fanon describes involved a twenty-year-old police officer (referred to by Fanon as 'A') who had been referred by his superiors because of his behavioural problems. Fanon established what he himself describes as a good rapport with his new patient, who explained that he was having difficulty sleeping at night because he kept hearing screams. They were the screams of the suspects he had tortured. He told Fanon that he could tell just which stage an interrogation had reached by the quality of the screams: 'A guy who has been punched twice in the face has a certain way of talking, screaming and saying that he is innocent. After he has been hanging by his wrists for two hours, his voice changes. After the bathtub, a different voice. And so on. But it's after the electricity that it becomes unbearable. You'd think he was going to die at any moment.' The young policeman was 'sick of it'. If Fanon could cure him, he would request a transfer to France; if he was refused his transfer, he would resign. Fanon put him on sick leave and then began to treat him as a private patient. They met in Fanon's home. Just before one session was due to begin, Fanon was called back to the ward by an emergency. Josie told 'A' that he could wait, but he replied that he would rather go for a walk in the grounds, thinking that he would meet Fanon on his way back from the ward. Fanon eventually found 'A' leaning against a tree, covered in sweat and obviously having a panic attack. In the course of his walk, he had encountered one of the prisoners he had tortured and who had been admitted to the hospital suffering from post-traumatic shock. Fanon treated 'A' with sedatives and went to the ward where his victim was being treated. The man was nowhere to be found, but was eventually discovered hiding in a toilet. He had tried to commit suicide because he had recognized 'A' and was convinced that he was about to be tortured again. 'A' saw Fanon on a number of occasions. His condition improved rapidly and he was eventually repatriated to France on medical grounds. It took a long time, remarks Fanon, to convince his Algerian patient that he had been mistaken, that the police could not enter the hospital at will, that he was 'tired' and that he was here to be cared for.[150]

Fanon's notes on the effects of torture on its perpetrators are rare and precious documents. They also paint an extraordinary picture of an extraordinary situation. A doctor who was quite possibly already under suspicion of being at least sympathetic to the FLN is consulted by a policeman, and another is referred to him by the police; Fanon establishes a 'good initial rapport' with a man who has tortured his comrades, and who could well have tortured him, had the circumstances been different. Case notes destined for hospital files were obviously not the place for political statements or comments, but there is no reason to doubt that Fanon was still trying to work as a psychiatrist who treated all his patients with the same concern. The very fact that he was able to go on treating anyone suggests either that his cover was very effective, or that the local intelligence services were quite ineffective.

The diagnostic accuracy of Fanon's notes has been confirmed by the author of one of the very few studies to have been made of the Algerian war's effect on French servicemen. In 1987, Bernard Sigg circulated an appeal asking those who had experienced psychical difficulties as a result of their actions in Algeria to contribute to a study he was making. He received very few replies, but they demonstrate the general tenor of Fanon's notes: torturers often suffer from a form of war neurosis. Sigg's informants also confirm what Fanon says in the fourth chapter of *Sociologie d'une révolution* about what doctors were expected to do, and did, during the war. A 'Dr P' is quoted as saying: 'In the space of a few months, I committed all kinds of violence, including the even more intolerable form of violence involved in the treatment and fate of a few "suspects" held captive in army posts, abandoned in cellars with no light and then "worked over" for information . . . when they were *in extremis*, we were asked to get them back on their feet.'[151] Sigg himself was a navy doctor who served in Morocco. When his predecessor told him that one of his tasks would be to keep tortured suspects alive for further 'interrogation', he deserted.

It would have been relatively easy for Fanon to have passed on the names of his torturer-patients to his FLN contacts, but he did not do so. It was only in connection with the Achiary affair that he broke doctor–patient confidentiality by informing Mandouze of how Achiary had plotted to disrupt Mollet's visit to Algiers. According to Geronimi, there was, however, more to the breach of confidentiality than a telephone call to André Mandouze. It was Achiary himself who drove his wife to Blida for her therapy sessions, and it was Fanon who set the date and time for them. There are unconfirmed reports that he informed the FLN of Achiary's movements so that a 'punitive action' could be organized. Deeply implicated in the rue de Thèbes bombing, Achiary had been sentenced to death by the FLN and had already escaped one assassination attempt.[152] He survived another in 1957.[153] The first attempt on Achiary's life took place in a street in Algiers and not in Blida, and there is no suggestion that Fanon had any hand in it. Whilst there is no independent confirmation of the story of Fanon's breach of confidentiality, it is by no means improbable. Extreme tension takes its toll on psychiatrists as well as their patients, and Fanon's next and totally irrevocable decision signalled that he had finally reached breaking point.

Much more exposed than Fanon, Mandouze had now become a hate figure in Algeria and was in a dangerous position. His dealings with Mendès France and the telephone conversation with Fanon were obviously not public knowledge, but his other actions were. In January, he had addressed the public meeting organized in Paris by the Intellectuals' Action Committee Against the Continued War in Algeria with the words: 'I was still in Algiers this morning, and I bring you greetings from the Algerian Resistance . . . I have come from the theatre of operations. It is everywhere, even in Algiers itself. There are still people who do not believe that they are passing the National Liberation Army in the streets.' And he concluded: 'If you are willing to demand it, negotiations can begin tomorrow, the fighters can hold discussions with the French government tomorrow, and two peoples can be reconciled tomorrow.'[154] This statement eventually won him a short term in prison. It could easily have cost him his life. In Algiers, a mob prevented him from entering the church where he had regularly attended mass for ten years and told him to go to the mosque if he loved Arabs so much. At the university, his students appeared with a rope, and every intention of hanging him.[155] At the beginning of April, Mandouze was transferred by the Ministry of Education to the University of Strasbourg for his own safety.

The Blida hospital was now the object of serious suspicion. Geronimi had been warned by one of his many Corsican cousins who, somewhat incongruously, worked for the police, that a major raid was being prepared, and left for Paris. Alice Cherki has recalled that Lacaton had been told by someone working in the Gouvernement-Général offices that she was to be expelled from Algeria and that Lacaton and Fanon were about to be arrested.[156] Fanon himself had begun to receive death threats from anonymous sources. He now wrote to the Resident Minister in Algiers to tender his resignation in very formal and dignified terms. Although he was about to 'become' Algerian, he addressed the Minister as an outraged French citizen. On arriving in Algeria he had, he said, already realized that objective conditions in that country meant that any attempt to practise psychiatry there would be doomed to failure. He now knew that he had been correct:

For almost three years, I have devoted myself completely to the service of this country and to the men who inhabit it. I have not been sparing in either my efforts or my enthusiasm. Every aspect of my actions demanded as its horizon the universally hoped for emergence of a viable world.

But what is enthusiasm and what is a concern for men when, day by day, reality is being torn apart by lies, acts of cowardice and scorn for man? What are intentions when their embodiment is made impossible by emotional poverty, intellectual sterility and hatred of the people of this country?

Madness is one of the ways in which man can lose his freedom. And being placed at this intersection, I can say that I have come to realize with horror how alienated the inhabitants of this country are.

If psychiatry is a medical technique which aspires to allow man to cease being alienated from his environment, I owe it to myself to assert that the Arab, who is permanently alienated in his own country, lives in a state of absolute depersonalization.

The status of Algeria? Systematic dehumanization . . .

For long months, my conscience has been the seat of unforgivable debates. And their conclusion is a will not to lose hope in man, or in other words myself.

I have resolved that I cannot face my responsibilities at any cost on the fallacious grounds that there is nothing else to be done. For all these reasons, Monsieur le Ministre, I have the honour of asking you to accept my resignation and to bring my mission in Algeria to an end.

The ministerial response came quickly. Prefectoral decree no. 3734-UR signalled Fanon's expulsion from Algerian territory.[157] There was no 'Fanon affair'. He did not attempt to publicize either his resignation or his expulsion, and nor did the authorities. The *Journal officiel* or government gazette simply noted without comment that, as of 1 February 1957, Dr Fanon had taken a year's leave of absence for personal reasons.[158]

The expulsion order may have saved Fanon's life. His departure from Blida was hurried, but its precise circumstances remain obscure. According to Geronimi, there was time for a brief clandestine meeting with Abane Ramdane and Ben Youssef Ben Khedda, but nothing is known of what was said. Such a meeting, if it did take place, would have been significant indeed as being admitted to a meeting with them signalled that the FLN's confidence in Fanon was now total; his acceptance of the invitation signalled an equally total commitment. Josie Fanon has left no account of the departure from Blida, and her son has no clear recollection of it, or even of whether the family all left together. He does recall the bomb that exploded outside their house, causing some material damage but no human casualties. He does not know who planted it. The army and police are unlikely candidates as they could simply have arrested Fanon, interrogated him and disposed of him at their leisure, but any one of the many freelance terrorist groups from the European community could have thought Fanon and his colleagues an attractive target. If Fanon's breach of confidentiality had come to Achiary's notice, he would have had no qualms about having a bomb planted but there is nothing to prove that this was the case. The major raid predicted by Geronimi's cousin came in January 1957 and within weeks of Fanon's departure in December, the Blida experiment was finally over. Some of the personnel were arrested, whilst others escaped to the mountains and began to make the painful journey on foot to Tunisia. Fanon himself went to Paris and from there, into exile.

# 8

# Exile

T HE DECISION TO resign from his post in Blida was even more irrevocable than Fanon's other sudden decisions. Despite the official
euphemisms about 'leave of absence', he was well aware that his career
as a psychiatrist in France, and even its overseas *département* of
Martinique, was over. He could not set foot in Algeria. The logical solution was either to work for the FLN in some capacity or to practise as a
psychiatrist in another French-speaking African country. Fanon did
both by going to Tunis, which was now the FLN's capital in exile.
Here, he would work as a psychiatrist and lecture on his specialism,
write for the FLN's paper *El Moudjahid* and become one of its international spokesmen, but not a member of its leadership.

Actually getting to Tunisia in the first place was no easy matter. On
leaving Blida, Fanon went to Paris after, according to one account,[1]
making a brief visit to Josie's family in Lyon. Paris was not the safest
place for someone who had made his position so clear to the French
authorities and Fanon could not stay there for long, but Marcel
Manville's apartment near the Porte de Champerret in the west of the
city provided a temporary haven. Manville recalled that the Fanon
family spent about a month there and that he did his best to persuade
his old friend not to go to Tunis. He had taken enough risks, argued

Manville, and should reserve his energies for the coming struggle in Martinique.[2] Not convinced that there was going to be any struggle in Martinique, Fanon ignored the advice, just as he had ignored that of the teacher who told him in 1943 that war burns and the widows of dead heroes marry living men. He was taken in hand by Salah Louanchi, who had been dispatched by Abane Ramdane to head the FLN's clandestine Fédération de France. Its main function was to raise funds for the war effort by taxing the Algerian community in France, but it was also fighting a vicious war against the Messalists of the MNA. The funds were smuggled by couriers into Switzerland, and FLN agents used the same routes. FLN propaganda material also found its way into France via Italy and Switzerland. Switzerland offered only relative safety; the war between the French secret services and the FLN was being fought there too.

During his short stay in Paris, Fanon had a brief encounter with Daniel Guérin, whose meeting on the West Indies he had been both unable and unwilling to attend in November 1955. He was, according to Guérin, being actively sought by the police because he had given medical aid to the FLN and had sheltered its fighters in both the hospital wards in Blida and his own quarters there. Fanon had now dedicated himself 'heart and soul' to the Algerian cause and Guérin's impression was that the adverb 'fanatically' would not have been inappropriate, especially when he heard him 'damning Messali to the flames of hell'.[3] There was also time for a short meeting with Francis Jeanson. Jeanson thought that Fanon was less of an *écorché vif* than he had been when they first met in Seuil's offices in 1952, but found him as difficult as ever and described him as 'haughty'. Fanon spoke eloquently of the terror he had experienced in Blida, where he had divided his days and nights between dealing with real madmen and false madmen, or in other words between those who had been both alienated and driven mad (*aliénés*) by colonization, and fighters who were seeking a temporary refuge. To Jeanson's annoyance, Fanon was scornfully dismissive of what was happening in France and even of the organization that was looking after him: 'He was going to Tunis and we did not exist.' Fanon's impatience to serve the Algerian cause was now so great that he saw Jeanson and his associates as no more than useful intermediaries.[4] The two men subsequently met by chance in Madrid airport and spent a long evening together in May 1959. Fanon now described Jeanson's efforts to support the FLN as 'futile' and claimed in obscurely menacing terms that he and his comrades were being manipulated by 'a military leader' they would never know. According to the philosopher, Fanon had a 'terrible need' to take the most radical option and to reject any form of action that did not have an immediate influence on the direction of the struggle.[5] In a retrospective interview, Jeanson interpreted Fanon's remarks as implying that nothing meaningful could be done by the Fédération de France until such time as it functioned as a real *wilaya* and brought the war home to France itself.[6]

The FLN was in fact already fighting a war in France, but for the moment it was a war against the Messalists, and they were fighting back. In the first nine months of 1956 alone, forty-two murders 'of a political nature' occurred in metropolitan France, and a further 618 non-homicidal attacks were reported.[7] In the first eight months of 1958, there were forty-seven killings in Lyon; in France as a whole, there was an average of two murders a day. The press regularly carried reports of machine-gun attacks on cafés frequented by Messali's supporters, and the inside pages of *Le Monde* ran two-line stories of Algerians whose throats had been cut and whose bodies had been stuffed into sacks being found in the grim streets of Paris's Goutte d'Or area. Not all of them were victims of the ongoing Algerian civil war. A student arrested and tortured by the Paris police in December 1958 was told by his captors that, should he be 'badly damaged', his body would be found in the Seine with a placard tied around his neck reading 'Traitor to the FLN'. A second student arrested at the same time reported the dialogue between the officers who had arrested him: '"What shall we do with him?" "Throw him in the Seine?" "Gangland killing." "State he's in, we'd do better to stuff him in a dustbin".'[8]

In 1956, Fanon probably knew little about the full extent of Jeanson's commitment to the Algerian struggle. When the Revolution began, the philosopher was contacted by people he had met in Algiers during his travels in 1948–9 and used them to learn more about what was happening. His wife Colette then travelled to Algeria to make 'certain contacts', which were arranged through the Chaulets. The result was a collaborative book entitled *Algérie hors la loi*, published by Seuil in the autumn of 1955. It was a solidly documented study which argued the case for Algerian independence on historical and political grounds and was one of the first to reproduce FLN leaflets and an interview with an anonymous FLN spokesman, but it was not an easy book to publish. Jean-Marie Domenach, Jeanson's fellow editor on the 'Esprit' series and soon to become a prominent figure in the campaign against the army's use of torture in Algeria, was actually opposed to its publication.[9] Domenach's objections to publishing a pro-FLN book were an index of the problems the French left had in coming to terms with the Algerian war, and of what Fanon saw as its impotence and irresponsibility.

The publication of the book inevitably led to greater involvement. FLN organizers in France were finding it extremely difficult to move around Paris and, as Jeanson put it in an interview, 'I began to act as their taxi driver. So that is how it started. It was quite simple: I helped them to move around Paris without difficulty, without running the risk of being arrested by the first traffic cop that came along. And then I gradually began to provide them with places to meet, places to stay by appealing to friends, to people I knew.'[10] In most cases, he never knew the names of the 'brothers' he was ferrying around the city. The eventual outcome of these minor but potentially dangerous activities was the formation, in October 1957, of the 'Jeanson network', which was the most important of the few small organizations that actively supported the FLN in France. The network carried suitcases for the FLN, and the suitcases were full of money collected by its tax-gatherers.[11] Jeanson became its full-time organizer, giving up teaching and going underground to live the nomadic and precarious life of the professional revolutionary. The Jeanson network did not smuggle arms for the FLN: their Algerian comrades never asked them to do so.

Given the increasing level of police repression and harassment, no Algerian could have carried a case filled with crumpled low-denomination notes and even coins. Young French volunteers could do so, albeit at considerable risk to themselves, and the money eventually found its way to accommodating Swiss banks. By the end of the war, many of these young people would identify with either Fanon himself or the composite Fanon–Nizan figure discussed in Chapter 1 above. Fanon did not identify with them. Jeanson's comment that 'he was going to Tunis and we did not exist' was an accurate insight into Fanon's state of mind in late 1956. It might, however, be more accurate still to say that it was France itself that 'did not exist' for him. Fanon never set foot in France again. Europe was no more than a staging post on journeys between African countries. Fanon's gaze was turned south to Algeria, Tunisia and beyond. In his own eyes, he was no longer French. Even in the professional domain, he had turned his back on France. He never again published in the French medical press and his clinical papers now appeared in Tunisian and Moroccan journals.

Fanon's dismissive comments to Jeanson may have been the effect of his ignorance of just how the Fédération de France operated and of the importance of its work. If that was the case, his ignorance is understandable. The FLN did not readily share its many secrets. Although it did receive financial aid from Egypt and the Arab world, the Algerian revolution was largely self-financed. In the early stages of the war, every FLN activist, member or sympathizer was required to contribute at least 1,000 francs per month; this later rose to 3,000. Algerian shopkeepers and café-owners paid at least 5,000 francs plus a percentage of their turnover. This was at a time when the average monthly salary was roughly 60,000 francs. According to the French authorities, this was extortion backed by the threat of death, and a degree of coercion was no doubt used. But it would have been impossible to coerce all of the 300,000-strong Algerian population and the FLN obviously enjoyed widespread passive support. Large sums of money were raised in this way: it is estimated that the FLN collected 463 million francs in the second quarter of 1957 alone.[12] A significant change was occurring within the Algerian community in France, and Simone de Beauvoir noticed it. She had been living for some years in a room in the rue de la Bûcherie, a narrow street in the Latin Quarter. The Café des Amis opposite her room was frequented mainly by Algerians, and fights often broke out. By 1955, the physiognomy of her street had changed: 'Well-dressed Algerians in leather jackets often visited the Café des Amis; alcohol was banned; through the windows, I could see customers sitting with glasses of milk in front of them.'[13] Some of those smart young men were collecting taxes. There were no more fights. Fanon too remarks that the crime rate amongst the Algerian community in France fell during the war and that the energies that had been wasted in minor but potentially murderous quarrels were now been channelled into the war effort.[14] He obviously had no first-hand experience of the war in France, and must have been drawing here on second-hand reports.

An incident that occurred shortly before Fanon left Algeria had revealed just how dangerous travel could be for anyone associated with the FLN. It also indicates something of the tensions that existed with the supposedly monolithic front. Ben Bella was furious at the decisions taken at the Soummam Conference and particularly at the insistence that the forces of the interior took priority and that recognition of Algeria's independence was a precondition for peace negotiations. Abane's triumph was Ben Bella's political defeat. His response was to begin to organize a summit conference which would allow the Tunisian and Moroccan governments to mediate with the French and to broker a compromise peace. He and the other three members of the external delegation were due to fly from Rabat to Tunis in the personal aircraft of the King of Morocco on 22 October 1956. At the last moment, there was a change of plan. There was, they were informed, no room on the royal plane and they would have to take an Air Maroc flight. The news that the DC3 was French-crewed did cause them some misgivings, but Ben Bella, Boudiaf, Khider and Aït Ahmed finally boarded the flight, together with the historian Mostefa Lacheraf. When he was in international airspace, the pilot received radio orders to change his course, and the DC3 made for Algiers, where all five Algerians were immediately arrested. They spent the remainder of the war in French prisons.

When the news of the hijacking was released, European Algeria exploded with joy.[15] Fanon was in the little town of Birtouta when he heard the news. A tobacconist suddenly burst out of his shop brandishing photographs of the five men and shouting: 'We've got them, and now we'll cut off their you-know-whats.'[16] The French intelligence services had certainly scored a victory, but it was an ambiguous one. The international press printed hostile reports of a breach of international law that would now be described as an act of state-sponsored terrorism. Both Tunisia and Morocco had been deeply offended, and the possibility of negotiations now looked more remote than ever. And, although they expressed outrage in public, Abane Ramdane and the 'interior' were no doubt delighted: there could be no splits between the interior and the exterior, now that the latter did not exist.[17]

The hijacking incident made it clear that air travel was dangerous. Communications between Tunisia and Morocco, which were the FLN's main foreign bases, were difficult. For anyone associated with the FLN, a stopover in Algiers would have been almost suicidal. The normal route therefore became a tortuous series of flights between Tunis and Rome, and then from Rome on to Madrid and finally Casablanca or Rabat. Fanon would take it on a number of occasions, but this was not his itinerary for the moment. For security reasons, taking a direct Air France flight to Tunis was out of the question. Fanon travelled through Switzerland and then on to Italy and Tunis, arriving there on 28 January 1957.[18] His timing was good and he was fortunate enough to get out of France before Louanchi was arrested on 26 February, when a meeting of the Fédération's Federal Committee being held in the smart sixteenth arrondissement was raided by agents of the Direction de la Surveillance du Territoire (DST) or internal counter-espionage service. Louanchi soon found himself in Fresnes prison; Fanon could easily have been there with him. The press crowed that the FLN in France had been decapitated but, like the political hydra it was, it soon grew new heads.[19]

The DST did not pose a threat in Tunis though agents working for its 'foreign' counterpart, the Service de documentation Extérieure et de Contre-espionnage, were certainly active there. The FLN operated openly and legally in the capital of the newly independent Tunisia where it functioned almost as a state within a state. The Conseil National de la Révolution Algérienne itself met in Cairo but most of the FLN's growing bureaucracy was based in Tunis, with outposts in Tripoli. In Tunis, Fanon could take part in political discussions in cafés and not behind locked doors. Yet even here, a certain discretion was necessary. The FLN's internal security service was controlled by Abdelhafid Boussouf and Fanon, like everyone else, soon learned to be very careful what he said when 'Boussouf's boys' were around.[20] Most of the 'external' military forces were in Tunisia and outnumbered those based on the western front on the Moroccan border. The war was not far away. Tunis itself is no more than 130 kilometres from the frontier and, until the Ligne Morice was completed in 1959, border clashes between the ALN and the French army were frequent. When it was completed, the impotent ALN became a permanent presence on Tunisian soil. Although Tunisian intelligence kept a cautious eye on the FLN, it could have done little to control it as President Bourguiba's armed forces, including national guardsmen, numbered no more than 18,000.[21] The Algerian forces were based in camps on the frontier and rarely ventured into the towns, but their presence was both palpable and a potential security threat. Tent cities along the border were home to tens of thousands of Algerian refugees who received some aid from the International Red Cross, but most of whose needs were met by the FLN itself. The Tunisian government had little option but to tolerate the Algerian presence, but it did issue periodic warnings about the need to respect Tunisian sovereignty. The Algerian troops were not the only potential threat to Tunisian security. When the country gained its independence, the French retained control of the important naval base at Bizerte and President Bourguiba's repeated demands for it to be handed back led to a tense relationship with Paris.

In Tunis, Fanon was able to work openly with the FLN and no longer needed to lead the stressful double life he had been living in Blida. He had, on the other hand, no real contacts with the FLN's representatives in Tunisia and they presumably knew relatively little about him. His only direct contacts with the FLN had been with the men of *wilaya* IV who were still in Algeria, and, briefly, with the Fédération de France. It took time to build contacts and to gain trust, and it was not until May 1957 that Fanon emerged as a public spokesmen for the FLN. Most of his first year in Tunis was dedicated to psychiatry.

Two days before Fanon's arrival in Tunis on 28 January, Yacef's bomb network struck at civilian targets in Algiers once more. The bombs were again planted by young women and they exploded in the very heart of the European city. The targets were the Otomatic, a bar on the rue Michelet that was popular with students and a nearby brasserie called the Coq Hardi. The caféteria was bombed for the second time. Diners in the Coq Hardi were caught by the classic terrorist tactic; as they rushed to the windows to see where the first explosions had occurred, the third bomb went off under a cast-iron table in the caféteria and hurled deadly fragments of glass and metal across the room. In all, sixty people were wounded and five killed, one of the dead being a young Muslim who was lynched by the furious mob. A fortnight later, more bombs exploded in the city's two football stadia, killing ten and injuring forty-five.[22]

There were two reasons for this new outbreak of urban terrorism. In military terms, 1956 had been a fairly good year for the ALN, which had succeeded in spreading the 'rot', and the bombings were part of the attempt – urged by Abane – to bring the war into the cities. They also coincided with a week-long strike called for the end of January. Interpretations of the strike vary. Abane himself certainly saw it as the prelude to an urban insurrection, but others claim that it was intended to focus the attention of the forthcoming UN session on Algeria. When the journalist Edward Behr, who covered the Algerian war for *Time* and *Life*, asked an FLN representative at the UN about the advisability of the bombing campaign, he was coldly told: 'You must realize that every time a bomb explodes in Algiers, we are taken more seriously here.'[23]

Leaflets distributed at the beginning of the month had urged the population of Algiers and other cities to demonstrate total support for the FLN and to prove to the UN that the Front was the sole authentic representative of the Algerian nation.[24] The strike seemed initially to be a success. On Monday 28 January almost all Muslim-owned shops remained closed behind their steel shutters. Workers in the public sector remained at home and schoolchildren were on strike. Even the street beggars and shoeshine boys had disappeared from the streets. European Algiers was living in fear. Tanks were stationed outside important buildings, and barbed wire entanglements and roadblocks made it difficult to move across the city. There was now almost no contact between the two communities. Cafés and bars remained open in the European areas, but the possibility of grenade attacks meant that customers drank behind half-closed steel shutters. Sales of handguns soared, and tailors were doing a good trade in bullet-proof vests.[25]

Calling the strike was a gamble. It laid down a direct challenge to the French government, and there could be only one winner in the coming contest. The French government now took a gamble of its own by giving full police powers to the army. At the beginning of January, General Jacques Massu, the Commander of the Tenth Parachute Division, was given full responsibility for security in Algiers. The army now had a dangerous degree of power. One of Massu's powers was that of *assignation à résidence*. In normal circumstances, the expression means 'house arrest'; in the Algerian context, it meant that a suspect could be held for an indefinite period in premises controlled by the army. Suspects did not have to be brought before a court and did not have the right to see either a lawyer or a doctor. Paul Teitgen, who was secretary-general of the Préfecture and in nominal charge of the Algiers police, agreed to place suspects under 'house arrest' at Massu's request. The civil power was now a servant of the military.[26] Accountable to no one outside the military command structure, the torturers had been given carte blanche. Massu and his men were both resolute and angry. On 5 November, they had been part of the airborne force that jumped at Port Said during the unsuccessful campaign to prevent Nasser taking control of the Suez Canal. They were pulled out the next day when France and Britain backed down in the face of strong protests from the Soviet Union, whose tanks had just rolled into Budapest, and silent disapproval from the United States.

The orders given to Massu by Resident Minister Lacoste were clear: the strike had to be broken. Massu had previous experience of this, as he had played a part in breaking strikes in the mining districts of northern France in 1947. The means at his disposal were formidable, and six full regiments were committed to the Battle of Algiers. Helicopters hovered menacingly over the Casbah and dropped leaflets orderings its inhabitants back to work. The shutters were ripped from shopfronts by steel hawsers attached to trucks and armoured cars. Shopowners were forced to open their premises at gunpoint and under threat of imprisonment or worse. Trucks collected strikers from their homes and physically bundled them into their workplaces. The schoolchildren were rounded up and taken bodily to school in fleets of army vehicles. Within two days, the strike was effectively over, despite the unconvincing claims in the FLN's press that it had been a total victory.[27]

The decision to call a long strike had been a bad miscalculation and its failure had disastrous effects. What has come to be known as the 'Battle of Algiers' now began in earnest. The so-called 'battle' was not a set-piece engagement but a bloody episode of urban guerrilla warfare between Massu's paratroopers and Yacef's *fidayine*. Massu's goal was to dismantle the FLN's cell structure piece by piece and his men achieved it with savage efficiency. The Casbah was ringed with barbed wire and all entrances and exits were tightly controlled. Metal detectors were used to stop the smuggling in or out of weapons. Algiers was divided into sectors and sub-sectors as a form of urban *quadrillage* was introduced. The Casbah was the responsibility of Colonel Marcel Bigeard's Third Regiment of Colonial Paratroopers. Checkpoints that had been manned by conscripts in ill-fitting uniforms were taken over by hardened paras wearing 'leopard' combat fatigues and distinctive long-peaked forage caps. An identification number was painted on every building in the labyrinth, and a warden-informant was assigned to each block. This was the work of Colonel Roger Trinquier's Dispositif Urbaine de Protection. The *quadrillage* of the Casbah was a re-enactment of an earlier episode in the military's relationship with Algiers. In the 1850s, the French had appropriated the urban space of the Casbah by giving names to streets that had none and numbers to buildings that had never been numbered.[28]

Bigeard used spies and informers but his real weapon was torture. From the intelligence-gathering point of view, most of the torture carried out in Algeria was not truly productive and its real function was to terrorize the population. During the Battle of Algiers, however, intelligence-gathering was its real purpose. Each name extracted from suspects who had been half-drowned and tortured with the *gégène* was added to the diagram being constructed on a blackboard by Colonel Yves Godard, Massu's Chief of Staff and the calculating brain behind the *quadrillage*. Henri Alleg describes the process:

> Massu's paratroopers had been ordered to round up hundreds of Algerians and, as they knew that a large proportion of them paid dues to the FLN, they began by torturing them to find out who it was in their neighbourhood that they paid the money to. Then they would arrest the collector and torture him to find out who he passed the money on to. In that way, they gradually built up an organization chart and identified those in charge.[29]

The shape of the pyramid command structure began to emerge. Yacef had been identified as the commander of the bomb network by numerous cross references, but the man himself remained elusive. He could not be found though the FLN was suffering very heavy losses and its organization was crumbling. On 15 February, Abane Ramdane and the surviving members of the FLN command had to admit to themselves that they were losing the battle and accepted that they would have to abandon the city, leaving Yacef in sole command. The bomb factory in the aptly named Impasse de la Grenade was discovered four days later and most of the network's members were soon in the hands of the French. Just as he was preparing his escape from Algiers, Larbi Ben M'Hidi, one of the chief military commanders in Algiers, was captured on 25 February by paratroopers acting on information supplied by an informer. On 6 March, it was officially announced that he had hanged himself by tearing his shirt into strips and using them to make a noose. He had been 'suicided'.[30] The FLN's organization had been largely destroyed. Krim and Abane Ramdane were smuggled out of the city in Claudine Chaulet's car and made their slow and painful way on foot to Morocco. Abane then flew via Madrid and Rome to Tunis, whilst Krim made his way east on foot.

Not a man to admit defeat easily, Yacef reorganized what forces he had left. In May, two paratroopers were shot dead by his men. In reprisal, their comrades raided a *hammam* which, according to an informer, was an FLN hideout. The information proved to be inaccurate, but almost eighty Muslim men were shot dead. There was no official inquiry. To avenge the dead and to reassert the FLN's presence, Yacef used *fidayine* dressed in the uniforms of the electricity and gas board to plant bombs in lamp standards in the city centre. They exploded during the rush hour but caused surprisingly little loss of life. Many of the eighty injured by shrapnel outside the main post office were, however, Muslims and Yacef soon realized that he had made a serious error. On 9 June, he reverted to his old policy of striking at purely European targets and of using women to carry the bombs. His chosen target was the Casino, a gambling establishment and dance hall on the western edge of the city. Nine died as the bomb went off in the early evening, and over eighty people were injured. As the bomb had been placed beneath the stage, the direction of the blast ensured that many of them lost their legs. The *ratonnade* that followed was the worst yet. Shops owned by Muslims were looted. Arabs were beaten with iron bars. One eye-witness saw the bodies of young Muslims hanging from meat hooks. Two hundred European rioters were arrested, but only four were held. They were released after only a short time.[31]

The hunt for Yacef was now the army's top priority. Turncoats – some of whom had been 'turned' by torture – were dressed in blue workmen's overalls and sent to mingle with their former associates in the Casbah. They eventually led the paratroopers to the hiding place of the new head of the bomb network and his deputy. Both were killed on 26 August. On 24 September, Yacef himself was finally captured. Two weeks later Ali La Pointe died when paratroopers placed small charges to bring down a false wall in the house in the rue des Abderames where he had taken refuge. The charges detonated a cache of bombs and brought down the entire house in an explosion that rocked the whole Casbah. The Battle of Algiers was over.

The balance of power within the FLN was now shifting. Abane's departure from Algiers and the collapse of the Autonomous Zone meant that, whatever the Soummam Conference may have decided, the politicians and soldiers outside Algeria were becoming much more important than the fighters within the country. There was now no unified command structure inside Algeria and the *wilayas* were isolated from one another. In military terms, the frontier armies and their colonels were becoming more important than the rural guerrillas. In political terms, the alliances and clans that were constantly being formed and reformed in Tunis were becoming more important than fighters in the Aurès. Men like Abane Ramdane would now become isolated and marginalized, whilst Colonel Boumédienne began his rise to power. Massu's victory also had implications for the European population. The 'paras' now became the darlings of French Algeria, and especially of those who had begun to flex their muscles during Mollet's disastrous visit to Algiers in February 1956. The popular cult of the para – which easily fed into their self-image as the saviours of Algérie française – contained the seeds of some alliances that would be as threatening to Paris as they were to the FLN.

After the FLN's defeat in Algiers, large numbers of students and city intellectuals, including many women, fled into the countryside to join the guerrillas. Their numbers included individuals who had been turned by Colonel Godard and Captain Léger during mopping-up operations, and they were joined by men claiming to have deserted from Algerian units in the army. The deserters were Godard's men. Godard and Léger (an expert on subversive warfare, who was now running a network of Muslim agents) were mounting a complex exercise in psychological warfare designed to spread 'blueitis' or 'spy-fever' amongst the ranks of the FLN – the term originally derived from the blue overalls worn by the spies in the Casbah. Their main target was Colonel Amirouche, the commander of Wilaya III. Forged letters and planted documents convinced him that he was surrounded by spies and traitors, and it was not difficult to play on the peasant's traditional distrust of city dwellers, intellectuals and especially educated women. Estimates of how many were killed in Amirouche's attempt to purge his *wilaya* of traitors vary considerably, but it is certain that hundreds died. In his memoirs, Azzedine cites the words of an old villager: 'Every people, every society has its traitors, and fortunately we have Amirouche here to prevent them doing any harm. But the Revolution must not drag on for too long; on independence day, only Amirouche and God will be left in Algeria.'[32] In *Les Damnés de la terre*, Fanon speaks in almost romantic terms of how the Algerian peasantry welcomed their brothers and sisters from the cities. Highly educated, urban to his fingertips and black, he would not have survived for long in Amirouche's *wilaya*.

The gains made by the FLN in 1956 were now threatened. The historic chiefs were either dead or in prison. The Algiers Autonomous Zone had effectively ceased to exist. The *wilayas* were isolated and had no coordinated policy. Amirouche's bout of blueitis was taking a cruel toll. In the countryside, *quadrillage* had reduced the ALN's freedom of movement even though the army could not, despite its ten-to-one superior force ratio, eradicate its Military-Political Organization or neutralize all its fighters. Strategic attention was now focused on the frontiers. In 1956, a 250-kilometre barrier had been constructed near the Moroccan border, initially to curb ALN activity in the mountains above Tlemcen and to prevent incursions. In 1958, work began on a similar line of defence just inside the border with Tunisia. Named after the Minister of Defence, the Morice Line consisted of parallel lines of barbed wire interspersed with manned blockhouses. Minefields were laid both inside and outside the lines of wire. Constant patrols, radar and floodlights made the line virtually impossible to cross, and the ALN took heavy casualties in trying to do so. Its forces in Tunisia were now hemmed in and could neither reinforce the forces of the interior or supply them with arms. The *wilayas* were being starved of both men and weaponry.[33] Although he had little choice in the matter, Fanon had not picked a good moment to join the FLN in Tunis. For the next three years, he would insist that the final victory was at hand and no doubt believed what he said.

Whilst Fanon would have found it impossible to find a clinical post in France, finding a position in Tunisia was not difficult. He was well-qualified, experienced and extremely gifted. He had published quite widely for someone who was still only thirty-one and working at a time when the 'publish or perish' ethos was not yet prevalent. There were few psychiatrists of Fanon's calibre in North Africa and he easily found a post at the Clinique Manouba, a public-sector institution in the suburbs of Tunis where he worked under the name of 'Dr Fares' as one of four *chefs de service* or consultants. Two of his colleagues were Tunisians, and two came from the North-African Jewish community. Fanon got on better with his Jewish colleagues than with the Tunisians, and came particularly close to the communist Lucien Lévy, with whom he collaborated on two clinical papers.[34]

Fanon and his family had arrived in Tunis in some haste, and one of the advantages of the Manouba was that it offered accommodation in the form of a large apartment in the administration block adjacent to the entrance. By taking up a position here, Fanon was, as he well knew, following in the footsteps of someone he had so often criticized: the Manouba clinic, technically described as 'a mixed and international asylum' attached to Tunis's civilian hospital, had been built in 1912 largely at the urgings of Antoine Porot, whose first major post had been in Tunis.[35] Like the hospital in Blida, the Manouba was set in extensive grounds with large trees shading the well-kept lawns and neat flower beds.[36] The physical environment was pleasant and the hospital was well equipped. Whilst many patients enjoyed freedom of movement and could take part in occupational therapy, the more radical innovations made by Fanon in Blida had not been imitated here. There was a newspaper but no café, and the more advanced facilities were enjoyed by only a minority of patients. The Manouba also had a large population of 'long-term' patients who had been effectively incarcerated for life.

Fanon's first attempts to introduce a programme of reform met with immediate opposition from the clinic's director, Dr Ben Soltan. His hostility to Fanon was not based solely on differences of opinion about policy. The director had a good track record in the Tunisian nationalist movement, dating back to his student days, but he was also a conservative who saw no need to make any changes in what he believed to be a well-run institution. He has been described as both an anti-Semite and an anti-black racist who referred to Fanon as a *nègre* and questioned his professional capabilities on the grounds that he could not speak much Arabic and that it was impossible to understand Arabs without knowing their language.[37] Fanon would no doubt have agreed that his lack of Arabic was a serious professional handicap, but he was no one's *nègre*. Anti-Semitism was by no means unusual in North Africa and nor, despite all the talk of African and Afro-Arab unity, was anti-black racism. In both Algeria and Tunisia, black people were commonly referred to as *Al-âbid* (the singular is '*Ab'd*'), meaning 'slaves' – a reminder that the corsaires of the Barbary Coast had enslaved blacks as well as whites.[38] Fanon was quite familiar with North Africa's hierarchy of racist attitudes – this was a place where, as the saying went, the French spat on the Jews, who spat on the Arabs, who spat on the negroes – but there is no record of his encountering open hostility in Blida. As he walked through the streets of Tunis, he often found that he was the object of a silent collective gaze and sensed its sullen hostility.[39] Ben Soltan was also one of those Tunisians who had no instinctive sympathy for his Algerian 'brothers', and he certainly did not welcome their presence in his hospital, where half the patients and a lot of the nurses were now Algerian. The arrival of a black consultant with both close links to the FLN and plans for reforms was decidedly unwelcome. The Tunisian writer Albert Memmi, who knew Ben Soltan well, describes him as 'very pleasant and jovial' but confirms that he was not pleased by the arrival of a younger man familiar with up-to-date therapies and intent upon changing things. The director had, he adds, been trained by the previous French director and had waited long years for his promotion.[40] Fanon's arrival simply added to his sense of frustration and discontent.

Ben Soltan greeted Fanon's first request for extra funding to introduce more occupational therapy with the stock answer of the bureaucrat: there was no money available. The budget for the coming year had already been drawn up, and the hospital had to work within its limits. This was not a problem Fanon had faced in Blida, where money had been readily available and where, whilst his senior colleagues may not have approved of what he was doing, he had been left to do largely as he pleased. This was obviously not going to be the case at the Manouba. Fanon went over Ben Soltan's head and, exploiting political contacts between the FLN and the Tunisian government, arranged to see the Minister for Health, Hammed Ben Salah – a sympathetic figure belonging to the left wing of the ruling Néo-Destour party – who told him that there was indeed a shortage of funds but that it might be possible to reallocate some of the money to the occupational therapy project. Fanon still did not give up and somehow obtained a copy of the Manouba's budget. The figures showed that most of the available funds were being spent on the long-term patients, and a series of interviews indicated that a significant number of them could in fact be safely released. The money saved could be spent on his projected reforms. Fanon went back to the Minister and finally obtained a promise of support.[41]

Ever since the days when, at Saint-Alban, he had persuaded the bursar's wife to lend him her precious piano, Fanon had displayed a talent for getting his own way and obtaining the unobtainable. He had done it again, but he had also made a potentially dangerous enemy who did not easily forget old scores. Unable to rid himself of Fanon by administrative methods, Ben Soltan turned to politicking. In 1959, he began to accuse Fanon and Geronimi, who reached Tunis in June 1958, of being undercover agents for Israel, and even of maltreating Algerian and Tunisian patients on Israeli orders. 'Zionism' was a potentially damning accusation in the Arab world of the late 1950s, but when Ben Soltan formally took his case to Minister Ben Salah and demanded the expulsion of the 'Zionists', he was simply laughed out of court.[42] He had, however, made Fanon's position at the Manouba so uncomfortable that the family moved out to live in premises owned by the FLN, which had bought and rented properties throughout Tunis (and which had no scruples about requisitioning houses belonging to individual Algerians when the need arose).

While Ben Soltan fumed and plotted, Fanon, whose capacity for work was little short of astonishing, began to combine his duties at the

Manouba with a commitment to a second institution. The Hôpital Charles-Nicolle was not a psychiatric institution but a general hospital with a neuro-psychiatric unit that had been in existence for some forty years. With the official blessing of the Tunisian authorities, and drawing on the lessons learned in Blida, Fanon now began to transform it into Africa's first psychiatric day clinic. He described his work there in a long two-part article; the second part was written in collaboration with Charles Geronimi,[43] who had been obliged to leave France in June 1958 faced by the imminent threat of being called up into the French army. He had hoped to find some peace in Paris but he found only a bad conscience. The newspapers were full of reports of his friends in Algeria, but when he tried to discuss this with Parisian acquaintances, they simply went on talking about their trips to the theatre and their holiday plans. He began to despise the French and the threat of his call up was the final blow. He decided that he was no longer a member of the French nation and left for Tunis.[44]

This was the first time that Fanon had worked in a unit attached to a general hospital and he found that it had distinct advantages. The availability of radiological services, pathology laboratories and bio-chemistry laboratories facilitated diagnostic work. Patients could easily be transferred to the neurological ward for appropriate treatment. The individual psychiatrist was no longer isolated in the asylum with 'his madmen' and was in frequent contact with surgeons and other special-ists. This was to the psychiatrist's advantage, but it also helped to demystify his role by removing the sinister aura that so often sur-rounded it. For patients, going into a ward in a general hospital was a much less traumatic experience than going into one of the old-style cap-itals of madness. Making psychiatry part of general medicine 'did a lot to correct the prejudices that are usually rooted in public opinion and transform the madman into a sick patient'.[45] Fanon was now convinced that this was the model for the future: relatively small psychiatric units attached to general hospitals should replace the big asylums of the past.

The advantages of an 'open-door' day clinic were many. For six days of the week, patients came to the hospital from seven in the morning onwards and remained there until six in the evening. Not being hospi-talized, they remained in contact with their families and, in some cases, with the world of work. In a psychiatric hospital, the patient was removed from the environment with which he or she was in conflict, and it was therefore possible for symptoms to disappear 'magically'. Commitment to an institution could also provide an illusory protection by allowing the patient to vegetate in a sort of waking sleep. Patients attending a day clinic, in contrast, were still in contact with the social or family conflicts that had made them ill, and could be helped to come to terms with them by doctors who could study their reactions in their 'natural environment'.[46] The open-day policy also had advantages that Fanon and Geronimi did not discuss in public. At the Blida hospital, it had been possible – at considerable risk – to harbour fighters, to give them rest and to treat their minor injuries. At Charles-Nicolle, it was possible to treat fighters quietly and with discretion. Not all the casualties taken by the ALN in its futile attempts to breach the Morice Line were physical. Stress, exhaustion, war neuroses and reactive psychoses all took their toll, particularly on the young liaison agents, scouts and runners.

Many of these casualties were now housed in barracks in and around Tunis, and they were difficult to deal with. Some were very reluctant to be treated by Tunisians and insisted on being seen by brother or sister Algerians. Others refused to surrender their personal weapons and had to be forcibly relieved of them before they could be admitted to any hospital. The facilities at Charles-Nicolle offered a solution to their problems. They could be brought in under guard in army trucks for a day's treatment and then safely returned to their barracks in the evening. In many cases, these semi-clandestine patients required little more than extended periods of sedation or at worst narcotherapy. Others needed quasi-psychoanalytic treatment to help them to come to terms with their traumas and, in some cases, their burden of knowledge about the grim secrets of the Algerian revolution.[47] By the end of 1957, Fanon was also treating some of the nurses who had worked in Wilaya IV's improvised health service. The military situation had deteriorated in the summer and they had been told by 'the brothers' to get out while they could. They protested that they were willing to die in Algeria, but were firmly told that they should go to Tunis, eat croissants, drink café au lait, and do their crying in a comfortable café. The twenty-year-old Kheira Bousafi was one of the small group who made their painful way – on foot and by night – to Tunisia, where she was hospitalized for two months in Fanon's ward.[48] In February 1958, more stragglers from the Blida area arrived, including a nurse identified only as 'A.C.' who already knew Fanon. She and her colleagues were found accommodation by Fanon and Ben Salah and, once they had recovered from their journey, were found jobs. Working part-time with Tunisian patients and part-time with their fellow Algerians, they were paid on a pro rata basis by the Ministry of Health and the FLN.[49]

Fanon no longer had to treat French torturers but he did treat their victims. Some suffered from anorexia and others – victims of the *gégène* – were so afraid of electricity that they were quite unable to turn on a light or a radio.[50] One patient was brought in in handcuffs. He was a survivor from a massacre in which twenty-nine of his comrades died, and he had attempted to fire on the ALN unit that had rescued him. In hospital, he declared that he was going to kill everyone and he attacked fellow patients with anything that came to hand, convinced that all Algerians were Frenchmen in disguise. After a three-day period of narcotherapy, it became possible for Fanon to talk him through his aggressive fantasies and the bout of manic agitation gradually diminished. The patient's reluctance to talk and his reclusiveness still worried Fanon, but the man was found a job and put under the supervision of the FLN's social services. Six months later, he was doing well.[51] During visits to the refugee camps, Fanon encountered women suffering from puerperal psychoses. Women who had recently given birth suffered depression, delusions of persecution and high levels of anxiety. Suicide attempts were common. Sedatives could do little for these women and, even if they did make a recovery, their symptoms were reactivated by the conditions in which they were living.[52] In Tunis, he encountered a nineteen-year-old ALN fighter who was convinced that he was being 'vampirized' or bled to death, as well as being persecuted by women who came to haunt him at night. Fanon initially thought that the hallucinations related to the image of the man's mother, who had been killed by a French soldier, and his two sisters, who had been taken away by the French; they proved to refer to a French woman he had stabbed to death in the course of a raid on a farm. In his nightmares, she came back with a gaping hole in her stomach, and demanded that he give back her blood. Fanon finally reached the non-scientific conclusion that time alone might do something to heal the man's dislocated personality.[53]

The first task was to transform the building itself. Handles were fitted to the doors so that they could be opened from the inside. The bars were removed from the windows and the straitjackets and other physical restraints were taken away. Patients were employed to knock down the walls of the old isolation units, which resembled punishment cells rather than hospital rooms. The entire building was repainted to make it look less forbidding.[54] After its physical transformation, the unit could admit forty male and forty female patients. The inclusion of a six-bed side ward for children in the female ward was, for the time, a particularly innovative move. Attitudes had to be transformed as well as the physical environment, as the usual inversion had occurred: far from being the beneficiaries of hospitalization, the patients had simply become, in Fanon's words, 'the enemies of the staff's tranquillity'. Lecture courses were introduced to help the eleven nurses (five female and six male) to adapt to the new regime. Some proved unable to adapt and requested to be transferred to other duties. They were replaced by younger people who had never been in contact with the mentally ill and who could therefore, Fanon claimed with great optimism, be trained *ab initio*.[55] The experiment was a success. In the sixteen-month period leading up to the publication of Fanon and Geronimi's paper, over one thousand patients were admitted to Charles-Nicolle and treated with a high rate of success; less than 1 per cent had to be committed to the Manouba for institutionalized care.[56]

Accounts of psychiatric therapy are almost always written by the doctors. Whilst Fanon describes in his own terms both his institutional reforms and the techniques he used, it is unusual to find a description from the patient's point of view. One such description does survive. Boukhatem Farés was hospitalized in Tunis in 1958 after being badly wounded in a battle, and had narrowly escaped having his legs amputated. He was an amateur artist and when Fanon heard this, he brought him a little book about Van Gogh. He began to visit Farés regularly, popping into the ward after he had finished his shift and before he went to *El Moudjahid*'s offices. The *moudjahid*-painter found to his surprise that Fanon had an interest in art.[57] Farés was working on a series of drawings and water colours entitled 'Screams in the Night' and Fanon was particularly taken with a drawing of a child waving an Algerian flag against the background of a sky filled with bombers. He encouraged the artist to use more colour, and to add crosses and roundels to the planes to make the scene both more vivid and more violent. Fanon was accustomed to using TATs and other forms of visually based tests, and now encouraged Farés to use painting as a means of exploring and 'visualizing' his own fears and anxieties. He was speaking as a psychiatrist eager to reorient his patient's attitude to the real world, and not as a psychoanalyst intent upon uncovering the unconscious origins of his fears. He also helped him to discover that he had a real talent. He told Farés that 'Drawings, art and painting complemented the armed struggle.' After his recovery, Farés joined the propaganda service attached to the Etat-Major's Political Commissariat: 'Fanon's advice was a great help to me in producing leaflets for the psychological struggle against the enemy, and for raising the morale of the ALN's troops.' Some of the drawings and water colours produced with Fanon's encouragement were subsequently acquired by the FLN leadership and presented to representatives of friendly foreign delegations.[58]

As at Blida, Fanon's goal was to create a therapeutic 'neo-society' in which patients could establish a multiplicity of social bonds, fulfil a variety of functions and act out a variety of roles. The symptomatology to be observed in the traditional hospital – the appearance of 'pure' or desocialized symptoms at the physical level – began to change. The patients had to verbalize their symptoms, explain themselves and return to a world of objects which now acquired a new density: 'Social therapy wrenches the patient away from his fantasies and forces him to confront reality on a new basis.'[59] Occupational therapy and forms of psychodrama were introduced to further the creation of the neo-society, whilst visits to the cinema or even a café helped the outside to filter back into the hospital. A wide variety of therapies was used. Although the unit used narcotherapy (now facilitated by the availability of new neuroleptics) and ECT treatment to break 'anxiogenic circuits that became too painful', therapy was primarily oriented towards verbalization, explanation, *la prise de conscience* and the strengthening of the ego.[60] The range of therapeutic techniques in use reflected the variety of patients admitted. This was a clinic that dealt with everything from stammers to delirious erotomania, from schizophrenia to attempted suicide and acute psychoses. It also reflects Fanon's own pragmatism. Like his mentor Tosquelles, he was less concerned with the niceties of theoretical constructs or doctrinal purity than with the efficacy of the techniques he used. The lack of concern for theory in the abstract, or even a degree of theoretical confusion, is most obvious in the brief mentions of psychoanalysis. Although Lacan is not mentioned in this paper, Fanon had read at least some of his work as a student in Lyon. He departs, however, from the most basic tenets of Lacanian psychoanalysis by referring to the need to strengthen the ego – which Lacan regarded as the capital sin of American ego-psychology. Fanon consistently described mental illness as a form of alienation from the world and as a loss of existential freedom. As a therapist, his goal was to 'consciousnessize' (*conscienciser*) his patient's conflicts so as to establish a new and more positive relationship with the external world. Fanon always stresses the sociogenic aspects of symptomatology: symptoms did not, in this view, originate from the personal unconscious or repressed sexual impulses so much as from a distorted dialectic between the ego and the world and from the internalization of social conflicts. Farés's warplanes were not symptoms of inner conflict, but images of the real world and they could be used to strengthen the painter's relationship with that world by helping him to master his fears.

Psychoanalytically inspired methods of treatment were used in Tunis, just as they had been in Blida, but Fanon admitted that he found it difficult to establish the 'transference' that allows the patient to project past conflicts on to the figure of the analyst and then to verbalize them through a 'talking cure'. He thought that he could not establish it because no money changed hands. Whilst the payment of fees does have great symbolic importance in psychoanalysis because it establishes a network of exchange between patient and analyst, the more obvious and simpler explanation is that Fanon, not having trained as an analyst, did not possess the requisite technique. Fanon's relationship with psychoanalysis was always a strained one, and not only for theoretical reasons. In Tunis, even more so than in Blida, he was beginning, probably without even realizing it, to go in the opposite direction to psychoanalysts in France where, thanks to the influence of Lacan, the dominant tendency was to 'demedicalize' psychoanalysis by transforming it into an autonomous science which borrowed from linguistics and anthropology to create a theory of a symbolic world that owed little to theories of sociogenesis. Fanon, in contrast, was trying to relate psychiatry to general medicine and using psychoanalysis as part of a therapeutic armoury that included everything from ECT to neuroleptics and narcotherapy. Fanon's belief that psychiatry should be more closely related to general medicine explains why he produced two papers in collaboration with Lucien Lévy. Both are typical clinical papers and, like that on the abandoned experiments with lithium citrate, they deal with topics much less glamorous than the creation of Africa's first day clinic.

The first joint paper deals with a twenty-one-year-old patient called 'Antoine' who was admitted to Charles-Nicolle in October 1956. He was suffering from dysbasia tordotica or Schwalbe-Ziehen-Oppenheim's disease. This is a form of spasmophilia characterized by undue contractions of the muscles, and is often associated with a deficiency of ionic calcium in the blood. Antoine had often gone into convulsions as a child and had gradually adopted a posture which made him look like a macabre clown. He had recently begun to have epileptic fits. As he walked, nervous spasms affecting his head, torso and arms gave him the appearance of a broken puppet. There was, it seemed, little that could be done for Antoine except to use the standard remedies of hyoscine (also known as scopalomine), atrophine or even morphine to induce narcosis and 'twilight sleep' in order to ameliorate at least the symptoms.[61] The case was of interest primarily because Antoine's condition was unusual and because the literature on it was not extensive. It had, however, been the subject of much discussion at the International Congress on Neurology, held in Brussels in 1957, where it was argued that recent advances in neurosurgery might be paving the way for new forms of treatment. Fanon and Lévy had had the good fortune to come across an example of a rare condition which was the subject of contemporary debate. And they did what any ambitious doctor would have done in the circumstances: they read the available literature, discussed its findings, made a detailed diagnosis of Antoine's condition and prognosis, and submitted their paper to *La Tunisie médicale* as a contribution to the ongoing debate.

At roughly the same time, Fanon and Lévy were also running clinical trials of a new drug which had first been tested in 1957 and had yet to come on to the market. Meprobamate, which was eventually commercialized as Equanil, is a muscular relaxant that is now normally administered in tablet form for the treatment of motion sickness and some stages of alcoholism.[62] After a series of classic trials, Fanon and Lévy concluded that, whilst the product had no effect on hypochondriac patients who presented conversion hysterias, or who literally converted an inner conflict into a physical symptom such as a persistent cough, it was useful for treating minor depressions associated with purely physical symptoms such as fatigability, insomnia, persistent headaches and buzzing in the ears. Daily doses of four to six ampoules of injectable meprobamate were, in their opinion, indicated for minor forms of hypochondria resembling what used to be known as neurasthenia.[63] The passing reference to conversion hysteria and neurasthenia are significant; Fanon and Lévy were recommending the use of drugs in territory that had been annexed by psychoanalysis. It is unlikely that any apprentice psychoanalyst would have made that recommendation, or carried out these clinical trials; this is precisely what Lacanians were rejecting. Like the publication of clinical papers, participation in clinical trials is an important feature in the curriculum vitae of an ambitious doctor of medicine. Fanon clearly still had medical ambitions and was not about to become a full-time professional revolutionary. There are two ironic aspects to the Fanon–Lévy papers. They were published in *La Tunisie médicale*, which was founded by the Antoine Porot of whom Fanon was so critical, and the Fanon who had turned his back on France was testing with drugs supplied by the French pharmaceutical company Clin-Byla.

Although the article he co-authored with Geronimi provides an accurate account of Fanon's clinical work in Tunis, it does no more than hint at the thinking behind it. A more detailed picture of his theoretical views emerges from the brief notes that have survived from a series of lectures given by Fanon at the University of Tunis in 1959 and 1960 and made available for publication in 1984 by Lilia Bensalem, who was taught by Fanon.[64] Although it is unclear whether these are Fanon's original notes or notes taken at his lectures by Lilia Bensalem, they provide an invaluable complement to the materials published in his lifetime.

Following Tosquelles and others who worked at Saint-Alban, Fanon describes mental illness as a loss of individual freedom that results in the social exclusion and alienation of the sufferer. The goal of what he calls social therapy is to create a neo-society within the hospital, and it follows that madness is 'forbidden' there. The patient is required to

behave in a socially acceptable manner by becoming part of the therapeutic community. There is very little discussion of psychoanalysis in
these lectures. Fanon does mention Lacan's mirror phase, but immediately strays far away from psychoanalysis by describing the child's
recognition of the human face as a 'conditioned reflex'. The longest of
the lectures deals, surprisingly, with the effects of the surveillance of the
workforce in factories and with the neuroses suffered by shop workers
and telephonists who were under constant observation. This is of no
obvious relevance to either Algeria or Tunisia, but suggests that Fanon
was becoming much more interested in social and industrial psychology
than in any form of Freudianism. In the final discussion of racism in
colonial societies and in the United States, Fanon returns to familiar
themes as he discusses how black aggressivity is turned against blacks as
they introject white society's condemnation of them. As in *Peau noire,
masques blancs*, the source of his information about the United States is
literature, and he cites both Richard Wright and Chester Himes. When
it comes to Himes, he misreads him badly. In *Peau noire*, Fanon refers
to *If He Hollers, Let Him Go*, but in his lectures he refers to *A Jealous
Man Can't Win*, which was translated as *La Reine des pommes* in 1948.
Written purely for the money, this is the first of Himes's 'Harlem
thrillers' and it introduces those very hard-boiled detectives Grave
Digger Jones and Coffin Ed Johnson. Fanon reads it as a realistic portrayal of Harlem life, but Himes always insisted that the Harlem of his
books was never real: 'I never called it real: I just wanted to take it away
from the white man, if only in my books.'[65]

Fanon continued to work as a psychiatrist but the few years he spent
in Tunis transformed him into a political militant and an intransigent
spokesman for the FLN. He also became an effective polemicist and a
contributor to *El Moudjahid*. This was 'the central organ of the FLN'
and it appeared between 1956 and 1962, at which point it became the
official daily paper of the new one-party state.[66] It replaced an earlier
journal entitled *Résistance algérienne*, which published little more than
military communiqués announcing ALN victories and overstating their
importance. Early issues of *El Moudjahid* were produced sporadically in
Algiers in 1956, but the repression that followed the Battle of Algiers
meant that production had to be transferred to Tunis, where the journal finally settled into a rhythm of fortnightly publication from 1957

onwards. Fanon's first contributions appeared in September of that year. Ninety-one issues were published between then and independence. The originals are now impossible to find, though they no doubt exist in private collections. A three-volume collected edition was published by the Yugoslav government in June 1962. Whilst this is the only available version, it has to be treated with some caution as some issues are said to have been 'retouched' before they were republished. The Yugoslav edition served the ideological needs – no doubt both Yugoslav and Algerian – of the moment rather than providing a full historical record.

Both Arabic and French editions of *El Moudjahid* were produced under the general editorship of Redha Malek who was himself responsible to Ahmed Boumendjel and to M'Hamed Yazid, the FLN's Minister for Information. Boumendjel, Yazid and Fanon were to become an effective team who would represent the GPRA at Pan-African conferences; for the moment, they collaborated on the newspaper. Boumendjel and Yazid were both much more experienced than Fanon. Between 1955 and 1957, Yazid had been based in New York, where the FLN had offices on East 56th Street,[67] and, together with Abdelkader Chanderli, had been a very effective lobyist at the UN. Yazid married an American called Olivia, and her presence at his side made him a very acceptable face of the FLN.

Boumendjel was a Parisian-trained lawyer whose political history went back to the pre-war Etoile de l'Afrique du Nord. He once acted as a lawyer for Messali but subsequently became close to Ferhat Abbas and was now a member of the CNRA. Although Boumendjel was less opposed to negotiations with the French than some in the FLN, he had very personal reasons for loathing French colonialism. On 9 February 1957, his brother Ali, also a lawyer who worked for the Shell oil company, was arrested on suspicion of being a senior figure in the FLN's bomb network and handed over to the 2nd RCP for interrogation. On 23 March or forty-three days after his arrest, the radio announced that he had died after flinging himself from the terrace of a high building occupied by the paratroopers in the El Biar area. For the official record, he had committed suicide in order to avoid another round of interrogation.[68] This was his second 'suicide attempt'. On 11 February, he had been hospitalized with a supposedly self-inflicted wound to the throat.

He had, explained the authorities, broken the lenses of his spectacles and used them to cut his own throat. The incident occurred shortly after he had been interrogated by Lieutenant-Colonel Fossey-François.[69] A clandestine publication explained how prisoners harmed themselves in this manner: 'One of the forms of torture often used by the paratroopers consists in holding a dagger to the throat of the person under interrogation and striking the back of his head so that his throat hits the dagger and is cut.'[70] Boumendjel had been a popular figure at the Paris bar and his 'suicide' caused a scandal. René Capitant, Professor of Law at the Sorbonne and one of de Gaulle's former ministers, cancelled his lectures and wrote in protest to the Minister for Education. The writer Vercors returned his Légion d'honneur insignia to President Coty. This was a highly significant gesture. Vercors's *Le Silence de la mer* (1942) is the classic novel on the French resistance. Vercors had been decorated for his resistance work, but felt that he 'could no longer remain in the Légion when my country is no longer covered with glory, but with shame'.[71]

A radio journalist who worked in Tunis between 1960 and 1962 has described how Yazid's Ministry for Information dealt with journalists. The Ministry provided journalists with their only real contacts with the Revolution. The FLN's senior leaders remained in the shadows, leaving Yazid and his colleagues to deal with the press. Half-truths, false trails and snippets of real information were imparted to journalists as though they were great secrets. Sometimes the information was accurate and sometimes it was false, and Yazid and Boumendjel exploited it to entice journalists into their web. Yazid, who was born in Blida in 1923, was a past master at this game. When he gave official press conferences, he adopted a relaxed 'American' style, but he preferred to meet journalists on a one-to-one basis in his little office in the rue des Entrepreneurs. Always addressing them as *tu*, he would say that he was ready to talk, and then add that everything was off the record and could not be printed. Journalists who had been entrusted with his 'secrets' then had to try to sort the truth from the lies and to match his statements with information gleaned from other sources. Nedha Malek, in contrast, tended simply to paraphrase official FLN statements, whilst Boumendjel kept hinting that negotiations with the French were still possible but always refused to say just what the conditions for those negotiations might be.[72]

In Tunisia, *El Moudjahid* was on open sale. Copies printed on thin paper were smuggled into Algeria itself and circulated clandestinely; being caught in possession of one was dangerous in the extreme as it was conclusive proof that the reader was at least an FLN sympathizer. The paper was not really intended for distribution in the Algerian maquis; most fighters were illiterate and the *wilaya* produced their own propaganda material.

Inside Algeria itself, radio was a much more effective propaganda medium than the written word. After 130 years of the French civilizing mission, the illiteracy rate was astonishingly high: in 1954, 86 per cent of Algerian men and 95 per cent of Algerian women could not read.[73] Even those who could read found it very difficult to obtain accurate information about what was going on in the country. The local press was firmly under the control of *pied noir* barons. Censorship was much more heavy-handed than it was in metropolitan France and offending issues of newspapers and magazines were regularly seized. The best sources of information were *Le Monde* and *L'Humanité*, and the weeklies *L'Express* and *France-Observateur*. One of the photographs reproduced in Jacques C. Duchemin's history of the FLN shows Mohammed Said and Belkacem Krim dressed in uniform with a sten gun at their feet.[74] They are drinking coffee and reading *Le Monde*. As Fanon points out, even attempting to buy the democratic metropolitan press could be dangerous. Local newspapers were delivered to homes in Algeria, but the French press could be bought only from newsstands and most newsstands were owned by army veterans. An Algerian who bought a French paper was immediately suspect. His purchase of a French newspaper was automatically interpreted as a declaration of solidarity with the Algerian Revolution.[75]

The first news of the Algerian Revolution had come from Radio Cairo in November 1954, and stations in Egypt, Tunisia and Morocco provided the only alternative to Radio-Alger. In late 1956, leaflets appeared, announcing that 'The Voice of Algeria', also known as the 'Radio of Free Fighting Algeria', was about to begin broadcasting 'from the mountains'. Its transmitters were in fact in Nodor, just across the Moroccan border. Despite repeated attempts on the part of the French to jam it, the station succeeded in broadcasting between December 1956 and September 1958, and then from July 1959 onwards. Fanon was never involved with the broadcasts, but the second chapter of his *Sociologie d'une révolution*, which deals with radio broadcasting, has been recognized as an important study of a relatively neglected aspect of the war.[76]

In 1954, 20,000 licensed radio sets were owned by Algerians, giving Radio Cairo an estimated potential audience of 100,000 people; by June 1958, sales of radios had risen by 30 per cent.[77] The authorities made repeated attempts to control sales, and eventually banned the sale of both battery-powered models – these were particularly important in rural areas where electricity supplies were poor or non-existent – and replacement batteries. The only effect of these measures was to stimulate a flourishing black market. According to Fanon, supplies were regularly smuggled into Algeria from Tunisia and Morocco from 1957 onwards.[78] The radio that had once been part of a repressive cultural arsenal suddenly became a channel of communication for the Revolution. The FLN's radio broadcast in demotic Arabic, the Berber languages of Kabylia and French. Listening to broadcasts in French had once meant Europeanization and cultural alienation; it was now a way of becoming part of the new Algeria that was coming into existence. Fanon draws the obvious parallel with listening to the Free French radio in occupied France, and must have recalled his own experience of listening to the BBC in Fort-de-France during '*tan Robè*'.

Fanon's descriptions of the importance of radio are couched in the language of revolutionary romanticism: 'The Algeria who wishes to live on the same level as the Revolution at last finds it possible to hear an official voice – that of the fighters – explaining the fight to him, telling him the history of the ongoing battle, and incorporating him at last into the Nation's new breath.'[79] But during his research trips to Kabylia, he had seen groups of dozens of peasants clustered around a radio set and listening in religious silence to Cairo Radio. Few of them understood the literary Arabic used in these broadcasts, but they could all recognize the word '*Istiqlal*' ('independence') and it was enough to sustain the conviction that they would win. In the hospital in Blida, Fanon had also noticed that a psychological change had occurred. Arab patients whose auditory hallucinations seemed to come 'from the radio' once described the French voices they heard as aggressive and hostile. The radio itself was a bad object that was both anxiogenic, or a cause of anxiety, and accursed. Fanon's patients still experienced hallucinations, but the voices were now protective and reassuring. Conversely, European patients suffering from depression thought that Arab voices on the radio were issuing them with death threats.[80]

Most copies of *El Moudjahid* found their way to France and other countries via the Moroccan city of Tetouan. They were addressed to a selected list of politicians, journalists and opinion-makers around the world, and to anyone else sympathetic to the cause and in a position to further it by publishing the FLN's position. Copies were, for instance, sent under plain cover to François Mauriac in Paris,[81] and much of the material published in André Mandouze's *La Révolution algérienne par les textes* first appeared in *El Moudjahid*. The events of February 1956 and the dispatch of the contingent to Algeria had signalled that there would be no rapid end to the war, and the heavy defeat suffered by the FLN during the Battle of Algiers meant that propaganda now took on a new importance. Winning support abroad and at the UN was vital, and *El Moudjahid* was designed to win that support. Articles were unsigned and no editorial team was ever listed and it is therefore difficult to determine whether the paper had a permanent staff. Fanon, Mohamed Harbi, Pierre Chaulet and Abane Ramdane are all known to have collaborated on *El Moudjahid* at various times, and other temporary contributors were no doubt recruited on an ad hoc basis. Although such figures are impossible to verify, the claimed print run was 10,000 copies per issue. According to its editor, the function of *El Moudjahid* was give 'a face' to the FLN movement.[82] Not everyone was impressed by the results. Meloud Feraoun, for one, found its style reminiscent of a 'regional weekly' and complained about its combination of 'demagogy, pretentiousness and naivety'.[83] The newspaper – and FLN propaganda in general – reminded Edward Behr of 'a Soviet-made film of the Stalin era', and he commented sharply on 'the idealized image of exiled revolutionaries'.[84] *El Moudjahid* was an improvement on *Résistance algérienne* but, like most revolutionary papers, it preached mainly to the converted.

Fanon was not a professional journalist and had no intention of becoming one, but he was more than willing to serve the cause of independence in any way possible. He was in fact an unlikely journalist in that he had still not learned to type and had to dictate his copy to a secretary, which is not exactly the norm on the news desk. His articles show little talent for, or interest in, hard news-gathering and a heavy reliance on agency reports and wire services. This was not necessarily a' disadvantage; *El Moudjahid* was much less interested in gathering news than in interpreting it.

Fanon's articles could have been and probably were written without leaving the FLN offices at 24–26 rue Sadikia, where a Swiss journalist with good Algerian contacts recalled encountering an angry Fanon and concluded somewhat cynically that he was trying to look and sound even more committed to the struggle than the actual fighters in the maquis.[85] It might have been fairer to have spoken of frustration. The office in Tunis was not always an exciting place to be and Fanon would no doubt have preferred to have been closer to the front. Fanon's visitor also failed to take account of the fact that he himself was a European, and that Fanon had little reason to trust white Europeans. Other visitors got a similar reception. In 1959, the Italian Giovanni Pirelli visited Tunis to collect material for a book on the Algerian revolution, and asked to meet Fanon. An FLN official told him that the request was pointless: Fanon had no time for white Europeans. Pirelli persevered and, after some hostile exchanges, won Fanon's confidence. The two became quite close, and Pirelli subsequently appended a useful biographical note to an Italian edition of *Les Damnés de la terre*.[86] Pirelli thought of writing a full-scale study of Fanon but never did so because, every time he sat down to write it, he imagined Fanon staring at him in anger. He told Peter Geismar: 'It's those glaring eyes – I'm never able to go on.'[87] Stories of Fanon's hostility to Europeans are not uncommon, but he did work closely with them in Tunis and was of course married to a European. The initial hostility was real enough, but could be overcome by establishing a political rapport.

'El Moudjahid' was translated on the cover as 'the warrior', but the editorial in the first issue gave a better translation and explained why this title had been chosen:

Because of an anti-Islamic prejudice dating back to the Crusades, the word *djihad* (holy war), from which *el moudjahid* (warrior of the faith) derives, has always been understood in the Christian West in a restrictive and limited sense. It is thought to be a symbol of religious aggression. This interpretation is already made absurd by the fact that respect for religions, and especially Christianity and Judaism, is of its basic prescriptions, and it has been put into practice for centuries.

Reduced to its essentials, *djihad* simply means a dynamic manifestation of self-defence designed to preserve or recover a heritage of higher values that are indispensable to both individual and community. It also means the will to constantly perfect oneself in every domain. *Djihad* is the quintessence of liberal and open patriotism. In a word, it means all the efforts that are driven by the wheel of history and guided by the FLN, and which converge towards a single goal: the independence of the country.

The appeal to Islamic tradition must have meant little to Fanon who was, he thought, fighting for a free and secular Algeria and who does appear to have underestimated the Islamic component in Algerian nationalism, but references to a *djihad* were powerfully evocative in a country where, in popular usage, any French person could be pejoratively described as a *Roumi* or 'Christian'. The way in which the *moudjahid* was described was a different matter, and did conform to Fanon's vision of the revolution. The *moudjahid* was 'The ALN soldier, the political militant, the liaison agent, the little shepherd, the housewife discussing the news in the casbah, the little schoolboy who is on strike in Algiers, economic sabotage, the student who takes to the maquis, the man who distributes leaflets, the fellah who suffers and hopes together with his family'.

*El Moudjahid*'s masthead was the slogan 'Revolution by the people and for the people'. The Algerian revolution was a revolution without a name, fought by an anonymous 'people' and led collectively rather than by any one charismatic figure. The decision not to reveal the name of individual journalists was in part a security measure, but it also reflects the FLN's conviction that individuals were subordinate to the collectivity. It also means that it is difficult to be specific about the nature or extent of Fanon's involvement with the paper. In 1964, Josie Fanon identified twenty-one articles as having been written by her husband, and they are included in *Pour la Révolution africaine*. Whilst they were certainly 'by' Fanon in a sense – no one else in Tunis was qualified to write the two pieces on the West Indies[88] – these articles were subject to collective editing, and are therefore not expressive of individual positions or views. There were occasions on which Fanon's more extreme turns of phrase had to be toned down by his colleagues. Writing an article on torture, he slipped in a reference to 'a nation as perverted as France'. This was thought unacceptable, as the FLN claimed, somewhat disingenuously, to be fighting a war against French colonialism and not the French people. The paper had already gone to the printer, but printing was halted to allow the removal of Fanon's unfortunate choice of words.[89] Professional journalist or not, Fanon was a loyal member of the team until other responsibilities began to take up more and more of his time from 1959 onwards. Even taken as a whole, Fanon's articles do not provide a coherent or complete history of the Algerian war. Major events are overlooked or mentioned only in passing. There is, for instance, no real discussion of the events that led up to de Gaulle's return to power in May 1958, but Fanon devotes an article to outbreaks of racist violence in France in May 1959. It discusses the repression directed against the FLN's commandos in France, but appears to have been inspired by the incident in which the Cameroonian novelist Ferdinand Oyono was stabbed by a racist mob when in the company of a white woman and by an attack on a cinema showing an anti-racist film. These incidents were certainly ugly but they were not of any great historical importance. Fanon's information came from the wire services, or even *Le Monde*, and he exploits it for polemical purposes.[90] Yet this was not great journalism.

Perhaps inevitably, Fanon's main polemics were directed against what he saw as the failings of the French left. Despite the dismissive remarks he made to Jeanson about what could or could not be done in France and his professed disdain for Jeanson's activities, Fanon actually shared the basic insight that spurred the philosopher to action: 'The starting point was the impotence of the left. Its glaring impotence.'[91] Although he cannot have hoped to get a positive response, Fanon addressed the French left in a three-part article published in *El Moudjahid* in December 1957.[92]

Fanon was quite unequivocal about where the duty of French intellectuals and democrats lay: they should unconditionally support the national demands of the Algerian people. Tracing an outline history of the 'intelligentsia's attitudes towards the liberation struggle', he described the period before the launch of the armed struggle as one in which a few solidarity meetings were held and in which the response to periodic repression was the publication of appeals and warnings of what was to come. The relative isolation and introversion of the left meant, however, that no real attempts were made to explain the situation 'to the whole population of the colonialist country'. When the pre-insurrectional phase became acute, the left found itself confused and helpless. Although it knew what was happening, it was unable to communicate its knowledge and was reduced to muttering to the government: 'You were warned; what is happening is all your fault.' There was still some communication between a people in revolt and 'the democratic elements'; many intellectuals and democrats were personally acquainted with the leaders of the armed struggle, but the apparent solidarity faded as violence and repression increased. In the colonialist country, chauvinist propaganda began to 'mobilize the racist elements implicit in the collective consciousness of the colonialist people'. It was now impossible to support the struggle of the colonized without opposing the colonizing nation. In the case of Algeria, this point was reached when the contingent was sent to North Africa in March 1956; since that date France had 'accepted the war in Algeria'. Many democrats then fell silent or retreated into an elementary 'patriotism'. The FLN's use of terror now allowed the colonial government to claim that it was fighting 'barbarism', and the left began to make its solidarity conditional: condemn the bombings and we will give our friendly support.

As to the nature of colonialism in Algeria, Fanon argued that the distinction between the working class and 'bourgeois capitalism' did not apply: the colonial situation was one of permanent military conquest and oppression by a foreign power; the status of 'the foreigner, the conqueror, the Frenchman' in Algeria was that of 'an oppressor' for whom neutrality or innocence was not an option. The left had failed to understand this and still claimed that the colonized people and the working class of the colonialist power had common interests. Given that Algeria was a 'settler colony', all French people were complicit in its oppression;

there could be no innocent or neutral Europeans there. The non-communist left, according to Fanon, was worried that an 'independent Algeria' would become part of either a communist bloc or a 'neutralist' bloc: red or Nasserite colonialism would, it feared, replace French colonialism. The Communist Party, for its part, feared that the spread of American influence in the Mediterranean would damage both French and Soviet interests in the area. No section of the left would fully support Algeria's demand for independence. The non-communists spoke of a federal solution to the Algerian conflict; the communists of the need for special links with France. Fanon ended his article by defining what he saw as the task of the French left:

The FLN appeals to the whole of the French left and, in this fourth year, asks it to make a concrete commitment to the fight for peace in Algeria.

There can be no question at any moment of French democrats joining our ranks or betraying their country. Without renouncing its own nation, the French left must struggle to make the government of its country respect the values known as: the right to self-determination, recognition of the national will, liquidation of colonialism, reciprocal and enriching relations between free peoples.

The FLN addresses the French left and French democrats, and asks them to encourage all strike action taken by the French people against the rising cost of living, new tasks and restriction of democratic freedoms in France: these are direct results of the war in Algeria.

The FLN asks the French left to do more to spread information and to go on explaining to the French masses the characteristics of the Algerian people's struggle, the principles that inspire it and the goals of the Revolution.

The FLN salutes those French people who have had the courage to refuse to take up arms against the Algerian people, and who are now in prison.

There must be more such examples in order to make it clear to the whole world and to the French government in particular that the French people rejects the war that is being waged in its name

against the right of peoples, for continued oppression and against
the rule of freedom.

The second part of this article, which describes the influence of the
*Algérie française* myth on the left, was reprinted in the weekly *France-
Observateur* but there was nothing to identify Fanon as its author.[93]
The headline was 'FLN attacks the French left'. An editorial note
described the article as representative of the views of a broad fraction of
the nationalist movement and especially of 'the men grouped around
Ramdane Abane'. It regretted the fact that the French government's
stubborn insistence that 'pacification' was the priority of the moment,
together with the FLN's hard line, meant that a negotiated settlement
was a very long way off. If he did read *France-Observateur*, which is
highly probable, Fanon must have taken this as confirmation that no
real support would be forthcoming from the French left. Further confirmation came in the next issue, in which Gilles Martinet, a prominent
member of the non-communist 'new left', insisted on the need for
'necessary compromises' and negotiations, rejected Fanon's definition
of colonialism, worried about the fate of the European minority in an
independent Algeria and insisted that Algerian nationalists and the
French working class did have interests in common and should work
together. Martinet speculated that the outline history of the intelligentsia had been written by a recent recruit to the FLN who had a taste
for 'outrageous language' and who was performing a 'psychological
strip-tease' (sic), whereas the final part was the work of a seasoned
politician with a sense of responsibility. He added, with some perspi-
cacity, that such intransigence might have been justified if an FLN
military victory seemed imminent; as no such victory seemed likely,
compromise was essential. It was not, he concluded, so much a matter
of a debate between Algerian nationalism's French friends and the
French left's Algerian friends, as one between French and Algerian
people who wanted to find a path that would lead to 'true friendship'
between the two peoples.[94]

Martinet's speculation that the article was written by someone close
to Abane Ramdane was not inaccurate. According to Mohammed
Harbi, who knew both men, Fanon grew close to Abane during the
latter's eight-month stay in Tunis.[95] They worked together on *El*

*Moudjahid* and shared the view, so often expressed in the paper, that there could be no peace negotiations before Algeria's independence was recognized. Both men belonged, that is, to the 'hard-line' faction within the FLN.

Abane was a dangerous man to be associated with. Many within the FLN leadership blamed him personally for the defeat suffered in Algiers. Others thought him arrogant and suspected that he was seeking personal power. A blunt and outspoken man who was prone to create angry scenes in public, Abane was on very bad terms with men like Boussouf, who was in charge of internal security, and Krim, and regarded Ben Bella as a traitor whose close ties with Nasser were suspicious. Ben Bella was, he thought, a dictator in the making.[96] Public expression of such views was highly dangerous in the FLN's Tunis, where Boussouf's boys were always on the alert.

In Paris, a rare Algerian voice now joined in the debate about the French left and the Algerian war. It was that of Jean El-Mouhoub Amrouche, a Catholic Kabyle born in 1906 and in many ways the prototypical 'assimilated Algerian'. Amrouche was a French citizen; he had been educated in French schools in Algeria, had attended the Ecole Normale Supérieure in Saint-Cloud and had taught in a French school in Tunisia. He had published two volumes of hermetic poetry in French, as well as a collection of traditional Kabyle songs in translation (his sister Taos's unaccompanied recordings of them have a spine-chilling beauty).[97] He was the author of a considerable body of literary criticism. As a radio broadcaster, Amrouche was famous for his interviews with French literary figures such as Paul Claudel, François Mauriac and André Gide, and his weekly programme 'Des Idées et des hommes ('Ideas and Men') enjoyed a good audience. During the Second World War, Amrouche had worked for the Gaullist Ministry for Information. Never a member of the FLN and mandated, as he put it, only by himself, he spent the war trying to explain the French to the Algerians, and the Algerians to the French. Amrouche was one of the negotiators who mediated between de Gaulle and Ferhat Abbas, but his political views cost him his position at the ORTF in 1959. This was a man who, in 1946 or fifty years before post-colonial theory made the term fashionable, called himself a 'cultural hybrid'.[98]

Like Fanon, Amrouche did not live to see an independent Algeria and died of cancer of the pancreas in April 1962. The poet Kateb Yacine paid tribute to them and the novelist Mouloud Feraoun, who was murdered by an OAS commando three days before the ceasefire in Algeria, thus:

> *Fanon, Amrouche and Feraoun*
> *Three broken voices that surprise us*
> *Closer than ever*
> *Three living springs who did not see*
> *The light of day*
> *And who made us hear*
> *The anguished murmur*
> *Of subterranean struggles*
> *Fanon, Amrouche, Feraoun*
> *They learned*
> *To read in the shadows*
> *And, eyes closed,*
> *Did not cease writing*
> *Bearing at arm's length*
> *Their works and their roots*
>
> *To die in this way is to live*
>
> *War and cancer of the blood*
> *To each his death, slow or violent*
> *And it is always the same*
> *For those who have learned*
> *To read in the shadows*
> *And who, eyes closed,*
> *Did not cease writing*
> *To die in this way is to live.*[99]

Writing in January 1958, Amrouche accepted that the FLN's position, as expressed by the unidentified Fanon, seemed harsh and that the comments on the stance taken by the left were both wounding and intended to wound, but went on to explain that:

An Algerian patriot, whatever he may be, is not an anticolonialist in the same way as a French man of the left. The experience of the colonized man is a specific experience. Even when it is expressed in doctrinal language, it still has an irreducible affective charge. The French man of the left knows of it, imagines it and empathizes with it out of human sympathy. But, in general, he himself has not suffered the scorn of colonial humiliation. The Algerian consciousness, collective or personal, is a traumatized consciousness. It has difficulty in escaping the tragedy into which it has been so completely plunged. For the French left, the Algerian tragedy is certainly real, but it is as though it were an ordeal, a set of political, social and economic problems that is less easy than others to formulate and solve. The French left is involved in the Algerian tragedy in the way that a doctor watches over his patients. It is not living it. For the Algerian, the Algerian war is not an armed conflict like any other. It is a holy war that calls into question his whole being, his very existence and the basis of that existence, and not simply certain modalities of his existence.[100]

Amrouche also agreed with Fanon that no French person in Algeria could be innocent or neutral. There was no denying that there were rich and poor French people in Algeria, or that 'tens' of them were decent people with many private virtues (sic: the European population was over a million-strong), 'but all these decent people are involved in the oppression, the repression and the application and justification of the colonial system'.[101] For Amrouche, it was the task of the French left to say out loud that France had been deceived by her leaders, that France was being compromised by an unjust and stupid war, and that the cause of the Algerian people was a just cause. The French left proved not to be up to that task.

Fanon was correct in saying that the voting of special powers signalled an acceptance of the war and a decisive break between the French left and the Algerian nationalist movement. As the debate went on calmly in the Assemblée Nationale on 9 March 1956, Algerian workers in Paris called a twenty-four-hour strike in protest. In the afternoon, ten thousand of them demonstrated in the streets. No organization on the

French left called out its troops to support them, and there were no protests when a violent police charge dispersed the demonstration outside the Hôtel de Ville.[102]

The French left's record on Algeria is not an inspiring one, and Fanon's criticisms are not as caricaturally extreme as they may seem. There had indeed been 'warnings' of what was to come in *Esprit* and elsewhere, but they had been given by a tiny minority of men such as Jeanson and Mandouze. In 1954, that Algeria was part of France was a fact of political life for right and left alike. Although the governments of the Fourth Republic were unstable and ramshackle coalitions, they were not of the far right. On the contrary, Mitterrand, Mollet and Mendès France were on the democratic left, but their position in 1954 was quite clear: Algeria was and would remain French. When Mollet's special powers were voted in 1956, it was clear that there would be no parliamentary opposition to the war in Algeria. And the one party that might have been expected to provide, or at least support, extra-parliamentary opposition, failed to do so.

It was not that the French Communist Party (PCF) was indifferent to the Algerian question. Between 1950 and 1955, it produced a monthly paper called *L'Algérien en France*, though it did little more than reproduce material from *L'Humanité*, interspersed with items of 'news from home'. The Party made serious attempts to recruit Algerians and to unionize those who worked in the factories and mines of France, but it always assumed that their 'class' interests outweighed their 'national' interest. A number of factors combined to shape the PCF's position on Algeria.[103] Ever since its foundation in 1920, it had always had difficulty in supporting the Leninist line that communist parties had an overriding duty to support liberation movements in the colonies, and had argued that colonized peoples would receive their deliverance thanks to – and after – the advent of socialism in the metropolis. Even less attention was given to the 'colonial question' after the adoption of the 'popular front' strategy, which subordinated everything to the struggle against fascism and called for an alliance of all the forces of the left, regardless of their ideological affiliations. In his report to the Ninth Congress of the PCF, which met in Arles in December 1937, Secretary General Maurice Thorez accepted the need to satisfy the demands of the peoples of French colonies by introducing major reforms, but added that it was in France's interests to do so because a failure to implement reforms would play into the hands of fascism, which would use demagogic arguments to turn certain strata of the native populations against France. Whilst he acknowledged the right of self-determination, he insisted that 'the *right* to divorce does not mean an *obligation* to have a divorce'. The decisive question of the moment was 'the victorious struggle against fascism' and it followed that 'the interest of colonial peoples' lay in 'union with the people of France and not in an attitude which might encourage the manoeuvres of fascism and put, for example, Algeria, Tunisia and Morocco under the yoke of Mussolini or Hitler'.[104] In the post-war period, the terms of the argument shifted slightly, but the implications for Algeria remained strikingly similar: the independence of both France and her colonies was now threatened by US imperialism rather than fascism. The interests of Algeria therefore once more coincided with those of France.

The refusal to support any demand for independence was not merely an instance of a general line on the colonial question, but of the representation of Algeria constructed by the PCF, and here Fanon is not mistaken when he insists that even the left had been influenced by the 'Algérie française' myth. Speaking in Algiers in February 1939, Thorez introduced the very influential notion of an 'Algerian nation in formation':

> When I speak of Frenchmen from Algeria, I mean all of you present here, all of you who are French of origin, French through naturalization, those of you who are Jewish and also those Arab and Berber Moslems, you are sons, if not by blood then at least in your hearts, of the great French Revolution.[105]

This is a 'leftist' version of the argument that Algeria was to be the birthplace of a new race formed from both an ethnic merger and the assimilation of French culture. The weakness of the argument is of course that virtually no mixed marriages were celebrated in Algeria, and that any form of sexual contact across the racial barrier – other than prostitution – was almost unknown. This is the obvious reason why there are no Algerian equivalents to Mayotte Capécia's tales of the torments of love across the barrier, and why the Fanons were a very odd couple in the Algerian context. As a very official publication from the Gouvernement Général in Algiers put it two years before Thorez spoke: 'One of our civilization's other successes is that it has facilitated the formation of a new people, European in origin and essentially Latin, which constitutes the most original and perfect synthesis ever to have existed in a Mediterranean country.'[106] The 'new race' concept was in part a literary construct, and the novelist Yvon Evenou-Norves was more outspoken in an article on 'the province of Algeria' published in 1922: 'A new people has taken shape here, and that people is French.'[107]

In 1956, a new phrase was coined to describe this stage in the formation of a new nation: 'the Algerian national formation'. As Thorez himself put it in 1957: 'We have modified our form of words and we speak quite rightly of the Algerian national phenomenon, of the constituted Algerian nation whose reality rests upon the merging of elements of varied origins.'[108] Two years into the war, the PCF was still arguing, despite all the evidence to the contrary, that settlers and Arab-Berbers were merging to form a new Algeria, and that the USA would move in if France moved out. From this perspective, it was self-evident that the explosions of November 1954 were the work of provocateurs, fascists or even reactionary settlers. Despite the PCF's construction of its own 'Algérie française' mythology, its press did cover the war well and was highly critical of the effects of the French army's actions.[109] Individual communists risked, and sometimes lost, their lives for the Algerian cause. The Party's general line was, however, 'peace in Algeria' and not 'victory to the FLN'.

The PCF's reluctance to oppose the war was also influenced by its attitude to the military, and its views on the army reflected the ambiguous nature of that institution itself. The army was both a professional army of enlisted regulars, and a conscript army in which all young men did a period of military service. The Party was always hostile to the professional regular army, and especially to its officer class – viewed as an appendage of a bourgeoisie that had become detached from the true or 'popular' French nation. On the other hand, it took a very positive view of the *contingent* of conscripts, in accordance with the republican view that military service was one of the ties that bound together the nation. The old image of the citizens' armies of the Revolution was still a powerful force. A communist's place was in the army, and his role was to try to argue the Party line to his comrades. The PCF did not condone desertion or *insoumission* (refusal to report for military service and to bear arms) and it certainly did not condone the actions of those who carried suitcases: communists who did so were expelled from their party. When, in September 1961, 121 intellectuals signed a public statement on the 'right' not to bear arms or to serve in the Algerian war, only two PCF members – the painter Edouard Pignon and the novelist Hélène Parmelin – added their names to the list and they did so without their party's approval.[110]

When the *rappelés* were called up in April 1956, there was significant and largely spontaneous popular opposition but this was not synonymous with support for the FLN and its revolution. Nor was it an expression of some Leninist revolutionary defeatism. It was symptomatic of a reluctance to serve – and quite possibly die – in a war that meant nothing to those who had to fight it. Attempts were made to stop the troop trains leaving. In Grenoble, cement was poured into the points to block their passage. That the protests came from *rappelés* is not surprising. They were significantly older than the nineteen- and twenty-year-olds of the *contingent*, and many had wives, children, jobs and financial commitments. They did not want to serve in Algeria, but they were not natural supporters of the FLN. Nor were France's students. In theory, France's conscript army represented the entire nation but its war in Algeria was fought mainly by the sons of workers and peasants. Middle-class students could defer their period of military service until after the completion of their studies, and it was not difficult to prolong those studies almost indefinitely. As the hero-narrator of Philippe Labro's semi-autobiographical novel remarks: 'Thanks to one deferment after another, one fiddle after another, I almost escaped Algeria.'[111] It was only when the government tried – unsuccessfully – to alter the deferment system in April 1960 that student opposition to the war became a major force.[112] By then, the political situation was very different and very dangerous.

Fanon was quite right to say that the left was 'confused' – in an unsigned article that found its way into *France-Observateur* in December 1957. One of the first manifestations of extra-parliamentary opposition to the war was the meeting in the Salle Wagram to which Mandouze somewhat rashly brought his 'greetings from the Algerian

Revolution' on Friday 27 January 1956. It was organized by an ad hoc 'Comité d'action des intellectuels contre la pursuite de la guerre en Afrique du Nord' formed the previous November and active until the summer of 1956. The organizers were opposed in principle to colonial wars and in favour of the right of self-determination, but soon found that they knew lamentably little about Algeria. The sociologist Edgar Morin, a refugee from the PCF who helped organize the meeting, later recalled that they were not even clear as to the distinction between the FLN and Messali's MNA.[113] If this was an attempt to interest France, or at least sections of the French left, in the Algerian question, it got off to a poor start. The French left simply did not come en masse, and three-quarters of those present in the Salle Wagram were Algerian.[114]

The main speakers were Mandouze, Sartre, Aimé Césaire and Jean Amrouche. Of those on the platform, Amrouche was, apart from Mandouze, by far the best informed about Algeria and his analysis of the colonial system was surprisingly close to Fanon's. Sartre, in contrast, knew relatively little about Algeria in 1956. He had been there with Simone de Beauvoir in 1948 and again in 1950. In 1948, they had gone because 'we wanted some sun and we loved the Mediterranean', but they had been disappointed: far from being the picturesque back-drop to films like *Pépé le Moko*, Algiers's Casbah was a place of 'wretchedness and rancour'.[115] Beauvoir remarks of their second visit in 1950, which took them across the Sahara: 'We were opposed to the colonialist system, but had no a priori prejudice against the men who administered native affairs or who were in charge of building the roads.'[116]

Sartre's presence at the Salle Wagram meeting was the first indication of his solidarity with the Algerian cause and of the commitment that would lead him to preface Fanon's *Les Damnés de la terre* in 1961. It would make him one of the most hated men in France. Armed with a battery of economic and demographic statistics, probably culled from the Jeansons' *L'Algérie hors la loi*, he argued that colonalism in Algeria was an all-pervasive system and warned against the 'neo-colonialist' illusion that the situation had degenerated simply because some elements within the system were rotten. The history of Algeria had, he said, been the history of the concentration of land ownership into the hands of the colonists. The Algerian economy and political system could not be reformed: 'The only thing we can and must do . . . is to struggle alongside the Algerian people to free *both* the Algerians and the French from colonial tyranny.'[117] His reference to freeing both the Algerians and the French inadvertently reveals the greatest weakness in the French left's stance on Algeria: it laboured under the illusion that the FLN was in some sense fighting a war on *its* behalf and not simply its own war of national liberation. The politics born of that illusion would prompt Fanon's harshest comments about the French left's concern for the victims of torture. He was to argue that they were more worried about the damage being done to France's honour and soul than about shattered Algerian bodies. In that sense, even Sartre was not beyond criticism and reproach. For his part, Césaire, who admitted to knowing little about North Africa, invoked the spirit of the Bandung Conference of 1955 which had, he said, signalled the end of Europe's unilateral domination of the world, and called for the abolition of the colonial regime. He looked forward to the birth or rebirth of an Algerian state 'united to France by the laws of friendship and solidarity, and no longer by the bonds of subjection and domination'.[118]

Amrouche's stinging words were closer to the analysis Fanon would make in *Les Damnés de la terre*:

> The colonial state makes the colonized native (whatever he may be, and even when he is integrated into the repressive apparatus and has at the same time become the despised and most odious tool of the profiteers) a foreigner who has no roots in his own land. He is reduced to the role of someone who lives on hand-outs, of a perpetual beggar who is fed on the relief that his masters give him as charity, who is on the margins of economically normal activities. He feels all the effects of the colonial conquest and despoilment that are supposed to be being transfigured into a civilizing epic weighing down on him so heavily that he is suffocating and that the air is physically unbreathable.

He ended with an anecdote. Two Kabyle peasants had told him 'In 1945, we were still afraid. Since then, we have learned that we must not be afraid any more. What can they do to us that we have not experienced already? Prison? We've been there. Poverty? We were born in poverty. Death? We are ready to die.' And he recalled the fable he had been told by an old relative. A peasant and his son were coming home from market. They were attacked by bandits, beaten and robbed. The son said: 'Father, they beat us.' His father replied 'They recognized us, son.' The bandits had beaten them because they recognized them as men who would not resist. Amrouche concluded: 'Ladies and gentlemen, it is that time, the time when the men of Algeria could be beaten with impunity, that is now behind us. There are no more natives . . . in Algeria. From now on, there are Algerians there.'[119] These were strong words from a man who had once considered himself honoured to be a French citizen.

The revelations about the massacres and the tortures, about the horrors of 'pacification', about the burning villages and about the prisoners shot while trying to escape that had begun with the publication of articles in *Les Temps Modernes* and *Esprit*, continued with the appearance of *Des Rappelés témoignent* in the autumn of 1957.[120] This was not 'the official face of the war'. The journalist Jean-Jacques Servan-Schreiber, who spent a tour of duty as a lieutenant in Algeria, describes that face: 'the daily dispatches' that read so flatly and repeated the now familiar place names: '"M. Boualem, owner of a plumbing business in L'Arba, seriously wounded", "Infantry unit takes out a rebel band near Palestro", "Muslim found with his throat cut in Ménerville", "Farm laid waste in Foundok", "Clash to the north of Tablat; no further information available" . . . These monotonous reports, day after day for months, for years, almost – who still reads them?'[121] The main thrust of Servan-Schreiber's argument – that France was turning a rebellion into a revolutionary war – was largely ignored.[122] Resolving the 'Algerian question' was not high on the average citizen's list of priorities.

The historian Pierre Vidal-Naquet, who was to become one of the most eloquently damning critics of French policy in Algeria, describes the opponents of the war as being a combination of Dreyfusards, Bolsheviks and Third Worldists.[123] The Dreyfusards were the linear descendants of the intellectuals who, like Zola, had accused the Republic of betraying its own principles when it allowed an innocent Jewish officer to be sent to Devil's Island for treason. The Bolsheviks – mostly Trotskyites and disgruntled refugees from the PCF – thought that they had rediscovered in the Algerian revolution a purity that had been stained by Stalinism, whilst the Third Worldists saw anti-colonialism as a new internationalism and as an alternative to the stagnation of the European left. His categorization of the opposition is broadly accurate, though it should be added that many, like André Mandouze, also believed that they were heirs to the wartime French Resistance. The back covers of the many documents published by Minuit bear the legend 'Editions de Minuit founded in clandestinity in 1942'.[124] Nor are Vidal-Naquet's categories completely watertight; Sartre, in particular, sometimes appeared to belong to all three at once. The Third Worldists had not really emerged in 1956, and were in part a product of Fanon's writings. The Dreyfusards were in the majority.

For the Dreyfusards, torture was the primary issue. That the French army could use torture in Algeria was a scandal because it meant that it was using the very methods that the Gestapo had used against the wartime resistance. In 1959, Minuit's publication of *La Gangrène* made it clear that torture was not confined to Algeria. The little book contained first-hand account of their treatment by Algerians who had been tortured in the headquarters of the DST in the rue des Saussaies. This was in the heart of Paris, and almost next door to the Elysée Palace. The gangrene was eating into the heart of France. For some, like Vidal-Naquet, this recalled horrors that were very close to home: his father Lucien had been tortured by the Gestapo in Marseille in 1944.[125] He was then deported for his resistance activities and murdered in Auschwitz. Marguerite or 'Margot' Vidal-Naquet also died in a gas chamber. Vidal-Naquet's father 'died for France'; his mother was murdered because she was Jewish.[126] A classicist by profession, Vidal-Naquet is convinced that the task of the historian is to establish and tell the truth, and he is now one of the most acute critics of the 'revisionism' that seeks to deny the existence of the Nazi death camps or to diminish their importance.[127] During the Algerian war, his main concern was to tell the truth about torture and doing so was not easy.

On 12 June 1957, Henri Alleg, a member of the PCA and the editor of the left-wing newspaper *Alger républicain*, was arrested at the home of his friend and comrade Maurice Audin, a young lecturer in mathematics at the University of Algiers. Alleg was taken by the paratroopers of the First Regiment of Colonial Paratroopers to an unfinished block of flats in the El-Biar district of Algiers. This was where Ali Boumendjel had 'committed suicide' in February. Alleg was beaten, stripped naked and tied to a plank before being tortured with electricity. He refused to answer his torturers' questions about where he had been staying. After the first 'session', Audin was brought into the room and told to tell Alleg what to expect. He merely said: 'It's hard, Henri' and was then taken away.[128] He was not seen again. Audin had been arrested the previous day and the army had been waiting in his flat for anyone who might turn up. Alleg had simply blundered into the trap. The paratroopers were looking for Paul Caballero, the Secretary-General of the PCA, and Audin was suspected of harbouring him. On 25 June, it was officially announced that Audin had escaped from custody while being transferred to another building.

After fourteen days in the hands of the paratroopers, Audin had been able to leap from a jeep as it slowed to take a tight bend, to scale a fence and avoid pursuit. One of his escorts opened fire with a sub-machine gun but presumably missed him as no bloodstains could be found. Maurice Audin had simply vanished.[129] His wife refused to believe this and quickly became convinced that he was dead. She went to court, laying charges of murder against 'persons unknown'. A Comité Audin was formed to investigate the circumstances of the man's death and the slow, careful search for the truth began. It became the main focus for the campaign against torture. The Audin campaign did not end with the end of the Algerian war; it was only in 1963 that the French government even admitted that he was dead. His body has never been found, but the evidence slowly assembled by Vidal-Naquet and the Comité Audin indicates that Maurice Audin was strangled by Sergeant Charbonnier from 1 RCP. In the meantime, Alleg went through the full gamut of horrors. He was beaten, half-drowned over and over again and repeatedly tortured with electricity. He was made to take sodium penthatol, or the so-called truth serum. When he was first taken to the interrogation centre, he was told by his captors that they reserved special treatment for Europeans who had taken the side of *les ratons*, and they kept their word. Alleg never talked, and was eventually sent to Barberousse Prison, guilty of having 'reconstituted a proscribed organization'.[130] His *La Question* was originally written as a letter of complaint to the *procureur général* while being held in a detention camp before being transferred to prison. Two copies were smuggled to Paris by members of the PCA. When *L'Humanité* published extracts from the document, it was seized by the police. Jérôme Lindon, the owner and editor of Editions de Minuit, published the full text in December. The book was promptly seized, but reprint after reprint ensured that it had sold almost 90,000 copies by the end of 1962.[131]

*La Question* is one of the most important – and most harrowing – books to have emerged from the Algerian war, and the Audin affair was in French terms one of that war's most significant events. For intellectuals, it still has immense symbolic power. One memory is particularly powerful. Maurice Audin was due to defend his doctoral thesis in public at the Sorbonne in the first week of December. The *soutenance* went ahead. The chairman of the jury asked 'Is M. Audin there?' and then said 'In the absence of M. Audin . . .' The thesis was defended by Maurice Audin's supervisor. When the jury returned to announce that Audin had been granted his doctorate, the crowded lecture hall rose to its feet. The chairman shouted: 'Do not applaud' and called for a minute's silence. The Minister for Education had argued that the *soutenance* should not go ahead; the Sorbonne's Dean of Science replied that it was 'normal pedagogic action'.[132] The Sorbonne's honour was intact.

Fanon never mentions the Audin case, but he did read *La Question* and was familiar with the work of the Paris-based campaigns against torture. He was interested in *La Question* only because it confirmed what he already knew, namely that French doctors and nurses were deeply involved in the war, that they administered truth drugs and that they revived torture victims so that they could be tortured anew.[133] In his article on Algeria and the French torturers, Fanon argued in brutal terms that French democrats who protested about torture in Algeria reminded him of Hegel's 'beautiful souls'. Reports like Louis Martin-Chauffier's book *Contre la torture* (1957) and articles like Georges Mattéï's 'Jours Kabyles' proved that all 'these humanists' were concerned about was 'the moral effects of these crimes on the souls of the French'. The tortures, the 'wood chores' and the rape of young Algerian girls were seen as a threat to 'a certain idea of French honour'.[134] This was a harsh judgement, but Georges Mattéï's article, which graphically describes the brutality of the so-called pacification of Algeria, ends thus:

> The young men who are fighting in Algeria today are twenty years old; they will all do eighteen months in French North Africa. What generation is being prepared in the culture-medium of modern Algeria? Plans are being made for the Nazification of my comrades. They are at an age when violence can easily act as a catalyst and teach reflex racism, the omnipotence of strength and what the paratroop officers call the 'shock unit spirit' – hatred of intellectuals, scorn for human thought: *the philosophy of the sten gun*. What is going on in Algeria today is a large-scale attempt to dehumanize French youth.[135]

Alleg himself made the same point when he observed that the building in El-Biar was 'not only a place where Algerians were tortured, but also a school for the perversion of young Frenchmen'.[136] Fanon comments on Mattéï's article thus: 'It is worth thinking about this attitude. Such exclusion of Algerians, such ignorance about the men being tortured or of the families that are being massacred constitutes a completely new phenomenon. It is related to the egocentric, sociocentric form of thought that has become characteristic of the French'.[137] For Fanon, torture was not an aberration but an integral part of a colonial system which had always been based upon brutality and extreme violence. It was a *normal* facet of colonialism. Whilst Fanon was in a sense right – the use of torture in Algeria did not begin in November 1954 – his polemic overlooks the fact that stories of atrocities could be exploited by the FLN's advantage and to turn international opinion against France. The FLN's overseas delegations did not make the same mistake.

The same argument surfaces in Fanon's comments on the case of Saadi Yacef's runner Djamila Bouhired, who had been arrested for her part in the Battle of Algiers. She had been picked up in February 1957 after a gunfight in which she was wounded, and had been badly tortured. When it was announced on 15 July that she had been sentenced to the guillotine, ten bombs shook Algiers. In France, protests were organized against the execution of the twenty-two-year-old woman and she became something of a *cause célèbre*, not least because the bomb she had planted failed to explode. The murder of Djamila Bouhired did not, wrote Fanon, pose any problem for the Algerian people; she was not the poor victim of some evil act, but a self-conscious Algerian patriot. By concentrating on individual cases, the conscience of the French left had simply shown that it was behind the times and that it had failed to realize that the struggle to defend individual freedoms and human rights had given way to the struggle to defend the rights of peoples. Even if Bouhired were pardoned, neither the struggle of the Algerian people nor the repression being carried out in the name of the French people would change.[138] Bouhired herself told the court;

> The truth is that I love my country and that I want to see it become free, and that is why I support the FLN's struggle. And that is the only reason why you are going to condemn me to death . . . But when you kill me, do not forget that you are also murdering your country's tradition of freedom, that you are compromising its honour and putting its future in danger, and that you will not prevent Algeria from becoming independent. *Inch'Allah.*[139]

Vidal-Naquet's 'Dreyfusards' were courageous and worked in a very honourable tradition. Some lost their jobs and they all risked prison on charges of sedition. They did not denounce torture in the abstract; they named names, gave details and accused officers and politicians of lying. Yet they were not fighting the same war as Fanon. Their points of ideological reference – the Dreyfus affair, the Resistance – were inevitably French and not Algerian. As Jérôme Lindon, who was until François Maspero and the 'Third Worldists' appeared on the scene from 1959 onwards the only publisher to print these books, put it after the war: 'I did it for France, not for Algeria.'[140] The Dreyfusard's opposition to the war was principled and brave but it did not satisfy Fanon, whose own position seems to have blinded him to the obvious: they were not Algerian nationalists, but French citizens who saw themselves as patriots and who were understandably fearful for the future of their own country.

The anonymity of its contributors ensured that *El Moudjahid* always spoke with one voice, and it always spoke in the name of a united organization. No hints of any schisms or even differences of opinion within the FLN were permitted: the façade of unity had to be preserved at all cost. The FLN had to be presented as the guide and guardian of the revolution, even if this meant the suppression of knowledge of the real nature of its actions. Two instances of the economic handling of the truth are of direct concern to any account of Fanon. The first was the Melouza incident of May 1957. On 31 May, the Gouvernement Général in Algiers announced that French troops had discovered evidence of a massacre that had taken place in the extreme south of Kabylia. Three hundred corpses were found in the houses of a hamlet known as Mechta-Kasba, some distance from Melouza itself. All were the bodies of men of fighting age, and they had been hacked to pieces and mutilated. It was obvious that those who had tried to escape had been machine-gunned. Realizing that the army had stumbled on a remarkable propaganda opportunity, Resident-Minister Lacoste sent in photographers and journalists to record the evidence of the FLN's brutality towards its own people.[141]

In one of its last issues, *Résistance algérienne* offered a different interpretation: 'Given the internal and external conjuncture in which this war has placed France, Melouza was a predictable event which was both indispensable and necessary to the French colonialists. On the night of 28–29 May 1957, five hundred Algerians were murdered in cold blood. It should be noted that the victims were chosen: they were all adult men or men in a condition to bear arms.'[142] In New York, the FLN's delegation to the UN sent a telegram to the Secretary General, demanding an impartial inquiry into the methods being used by both sides in Algeria. This would, it was claimed, demonstrate that the French were lying.[143] In France, the FLN's Fédération was distributing leaflets making the same claim.[144] Fanon's first public statement following his arrival in Tunis was made in the course of an FLN press conference about this incident. Describing him as a psychiatrist of West Indian origin who had practised in Algeria for a few years before taking to the *maquis* and as the author of a study entitled *Peau noire, masques blancs*, *Le Monde* reported without comment the statement he read out:

The foul machinations over Melouza, which are intended to discredit the National Liberation Front in the eyes of the civilized world, show the extent of the French authorities' cynicism and monstrous perfidy. The description of the Melouza massacre suggests that it was carefully stage-managed. And we would not be surprised if the French authorities were planning to make a film about the 'martyred village' in preparation for the forthcoming session of the UN . . . there is an obvious wish to blame the FLN for an absurd and horrible massacre.[145]

He added that the entire population of Melouza had been helping the forces of the Liberation Army and that the area had never been 'won over to Messalism'.[146] Fanon's press conference was the last shot in a propaganda war that had been lost; for two days *Le Monde* had been running headlines about the atrocity committed by the FLN. Shortly after these events, *wilaya* III's Colonel Mohammedi Saïd was quietly recalled in Tunis.[147] In October 1988, Saïd admitted in an interview on Algerian television that he had ordered the Melouza massacre.[148] The Melouza incident caused a degree of soul-searching on the part of the French left, with some asking the FLN to supply proof that it was not responsible and others trying hard to convince themselves that the killings were 'individual acts' born of despair and fanaticism or acts of cruelty on the part of individuals driven mad by rage at the atrocities that had been inflicted on them in the course of the war.[149] The FLN remained silent.

The massacre was one of the ugliest incidents in the ongoing war between the ALN and Messali's MNA. Fanon was not mistaken in saying that the villagers of Melouza had rallied to the FLN. As so often, their support for the FLN was the direct outcome of French repression; after the murder of a captain, the French army had summarily executed suspects and left their corpses exposed on the road as a warning. When the army moved out, the FLN moved in.[150] The sequence of events that led up to the massacre began when Amiroche wiped out an MNA unit commanded by Mohamed Bellounis. Bellounis and a small group escaped and eventually reached Melouza, where they found some support amongst local people. It was this group and its supporters who were massacred in a well-planned operation ordered by Saïd and carried out by Commandant Arab. Bellounis somehow survived and went over to the French. Alert to the possible utility of using a private army, they made him a general and gave him command of a 3,000 strong Armée Nationale. It proved to be so troublesome and made so many heavy demands on the villages where it operated that it was physically liquidated by its sponsors in July 1958. Its liquidation did not cause any outcry.

Whether or not Fanon knew what actually happened at Melouza, or whether or not he believed what he told the press conference, cannot be established with any certainty. Other episodes reveal a considerable discrepancy between what he said or endorsed in public and what he said in private, and indicate that his definition of 'true' was decidedly instrumental. In *Les Damnés de la terre*, he argues that there is no such thing as 'absolute truth': 'Truth is that which precipitates the dislocation of the colonial regime, that which promotes the emergence of the nation. Truth is that which protects the natives and destroys foreigners. In the colonial context, there is no truthful behaviour.'[151] This is scarcely surprising: anyone working on propaganda is less concerned with objectivity than with the way events can be manipulated to the desired end. The French played the same game, producing fake editions of *El Moudjahid* and planting disinformation wherever possible. It is difficult to believe the Algerian casualty figures that appeared day after day in the French press, and there is no doubt that dead peasants were posthumously transformed into dead ALN fighters and auxiliaries on a regular basis.

The FLN's attempt to pass off the Melouza massacre as the work of the French army may look crude, but it was effective in a country where French forces did commit massacres and where it was all too easy to believe the worst of them. No one had forgotten Sétif or the football stadium in Philippeville. Charles Geronimi is convinced that Fanon did know what happened in Melouza. Some of Fanon's psychiatric patients in Tunis were young liaison agents and scouts who worked clandestinely under terrible pressure and suffered the effects of heavy stress. As they well knew, capture meant torture and death. They also knew that they were working for an organization that could be ruthless in the extreme. Some of these young men and women knew where the bodies were buried, and that many Algerian bodies were victims of the FLN itself.

They could well have confided in a sympathetic psychiatrist who was prepared to listen. One of the bodies Fanon almost certainly knew about was that of Abane Ramdane.

On 24 May 1958, *El Moudjahid* featured Ramdane's photograph on its front page. It was framed in black, and the headline read: 'Abane Ramdane dead on the field of honour'. When this appeared, Abane had already been dead for five months and he did not die in battle. He had not been wounded in a fire fight that lasted for hours and the FLN leadership had not been hoping for months that he would recover. And nor was it a haemorrhage that finally killed him. Abane Ramdane was strangled with a length of rope in a villa outside Tetouan, having been lured to Morocco on the pretext that there was important business to be settled there. His assassins were two of 'Boussouf's boys',[152] and his murder was the result of long-standing political differences that came to a head at a CNRA meeting held in Cairo in August 1957. This was marked by violent exchanges between Abane, Boussouf and Belkacem Krim, and Abane lost the argument. The meeting resolved that politics did not take priority over military issues, that there was no difference between the interior and the exterior, and that the definition of the goals of the Revolution should refer to the 'creation of a democratic and social Algerian Republic that was not in contradiction with the principles of Islam'.[153] All these shifts of policy represented a reversal of the decisions of the Soumman conference, at which Abane had been a major force. An expansion and reorganization of the CNRA itself made it clear that the real power now lay with the military. Abane had been dangerously marginalized and the age of the 'war lords' had begun. Abane had lost his battle to politicize the Revolution and he lost his life as a result.

This could not be admitted. For official purposes, Abane had died a hero's death and Ali Boumendjel wrote the appropriate obituary for *El Moudjahid*. Fanon said nothing. He had good reason to remain silent. According to Mohammed Harbi, Fanon's name was on the list of those who were to be eliminated in the event of a violent reaction to Abane's liquidation.[154] Fanon was close enough to the 'information services' to know the truth about Abane's death, and probably to know of the existence of just such a list. When they met in Rome, Fanon told Simone de Beauvoir that he had two deaths on his conscience and could not forgive himself for them. One was that of Patrice Lumumba, and the other that of Abane Ramdane.[155] He did not expand. He had met and admired him, but Fanon obviously had no part in the death of Lumumba, who was murdered by domestic political rivals. He clearly felt some responsibility for the fate of Abane. This implies that he thought that he could have prevented him from going to Morocco, and that in turn implies that he knew or strongly suspected what was going to happen there. Beauvoir certainly gained the impression that he knew far more than he would or could say about the grimmer secrets of the Algerian Revolution. Fanon was not alone in keeping silent. The story of Abane's murder was told for the first time in Yves Courrière's history of the Algerian war, published in 1970.[156] As late as the beginning of the 1990s, schoolchildren in Algeria were still being taught that Abane Ramdane was one of the Revolution's martyrs.[157]

Writing for *El Moudjahid* was by no means a full-time occupation and it was not difficult for Fanon to combine it with his clinical work. The longest of his articles were no more than 3,000 words long, and writing – or at least dictating – 3,000 words once or twice a month was scarcely taxing. Fanon's appearance at the press conference on Melouza was the first indication that he was to become a significant spokesman for the FLN, but it was only at the end of 1958 that he began to represent the organization in the international arena at the All-African People's Congress in Accra.

# 9

# 'We Algerians'

FANON'S CLINICAL WORK at the Manouba, the reforms he instituted at Charles-Nicolle and his collaborative work with Lucien Lévy are indicative of his full professional commitment to psychiatry and medicine. He was also fully committed to the cause of Algerian independence, and the double obligation soon resulted in a punishingly hard schedule of activity. The spokesman who now began to represent Algeria on the international stage in sub-Saharan Africa would return to his clinical work and to *El Moudjahid*'s office whenever he was in Tunis. He was now acquiring new responsibilities, and he assumed a new identity to go with them. In the summer of 1958, Fanon was issued with a passport by the Tunisian consulate of the United Kingdom of Libya. Delivered on 10 August and valid for all countries, passport number 018728 identified him as Omar Ibrahim Fanon, born in Tunis in 1925, 165 centimetres in height, with black eyes and black hair, and domiciled in Tunis.[1] The document was what has come to be known in French as *un vrai faux passeport* – a 'real false passport' – or a genuine document issued under a false identity as opposed to a forgery. It was valid until August 1963. The adoption of the somewhat transparent pseudonym was obviously a security precaution. FLN members often used aliases for security reasons but the practice also had symbolic overtones: they were the anonymous servants of a revolution without a face. Fanon's adoption of a new name also had unexpected long-term repercussions when his mother died in 1981. Her property and the proceeds from the sale of the house in Redoute were bequeathed to her children and Frantz's share should have automatically gone to his only son. The bureaucratic French *état civil*, however, held no record of the death of Frantz Fanon and, even though knowledge of his father's demise was very much in the public domain, Olivier therefore had to provide documentary proof that he was no longer alive before he could inherit the small amount of money involved.[2]

The passport was first used on a mysterious trip to Rome in September 1958. An entry stamp in it indicates that Fanon landed at Elmas airport in the Sardinian capital of Cagliari on 14 September and then travelled on to Rome. No details have emerged about this visit to a city which Fanon would come to know well, but the circuitous route he took suggests that secrecy was a priority. It can, however, be safely assumed that the trip to Rome was not unrelated to the establishment of the Provisional Government of the Republic of Algeria (GPRA).

At 13.00 (Algerian time) on 19 September 1958, the same statement was read out in both Arabic and French in Tunis, Cairo and Rabat:

The CEE . . . has resolved to form a Provisional Government of the Republic of Algeria. The GPRA will take over the executive powers of the Algerian State until the liberation of the territory and the establishment of its definitive institutions. Answering to the CNRA, it is responsible for the conduct of the war and for the management of the interests of the nation. It takes office as of today.[3]

Ferhat Abbas was appointed President, with Belkacem Krim and Ben Bella as his Vice-Presidents. Although they were still in prison in France, Hocine Aït Ahmed, Rabah Bitat, Mohamed Boudiaf and Mohamed Khider were made Ministers of State. A full cabinet of nine ministers and three secretaries of state was created. Frantz Fanon had no position in the Provisional Government. The real power was in the hand of Krim, Ben Tobbal and Boussouf who were, respectively, Minister for the Armed Forces, Minister of the Interior, and the Minister responsible for communications and weapons-procurement. Within hours, the GPRA had been recognized by Iraq, Egypt, Pakistan, Libya, Yemen, Morocco, Tunisia, Saudi Arabia and Sudan. Within days, it was also recognized by China, Mongolia, North Korea, North Vietnam and Indonesia. Although the CNRA remained in Cairo, the GPRA was based in Tunis. This brought it closer to the front line but it also loosened the embrace of Gamal Abdel Nasser, which was beginning to feel suffocating rather than fraternal.

The establishment of the GPRA was a response to developments both inside and outside Algeria. The defeats of 1957 had pointed to the need for the reorganization and consolidation of the FLN's leadership and structures. As it became increasingly obvious that an outright military victory on the ground was unlikely, the diplomatic front became more important. The Algerian struggle had to be internationalized so as to isolate France at the UN and elsewhere. The GPRA had delegations in all the Arab countries, but needed to expand its network of representatives. Diplomatic missions were eventually established in New York, Rome, Bonn, Geneva, Madrid, Stockholm and London, where the MPs Anthony Wedgwood Benn, Barbara Castle and Fenner Brockway organized a 'Free Algeria' campaign.[4]

The official FLN position was that the formation of the GPRA was proof of the nationalist movement's new maturity. *El Moudjahid* insisted, as always, that the movement was monolithic and that the GPRA was an expression of the sovereignty of the whole people and not of the opinion of one fraction within it.[5] Not everyone within the FLN agreed. Furious that the principle of 'priority to the forces of the interior' appeared to have been flouted, Amirouche called a meeting of the *wilaya* colonels for December. They reasserted the old principle, complained bitterly that they were not receiving enough arms and spoke of the need for further purges within their own ranks. This was a direct challenge to the authority of the GPRA, which summoned the colonels to Tunis for consultations. Amirouche and two of his comrades died in French ambushes as they tried to make their way there in early 1959. It is said by some historians that the French army somehow knew in advance of the route Amirouche was taking.[6]

France had already made its own contribution to the internationalization of the Algerian question and had set in train a sequence of events that were to have momentous consequences. In early January, there was a serious clash between the ALN and a French patrol on the Tunisian border. The French response was to exercise the right of pursuit by bombing a disused mine just across the border that was being used as an ALN base on 8 February. The base was destroyed but, either by accident or design, the neighbouring village of Sakiet Sidi Youssef was also bombed on the very day that a Red Cross team was distributing food to the refugees living there. At least seventy civilians died in the raid, and a further one hundred and fifty were injured. The victims included Tunisian schoolchildren. Tunisia immediately recalled its ambassador from Paris, closed France's consulates and brought the incident to the attention of the UN's Security Council.

According to Fanon and *El Moudjahid*, the Sakiet incident was France's way of punishing Tunisia for its solidarity with the Algerian people, but also the prelude to the reconquest of Tunisia in order to put the whole of the Maghreb under French domination.[7] Fanon, whose tendency to think in apocalytic terms was becoming more and more pronounced, may well have believed this; the more skilled operators on the paper certainly realized that the incident offered a propaganda opportunity that was not to be missed. The French action was widely condemned around the world, and a new stage in the internationalization of the war came with an Anglo-American offer of 'good offices'. Accepting the offer would have meant admitting that Algeria was not an internal French matter. Fanon and *El Moudjahid* interpreted it as an attempt to throw the 'anti-colonialist world' into confusion.[8] The proposal came to nothing, as President Bourguiba would not accept the plan to put the frontier zone under international control, but it did cause a ministerial crisis in Paris, where there was panicky talk of a coming 'diplomatic Dien Bien Phu'. This was the twentieth ministerial crisis in the Fourth Republic's history and the government fell on 15 April. President Coty was faced with a difficult choice. He could either appoint a right-wing prime minister and adopt the 'Public Safety' policy being demanded in Algiers, or he could appoint someone who favoured a negotiated solution and face a possible rebellion on the other side of the Mediterranean.[9] There was a growing sense that a man of providence was needed. The name of Charles de Gaulle was being mentioned more and more often.

In Algiers, the atmosphere was feverish and the panic fear that the interests of *Algérie française* were about to be sold out was spreading. On 9 May, General Salan telegrammed his superior officer in Paris to warn him that the army was demanding a government that would permit it to win a total victory over the FLN; if there was even a hint that Algeria was going to be abandoned by France, there was no telling how the military would react. The plotters were hard at work again. Massu had declared that he personally wanted de Gaulle to return to power as he was the only man who could guarantee that Algeria would remain French. Governor-General Lacoste was under pressure to declare where his sympathies lay. The Socialist Party had stated that it would not be part of the coalition government Pierre Pflimlin was trying to put together, and Lacoste was being urged to leave his party. He fled Algiers instead, leaving the city with no civil power and creating a dangerous vacuum. At this point, the FLN announced that it had executed three of its French prisoners of war. Two demonstrations were immediately called for 13 May. One, headed by Salan, was a protest against the executions; the second was meant to be a display of the *pied noir* population's insistence that Algeria was and would remain French. Trinquier's Third Regiment of Colonial Paratroopers was brought into Algiers to maintain order.[10]

Huge crowds gathered around the war memorial where Mollet had been so humiliated in February 1956.[11] Suspected of wanting to sell out Algeria, Salan was greeted with boos; Massu was cheered. Urged on by Pierre Lagaillarde in the para uniform he had no right to wear, a group of young activists began to encourage the crowd to storm the Gouvernement-Général building. The CRS and Trinquier's men offered only token resistance. The demonstrators invaded the building, locking frightened civil servants in their offices, and flung armfuls of documents from the windows. In the midst of the confusion, Salan appeared on the balcony and asked the crowd to disperse. He was again booed. Massu then appeared and harangued the crowd with an improvised speech in which he promised the demonstrators the support of the army. Hours later, the formation of a Committee of Public Safety was proclaimed. It was headed by Massu. Salan backed his subordinate's act of sedition. A telegram was dispatched to President Coty: the CPS was vigilantly awaiting the formation of a government of public safety to ensure that Algeria remained an integral part of the metropolis.[12] The Committee consisted of three colonels and seven civilians. Algiers was in open rebellion, and it had the support of the army. The cover of the 13 May issue of *Le Bled*, which had a print run of 200,000, announced that keeping Algeria French was 'the army's number one mission'.

In Paris, the Pflimlin government proclaimed a state of emergency but tacitly accepted that it no longer had any authority in Algiers. Two days after the rebellion began, Salan appeared on the balcony of the Gouvernement-Général and cried '*Vive de Gaulle*!' The General had intimated that he was willing to assume power. Salan, in the meantime, was planning Operation Resurrection. If necessary, paratroops would be dropped on Paris to use force to return de Gaulle to power. Committees of Public Safety had already been established by paratroops in Corsica, and civil war or even a military takeover began to look distinctly possible. On 27 May, de Gaulle announced that he was forming a republican government capable of guaranteeing the unity and independence of France. Prime Minister Pflimlin tendered his resignation the next day. On 1 June, de Gaulle became the head of the government. Two days later the Assemblée nationale granted him full powers for a period of six months, and special powers in Algeria. A referendum to ratify de Gaulle's constitutional proposals was promised for September. Coty remained President in name, but was really only a symbolic figure. No one knew what de Gaulle's Algerian policy would be. Some within the FLN, including Ferhat Abbas, entertained the hope that it might be possible to negotiate a peace settlement with him. Informal contacts were established through Jean Amrouche and, whatever was said in public by either side, secret negotiations did go on throughout the last four years of the war.[13]

Three days after his investiture, de Gaulle was in Algiers. The city was decked out with red, white and blue banners and the road from the airport was lined with delirious welcomers. On the evening of 4 June 1958, de Gaulle addressed the enormous crowd packed into the Forum. Raising his arms above his head in a 'V for victory' gesture, he told the *pied noir* population of Algiers: '*Je vous ai compris*' ('I have understood you'). This was immediately interpreted as an expression of unconditional support but, in the storm of applause that followed, it was difficult to hear what de Gaulle was actually saying. He went on to say that the population of Algeria was composed of French citizens: 'French wholly and entirely, in a single college, and in less than three months' time, all the French, including ten million French citizens, will have an opportunity to decide their own destiny.'[14] Talk of a single college and of Muslim participation in a referendum was not what the crowd wanted to hear, but it was the *je vous ai compris* that dominated their memory of the speech. In the speaking tour that followed, de Gaulle used the hallowed phrase *Algérie française* only once.[15] The promised referendum would be the final stimulus for the formation of the GPRA, but the FLN leadership was not, for the moment, impressed. On 10 June, a communiqué insisted that the FLN would have independence, whatever the cost. And it called upon its supporters to attack the French wherever they could, to seize French arms and to strike at every possible opportunity.[16]

The FLN now activated the Fédération de France's 'special sections' and carried the war to the metropolis. The war with the Messalists was still going on, and there had been attacks on police and military targets. The FLN's gunmen had also shown themselves capable of remarkable discipline and restraint. On 19 May 1957, Ali Chekkal, a former Vice-President of the Algerian Assembly and, in the FLN's eyes, a traitor, was assassinated by Mohammed Ben Sadok while he was watching the French cup final. Chekkal had been standing beside René Coty but Ben Sadok made no attempt to harm the President of the Republic and quietly gave himself up to the police. In the wave of repression that followed, over 2,000 arrests were made in the narrow streets around the place Maubert alone.[17] On the 'Red Night' of 25 August 1958, restraint was thrown aside.[18] An annexe of a police station on the boulevard de l'Hôpital in Paris was machine-gunned, killing two policemen and injuring a third. A police station in the thirteenth arrondissement was also attacked. An attempt to blow up the cartridge factory in the Bois de Vincennes ended in failure, and in a fire fight one policeman and two FLN men died. In the suburbs, oil-storage facilities in Gennevilliers and Ivry were set ablaze. Elsewhere, there were further acts of sabotage: bombs went off in La Rochelle and at oil refineries near Montpellier and Marseille. Police vehicles were machine-gunned in central Paris. Over the next month, there were fifty-six acts of sabotage and over 200 gun attacks; eighty-two people died. The police crackdown was immediate and heavy. In Paris, thousands were arrested and herded into the Vélodrome d'Hiver. This oval building on the left bank was an indoor cycle track, often used for other sporting events as well as for political rallies. It had also been used for other purposes. In July 1942, it had held 12,000 of the Jews, including 4,000 children, who were picked up in the first of many raids. Most later died in Auschwitz.[19] The Algerians arrested sixteen years later were officially 'returned to their home villages'. But those villages were internment camps in the southern desert.

The FLN could not and did not want to fight a sustained war inside France. To do so would have inevitably led to the destruction of the Fédération, and that would have made it much harder to finance the war in Algeria and the diplomatic offensive abroad. The flurry of violence demonstrated, on the other hand, that whatever the outcome of the referendum and whatever the possibility of negotiations, the war would go on until independence was achieved. The FLN was also anxious to show that it was at war with the French state, and not the French people. No bombs were planted in the Métro, no crowded cafés were sprayed with machine-gun fire, and there was none of the random terrorism that had become commonplace in Algiers.

In the September referendum, de Gaulle won a huge 'yes' vote, with even the Socialist Party voting in favour of his proposals for a Fifth Republic and a constitution that gave the President extensive powers. He also won a 'yes' vote in Algeria, despite the FLN's call for Algerians to abstain. For once the PCF and the FLN were in agreement. The PCF had called for a 'no' vote and saw de Gaulle as a dangerous authoritarian or even a proto-fascist; Fanon and *El Moudjahid* described the 'saviour of France' as a pre-fascist who had now become a complete fascist.[20] With one exception, the African colonies voted for the establishment of a French Community that would give them internal autonomy. According to Fanon and the *El Moudjahid* team, they had freely consented to their indefinite 'domestication' by France.[21]

De Gaulle's most pressing concern was of course with Algeria. Early in October, he returned there and, in a major speech given in Constantine, spoke of land distribution, the development of the Saharan oil and gas reserves and of the need to reduce the economic gulf between the European and Muslim communities. Huge sums of money were, he announced, to be made available for the creation of new industries. The end of the speech marked a significant shift of position: '*Vive l'Algérie et la France!*'[22] Limited reforms were introduced. Military men with public administration responsibilities were replaced by civil servants and the Commitees of Public Safety, which had been designed to provide a shadow government, were disbanded. Salan was quietly recalled to France. At a press conference held on 23 October, de Gaulle made his first direct appeal to the newly created GPRA by offering them 'the peace of the brave': those who had opened fire could now cease fire and go home without being dishonoured. The ALN's fighters were invited to meet France's military leaders; the FLN leaders were invited to contact the French embassies in Tunis and Morocco. The GPRA rightly interpreted this as a demand for a complete surrender and rejected the offer.[23] As always, de Gaulle's words were ambiguous. On the one hand, he had demanded a surrender; on the other, he had tacitly acknowledged that the ALN was not a band of rebels and outlaws, but an army that had fought bravely. He had sensed that the existence of the GPRA meant that there was at last someone it might be possible to talk to.

On 1 December Fanon flew directly to Rome's Ciampino airport. He was travelling on a transit visa and was also in possession of a visa issued by the British Embassy in Tunis and stamped 'seen by' the embassy in the Italian capital two days after his arrival in Rome. Valid for twenty-eight days, the document issued in Tunis was good for a single journey to Nigeria in direct transit to Ghana. The Republic of Ghana, made up of the former British territories of the Gold Coast and Togoland, had become independent in 1957 and, under the presidency of Dr Kwame Nkrumah and the leadership of the Convention People's Party, had embarked upon a policy of 'African Socialism'. In international terms, the young republic had become the main focus for Pan-Africanism. Pan-Africanism already had a long history dating back to the beginning of the twentieth century, when men like the American Du Bois first began to regard Africa as one great territorial unit. It took on a new impetus when a sixth Pan-African Congress was held in Manchester in 1945 and demanded 'autonomy and independence' for the whole of Africa. The conference also resolved for the first time that 'We are determined to be free', adding the rider: 'if the Western world is still determined to rule Mankind by force, then Africans, as a last resort, may have to appeal to force in the effort to achieve freedom'.[24] The independence of Ghana and the prospect of independence for other states seemed to have transformed the old dream of continental unity into a utopia that could finally be realized.[25]

This was Fanon's first visit to sub-Saharan Africa and it was occasioned by the All-African People's Congress, held in Accra from 8 to 12 December 1958. Attended by some 200 delegates from twenty-five countries, the Congress was seen by its organizers as a first step towards a Pan-African Commonwealth of a free and independent United States of Africa.[26] The nucleus of that Commonwealth had, it was claimed, already been formed by the short-lived union between Ghana and Guinea. The Congress opened on 8 December in the Ambassador Hotel, where the first session was addressed by Nkrumah himself. Speaking from a rostrum backed by a banner showing a flaming torch superimposed on a map of Africa and emblazoned with the slogan 'Hands off Africa', he spoke of the need for the 'total liberation of Africa': 'We have a continent to regain. We have freedom and human dignity to attain.'[27] Some of the obstacles to total liberation and unity were already apparent. Senghor was not present in Accra, but came under attack for taking Senegal into the 'Community', made up of France and twelve African countries that had come into being in October. The formation of the Community was de Gaulle's initial response to the growing demand for independence. The individual states enjoyed internal self-government, but the 'Community', or in other words France, was responsible for foreign policy, defence, economic policy, education, justice and transport and communication. French troops remained in these autonomous states and were usually stationed near the airports and other transport facilities. Their ostensible role was to protect French nationals, should the need arise, but they could also be used to suppress internal dissent. Only Guinea had voted 'no' in the referendum held on 28 September. Most of those present in Accra viewed the Community, which existed only until 1960, as a 'new form of French imperialism' or an Empire by another name.[28] Fanon scornfully described it as something that appealed to 'all the specialists in colonial lethargy'.[29] The ominously heavy police presence outside the conference was, however, a reminder that there were also purely African obstacles to African unity. There had been a bomb threat from those demanding the release of some of Nkrumah's political opponents,[30] who had been held without trial under the Preventive Detention Act of July 1958 on the grounds that they had engaged in 'dangerous political activity' whose very nature meant that no court would be able to prove a case against them.[31]

Fanon was part of a four-man delegation. Although the London *Times* described 'Dr F. Omar' as the leader of the 'Algerian Liberation Front delegation',[32] Fanon was not the senior figure. He had clearly moved up in the GPRA's diplomatic hierarchy but the delegation was headed by Ahmed Boumendjel. Boumendjel addressed the Congress on 11 December, speaking emotionally of the 'affection and fraternal support' that had been displayed by the whole of Africa and of his conviction that Algeria could expect the 'capitulation of the forces of oppression'.[33] Fanon had, however, inadvertently upstaged him the previous day when, to a standing ovation, he told the delegates that the struggle for liberation could never rule out recourse to violence. Freedom fighters and nationalist leaders had to adopt *all* forms of struggle and could not rely on peaceful negotiations alone. Although Fanon received wild applause when he said this, he had displayed a remarkable lack of tact. He had gone against the general ethos of the conference and was in effect openly criticizing Tom Mboya who, chairing the session and representing Kenya, had placed the emphasis on non-violence and negotiation. To make matters worse, it was well known that Nkrumah himself was no believer in violence and that his theory of 'positive action' emphasized non-violent means of struggle.[34] In an attempt to avoid an embarrassing confrontation with the Algerian delegates, Mboya called a press conference and stated that, whilst nobody liked to employ violence, 'the actions of colonial powers, especially in Algeria, will eventually determined whether we should use force, and when that time comes we should not be blamed'.[35] The FLN position proved popular: Boumendjel was elected on to the Conference's steering committee, and the other Algerian delegates on to various sub-committees.

The few days he spent in the capital of Ghana allowed Fanon to establish direct personal contact with nationalists all over the continent, from South Africa, whose policy of apartheid was denounced with a call for sanctions, to Cameroon and the Congo. Some of those contacts were to have great personal significance as well as important political implications. Fanon was elated by the Accra conference and wrote, presumably in collaboration with Boumendjel, two enthusiastic pieces about it for *El Moudjahid* on his return to Tunis.[36] The hour-long private discussion the Algerian delegates had had with Nkrumah, who intimated that Ghana would soon recognize the GPRA, had been a concrete gesture of solidarity and had placed Algeria high on the Pan-African agenda. More generally, the euphoric atmosphere in the Ambassador Hotel had convinced Fanon that almost sixty million Africans would be free 'by 1960'. Turning to the issue of violence, Fanon argued that the 'successive defeats' it had experienced in 'other territories' (meaning Algeria, Morocco and Tunisia) had allowed or obliged France to begin a peaceful decolonization elsewhere in sub-Saharan Africa. The ongoing war in Algeria meant that France was simply not capable of fighting colonial wars elsewhere. In Fanon's view, Algeria was the 'guide-territory' and was leading what would become a continent-wide revolution,[37] and the reception he and his fellow delegates had received in Accra was proof that its leading role had been recognized. The Conference had debated and endorsed, at least in principle, the creation of a new agency of international struggle, namely an 'African Legion' that would fight in Algeria:

> By deciding to create in all territories a corps of volunteers, the peoples of Africa are making a clear demonstration of their solidarity with other peoples and have thus expressed the view that national liberation is bound up with the liberation of the continent . . . In popular meetings organized in Ghana, Ethiopia, and Nigeria, hundreds of men have sworn to aid their Algerian or South-African brothers when they ask for it.[38]

Even in 1958, such words must have sounded utopian in the extreme, but the idea of an 'African Legion' came to mean a great deal to Fanon, who concluded in 1960 that troops based south of the Sahara could be used to open up a second front within Algeria itself. Although Fanon always refers to this project as an intensification of the struggle, it in fact revealed a weakness. It was only because the ALN's fighters of the interior found themselves increasingly isolated and immobilized that a southern front was necessary.

Fanon did not return directly to Tunis, and travelled back via Lisbon where he spent the night of 14–15 December. The stopover in Lisbon is as mysterious as the trip to Italy in September, but Fanon may have been following up some Angolan contacts he had made in Accra. He had met members of the Popular Movement for the Liberation of Angola or MPLA at Présence africaine's Paris Conference in 1956, but in Accra he encountered someone from a different Angolan organization. Roberto Holden was not an official delegate to the Conference but had somehow smuggled himself into the Ambassador Hotel. Born in 1923, he was the leader of a self-styled Union of the Peoples of Northern Angola. Founded in July 1956, it was calling for the restoration of the old Kongo kingdom, claiming that it had always been a separate political entity and had never been part of the Angola defined by Portugal. Holden had appealed to both the UN and the USA for support. In Accra, he was firmly told that the idea of the restoration of the state of Kongo was a 'tribal anachronism' and, with remarkable alacrity, responded by drafting a manifesto calling for the liberation of the whole of Angola and rebaptizing his organization the Union of the Peoples of Angola. Despite the new name and manifesto, the UPA remained a regionally based party, or rather a pressure group which was at this stage still hoping to persuade Portugal to introduce a programe of reforms. It was also hostile to the older and more broadly based MPLA.[39] The GPRA was pressing the case for armed insurrection in the hope that its own struggle for independence would be emulated on a continental scale. For the moment, it was somewhat wary of Holden, not least because of his American connections and rumoured links with the CIA, and was more sympathetic to the MPLA. Within the space of a year and largely at Fanon's urgings, it gave its support to Holden and his UPA. The effects of this change of political heart were to be disastrous in both the short and the long term.

The Accra conference did much to cast Algeria in the role of what might be termed Africa's senior revolution: apart from the so-called 'Mau Mau' (more properly known as the Land and Freedom Army), which had launched an insurrection in Kenya in 1952,[40] Algeria's FLN was the first revolutionary organization to use violence on such a scale and, eventually, with success. The attempt to export the Algerian model to other countries, which was actively promoted by Fanon from 1959 onwards, did not, however, always have positive results. His hugely successful performance in Accra also helped to promote the image of Fanon as the apostle of violence three years before the publication of *Les Damnés de la terre*. When she met him in Rome in the summer of 1961, Simone de Beauvoir knew little about Fanon himself, though she had recently read his books, but she did know that this was the man who had been applauded in Accra for the 'impassioned speech on the necessity for and value of violence' and for his criticisms of Nkrumah's 'pacifist theses'.[41] Fanon's reputation had also come to the notice of *L'Express*'s Jean Daniel. Daniel was not present in Accra himself, but he had, he recalled in 1961, heard many of those who were there speak of the 'poignant speech' in which Fanon justified the use of violence 'with accents that reduced him to tears and made his audience feel a sort of communion'.[42]

From Lisbon, Fanon went back to Tunis but his clinical work was soon interrupted by a long-standing engagement to speak at Présence africaine's Second Congress of Black Writers and Artists, which was held in Rome from 26 March to 1 April 1959. Fanon was now quite familiar with the city, and he already knew Taleb Boulharouf (also known as 'Pablo'), who had headed the FLN delegation there since October 1958. Although its activities were shrouded in secrecy, the FLN was not forced to work in total clandestinity in Rome and had even been provided with offices by an Italian Communist Party rather more sympathetic to the Algerian cause than its French counterpart. The government tolerated the FLN presence and gave Boulharouf's delegation de facto recognition.[43] Fanon himself did not feel too comfortable in Rome as he suspected that he was perceived as a *nègre* in that city too. When she was with him, it was always Josie who took care of their hotel arrangements. Fanon thought, rightly or wrongly, that if he tried to book a hotel room, he would be turned away on the grounds that his presence might 'disturb the American guests' or 'cause trouble'.[44]

Although everyone at the Congress was perfectly well aware of who and what he was – his speech in Accra had been widely reported in the international press – Fanon had not been invited to Rome to speak on behalf of the GPRA. At the Paris Congress of 1956, speakers had been representatives of national delegations; on this occasion they spoke either in their individual capacity or as members of the various working commissions set up in 1956. As in Paris, this was a cultural rather than a political gathering and, although the final motion did condemn colonial wars, no one actually spoke in the name of those fighting them. No political parties were represented. The theme was not national liberation but 'the unity of Negro-African cultures'.[45] According to the general preamble, the 1956 Congress, which was devoted to the 'crisis in culture', had had a diagnostic role; the role of the Rome Congress would be to outline a solution in the form of 'solidarity between peoples'. One of the most harmful of the West's 'cardinal sins', it went on, was the notion of 'peoples without culture'; now that the peoples of Africa were either gaining or on the point of gaining their political independence, their economic and cultural independence must also be guaranteed. As before, the 'peoples' represented were primarily those of the French-speaking Caribbean and Africa, Madagascar and the United States, though all the proceedings were in French. Fanon was the only speaker from the Maghreb.

To the disappointment of its organizers, not all those billed to speak at the Congress were actually present. Although their contributions were included in the published proceedings, neither Sekhou Touré nor Senghor could attend and sent their apologies from Guinea and Senegal respectively. Présence africaine's second conference was less well attended than the Paris conference – according to Le Monde the opening session was attended by only 150 people[46] – but proceedings began in style with a reception in the Capitole. Formal speeches of welcome were made by representatives of the Italian government, Prince Alliata di Montreale, the acting president of the Istituto Italiano per l'Africa, Ignazio Silone, representing the Union of Italian Writers, and a representative from UNESCO. The Congress then transferred to the Istituto to begin its working sessions.

Alioune Diop set the tone in his opening address when he defined negritude as both 'the negro genius' and 'the desire to reveal its dignity'.[47] He spoke of the need to 'dewesternize' Africa, taking care to add that this did not mean dewesternization for the sake of it: 'We are resolved to conserve the gifts of the West, provided that we can use them in accordance with our own genius and our own situations.'[48] One of the 'gifts' of the West was apparently Catholicism: the delegates were granted a formal audience with Pope John XXIII. Senghor, for one, never had any difficulty in reconciling his negritude with his Catholicism. Papers on Christian theology were presented to the Congress, but there were none on Islam even though it was the majority religion in most of the African countries represented. The repeated references to an 'African genius' in Diop's address indicated that the conference would be dominated by the theme of the negritude that had emerged in the 1940s. Jean Price-Mars, who was now Haiti's ambassador to Paris, invoked palaeontology, prehistory and archaeology, as well as UNESCO's 1952 reports on race and biology,[49] to demonstrate that Africa was humanity's original cradle and that, far from being the 'dregs of humanity', the innumerable branches of the 'melanic type', which represented the majority of the world's population, had a legitimate claim to a glorious past and the right to a dignified future. The melanic race was, argued Price-Mars, now embarking on a crusade for justice and fraternity and appealed to all men 'whatever the colour of their skin, the texture of their hair or the shape of their nose' in the name of the unity of the human race.[50] Cheikh Anta Diop reiterated his theses about the black-Egyptian origins of Greek culture and argued that a traditionally peaceful and matriarchal Africa had, from the time of the Acheans to the contemporary period, constantly been invaded from the north and robbed of its natural riches.[51] Diop's sub-text helps to explain some of the tensions between North Africa and the regions to the south of the Sahara and to clarify why the Maghreb never became an important issue for *Présence africaine*: some of the invaders and robbers from the North were Bedouin and Arab traders and slavers.

Amadou Hampaté Bâ, the Senegalese writer, described the traditional animism of the French Sudan in poetic and almost mystical terms, reminiscent of Placide Tempels's account of Bantu philosophy, and concluded that Black African traditions were the very basis of 'our intellectuality': 'We must build our modern culture on the age-old traditions of our ancestors.' That modern culture would then be the creation of Africans themselves and a distinctive contribution to world culture.[52] Black American literature was discussed at some length,[53] as was the issue of racial discrimination and the US Supreme Court,[54] but the focus was, as it had been in Paris, mainly on Francophone Africa. There were, however, differences between the two conferences. Although speakers like Bâ and Diop were still celebrating the Senghorian version of negritude, others concentrated on the responsibilities of the intellectual. As a historian of Francophone African writing puts it: 'From 1959 forward, the role of Présence africaine and SAC-sponsored conferences was to form a socially responsible and politically conscious elite primed to bring about cultural change in Africa.'[55] Reclaiming and celebrating the pre-colonial past was now less important than preparing for the post-colonial future.

The resolution adopted by the Commission on Literature gives a good sense of the general mood of the conference:

> Black peoples have endured a number of historical atavars which, in the particular form of a total colonization implying both slavery, deportation and racism, has, in the objectively known historical period, been imposed only on those peoples and on those peoples alone.
>
> The existence of a Negro-African civilization that transcends national or regional cultural particularisms, therefore appears to be historically justified, and it is legitimate and enriching to refer to that civilization.
>
> That must be the basis for the unity and solidarity of the various Negro peoples, without it being necessary to reduce those peoples, and especially their men of culture, to the sterile uniformity of a corpus of precepts, doctrines and imperatives.[56]

The paper Fanon read to the Congress struck a rather discordant note in that it rejected the continent-wide perspective of most of the participants and, despite his own interest in the very different form of Pan-Africanism symbolized by the African Legion, focused on the nation-state. His theme was 'The Reciprocal Foundation of National Culture and Liberation Struggles'. His title is of particular significance: although he had long had doubts about the existence of 'one black people', but had been willing to concede in 1955 that West Indian and African peoples did exist,[57] he was now concerned primarily with the nation as a political and cultural unit: any authentic culture was, he contended, by definition a *national* culture. When deprived of the twin supports of the nation and the state, cultures perished and died: national liberation and the renaissance of the state were the preconditions for the very existence of a culture.[58] No national culture, no national cultural life and no cultural innovations or transformations could exist under colonial domination.[59] To try to 'miss out' the national stage of development would be a disastrous error. Whilst some proponents of Pan-Africanism were thinking in terms of supranational states, Fanon was thinking in terms of alliances between nation-states.

Fanon's speech was included in *Les Damnés de la terre*. There are some reworkings – the first two paragraphs are omitted – but they are minor and take the form of the introduction of paragraph-breaks into what was originally a monolithic slab of text. More important is the addition of a long 'preface', which is clearer on some points than the version read out in Rome. Written in the spring or early summer of 1961, it is also much harsher and says things that could scarcely be said on a public platform by someone whose main concern was to rally support for the GPRA and the Algerian cause. Fanon had already rejected negritude as a 'great black mirage' in his 1955 article on 'West Indians and Africans', but he said relatively little about it to the Congress. In *Les Damnés de la terre*, he returned to that topic in more detail. He now argued that the doubts about the existence of a universal black culture expressed by Richard Wright and others in Paris demonstrated that cultures always existed in national contexts, and that the problems faced by Wright or Langston Hughes were therefore not the same as those facing Senghor or Jomo Kenyatta.[60] In the underdeveloped countries, national culture meant the struggle for national liberation, not folklore or an abstract populism. Those who were still fighting in the name of Negro-African culture and organizing conferences dedicated to the unity of that culture should realize that they had all been reduced to comparing coins and sarcophagi.[61] A footnote picks up the fact that Senghor had decided that negritude should be included in Senegal's school curriculum. If, adds Fanon, this was an exercise in cultural history, the decision could only be approved; if it was a matter of shaping black consciousnesses, Senghor was turning his back on history, which had already noted the fact that most *nègres* had ceased to exist.[62]

*Nègres* had ceased to exist, or were ceasing to exist, in the sense that 'those who created them are witnessing the dissolution of their economic and cultural supremacy'.[63] The emergence of black national movements and nation-states meant that the black man was no longer created by the white man in the way that the Jew was created by the anti-Semite. The black man was escaping the mode of being-for-others. Fanon had reached, or perhaps returned to, the Sartrean position of which he had been so critical in *Peau noire, masques blancs*; negritude had been no more than a 'racist anti-racism' that had to be transcended. Negritude could exist only in the context of white domination: blacks from Chicago and blacks from Nigeria or Tanganyika were the same *only* to the extent that they defined themselves in relation to whites.[64] It was the dominant white culture that had described all the inhabitants of Africa as 'negroes' and the people of Algeria as 'Arabs' or 'natives'. The history of slang corroborates Fanon's argument. *Bougnole* derives from a Wolof word meaning 'black' but was, from the nineteenth century, used in French as a pejorative term applying to all the black peoples of Senegal and West Africa in general, regardless of their ethnicity. It was subsequently applied indiscriminately to the Arab-Berber population of the Maghreb when individuals were reduced to a collective 'essence of Arab', as Francis Jeanson once put it. Something had begun to change when 'the negroes' began to describe themselves as 'Angolans' or 'Ghanaians'; as Amrouche had remarked in 1956, Algeria was beginning to be inhabited by 'Algerians' and not stateless 'natives'. The theorists of negritude had, according to Fanon, failed to register that change.

The real venom was reserved for the final paragraphs of *Les Damnés de la terre*'s chapter on 'national culture'. Jacques Rabemananjara, bard of cultural unity, once a political prisoner in French jails and now a Minister in Madagascar, was, Fanon stressed, a member of a government that voted against the Algerian people in the UN's General Assembly. Léopold Sédar Senghor, President of a Republic of Senegal that was still part of a French-defined 'Community', poet of negritude and member of the Société Africaine de Culture, had also ordered his delegates to vote with the French.[65] When it came to solidarity with the Algerian Revolution, those who spoke of the unity of African culture were as ineffectual as a French left that worried about universal values and French honour rather than shattered Algerian bodies. The harshness of Fanon's comments no doubt goes some way to explaining why, when a brochure was published to celebrate the first ten years of *Présence africaine*'s existence, it made no mention of Fanon, and why, in an article published to mark its fortieth anniversary, Rabemananjara himself fails to signal Fanon's presence in either Paris or Rome.[66]

The description of the emergence of a national consciousness is remarkably unspecific, partly because of Fanon's undoubted tendency to generalize but also, surely, because it is more difficult to speak of colonialism in general than of colonies in particular. Fanon identifies three stages in the history of the national culture of the colonized country – culture being defined in terms broad enough to include everything from ceramics and woodcarving to literature. Colonial domination results in the obliteration of the reality of the nation and obliges the colonized to recognize the inferiority of their culture. Traditions decline, and the intellectual frantically tries to acquire and identify with the culture of the colonizing power. There is, in other words, a relationship of mutual dependency between the withering away of the reality of the precolonial nation and the death-throes of the national culture.[67] In literary terms, this stage is, paradoxically, characterized by 'relative over-production' that expresses a gradual differentiation and a 'particularizing will' that marks the beginning of something new: 'Whereas the colonized writer began by producing exclusively for the oppressor, either in order to charm him or to denounce him by using ethical or subjectivist categories, he gradually adopts the habit of addressing himself to the people. It is only from this point onwards that one can speak of national literatures.'[68]

The schema is in fact clearer in the additional material included in *Les Damnés de la terre* where Fanon speaks of an assimilationist period in which colonized writers imitate or mimic Parnassianism,[69] symbolism and surrealism, followed by a 'pre-combat' period in which they 'decide to remember' and reclaim their past, and finally the period of combat in which a national culture and literature finally emerge.[70] Laments and indictments give way to appeals to the people and calls for revolt: 'This is combat literature in the true sense of the word, in the sense that it calls upon a whole people to join in the struggle for the existence of the nation . . . because it informs the national consciousness . . . because it is a temporalized will.'[71] For Fanon, the nation is a product of the will, and a form of consciousness which is not to be defined in ethnic terms; in his view, being Algerian was a matter of willing oneself to be Algerian rather than of being born in a country called Algeria. His description of the emergence of the national consciousness in *Les Damnés de la terre* is couched not in ethnic terms, but in Sartrean and phenomenological terms.

Although the Fanon who spoke in Rome can in a sense be regarded as speaking on behalf of the GPRA, there is surprisingly little in his speech that is specific to Algeria. It seems almost self-evident that when he speaks of 'the nation' or 'Africa', Fanon means 'Algeria'.[72] A closer examination of both the Rome speech itself and the material added to it in *Les Damnés de la terre* makes that assumption look surprisingly problematic. Algeria is in fact mentioned only once, when Fanon, thinking of his experiences in Blida, refers to the changing role of traditional story-tellers. Whereas they used to recite 'inert episodes', they had now begun to update their stories, to use the names of modern heroes in the new epics they were creating.[73] Fanon's brief comments on jazz and the blues provide a rare insight into his musical tastes, but are not at all pertinent to Algeria.[74] The audience for jazz in Algeria was drawn from a minority of Europeans – Geronimi, for instance, was a reader of *Jazz Hot* magazine – and, whilst it also included a Martinican who liked Stellio, it cannot have comprised many Algerians. The making of masks which he discusses is surely typical of sub-Saharan Africa rather than the Maghreb.[75] A literary historian points out that there were no imitations of Parnassianism, symbolism and surrealism in colonial Algeria, not least because those schools of writing were not studied there.[76] Negritude is, for obvious reasons, largely irrelevant to Algeria, though Jean Amrouche did once suggest with bitter humour that, when he rebelled against assimilation, the *bicot* should freely assume his *bicoterie* ('wogginess' might be an approximate translation), in the same way that the *nègre* had assumed his negritude.[77] Whilst imitations of surrealism and negritude meant little in the Algerian context, they had been significant factors in Martinique. To speak of a transition from 'assimilationist' rhymed verse to 'the rhythm of the poetic *tam-tam*' recalls not the poets of the Maghreb, but rather Aimé Césaire and the Fanon who edited a little magazine called *Tam-tam* in Lyon. Fanon's Rome speech and the related chapter of *Les Damnés de la terre* are, in a very real sense, a recapitulation of his own experience. His early work and indeed experience is characterized by a tension between being the object of the white gaze and proclaiming, like Aimé Césaire, that it is 'good and fine to be a *nègre*'; from 1959 onwards, that tension was overcome by the will to be Algerian.

What Fanon calls laments and indictments had indeed been heard in Algeria. One of them was a lengthy poem by Aït Djefar which circulated in student circles from 1951 onwards. The 'Lament of the Arab Beggars of the Casbah and of little Yasmina, Killed by her Father' tells the true story of Ahmed Kuani, a forty-two-year-old beggar who looked seventy, and his nine-year-old daughter Yasmina. They had nothing to eat and Ahmed was suffering from tuberculosis. As they walked hand in hand through the streets of Algiers, he suddenly pushed his daughter under the wheels of a heavy truck. She somehow fell between the kerb and the truck, and so he pushed her again. This time, she died almost instantaneously. A psychiatric report reproduced at the end of the poem described Kuani as 'mentally feeble' and as suffering from severe neurasthenia and melancholia which made him prone to bouts of dementia. The 'North-African syndrome' had struck again. Judged to have acted in a state of diminished responsibility, Ahmed Kuani was committed to Blida for life. The 'Lament' is dedicated to 'those who have never been hungry', and begins thus:

> *Crowd*
> *Individuals*
> *Audience*
> *Spectators*
> *Onlookers*
> *Readers*
> *I raise*
> *My blood-filled glass*
> *To the health*
> *Of those who are in good health*
> *I raise it*
> *And I break it*
> *Angrily on the pavement*
> *Of my anger*
> *And grind the shards into my fingers*[78]

The *pied noir* poet Jean Sénac also wrote laments for the children of Algiers:

> In the rue de Chartres
> they sleep in the mud
> tender cockroaches on their cheeks
>
> Torn feet
> cold eyes
> beautiful, smiling
> crammed together
>
> In the rue de Chartres
> the children
>
> In our tender beds
> shame
>
> In the rue de Chartres certainty
> has violet lips
>
> They cannot sleep on they cannot sleep
> all the clubs in the world have been let loose on them
> Order is building peace
> with kicks to blonde heads
>
> Do those bags of nerves have souls
> beneath their skulls of cotton
> cheap torturers
> taking their revenge on our children
> because they are not men
>
> Sacred sleep
> sleep soiled in its praise
> midnight a dozen blows from a truncheon
> a dream bleeding from the throat

*Hot bread rises from the oven*
*mint from the near-by café*
*sacks, an alarming*
*bed*
*in the coughs*
*in the fleas*
*hunger bivouacs*
*anger bares its throat*

*The dawn following the insomnia will be cruel*
*the lyre is broken*
*the earth is absent*
*a hunted life invents*
*a different life*

*With the children*
*awoken, beaten*
*with the beggars*
*kicked and chased away*
*sharpen our cry*

*We are on our feet to bear witness*
*to scratch the wound*
*till it is healthy*
*till men who are good and just appear.*[79]

Fanon did not know either of these laments. Had he done so, he could have cited them alongside Jacques Roumain's 'Sales Nègres'; they too speak for the wretched of the earth.

There is a wide consensus that a new 'Algerian literature' began to emerge in the 1950s.[80] 'Algerian literature' originally meant the literature that both reflected the existence and values of French Algeria and helped to create them by celebrating the birth of the 'new Latin race'.[81] This was to change. Reviewing a group of 'novelists from North Africa' in 1953, the critic Maurice Nadeau remarked that whereas the term had hitherto applied to Camus, Jules Roy and Emmanuel Roblès, it could now reasonably be applied to the Algerians Mohammed Dib and

Maloud Mammeri, and the Tunisian Albert Memmi.[82] The names of Kateb Yacine, whose work constantly evokes the 1945 massacres in Sétif and who spoke in a novel published in 1956 of the 'indestructible seed of a nation torn between two continents',[83] and Mohammed Feraoun would soon be added to the list. In terms of Fanon's schema, the most significant is probably Dib, born in the western city of Tlemcen in 1920. The trilogy of novels he published between 1952 and 1957 is simply entitled '*Algérie*' and describes the country in the years leading up to the Second World War.[84]

The dominant images of the Algeria of the young Omar, who is the principal character, are of hunger, poverty and oppression. In a class-room in pre-war Tlemcen, Monsieur Hassan asks his pupils what they understand by the nation ('*la patrie*'). The first and obvious answer is 'France'. The teacher eventually answers his own question: '*La patrie* is the land of our fathers. The country where we have been settled for generations . . . *La patrie* is not simply the land of which we live, but also all of its inhabitants and everything found in it . . . When foreign-ers come from the outside and claim to be the masters, *la patrie* is in danger. These foreigners are enemies and the whole of the population must defend the endangered *patrie* against them. It is now a matter of war. The inhabitants must defend the *patrie* at the cost of their lives.'[85] It is difficult to imagine a teacher actually pronouncing these words in the Algeria of the time, but Dib's novel clearly signals the emergence of a new national (and nationalist) consciousness.[86] For a 'native' to use 'Algeria' in this sense was provocative in the extreme. In view of what was to come, the reference to 'a matter of war' is both grimly prophetic and a reminder that the Fanon of *Les Damnés de la terre* was by no means alone in insisting that the birth or rebirth of a nation in Algeria would be a violent process.

The second volume of the trilogy, which appeared in the autumn of 1954, is even more explicit. It deals with a strike by rural workers who have lost their own land and are forced to work for French *colons* in the hinterland of Tlemcen, and who are finally provoked into action by their starvation wages. A mysterious fire breaks out and destroys the wretched huts in which they live. It is made quite clear that the work-ers did not start it, but they are nevertheless imprisoned and beaten. The flames become a metaphor: 'A fire had been lit and it would never go out again. It would gradually spread; the flames of blood would not go out until they had spread their sinister brightness across the whole country.'[87] In the course of an angry meeting one of the strikers says, 'They tell us we should form a single movement with the goal of shaking off all the vermin that is eating us.'[88] The same imagery appears at the end of 'Le Compagnon', a short story published in 1955: 'Have our brothers over there in the mountains finally taken up arms against the vermin that have eaten the inside of our eyes? And what do you think will happen from now on? Every day will see new fighters joining them.'[89]

In Fanon's terms, Dib's early fiction corresponds to the transition from a literature of indictment to one of revolt, and Dib himself saw it in those terms: he and his fellow Algerian writers were 'actors in this tragedy . . . It seems to us that we are bound to our people by a contract. We could call ourselves public writers.' In his first novels, he wanted his voice to 'merge into the collective voice', but by 1964 he had come to the conclusion that the time for commitment was over.[90] Dib was never a political activist in any real sense, but he did collect funds for the FLN and was expelled from Algeria for doing so; he did not return after independence. Speaking to the people and becoming part of a collective voice was, however, difficult. All the new Algerian novelists wrote in French and were published in Paris, not Algiers. Algeria's appalling illiteracy rate ensured that they found few, if any, readers in their own country.

Astonishingly, Fanon does not mention any of these manifestations of the very Algerian nationalism to which he was so dedicated, the only possible explanation being that he had simply not read the authors and books in question. His chosen example of *littérature de combat* comes not from Algeria, but from Guinea. Guinea became independent on 30 September 1958 and President Sekou Touré's refusal to join de Gaulle's proposed 'Community' gave him heroic status in Fanon's eyes. Guinea would, he believed, crystallize the revolutionary potential of the neighbouring territories of Senegal, the French Sudan and the Ivory Coast.[91] Fanon was badly mistaken. Sekou Touré's Guinea was a classic one-party state and the Democratic Party of Guinea tolerated no opposition. Far from crystallizing the revolutionary potential of its neighbours, the country existed in virtual diplomatic isolation until the mid-1970s. The poet Fanon chose to illustrate what he meant by *littérature de combat* was Kéita Fodéba, once the director of the Ballets Africains troupe which sought to unite African and European traditions, and at the time Sekou Touré's Minister for the Interior. Little is known of him, except that he was born in 1921 and educated in Dakar and Paris, where he studied law.[92] Fanon describes Fodéba as helping to outwit the plots organized 'by French colonialism'; in May 1969, the poet-minister was himself executed for allegedly plotting against the regime.[93]

Keita Fodéba's poem 'Aube africain' ('African Dawn') is a long prose poem intended to be performed to the accompaniment of a guitar and a kora, which is a traditional stringed instrument resembling the European harp. The poem tells the story of a young Mande called Naman, who was selected to fight in the Second World War and who serves in Corsica, Italy and Germany, where he is taken prisoner. He survives the war, but is killed in a dispute between African soldiers and their 'white chiefs'; this is a reference to the massacre of Senegalese troops by French soldiers in Thiaroye (Senegal) in December 1944. At the end of the poem a giant vulture hovers over Naman's body and seems to say 'You have not danced the dance that bears my name. Others will dance it.'

Fanon comments:

To understand this poem is to understand the role we have to play, to identify how we should act and to supply arms. There is not one colonized man who will not receive the message contained in this poem. Naman, hero of the battlefields of Europe, Naman who always ensured that the metropolis would have power and would last, Naman shot down by the police at the moment when he makes contact with his native land, this is Sétif in 1945, Fort-de-France, Saigon, Dakar, Lagos. All the *nègres* and all the *bicots* who fought to defend France's freedom or British civilization will recognize themselves in this poem by Kéita Fodéba.[94]

The Fanon who had, like Naman, fought in the Second World War, certainly recognized himself in it, but he misrecognizes certain other things and imagines others: there were no massacres in Fort-de-France in 1945. As the American academic Christopher L. Miller has pointed out, Fanon fails to recognize that the symbolism of the poem is rooted in the ethnic culture of the Mande people and that it celebrates the traditional ethnic identity of that culture rather than a Guinean national identity.[95] By insisting that *all* the *nègres* and *bicots* will recognize themselves in it, Fanon universalizes the poem and ignores its ethnicity. His misreading of the poem does, on the other hand, confirm that his own theory of the nation and national culture is not based upon ethnicity. Indeed, one of his harshest criticisms of negritude was that it racialized thought.[96]

In calling for a *littérature de combat* – a phrase which, for any French reader, automatically evokes the literature of the wartime resistance – Fanon is echoing the call for 'plays extolling the patriotic struggle for independence' made in the Soummam 'platform' of August 1956.[97] The call was not really answered. Fanon's speech in Rome was published in *El Moudjahid* (no. 39, 18 April 1959) as 'Culture nationale et guerre de libération', but this was the first time the paper had dealt with cultural politics. It had certainly spoken of the importance of Algeria's Arab-Islamic culture, but defined that culture in terms of an awareness of national identity and rarely spoke of cultural production in the literary sense. Early in 1958, it described the 'new Algerian culture' as the 'fruit of the national Algerian spirit and as a creation of the entire nation', but went no further than that.[98] *El Moudjahid* occasionally published documents such as 'The diary of a woman resistance fighter',[99] but these are not necessarily genuine, could easily have been written in Tunis and have little literary value. The FLN did have its cultural workers, and a drama troupe had been formed in Tunis. In May 1959, its director Mustapha Kateb explained what he meant by 'committed culture'. He was describing a play entitled *The Children of the Casbah*, which dealt with the urban struggle in Algiers: 'For us, theatre is a form of struggle. Theatre is committed. It is at the heart of the revolution. We are the theatre of a people at war. For us as artists, it is quite natural to think and act as militants. In this phase of the struggle, our realist theatre must be an FLN theatre.'[100] Fanon enjoyed the theatre, had once tried to write plays and, according to Geronimi, attended every theatrical performance he could in Tunis. He may well have seen *The Children of the Casbah*.

Little fiction was produced during the war itself, and none of it was produced by the fighters. Of the twenty-one novels by Algerian writers between 1954 and 1962, only eight dealt with the war and most, like Malek Haddad's *Le Quai aux fleurs ne répond pas* (1961), feature heroes who are living in France and who are torn between their love for Algeria and their love of French women.[101] The 'war novel' is very much a post-independence genre and soon became so conventional and cliché-ridden as to provoke the poet Ahmed Azeggagh to cry out:

> *Stop celebrating the massacres*
> *Stop celebrating names*
> *Stop celebrating ghosts*
> *Stop celebrating dates*
> *Stop celebrating History*[102]

Fanon's outline history of the emergence of a national culture is, then, somewhat at odds with the actual cultural history of Algeria and greatly influenced by his personal history. Insofar as they can be reconstructed, his personal enthusiasms also appear to be somewhat out of step with those of the FLN, few of whose members can have shared his taste for Chester Himes, Richard Wright and Aimé Césaire. He may have called for a *littérature de combat* , but his actual tastes were broader than the phrase might suggest.

Assia Djebar arrived in Tunis in May 1958 and began to move in the *El Moudjahid* circle. It was here that she met Fanon, and became close to Josie Fanon, who was now writing unsigned articles for the Tunisian journal *L'Action*. Djebar did not make a major contribution to *El Moudjahid*, but she did lend her pen to the attempts to counter the French propaganda which purported to describe how nurses working for the FLN tortured French captives. The daughter of a fairly wealthy family, Djebar was the first Algerian woman to attend the Ecole Normale Supérieure des Jeunes Filles outside Paris but failed to complete her *agrégation* in history because she joined the strike called by Algerian student organizations in May 1956. Still in her early twenties, she had already published two novels,[103] and had inevitably been dubbed the 'Algerian Françoise Sagan'. Her first novel, *La Soif*, could scarcely be described as an exemplary piece of *littérature de combat*; it is a psychological novel concerned mainly with the individual problems and emancipation of a young Algerian woman, and makes no real allusions to the war. The first-person narrator, the daughter of a French mother who has been brought up in the European manner but still feels that she is 'one of theirs' or in other words a Muslim, is much given to such statements as 'My life was peaceful, superficial and empty. Just the thing to make you cynical and disillusioned when you are twenty. That was what I was thinking and the only thing that satisfied me was my lucidity. I'd even become tired of my car for some time. Speed is a form of alcohol that quickly tires you out.'[104] Although she had not yet written about it, even this middle-class young woman had been touched by the war: her brother had been imprisoned in France at the age of seventeen and would not be released until 1962.[105]

Djebar found to her surprise that Fanon was the only person associated with the GPRA in Tunis who was willing to discuss her books and her plans for future novels on her own terms. The others wanted her to write edifying tales about heroic guerrillas in the *djebel*, but Fanon was prepared to listen to her,[106] just as he was willing to discuss Van Gogh with a hospitalized *moudjahidine*. In her third novel, *Les Enfants du nouveau monde* (1962), Djebar begins to deal with the war and to find her own very distinctive voice – or voices – and it was to make her one of Algeria's most important writers and certainly its most important woman writer.[107] It deals with the very different attempts made by a group of women to come to terms with the war in the spring of 1956, is set in a thinly disguised Blida, and marks the emergence of Djebar's mature polyphonic style, in which women's voices mingle in the absence of any one omniscient voice. Even this did not satisfy the FLN's harder ideologues. In an interview about the future of Algerian culture, Mostefa Lacheraf was scathing about her work, claiming that she knew nothing about Algeria's problems, except insofar as they affected the petty bourgeoisie, and she, like Haddad, concealed Algerian realities behind a poetic façade that was designed to appeal to no one but French critics.[108]

Fanon consistently argues that the birth or rebirth of the nation is a necessary precondition for the development of a culture and speaks of 'reestablishing the sovereignty of the nation',[109] and thus reiterates the claims put forward by the FLN in both its 'proclamation' of November 1954 and the Soummam Conference documents. The war of independence was, it was argued, a struggle for the recreation and recognition of an Algerian state that had existed before 1830. This claim was a response to the French claim that Algeria itself was the product of the colonial and civilizing mission. As Fanon puts it, colonialism meant the 'negation' of Algeria's 'national reality' and even the non-existence of the nation.[110] The idea that there had never been an Algerian nation so internalized by the colonized meant that in 1936 Ferhat Abbas himself would write in despair: 'I will not die for the Algerian nation because that nation does not exist. I have not found it. I have questioned history, I have questioned the living and the dead, and I have visited the cemeteries. No one has told me of it.'[111] The issue of the existence or non-existence of a pre-colonial state remains controversial. Ahmed Mahsas, once a member of the Organisation Spéciale and Minister for Agriculture from 1963 to 1966 (at which point he was forced into exile), argues that the Regency or Beylik of Algiers was a regional state within an international Muslim community (*Umma*) and that it had all the attributes of a state, as understood at the time.[112] A French specialist, in contrast, argues that the Beylik of Algiers was neither a centralized state nor an Ottoman colony but a military power established by a handful of janissaries who had succeeded in imposing their authority on a fragmented tribal society by using a policy of divide and rule.[113] The precise nature and status of the Regency or Beylik in 1830 are obviously of much less importance that the ideological significance of the supposed pre-colonial state. Insofar as they are 'imagined communities' rather than natural entities, all nations appeal to foundation myths in order to assert their legitimacy.[114] This is precisely what France did in 1996, when the nation celebrated the 1,500th anniversary of the baptism of Clovis I (465–511), who is traditionally regarded as the first monarch to reign over a united France.

Whilst Fanon does subscribe to the notion of resurrecting a state or nation that once existed and had been destroyed by colonialism, he also argues that the struggle will end with the disappearance of both colonialism and of the colonized, and with the creation of a new man and a new humanism.[115] This too could be reconciled with the FLN's official position, but Fanon departs from its thinking in that he makes no mention of the Arab-Islamic component of the culture of an independent

Algeria, even though the FLN had been stressing its importance since 1954. He does not discuss the language issue, whereas much of Lacharef's discussion of the future of Algerian culture is devoted to the linguistically and culturally Arab dimension and to the need for a future Arabization of Algeria, or in other words to base its culture on a linguistic-ethnic identity (which inevitably raises the thorny issue of the minority Berber communities who do not speak Arabic).

Fanon speaks of a 'nation born of the concerted action of the people'[116] but does not define that people in either religious or ethnic terms. In his remarkably generous discussion of the role and fate of Algeria's European minority in *L'An V de la Révolution*, Fanon is quite explicit about what he understands 'Algerian' to mean: any individual living in Algeria was a potential Algerian and could decide to be a citizen of the nation of the future.[117] Fanon's 'nation' is the dynamic creation of the action of the people, and his nationalism is a nationalism of the political will to be Algerian, not of ethnicity. And it is this nationalism of the will that allows him to speak in *Sociologie d'une révolution* and *Les Damnés de la terre* of 'we Algerians'. It had required the gaze of a white child to teach Fanon that he was a *nègre*; he needed no one to tell him that he was Algerian – he was Algerian because he willed himself to be Algerian. The official FLN position in 1954 was that Europeans would be free to opt for either French or Algerian nationality; there was no provision for dual nationality. In practice, the Code of Nationality adopted in 1962 defined Algerian nationality in both ethnic and religious terms and made Islam the state religion, though it also specified that citizenship could be granted by decree to non-ethnic and non-Muslim 'Algerians'.[118] It was granted to only a tiny number of Europeans. Had he lived, Fanon would no doubt have been granted Algerian citizenship and an Algerian passport, but in a sense he would always have remained an honorary Algerian.

Bernard Dadié, a novelist from the Ivory Coast, was present at the Rome Congress and later recalled that 'Fanon came and gave his speech, then he left right away'.[119] Yet more discussion of negritude, or more comparisons of sarcophagi, had little appeal for Fanon and, as at all conferences, what was going on in the wings was at least as important as what was being said on the official platform. Rome provided Fanon with a further opportunity for a meeting with representatives of the MPLA but not, it would appear, with Roberto Holden's UPA. Acting as an adviser to the GPRA, Fanon had discussions with an MPLA delegation consisting of Mario de Andrade, Secretary-General Viriato da Cruz, and Lucio Lara. The main topic for discussion was the advisability of launching an armed struggle in Angola. Fanon was convinced that the opening of a new front would weaken the imperialist forces in Africa as a whole and that this would do something to relieve the burden on the ALN, currently the only force on the continent that was actually fighting a war of national liberation. This suggests that he was anticipating a continent-wide struggle against imperialism as such and saw the Algerian war as its prelude. The MPLA representatives were in agreement in principle, but differences arose when it came to discussing the practicalities. Fanon had a concrete proposition to make: the FLN would train a small group of cadres in its camps on either the Moroccan or Tunisian frontier and they would form the first units of a liberation army. The difficulty was that the only suitable candidates were working underground inside Angola and that it would be very hard to get them out. According to Mario de Andrade, the task of contacting them was entrusted to Amilcar Cabral, the founder and Secretary-General of the Partido da Independencia da Guiné e Cabo Verde which was preparing to launch a war of independence in Portuguese Guinea.[120] When Cabral reached Luanda in August, the situation had deteriorated badly. Alarmed at developments in the neighbouring Congo, the Portuguese had adopted a policy of preventive repression and many of the MPLA's cadres were in jail.

When they met in Tunis in February 1960, Lara informed Fanon of what had happened and concluded that the agreements reached in Rome would have to be cancelled. Fanon retorted that the important thing was to begin the struggle, but the MPLA's representative insisted that it needed time to regroup its forces and to plan the insurrection properly. The MPLA also stressed the importance of the struggle in Luanda and Angola's other urban centres and of uniting all social groups in the fight against Portugal, whilst Fanon insisted that, as in Algeria, the only true revolutionary force was the peasantry. The negotiations broke down, and the GPRA offered its aid to the UPA.[121] Ferhat Abbas recognized the shadowy organization set up by Holden as an Angolan provisional government, which was tantamount to giving it the GPRA's official blessing. Fanon is reported to have explained to his Algerian associates that 'I know Holden is inferior to the MPLA men. But Holden is ready to begin, and they are not. And I am convinced that what is necessary is to begin, and that an Angolan revolutionary movement will be formed in the ensuing struggle.'[122] For his part, Mohammed Harbi contends that Fanon favoured the UPA 'for doctrinal reasons' and because he regarded the MPLA as a purely urban party with no interest in the peasantry.[123]

Holden was in agreement about the need to begin the armed struggle and was already infiltrating young Kongo men into Angola to prepare for a rising. Some of his young fighters were briefly trained by the FLN at its Wadi Melleg camp in Tunisia[124] and arms supplied by the Algerians found their way into Angola by devious routes. On 14 March, an unidentified Angolan in North Africa was told by an Algerian contact that the war would begin 'tomorrow'.[125] There had already been a more or less spontaneous uprising in Luanda in February, and it had been met with brutal repression. Holden's men crossed the Congo frontier on 15 March and found northern Angola in tumult. No one knew what was happening and no attempt had been made to build guerrilla bases for what was obviously going to be a long war: 'The whole affair was conducted in a nightmare of confusion, messianic dreams, bloodshot revenge.'[126] Although Holden had claimed to be acting in the name of the whole of Angola, his forces were regionally based, ill-trained and bloodthirsty, and brutally attacked the civilian population – black and white. The repression that followed the revolt in the north was savage and the Portuguese army soon gained the upper hand over the guerrillas, who lacked weapons, experience and a political base. In March, rebels under the nominal command of the UPA had hunted down whites and *assimilados*; until June, the army and civilian militia groups hunted down and killed blacks with any kind of education, however minimal. Estimates for the death toll range from twenty to thirty thousand.[127] Most of the membership of the original MPLA were killed, but it was gradually rebuilt under the leadership of Agostinho Neto and Mario de Andrade from late 1962 onwards. Holden rejected proposals for joint action. In 1966 a third force emerged when Jonas Savimbi, once foreign minister in Holden's 'government', founded UNITA which received support from both the West and South Africa.

A civil war began within the war of liberation and it continued long after independence. Some of the seeds of that civil war were sown by the FLN and Fanon when they agreed to lend their support to Roberto Holden. Over-confident and over-optimistic, insisting on 'beginning now', and convinced that the Algerian model of the uprisings of 1956 could be exported to a country of which they had little concrete knowledge, they had made a disastrous political miscalculation. Mario de Andrade was one of the speakers at the Mémorial International held to honour Fanon's memory in Fort-de-France in 1982. He was extremely critical of the advice Fanon had given the MPLA in Rome twenty-six years earlier but, with quite remarkable generosity, also spoke of his ability to 'capture the anger of the world'.[128]

Just over a month after the Rome Congress, Fanon began to plan a trip to Morocco to help with the reorganization of the FLN's medical services on the Algerian–Moroccan border. The journey was, as always, complicated and circuitous. An exit visa from Tunisia had to be obtained; entry visas for Spain and Morocco had to be collected from the relevant consulates. The Moroccan visa, issued in Tunis on 22 May, granted him permission to stay in the country for a month. Having travelled via Rome and Madrid, Fanon finally reached Rabat and then travelled overland to the border area. His final destination was the Ben M'Hidi base, some miles from Oujda and the headquarters of the western Frontier Army. Here he was met by the twenty-four-year-old Amar Boukri. A member of the ALN since 1955, Boukri had been invalided out of active service and had retrained as a paramedic. He now became Fanon's assistant. In 1992, he talked about their work to an Algerian journalist.[129] A hospital equipped by Yugoslavia and East Germany had been established in the hamlet of Medagh, and the two men shared a room there. They spent a lot of time together, and Boukri later recalled their evening walks, with Fanon in his khaki shirt, overalls and, somewhat incongrously for someone who was usually so concerned about his appearance, carpet slippers. According to Boukri, Fanon received a number of important visitors, including Colonel Houari Boumédienne who was in the process of reorganizing and uniting the ALN's Eastern and Western commands.

As usual, Fanon slept little, rose early and often read until one or two in the morning. Boukri also reported that Fanon was writing a great deal: it is possible that he was still completing the preface to *L'An V de la révolution*. Most of his patients were fighters from the mountains who were suffering from mental and physical exhaustion, and Fanon treated them by putting them into what he called 'artificial hibernation'. That is, he used narcotherapy, employing mild and non-addictive sedatives to send them to sleep for long periods. The therapy was not particularly sophisticated, but it was effective and allowed the fighters to recover their strength and energy.

Towards the end of the month, Fanon was asked to go to the village of Kobdara to bring back some new patients and climbed into an Opel driven by one Mokhtar Bouizem. As they were leaving Berkhane, the car skidded on gravel and Bouizem lost control of it. Fanon was thrown out of the moving vehicle and landed on his back, badly damaging several vertebrae.[130] He was unable to move and had to be taken on a stretcher to a hospital in Oudja. One of those who ran to help him was young Abdelaziz Bouteflika, who later served as a minister under Boumédienne and became President of Algeria in 1998. For anyone even vaguely acquainted with the manner of Abane Ramdane's death, news of 'an accident in Morocco' had a sinister ring to it, and an alarmed Josie Fanon made her way to Oudja to make certain that it was indeed an accident.[131] Even in hospital, Fanon's first concern was for his patients and he gave careful instructions on how they should be treated. His own injuries were too bad to be treated there, and someone took the decision to send him to Rome. Even in this condition, Fanon needed visas to travel. A two-month visa for Italy was issued in Rabat on 2 July and Fanon left Tangiers for Spain a day later. On Sunday, 5 July, he finally reached Rome. Josie did not travel with him.

Fanon and his bodyguards – one Moroccan and one Tunisian – had expected to be met in Rome by Taleb Boulharouf. They were in fact met by the police. The police were not there to arrest them, but to take the little group under their protection. There had been a bomb. As Boulharouf left his home and walked towards his car, a group of children kicked a ball towards it. The ball rolled under the car and it exploded in flames, killing a boy called Rolando Royal and badly injuring his playmates. The police picked up Boulharouf, who described himself as a Tunisian national who worked for his country's embassy,[132] and sent officers to the airport, where they collected the 'Libyan' – 'Dr

Ibrahim Omar Fanon' – and his two companions. The 'Libyan', bandaged from the neck to the pelvis, was taken to hospital and an armed *carabiniere* was placed outside the door of his room. He had, according to press reports, recently been shot in the back in a clash on the Moroccan–Algerian border.

Although the police and counter-espionage service released little information, the Italian press was eager to speculate about what had happened and the story was picked up by both Reuters and AFP. For some, Boulharouf was obviously an FLN leader who had narrowly escaped an assassination attempt at the hands of enemies within that organization; for others, the attack had been planned by the French secret services. On 8 July, the FLN's Cairo office issued a statement blaming the French. Boulharouf now described himself to the police as an Algerian-born naturalized Tunisian. After questioning and the seizure of some papers, he was eventually released. Forensic examination of what was left of his car showed that it had been destroyed by a powerful charge of plastic explosive placed immediately beneath the driver's seat.[133] A bouncing ball had been enough to detonate it. As he was reading a newspaper report of the car bomb, Fanon noticed that his presence – or at least that of a mysterious Libyan – in the hospital had been mentioned in print and insisted on being moved in secret to another room. He was right to do so; a gunman succeeded in gaining admission to the hospital and found his original room. Had he not read the newspaper, he could well have been killed.[134]

The incident remains mysterious and will probably never be fully explained. The original press reports speculated that the assassination attempt was the work of a shadowy 'Red Hand' organization. The same explanation is given by Maurice Maschino, in his *Le Déserteur* and by Renate Zahar,[135] and it has since been repeated by both Geismar, who describes the Red Hand as 'an organization of right-wing settlers from Algeria', and Irène Gendzier.[136] A series of bombs and attacks on figures connected with the FLN had been occurring since the end of 1957. In December of that year, a car belonging to the arms dealer Otto Schutler had been exploded in Hamburg, killing his mother and badly injuring him. Eleven months later, the car of Aid Ahcene, who represented the FLN in Bonn, was machine-gunned on the road between Bonn and Bad Godesberg, and Ahcene subsequently died of his wounds. After premises in Godesberg and Frankfurt had been searched, state prosecutor Heinz Wolf concluded that an organization calling itself the Red Hand was responsible. In January 1959, an FLN representative was killed in Saarbrücken; his murderers were not found. Three months later, another German arms dealer was killed by a car bomb.[137] At the end of 1959 a certain Christian Durieux made a statement to the *Daily Mail*'s Paris correspondent, describing himself as a member of the Red Hand, and claiming responsibility on its behalf for the attacks in Germany which, being one of the main sources of the FLN's weaponry, was an obvious area for such operations, but not for the bomb in Rome.[138] 'Durieux' was presumably a pseudonym and there is no way of verifying his claims. All the attacks he mentioned had been reported in the press and any mythomaniac could have claimed responsibility for them. An organization calling itself La Main Rouge did at one point exist in Morocco, but the well-informed Yves Courrière argues that the name simply became a flag of convenience used by the French secret services, who were quite happy to allow gullible journalists to fantasize about a mysterious freelance operation.[139]

The Rome bombing was certainly a professional job, and probably the work one of SDECE's 'action units' rather than a group of *pied noir* terrorists. 'Plastic' explosive – presumably meaning Czech-made Semtex – was difficult and expensive to obtain and whilst both the FLN and the French secret services used it, amateur terrorists are unlikely to have had access to it. It is also improbable that Fanon was the primary target. The bomb was of the same type as those used in Germany, and they were designed to explode when the ignition key was turned. This was not a bomb that was intended to go off at the airport. It seems, then, that Boulharouf was the target, and that the attempt to kill the hospitalized Fanon was an opportunist act of terrorism rather than part of a more complex plot directed specifically against him. SDECE would have been perfectly happy to kill him, but its agents are unlikely to have gone to Rome with the express purpose of doing so. Fanon had escaped with his life, but remained helpless in hospital for several weeks.

Fanon's injuries were not so serious as to prevent him from taking part in an important, if ill-documented, series of meetings in Tunis in

August. This was the only occasion on which he had any direct influence on FLN policy. The purpose of the meetings was to draw up a political programme and proposals for the FLN's statutes to be approved by the CNRA, which was due to meet at the end of the year. A meeting of military leaders had set up two commissions, one consisting of 'specialists' and the other of 'organizers', or in other words, military men. Fanon was appointed to the 'specialist' commission, along with Omar Oussedik, Abderrazack Chenlouf and Mohammed Seddick Bennyahia; the 'organizers' were Ben Khedda, Moubrouch Belhocine and Lamine Khène. According to the specialists, the goal of the war was 'the liberation of the national territory' and 'the social and economic revolution form a whole . . . and do not constitute two distinct stages'. The force leading the Revolution was the peasantry: 'It is still the most revolutionary section of the population and contains inexhaustible forces.'[140] Workers were said to be 'the most dynamic elements in the towns'; their importance meant that trade unions should be given a more important role in the leadership. The defeats of 1957 and the decline in the political importance of the towns meant, however, that union delegates should go to the countryside and work in the *wilayas*. The role of students and intellectuals was defined in contradictory terms. On the one hand, it was argued, given that winning the war was the essential priority, they were needed in that war; it was a mistake to argue that they should not be directly involved in the struggle on the grounds that they would be more useful to the Algeria of the future. On the other hand, it was also claimed that an independent Algeria would need technicians and that the students should be sent outside the country. Mohammed Harbi explains the obvious contradiction between the two theses in terms of a long-standing difference of opinion between the ALN and the FLN. The insistence that the peasantry was the driving force behind the Revolution is recognizably 'Fanonist' and would provide the basic arguments of *Les Damnés de la terre*. This view was obviously shared by elements within the leadership; the need for debate indicates that not everyone agreed.

At the international level, priority was to be given to acquiring the material and financial means to strengthen the Revolution's military and diplomatic position. Whilst the support of the socialist bloc was important – a delegation had just been sent to China – the GPRA was hostile 'to colonialism and not the West'. The draft programme also ruled out 'alliances with groups like those which take part in Afro-Asiatic-type conferences in Cairo, and which are often in opposition in other countries'.[141] The Algerian concept of 'internationalism' was, in other words, purely instrumental, not to say cynical. Although the GPRA sent delegates to the very conferences that were condemned in these discussions, it did so in order to rally support for its own nationalist struggle. Neither Pan-Africanism nor Pan-Arabism was on its agenda.

Fanon's own contribution to what he called Algeria's *littérature de combat* was *L'An V de la Révolution algérienne*, which was published in the autumn of 1959. There had been an earlier plan to write a book on Algeria in collaboration with Lacheraf but it came to nothing. Mostefa Lacheraf states that he met Fanon at Francis Jeanson's home just outside Paris in August 1955 and that they discussed the possibility of working together. Fanon declined the suggestion, which seems to have come from Lacheraf, on the grounds that he thought he was still thinking in 'European terms'. Lacheraf, who takes the view that Fanon owed a great deal more to Algeria than Algeria owed to Fanon, explains that, before he went to work in Blida, Fanon knew almost nothing about Algeria and that in 1955 he was still, in terms of his thinking, a 'hostage to the European milieu', adding that, despite his political sympathies, Fanon was an '*assimilé*'.[142] The comment is an interesting reflection on race relations in Algeria in that Lacheraf seems to have perceived Fanon as a European and not a black Martinican.

There is no independent confirmation that this meeting did in fact take place, but the date is plausible. Any meeting must have taken place before October 1956, as Lacheraf was one of those on the hijacked aircraft and he spent the next five years in prison even though he was of little political significance at the time. In the summer of 1955 he was still based in Paris, where he taught at the Lycée Louis-le-Grand and he had made major contributions to the history of Algeria and Algerian nationalism in a series of articles published in *Les Temps modernes* and *Esprit*.[143] Any collaboration between Fanon and Lacheraf would probably have ended in disaster, as it is obvious from a comparison of Fanon's writings on culture and nation and Lacheraf's 1963 article on 'The Future of Algerian Culture' that they interpreted 'Algerian' in very different senses.

'Year V of the Algerian Revolution' was not Fanon's original choice of title for his new book. He at first intended to call it *Réalité d'une nation*,[144] but a book with a very similar title and a very different line on Algeria was already on sale: Marcel Egretaud's *Réalité de la nation algérienne*, published by Editions Sociales in 1958, was a defence of the PCF's position on the Algerian 'nation in formation'. Fanon's second book is in fact known by two titles. The second edition of 1966 was rather misleadingly entitled *Sociologie de la Révolution algérienne*, even though it is obviously not an exercise in sociology in any real sense and is more accurately, and more modestly, described by Fanon himself as an examination of 'some aspects of the Algerian Revolution'.[145] The change of title also obscures an important historical allusion. 'Year V' alludes to the revolutionary calendar that made 1789 'Year I of the French Revolution' and expresses Fanon's conviction that a new historical era had begun on 1 November 1954.

The edition published in the 'Petite Collection Maspero' in 1968 gives the original title in parentheses.[146] This is the only complete edition as the first two appeared without Fanon's original preface. Fanon had approached Ferhat Abbas with a request that he should preface the book. This was apparently a shrewd move; of all the leading figures in the FLN, Ferhat Abbas was the best known to the French public, even though he had very little real power. Fanon's name, in contrast, was virtually unknown to his potential readership. *Peau noire, masques blancs* had attracted little attention in 1952 and had now been out of print for years. The contributions to *El Moudjahid* were unsigned and Fanon had not been identified as the author of the article on the French left that gave rise to the debate in *France-Observateur*. Fanon's name was quite well known in psychiatric circles and in the *Présence africaine* milieu, but not elsewhere. Only attentive readers of the French press knew him as a spokesman for the FLN. He was not, in other words, particularly well known and being prefaced by Ferhat Abbas would have brought welcome publicity. That publicity was not forthcoming. Abbas, who is quite possibly the only person ever to have regarded Fanon as 'an authentic Marxist', told him that, in approaching him, he had made a psychological misjudgement and that any preface he wrote would harm the success of the book. He then advised him to approach 'a colonel'.[147] This was a polite way of saying that he did not like the book or its content; Ferhat Abbas did not share Fanon's views on violence. Although he greatly admired the fighters of the ALN, Fanon had, for his part, little love for 'colonels' and, according to Abbas, thought that Boumédienne's appetite for power bordered on the pathological. He did not approach any of the colonels. He wrote his own preface and in doing so created new problems.

This was not an easy book to publish and could not conceivably have appeared in Seuil's 'Esprit' collection. Although highly critical of the war and indignant at the army's use of torture, Jean-Marie Domenach and his colleagues could not publish it. Seuil provided a platform for the Dreyfusards of the 'French Resistance', not the FLN. *L'An V de la Révolution* appeared as the second volume in the 'Cahiers libres' series produced by François Maspero's new publishing house, which soon became the main sponsor of Vidal-Naquet's 'Third Worldists'.[148] The 'Cahiers libres' series sold both through bookshops and on a subscription basis. The subscription system was advantageous to both publisher and reader. It provided Maspero with a stable source of revenue, but it also put the books beyond the reach of the censor once they were in the post. Readers received their books on a regular basis and saved money; *L'An V*'s cover price was 7.80 francs, but a subscription for twelve volumes cost fifty-nine francs, and twenty-four 110 francs.

Even with Maspero, there were problems. François Maspero has never explained why the preface was not included in the first edition, but one sentence must have caused him problems: 'The death of colonialism means both the death of the colonized man and the death of the colonizer.'[149] This was a variant on what Fanon said in Rome when he said that the struggle would end with the disappearance of colonialism, but also with the disappearance of the colonized.[150] *Disparition* is an ambiguous word. It means 'disappearance', but is also frequently used as a euphemistic synonym for 'death'. The only ambiguity about the phrase 'the death of the colonizer' is whether or not it constitutes an incitement to murder. In his preface to *Les Damnés de la terre*, Sartre removed any possible ambiguity: 'In the early stages of the revolt, there has to be killing. To kill a European is to kill two birds with one stone: it does away with both an oppressor and an oppressed man, and leaves one man dead and one man free.'[151]

If it was this sentence that troubled Maspero, he need not have worried as the omission of the preface did not stave off the inevitable. Fanon's second book was seized by the police three months after its publication. Censorship during the Algerian war was not terribly systematic but it could be both very effective and costly to publishers and booksellers alike. Books did not have to be submitted for vetting prior to publication and there was no official index of prohibited books. Books and pamphlets that were deemed to pose a threat to national security were physically seized by the police, acting on orders from either the Ministry of the Interior or the Prefect of Police. Such seizures were not dramatic affairs and did not normally result in the pulping of entire print runs. Copies continued to be sold and to circulate clandestinely, and some titles were quietly reprinted in Lucerne by Nils Anderson's 'La Cité'. According to one account, some of the Swiss versions were actually used by the French secret services to make parcel bombs addressed to foreigners who had 'displeased them'.[152] Commissaire Mathieu's officers, who carried out the raids in Paris, were unfailingly courteous, and both Editions de Minuit's Jérôme Lindon and François Maspero eventually reconciled themselves to making up small parcels of books for them to take away. It saved time.[153] After one encounter with Mathieu's men, Pierre Vidal-Naquet concluded that they were both 'very polite' and 'not in favour of continuing the war in Algeria'.[154] There was little scandal or protest about the seizures; only a two-line report on an inside page of *Le Monde* indicated that another act of censorship had taken place. *L'An V* and *Les Damnés de la terre* were two of the twenty-three books published between 1957 and 1962 to suffer this fate; twelve were Maspero titles and ten were published by Minuit.[155] The first to be seized was Alleg's *La Question*.

Fanon's *L'An V* comprises short studies of five 'aspects' of the Algerian Revolution: the changing role of women, the FLN's use of radio propaganda, the effects of the Revolution on the Algerian family, medicine and colonization, and the position of the European minority. Two appendices – one by Geronimi and the other by Yvon Bresson – are included to demonstrate that there was a role for Europeans in the Revolution. The book says little about the structure or policies of the FLN – except to stress again and again that it was the sole legitimate representative of the Algerian people and that its demand for independence was non-negotiable – and concentrates on describing the impact of the Revolution on Algerian lives. The general tone is captured in the suppressed preface: 'We want an Algeria that is open to all, in which every kind of genius can flourish. That is what we want and we will create it. We do not think that any force that exists anywhere is capable of stopping us.' Whatever Lacheraf may have thought of him in 1955, Fanon speaks in 1959 as an Algerian convinced that victory is at hand and as believer in a nationalism of the will and not of ethnicity. The style is, however, very different to that of the articles written or co-written for *El Moudjahid*. The tone is more muted, and Fanon writes quite plainly and simply, with none of the baroque flourishes and neologisms that characterized *Peau noire, masques blancs*. This was a book designed to inform and to persuade, and it played an important role in shaping the left's perception of the Algerian Revolution.

The chapter on the European minority was first published in the May–June issue of *Les Temps modernes*, where an editorial note remarked that 'the personality of its author gives it a particular political importance'. Its 'particular importance' is perhaps that, in this chapter, Fanon adopts a much more conciliatory stance towards the French left than he did in late 1957. He speaks in very positive terms of men like Bourdet and Domenach, of French public opinion's revulsion about their revelations about torture in Algeria and of their success in unmasking the 'ultras' in the metropolis.[156] Fanon's position on the European minority in Algeria is also more moderate than might have been expected from someone so often and so easily associated with a Manichaean fanaticism. He stresses that those Europeans who had been arrested and tortured because of their involvement with FLN networks had behaved as 'authentic militants' who had not talked.[157] He insists that Europeans and Jews did have a role to play in the revolution because 'any individual living in Algeria is an Algerian. In tomorrow's independent Algeria, it will be up to every Algerian to take on Algerian citizenship or to reject it in favour of a different citizenship.'[158] His position here is based upon the FLN's proclamation of 1954 and the Soummam Conference document, both of which offer a choice of nationality and exclude the possibility of dual nationality. Fanon greatly exaggerates the number of Europeans involved with or sympathetic to the FLN, and his reference to meetings between Muslim Algerians and European Algerians and to Europeans reaching the conclusion that armed struggle is the only way out of Algeria's desperate situation,[159] seem to refer to the early stages of the war rather than to the situation in 1959. Men like Chaulet, Geronimi and Bresson, a police officer who passed on intelligence and police records to the FLN, were rare individuals indeed and by 1959 most of them were either dead or outside Algeria. Fanon's exaggerated picture of European involvement is obviously influenced by his own concept of Algerian 'nationalism of the will', but it also reveals the over-optimism and even idealism that is the obverse of his vision of an imminent and destructive apocalypse.

Although it draws on notes and drafts made in Blida, the book was composed and dictated in Tunis in the spring of 1959, and, according to Geronimi – to whom Fanon read long extracts – it was begun and finished within a matter of weeks. Fanon's haste is the likeliest explanation for the extraordinary slip over one important date: he confuses 13 May 1958 and 16 May.[160] According to Fanon, 13 May was the date of one of the strangest episodes of the entire war: the strange day of 'fraternization' that occurred in central Algiers when thousands of Algerians were brought in by truck, stewarded by squads of Algerians working for the French army, and shouted *Algérie française* alongside their *pied noir* 'brothers'. This actually took place on 16 May; 13 May was the day on which Massu and his officers established their Committee of Public Safety.

Fanon rarely indicates his sources, and this makes it difficult to verify the accuracy of what he says. Some sections – notably that on medicine and colonialism and presumably that on radio – obviously draw on his experience in Blida. The anecdote about the tobacconist in Birtouta running out of his shop brandishing a photograph of the hijacked FLN leaders has all the vividness of something that Fanon actually witnessed in October 1956.[161] The account of peasants clustering around radio sets in Kabylia is also based upon personal experience. Other sections of the book describe things that Fanon cannot possibly have seen for himself.

The best-known chapter of the book is the first. The chapter title 'L'Algérie se dévoile' has been translated as 'Algeria Unveiled', but 'Algeria Unveils Herself' would be more accurate as the original French describes a process that is taking place and not something that has already happened. This is also the most problematic chapter. Fanon's bald and apparently authoritative statement that 'until 1955, the battle was fought exclusively by men' and that the FLN then took a deliberate decision to recruit women has been openly contradicted. Djamila Amrane (née Danièle Minne), states categorically in her very important studies of women in the Algerian war that there is no trace of any such decision in either the FLN's official texts or in the files of the Ministry of War Veterans, to which she has had privileged access.[162] According to her research, there is no basis for Fanon's claim that the FLN began by recruiting older married women and turned to young women only at a later stage in the war. The percentage of the female population involved seems to have remained almost constant – 3 to 5 per cent – throughout the war and women's involvement appears to have been as spontaneous as that of men. Amrane is certainly in a position to know what she is talking about: she planted the bomb that ripped apart the Otomatic in January 1957.

It is difficult, if not impossible, to explain why Fanon made these erroneous statements. Working on *El Moudjahid*, he was part of the FLN's information service and had ready access to very well-informed sources. In his haste to complete the book, he may have simply omitted to check his information. What is more likely is that his own perception of the role of women obscured the more objective facts. He is in fact less interested in women's general commitment to the war effort than in 'the instrumentalization of the veil'.[163]

Thanks to Gillo Pontecorvo's film *The Battle of Algiers*, the image of a young woman slipping a gun to a *fidai* seconds before the assassination takes place, or carrying a beach bag with a primed bomb in it, has become so familiar as to be one of the dominant images of the Algerian war. *L'An V* did a lot to create that image. Fanon describes the 'young girl, who was wearing a veil only yesterday, going through a European town swarming with policemen, paratroopers and militia-men'.[164] He describes young women carrying guns and grenades in their bags or beneath their voluminous veils and slipping them to an accomplice at the opportune moment. He describes young women in European dress being allowed through the barbed wire entanglements that blocked off the Casbah and going into the European city to wreak destruction.

Some of his descriptions are simply confused because they deal with events that are still difficult to elucidate. When he mentions the assassination of Amédée Froger, the mayor of Boufarik and former chairman of the powerful Association of Mayors, Fanon suggests, for instance, that the gun used was carried by a woman and then slipped to Froger's killer.[165] There are conflicting accounts of just how Froger died on 28 December 1956, but none of them suggests that a woman was involved.[166] Saadi Yacef, who organized the assassination, certainly does not say so.[167]

If anything, Fanon underestimates women's role by failing to mention that the first bombs used by the FLN in Algiers were *planted* and not merely transported by women. Women were involved in the Battle of Algiers from the start, but there were no eye-witnesses present when Yacef handed the primed bombs to Zohara Drif, Samhia Kakdari and Djamila Bouhired on 30 October 1956. Until it was prised open by Massu's torturers, the FLN's organization in Algiers was watertight; the cells acted independently and their members did not know who was in the other cells. Yacef's bomb network was a watertight structure within a watertight structure, and Fanon certainly did not have privileged information about how it was organized or how it operated. Fanon is describing something he has been told about. One of his patients in Tunis was Kheira Bousafi, who had served as a nurse in *wilaya* IV. At the age of twenty she had carried guns in Algiers: 'I had taken off my veil, I was young and dark, and people took me for a European girl. They often called me "the little Spaniard". I played at being the free woman who received men at home, as though I were not a good Muslim.'[168] Bousafi was eventually betrayed and fled to the mountains to work as a nurse. She eventually reached Tunis at the end of 1957, spent two months in Fanon's care and was presumably one of his informants.

Although he is relaying what he had been told by others and not describing what he had seen, Fanon's account of how dress codes were used to outwit the French army is not entirely inaccurate. Malika Ighilhariz was a twenty-year-old lycéenne during the Battle of Algiers. Unusually for a young woman, she could drive:

I had false papers in the name of Martine, can't remember what the patronymic was. I could pass myself off as the daughter of a *colon*; I looked the part in the big De Soto. I wore my hair loose, and got broad smiles when I went through all the road blocks. To go back into the Casbah, I would park near the Gendarmerie on the boulevard de la Victoire. People would see me getting out of the car just like a Frenchwoman. I would go into a block of flats and put on my veil and my face veil, come out veiled and go down into the Casbah. I would leave what I had to leave and pick up whatever – messages, weapons – had to be got out of the Casbah. and then I would pull off the same trick. In the entrance to a block of flats, I took off the veil, put on my lipstick and my sunglasses, came out and got back into my beautiful car.[169]

Fanon also describes how women ran the safe houses in which fighters being sought by the police took refuge. The woman of the house would provide food, carry messages and communicate with the outside world on their behalf. The presence of the *fidayine* led to changes within the family as her husband or father had to overcome his 'congenital' jealousy.[170] Yacef had personal experience of similar situations. During the Battle of Algiers, he was housed by an old *maraboutique* family whose fourteen-year-old daughter was not normally allowed to go out into the street alone; her father was happy to allow her to mix with men from the ALN and to face the same dangers as them. He comments: 'a mental revolution had taken place in this venerable family where the women (who had long been kept in the background) showed their desire to take an active part in the liberation struggle . . . Who could have imagined this only two years earlier?'[171] Fanon himself was convinced that 'the liberation of the Algerian people was identical with the liberation of women, and with their entry into history. The destruction of colonization is the birth of a new woman.'[172] Neither Fanon nor the FLN understood 'women's liberation' in the sense in which it came to be used by the 'second-wave' feminists of the late 1960s and 1970s. The delegates to the Soummam Conference saluted the courage of those women who had actively joined the 'sacred struggle for the liberation of the fatherland', but the final document effectively defined women's role as providing moral support for the fighters, helping to supply information, supplies and refuges, and helping the families and children of the fighters, the prisoners and the internees.[173]

405

Baya Hocine, born in the Casbah in 1940, acted both as a liaison agent and as a house-mother to a group of *fidayine*, all of whom had a criminal background. They found it quite normal for her to cook for them and to transport arms on their behalf. She did all the housework, and they found that normal too. What had changed was that, unlike her brothers and cousins, they never *ordered* her to do their washing. They had, she recalls, found 'new and very natural ways of relating to one another, at a time when the situation was anything but normal. We related in ways that did not exist in normal times.'[174] Claudie Duhamel, who was arrested in November 1961 on suspicion of carrying suitcases between Lyon and Paris,[175] thought that Fanon's writings conveyed the impression of a movement that was 'secular and socialist, overturning traditional values'. She found that the depiction of the changing role of women was particularly inspiring, and that impression was confirmed when she found herself alongside some of them in prison.[176] She, and no doubt many of her sisters, was to be disappointed. They had, states Baya Hocine, begun to break down the dikes, but the dikes were rebuilt after 1962. She then became the victim of a terrible exclusion; she had broken with tradition and felt she was being rejected for having done so.[177] The historian Mohamed Harbi adds that women with political ambitions, or who wanted to be the equals of their 'brothers', had a particularly hard time of it. Their desire for equality was interpreted as meaning that they were 'loose women'.[178] After the Battle of Algiers, an unknown number of these ambitious young women became victims of Amirouche's blueitis, and were massacred by their 'brothers'. Like some of his informants, Fanon mistook temporary changes born of extraordinary circumstances for a permanent revolution.

Fanon reportedly told Lacheraf that he could not collaborate on a book on Algeria because he was still thinking like 'a European'. Some of his comments on women indicate that, whatever he was *thinking*, he was still *seeing* as a European in the spring of 1959. He was also seeing as a man. In the second paragraph of 'Algérie se dévoile' he observes that

In the Arab world . . . the veil in which the women are draped is immediately perceived by the tourist . . . In the Arab Maghreb, the veil is part of the traditional dress of the national societies of

Tunisia, Algeria, Morocco and Libya. For the tourist and the foreigner, the veil delimits both Algerian society and its female
component . . . The woman wrapped in her white veil unifies the
perception one has of female Algerian society. What we are dealing with here is quite obviously a uniform which tolerates no
modification, no variation.[179]

No Algerian woman would find any of this 'obvious'. Rachida Tita, for
instance, points out that the *haïk*, or the square of white cloth that veils
a woman from head to foot, is indeed subject to modifications. A *haïk*
can be made of plain cotton, of silk or of a man-made fabric. It can be
held around the body and drawn across the face in different ways. It can
be held beneath the chin, and a smaller veil can be fastened below the
eyes. There can be variations in the stitching, and there are regional
variations. It is the tourist (there is something truly odd about Fanon's
mention of 'tourism' in the context of the Algeria of 1959) or the foreigner who sees an anonymous veiled woman. Her sisters recognize an
individual by the way she holds herself and wears her *haïk*; Algerian men
learn to do the same.[180] Fanon was not looking as an Algerian would
look. And although he refers in phenomenological terms to the
Algerian woman's lived experience and even her 'lived body' (*corps
vécu*), he makes no attempt to understand what wearing a veil might
mean for her or what its symbolism might be. Just how closely Fanon
reproduces the European image of the anonymous Algerian woman is
apparent from Albert Camus's description of 'Their women, whom
you never saw. Or if you did see them in the street, you did not know
who they were, with their veils covering half their faces and their sensual, gentle eyes showing above the cloth.'[181]

Fanon's description of the Algerian revolutionary who takes off her
veil and walks 'naked' into the European city is couched in terms drawn
from Merleau-Ponty and Lhermitte. He speaks of her lived experience,
of her lived body and her corporeal schema. His actual description of
the unveiled woman suggests something more than a phenomenological interest:

The shoulders of the unveiled Algerian woman are bare. Her
stride is lithe and measured: neither too fast nor too slow. Her legs

are bare, and not caught up in the veil and her hips are exposed to the air . . .The absence of the veil alters the Algerian woman's corporeal schema. She has to rapidly discover new dimensions to her body, new means of controlling her muscles. She has to create for herself the gait of an-unveiled-woman-outside . . . .. The Algerian woman who walks quite naked into the European city relearns her body, and resituates it in a totally revolutionary way. In the case of women, this new dialectic between the body and the world is of capital importance.[182]

Fanon is not describing a woman who has unveiled only her face. He is describing – or imagining – a woman who appears to be wearing a short and sleeveless summer dress. He is unlikely to have actually seen a young woman dressed like this in Algiers, but he is certainly imagining her the way a man would imagine her. Perhaps this is what he wanted to see: the body beneath the veil.

Despite his political commitment to Algeria and despite his own intentions, Fanon comes dangerously close to reproducing the stereotypes of the very colonialism he was fighting. He speaks, for instance, of the cloistered lives of Algerian women who never leave the house unaccompanied and whose every movement is known and predictable.[183] He conspicuously fails to note that women did go out, usually veiled, to shop, to the *hammam* ('Turkish' baths) and to visit relatives, or that girls walked to school.[184] His comments on the cloistered lives of women who never went out are actually subverted by his own narrative. If women *never* went out, no woman in a veil could possibly have carried a concealed sten gun; the whole tactic depended for its success on her ability to look inconspicuous on a street where there were other women and where, until they realized what certain women were doing, French troops followed the advice given to their officers in an official guide to 'understanding Algeria': show great discretion in dealing with Muslim women.[185] Fanon also contradicts himself quite openly by remarking that groups of women did go out on Fridays to visit local cemeteries or sanctuaries.[186] He had probably seen this for himself: Blida's *bois sacré* was a typical destination for such excursions.

Fanon is quite right to note that what might be described as the French cult of the veil, which did govern European perceptions of

Algerian women, was 'a romantic exoticism, strongly tinged with sen-
suality'.[187] The assumption that the veil concealed a beautiful woman
was a widespread fantasy central to a whole sub-culture comprising literature, painting and photography.[188] Most Orientalist painting from
Delacroix's *Women of Algiers in their Apartment* (1832, Paris, Musée
du Louvre) onwards is organized around the depiction of unveiled
women in a 'harem'; as Titah remarks, the groups of women were more
likely to be sisters, aunts and cousins rather than the co-wives they were
imagined to be but the mythology of the harem was powerful enough
to overcome mere reality. There was, in nineteenth-century Algeria, a
flourishing trade in exotic photographs of unveiled women who look
directly at the camera, and who were presumably paid to overcome
their reluctance to pose in this state; a further frisson was obtained
when European women dressed up in 'local costume' and posed for
similar photographs. The production of postcards was almost an industry in itself, and their depiction of Algerian women ranged from the
exotic to the pornographic.[189] In *L'An V*, Fanon is describing aspects of
a revolution and neither literary history nor the visual arts, but the fantasies he describes fit into a definite tradition. His male patients
dreamed of 'tearing the veil', which is a fairly obvious metaphor for pen-
etration or rape. They also dreamed of penetrating groups of women,
and always with great violence. The aggressivity is then projected:
Algerian women thus become hypocritical, perverts or nymphomani-
acs.[190] Some of these dreams could have originated in a pornographic
postcard bought on the fringes of the Casbah.

On 14 November 1959, Maspero sent a copy of Fanon's new book
to Daniel Guérin, asking him if he would be willing to write something
about it 'before too long'. He was, he said, worried about the 'unjustified' silence about the book and hoped that Guérin would help to
break it.[191] Maspero had good cause to be worried, as he had ordered
a very ambitious print-run of 14,000 copies.[192] Guérin's review, published in the December issue of *Correspondence socialiste internationale*,
was elogious, though the paper's limited circulation meant that it probably did little to increase sales. He had, he wrote, rarely read such a rich
and overwhelming book, and described it as 'an inexhaustible source of
reflections not only for anti-colonialists, but also for the international
proletariat, sociologists, psychologists and, finally, humanity as a whole'.

Fanon had succeeded in describing the Algerian people's revolution from within; this was a book that would be read long after the war was over, and it was already 'one of the classics of free Algeria'.[193]

A book like this was never going to be a popular bestseller, but it proved to have a great appeal for some readers and helped to shape the thinking of the new Third Worldists. For the leftist lawyer Pierre Stibbe, writing in *France-Observateur*, Fanon's book was a 'document of great value' and 'both an autopsy of *l'Algérie de papa* and a revelation about the Algeria of tomorrow'.[194] Maurice Maschino, whose account of his desertion from the French army was also published by Maspero, agreed: 'It is an extremely dense and rich book by an Algerian psychiatrist who is committed to the struggle for national liberation, and it explains, from the inside so to speak, what Algerian society has become since the Revolution began, and the transformations and mutations it has undergone. This aspect has, with good reason, usually been overlooked; hence the originality and importance of *L'An V*.'[195]

The few reviews that appeared rightly stress the novelty and originality of Fanon's book. Even in this, the fifth year of the war, there were few inside accounts of Algeria, and none by Algerians. The issues of torture, human rights and the general conduct of the war had now been raised in books and pamphlets, as well as in the press, but few readers had any clear idea of the nature of the Algerian Revolution itself. In retrospect, Fanon's account does seem idealistic in the extreme and even dangerously confused in some respects; at the time of its publication, it had a major impact on a certain readership. Martin Evans's *Memory of Resistance* is based upon lengthy interviews with some of the young people who 'carried suitcases' or aided the FLN in other ways. A number of his informants cite Fanon, together with Albert Memmi and Mohammed Dib, as having helped to shape both their perception of themselves as 'Third Worldists' and their perception of the Algerian struggle as a socialist revolution. Gérard Chaliand recalled:

> I read *L'An V* as soon as it came out. As we had no other sources, we found that what Fanon had to say about the emancipation of women, the new stance adopted by young people regarding the traditional authority of their elders, the changes in social structures brought about by the revolutionary process – we found it all

highly likely, if not certain. Let's say that the picture of the revolution in the circles I'm talking about was perceived through the perception depicted by Fanon.[196]

The deserter 'Maurienne' remembered: 'My vision of the world was Fanonist . . . that is, the reawakening of the wretched of the earth. In so thinking I had a romantic and almost mystical vision which was that the salvation of the world would perhaps come from the Third World.'[197] 'Fanonism' had come into being.

# 10

# The Year of Africa

SPEAKING IN CAPE Town on 3 February 1960, British Prime Minister Harold Macmillan referred to the 'wind of change' that was blowing through Africa. It was blowing particularly strongly in France's African colonies. By the end of the year, all of the sub-Saharan territories would become independent states as the Community established in 1958 died a quiet death. In Algeria, the war without a name was still in progress and, despite Fanon and *El Moudjahid*'s regular predictions of imminent victory, it was not going well for the ALN. The completion of the Morice line had sealed the frontiers and starved the forces of the interior of both weapons and men. The frontier armies in Morocco and Tunisia were increasingly frustrated by their failure to penetrate the French defences. Amirouche's bout of 'blueitis' had taken a heavy toll on the forces of the interior. De Gaulle's appointment of General Maurice Challe as Commander-in-Chief in December 1958 now resulted in a change of tactics on the part of the French army. Challe was an air force officer and approached the Algerian situation with fresh eyes. In his view, the *quadrillage* tactic had allowed the army to grow fat and lazy, but had not prevented the ALN from operating effectively. It was still relatively safe in the mountain fortresses of Kabylia and the Aurès, and its Politico-Administrative

412

Organization was functioning as a parallel administration in much of the country.

Challe realized that the ALN could be completely defeated only if the French adopted its tactics, pursued its *katibas* into their sanctuaries and remained there long enough to eliminate them. To do that, the army needed both reinforcements and new equipment. The old GMC trucks, which were no longer being produced in the USA, were replaced by Berliet all-terrain vehicles. The gradual introduction of big Boeing troop-carrying helicopters – known as 'bananas' because of their shape – gave Challe's troops greater mobility than ever before and made it possible to have whole battalions in action within a quarter of an hour. By the summer of 1959, there were 400,000 troops on the borders. Challe also established a 'general reserve' of two divisions, made up mainly of paratroopers and legionnaires. The reserve troops were used to split up or destroy the ALN's *katibas* in steam-roller operations; *commandos de chasse* were then deployed in close-quarter counter-insurgency operations against the survivors, the ultimate plan being to drive them towards the Morice line, pin them down and eradicate them. The commandos lived in the field for extended periods and could be supplied, reinforced or redeployed by helicopter. Much greater use was now made of the *harkis*, the Algerians who had either rallied to the French of their own accord or who had been 'persuaded' – often by violent means – to do so. Many of them were captured ALN fighters whose local knowledge of the terrain and familiarity with ALN tactics proved to be invaluable assets. Unlike the clumsy sweeps of 1954 and 1955, the operations launched from early 1959 onwards were classic exercises in counter-insurgency warfare. Vulnerable to air-strikes, conspicuously visible to spotter-planes and harassed by the big 'reserve' units, the *katibas* were forced to split up into small groups that could be hunted down by the *commandos de chasse*. During the *Couronne* ('Crown') operation of February 1959, 1,600 ALN fighters were killed in the hinterland of Oran; almost 4,000 were killed in July as operations Jumelles ('Binoculars') and Etincelles ('Sparks') swept through Kabylia.[1] Although the ALN could not be physically eradicated down to the last man, it could scarcely go on taking this rate of casualties.

As the military situation inside Algeria deteriorated, the diplomatic front became more and more important to the GPRA. The diplomatic offensive had begun in 1957 and had then been consolidated by the establishment of the network of foreign delegations. Co-ordinated from Cairo by Lamine Debaghia, the offensive was now expanded to Africa. Omar Oussedik was dispatched to Conakry in Guinea and Boualem Oussedik to the Malian capital of Bamako.[2] In February, Fanon became the GPRA's permanent representative in Accra and thus acquired quasi-diplomatic status; the Ghanaian government regarded the permanent delegation as an embassy and Fanon as an ambassador. The premises used by the delegation in Accra were provided by the Ghanaians, and Nkrumah's government paid all its expenses.[3] This was not a high-profile diplomatic mission. The main purpose of the African delegations was to rally support for the GPRA within the Afro-Asian bloc at the United Nations, but they did not have the same importance as those in Europe, the Eastern bloc or the Arab countries. Being an ambassador for a provisional government recognized by only a few Third World countries and, as of October 1960, the Soviet Union, was both less exalted and less glamorous than it might sound. It meant spending a lot of time in planes – and even more time in airports – and often meant living in hotels or borrowed accommodation. Despite his promotion, Fanon did not have diplomatic status and still travelled on his Libyan passport and still had to obtain tourist visas before he could travel.

Fanon enjoyed Accra, and he liked the company of the African nationalists and revolutionaries he met there. It was here that he acquired his rather incongruous taste for the British Empire's favourite drink of gin and tonic.[4] He clearly made an impression on Nkrumah, who later described him as 'ideologically sound' and grudgingly praised *Les Damnés de la terre* as 'a powerful book but without a practical revolutionary philosophy'.[5] Other acquaintances made in Accra included Félix Moumié from Cameroon, the Congolese Patrice Lumumba, the Kenyan Tom M'Boya and the UPA's sinister Roberto Holden. Theirs was a world of plans for the future, but also a dangerous world of intrigue, plots and intense rivalries. Some of Fanon's new acquaintances were sincere nationalists; others were adventurers or worse. Arms dealers, mercenaries, spies and dubious journalists were never far away. It is improbable in the extreme that Fanon's movements and contacts were not being observed by the French intelligence services, and by agencies from further afield. There had certainly been an intelligence presence at the 1958 conference in Accra. The kindly American who offered to act as an informal intepreter for Patrice Lumumba, who had no English, proved to be a CIA agent.[6]

Fanon could now devote all his considerable energies to promoting the cause of Algerian independence in black Africa – though his 'black Africa' was in fact limited to the few French-speaking countries he visited: Guinea, Ivory Coast, Congo and Mali. Ghana was the only English-speaking country in which he had any real contacts. He was not a natural diplomat. His commitment to Algeria and to his own vision of African unity was total, but his faith in Sekou Touré and the confidence he placed in men like Roberto Holden points to a certain lack of both political judgement and political experience. Fanon was a good propagandist, but not a subtle one. A more skilled operator like Yazid could use reports of torture to turn international public opinion against France; Fanon simply used them to flagellate the French left for its failings. Intolerant and much given to making sudden but irreversible decisions, he was not a master of the art of compromise and it is very hard to imagine Fanon exchanging small talk over the canapés at reception after reception. To make matters worse, his English was poor and French was not widely spoken in Accra. Promoting the Algerian cause was not always easy, and in late 1960 Fanon would complain that: 'For almost three years, I have been trying to drag the woolly-minded idea of African Unity out of the subjectivist or even woolly-minded swamps in which the majority of its supporters live.' Contradicting the views on the need for national cultures he had expressed in Rome in 1959 (and which would be reiterated in *Les Damnés de la terre*), he now argued that African unity was a prelude to the creation of a United States of Africa that bypassed the 'national chauvinist bourgeois phase'.[7]

Shortly before Fanon took up his post in Accra and uprooted his family yet again, Martinique forced itself upon his attention once more. In January 1958, he had written an article for *El Moudjahid* about the Caribbean on the eve of the formation of the Federation of the West Indies.[8] This was little more than a survey of the general situation intended for readers with little or no knowledge of the region and, in terms of Fanon's own development, its real significance is that it is here that he first cites Jacques Roumain's 'Sales nègres', the last lines of which eventually supplied him with the title *Les Damnés de la terre*. It was an optimistic article in that Fanon sensed that a cultural renaissance was taking place in the Caribbean. The rediscovery of West Indian history, the rehabilitation of local traditions and non-Christian religions (notably in Haiti), and pride in being black all pointed to the emergence of a 'West Indian consciousness' which found its primary expression in the use of Creole. Creole and the national consciousness that went with it, he suggested, could be the basis for the eventual emergence of a West Indian nation. That nation would, Fanon believed, gradually emerge as newly independent countries came together in a confederation of states prepared to defend one another's freedom and to give each other economic aid. Even when Martinique voted in 1958 to remain part of the French Community, Fanon still seemed to believe that Martinican independence within a West Indian Federation was at least a possibility.[9] Here, Fanon's optimism, combined with his lack of knowledge about the English-speaking islands, leads him somewhat astray. Language alone was unlikely to have provided the basis for federal unity between the scattered islands of the archipelago. The Creole spoken in Martinique is very similar to that used in Guadeloupe, and both are understood in Dominica and St Lucia, but the 'patois' of Jamaica, for instance, is much more English-based. The hopes of 1958 notwithstanding, the Federation, which included ten English-speaking islands, ceased to exist in 1962 when first Jamaica and then Trinidad and Tobago withdrew.

Fanon's second *El Moudjahid* article on Martinique appeared the first week of January 1960 and was entitled 'Bloodshed in the French-dominated West Indies'.[10] It dealt with the riots that suddenly broke out in Fort-de-France in the third week of December 1959. They began with a banal incident. At about eight in the evening of Sunday 20 December, a white incomer who had been repatriated from Morocco accidentally backed his car into a badly parked Vespa scooter belonging to a black docker. Angry words and then blows were exchanged, and the incident rapidly acquired racial overtones. All this took place on the edge of the Savanne, which was full of strollers, and a crowd began to gather. The mood soon turned ugly. The day ended with a serious outbreak of violence.

Martinique had changed since Fanon had left, and the changes had not all been for the better. Since 1946, it had been an overseas *départe-ment* rather than a colony, but the socio-economic climate was difficult and tensions were rising. The sugar industry was in crisis. Rum exports were falling. Forty-six per cent of the population was still working in the primary sector, but had stable work for less than half of the year.[11] As the island produced and exported less and less, it was forced into new forms of dependency as grants and welfare payments from the metropolis became a major source of revenue. Rural unemployment fuelled rural depopulation, and migration into the suburbs of Fort-de-France forced up property prices and rents. The shanty towns of Volga-Plage and Texaco were growing like urban mangrove swamps on the edges of the capital. It has been estimated that the price of basic foodstuffs such as rice and fish had risen by 40 per cent since 1956. Tourism was just beginning to develop; the Lido hotel opened in 1959 and souvenir shops catering for tourists were appearing in the rue de la Liberté on the edge of the Savanne. Tourism provided few benefits for most of the population and generated resentment rather than prosperity. The internal racial balance had begun to shift slightly but significantly with the arrival of *pieds noirs* who had left Tunisia and Morocco after independence or who had decided that there was no future for them in Algeria. They were not popular, especially when they began to regard and speak to black Martinicans as though they were *bicots*. Martinicans were well aware that a war was going on in Algeria – some of them had served in it. Departmentalization had also had unfortunate side-effects in that it brought an influx of civil servants from France who were paid much better salaries than locals; many a second home was bought *en métropole* with savings accumulated during a 'hardship' posting in Martinique or the other DOMs.

The underlying crisis turned a minor accident into an explosion of violence. The actual sequence of events is still not entirely clear. According to some accounts, the initial dispute between the white driver and the docker was quickly resolved and the two men involved even went for a drink together. It was only later that the crowd began to turn ugly, especially when it was swelled by people from the slums of the Terres-Sainville, Sainte-Thérèse and Morne Pichevin districts – described by Patrick Chamoiseau as 'places where people chewed pebbles without bread on the side'[12] – flooding into the town centre. At this point, someone phoned the police from the Hotel Europe, where a group of *pieds noirs* had gathered. Without warning, a squad of CRS riot police fired teargas grenades into the crowd and then waded in with their long batons. The crowd responded with whatever missiles came to hand and drove the tough CRS back into their barracks in the Fort Saint-Louis. Three nights of violent riots followed. The Hotel Europe was wrecked. Police stations were attacked with improvised fire bombs and police cars were burned out and then pushed into the Canal Levassor. The windows of Martinique's first Prisunic supermarket were broken, as were those of the luxury 'Roger Albert' shops that sold (and still sell) tourist goods on the rue de la Liberté. Whites – and especially whites who could not speak Creole – were in considerable danger. Three young men – Christian Marajo, a sixteen-year-old *lycéen*, a twenty-year-old identified only as Rosile and a nineteen-year-old electrician called Julien Betzi – were shot dead by the CRS during the riots. The situation appeared to be getting out of control. After a panicky debate in the Assemblée Nationale in Paris, the cruiser *de Grasse* was ordered to make for the troubled island, but her orders were countermanded almost immediately.[13] By the end of the week, a curfew had been imposed and the CRS had been withdrawn to barracks before being repatriated to France (they have not been used in Martinique since 1959).[14] An uneasy calm was gradually restored.

Fanon speaks in *El Moudjahid* of 'fifteen dead' and 'many wounded', and describes the riots as an embryonic revolution: some Martinicans had at last dared to take up arms and occupy Fort-de-France for a few hours.

> The old assimilated politicians who are rotting from within and who, for a long time, have represented only their own mediocre interests and their own mediocrity, must be very worried today. They have suddenly discovered that Martinicans can indeed be treated by France as rebels. They are also discovering the existence of a rebel spirit, of a national spirit . . . The West Indian question, the question of the Caribbean Federation cannot be concealed for much longer. The former Dutch and British Guyanas which are now independent, are exercising their attraction on French-dominated Guyana. The British-dominated West Indies are

achieving independence. In Cuba, Castro is giving the Caribbean islands a new face. Yes, the question has been raised.

Fanon accepted that 'this first manifestation of the Martinican national spirit' would, in the short term, be repressed by the French forces and their local allies, but forecast that Guadeloupe, Martinique and Guyana would eventually become independent:

> The Algerian people assures the West Indians and Guyanese peoples of its fraternal sympathy and urges them to sharpen their combativity. Those West Indian soldiers, NCOs and officers who are fighting their Algerian brothers while French troops are machine-gunning their people in Fort-de-France and Basse-Terre must refuse to fight and must desert.
>
> We now know that links exist between the war in Algeria and the recent events that have stained Martinique with blood. The riposte of the Martinican masses was provoked by former French civil servants from North Africa, by those who have been expelled from Morocco and Tunis, by those who compromised themselves too much in Algeria.

He dismissed out of hand the 'official explanation' that the riots were a reaction to 'a banal traffic accident'. That expression was indeed used by Jacques Soustelle, who was now Minister of the Interior, when he spoke to the Assemblée on 30 December, but it was not 'the official explanation' and appears to originate from the original AFP report picked up by *Le Monde*, which was no doubt Fanon's main source of information.[15]

In private, Fanon gave a very different interpretation of the events in Fort-de-France. Bertène Juminer, a doctor and political activist from Guyana, met Fanon in Tunis in 1958 and later recalled the cold welcome he received: 'So you're still in *politics* in the West Indies and Guyana? One of these days, it will be by kicks in your arse that France will force you to take your independence. And you will owe it to Algeria, our Algeria, which has been the whore of the colonial French Empire.'[16] The brutality of the CRS might have been seen as one of the 'kicks in the arse', but Fanon was dismissive about the likely reaction to the December events. He subsequently told Juminer that the people of Martinique should have gathered their dead, disembowelled them and paraded them through the streets crying for vengeance. Then he shrugged his shoulders: 'They are not going to do anything about it. They'll probably vote for some symbolic motion and then begin all over again to croak from misery. In reality, a flash of anger on their part reassures the colonialists. It will be a question of a manifestation and nothing more, somewhat like an erotic dream. One makes love to a shadow, soils the bed and the next morning everything is back in order again and soon forgotten.'[17]

In public, Fanon grossly overstates the importance of the riots; in private he describes them as a failure. In some respects, he was simply misinformed. According to Raphaël Confiant's reconstruction of events, which is based on contemporary reports in the local press, the crowd did attempt to carry the body of Marajo through the streets, but was dissuaded from doing so by a member of the municipal council anxious to defuse the situation.[18] Fanon was, on the other hand, quite right when he remarked that nothing would happen and that only symbolic motions would be passed. The PCM and PPM issued a joint statement calling for calm and stating that demonstrations of this kind were both sterile and dangerous.[19] In Paris, Manville helped to organize a protest meeting in the Mutualité hall and argued that relations between France and Martinique now had to be defined in terms other than dependency, whilst Michel Leiris explained the violence as a reaction to the racism of 'certain Europeans', the violence of the police and the difficult economic and social situation.[20] The meeting did not succeed in making Martinique a major political issue. Within a month, very different issues would come to the fore and make it impossible to sustain any public interest in the island.

The riots do appear to have been spontaneous, but the targets attacked were well chosen. The hotels and souvenir shops were, as a Martinican historian puts it, symbols of a 'new modernity' from which most of the population was being excluded. The rioters attacked the new order and the institutions of the French state, but not the property of the béké-Martinique. The December events did not signal the beginning of a revolution but they did mark the beginning of a troubled period of strikes, unrest and repression during which Fanon's name was, thanks to the short-lived Organisation de la Jeunesse Anti-colonialiste de la Martinique (OJAM), briefly linked with Martinican nationalism. In April 1962, a special issue of *Esprit* was devoted to the French West Indies. In his editorial, Jean-Marie Domenach evoked the spectre of serious unrest and insisted that reforms, including greater autonomy for the DOMs, had to be introduced 'before it was too late'.[21] In an article on the social climate, Yvon Leborgne described Martinique's and Guadeloupe's problems in terms that are strikingly reminiscent of *Peau noire, masques blancs*, even though he does not mention Fanon by name. The heritage of slavery meant that the absolute superiority of whites was still based upon the assertion that blacks were not human. The fundamental contradiction was, he wrote, expressed perfectly by the role of schools in colonial society. On the one hand, the content of education constantly stressed the superiority of the colonizer and the eternal inferiority of the colonized; on the other, it encouraged 'assimilationist tendencies' by inculcating the moral and cultural values of the colonizer to the exclusion of everything else.[22]

Like René Ménil and Fanon, Edouard Glissant stressed the alienating effects of a culture in which the imitation of France – the wearing of the mask – was the rule.[23] His vision of the future was that of a federation uniting Martinique, Guadeloupe and Guyana, and he invoked Fanon's name. Césaire's *Cahier d'un retour au pays natal* had provided a 'spiritual charter' for Africans and West Indians alike and Fanon had foreseen their political destiny: 'He died in the service of Algeria. He died Algerian, totally Algerian. And the West Indian people will cherish the memory of that Algerian because they can see in him the most exalted and sublime image of their own vocation.'[24] The young founders of OJAM were thinking along similar lines but were unable to realize their project.

Simone de Beauvoir reports Fanon as saying in the summer of 1961 that Martinique was not 'ripe' for an uprising, but also as remarking that the victory that was being won in Algeria would help the West Indies. Even so, she sensed that he was frustrated at not being able to be politically active in his own country.[25] Others suggest that his commitment to Algeria was a form of compensation for his frustration and disappointment with Martinique. The argument was originally put forward by the Tunisian Albert Memmi, whose analysis of the relationship between colonizer and colonized is not dissimilar to Fanon's. The question of mutual influence does not arise. Memmi's 'portrait of the colonized' was first published in 1957, but he had not read *Peau noire, masques blancs* at that time;[26] there is not any indication in *Les Damnés de la terre* that Fanon ever read Memmi. The two men never met, and Memmi's knowledge of Fanon derived from Peter Geismar's biography of him. The similarity between their respective analyses of the colonial situation derives from their common debt to Sartre and, in particular, to the argument of his *Refléxions sur la question juive*: colonial racism creates the colonized, just as anti-Semitism creates 'the Jew'. Like Fanon, Memmi held that colonialism induces a profound sense of depersonalization by drowning the individual in 'an anonymous collectivity' ('They're all the same').[27] Memmi's analysis reveals that colonial racism explains, justifies and maintains the colonial system by

1. Discovering and stressing the *differences* between colonizer and colonized.
2. Valorizing those differences for the benefit of the colonizer and to the disadvantage of the colonized.
3. Making those differences *absolute* by asserting that they are definitive and acting in such a way that they become definitive.[28]

In this situation, the colonized can react in one of two ways. He can 'change his condition by changing his skin' or,[29] in Fanon's phrase, by putting on the white mask. This internalization of the oppressor-other inevitably induces self-hatred and is the source of 'the negro's negrophobia and the Jew's anti-Semitism'.[30] The alternative to self-hatred is rebellion:

Rebellion: the very existence of the colonizer creates oppression and only the complete liquidation of colonization will bring about the liberation of the colonized . . . Revolution: we have noted that colonization kills the colonized in material terms. It should be added that it kills him in spiritual terms. Colonization perverts human relations, destroys institutions or makes them sclerotic, and corrupts men, both colonized and colonizing. In order to live, the colonized must suppress colonization. But in order to become a man, he must suppress the colonized man he has become. Whilst the European must annihilate the colonizer inside himself, the colonized must transcend the colonized man.[31]

In 1971, Memmi argued in a lengthy – and by no means unsympathetic – article that Fanon's life had been 'impossible'. The 'specific destiny of Frantz Fanon, his future and definitive intellectual and political physionomy' emerged when he discovered that assimilation was a deception and 'broke with France and the French with all the passion that fiery temperament was capable of'.[32] His rejection of France meant the rejection of his first love, and also the rejection of part of himself. At the same time, he could no longer identify with the 'black mirage of negritude', and Martinique's failure to rise up in arms in December 1959 completed his disillusionment with his native island. Fanon's identification with the Algerian nation was therefore a psychological substitute for 'an impossible identification with the Martinican nation'. Fanon had, according to Memmi, categorically rejected Martinique and the West Indies and he identified with Algeria primarily because it was neither France nor Martinique.[33] Memmi notes that Fanon addresses his 'fellow' Martinicans as though he were an Algerian and takes this as proof that he had abandoned his Martinican identity, but the argument must surely be qualified: Fanon was writing not in his own name, but as one of a team of propagandists who were quite definitely Algerian.

Françoise Vergès advances a more sophisticated and psychoanalytically inflected version of this argument by contending that Fanon 'disavows' Martinique and constructs a family romance centred on Algeria.[34] 'Family romance' is Freud's term for the very common fantasy in which a child imagines that it is not being brought up by its real parents and that its 'true parents' are of noble birth. In some variants, the child fantasizes that it is illegitimate and has been abandoned by one of its parents, usually that of the same sex.[35] Vergès has used the 'family romance' theme to analyse France's relationship with the old colonies, which were indeed infantilized by being turned into the 'children' of La Mère-patrie, with particular reference to her home island of Réunion.[36] The result is a fascinating analysis which can also be applied to Martinique, but it does rest upon the unproven assumption that the life of a collectivity – a nation, an island – can be unproblematically described by using the categories of a depth psychology designed for the psychoanalysis of individuals.

Vergès quite rightly remarks that Fanon's relationship with Martinique was ambivalent, and goes on to argue that he disavows it, by recreating his family and locating his 'symbolic ancestry' in Algeria.[37] In Freudian terms, 'disavowal' is a mode of defence in which the individual refuses to recognize the reality of a traumatic perception, the classic example being the child's refusal to recognize that a woman does not have a penis.[38] For Vergès, Fanon disavows the 'Creole filiation', or the rape of the Martinican mother and the emasculation of the Martinican father. He refuses to recognize that they are his parents and, rejecting the weak men of Martinique, he makes the FLN's virile fighters his symbolic father and brothers. She further contends that the identification with Algeria helps Fanon to come to terms with a psycho-sexual problem: 'It was in Africa that Fanon found the virile male that would belie the colonial construction of emasculated masculinity.'[39] Like so many psychoanalytic readings, the analysis is seductive but it relies on some rather heavy-handed symbolic interpretations. 'Brother' (*frère*), for instance, was a normal form of address in FLN circles and was the equivalent to the communist 'comrade'. It does not necessarily have the connotations Vergès lends it.

Such interpretations are brusquely rejected by Marcel Manville and Joby Fanon who obviously have reasons of their own to reclaim Fanon for Martinique. Edouard Glissant also insists that Fanon developed a new interest in Martinique in the last months of his life. The relevance of Fanon's supposed problems with psycho-sexual identity is perhaps not as obvious as it may seem to post-colonial theorists who rely heavily on wild – and almost exclusively textual – psychoanalysis. There were, after all, enough purely political reasons to despair of Martinique and of Césaire. It is true that Fanon wrote very little on Martinique and that he never returned there after the unsatisfactory experience of 1952. There is, however, evidence to suggest that the memory of Martinique returned to haunt him in the last weeks of his life.

The arguments of both Memmi and Vergès rely for their coherence upon a strange blindness to certain features of *Les Damnés de la terre*. The title itself derives not from any text produced by the FLN, but from

a defiant expression of West Indian negritude as revolt. The first chapter on violence includes a long quotation from Aimé Césaire which also
appears in *Peau noire*. This was not included in the version that
appeared in *Les Temps modernes* in May 1961, but was inserted as Fanon
made his final revisions of the text, or in other words as he was dying of
leukaemia later that summer. Written in 1946, Césaire's *Et les chiens se
taisaient* ('And the Dogs Fell Silent') is a tragedy in the form of a
lengthy oratorio telling of a slave revolt that occurred in Martinique at
an unspecified date. It begins with an echo speaking as the curtain
slowly rises on the stage: 'Of course the Rebel is going to die . . . Of
course the Rebel is going to leave your world of rape where the victim
is, by your grace, a brute and an unbeliever.' The passage cited by
Fanon begins with an exchange between the anonymous Rebel and his
mother:

The Rebel
NAME: offended; forename: humiliated; status: in revolt; age: the
    stone age.

The Mother
RACE: the human race. Religion: fraternity.

The Rebel then describes the murder for which he will die:

My heart, you will not deliver me from my memories.
It was one evening in November
And suddenly a clamour lit up the silence.
We leaped – we, the slaves, the shit, we the animals shod with
    patience.
We ran like maniacs; shots rang out. We struck blows. The sweat
    and the blood cooled us down. We struck blows in the midst of
    the screams
and the screams became more strident and a great clamour rose in
    the east.
The outhouses were burning and the flames gently licked our
    backs.
Then came the assault on the master's house.

They were firing from the windows.

We forced the doors.

The master's bedroom was open. The master's bedroom was
   brightly lit

and the master was there, very calm . . . and our men halted . . .
   it was the master.

I went in. It's you, he said to me very quietly. It was me, it was
   indeed me,

I told him, me, the good slave, the faithful slave, the slavish slave,

and suddenly his eyes were like two frightened roaches on a rainy
   day . . .

I struck a blow and blood flowed: that is the only baptism I can
   remember today.[40]

Fanon cites Césaire's oratorio because of its 'prophetic significance'
and because it exemplifies the central thesis of *Les Damnés de la terre*:
'The colonized man liberates himself in and through violence.'[41] The
very late insertion of the quotation makes it difficult to accept the claim
that Fanon disavowed his Martinican past. On the contrary, he returns
to it as he is dying. The final image of the revolt of the wretched of the
earth is not that of an Algerian freedom fighter carrying a gun, but of
a doomed Martinican *marron* with a blood-stained machete in his
hand.

At the beginning of 1960, Fanon's attention was, for fairly obvious
reasons, focused not on Martinique, but on sub-Saharan Africa. The
transfer to Accra was certainly a promotion in one sense, but in another
sense it marginalized and isolated Fanon. The FLN's power – and the
struggles for power that went on within the FLN – was centred on
Tunis and Cairo. Most of Fanon's activities related to the development
of the 'African Legion' project that had first been mentioned at Accra
in December 1958. The project may well have been Fanon's own
brainchild, but he was not free to act on his own initiative. In March
1960, he therefore travelled to Cairo to win the approval of the GPRA
and the newly formed *Etat Major*, which brought the Eastern and
Western frontier armies under a single command for the first time. But
although officially approved, the African Legion was never to be a
major topic of discussion in North Africa and it does not figure greatly

in standard histories of the Algerian war. In the oration he gave at Fanon's burial, Belkacem Krim, then Vice-President of the GPRA, paid due tribute to Fanon's role in revealing 'the true face of our Revolution' at so many conferences in Africa but not once did he mention the African Legion project.[42] Whilst the FLN obviously welcomed expressions of solidarity from south of the Sahara, and needed that solidarity on the international diplomatic front, the discussions of August 1959 had made it quite clear that the revolution it was leading was first and foremost an Arab-Islamic affair and not part of a pan-African movement. The GPRA was reluctant to admit foreign fighters into its ranks and, whatever Fanon himself may have believed, the African Legion project does not appear to have been high on its list of priorities.

The speeches Fanon gave to the conferences he attended have never been published in their entirety, and would probably make for very repetitious reading if they were. Their content can be reconstructed from contemporary press reports and from comments made elsewhere by Fanon. Although they were euphoric experiences for the participants, the conferences themselves were relatively minor events given the scale of the changes that were occurring in sub-Saharan Africa. In retrospect, the dominant themes of continental or pan-African solidarity and even union seem naively optimistic. For those involved at the time, this was one of those dawns in which it was a joy to be alive. But Fanon also had his doubts and fears about the future, and warned against the threats posed by tensions between Ghana and Senegal, Somalia and Ethiopia, and Morocco and Mauritania.[43]

Fanon's round of conferences began in Tunis itself when President Habib Bourguiba opened the Conference of African Peoples on 25 January 1960. Predictable demands were put forward, demanding a halt to plans for nuclear testing in the Sahara, where France was planning to explode its first atom bomb in mid-February, and the return of Bizerte to Tunisia,[44] and it was at this conference that the agreement with Roberto Holden was quietly finalized. The meeting in Tunis was, however, completely overshadowed by events in Algeria itself and received little coverage in the international press. The week of 24 January to 1 February has become known as the 'week of the barricades' and it precipitated a major political crisis in both France and

Algeria. The forces that had sensed their strength in February 1956 and flexed their muscles in May 1958 now made a real bid for power.

The events of January 1960 were precipitated by de Gaulle himself. In May 1958, he had appeared to be the saviour of *Algérie française* and the man who had 'understood' its supporters. A year and a half later, he finally expressed in public his long-held private view that there was no real alternative to self-determination for Algeria, though 'self-determination' was by no means synonymous with independence under the GPRA, and de Gaulle's definition of 'Algerian' included the European minority. Speaking on television on 16 September 1959, he outlined the alternatives: complete Francoization with complete equality of rights for everyone in Algeria, or 'a government of the Algerians by the Algerians' and close union with France. Complete secession would, he argued, lead to terrible chaos and a communist dictatorship.[45]

Although the French army was still fighting a war of attrition against the ALN, it was now clear that some form of self-determination was on the political agenda. De Gaulle's military strategy was designed to ensure that, should it become necessary to do so, he could negotiate from a position of strength. A week later, the GPRA responded to his statement by insisting that there could be no return to peace prior to recognition of the right to self-determination, but also indicated its willingness to discuss the military and political conditions for a ceasefire. Whatever Fanon may have thought and said, the provisional government he represented had concluded that an outright military victory was impossible.

The very mention of self-determination provoked consternation in Algiers, where the European population understandably leaped to the conclusion that their interests were about to be sold out and that they would indeed have to choose between the coffin and the suitcase. Men like Jo Ortiz and Pierre Lagaillarde, who had helped to overthrow the Fourth Republic, began to plot against the Fifth. Formed in late 1956, Ortiz's neo-fascist militia, the Front National Français, was now a force to be reckoned with and its young shock troops were a visible presence on the streets. It was no secret that it enjoyed the support of sections of the army and particularly of the locally recruited Unités Territoriales.

It was not only the civilian population that was alarmed by the mention of Algerian self-determination. In an interview with a German journalist, General Massu – a brave soldier but never the most tactful or astute of men – carelessly admitted that the army 'no longer understood' its President's policy on Algeria. He went on to say: 'Our greatest disappointment has been to see General de Gaulle become a man of the left' and confided that the army was both urging Europeans to form paramilitary organizations and supplying them with arms. Massu's interview was published in the Munich-based *Süddeutsche Zeitung* on 18 January and was immediately reproduced by all the major press agencies.[46] The General was promptly recalled to Paris, relieved of his command and posted to Germany. Their victory in the Battle of Algiers and the events of 13 May had made Massu and his men popular heroes, and his removal led to widespread resentment and anger. A direct confrontation between Paris and Algiers was now inevitable.

A general strike was called for Sunday 24 January and, safe in the knowledge that the army would let them act with impunity, uniformed youths from Ortiz's private army ensured that the city closed down. Crowds began to gather around the war memorial on the plateau des Glières and at the foot of the monumental steps leading up to the Forum. The slogans called for the resignation – or even the death – of de Gaulle and for the return of Massu. Lagaillarde and a small group of confederates had occupied part of the University overnight and were now turning it into a fortified position. Weapons and uniforms were smuggled in by members of the Unités Territoriales and machine guns were placed on the roof. Ortiz established his own command post in a building overlooking the plateau des Glières and opposite the main post office. Barricades were built to block the surrounding streets. At eight in the morning, Ortiz appeared on the balcony of the University, with Colonel Jean Gardes in full uniform at his side. It seemed that the army had taken the insurgents' side and that a full-scale coup was in progress.[47]

At six in the evening, a squad of gendarmes began to move slowly down the steps from the Forum to disperse the crowd. In accordance with regulations, their weapons were unloaded. The barricades were opened to let them through but it immediately became obvious that they had walked into a trap. Projectiles of all kinds rained down on them and then a shot rang out. Machine-gun fire came from

Lagaillarde's rooftop positions. Tyres packed with explosives were sent rolling down to the steps into the ranks of the gendarmes, who were now desperately trying to load their guns. In the mayhem that followed, fourteen of the gendarmes were killed and a further 123 were wounded. One was found hanging by his feet in a stairwell. Six demonstrators were also killed. The firing went on for an hour. Units from the Foreign Legion's First Parachute Regiment and the First Colonial Parachute Regiment were stationed only a few hundred yards away but did not intervene until the firing stopped. They did not move against the insurgents and it was clear where their colonels' loyalties lay. On the morning of 25 January, metropolitan France was astonished to learn from the news that the barricades were still in place. It was obvious to all that, had the army wanted to, it could have put down the rebellion overnight. Fearing a possible military coup, the left, and the PCF in particular, now began to mobilize in France and to call for negotiations with the FLN, a ceasefire and recognition of Algeria's right to self-determination.

The rebellion found little support outside Algiers. Although there were minor incidents in Oran and elsewhere, it was becoming obvious that the men of the *contingent* who, just like the ALN fighters and sympathizers described by Fanon in *L'An V*, had been following events by listening to transistor radios, would not follow the paratroopers. They were more concerned with their longed-for demobilization than with joining in a coup. Most officers also took a dim view of events in Algiers. In the Constantinois, General Gandoët told local activists that if they built barricades, his tanks would flatten them, and warned them that if the agitation continued, he would pull out his troops and leave them to deal with two million Muslims as best they could.[48] On 29 January, de Gaulle appeared on television in full uniform and again spoke of self-determination for Algeria but still rejected the GPRA's insistence that recognition of Algeria's independence was a precondition for a ceasefire. De Gaulle wore uniform – and de Gaulle in uniform was an impressive sight – to remind the army that he was its supreme commander. He warned the army that it was in danger of disintegrating into an anarchic mass controlled by feudal lords. He had played a dangerous waiting game and he won it. By 1 February, the ultras had surrendered. The threat of mutiny faded.

The fragmentary writings of Fanon's last years do not provide any general overview of the Algerian war and they contain no discussion of barricades week. Fanon himself was far away from Algiers and Tunis, was primarily concerned with the Legion project and was still predicting a military victory for the ALN even though he must by now have had private and unspoken doubts about its likelihood. In April, he was in Conakry to speak at the Afro-Asiatic Solidarity Conference. The conference was formally opened on 11 April 1960 by Sekou Touré, who described the delegates as representing a world of hunger, poverty and ignorance which had been denied any kind of human rights by an imperialism that had exploited it as an immense reservoir of men and commodities.[49] Algeria was obviously a major issue and the film *Héroïne algérienne*, which tells the story of Djamila Bouhired's role in the Battle of Algiers, was shown. Speaking on 13 April, Fanon spoke of the GPRA's determination to pursue the war of independence until the final victory was achieved and sternly denounced countries whose 'negative neutralism' had led them to sign treaties with France, the main targets of such criticism being Senghor's Senegal and Houphouet-Boigny's Ivory Coast. Such treaties were, he argued, to be regarded with distrust and suspicion by all those who were fighting for the right to self-determination, for human rights and for freedom and dignity.[50] The final resolution adopted on 16 April called for intensified action at the international level to bring about the triumph of the Algerian cause. The attention of the heads of state present was drawn to the gravity of the situation in Algeria and to the threat it posed to peace and security throughout North Africa. The conference solemnly resolved to use all possible means to make Algeria's national independence a concrete reality.

It was presumably this conference that Fanon reported to Simone de Beauvoir who, although a reliable witness in many respects, can be infuriatingly vague about dates. Fanon described to her the embarrassing incident that occurred when he escorted an Algerian delegation to an evening of entertainment laid on for them by the Guinean government. The Algerians were scandalized and shocked to see bare-breasted women dancing in public and asked: 'Are they decent women? And is this country socialist?' To judge by Beauvoir's account, Fanon was scandalized too, as – two years after the event – he kept muttering: 'Bare breasts. They have breasts, they're showing them.'[51] Fanon was neither puritanical nor prudish; this was simply a spectacle he would never have seen in Martinique,[52] much less in Algeria.

In the same week, Fanon returned to Accra for the Conference on Positive Action. Again, there were condemnations of France's use of the Sahara for nuclear tests and calls for the withdrawal of French troops from Algeria. The Committee on Algeria elected by the conference now suggested that the heads of independent states should meet to organize a corps of African volunteers to support the ALN.[53] A local official called Ackah had already announced that he was in charge of recruitment and that 500 Ghanaian volunteers were currently in training, and the GPRA had recently signalled for the first time that it was ready to accept their services.[54] Whether or not these volunteers ever existed other than on paper is not certain; what is certain is that they never fought in Algeria.

The audience in Accra included Peter Worsely, Professor of Sociology at the University of Manchester. When the GPRA's ambassador stood up to speak, Worsely expected to hear an address by a diplomat – 'not usually', he adds, 'an experience to set the pulses racing'. To his surprise: 'I found myself electrified by a contribution that was remarkable not only for its analytic power, but delivered, too, with a passion and brilliance that is all too rare.' At one point, Fanon seemed almost to break down. Worsely approached him afterwards and asked what had been wrong:

> He replied that he suddenly felt overcome at the thought that he had to stand there, before the assembled representatives of African nationalist movements, to try and persuade them that the Algerian cause was important, at a time when men were dying and being tortured in his country for a cause whose justice ought to command automatic support from rational and progressive human beings.[55]

Just over a month later, Fanon travelled to the Ethiopian capital for the Conference of Independent African States, which met from 14 to 20 June. The GPRA, which had had observer status at most of the conferences attended by Fanon, was treated as a legitimate government, as were the delegates from Nigeria and Somalia. The Belgian Congo had become officially independent at the beginning of the month and the delegates from the young but dangerously weak République du Congo were given a particularly warm welcome. Previous conferences of this kind had passed off without incident, but that in Addis Ababa was the scene of a minor diplomatic scandal. The delegations had been seated in alphabetical order, which put the Algerians in the front row in the parliament building. When the French Ambassador entered the building, he suddenly realized that he would have to sit next to representatives of the GPRA. To compound his embarrassment, a green and white Algerian flag was suddenly unfurled. Ambassador Juniac turned on his heel and left the conference. The provocation was deliberate: the GPRA had brought its own flag from Cairo as there were no Algerian flags in Addis. The main GPRA speaker was not Fanon but M'Hammed Yazid, who had gained considerable diplomatic experience as an FLN spokesman in New York, and he succeeded in persuading the conference to call for a boycott of all French goods. There was another call for an end to the war. The last day was dominated by a discussion of Cameroonian independence.[56]

It was in Addis Ababa, he thinks, that Jean Daniel had his only meeting with Fanon, though he had been told about him by the psychiatrist Suzanne Taïeb. Taïeb had apparently mentioned the presence in Blida of a very welcoming 'visionary', and Daniel was under the illusion that *Peau noire* – which he had clearly not read – was based on Fanon's experiences in Algeria. When he learned of Fanon's death, he recalled that he had great respect for the man, even though he did not like *Les Damnés de la terre*. Daniel's memories are strangely confused and may have been influenced by the fact that he was writing after Fanon's death. In December 1961, he recalled:

> As his face became more hollow and as his eyes seemed to devour it, he seemed to internalize everything. His handshake became more urgent and always seemed to have a message. The way he met your gaze was both sharp and indulgent. You always hesitated for a moment before knowing whether you had been admitted to the demanding universe into which he had withdrawn, and where he remained to think about the condition of

his people – a condition that was, for him, still not the human condition.[57]

Daniel, a *pied noir* born in Blida who was to become the powerful editor of *France-Observateur* and then *Le Nouvel Observateur*, was at this point still working as a reporter for *L'Express* and these words, not published at the time, were written in a hospital bed in Algeria. He had been wounded while covering the fighting that broke out when lightly armed Tunisian forces unsuccessfully attempted to seize the naval base at Bizerte, and was now convalescing. In a published discussion of *Les Damnés de la terre*, he gives a slightly different version of his meeting with Fanon which suggests that they met at a later date. He describes Fanon in almost exactly the same terms, but claims that they met after Fanon's return from Accra, or in other words at the end of 1960.[58]

At the end of August Fanon, Oussedik and Yazid travelled to Léopoldville (now Kinshasa) to attend the Pan-African Congress convened at the suggestion of Patrice Lumumba. They clearly had difficulty in getting there, as *Le Monde* twice reported the Algerian delegation as 'expected to arrive'.[59] In the circumstances, it is surprising that they got there at all. This was neither a good time nor a good place for a conference about African unity. The République du Congo (now the Democratic Republic of the Congo, and formerly Zaïre) had been independent only since June. Its independence was nominal rather than real. The administration was still Belgian-controlled, and so was the army, which was in a state of mutiny. There were serious conflicts between Prime Minister Lumumba and the head of state, Joseph Kasavuba. The mineral-rich southern province of Katanga had seceded under the leadership of Moise Tschombe, and fighting had broken out. The crisis in the Congo was violent and messy, and came to involve Belgian troops, white mercenaries and UN forces.

When the Algerian delegation finally arrived on 1 September, the conference itself was in chaos. On the opening day, banners denouncing Lumumba were unfurled and the photographers who tried to take pictures of them had their cameras seized. Lumumba himself was not present, having gone to his home town of Stanleyville (Kisangani) in an attempt to rally support. He needed it badly. All available troops had been committed to fight the secessionists and Lumumba's own position was far from secure. He returned to the capital to give the closing speech. Uncompromising, idealistic, brave and angry, the speech was typical of the man:

> The colonialists have created a completely false problem. That problem, as you all know, is the tragedy of Katanga, behind which lies concealed a whole organization for sabotaging our national independence. That organization, which is now acting in devious ways, through intermediaries, has but one aim in view: to foment disturbances, to create problems for the government and discredit it in the eyes of other nations through a carefully prepared propaganda, and so reconquer the Congo . . . It is not Africa itself that the colonialists are interested in, but the wealth of Africa; and everything they do in Africa is determined by what is best for their own financial interests, at the expense of the African people. They will stop at nothing to get hold of that wealth.[60]

The resolutions calling for the unity of the Congo and condemning French nuclear policy in the Sahara, and Yazid's speech stressing the importance of Algerian–Congolese friendship, meant little. Lumumba was murdered by his political opponents on 17 January 1961. Like Fanon, he was thirty-five. For Fanon, Lumumba's death was one of Africa's great tragedies but there was a lesson to be learned from it. Lumumba had made a serious error by appealing to the UN for help. The UN was no more than a tool of the great powers that were intent on dividing the world between them: 'Africans must remember this lesson. If we do need external help, let us call on our friends. They alone can give us the real and total help that will enable us to realize our objectives because the friendship that binds us together is, of course, a militant friendship.'[61]

Fanon began to organize external help for the Algerian Revolution. The 'African Legion' project now became a matter of actual planning rather than conference motions. A stamp in Fanon's passport indicates that on 12 September, he took an internal flight from Conakry to the town of Kankan, where he reported to the police on arrival. Kankan is some 400 kilometres from the capital of Guinea and quite close to the border with Mali. There was no diplomatic reason for going there, but there was a road leading north to Bamako. The only possible explanation for Fanon's presence in Kankan is that he had begun to reconnoitre a route north to Algeria. There was in fact no real need for reconnaissance in the sense of exploration. Kankan was a staging post on one of the ancient trade routes between West Africa and the Maghreb. For centuries, it was used by camel-trains carrying handicrafts from the Mediterranean cities of the Maghreb and salt from the fringes of the Sahara to the kingdoms of Black Africa; they returned north carrying gold. Although difficult and potentially dangerous, the route was by no means unknown; what Fanon did not know was whether or not it could be used by an African Legion to enter Algeria from the south and to relieve the beleaguered fighters of *wilaya* V in the south of the Oranois and VI in the southern Sahara.

Fanon's movements now become difficult to trace, but it is clear that on 30 September he met the Cameroonian Félix Moumié at Accra airport, from whence they flew to Tripoli. As they approached the Libyan capital, thick fog made it impossible to land and their plane had to circle the field. Eventually, the pilot ignored air-traffic control's instructions and succeeded in landing. Moumié remarked to Fanon that pilots like that were 'gambling with people's lives'.[62] Fanon later remarked that whilst this was true, it was also true that they themselves were gambling with their own lives. They both lost the wager. From Tripoli, Moumié flew on to Geneva for what Fanon called 'very important discussions'. He had arranged to meet Fanon a fortnight later in Rome on 15 October, but never arrived there. Roland Félix Moumié died at the age of thirty-four. The manner of his death was as mysterious as the man himself.

Moumié was a controversial figure in the Union of the Cameroonian People (UPC), which was founded in 1948 by Um Nyobe to fight for the reunification of Cameroon. Until 1918, the country had been a German colony known as Kamerun. When Germany lost its African colonies under the terms of the Treaty of Versailles, Kamerun was partitioned into French and British mandated territories. In May 1955, the UPC had launched an armed insurrection which was seen by many as 'tribally' based. This was supposedly masterminded by Moumié, who was later reported to have gone into exile in first Cairo and then Conakry. He was said to have the sponsorship of Nkrumah and Sekou Touré, and to have good contacts with Bourguiba in Tunisia. Nyobe was killed by a French patrol on 13 September 1958, leaving Moumié in nominal command of the UPC. Cameroon became independent in January 1960, but the UPC remained a proscribed organization until August, when it was legalized by President Amhadou Ahidjo. In March, Moumié announced that he had formed an alternative government in exile in Conakry.[63] According to at least one historian, he was a charlatan. His claim to be a doctor of medicine was reportedly baseless, as was the story that the money he received was being used to supply weapons to fighters in the forests of Cameroon. Some of the guns apparently found their way into the hands of opposition groups in Ghana and Guinea, whilst most of the money is said to have found its way into Moumié's many bank accounts in Europe.[64]

The precise nature of Moumié's 'very important discussions' in Geneva remains a mystery. What is known is that he gave a party for a group of friends there on 12 October. At some point he left the room and while he was absent, something was slipped into his glass of wine and that of the European woman who acted as his secretary. Moumié had been poisoned, went into a coma and died on 4 November 1960 after having been in an iron lung for over a fortnight. The substance slipped into his drink proved to be a derivative of thalium, a malleable white metal whose highly toxic compounds are used in the manufacture of rat poison.[65] There was the inevitable speculation in émigré circles that he had been killed by the Red Hand, but Moumié was not short of enemies either at home or abroad. A historian cites Swiss sources identifying the killer as William Betchel of the French secret service.[66] The details are still confused. Press reports of the day spoke of a mysterious blonde trying to reclaim papers from Moumié's hotel room by claiming to be his wife, and then disappearing, never to be heard of again.

The story of Moumié's death could have come from the pages of a bad spy story, but Fanon describes this strange character in very positive terms. He was, he wrote, 'Aggressive, violent, angry and with a great love for his country. He hated cowards and manoeuvrers. Austere, hard, incorruptible. The essence of revolution packed into sixty kilos of muscle and bone.'[67] Like Roberto Holden, Moumié was – or at least claimed to be – an advocate of immediate and violent action. In October 1959 he had published a pamphlet in Rabat entitled 'La Révolution Kamerounaise et la lutte des peuples africains' which advocated the use of violence on the grounds that non-violent modes of struggle had proved futile.[68] This was precisely the message Fanon had been preaching at so many conferences and he no doubt believed that he had found both an ally and a kindred spirit. As in the case of Roberto Holden, he had judged his man very badly, though he was by no means the only one to have been taken in by him.

Fanon heard of Moumié's death a few days after the event and spent some time with the dead man's comrades and parents. The death – 'a murder in which no blood was spilled' – was difficult to comprehend. Moumié's father listened to Fanon talking about his son, his face inexpressive and immobile. Fanon was reminded of the Algerian parents who listened in a stupor to the stories of how their children had died, asked a few hesitant questions and then lapsed back into a sort of inertia that allowed them to commune with the dead. Gradually, the militant spirit overcame the father and he agreed that the fight had to go on. The next day, Fanon set off for the north.

During his reconnaissance trip, Fanon kept a log or *journal de bord*, partly so that he could make a full report to the Etat Major or High Command in Cairo.[69] This was the only occasion on which he kept any kind of diary and it is the only manuscript by him to have survived. It is contained in a 'Teacher's Note Book No 3' issued by 'The Ghana Schools', but the physical document looks strangely familiar to anyone educated in the British school system in the 1950s or 1960s. It is a clothbound hardbacked 'Lion Brand' note book with a mottled blue-back cover measuring seven inches by nine, and printed by John Dickinson & Co Ltd, London. Twenty-three of the lined pages are filled with Fanon's scrawled handwriting. There are a number of deletions and crossings-out in the original, and these have not been reinstated in the version published in *Pour la Révolution africaine* in 1964 as 'Cette Afrique à venir'. They are not particularly significant, and are merely the minor revisions made by someone scribbling down notes in haste and in difficult circumstances. Obviously not written with publication in mind, the document is somewhat vague about dates and distances travelled. Fanon presumably intended to revise it and turn it into something more substantial.

The manuscript begins thus, and Fanon's sense of excitement is almost physically palpable:

438

Get Africa moving, collaborate in its organization, its regroupment, on revolutionary principles. Participating in the coordinated movement of a continent; that, definitely, is the task I had chosen. The first starting point, the first platform, was represented by Guinea. Then Mali, ready for anything, fervent and brutal, coherent and particularly scathing, offered a bridgehead and opened up precious perspectives. To the East, Lumumba was making no progress. The Congo, which was the second invasion beach for revolutionary ideas, was caught up in a painful tangle of sterile contradictions. We still had to wait before we could effectively besiege the colonialist citadels known as Angola, Mozambique, Kenya and the Union of South Africa.[70]

Fanon spoke with deep emotion of Africa:

Day to day Africa. Oh, not the Africa of the poets, the Africa that is sleeping, but the Africa that stops you sleeping because the people are impatient to be doing something, to speak and to play. The people who are saying: 'We want to make ourselves a people, we want to build, love, respect and create.' The people who weep when you say 'I come from a country where the women have no children and children who have no mothers.' The people who sing 'Algeria, our brother country, a country that is calling out, a country that hopes.'

The tone implies an enormous, even reckless, optimism of the will:

Tomorrow, we must immediately take the war to the enemy, leave him no rest, harass him, cut off his breath. Let's go. Our mission: to open up the southern front. To bring in arms and munitions from Bamako. Stir up the population of the Sahara, infiltrate our way into the high plains of Algeria. Having taken Algeria to the four corners of Africa, we now have to go back with the whole of Africa to African Algeria, towards the north, towards the continental city of Algiers. That is what I want: great lines, great channels of communication across the desert. To wear out the desert, to deny it, to bring together Africa and to create the continent. Let Malians, Senegalese, Guineans, Ivoirians and Ghanaians flood into our territory from Mali, and men from Nigeria and Togo. Let them all climb up the slopes of the desert and pour into the colonialist bastion. Take the absurd and the impossible, rub it up the wrong way and hurl a continent into the assault on the last ramparts of colonial power.[71]

A commando of eight men set out on this apocalytic mission: two soldiers, two signals experts, two political commissars and two medics. Fanon describes only one of his companions in any detail. He was the ALN's Commandant Chawki, a small, hard man with pitiless eyes. Fanon had known many men with eyes like this:

> I've long been able to tell how long a guerrilla has been fighting by the look in his eyes. Eyes like this do not lie. They say quite openly that they have seen terrible things: repression, torture, shelling, pursuits, liquidations . . . You see a sort of haughtiness in such eyes, and an almost murderous hardness. And intimidation. You quickly get into the habit of being careful in dealing with men like these. You can tell them everything, but they have to be able to feel and touch the Revolution in the words you use. Very difficult to deceive, to get around or to infiltrate.[72]

Chawki had, according to Fanon's account, studied at the Islamic University of Zitouna in Tunis, but then moved to Algiers to learn French and study European culture. The atmosphere in Algiers, the scornful attitude of the *colons* and the hermetic closure of the European community there had depressed him so much that he then left for Paris, where he could move more easily in European circles, haunt the libraries and read widely. He finally returned to Algeria, intending to work his father's land, but in 1954 picked up his shotgun and joined the 'brothers' in the mountains. He had come to know the Sahara well, and Fanon was in awe of his understanding of that inhospitable environment. The two spent a lot of time talking and Fanon clearly admired and even idealized the Commandant. His remark that 'for the moment, we are sharing the same bed' has, however, been over-interpreted as an expression of a need for homosociality or even a repressed homosexuality. It has, for instance, been claimed that: 'Fanon recalls one of his central experiences as a time when he and an FLN major shared the same bed. It seems to be a bonding movement which made him part of the Algerian revolution.' The same author goes on to remark that 'male bonding is consistently the central energy' in *Les Damnés de la terre*.[73] Fanon's comments are much more neutral than this description might suggest, and they refer to a banal situation: two men sharing a camp bed in a tent is surely an unexceptional aspect of military life. Fanon had shared tiny tents and probably beds in an earlier war. In the circumstances of a trek across Mali, it would be considerably more surprising to learn that Fanon had shared his bed with a woman. And he bonded with the Algerian revolution long before he met Chawki.

The mission could well have ended in the interrogation rooms of Algiers. At Accra airport, Mensah, an employee of Ghana Airways who always demanded several thousand francs for making reservations, had confirmed that Fanon and his companions had seats on the flight from Monrovia to Conakry, but in the Liberian capital Fanon and his comrades were told that the flight was full and that they would have to wait for the next day's Air France flight. The airport staff, some of whom were French, were unusually solicitous and offered them overnight accommodation at Air France's expense. The proposed change of plan sounded ominously like the one that had resulted in the hijacking of Ben Bella and his companions in 1956. The little commando decided to leave by road and to travel overnight, entering Mali via the border towns of Diéké and N'Zérékoré. They later learned that the plane had been diverted to Abidjan, where it was searched by members of the French forces still based in the Ivory Coast; Fanon was convinced that this could not have been done without the knowledge and complicity of Houphouet-Boigny.

Once inside Mali, the eight made for Bamako, where they had urgent discussions with President Mobido Keita, who readily agreed to let them establish a listening post in Kayes. For the moment, they were billeted in Bamako's main barrracks. There was still a noticeable French presence in the capital of Mali, where most shops were still owned by the French. Some French soldiers were still around. On Sunday 20 October, Fanon and his comrades were approached by a French warrant officer who had just returned from Segou with his company. He politely introduced himself, shook their hands and asked if they could give him a bed for the night. As Fanon remarked, a sense of humour did help in such circumstances, but his commando took the precaution of mounting guard from 8 p.m. onwards.

Two days later they set off at five in the morning for Segou, armed with official papers issued by the Minister of the Interior. Rain and flooding had made the northern route via Timbuktu impassable, and they had to travel by the road leading to the south of the Niger to Segou, where they filled up with petrol, and then on to San and Mopti. They were travelling fast and covering up to 200 kilometres at a stretch on very poor roads. It was in Mopti that the only difficult incident occurred. They were stopped at a checkpoint where the gendarmerie demanded to see their papers. Despite seeing the papers that had been issued in Bamako, the guards wanted to see individual passports. A senior officer finally arrived and insisted to Fanon that he needed to know the nature of his mission and the names and functions of his companions. Suspecting that the man was in the pay of the French, Fanon lost – or pretended to lose – his temper and demanded to be arrested for failing to show his papers. The officer backed down. Not for the first time, Fanon got what he wanted thanks to a calculated display of anger.

The road from Mopti to Douentza was, said Fanon, a joke. The commando was now travelling through thick tropical forest and trying to follow the tracks of a vehicle that had passed that way months earlier. They lost their way more than once, but finally reached their destination at two in the morning, after having travelled over 250 kilometres. The local military commander was away, and his wife directed them to a camp which proved to be closed. They slept as best they could in their Land Rovers and set off for Hombori and then Gao, where they could cross the Niger river. The route was then almost due north towards the Algerian border. They reached Gao at nine in the evening and immediately entered into discussions with the local commander, who was more than willing to offer all the help he could, including access to confidential documents that had been left behind by French intelligence officers.

After two days' rest, now dressed in 'colonial' uniforms supplied by the Malian army and armed, they set off for Aguerhoc and Tessalit, the last Malian settlement before the border. The journey was without incident. The weapons were used only to kill a bustard and some gazelles for food. As they passed through a French outpost in Tessalit, a bare-chested soldier gave them a friendly wave. Fanon's sense of excitement was now palpable: it was possible to gather intelligence about French troop movements from Malian nomads. Across the border lay Bordj le Prieur, and Tir Zaouten; Algeria's border with Morocco was a further 1,000 miles to the north. They had done what they wanted to do and had proved that the route was navigable. The return trip was more relaxed; in Kidal, Fanon found a collection of books on the history of the area, and plunged himself into reading epics about the empires of Mali, Ghana and Gao.

Fanon's narrative is rapid and breathless. Although he had travelled from tropical forest to savannah and then desert, he never describes the landscapes he had seen, even though their physical geography would have been of strategic importance to any expeditionary force. He mentions only the sunsets that turned the Saharan sky purple and dark red.

The *journal de bord* concludes with some schematic plans for the consideration of the Etat Major. There were a number of possibilities: supplying arms to the ALN forces that already existed in the Sahara; supplying *wilayas* I and II and what remained of *wilaya* VI; or creating lines of attack at ninety degrees to the line of the Tellean Atlas and then moving east to link up with the *wilayas*. Fanon was in favour of the latter option and envisaged small groups of locally recruited men moving north in an ordered sequence. The immediate priority was weaponry and Fanon was thinking on the grand scale: 10,000 rifles, 4,000 sub-machine guns, 600 heavy machine guns, and 300 to 400 rocket-launchers would have to be transported to the border within two months. By mid-January 1961, it should be possible to have between 500 and 800 armed men inside Algeria.

Fanon had seen combat and in that sense was not merely an armchair strategist, but he *was* an amateur strategist. In his enthusiasm, he overlooked some important details. The southern Sahara had never been an important combat zone for the ALN. This was partly for strategic reasons, but the lack of interest in the Sahara was also influenced by cultural and historical factors. Until the oil and gas reserves were discovered, few Algerians gave a thought to the vast emptiness of the desert. Most Algerians looked down on the nomadic tribes of the interior, regarding them as primitive and barbaric.[74] A Saharan Front was opened in October 1956, but it was much further to the east and closer to the line of the mountains of the Saharan Atlas. There were attacks on convoys of vehicles belonging to oil companies and occasional acts of sabotage. The power-station in Laghouat was a target, but the area was never a major theatre. ALN fighters also operated on the border with Morocco in the Figuig area, but here too they were close to the mountain terrain they favoured for their brand of guerrilla warfare. Fighting in the desert itself was difficult. There was little water and supply lines would have been very hard to maintain. All but the smallest units would have been terribly vulnerable to attack from the air. The French army had succeeded in retaining the loyalty of most of the nomadic tribes – the only source of guides. It is possible to fight a war in this terrain, and POLISARIO did so during its war of independence against Morocco in the Western Sahara in the 1970s. POLISARIO had light all-terrain vehicles and long-range Land Rovers; these were not available to the ALN in 1960.

No African Legion ever marched from Bamako to southern Algeria, but Fanon's plans did in a sense come to fruition. Relations between France and Mali were not good and Mobido Keita did collude in the establishment of a southern front in the summer of 1961. Small groups of fighters did operate in the Adrar des Iforas area, which Fanon had crossed the previous year. The operations were, however, on a minor scale and were not seen as a prelude to a great invasion from the south. Some local forces were recruited, but major lines of communications across the Sahara were never established. That the leaders of the ALN forces in the area were posted there as a sanction (a mild one by Algerian standards) for having been rather too sympathetic to a group of colonels who had plotted against the GPRA suggests that the southern front was never taken very seriously in military terms.[75]

The expedition across Mali to the Algerian border left Fanon exhausted. The travelling had been hard and Fanon and his comrades had covered over 2,000 kilometres. Fanon had no previous experience of desert conditions. He had lost a lot of weight and his face now looked gaunt. Despite his poor physical condition, he continued to try to work and made a final contribution to the English-language information bulletin produced by the GPRA's 'Mission in Ghana'. The issue in question is dated '14 December 1960' and it is the only means of estimating how long Fanon remained in Ghana after his return from the Malian expedition in late October. Fanon's short two-page article has been transformed by a generation of bibliographers into a text called 'The Stages of Imperalism', but it is in fact entitled 'The Stooges of Imperialism'. It is a spirited polemical attack on the French 'Community' and on France's unsuccessful attempts to use the 'puppet states' in it to frustrate Algeria's struggle for support and recognition at the UN.[76] It is possible that Fanon was also the author of the accompanying piece on 'General de Gaulle's Trip to Algeria', which calls for a UN-sponsored referendum in Algeria and insists that de Gaulle's dream of an Algeria that was Algerian 'in form only . . . an Algeria shorn of the FLN and the Algerian Revolution, a very French Algeria' was no more than a figment of his imagination: 'There is no place for an Algeria shorn of the FLN, because the FLN is nothing less than the regrouping of the Algerian people imbued with the resolute desire to achieve independence.'

Fanon was a fit man who had never been seriously ill in his life, but he had to admit that he was suffering from more than physical exhaustion. An initial consultation with a doctor in Accra revealed a disturbingly high level of leucocytes or white corpuscles in his blood, but the initial diagnosis was inconclusive. At Josie's insistence, Fanon returned to Tunis and underwent further tests. This time, the diagnosis was unforgiving: leukaemia. The prognosis was not good and Fanon knew it. His body was producing a surplus of leucocytes and they were suppressing the production of other blood cells. There was a real danger that the cancer of the blood would spread to his spleen and his liver. Fanon did not have long to live.

Fanon's situation was now very difficult. Although the medical care available in Tunis was, by the African standards of the day, good, the hospitals there could do little to help him. The advanced treatment he required was certainly available in Europe, but hospitalization in France was clearly out of the question and even a hospital in Rome had already proved to be a very dangerous place. Fanon was adamant that he would not go to the United States for treatment, arguing that it was a land of

445

racists and lynch mobs. The only solution was to turn to the socialist countries. Fanon was finally flown to Moscow for treatment. Very little is known about this episode, but the very fact that the GPRA was willing to arrange for Fanon to go there is an indication of the high esteem in which it held its ambassador. Fanon mentioned his trip to the Soviet Union to Simone de Beauvoir but did not go into detail. Peter Geismar describes how Fanon was flown to Moscow but does not identify the source of his information and supplies no dates. Other evidence about Fanon's movements strongly suggests that it was in the spring of 1961 that Fanon was treated at a clinic outside Moscow. Still in Accra in December, he is known to have been back in Tunis by early April. When he wrote to his publisher on 7 April, he told him that his health had improved slightly, presumably as a result of the treatment he had received in the Soviet Union.[77]

According to Geismar, Fanon was treated with Myleran.[78] Developed by the Wellcome Medical Division, Myleran is indicated for the treatment of the chronic phase of myeloid leukaemia and is taken in the form of either two- or five-milligram white tablets. The active ingredient is busulphan, a powerful cytotoxin which destroys the white blood cells but also interferes with the reproduction of other cells. It can also damage the patient's DNA. The drug has many unpleasant side-effects, ranging from nausea, vomiting and diarrhoea and a persistent cough to hyperpigmentation, or darkening of the skin, and it is not a cure for leukaemia. It does have the palliative effect of relieving the symptoms, reducing the total granulocyte mass and improving the patient's clinical state.[79] In Fanon's case, the drug brought on a brief period of remission. It also allowed him to write *Les Damnés de la terre*.

# 11

# The Wretched of
# the Earth

S ARTRE'S SPEECH TO the meeting in the Salle Wagram in January 1956 marked the beginning of a long and deeply serious commitment to the cause of Algerian independence. His journal *Les Temps modernes* became a major platform for Vidal-Naquet's 'Third Worldists', who became an increasingly significant – if numerically small – force in the last years of the war. Their perception of Algeria had been greatly influenced by Fanon's *L'An V de la Révolution algérienne* and their image of the Third World would be shaped largely by his *Les Damnés de la terre*, which appeared at the end of 1961. Sartre himself was no political organizer but rather a symbolic pole around whom opposition to the war could coalesce. His lengthy reviews of the anonymous collection *Des rappelés témoignent* and Alleg's *La Question* did much to publicize the appalling violence that was a daily reality in Algeria and clearly touched a sore point with the government, which responded by seizing the issue of *L'Express* that carried the Alleg review.[1]

By the summer of 1960, Sartre had finally adopted the stance Fanon had demanded of the French left in late 1957. In an interview with K. S. Karol published in a semi-clandestine paper, he endorsed the actions of the young men who were reluctant to fight in Algeria and who were deserting or ignoring their call-up orders in increasing numbers,[2] and he recalled a 'truth that adults have completely forgotten: the violence of the left'. He went on

> The left is tired. Its cadres have grown old. Believe me, old age is a cause that Marxism has not envisaged, but it exists, as it is easy to grow old in our society. Young people are the only ones to have responded to mystification as they should respond, or in other words with violence . . . In my view, the only real men of the left in today's France are to be found amongst the twenty-year-olds.

Sartre's conclusion was that 'The French left must act in solidarity with the FLN. Besides, their fates are linked. The victory of the FLN will be the victory of the left.'[3] The paper was seized by the police on the grounds that Sartre's comments constituted an incitement to desertion and a breach of state security.

Sartre was not the only French intellectual to have reached the conclusion that the left had to demonstrate its solidarity with the FLN, but not all of those who did so were twenty-year-olds. In the summer of 1960, Dionys Mascolo and others began to float the idea of a manifesto supporting the actions of the *insoumis*, those who refused to serve the FLN in Algeria. Born in 1916 and the son of an Italian immigrant, Mascolo worked as a reader for Gallimard, and had been very active in the wartime resistance in Paris. After the war, he joined the PCF but his objections to the Rajk trial led to his expulsion for 'Titoism' in 1949. He then became active in anti-colonial movements, and was one of the organizers of the Salle Wagram meeting. He now began the slow task of collecting signatures with the help of Jean Schuster, a veteran of the surrealist movement.[4] Sartre promised his support and made the resources of *Les Temps modernes* available to them.[5]

A full list of 121 signatures had been collected by the beginning of October. The signatories included academics, writers and men and women from the world of the theatre and cinema. They ranged from the dramatist Arthur Adamov to the novelist Maurice Blanchot (who is said to have actually drafted the manifesto) and the composer Pierre Boulez, from Marguerite Duras to Françoise Sagan and Nathalie Sarraute. The figure of 121 had no particular significance or symbolism. The list was, according to Editions de Minuit's Lindon, closed at that point simply because the figure was 'aesthetically satisfying'.[6] The so-called *Manifeste des 121* was probably the most explosive petition to have been produced since Zola's *J'Accuse*, which launched the controversy over the Dreyfus affair, but it could not be openly published in France.[7] No newspaper could or would take the risk of publishing this, but the manifesto's existence was effectively made public when *Le Monde* ran the story '121 Writers and Artists Sign a Declaration on the Right to *insoumission* in the War in Algeria' on 4 September. The names of the signatories and the nature of the text were soon widely known. The manifesto stated quite openly that, for the Algerians, the war was a war of national independence. As for France, this was

> Neither a war of conquest, a war of 'national defence' nor a civil war, the war in Algeria has gradually become an action on the part of an army and a caste which are refusing to give way in the face of an uprising which even the civil power, having taken stock of the general collapse of colonial empires, seems ready to recognize as having a meaning.
>
> Today, it is primarily the army that is pursuing this criminal and absurd war. Because of the political role several of its highest representatives are making it play, this army is often openly and violently acting outside the law and betraying the goals the whole of the country has set it, and it is compromising and threatening to pervert the nation itself by forcing those citizens who are under its command to become accomplices in an action that is both factious and degrading. Does it have to be recalled that, fifteen years after the destruction of the Hitlerite order, French militarism has, because of the demands of a war of this kind, succeeded in reintroducing torture and has once more institutionalized it in Europe?
>
> Under these conditions, many French people have reached the point of challenging the meaning of traditional values and obligations. What does civic duty mean when, in certain circumstances, it becomes a shameful submission? Are there not cases in which saying 'no' is a sacred duty and when 'treason' means a courageous respect for the truth? And when, because those who are deliberately using it as an instrument of racist or ideological

domination, the army proves to be in a state of open or latent rebellion against democratic institutions, does not rebellion against the army take on a new meaning?

The manifesto ended by making three points:

- We respect and regard as justified the refusal to take up arms against the Algerian people.
- We respect and regard as justified the actions of those French citizens who think it their duty to give help and protection to Algerians who are being oppressed in the name of the French people.
- The cause of the Algerian people, which is making a decisive contribution to the ruination of the colonial system, is the cause of all free men.

The manifesto did not end with a defiant 'Victory to the FLN', but it marked a sea-change in left opinion. Like virtually all protests against the war, it had as much to do with developments in France as with Algeria. It was also, in other words, a manifesto against those who had been involved in barricades week. Signing it was a courageous act. Teachers and civil servants who signed, or who made their support for it known, were suspended from duty (usually on full pay) and threatened with prosecution. The state-run television and radio blacklisted the signatories, and actors and actresses suddenly found that work was difficult to obtain.

Those involved in the 'Jeanson network' fared much worse. The trial of those who had carried suitcases for the FLN began on Monday 5 September and lasted for almost three weeks. They were tried before a military court sitting in the old Cherche-Midi prison. Dreyfus had been tried in the very same building. During the Occupation, resistance fighters died there at the hands of the Gestapo. Throughout the trial, the presiding judge repeatedly interrupted the defence lawyers and witnesses to warn them not to speak of the 'Algerian war'. One lawyer was told: 'I would prefer you to speak of the "operations" in Algeria. I do not have the right to allow you to express your opinion about current events.'[8] Nine of the accused were acquitted. Six Algerians and eighteen French citizens were found guilty of offences against state security and received sentences ranging from eight months to ten years in prison. Heavy fines were also imposed. Francis Jeanson, who had escaped to Switzerland, was tried *in absentia* and sentenced to ten years in prison. All were finally amnestied in 1966;[9] by then, most Algerian political prisoners had already been free for four years.

Fanon exaggerated the numbers of those involved in the campaigns against the war, but he saluted them in this final book, believing that Algeria was now receiving the support he had been calling for since the end of 1958: 'Soldiers are deserting from the ranks of the colonialists, others are openly refusing to fight against the freedom of the people, and are going to prison in the name of that people's right to independence and to manage its own affairs.'[10]

Legal sanctions and even prison sentences were by no means the most serious threats they faced. Early in 1961, a new clandestine organization known as the Organisation Armée Secrète (OAS) began to make its presence felt.[11] It was originally a small organization based in Spain; by May, it had developed into a terrorist group organized on military lines and operating in both France and Algeria. Its leaders were the generals and colonels who led the failed coup against de Gaulle in April of that year. The OAS was fanatical, well armed and, for a while, devastatingly effective. Its weapon of choice was plastic explosive and, acting in the name of 'French Algeria', it was quite prepared to kill French citizens as well as Algerians. Paris had long been a war zone for Algerians; Parisians were now drawn into the conflict too and the more prominent of the 121 signatories were soon on the death lists.

Sartre was not the originator of the manifesto, but he was the most visible figure associated with it and he now became the most hated man in France. At the beginning of October, right-wing demonstrators who had gathered on the Champs-Elysées to honour those who had died in Algeria were calling for him to be shot. They broke the windows of *L'Express* – a symbol of political liberalism that now signified treason. The conservative press was howling for Sartre to be arrested and charged with sedition. In the conservative *Le Figaro*, Thierry Maulnier remarked that all Sartre had to do now was to join the ranks of the FLN and defend his stance 'with gun or bomb in hand; if he did that, he would at least be taking a risk'.[12] In the National Assembly, a *député* put down a written question asking if it was 'natural' for Sartre to be declaring his support for the FLN with impunity 'at a time when thousands of young Frenchmen were risking their lives to pacify Algeria'.[13] For a significant proportion of the population, Sartre was now 'public enemy number one'.[14] Sartre himself was defiant and demanded to be arrested if he had broken the law. De Gaulle finessed him by saying, with one of his better witticisms, 'One does not arrest Voltaire.'

This was the Sartre Fanon tried to contact in the spring of 1961: the Sartre who had come to symbolize Third Worldism and solidarity with the Algerian cause. He was also eager to meet the Sartre who had published *Critique de la raison dialectique* in May 1960. This is by far the most indigestible of all Sartre's philosophical writings but Fanon read it with passion and enthusiasm as soon as it appeared, and it was to be the main theoretical influence on his *Les Damnés de la terre*. Although his writings reveal a complex intellectual relationship with Sartre that goes back to his student days in Lyon, Fanon had never met him and appears to have made no attempt to do so, which is somewhat surprising given that Sartre was both very approachable and generous with his time. There is no indication that Sartre had read or even heard of Fanon until *Les Temps modernes* published the chapter from *L'An V* in May–June 1959. Their very short-lived collaboration was, however, to have extraordinary results.

Fanon did not write to Sartre directly and the first contacts were made through intermediaries. Claude Lanzmann and Marcel Péju were on the editorial board of *Les Temps modernes* and acted as its emissaries to a conference in Tunis.[15] Here, they met Ferhat Abbas who, to their mingled amusement and annoyance, mistook them for representatives of *Esprit,* spoke disparagingly of 'communist materialism' and bounced his young niece on his knee as he talked to them. Lanzmann and Péju rapidly reached the conclusion that, even though Abbas was the titular President of the GPRA, his role in the Algerian Revolution was now purely decorative. An FLN representative they met agreed: Abbas was old and, whilst he was a useful figurehead, he was not in command and would not be allowed to take command. There were, went on the unnamed FLN man, two tendencies within the Revolution. The 'politicians' were ready to collaborate with France and even to put an end to the Revolution, but the fighters and 'the base' were demanding agrarian reform and socialism. If need be, they would take to the mountains once more to defend their Revolution.[16]

Lanzman and Péju also met Fanon in Tunis, and they were shocked by the state in which they found him. He was in a room furnished only with a mattress on the floor and was visibly seriously ill, but refused to talk about his condition. Lanzmann and Péju quickly learned from Fanon, whose wife had left the room in tears, that he probably had less than a year to live. He then insisted on talking about something else. The 'something else' was Sartre and the *Critique de la raison dialectique*, and Fanon talked about them for hours.

He also talked at length about Algeria and Africa. His account of the Algerian revolution and the coming African revolution was visionary to the point of being idealist, and he tried to convince his visitors that the interior of Algeria was now a realm of pure freedom that had been cleansed of all prejudice. Fanon was, on the other hand, deeply worried about developments in Black Africa and profoundly depressed about the news of Lumumba's death. His dream of a united Africa had been shattered by the realization that black Africans were quite capable of murdering one another. Lanzmann and Péju also heard Fanon describe how he had gone to the Algerian forces based, or rather trapped, on the Tunisian border to give talks and lectures. His main subject was Sartre and the *Critique de la raison dialectique*.[17] That the lectures were given is confirmed by *El Moudjahid*'s report of Fanon's funeral: 'Three months ago, he came to spend several days with the ALN to do more work and to talk about Africa.'[18] The dates do not concur with those given by Lanzmann and are confusing, but *El Moudjahid*'s account does confirm that Fanon was in the frontier region in the summer of 1961, or in other words after his return from Moscow. The lectures or talks in question have never been published and nothing is known of their content, but they presumably related to both Sartre's *Critique* and Fanon's own *Les Damnés de la terre*. Sadly, one can only speculate as to how lectures on Sartre were received by the *djounoud* of the ALN's frontier army.

Lanzmann and Péju's visit to Tunis marked the initial forging of the Fanon–Sartre alliance. Fanon himself took the next step, but an intermediary was once more involved. On 7 April 1961, he wrote to his publisher in Paris to say that his health had improved slightly and that he was 'resolved to write something anyway'. He begged Maspero to get the manuscript he was preparing into print as quickly as possible: 'We need it in Algeria and Africa . . . Ask Sartre to write me a preface. Tell him that I think of him every time I sit down at my desk. The things he is writing are so important for our future but he still can't find readers who know how to read at home, and he just doesn't find readers here.'[19] Fanon's letter to Maspero eventually resulted in the publication of the most notorious of all Sartre's publications: the preface to *Les Damnés de la terre*.

*Les Damnés de la terre* is widely regarded as one of the classics of the literature of decolonization, but its composition and even its nature are strangely heteroclite. As his publisher remarks, Fanon's explosive text is actually made up of material dictated to his wife in the spring and summer of 1961, and supplemented by previously published and reworked material. The 'Bible of Third Worldism' was composed 'in pitiful haste' by a man who was dying but still trying to live up to the demands of a revolution.[20] Less than half the material included in the book was actually produced in 1961. The section on 'national culture' is an expanded version of the speech given by Fanon to Présence africaine's Rome congress at Easter 1959. The final section on 'colonial war and mental illness' consists mainly of case-notes made in Blida and Tunis between 1954 and 1959, supplemented by a short essay which takes up and revises both Fanon's 1952 essay on 'The North-African syndrome' and his one brief contribution to *Consciences maghrébines*. Here, he once more discusses the Algiers School's thesis that the 'criminal impulsiveness of the North African' was a 'behavioural transcription' of the organization of the nervous system, and refuted it by insisting that Algerian criminality was 'a direct product of the colonial situation'.[21] As the war progressed, the crime rate had fallen and the internalized alienation that had set Algerian against Algerian had been overcome: 'The national struggle seems to have channelled all the anger, to have nationalized all the affective or emotional tendencies.'[22]

The notorious first chapter on violence first appeared as a long – fifty-page – article published in *Les Temps modernes* in May 1961, and was subject to slight but significant revisions before its inclusion in the book: they indicate that the dying Fanon was still interested in

Martinique and that the psychological wound inflicted by his disillusionment during the Second World War had still not healed. There was
nothing in *Les Temps modernes* to suggest that the article was part of a
forthcoming book, as there had been when the extract from *L'An V* was
published. Internal evidence provides some proof as to how and when
it was written. Fanon's reference to the OAS's murder of the mayor of
Evian,[23] who was killed on 31 March, appears in both versions of the
text, and indicates that Fanon could not have completed this section
before early April. To get the chapter into print by May was no mean
achievement on the part of *Les Temps modernes*'s editorial team, to say
nothing of the printer. The short section on 'violence in the international context' did not appear in the *Temps modernes* version, and the
allusion to the opening of the Nazi war criminal Eichmann's trial in
Jerusalem on 11 April indicates that it was either written or revised after
that date.[24] The final version of the full text must have been completed
by July; when Sartre and Fanon met in the third week of that month,
the philosopher had read the book he then agreed to preface. When
they met in July, Fanon told Bertène Juminer that he had just completed *Les Damnés de la terre*, adding: 'I should have liked to have
written something more.'[25] Between April and the beginning of July,
Fanon worked fast against the clock. The final text reflects the speed at
which he worked. Little or no research was done. His impressions of
what he had seen of the newly independent states of Africa merge into
a nightmarish picture of colonial Algeria. Fanon's hopes and fears for
the future are expressed with powerful emotion, but he rarely justifies
them with hard facts.

Although it is not apparent from *Les Damnés de la terre*, a deadly
game was now being played out in both France and Algeria. Fanon
himself may have been opposed to a negotiated settlement and may
even have still believed in the possibility of a final military victory, but
it was increasingly obvious that there would be no such victory.
Contacts between the French government and the GPRA were now
well established and it was clear that de Gaulle's priority was to extricate
France from a war neither the French army nor the ALN could win on
the ground. ALN fighters inside Algeria could not be totally eradicated
but they had weakened to such a degree that they could not mount
major offensives. The frontier armies in Tunisia and Morocco were

impotent. Public opinion in France was now turning against a war which seemed to be going on for ever, and France was increasingly isolated at the UN and elsewhere. On 19 September 1959, de Gaulle had begun to speak of the existence of self-determination and even of the existence of a future 'Algerian Republic'. For the first time, he indicated a willingness to talk with the 'external leadership' of the GPRA. Algiers was seething with anger and the situation was volatile and dangerous.

De Gaulle went to Algiers on 9 December and his arrival provoked three days of serious rioting. The wind was changing: de Gaulle was now booed by crowds of *pieds noirs* and cheered by smaller crowds of Algerians. *Pied noir* activist groups and even some elements in the army were plotting his assassination. The December riots in Algiers were not spontaneous, but were deliberately organized by 'ultra' groups, including a recently formed Front d'Algérie Française which claimed to have half a million members. There were to be no mass demonstrations. Small groups of FAF shock troops had orders to attack the gendarmes and CRS in an attempt to provoke the paratroop regiments into intervening and taking full control of Algiers and other centres before kidnapping de Gaulle. On Friday 9 December, car bombs went off in the centre of Algiers and FAF gangs attacked the police and gendarmes with anything that came to hand. Edward Behr describes what he saw: 'The rue Michelet became a writhing mass of demonstrators and security troops. A car was overturned and burnt, and security squads moved in with armoured cars and tear-gas under a hail of paving stones and bottles.'[26] The battle resumed the next day. The FAF was not the only clandestine organization operating in the city. The FLN had succeeded in re-establishing its presence and it was now provoked into violent action. Racial violence had broken out in the mixed area of Belcourt when some deluded European groups attempted to persuade Muslims to demonstrate alongside them. On the Sunday, Algiers was festooned with the green and white flags of the FLN and thousands of demonstrators were on the streets. They swept out of the Casbah, brushing aside the thin cordon of gendarmes, and into the streets of Belcourt. Fanon had heard Algerian women ululating in Blida; French Algerians now heard the terrifying noise of their *you-you-yous* as they urged on the young men. European shops were attacked and pillaged; shots were fired from the tenement homes of the area's poor white population.

The FAF turned on the Muslims, and the FLN fought back. One hundred and twenty people died in the riots in Algiers and Oran; all but eight were Muslims. On that Sunday morning, Behr saw the extraordinary sight of a Muslim on a motorcycle, with a huge FLN flag tied to it. When a gendarme officer told him to put it away, he replied, 'We're doing nothing wrong. General de Gaulle said Algerian Algeria. We're Algerians, aren't we?'[27]

It was clear that the situation was drifting rapidly out of control and that urgent action was required. De Gaulle called a referendum for 8 January 1962. The electorate was asked if it approved the policy of self-determination for the Algerian population and the organization of public powers in Algeria before self-determination. In France, 56 per cent of the electorate voted 'yes'. De Gaulle won a majority in Algeria too, but the 42 per cent abstention rate amongst the Muslim population indicated solid support for the FLN, which had boycotted the referendum. De Gaulle had won a vote of confidence and a mandate with the GPRA as he saw fit. A week later, the GPRA indicated its willingness to enter into negotiations.[28]

The crisis came to a head on 22 April, when Generals Salan, Zeller, Jouhaud and Challe staged a coup in Algiers with the support of the Foreign Legion's First Parachute Regiment. Government buildings were taken over by armed extremists and the generals announced that they had taken full powers. Paris was in panic. This time, the Republic was indeed in danger. The great fear was that the paratroopers would make an airborne landing in or near Paris, and the civilian population was urged to occupy the airports and airfields. All the bridges in Paris were blocked by parked buses. Tanks were in position outside the National Assembly. Police stations were defended by sandbags and machine guns. Explosions were a nightly occurrence. De Gaulle's response was to appeal directly to the troops and the conscripts in particular. The coup leaders suddenly found that they had little support outside the Algiers military region and that the conscripts of the *contingent* would not move against the government. Army units stationed in metropolitan France did not do so either. By 25 April, the coup was over. Its leaders were either under arrest or in hiding, and a purge of the officer corps began. The Republic was saved, but the army was seriously weakened. The rebel generals went underground, joined the OAS and reorganized it on military lines. Salan, who had once decorated Fanon for distinguished conduct, became its commander. On 20 May, the GPRA and the French government began negotiations in Evian, but they rapidly broke down over the issue of the Sahara. The only hint of what was going on to be found in *Les Damnés de la terre* was the brief mention of the assassination of Evian's unfortunate mayor.

Fanon and Sartre finally met in Rome in the third week of July 1961. Sartre and Beauvoir had gone to Rome to escape the tensions and dangers of Paris. It was now obvious that the OAS was targeting the signatories of the 121 Manifesto and Sartre had been warned that he was on its death list. He took the precaution of leaving the appartment he shared with his mother in the rue Bonaparte, and moved in with Beauvoir whilst his mother went to a hotel. As they were packing their bags on the morning of 19 July, they received a phone call: a bomb had exploded in the entrance hall of 48 rue Bonaparte. It caused only minor damage but sent out a clear warning.[29] Rome, in comparison, was a haven of peace. Sartre and Beauvoir, who were accompanied by Claude Lanzmann, took adjoining rooms in a quiet hotel outside the city centre. They rose late and spent their mornings reading the newspapers and listening to music on the radio. Meals were leisurely affairs. Beauvoir had hoped that Sartre would work less in Rome and he did so, though his consumption of corydrane did not diminish. Corydrane was a mixture of aspirin and amphetamines which, until it was made illegal in 1971, was on open sale in French pharmacies. It had fuelled the writing of the *Critique de la raison dialectique* and was now having a bad effect on Sartre's health, not least because he was also consuming large amounts of alcohol. His pace of life did slow down somewhat in Rome but he continued to work and was now preoccupied with writing a long essay on Merleau-Ponty, who had died in May, for the October issue of *Les Temps modernes*.

Fanon had come to Italy to meet Sartre, but he also had other reasons for being there and did not stay long in Rome. He was on his way to the north-eastern spa town of Abano Terme to have what Beauvoir calls his 'rheumatism' – the lingering effects of the spinal injuries sustained in Morocco – treated. Shortly after their arrival in Rome, Beauvoir and Lanzmann drove out to Ciampino airport to pick up Fanon. They saw him before he saw them. Fanon was clearly very nervous, sitting down and then standing up again, picking up his luggage and then putting it down. He went to change money, his eyes darting around the arrivals hall.[30] Rome and its airport had uncomfortable associations. He had already survived one assassination attempt in the city and a second was not beyond the bounds of possibility. As the trio drove back to meet Sartre for lunch, Fanon talked with feverish excitement. On 20 July, lightly armed Tunisian forces had attacked the French naval base at Bizerte. Bourguiba had long been demanding its return and had finally taken military action in an attempt to regain it. The French response was to drop 7,000 paratroops to reinforce the base, and to bombard the Tunisian forces from the sea. As Fanon and Sartre talked, a vicious three-day battle was in progress. Fanon was convinced that this was a prelude to a full-scale invasion and that blood would flow. Seven hundred Tunisians did die, but the incident did not have the consequences he foresaw. Like the earlier Sakiet incident in February 1958, it did, on the other hand, lead to a breakdown of diplomatic relations between France and Tunisia. De Gaulle's militarism and use of overkill lost France an important ally. Bourguiba would no longer be a moderating influence on the GPRA. He would no longer support de Gaulle's attempts to 'internationalize' the Sahara and its oil and gas reserves in order to keep them out of Algerian hands.[31] Fanon's dire predictions did not come true, but they are indicative of his mood. He was living through an apocalypse of his own and told Beauvoir that, whilst victory was at hand, Algeria would pay a terrible price for its freedom. He believed that the cities would rise up, and that 150,000 people would die in the risings. At other times, he spoke of one million deaths.[32]

The conversation with Fanon began over lunch and continued until two in the morning, at which point a worried Simone de Beauvoir insisted as politely as she could that Sartre had to have some sleep. Fanon was outraged and told Lanzmann: 'I don't like people who spare themselves.' He then kept him up until eight. In more conciliatory tones, he also said that he would give 20,000 francs to be able to talk to Sartre from morning to night for a fortnight. They in fact talked for three days and met again ten days later when Fanon returned to Rome to catch his flight back to Tunis. Fanon certainly did not spare himself, and talked endlessly of his future projects as though he had years ahead of him. Beauvoir has little to say about the philosophical content of Fanon's discussions with Sartre, but it can be assumed that they centred on the *Critique de la raison dialectique* and particularly on the themes of fraternity and terror that are so central to *Les Damnés de la terre*. Her account does, on the other hand, contain what is in effect a miniature biography of Fanon, who spoke of Martinique, his war experience, his studies in Lyon and his clandestine work in Blida. He now identified himself as the author of the unsigned article denouncing the French left that had been reprinted by *France-Observateur*. It was most unusual for Fanon to talk about himself in this way, and Beauvoir and Sartre must have been both skilful and sympathetic interrogators. There is certainly no other record of Fanon speaking as openly as this to anyone. Beauvoir herself thought that Fanon was 'haunted by death' and speculated that this might explain his impatience, his loquacity and his sense of impending catastrophe. He was as reluctant to talk about his health as he had been in Tunis, but did admit that he had feared for his life when he lost his sight for two to three weeks and felt himself sinking into his mattress 'like a dead weight'. That he had already been to the USSR for treatment was mentioned almost as an afterthought.

On his return from Abano Terme, Fanon described an exchange he had had with a chambermaid in his hotel there. She had been watching him for days, and finally summoned the courage to ask: 'Is it true what they say? Do you hate white people?' Fanon reported the encounter in bitter terms: 'The truth of the matter is that you white people have a physiological horror of us blacks.' His conviction that this was the case did not make for an easy relationship with Sartre. Fanon did not hate white people as such, but he could not forget that Sartre was French and would not forgive him for it. He claimed that the Algerians had 'rights over Sartre' and that Sartre should repay them by doing something effective or becoming a martyr and getting himself sent to prison. Clearly unaware of de Gaulle's comments about the inadvisability of arresting 'Voltaire',[33] he was convinced that this would cause a national scandal and somehow sway public opinion in favour of the FLN. The demand for immediate and dramatic action on Sartre's part was typical of Fanon's impetuosity and intransigence, but it also indicates his ignorance of just how intellectual politics worked in Paris. The OAS might have been perfectly happy to kill Sartre, but no one was going to arrest him, put him on trial for sedition and give him a public platform in a court of law.

Fanon also had some difficulty in accepting the life-style of Sartre and Beauvoir, whose passionate discussions of the Cuban and Algerian Revolutions did not interrupt their round of visits to favourite cafés and restaurants. Taking Fanon to a trattoria on the Via Appia proved to be a mistake. He had absolutely no interest in Europe's past or in Roman ruins, and literally could not understand what they were doing there. It was only when they talked of Algeria and when Sartre asked him about his views of psychiatry that Fanon become animated. He was scathing about the carceral institutions he had seen during his brief visit to the Soviet Union and contrasted them with his own 'open door' policy, arguing that patients should be cared for without being removed from their social and family environment. Much more should be done, he believed, to relate psychotherapy to the 'civic education' of patients; in a curious turn of phrase, he said that political commissars should be psychiatrists too.

Despite some moments of tension, Sartre and Beauvoir got on well with Fanon, who could be seductively charming when he wished to be. To Beauvoir's surprise, he proved to have a personal horror of violence. Although he justified the use of violence both on the public platform and in print, he was obviously deeply distressed when he spoke of the violence inflicted by the Belgians in the Congo and the Portuguese in Angola. More surprisingly, he displayed the same emotion when he spoke of the 'counter-violence' of the colonized and of the settling of scores that had taken place within the FLN: he could not forgive himself for Abane Ramdane's death and hinted that he was in some sense responsible for it. He thought, however, that his personal dislike of violence was a failing that reflected his position as 'an intellectual'. Beauvoir found Fanon acutely intelligent and, despite his tendency to indulge in dire predictions for the future, full of life. He was a man with a grim sense of humour whose explanations, jokes, mimicry and stories brought whatever he was talking about to life. As she shook his hand when they parted, she felt that she was 'touching the passion that burned within him. He could communicate that fire; when you were near him, life seemed to be a tragic, and often horrible, adventure but also a priceless adventure.'[34]

July 1961 also provided the opportunity for what was to be a last meeting with Edouard Glissant. He was in Rome with Léon-Gontras Damas, whom Fanon had briefly met at Présence africaine's second congress,[35] and who was now working as a cultural adviser to France's overseas radio network. Glissant gives no date for the meeting but remarks that Fanon was being sought by the OAS, which came into existence only in February 1961. Anxious not to put Damas and Glissant in danger, Fanon insisted that they met at night and in a discreet place; Glissant later told friends that they met in a brothel, not because of the sexual opportunities on offer but because it had a number of different exits.[36] According to Glissant, Fanon was now very interested in what was happening in the West Indies and Martinique. Glissant is not very specific here, but Fanon was no doubt 'interested in' the aftermath of the riots of December 1959: 'He had changed again, now that a positive outcome to the Algeria business seemed to be in sight . . . I can testify to the fact that when we saw each other at this moment (the last moments of his life), he was concerned about the situation in the West Indies.'[37] The last-minute insertion of a long quotation from Césaire into *Les Damnés de la terre* suggests that Glissant's brief account of Fanon's concerns is an accurate one.

Sartre was more than willing to preface Fanon's book, which he regarded as an 'Extreme Third World manifesto . . . incendiary but also complex and subtle', but he was in no hurry to begin. He was tired of working against the clock and needed, he told Beauvoir, to 'recuperate'.[38] The combination of alcohol and corydrane had taken its toll and there was also the article on Merleau-Ponty to be completed. Now more closely identified than ever with the growing Third Worldist support for the FLN, Sartre was the obvious man to write a preface for the book. He was also one of the very few men, if not the only man, in France who would have been willing to do so. Agreeing to write it was an act of considerable courage. Sartre's position on Algeria was no secret, but associating himself publicly with Fanon meant going further than he had ever gone before. *Le Figaro*'s Thierry Maulnier had challenged him to take the risk of supporting the FLN with bomb in hand. In literary terms, that was precisely what he now did.

When it appeared in print, the preface was dated 'September 1961' and it was therefore presumably written in late July or early August.

According to one unconfirmed report, Sartre wrote a first draft 'and then systematically revised the style to make it more violent'.[39] Given that no manuscript appears to have survived, it is not possible to verify this claim but the short – seventeen pages – preface to *Les Damnés de la terre* is certainly one of the most violent texts ever written by Sartre. Neither the verbal violence of the text nor the real violence it condones is a product of the brief encounters with Fanon, who was a catalyst rather than a cause. The preface is the final product of a subterranean strand in Sartre's thought. It first appears in the incomplete notebooks written in 1947–8. These contain the preliminary work for the study of ethics announced in the final lines of *L'Etre et le néant*.[40] Like so many of Sartre's projects, the 'ethics' was never completed and the *Cahiers pour une morale* were not published until 1983. They can be regarded as the intermediary stage between *L'Etre et la néant* and *Critique de la raison dialectique*. And it is in the *Cahiers*, which are contemporary with both the essay on the 'Jewish question' and the 1948 preface to Senghor's anthology of negritude poetry, that Sartre first begins to take an interest in racism. That interest was not, however, prompted by the poetry itself.

In January 1945, Sartre had visited the United States with a group of journalists at the invitation of the Office of War Information, which wanted to publicize the American war effort. The group travelled widely, and learned more than the Office might have wanted them to learn. Sartre, for instance, discovered that in the south 90 per cent of the black population still did not have the vote.[41] This revelation inspired a short passage in the *Notebooks* that is of direct relevance to the Fanon preface. The blacks of the south had a formal constitutional right to vote, but did not exercise it because they had to pay heavy poll taxes before they could register as voters. The abstract freedom of the right to vote was negated by concrete material oppression. Sartre concluded: 'To change this situation, the oppressed has to use violence . . . The union of the oppressed will come about, therefore, through violence.'[42] The idea that violence might be the only thing that could overcome the oppression of racism (and by extension colonialism) was there *in nuce* long before Sartre met Fanon. By 1960, Sartre had reached the same conclusion with respect to Algeria. Total negation had to be met with total negation, and violence with equal violence:

the dispersal and atomization of the population brought about by 130 years of colonialism would be negated by 'an initially negative unity whose content would be determined in battle: the Algerian nation. The desperately violent nature of the Algerian insurrection is no more than an assumption of the despair in which the *colon* kept the colonized.'[43]

The preface to *Les Damnés de la terre* is, if anything, even more violent than Fanon's own text. Sartre wholeheartedly endorses the thesis that violence can be cleansing or even therapeutic, and that the colonized man cures himself of his colonial neurosis by driving out the *colon* by force of arms.[44] He had no doubt as to where the origins of the colonized's violence lay: in the century of violence that had begun when French forces first landed in Algeria. France had sown the wind, and Fanon's voice was the voice of the whirlwind.[45] Fanon's voice was that of 'an African, a man of the Third World, a former colonized man'; it was a voice through which 'the Third World discovered itself and spoke for itself'.[46] The book was not, in Sartre's view, addressed to white Europeans, but white Europeans would be well advised to read it:

Europeans, open this book, enter into it. After a few steps in the dark, you will see some foreigners gathered around a fire, move closer and listen: they are discussing the fate they have in store for your concessions and the mercenaries who defend them. They may see you, but they will go on talking amongst themselves, without even raising their voices. This indifference strikes at your heart: the fathers, creatures of the darkness and *your* creatures, were dead souls. You gave them light; they addressed themselves only to you, and you did not bother to reply to those zombies. The sons ignore you: a fire gives them light and warmth, and it is not your fire. Keeping a respectful distance, you will feel furtive, nocturnal and chilled to the bone. Each to his turn: in these shadows from which a new dawn will break, it is you who are the zombies.[47]

Sartre gives two reasons why Europeans should read a book that is not addressed to them. The first is that Fanon is explaining to his brothers the mechanism of European alienation; by showing Europeans what

they have done to the colonized, Fanon is also showing what the colonizers have done to themselves. The second is that, leaving aside the
fascist rantings of Georges Sorel, Fanon is the first person since Engels
to have discussed the role of the midwife of history. This is perhaps an
unfortunate comment in two ways. First, it obscures Sartre's own contribution to Fanon's stance on violence. Second, the reference to Sorel
is something of a red herring. The notion that Sorel's *Reflections on
Violence* of 1908 influenced Fanon has been taken seriously by Hannah
Arendt and others,[48] but whilst he had, apparently, read it, there is
little evidence that he was influenced by it. The second chapter of *Les
Damnés de la terre* describes the first as consisting of 'reflections on violence' and alludes openly to the title of Sorel's book.[49] Sorel writes of
violence in the sense of riots, violent strikes and, ultimately, the proletarian general strike. He does speak of the 'proletarian violence' that
'makes the future revolution certain',[50] but his violence is a mobilizing
myth which will eventually bring about an apocalytpic transformation of
society rather than a contemporary reality. Unlike Fanon, Sorel belongs
to the old syndicalist tradition. There was nothing mythical about the
bombs in the Caféteria and the Otomatic and Fanon had no need to
read Sorel to learn about violence. The situation in Algeria was such
that violence was simply a reality, even *the* reality. Abane Ramdane was
no philosopher, but he knew that violence would lead to counter-violence as the infernal spiral went on. Fanon himself justifies the violence
of the colonized by evoking the 'absolute wound'[51] that was first
inflicted when the eyes of the *béké* burned the eyes of the black man.
The ultimate reason for reading Fanon was, for Sartre, this: 'This book
had no need of a preface. But I have written one to carry the dialectic
through to the end: we too, the people of Europe, are being decolonized; this means that, thanks to a bloody operation, the *colon* that lives
within all of us is being extirpated.' France had to be decolonized too.

Inviting Sartre to preface *Les Damnés de la terre* meant taking a risk.
There was always the danger that the preface would overshadow the
text itself, and many reviews made it do just that. In *Esprit*, Jean-Marie
Domenach reviewed the preface and Fanon's own text in two separate
articles, devoting ten pages to Sartre and twelve to Fanon.[52] Sartre, he
wrote, was French and European and therefore did not have the right
to address other French Europeans in these terms until such time as he

chose exile. His comments on Fanon are not so tart, but they are not flattering: Fanon had, wrote Domenach, acquired a new identity by becoming Algerian, and wrongly believed that insurrectionary violence would have a similar effect on those who indulged in it.[53] *Le Monde*'s Pierre Viansson-Ponté telephoned Jean Daniel and urged him to read Fanon's new book, he said that everyone was talking about it but added that it was the *preface* that was the real event.[54] Daniel did not like the preface, and spoke scornfully of Sartre's 'masochistic fury' and 'verbal masturbation'.[55] He found the implications of the book itself terrifying. If this became a work of reference 'for a few great agitators or leaders, the whole of the third world might go into convulsions. Having found it necessary to kill the colonists, they will find it indispensable to kill those of their own who are reluctant to kill. This book by Fanon: a terrible book, a terrible revelation, a terrible portent of barbaric dispensers of justice. The disciples of these theses will be tranquil killers, self-justified executioners, terrorists whose only cause will be to assert themselves through the death of others. If the white man has to die for the black man to live, then we are going back to sacrificing scapegoats.'[56] But his real criticisms were reserved for Sartre:

> Here we have the great white sorcerer interpreting for his fellows the furiously vindictive warning about the great black rage, the powerful revolt of the alienated, and the sorcerer understands, approves, goes along and exhorts: he wants his own people to die, he wants to die himself, he will die from the blows of the humble, in order that others might live . . . It is not the advent of the new man that is being foretold here; it is the advent of the new torturer. A suicidal Prospero, a demented Scipio singing the praises of a new Caligula.[57]

Daniel misreads the text in spectacular fashion: Sartre speaks of colonizers and colonized, of Europeans and natives, but not of blacks and whites. Yet Daniel was a man of the left, a journalist working for *L'Express* which was one of the few magazines to be critical of French policy in Algeria. As Sartre puts it: 'The Metropolitan Left is embarrassed: it knows about the real fate of the natives, and about the merciless oppression they are subjected to. It does not condemn their revolt, knowing that we have done all we could to provoke it. But, it thinks, there are limits after all: these guerrillas should make a point of proving themselves chivalrous; that would be the best way of showing they are men. It sometimes scolds them: "You're going too far, we no longer support you".[58] This was precisely what Fanon had been saying in 1957.

It was as though Sartre's preface were taking on a life of its own, and it does have a history of its own. In 1968, *Les Damnés de la terre* was reprinted in the elegant Petite Collection Maspero but it appeared without the scandalous preface. This was at Josie Fanon's insistence. In June of the previous year, she had sent a telegram from Algiers to François Maspero in Paris: 'Please immediately omit from all future editions Jean-Paul Sartre's preface to Frantz Fanon's book *Les Damnés de la terre* because of the pro-Zionist and pro-imperialist position taken by its author with respect to Zionist aggression against Arab peoples.'[59] Sartre, who had long expressed pro-Israeli feelings, had publicly defended Israel's actions during the Six Day War of June 1967. More specifically, he had signed a petition which had described Israel as being under threat from its Arab neighbours and denying that the country was part of 'the imperialist camp'. Algeria was of course staunchly anti-Israeli. *El Moudjahid* was running stories about anti-Zionist demonstrations in Algiers and banner headlines reading: 'Anglo-American imperialists rush to help Zionists. Algeria breaks off diplomatic relations and puts Anglo-American assets under state control.'[60] It was in this climate that Fanon's widow published an article criticizing Sartre in very violent terms.[61]

All Algerians and all Arabs would, she wrote, understand why she had asked for the preface to be dropped: the Sartre who had, in 1961, wanted to be on the side of those who were making history had gone over to the other side – the side of the murderers who were at work in Vietnam, the Middle East, Africa and Latin America. Citing her late husband, she claimed that Sartre was now on the side of 'The Europe that never stops talking about man and at the same time massacres men wherever it finds them.'[62] She also cast doubts on the reality of Sartre's earlier commitment, suggesting that it had never really been 'concrete' and that he had always stood on the touchline. Sartre was just like all the other French leftists who had 'projected their dreams and disappointed hopes on to Algeria. They made revolution by proxy, but they did not neglect their role as "advisers" who were in possession of the truth, as the teachers of the poor illiterate colonized, who could obviously carry machine guns but who were completely inapt when it came to political analysis.' And now they were 'disappointed' with what was happening in Algeria. Speaking as a former member of the French left, she now claimed that 'All Europeans are born racists. It takes a hard apprenticeship for them to be reborn into the human fraternity. Fortunate circumstances may facilitate or accelerate the process, but they also have to make a personal effort.' A final anecdote (for which there is no independent corroboration) was particularly damning. On his return from Rome, Fanon reported Sartre as saying to him: 'You are the only black man in whose presence I forget that he is black.'

In Paris, Maspero both obeyed and ignored Josie Fanon's angry instructions. Sartre's preface was, after all, a major selling point. Maspero technically obeyed Josie by dropping the preface from the bound volume, but ignored her by reprinting it as a poster which was folded and inserted into the book as a 'supplement'. Entitled 'Frantz Fanon, son of violence', it is now a very rare item. It was not until 1985 that the preface was once more restored to its place in French editions of *Les Damnés de la terre*.

The coda to the history of Sartre's preface came in 1980, when Sartre gave a series of interviews to Benny Lévy, who was acting as his secretary. Pressed by Lévy, Sartre described the circumstances in which the text was written:

> We were in a difficult position, for in spite of anything, we were struggling *against* France and with the Algerians, who didn't care much for us even though we were on their side. That put us in quite a special situation, which found expression in the book, a situation of malaise, of greater violence, and, because it was easier, of intransigence. France is something that has real meaning for me. I found it unpleasant to be against my own country.[63]

There was no sign that he found it 'unpleasant' in 1961, when intransigence was anything but an easy option. Many doubts have been expressed about the value of the 1980 interviews, and even about their authenticity. Sartre was blind, seriously ill and died within weeks of their publication. Lévy has been accused of putting words into the mouth of a dying man and of seriously misrepresenting Sartre's views. Whilst he persuades Sartre to disown his Fanon preface, Lévy does not speak of his own former endorsement of revolutionary violence. Benny Lévy, the peaceful rabbinical student of 1980, was in the 1970s 'Pierre Victor', Maoist warlord and apostle of revolutionary people's justice.[64] It is hard to escape the conclusion that an old man in a pitiful state was being exploited by a younger man anxious to repress the memory of his own past. It is harder still to avoid the conclusion that Sartre's retraction, assuming it to be a real retraction and not one prompted by a very persuasive individual, is not an effect of the general occultation of the Algerian war and its extreme violence.

Unlike *L'An V de la révolution algérienne*, *Les Damnés de la terre* is not in any real sense a book about Algeria itself, even though that country and its revolution are obviously important referents. The 'Bible of Third Worldism' is not the manifesto of the Algerian Revolution. In his last book Fanon looks far beyond the horizons of Algerian nationalism and – especially in the chapter on 'the misadventures of the national consciousness' – departs significantly from the FLN line. In his preface, Sartre rightly speaks of a voice from the Third World, and not of a voice from Algeria. In his conclusion, Fanon speaks of the Third World as a 'colossal mass' facing Europe and states that its 'project' must be to resolve problems to which Europe has found no solutions.[65] Yet although *Les Damnés de la terre* helped to shape a generation's perception of the Third World, Fanon's own 'Third World' is a curious geographical entity. It apparently does not include Asia, and there is little mention in the text of Latin America or the Middle East. Fanon makes 'Third World' synonymous with 'Africa', and his Africa consists essentially of the Maghreb and the countries he had visited in West Africa on his round of conferences and as the GPRA's ambassador to Accra. There are critical references to South Africa, to its policy of apartheid, and to the Sharpeville massacres of 21 March 1960 when sixty-nine people were shot dead during mass protests against the pass laws, but they are not particularly 'Fanonist' and could have been made by virtually anyone to the left of that country's National Party. Despite his insistence on the importance of nationalism and his contention that a nation is a form of consciousness, Fanon rarely speaks of specific nations and in many ways paints a composite picture of a continent. Any reader who turned to *Les Damnés de la terre* for a description of Mali's political system, of the FLN's political programme or of Senegal's groundnut industry would be sadly disappointed. The actual content of the book is somewhat disparate, as it ranges from the issue of violence to the role of the national bourgeoisie in the post-independence period, from revolutionary spontaneity to the question of nationalism and culture, but it does have an underlying unity. That unity is supplied by a philosophical framework derived from Sartre, but it is not always visible in the text itself and disappears in the flawed English translation.

The composite image of the 'Third World' that emerges from the book is in part a product of Fanon's relatively limited experience, of the circumstances in which it was composed and of Fanon's style of working. There is no indication of extensive or original research on his part. There are no statistics on the demography or the economy of his Third World. Political policies are discussed in very broad terms, and with little sense of detail. Fanon's tendency to generalize was now exacerbated by his material situation: he was dying and writing against a clock that was ticking faster and faster. Hence the rapid shifts from Algeria to images culled from the relatively short time he had spent in sub-Saharan Africa. The picture is composite, and Fanon's analysis is multiple. He writes on the basis of his own personal experience, but also as a seasoned political militant. He occasionally speaks as a prophet, and often writes as a psychiatrist who is as intent upon analysing the psychological effects of the colonial situation as he had been in *Peau noire, masques blancs*. Psychiatry can also be a fertile source of metaphors. Only a practising psychiatrist would describe the 'nationalist reformism' of Gabon's President Léon M'Ba as a form of narcotherapy that puts the people to sleep and ensures that formal independence does not lead to any fundamental change.[66]

Fanon always tended to generalize, and he now does so on a grand scale, plucking images from his experience of Guinea, Ghana and no doubt Tunisia to produce a very broad picture of a national bourgeoisie that has little in common with the more conventional Marxist use of that term. Occasional memories of Martinique and Caribbean negritude flash past the reader's eye, especially in the quotation from Césaire in the opening chapter on violence and in the title itself. Césaire is no longer the major point of reference he had been in *Peau noire, masques blancs* but he has not been forgotten. When Fanon recalls that 'not so long ago, Nazism turned the whole of Europe into a veritable colony',[67] he is recalling both his own disillusionment in 1945 and the argument of Césaire's *Discours sur le colonialisme* of 1951: the one thing that the 'very humanistic and very Christian' bourgeois of the twentieth century could not forgive Hitler for was that he had humiliated the white man and 'had applied to Europe colonialist practices which had until then been reserved for the Arabs of Algeria, the coolies of India and the Negroes of America'.[68]

The description of the 'compartmentalized world' of colonialism applies to Algeria rather than to Martinique or to African countries that were not settler colonies with a large European population: 'The zone inhabited by the colonized is not complementary to the zone inhabited by the *colons* . . . The *colons*' town is a town of whites, of foreigners . . . The colonized's town is a town that squats down, a town on its knees, a town that wallows. This is a town of niggers, a town of *bicots*.'[69] This is not the Martinique of Fanon's childhood; it is Algiers, where the Casbah was an Arab town embedded in a European city. Built on an outcrop of rock overlooking the bay, the Casbah was originally the fortress-palace of the old city of Algiers. The modern city of *Alger la blanche* ('white Algiers' – the adjective refers to the colour of the buildings and not their inhabitants) – with its broad boulevards and avenues running parallel to the sea, was a French creation. It was also a European city; by the 1890s, two thirds of the urban population was of European origin. In 1926, almost 80 per cent of the Muslim population lived within the limits of the old city that had existed a hundred years earlier, and two thirds of the total lived in the Casbah itself. In the predominantly Spanish quarter of Bab El Oued, a total population of 28,500 included just 811 Muslims. In the most Europeanized and richest areas, less than 3 per cent of the population was Muslim.[70] When the first bombs went off in November 1954, almost no Europeans lived in the Casbah. As rural depopulation progressed, the area became more and more crowded. Rooms were subdivided, gracious old courtyards were transformed into dwelling places and precarious shacks were built on the roof terraces. The old Casbah could not contain all the new-comers, and it is estimated that by 1960 almost 90,000 people were living in the *bidonvilles* that had sprung up on waste land and demolition sites and in the ravines that ran down to the sea.[71]

Fanon is sometimes accused of being 'Manichaean', but colonial Algeria itself was planned and built on Manichaean lines. It was commonplace to refer to the Arab quarter of a city as the 'medina' or 'nigger town'. Not content with using the police and the gendarmerie to put physical limits on the 'colonized's space', colonial Manichaeanism also dehumanized the colonized: 'when he is talking about the colonized, the colonizer's language is a zoological language': 'They allude to the crawling movements of the yellow man, to the stench from the native town, to the hordes, the stink, the swarms, the milling . . .'[72] The vocabulary of racism turned the colonized into an animal. The Arab or the Berber was a *raton* (a young rat) or a *bicot*. The latter expression is said to derive from the Italian *arabico*, but a *bicot* is also a young goat and there was no doubt some semantic cross-fertilization at work. Other items in the colonial lexicon relegated him to the vegetable kingdom: *melon* ('melon') or even *tronc de figuier* ('the trunk of the fig tree' beneath which the lazy native sat all day). If the colonized are not human, it follows that the *colon* is the only real man.

Significantly, the epic of colonization left unfinished by Albert Camus when he died in a car accident in 1960 is entitled *Le Premier homme* ('The First Man'). It is in part an autobiography and it does provide a very rich evocation of a childhood in colonial Algeria but it relies for its cohesion on the myth of the *colon* as 'first man'. Camus was no ultra, but he shared the assumptions of most *pieds noirs* and 'Arabs' rarely even speak in his fiction.[73] In *Le Premier homme*, colonized Algerians are no more than part of the landscape. Fanon attacks this mythology in his denunciation of Algeria's profound alienation. According to the mythologies of *Algérie française*, it is always the *colon* who makes history: 'His life is an epic, an odyssey. He is the absolute beginning. A compartmentalized, manichaean and immobile world, a world of statues: the statue of the general who conquered the country, the statue of the engineer who built the bridge.'[74] The 'natives', in contrast, are simply part of the landscape: 'The Algerians, the women in their "haiks", the palm groves and the camels are part of the view, the *natural* background to the human French presence.'[75] The Algerian population is quite literally dehumanized.

All this is very Algerian-oriented, but Fanon rapidly moves to a composite picture and combines a psychiatric diagnosis with a sociological analysis. The compartmentalization of the colonial world and the confinement of the colonized in one zone stimulates 'muscular dreams, dreams of action, aggressive dreams. I dream of swimming, of running, of jumping . . . During colonization, the colonized man never stops liberating himself between nine in the evening and six in the morning.'[76] During the day, the aggressivity 'sedimented in the muscles' is turned against his fellow colonized in the displays of violence that so puzzled policemen and the psychiatrists of the Algiers school. The muscular tension finds expression in tribal struggles, struggles between *çofs* ('clans') and even individuals. The tendency towards violence is, however, inhibited by the 'terrifying myths that are so prolific in under-developed societies'. Leopard-men, snake-men, six-legged dogs and zombies establish a world of prohibitions and taboos that is much more terrifying than the colonial world itself. Possession cults provide one outlet: 'This muscular orgy in which the most acute aggressivity and the most immediate violence are channelled, transformed and conjured away, is the colonized's relaxation . . . It all has to come out: symbolic killings, figurative cavalcades, imaginary multiple murders.' Vampirism, possession by djinns, zombies, and the Voodoo god Legba are all described as ways of acting out the internalized violence, of finding a release.[77] The only creatures in this fantastic bestiary that are specific to the Maghreb are the djinns that slip into the body of anyone who is careless enough to yawn without taking the appropriate precautions. Fanon had seen possession cults during his travels in Kabylia, but his leopard-men and snake-men are from south of the Sahara. There are no zombies in North Africa, but the Fanon who remarks that 'Zombies are more terrifying than *colons,* believe me'[78] had heard stories of zombies in the Martinique of his childhood. The manner in which Fanon moves between levels of analysis, combining psychiatric diagnosis with sociology, and images of Algeria with memories of Martinique with nightmare visions from sub-Saharan Africa, is a source of both strengths and weaknesses. On the one hand, it allows him to paint a rich and evocative picture of a composite 'Third World';

on the other, it results in some remarkably non-specific generalizations.

According to Fanon's analysis, the liberation struggle leads to the decline of such cults as the violence is channelled into revolutionary action. 'With his back to the wall and a knife to his throat or, to be more specific, an electrode on his genitals', the colonized has no need to tell himself stories. He has discovered or rediscovered the real and 'transforms it in the movement of his praxis, in the use of violence, and in his project of liberation'.[79] The comment indicates how far Fanon's social psychiatry is removed from psychoanalytic theory. The encounter with the real world simply dissolves regressive fantasies which were grounded not in an individual unconscious, but in a collective alienation that misrecognized the real world. The dreams of the colonized are not what Freudian analysis calls the fulfilment of repressed wishes, usually of a sexual nature, but a reaction to the real frustrations of their lives. In the unpublished paper on sexual dysfunctionality he co-authored with Azoulay, Fanon took an understanding, almost sympathetic, view of the magical practices he had observed in rural Algeria; they are now seen as part of the past that is being swept away by the Revolution that began with Algeria's 'Year Zero'. Violence, and violence alone, can cauterize the absolute wound of colonialism.

In his articles in *El Moudjahid* and in his conference speeches, Fanon had insisted that the liberation of Algeria would come about only through violence or in other words through the armed struggle of a war of independence. *Les Damnés de la terre* now provides the historical-theoretical basis for that contention. 'Fanon and violence' is now such a spontaneous association in France that it trivializes what he is actually describing. A skinhead's talk of violence reminds a sociologist of Fanon.[80] An article in *Le Monde* in 1999 begins a discussion of urban violence by asserting: 'No thinker of note now endorses Sorel's texts or even Sartre's famous preface to Fanon's *Les Damnés de la terre*. Our prosperous societies no longer believe in the possibility of a violent revolution, either in the sense of fearing it or hoping for it. But at a time when they are actually becoming more peaceful and calmer, they have nightmares about violence.'[81] Their nightmares are about cars being taken for 'joyrides' before they are set on fire – a common enough event and a depressing one, but scarcely one that illustrates Fanon's theories. Fanon was not talking about urban vandalism, but about a broad historical process that necessarily involved violence: 'What, in reality, is this violence? . . . It is the colonized masses' intuition that their liberation must come about, and can only come about, through force.'[82] In a sense, it is the term 'violence' itself that is so scandalous; had Fanon spoken of 'armed struggle' the book would have been much less contentious.

Critics like Daniel and Domenach suggest that Fanon's theses on violence are an attempt to justify the unjustifiable. Hannah Arendt makes the same point and quite erroneously claims that he glorifies 'violence for its own sake'.[83] Fanon does not 'glorify' violence and in fact rarely describes it in any detail: there are no descriptions of what happens when a bomb explodes in a crowded café and when shards of glass slice into human flesh. The violence Fanon evokes is instrumental and he never dwells or gloats on its effects. In a sense, it is almost absurd to criticize Fanon for his advocacy of violence. He did not need to advocate it. The ALN was fighting a war and armies are not normally called upon to justify their violence. By 1961, the violence was everywhere. It had even seeped into the unconscious. A schoolteacher 'somewhere in Algeria' set his pupils, aged between ten and fourteen, the essay topic 'What would you do if you were invisible?' They all said that they would steal arms and kill the French soldiers.[84] The children of Algeria dreamed of violence, and two of Fanon's young patients in Blida acted out those dreams. 'Our prosperous societies' do not have nightmarish dreams about massacres in Sétif and Philippeville or torture in their schools. Algeria had been having those nightmares for over a century.

Fanon's initial contention is that decolonization is always a violent phenomenon.[85] It is violent in that it brings about a total change and the replacement of one 'species' of men by another. It is an encounter between two mutually antagonistic forces.[86] In the biblical phrase cited by Fanon: 'The last shall be first' (Matthew 19: 30). In its broadest sense, 'violence' is not synonymous with war or even armed struggle. Whilst he may have had doubts about its eventual outcome (and particularly the role played in it by the national bourgeoisie), Fanon had to accept the possibility that independence, or at least a formal independence, could be achieved without violence. Nkrumah's 'positive action' may not have appealed to him in either ideological or personal terms, but Fanon was well aware that Ghana had been decolonized without an armed struggle. He even suggests that France's military involvement in Algeria meant that it could not fight colonial wars elsewhere and that peaceful decolonization was possible in West Africa. Fanon's violence is primarily the violence of Algeria and its history. When he insists that a violent liberation struggle leads to a higher or purer form of independence, he is thinking of the future independence of Algeria. What he fails to recognize is that, in terms of the decolonization of 'French' Africa at least, Algeria was the exception and not the rule.

The conquest of Algiers began with violence: French Algeria was, to borrow the title of the Jeansons' book *L'Algérie hors la loi*, always 'outside the law'. In 1830, the Turkish rulers and defenders of Algiers capitulated to the French, who promptly disregarded the terms of the surrender that had been negotiated and looted the city. In 1832, an estimated 12,000 were killed during a single French 'expedition' into the interior. The aftermath was as brutal as the massacre itself. When the looted booty was put on sale in the market, it included women's bracelets still attached to severed wrists and earrings dangling from bits of flesh. When Constantine finally fell to the French in 1837, they took no prisoners. Senior officers paid their men for every pair of Algerian ears they collected.[87] Flying columns destroyed whole communities on their savage razzias. The worst atrocities occurred in 1845 when, on three separate occasions, fleeing civilians and fighters took refuge in caves. The orders given to the French troops were simple: 'Smoke them out like foxes.' Brushwood was piled up and fires were lit, but the foxes did not come out. Men, women, children and their livestock died of asphyxiation and smoke inhalation. This was almost exactly one hundred years before the massacres in Sétif, and one hundred and ten before the machine guns opened fire in the football stadium in Philippeville. In a largely pre-literate society with a strong oral culture, a hundred years is not a long time. The memory of the precolonial period was preserved. Mothers still told their children tales of the warriors who had resisted the French and, according to Fanon, such tales began to be told more often after the armed struggle began.[88]

Not all the tales that were told were of heroes. One of the architects of the conquest was Marshal Thomas Bugeaud (1784–1849), who served as Algeria's governor between 1840 and 1847. Algerian accents distorted his name to 'Bichou', and he became the bogeyman. Mothers would tell their children: 'Be quiet, or I'll get Bichou.'[89] Such threats had a very contemporary ring to them: in 1957–8, ALN fighters who had taken refuge in the limestone caves of the Aïn Mlilia region died asphyxiated by gas and fumes from smoke grenades.[90] The foxes were still being smoked out and shot when they emerged. If they did not come out, they died as their forebears had died.

In 1833, a royal commission appointed by Louis-Philippe reported on 'the real situation in the colony':

Acting on mere suspicion and without trial, we have executed people whose guilt subsequently proved to be more than doubt-ful . . . We have massacred people carrying safe-conducts; on the basis of suspicion, we have massacred whole populations, who later proved to be innocent. We have put on trial men who are regarded as the country's saints, men who are venerated because they had the courage to resist our rages . . . We have thrown tribal chieftains into dungeons because their tribes gave our deserters asylum. We have honoured treason by calling it negoti-ation, described shameful ambushes as diplomatic acts. In a word, we have outdone the barbarism of the barbarians we came to civ-ilize.[91]

The report changed nothing and critics were dismissed as 'philanthro-pists' who understood nothing of Algeria or Algerians. It was seriously suggested that France should emulate the pioneers who tamed America, and adopt a policy of genocide.[92]

In Algeria, violence was not just the midwife of history. Violence was Algeria's father and mother. As a character in one of Mohammed Dib's novels about the war of independence puts it, France had created 'an Algeria that has to be killed. Killed so that a cleaner one can come into the world.'[93] For his part, Sartre maintained that 'The colonial wars of the nineteenth century created for the *colon* a primal situation in which violence was his basic relationship with the native. This situation of violence was produced and reproduced as the result of a set of violent practices.'[94] French Algeria was the product of violence: 'For the son of the *colon*, violence is present in the situation itself; it is the social force

477

that produces him. Both the son of the *colon* and the son of the Muslim are sons of the objective violence that defines the situation itself.'[95] The logic of a situation created by a primal violence is such that it will eventually provoke the counter-violence of the colonized. For Sartre and Fanon, that counter-violence reveals the truth of the colonial situation: it was founded and perpetuated by violence. The violence of the Algerian revolution was a response to a history of violence: total negation had to be met with total negation.

When Fanon describes the Third World as a colossal mass with a 'project',[96] he is using the technical vocabulary of Sartre's *Critique de la raison dialectique* and it is that work which supplies the overall framework of his analysis of violence in Algeria. In Sartrean terms, a project implies a twofold relationship with an existing state of affairs. On the one hand, a project is negative in that it negates or destroys that which exists; in another sense, it is positive in that it opens on to that which does not exist.[97] It is both a rejection of the present and a leap into the future; it is the defining characteristic of human action which 'traverses the world', fully aware of its determinations, and 'transforms the world on the basis of given conditions'.[98] The counter-violence of the colonized is a form of praxis, or purposeful human action determined by a project, that responds to and negates the primal and endemic violence of colonization. At the same time, it negates the colonized created by colonization and allows a 'new man' to emerge. It is in that sense that Fanon can describe violence as 'absolute praxis'.[99] It negates the Manichaean action which, in the colonial situation, makes the Algerian something 'other than man'.[100]

Sartre's *Critique* both acknowledges that Marxism is the untranscendable philosophy of our time and criticizes most forms of Marxism for their failure to acknowledge that an individual's life does not begin when he or she first draws a pay-packet and is structured by an individual or collective project as well as by economic realities. Before going on to look at how the schemas of the *Critique* helped to structure Fanon's account of both the liberation of the Third World and the post-independence problems that await it, it is helpful to examine his relationship with a more conventional Marxism, not least because doing so raises the issue of the agency of the Third World's project.

Recalling the occasion when Fanon requested him to write a preface to *L'An V de la Révolution algérienne*, Ferhat Abbas said of him that he was an 'authentic Marxist'. The claim is difficult to accept. A lot has been written on Fanon and Marxism but the debate in a sense gets off to a false start.[101] Fanon shows little interest in Marxist theory and, whilst he had obviously absorbed its general principles, there is no sign that he ever studied it in any depth. It was, it has been reported, only because Rheda Malek gave him a copy of it that he read the chapters on 'the force theory' (*théorie de la violence* in French) in Engels's *Anti-Dühring*; he found it 'too mild' and inappropriate in the Algerian context.[102] In the text itself, Fanon dismisses as 'childish' Engels's speculations as to how the balance of power would change if Man Friday suddenly acquired a loaded revolver and forced Robinson Crusoe to be his drudge.[103] At the beginning of *Peau noire*, Fanon asks rhetorically how one can fail to hear that voice 'crashing down the steps of history: "The point is not to interpret the world, but to change it,"'[104] but the ability to cite the 'Theses on Feuerbach' does not necessarily indicate any great familiarity with Marx. Towards the end of the book, Fanon states that, for the black working in the cane plantations of Le Robert, the only solution is 'the struggle' and adds: 'And he will not begin and wage that struggle after making either an idealist or a Marxist analysis, but because he cannot conceive of his existence other than in terms of a battle that is waged against exploitation, poverty and hunger.'[105] These are the only substantive references to Marxism in the book. That there should be so few is not surprising. The Marxism of the early 1950s had nothing to say about the lived experience of the black man. Sartre and Merleau-Ponty were of much more use to Fanon. As Aimé Césaire remarked when he parted company with the PCF in 1956, it was obvious that 'the struggle of colonial peoples against colonialism, the struggle of people of colour against racism is much more complex – what am I saying? – of a completely different nature to the French worker's struggle against French capitalism and can in no way be regarded as a part or fragment of that struggle.'[106] By 1961, there can have been few issues over which Fanon and Césaire were in agreement, but this was one of them.

In *Les Damnés de la terre*, Fanon contends that, when one approaches the colonial situation, 'Marxist analyses have to be stretched a little,'[107] and few would disagree that classical Marxism cannot simply

be 'applied' to that situation. Indeed, a major strand within classical
Marxism holds that colonization is, for the colonized nation, an accelerated, if brutal, form of modernization and Marxists can easily come
up with their own version of the 'civilizing mission'. Marx applies the
argument to British rule in India.[108] Engels uses the same argument
with respect to Algeria and describes the conquest as 'an important fact
and favourable to the progress of civilization'. The Bedouins were, he
claims, no more than 'thieves', adding that 'the modern bourgeois,
with the civilization, industry and enlightenment that he carries, is
preferable to the feudal lord or plunderer and to the barbaric conditions
of the society to which they belong'.[109] Fanon was not, it seems,
acquainted with either of these texts, but they lend weight to his insistence that Marxism needs to be stretched somewhat.

Fanon 'stretches' Marxism in two directions at once. On the one
hand, he disputes the role that is traditionally given to the proletariat by
Marxism; on the other, he maintains that the peasantry (and perhaps
the lumpenproletariat) is the only revolutionary force in the Third
World and in Algeria in particular. Both claims are disputed by Marxists,
who object in particularly strong terms to the argument that 'in colonial
territories, the proletariat is the kernel of the colonized people that is
most pampered by the colonial regime'.[110] Writing in the PCF journal
*La Pensée*, a Vietnamese Marxist complained that, in order to advance
his theses about the peasant revolution, Fanon had denied that the
working class had any revolutionary potential, and insisted that peasants
could never develop a 'revolutionary consciousness': rural revolutionary
bases were never created by peasants. They were created by militants
from the cities who shaped the rural world in their image.[111] Defined
for all time and applicable to all situations, the categories of Marxist
analysis were clearly more on his mind than Algerian realities. In a
country such as Algeria, the primary contradiction is not, for Fanon,
that between the bourgeoisie and the proletariat, mainly because the
bourgeoisie is not defined by its ownership of property or factories but
by the fact that it 'does not resemble the natives, the "others"'.[112] Class
therefore cannot be the main factor in the analysis, though it does
prove to be a surprisingly important one for Fanon. A not dissimilar
argument was put forward by a member of Mandouze's *Consciences
maghrébines* group: 'In North Africa . . . there are two social classes –

the bourgeois and the proletarians – but there are also two peoples, two "races": the "Europeans" and the "Arabs". And the Europeans are bourgeois, and the Arabs are proletarian.'[113] Fanon himself puts it in more robust terms, which could also be applied to Martinique: 'In the colonies, the economic infrastructure is also a superstructure. The cause is an effect: you are rich because you are white, and you are white because you are rich.'[114] The Marxist response is that: 'Fanon . . . placed his faith in the spontaneous revolutionary attitude of the peasants and scorned the alleged conservatism of the urban workers . . . all his arguments have the effect of stoking up mistrust between workers and peasants, and of setting one against the other.'[115] The sociologist Pierre Bourdieu also criticized Fanon's theses, arguing that whilst the peasantry and the sub-proletariat of the cities might be a force for revolution, they could never be revolutionary forces in themselves.[116] Elsewhere, the same author accepted that the number of skilled workers in the modern sector was 'relatively small', but did enjoy privileges such as stability of employment, family allowances, pensions and schooling for their children.[117] Compared to that of the average fellah, theirs was a pampered existence.

A more realistic criticism of Fanon is made by Harbi in his comments on the discussions of 1959, when the 'Fanonist' line on the peasantry was endorsed. It was, he remarks, unrealistic to speak of the peasantry's inexhaustible resources at a time when 'The peasants have been shattered and uprooted. Between 1954 and 1960, two million of them were in resettlement camps and 300,000 were in refugee camps in Tunisia and Morocco. 731,000 have left the countryside for the towns. The number of emigrants to France doubled. Rural structures were no longer supported by peasant activity. This descent into hell destroyed the peasantry's grip on reality, and weakened its sense of identity or even of its dignity.'[118]

Fanon is, of course, not alone in disputing the central role of the proletariat. The FLN's analysis of Algerian society, such as it was, spoke simply of the 'people': the people was the sole hero of the revolution, though the FLN's position is rarely mentioned in discussions of Fanon and Marxism. It is true that Fanon's 'proletariat' is a strange animal in that it includes 'tram drivers, taxi drivers, interpreters, and nurses' as well as miners and dockers,[119] but it is also true to say that Algeria did

481

not really have a proletariat in the Marxist sense of an industrial work-force that exchanged its labour-power for a wage and generated surplus value. It is estimated that in 1954, some 146,000 unskilled workers were employed in construction, dock work, manufacturing and the service sector, whilst a further 72,000 skilled workers were employed in a variety of trades. This was a tiny proportion of a total population of over eight million. In 1950, Francis Jeanson remarked that there were 'few' Muslim workers and that they resembled a sub-proletariat rather than a true proletariat.[120]

There was a 'true' Algerian proletariat – but in France. Fanon does not mention the Algerian community in France, but the money sent back there financed many a family at home and the taxes it paid to the FLN financed the Revolution. The presence in France of 211,000 Algerians in 1954 and of 350,000 in 1962 was a reflection of both the labour shortage there – a shortage that increased dramatically when so many young men were conscripted into the army – and the underde-velopment of an Algeria which had not evolved a modern industry and where the primary sector (agriculture and extractive industries) was both dominant and the biggest employer.[121] Colonization did not lay the foundations of Western society in Algeria. It created a divided and unevenly developed society, segregated along ethnic lines. In the French scheme of things, the role of a colony or even three *départements* on the other side of the Mediterranean was to act as a supplier of raw materials and agricultural produce, and as a market for manufactured goods. As in Martinique (albeit it on a very different scale), Algeria's 'development' was actually an *under*development. It could not be per-mitted to compete with France, and even the cultivation of vines was reined back when Algerian wine seemed to pose a threat to the interests of growers in the south of France. Algerian wine was originally a sub-stitute. Vines began to be planted on a large scale only because the phylloxera outbreak of 1880 ravaged the vineyards of southern France.

In Marxist or Leninist terms, the small Parti Communiste Algérien should have been the vanguard of the proletariat and should have played a leading role in any revolution. Francis Jeanson remarked in 1950 that there 'was very little to say about' the PCA, mainly because it had no root in 'the Muslim masses'.[122] Most of its members were European and they closed ranks with their fellow Europeans when the demonstrators in Sétif began to demand independence in 1945. According to many sources, they participated in the repression that followed. This was not forgotten by the FLN.

For Fanon, the peasantry was Algeria's true revolutionary force. Although it did have its 'obscurantist tendencies',[123] it was also the authentic spokesman for the real Algeria. Fanon describes in lyrical terms what happens when the urban militants who have been driven out of the towns go to the countryside:

> These men get into the habit of talking to the peasants. They discover that the rural masses have never ceased to pose the problem of their liberation in terms of violence, of taking back the land from the foreigners, in terms of a national struggle. Everything is simple. These men discover a coherent people which perpetuates itself in a sort of immobility but keeps intact its moral values, its attachment to the nation. They discover a generous people that is prepared to make sacrifices, willing to give of itself, impatient and with a stony pride. One can understand that the encounter between militants who are being hunted by the police and these impatient masses, who are instinctually rebellious, can produce an explosive mixture of unexpected power.[124]

The urban equivalent to the peasantry is a lumpenproletariat that has been driven off the land and into the shanty towns of Algiers and the other cities. Fanon acknowledges that the lumpenproletariat can be manipulated by colonialism and even claims, without actually proving his point, that most of the *harkis* were drawn from its ranks, but he also insists that: 'The insurrection will find its urban spearhead in the people of the shanty towns, in the lumpenproletariat. The lumpenproletariat, this cohort of starving men who have been detribalized and declanized, constitutes one of the most spontaneously and radically revolutionary forces of a colonized people.'[125] These, and not the relatively pampered proletariat, are the wretched of the earth. That this is a highly idealized picture of both the peasantry and the lumpenproletariat goes without saying, though it is true that the criminal milieu of Algiers did supply some of Yacef's fighters – not least the Ali La Pointe of the Battle of Algiers. It is, however, impossible to reconcile Fanon's idealization of the peasantry with the reality of what happened to so many young people who fled into the countryside after the Battle of Algiers. They were killed by Amirouche and his men during the 'blueitis' episode. As a black outsider who was both intellectual and urbanized to his fingertips, Fanon himself would not have survived long in Amirouche's company.

Whilst the image of the peasantry is undoubtedly idealized, Fanon is remarkably consistent and also remarkably generous. The spontaneous violence of the countryside is no more than a starting point and as the struggle develops into a form of national consciousness, it will overcome or transcend the Manichaeism instilled by colonization and then internalized by the colonized.[126] Once more, Fanon describes the emergent Algerian nation in terms of will and consciousness, and not in ethnic terms: 'the racial and racist level is transcended'.[127] In Fanon's vision, there is a place for members of the European minority, provided that they 'become' negroes or Arabs in the sense of identifying with the insurgent wretched of the earth.[128]

The unifying factor is violence: 'the violence of the colonized unites the people. By its very structure, colonialism is separatist and regionalist. Violence in practice is totalizing, national.'[129] Fanon habitually equates 'nation' with a form of consciousness, but he shifts his ground somewhat in *Les Damnés de la terre*. His account of the emergence of the nation through the praxis of violence is modelled on Sartre's description of the group-in-fusion and its escape from seriality. The two are starkly contrasted modes of being. Sartre's classic example of seriality is that of a line of people queuing for a bus in St Germain-des-près. To the extent that they are waiting for and hoping to board the same bus, they share a common project. The bus can, however, take only a limited number of passengers and the project of each would-be passenger implies a conflictual relationship with that of every other would-be passenger. For the bus driver, they are all anonymous and interchangeable members of the series. Colonization reduced Algeria to the status of a serial: 'the repressive practices, the divide and rule politics and especially the dispossessions rapidly liquidate feudal structures and transform this backward but structured society into an "atomized crowd" . . . Muslim society's new form is an expression of the violence itself; its objective meaning is the violence inflicted on each of the serial

Others it has produced.'[130] A surprisingly similar analysis emerged from the deliberations of the Soummam Conference. According to the Soummam 'platform', the actions of the ALN had given the Algerian people a psychological jolt which freed it from its 'torpor, fear and scepticism' and had produced a 'psychopolitical union of all Algerians, the national unanimity that fertilizes the armed struggle and makes freedom's victory inevitable'.[131]

The function of the violence of the colonized is to negate and transcend the seriality created by the violence of colonization. In doing so, it creates a group-in-fusion with a common project and praxis. Sartre's examples of the workings of a group-in-fusion are mostly taken from the Revolution of 1789. A group-in-fusion suddenly emerges when the serial waiting outside a bakery is transformed by the anonymous cry that tells it to storm the bakery itself. The cry of 'To arms' or 'To the Bastille' turns a series of individuals into the group that storms the hated prison and creates history; whatever happens afterwards, 14 July will always be the day on which the Bastille was stormed.[132] The call to arms creates a fraternity based upon the terror that prevents anyone from breaking the oath. This is why Fanon attaches such importance to what he had heard about the Mau Mau in Kenya.[133]

> The Mau Mau . . . demanded that every member of the group had to strike the victim. Everyone was therefore personally responsible for the death of that victim. Working means working towards the death of the *colon*. Claiming responsibility for the violence also allows those members of the group who have strayed or who have been proscribed to come back, to retake their place and to be reintegrated. Violence can thus be understood as mediation par excellence. The colonized man liberates himself in and through violence.[134]

It is at this point that Fanon cites Césaire's tragedy *Et les chiens se taisaient* and in doing so links the violent past of Martinique to that of Algeria. The argument is certainly brutal, even blood-curdling, but it can scarcely be construed as a glorification of violence for the sake of violence.

The central category in Fanon's sociological analysis of the post-independence period is the 'national bourgeoisie' but his understanding

485

of that term is far from conventional. In the Marxist tradition, it is viewed as a class which shares with the proletariat and the peasantry an interest in the liberation of a colonial country. Unlike the comprador bourgeoisie,[135] which is directly linked to forces of colonialism or imperialism, it is 'a class with a dual character'. On the one hand, it is oppressed by imperialism and can therefore enter into an alliance with the revolutionary forces led by the proletariat and its party; on the other, its links with imperialism mean that it may follow the example of the comprador class and act as imperialism's accomplice.[136] Such a class did exist, at least in embryo, in Algeria and some of its members brought Fanon into contact with the FLN. There was a small Algerian elite of perhaps 6,000 owners of factories, commercial farmers, and higher level civil servants, but it would be difficult to describe it as an industrial bourgeoisie in possession of the means of production.[137]

For Fanon, the national bourgeoisie is an underdeveloped bourgeoisie which takes power at the end of the colonial period,[138] or in other words a post-independence phenomenon. Although he is vague, he is referring to what he had seen in newly independent states like Ghana, Guinea and Ivory Coast and to what he knew of Senegal. He is not speaking here of Algeria itself, but he is voicing forebodings about the future of an independent Algeria. His dismissive references to 'nationalist' parties that shy away from contacts with the peasantry allude to countries that were already independent or on the point of becoming independent, though they can perhaps be read as alluding to the pre-1954 period in Algeria. But when he describes the one-party state that had been established in countries like the Ivory Coast,[139] and contends that it is 'the modern form of the dictatorship of the bourgeoisie that has no mask, no make-up and no scruples',[140] he is seriously out of step with the FLN, which was certainly not prepared to share power before or after independence. In September 1963, a referendum approved the one-party system and it remained in place until another referendum introduced a multiparty political system in February 1989.

If it is truly to become part of the nation, the national bourgeoisie must, argues Fanon, be untrue to itself:

In an underdeveloped country, an authentic national bourgeoisie must make it its imperative duty to betray the vocation to which it is destined, and learn from the people, or in other words make available to the people the intellectual and technical capital it snatched when it went through colonial universities. We will see, unfortunately, that the national bourgeoisie turns away from this historic and heroic path, which is both fertile and just, and plunges, with its soul at peace into the anti-national, and therefore horrible, path of a bourgeois bourgeoisie that is unimaginably, stupidly and cynically bourgeois.[141]

There is a very Sartrean ring to the insistence that it is by betraying itself that the national bourgeoisie can be true to the nation of which it is part. It is a variant on the argument used by the *génération algérienne* who, in betraying France, betrayed those who had betrayed the true interests of both France and Algeria. The broader argument is Sartrean too. Like the 'pampered' Algerian proletariat, the national bourgeoisie is individualistic; its inability to see beyond its immediate interests makes it incapable of building national unity. As a result, the national front that had forced colonialism into retreat disintegrates and collapses.[142] The outcome is inevitable: 'Nationalism, that magnificent hymn that raised up the masses against the oppressor, disintegrates (*se désagrége*).'[143] *Se désagréger* is the term Sartre uses to describe the group-in-fusion's seemingly inevitable lapse back into seriality. The fundamental ambiguity of *Les Damnés de la terre* is that, whilst Fanon constantly prophesies the victory of the people, the theoretical model he adopts necessarily implies that the group unity on which that victory is based cannot be sustained. In a sense, Fanon foresaw that the post-independence period would be difficult and dangerous; he could not foresee that it was a bureaucratized army that would hold the real power in an independent Algeria. And he did not live to see it do so.

Although Fanon's theoretical model implies the inevitable disintegration of the national consciousness, he does propose an alternative: 'Today, arms factories are functioning several metres underground in the middle of the mountains; today, people's courts are functioning at every level; local planning commissions are organizing the break up of big farms, and are building the Algeria of tomorrow.'[144] He describes how an alternative economy was organized in the zones where freedom of movement had been severely restricted by the French army. Peasants could no longer go into the towns to buy provisions and a thriving black market developed. Unable to pay their debts in kind, the peasants began to mortgage their land or even to sell it to pay the few shopowners who could go into town. According to Fanon, 'the political commissars' now intervened to ensure that all supplies were bought from nationalist wholesalers in the towns, that fair prices were set. Heavy fines were imposed on those traders who tried to cheat; in extreme cases, an elected management committee took over the running of the business.[145] Fanon's self-management model clearly refers to the FLN's Political-Administrative Organization, which did function as an alternative administration in many parts of Algeria. As in his descriptions of the transformations that were brought about in the lives of Algerian women, he appears to have mistaken temporary transformations brought about by exceptional circumstances for permanent changes. Self-management (*auto-gestion*) was indeed a feature of post-independence Algeria, where elected committees did run factories and farms and it seemed to many to represent a decentralized and democratic socialism. *Auto-gestion* can be more accurately seen as a response to a difficult situation. When the *pied noir* exodus accelerated in the summer of 1962, many factories and farms were simply abandoned by their owners and were left without managers. Many factory workers established management committees to prevent plants from being taken over by individuals; in the countryside, peasants formed committees simply because the crops on the big *pied noir* farms had to be brought in. *Auto-gestion* was encouraged by Ben Bella and the self-managed sector was regulated and protected by law, but did not provide a lasting base for the economy. Self-management gradually gave way to centralization and state control.

At the beginning of October, Fanon suffered a serious relapse only weeks before his book was due to be published. He was now in desperate need of advanced forms of treatment that were simply not available in North Africa. Using a hospital in France was clearly out of the question and even hospitals in Rome were not safe, as Fanon knew from experience. He had already consulted Russian doctors to no avail. Fanon was reluctant to go to the United States, which he regarded as a land of lynch mobs, but was eventually persuaded that there was no alternative. As there were no direct flights, this meant one more stopover in Rome. Fanon was driven to the airport for the last time. Sartre, accompanied by Boulharouf, spent a few hours with him in his hotel room in the Italian capital. The once voluble Fanon had at last been silenced by his terminal illness. He lay flat on his bed, so exhausted that he was unable to speak. Yet he moved convulsively. At the end of *Peau noire* he had expressed the wish that his body would make him a man who always asked questions; its convulsive movements were now its only way of fighting the passivity to which it had been reduced.[146]

When he reached Washington on 3 October, Fanon did not receive the welcome he had expected and, rather than being hospitalized, he was left alone in a hotel room. He was joined by his wife and son. In the course of her research on Fanon, Irene Gendzier tried to clarify the details. She received a brief written reply: 'Ibrahim Fanon no. CC 03-86-00, was admitted to the Clinical Centre, National Institute of Health, Bethesda, Maryland, on October 10 1961 and expired on December 6 1961.'[147]

Fanon was hospitalized under the care of a Dr David Haywood. It was in hospital that he first met Abdelkader Chendli, the head of the GPRA's New York delegation, who visited him regularly and described him as a man 'who was already looking at the world and at men from the beyond'.[148] In a series of telephone calls to Simone de Beauvoir, Josie Fanon described how he had undergone an operation. His blood was changed completely in the hope that this would stimulate the production of new bone marrow. There was no possibility of a full recovery, but it was thought that he might live for another year. He received the first reviews of his book, but merely commented that 'That won't give me my bone marrow back.' At two in the morning on 6 December, Josie rang Lanzmann in Paris: Frantz was dead. He had succumbed to double pneumonia.[149]

Sensing Josie's desperation, Lanzmann flew to Washington, even though he did not know her well. He returned after a few days, badly shaken by what he had learned:

Fanon had lived his death minute by minute and had resisted it savagely; his prickly aggressivity found a release in the fantasies of a dying man: he hated those American racists, and distrusted all the hospital staff. When he woke up on his last morning, he betrayed his obsessions by saying to his wife: 'They put me through the washing machine last night.'

The treatment appears to have reactivated an old fear or fantasy: 'For a few years now, certain laboratories have been trying to discover a dene-grification serum; certain laboratories have, in all seriousness, rinsed out their test tubes, adjusted their scales and undertaken research that will allow those unfortunate negroes to turn white . . .'[150] The five-year-old Olivier had found his way into his father's room, where he saw him undergoing a transfusion. The tubes and bags of blood convinced him that his father had been cut into pieces. He was subsequently found waving a green and white Algerian flag on the streets.

Flying Fanon to the United States obviously involved some delicate politics. The CIA had to be involved and it appointed an agent called Ollie Iselin, officially a member of the diplomatic corps in North Africa, as his case-officer. CIA involvement was first revealed by Joseph Alsop in his syndicated column in the *Washington Post* on 21 February 1969 and the story was reprinted in the *International Herald Tribune* the next day. Alsop was careful to spread his story, even writing to the *New Statesman* to point out that David Caute's 'Modern Masters' study of Fanon omitted to mention the fact that 'Frantz Fanon died almost lit-erally in the arms of the CIA'.[151] *Le Monde* had run the original story a year earlier under the headline 'Did Frantz Fanon die in the arms of the CIA?'[152] The story was that Iselin was, apart from his wife, Fanon's 'only friend' in Washington. Alsop, who died in 1989, was a conserva-tive journalist with close links to the CIA,[153] and he seems to have wanted to imply that a hero of the left was involved – or worse – with the Agency. His article provoked a lengthy reply from M'Hammed Yazid, the former GPRA minister for information with whom Fanon had worked so often:

In the issue of *Le Monde* dated 23–24 February, you published *en encadre* an article entitled 'Did Frantz Fanon die in the arms of the CIA?'. Your article refers to a text by Joseph Alsop that appeared in the *International Herald Tribune*.

I must tell you that reading Mr Joseph Alsop's article made

such an incredible impression on me that I have difficulty in understanding the interest your paper seems to have taken in it.

Before re-establishing the facts concerning the conditions in which my brother Frantz Fanon died, I have to concede that it was only natural for the CIA to take an interest in an activist whose thought, writings and anti-imperialist actions have made a profound impression on the revolutionary movement of the Blacks of America. Such interest honours a great activist.

Having said that, Frantz Fanon was hospitalized in Washington's National Health Institute in September 1961. The decision to transfer him to that institution was taken after consultations with prominent figures in the medical world. The United States embassy in Tunis and the State Department offered to help to facilitate his admission to hospital.

During his hospitalization in Washington, and until his death, Frantz Fanon was surrounded by *la sollicitude* and the presence of members of the FLN's New York delegation, by that of members of the African diplomatic corps in Washington and by black American activists. His wife and his son, who were guests of the Guinean Embassy in Washington were present. Frantz Fanon died 'in the arms' of his wife and his brothers.

His body was transferred immediately to Tunis and was subsequently buried in liberated Algerian territory. The fact that a representative of the State Department was present at the funeral is no revelation. The Algerian information services made this known and distributed a set of photographs of the ceremony on the very day it took place.[154]

Yazid's account is inaccurate in some respects – Fanon was admitted to hospital in October and did not become a hero for black Americans until after 1965 – but he is surely right to play down the importance of Alsop's revelation. That an American had been present when Fanon was buried was obvious from the photographs published in *El Moudjahid*, and he was obviously no tourist. Alsop provided no documentary evidence to back up his allegations, and his motive appears simply to have been to stir up doubts about Fanon in the minds of his new admirers. Neither the CIA nor the State

Department is a philanthropic institution, and no doubt they had their reasons for wishing to get close to Fanon. It is also probable that the CIA already knew a lot about Fanon. His friendship with Holden and Moumié cannot have gone unnoticed, and nor can his recent activities in West Africa and the Sahara. Algeria was obviously on the verge of independence and, whilst Fanon was not a member of the GPRA, he had close contacts with it and could have been used to win friends. He was a potential asset, and there is nothing particularly shocking about an intelligence agency's attempt to use him as such.

On the day that the news of Fanon's death reached Paris, the French police began to seize copies of *Les Damnés de la terre* from the bookshops.[155] In New York, the GPRA's representatives at the UN gave copies of it to diplomats as a Christmas present.[156]

# 12

# Endgame

After the long and exhausting conversations with Sartre and Beauvoir in Rome in July, Fanon fell silent. He could no longer write and he did not comment on the endgame that was being played out in Algeria and France. Fanon did see copies of his last book but for its first readers, *Les Damnés de la terre* was a posthumous work. Francis Jeanson was putting the finishing touches to his *La Révolution algérienne*, which was published by Feltrinelli in Milan in March 1962, when he heard the news of Fanon's death. He added a boxed insert to the last page of his book. Jeanson and Fanon had had their political differences, but the taxi-driver and carrier of suitcases now wrote:

> It is not for me to say what this death represents for our Algerian comrades. But I met Fanon in 1952 and I saw him again on several occasions after that. I was always passionately interested in what he wrote and what he did, and I now have a feeling of irreparable loss. For the obvious personal reasons, but also because no man could be a more perfect symbol of the common struggle of peoples for their liberation. This Martinican, who was turned by his transition through French culture into an Algerian revolutionary, will remain for us a very living example of univeralism in

493

action and the most noble approach to the human that has ever been made until now in this inhuman world.

When Jeanson's book appeared it was quite obvious that Algeria was on the brink of independence. The French army was observing a unilaterally declared truce. Representatives of the French government and the GPRA had met in early February. The discussions were not easy, the main points of disagreement being the question of the Sahara – some French politicians were still thinking in terms of partition – the fate of the European minority, the organization of a transitional executive and the release of Algerian prisoners. After eight days of bargaining, a compromise solution was reached. During the interval between the ceasefire and the referendum on self-determination, a mixed High Commission would serve as an administration. French troop numbers would gradually be reduced and the *pieds noirs* would be free to opt for either French or Algerian nationality. A final round of negotiations would begin at Evian on 7 March. In the meantime, the violence went on.

Throughout the summer of 1961, the FLN went on waging its war against what remained of the MNA in France. Cafés and the *hôtels meublés* continued to be machine-gunned and attacked with grenades. Policemen continued to be killed. At the beginning of October, a curfew was imposed upon the Algerian population of the metropolis. Algerians were 'strongly advised' to stay off the streets of Paris and the suburbs between 8.30 at night and 5.30 in the morning. Those who had to break the curfew to go to work would be issued with special permits. Cafés and bars frequented by Algerians were ordered to close at seven. Those Algerians who did have to go out were 'very strongly advised' to do so alone. Groups of three or four could easily be mistaken for FLN commandos.

Fanon was admitted to the hospital in Bethesda on 10 October. A week later, the Fédération de France called demonstrations in Paris to protest at the curfew. The official rationale for the curfew was the need to halt the terrorism; it also made it almost impossible for the FLN to operate politically and, more important still, to collect the crucial taxes. The demonstrations were meant to be a peaceful and dignified protest, and the FLN's militants saw to it that no one was armed. On the evening of 17 October, they came from their *bidonvilles*, unarmed, dressed in their best clothes and in some cases accompanied by their wives and children. Many were excited: they had never been to central Paris before. An estimated 30,000 took part in the demonstrations. The marchers were quiet and disciplined, and they kept to one side of the road so as not to block the traffic. On the *grands boulevards* that run from the place de l'Opéra to the place de la République, on the pont de Neuilly, in the place de l'Opéra itself and in the Latin Quarter, the police opened fire. As the would-be demonstrators emerged from the métro station at the Etoile, they were beaten and bundled into buses. Algerians died in the courtyard of the Préfecture de Police in central Paris. Corpses floated in the Seine and bodies were found hanging from trees in the bois de Vincennes. Many of the 15,000 who were arrested were herded into the Palais des sports in the west of the city – the Vel d'Hiv had been demolished by now. Conditions inside were atrocious. A photograph published in *France-Observateur* on 25 October showed hundreds of men in the great sports hall, sitting, standing or milling around. The caption read 'Does it remind you of anything?' The prisoners were not held in the Palais des sports for long. Ray Charles was booked to play a concert there a few days later. Paris loved Brother Ray, and the concert went ahead as planned. Just how many Algerians died in Paris that October is still a matter for controversy. Prefect of Police Maurice Papon merely commented that the police had done what it had to do.

Another war was going on too. The leaders of the failed April putsch were either in jail or had gone underground and the OAS, now led by Salan, was fighting a desperate rearguard action to try to wreck the peace process. In July and August, it adopted a policy of systematic terrorism in both France and Algeria. The dull thud of plastic explosives going off became a familiar sound. In its leaflets, the OAS claimed that it could strike wherever it wanted and whenever it wanted. This was no exaggeration. The OAS described the army in Algeria as an occupying force and as a legitimate target. Civil service offices were attacked. The OAS also attacked Algerian civilians. On 9 September, de Gaulle narrowly survived an assassination attempt. By the end of the year, twenty people were being killed each day in Algiers. Europeans were afraid to leave their homes and the Algerian population cowered in fear in the Casbah and the *bidonvilles*. Children had stopped going to school. In

Oran, bloody clashes between Europeans and Algerians had become a daily occurrence. In Paris, thirty bombs went off in the second week of January alone. On 8 February, the PCF and the trade unions organized a 10,000-strong demonstration against the OAS. Despite being banned, it went ahead and ended in very violent clashes with the police. Nine people, including three women and a child, died on the steps of the Charonne métro station. Half a million people were present when they were buried in the Père Lachaise cemetery five days later. Only one of the speakers who addressed the crowd remembered to speak of the Algerians who had died in October.

The Evian talks began on 7 March. Eleven days later, de Gaulle announced that a ceasefire would come into effect on 19 March. Political prisoners and prisoners of war would be released within three weeks of that date. The army would remain in Algeria until the referendum that would decide the country's fate. The OAS reacted to the reopening of talks by launching 'Operation Rock and Roll': 120 explosions rocked Algiers within the space of a few hours. When the ceasefire came into effect, Salan declared war on the army in which he had served for so many years. Six conscripts were killed when they refused to hand over their weapons to an OAS commando. Squeezed between the Casbah and the sea, the poor white quarter of Bab El-Oued became an insurrectional zone. When the army and the gendarmerie tried to enter the area on 23 March they were fired on from the roofs and windows of the tenement buildings. Tanks were brought in and warplanes fired rockets into the narrow streets. The façades of the buildings were raked with fire from heavy machine guns. Tank rounds were fired at suspected sniper positions. It took three days for the army to bring the area under control. A protest demonstration was called for 26 March and some of those present were hoping to march on Bab El-Oued and to challenge the army. As the crowds massed by the war memorial where Guy Mollet had been humiliated in February 1956, the sound of gunfire was heard. In the rue d'Isley, which led to the plateau des Glières, the crowd trying to join the demonstrators had encountered an army roadblock. It was manned by an infantry unit made up of 'loyal' Algerian troops. They were young, inexperienced and frightened. When they were shot at from a rooftop, they opened fire. Forty-six people were shot dead and a further 200 were wounded.

The OAS now turned on the Algerian population. Its commandos attacked florists' stalls and grocery shops. They killed cleaning ladies and attacked medical centres. Completely terrorized, Algerians refused to leave their homes and Algiers ground to a halt. The *ratonnades* were now on a scale that had never been seen before. The European population was also afraid: the siege of Bab El-Oued and the massacre in the rue d'Isley had proved beyond doubt that the OAS was not its saviour. The Europeans also had good reason to fear the FLN. The *pieds noirs* had indeed to choose between the suitcase and the coffin, and brave – or reckless – Algerians were obligingly selling cheap suitcases on the street corners. The European population began to leave.

In the meantime, a Provisional Executive, in which the FLN was at last included, was trying to prepare for the referendum on 8 April. The European population did not have a vote, and a majority of over 90 per cent ratified the Evian Agreements that brought an independent Algeria into existence. Throughout the month of April, OAS commandos attacked the police, the army and the Algerian population. In one incident, sixty-two Algerians died when a car bomb exploded in the docks. Azzedine had by now succeeded in re-establishing the old 'autonomous zone' of Algiers and his men attacked OAS units. They also kidnapped, tortured and killed a number of Europeans. The OAS's response was as bloody as it was predictable, but the two organizations did eventually negotiate a ceasefire. There seemed to be an end to the horror. An estimated 100,000 Europeans fled from Algeria in May 1962. To do so, they had to defy the OAS, who had ordered them to stay. Some sold their property for derisory sums, others simply abandoned it. Some drove to the port in their cars and then set them on fire on the quayside.

There was a further upsurge of OAS violence in the period leading up to the July referendum on independence, but the terrorist organization had to accept that it had lost the battle. Salan and most of its other leaders had been arrested. On 3 July, Algeria was proclaimed an independent state. For a few brief days, the country was in a state of elation but on 5 July gunfire interrupted the parades being held to welcome Ben Kedda and the first members of the GPRA to Algiers. In the panic that followed, ALN troops, FLN activists and French troops all opened fire. Ninety-five people died. Violence continued in the countryside too. In the Mitidja, hundreds of Europeans were kidnapped. Europeans were tortured and murdered in Oran. In the course of the summer, a further 30,000 *pieds noirs* fled a country that was no longer theirs.

There was also serious conflict within the new Algerian government. Ben Bella and Ben Khedda were the respective leaders of the main factions. Ben Bella received a rapturous welcome when he reached Algiers on 12 July, but Ben Khedda accused him of wanting to establish a military dictatorship. A dangerous split between the two, which reflected the old divisions between the ALN and the GPRA, was narrowly avoided. Ben Bella's insistence that the *wilayas* should come under the control of a newly established central Political Bureau to prevent Algeria becoming a loose amalgam of feudal fiefdoms also met with opposition from *wilayas* III (Kabylia) and IV (Algérois). This led to armed conflict. In late August, Ben Bella left Algiers for Oran and ordered those troops loyal to him to march on the capital. Perhaps 1,000 died in the fighting. The arrival of Boumédienne's tanks in September put an end to the conflict, but it also left still more dead. The people – the sole hero of the Algerian Revolution – made no secret of what was needed. The popular cry was now '*Baraket*' – 'That's enough'. But the blood-letting was still not over. The *harkis* and the Algerians who had served in regular French units were the new victims. As early as March, SAS officers had been trying to transfer their *harkis* to France, but were warned that doing so was illegal. Some who had served with the French did manage to escape to the metropolis, but the army was forced to abandon the vast majority of its Algerian recruits. Tens of thousands of them were massacred and they did not die pretty deaths.

The independence of Algeria was formally proclaimed on 3 July 1962, but the country celebrates its national day on 5 July. It is the anniversary of the day on which the Bey of Algiers capitulated to the French in 1830.

# Afterword

I CANNOT RECALL JUST why I first read Frantz Fanon. Perhaps it was a recommendation from a friend, perhaps it was the Sartre connection. But I do remember where and when I discovered Fanon. I was twenty and spending a year in Paris as part of a degree course in French. It was a good year and provided an introduction to many things, but it began with a severe culture shock. When I went to the Préfecture de police on the Ile de la Cité to obtain a temporary resident's permit, I saw a group of Algerians – all men – being turned away from the counter on the grounds they had not filled in their application forms correctly. Individually, they were addressed as *tu*. Collectively, those men were treated with utter contempt by officials who knew a *bicot* when they saw one. It transpired that the Algerians simply could not read and write well enough to complete the forms.

To watch anyone being humiliated – to recognize the look of hurt in the eyes of the other – is distressing. I had rarely seen people looking so forlorn and lost, and I do not think I had ever seen such a naked display of racism. When my turn came to approach the counter, the photograph I tendered was rejected: my hair concealed too much of my face, and I had to have new photographs taken with it pulled back off my face. For a year, I therefore carried a resident's permit bearing a photograph in which I was almost unrecognizable. This was a source of amusement rather than humiliation. I was treated brusquely, even rudely, but not with contempt. After all, I was a white European, not a *bicot*, not a *bougnole*, not a 'Mohammed' and not a 'Sidi'. In the circumstances, it seemed only natural to at least try to help the Algerians with their application forms. I should have known I could never have been of any great help. Any encounter between undergraduate French and Gallic bureaucratese is always going to be an unequal struggle. I could not speak the language of these men and they could not speak mine. I could not help. I assumed that they were immigrant workers. If and when they did get their papers, they probably helped to build the rapid transport system that exiled most Algerians from central Paris by displacing them to distant suburbs. It was a good moment to encounter Fanon.

Now very battered, my old copies of *Les Damnés de la terre* (*The Wretched of the Earth*) and *L'An V de la révolution algérienne* (*Studies in a Dying Colonialism*) were bought in the spring of 1970 from François Maspero's La Joie de lire bookshop in the rue Saint Séverin. Maspero was Fanon's main publisher, and this was where *Les Damnés de la terre* first went on sale in late 1961. It is also where, on the very day that the news of Fanon's death reached Paris, copies were seized and taken away by the police because they were deemed seditious. My copies are not first editions but the reprints published in the Petite Collection Maspero edition. Copies of those elegant little books are now quite difficult to find, and the shop where I bought them has gone. The sites of its two branches – one on either side of the narrow street – are now home to a travel agency and a shop selling posters and cards. The bookshop's name meant 'the joy of reading', and I always find its absence depressing.

The Algerian war had been over for eight years in 1970; almost no one talked about it. It was still impossible for Gillo Pontecorvo's *Battle of Algiers* to be shown in a French cinema. It was to be almost thirty years before a French government could finally admit that what occurred in Algeria was indeed a war and not a police operation. No one talked about how, in October 1961 or only two months before Fanon's death, the police opened fire on unarmed Algerian demonstrators at the bottom of the boulevard St Michel. No one talked about how Algerians died in the courtyard of the Préfecture de Police. The memory of the student revolt of May '68 had eclipsed that of an earlier generation of twenty-year-olds, some of whom fought and died in a war that had no name, and some of whom refused to fight in it or even deserted from the army. Many of those who deserted, who refused to accept their call-up papers or who even joined the small groups that gave active and clandestine support to the Front de Libération National, were inspired to do so by Fanon, the black doctor from Martinique who resigned from his post in a psychiatric hospital in colonial Algeria to join the Front and who preached a gospel of violent revolution.

May '68 had come and gone, but Paris was still turbulent. The police presence around the rue St-Séverin was both permanent and heavy. Although it certainly helped a great deal, one did not need to be black or North African to be stopped regularly and asked for one's papers; being twenty and having long hair were perfectly good qualifications. It felt right to rebel, to be angry, even though our anger and our rebellion were largely symbolic. Running away from police charges during occasional demonstrations in the Latin Quarter was both frightening and exhilarating, but we were not facing machine guns. Was it really possible to believe that the CRS riot police were a latter day SS?

In 1970, the political horizon was dominated not by Algeria, but by the war in Vietnam that politicized so many members of a generation. There were some vague parallels with the experience of the so-called Algerian generation. They had dismissed talk of 'peace in Algeria' and calls for a negotiated settlement in favour of a much more militant commitment. In 1970, 'Victory to the NLF' felt a much more appropriate slogan than 'Peace in Vietnam'. At Christmas and the New Year, banners went up on the lampposts in the boulevard St Germain, courtesy of John Lennon and Yoko Ono: 'War is Over (if you want it)'. It went on, regardless of what we wanted.

It was a sign of the times that my acquaintance with Fanon began with *Les Damnés de la terre* and not *Peau noire, masques blancs* (*Black Skin, White Masks*). In many ways he seemed to have less to do with an Algeria that had been bureaucratized than with a very general image of the Third World – that colossus facing Europe. Fanon had spoken of setting Africa ablaze, and it was on fire. Vicious colonial wars were going on in Portugal's African colonies. A guerrilla war was taking place in a Rhodesia that would eventually become Zimbabwe. In South Africa, the armed wing of the Africa National Congress was waging its own struggle. It was possible to follow the wars' progress by browsing through the collection of papers and journals on offer in La Joie de lire's basement. This was as much a library as a bookshop and there was certainly no obligation to buy. Fanon fitted easily into the revolutionary pantheon of the day, along with Ho Chi Minh, Che Guevara, Amilcar Cabral, Samora Machel and the Mao of the Cultural Revolution. There was also a close perceived association between Fanon and the Black Power movement in the United States. Every brother on a rooftop who was taking care of business with a gun could, so it was said, quote Fanon. A lot of white students thought they wanted to be on the rooftops too. And so, we read Fanon. It was his anger that was so attractive.

I read a lot during that year in Paris. It was the beginning of the moment of theory, a time to read Althusser, Lacan and Foucault. Fanon began to look naive. His analyses were wrong so often, disastrously so when it came to Angola. It was obvious to any Marxist, to any Althusserian, that the peasantry could not lead a revolution, that the lumpenproletariat could not play a progressive role. Just look at Marx and Lenin. Just look at the state of Algeria. Fanon had feared that the national bourgeoisie would confiscate the revolution. But it was confiscated by the FLN and by the army that stood behind it in the shadows.

In October 1988, Algeria began to implode. Strikes and riots broke out as discontent with the FLN, corruption and the stagnation of what should have been an oil-rich economy turned to violent protest. Violence was met with violence and perhaps some 500 people died on the streets of Algiers when the army was sent in. According to some accounts, their deaths were a factor that contributed to the suicide of Fanon's widow. In February 1989, a multi-party system was introduced after a referendum. One of the new parties to emerge was the fundamentalist Islamic Salvation Front (FIS). Victorious in the local elections of June, it seemed poised to win the legislative elections of December. Within a month, the president had been deposed and the elections had been cancelled. The FIS turned to armed struggle. Policemen began to be assassinated and a civil war was soon underway. Over the next ten years up to one hundred thousand people would be killed. No one knows the exact figure.

The foreigners were ordered to get out of Algeria by the fundamentalists. Some were killed. The writers, the musicians and the intellectuals began to be murdered. The novelist Tahar Djaout spoke out: 'Silence is death, and if you say nothing you die, and if you speak you die, so speak and die.' He died at the hands of two gunmen. In a sense, Djaout spoke on behalf of – and died for – Fanon's wretched of the earth, on behalf of the thousands who were dying cruel and anonymous deaths. Other writers also spoke on their behalf. They have produced a literature of defiance and of terrible beauty. It is a good time to reread Fanon. Not to hear once more the call for violent revolution, but to recapture the quality of the anger that inspired it. Fanon does not speak for the tragic Algeria of today. The themes of Third World solidarity and unity, of a version of Pan-Africanism and of the liberating power of violence have not worn well. For a generation, Fanon was a prophet. He has become a witness to the process of decolonization but, whilst his discussion of racism remains valid, he has little to say about the outcome of that process.

Fanon was angry. His readers should still be angry too. Angry that Algerian immigrants could be treated with such contempt in a police station. Angry at the casual racism that still assumes that the black and North African youths of the suburbs are all criminals or at least potential criminals (which is not to say that they are all angels, merely that the repeated experience of poverty and exclusion does not make for good citizens). Angry at the cultural alienation that still afflicts the children of Martinique, so beautiful in their smart school uniforms and so convinced that they are just like other French children until someone teaches them otherwise. Angry at what has happened in Algeria. Angry that the wretched of the earth are still with us. Anger does not in itself produce political programmes for change, but it is perhaps the most basic political emotion. Without it, there is no hope.

To read or study the history of the Algerian war is to sup on horrors. To do so against the backdrop of contemporary Algeria was worse. I have read so many horror stories about contemporary Algeria, and I have been told many others. The Algeria with which Fanon identified so strongly had become a country in which police interrogators used blow torches in cellars and in which mass murder was committed in the name of a perversion of Islam. Several of my informants were forced to leave the Algeria where they had lived since independence in 1962, and where some had been born. Some simply left as the tide of intolerance and xenophobia began to rise faster and faster. Others had narrower escapes. One morning, a doctor was informed by the police that his name figured on a death list of several doctors who were to be killed by a group of self-styled Islamic fundamentalists. He was immediately put on a plane for Paris. The other doctors were killed. The list itself had been drawn up by one of the doctor's own students. I was told the story of what happened in a school in the Algerian countryside. A group of armed men burst into a classroom and cut the throat of the teacher. They then severed her head and left it on her desk. This occurred in front of a class of primary schoolchildren. I will never know the name of that teacher but I cannot – will not – forget the story of her death. Some things must not be forgotten. And whatever else happens in and to Algeria, it will take years for the trauma inflicted on those children to heal.

The violence in Algeria had its effects in France. Schoolgirls who wore 'Islamic headscarves' to school in defiance of the secularism of the French educational system were portrayed in the press as members of a fundamentalist fifth column, or even as potential Algerian terrorists. They proved to be Turkish. In the summer and autumn of 1995, bombs went off in Paris, with the shadowy Armed Islamic Groups claiming responsibility. Tension was high. From the window of a hotel room, I could watch the police stopping every car driven by anyone who looked even vaguely 'Algerian'. No doubt those stopped were addressed as *tu*. No doubt a few Martinicans were stopped too, only to be let go with the gruff apology: 'Sorry, thought you were Algerian . . .' It happened to Fanon too.

I half expected some hostility or at least suspicion from those I approached for information about Fanon. White liberals and white left-ists are, for understandable reasons, not welcome in all quarters. The Algerian war is still a delicate and difficult issue in France. I could, to some extent, empathize with the forlorn Algerians in the Préfecture, but no child has ever stared at me in a park and said 'Look a nigger. Mummy, I'm frightened.' I need not have worried. One or two people – white, as it happens – expressed amused surprise when they opened their doors and found that Fanon's would-be biographer was a white redhead. Most were only too delighted to find that *someone* was interested in Fanon, who is not now widely read in France. My most emotionally charged memory is that of a conversation with an elderly Martinican who played football with Fanon as a child and fought alongside him in the Second World War. He gently brushed his black fingers across my white wrist, looked at me and said 'Fanon . . . race . . . racism: it's nothing to do with *that*.'

Fanon has often been described as preaching a gospel of hate and violence. He certainly had a talent for hate and he did advocate and justify a violence that I can no longer justify. And yet, his first readers sensed in his work a great generosity. The combination of anger and generosity of spirit is his true legacy. In the introduction to his first book, Fanon writes that 'man is a *yes*'. The 'universal-inclusive' *man* grates, but it is rather pointless to reproach Fanon for not sharing the political sensibilities of a new millennium. In the final chapter he picks up the same argument: 'Yes to life. Yes to love. Yes to generosity. But man is also a *no*. No to scorn for man. No to the indignity of man. No to the exploitation of man. To the murder of what is most human about men: freedom.' *Fanon, pas mort.*

# Notes

## 1 Forgetting Fanon, Remembering Fanon

1  Guy Sitbon, 'Les officiers de l'ALN ne cherchent pas à prendre le pouvoir, mais à le constituter étroitement au nom du peuple', *Le Monde*, 3 May 1962, p. 2.

2  Jean-François Khan, 'Les Conjurés voulaient défiler jeudi à Alger', *Paris-presse*, 3 July 1962, pp. 1, 2.

3  Ferhat Abbas, *L'Indépendance confisquée,* Paris: Flammarion, 1984, p. 59.

4  'Frantz Fanon, notre frère', *El Moudjahid,* 21 December 1961.

5  'Un Example toujours vivant', ibid., pp. 648–9.

6  'Sa Dernière Victoire' in *Pour Fanon: Rencontre Internationale d'Alger, Centre des Arts Riahd El Feth, 10 au 15 décembre 1982,* p. 31.

7  François Maspero, 'Pour étouffer un homme libre', *Tribune socialiste,* 16 December 1961.

8  'Lettre de Ain-Kerma', *El Moudjahid,* 11–12 December 1987, p. 24.

9  Josie Fanon's suicide is movingly described by her friend Assia Djebar in her *Le Blanc de l'Algérie,* Paris: Albin Michel, 1995, pp. 210–11. Djebar recalls (ibid., pp. 106–7) talking to Josie Fanon in October 1988, when demonstrations in Algiers were ferociously put down by the army. From the balcony of her flat in the El Biar district, Josie Fanon watched the youths of Algiers setting police vehicles on fire, and the troops opening fire on them.

Speaking on the telephone to Djebar, she sighed: 'Oh Frantz, the wretched of the earth again.'

10  Frantz Fanon, *Peau noire, masques blancs*, Paris, Seuil, collection 'Points', 1975, p. 188. The epitaph is in fact an abridgement of the original text, which reads: 'My final prayer: oh my body, make me always a man who asks questions.'

11  François Bondy, 'The Black Rousseau', *New York Review of Books*, 31 March 1966.

12  *Témoignage chrétien*, 17 December 1964; *Alger-républicain*, 10 February 1964.

13  Gilles Manceron and Hassan Remanoun, *D'une Rive à l'autre: la guerre d'Algérie de la mémoire à l'histoire*, Paris: Syros, 1993, p. 227.

14  'Reconnaissance de Frantz Fanon', *Partisans* 23, June–July 1965, pp. 90–1.

15  'Relire Fanon', *Algérie-actualité*, 30 September 1982. The papers presented at the conference held to remedy this ignorance are published in *Kalim* 4, 1982.

16  F. Kader, 'Le Visionnaire d'un monde nouveau', *El Moudjahid*, 14 October 1982.

17  Interview with Fanny Colonna.

18  See in particular Mohammed Harbi, *Le FLN: Mirage et réalité. Des Origines à la prise du pouvoir*, Algiers: NAQD/ENAL1993 (revised edn); Khalfa Mameri, *Abane Ramdane, héros de la guerre d'Algérie*, Paris: L'Harmattan, 1988.

19  Malek Bennabi, *Perspectives algériennes* (1964), cited Monique Gadant, *Parcours d'une intellectuelle en Algérie: Nationalisme et anticolonialisme dans les sciences sociales*, Paris: L'Harmattan, 1995, p. 45.

20  'Frantz Fanon et la Révolution algérienne', *El Moudjahid*, 20 March 1971; Mohammed Amghar, '"*El Thaqafa,*, Fanon et la pensée occidentale" de Mohammed El Milli,' *El Moudjahid*, 2 June 1971, p. 5. El Milli's original articles appeared in Arabic in *Al Thaqafa* in March and May 1971.

21  Lewis R. Gordon, *Fanon and the Crisis of European Man: An Essay on Philosophy and the Human Sciences*, New York and London: Routledge, 1995, p. 1.

22  Lewis R. Gordon, T. Denean Sharpley-Whiting and Renée T. White, 'Introduction: Five Stages of Fanon Studies', in *Fanon: A Critical Reader*, Oxford: Blackwell, 1996, p. 3.

23  See, *inter alia*, Serge Bromberger, *Les Rebelles algériens*, Paris: Plon, 1958; Jacques C. Duchemin, *Histoire du FLN*, Paris: La Table Ronde, 1962; Francis Jeanson, *La Révolution algérienne*, Milan: Feltrinelli, 1962; Mostefa Lacheraf, *L'Algérie: nation et société*, Paris: Maspero, 1969; William B. Quandt, *Revolution and*

*Political Leadership in Algeria 1954–1968*, Cambridge MA and London: MIT Press 1969; Henry F. Jackson, *The FLN in Algeria: Party Development in a Revolutionary Society*: Westport, Conn: Greenwood Press, 1977; Henri Alleg (ed.), *La Guerre d'Algérie*, Paris: Temps actuels, 1981, three vols; Alistair Horne: *A Savage War of Peace: Algeria 1954–1962*; London: Papermac, 1987 (revised edn); Rachid Tlemcani, *State and Revolution in Algeria*; Boulder, Col. and London: Westview Press and Zed Books, 1986; Yves Courrière, *La Guerre d'Algérie*, Paris: Robert Laffont, Collection "Bouquins", 1991, two vols.; Bernard Droz and Evelyne Lever, *Histoire de la guerre d'Algérie 1954–1962*, Paris: Seuil, Collection "Points", 1991 (revised edn); Mohammed Harbi, *Le FLN: Mirage et réalité*; Benjamin Stora, *Histoire de la guerre d'Algérie (1954–62)*, Paris: La Découverte, 1993.

24  Ferhat Abbas, *Autopsie d'une guerre: l'aurore*, Paris: Garnier, 1980, pp. 316–17.

25  Interview with Charles Geronimi.

26  Garcia Malsa, 'La Chose la plus essentielle', *Antilla* 23, November–December 1991, p. 35.

27  Aimé Césaire, *Cahier d'un retour au pays natal*, in *La Poésie*, Paris: Seuil, 1994, p. 11. On Schoelcher, see Nelly Schmidt, *Victor Schoelcher et l'abolition de l'esclavage*, Paris: Fayard, 1994.

28  Fanon, *Peau noire*, p. 178.

29  Mayotte Capécia, *Je suis Martiniquaise*, Paris: Éditions Corréa, 1948, p. 113.

30  Césaire, *Cahier*, ibid.

31  *Marron* and the English 'maroon' derive from the Spanish *cimarrón*, originally used to describe imported domestic animals from Europe that had escaped and gone wild. See Eric Hobsbawm, 'Postmodernism in the Forest', in *On History*, London: Weidenfeld and Nicolson, 1997, p. 192.

32  See Armand Nicolas, 'La Révolution anti-esclavagiste de mai 1848 à la Martinique', supplement to *Action* 13, May 1967.

33  *Peau noire*, pp. 178–9.

34  Robert Aldrich and John Connell, *France's Overseas Frontier: Départements et Territoires D'Outre-Mer*, Cambridge: Cambridge University Press, 1992, p. 218; Richard D. E. Burton, 'Towards 1992: Political-Cultural Assimilation and Opposition in Contemporary Martinique', *French Cultural Studies* 3, 1992, p. 74.

35  *Le Monde*, 3 June 1997.

36  Annick Cojean, 'Alfred Marie-Jeanne, habile et étrange "nègre marron" de la Martinique', *Le Monde*, 5–6 April 1998.

37  See Eric Conan, 'Martinique, ce département dont le patron est indépendantiste', *L'Express* 4 March 1999, pp. 47–53.

38   Alain-Philippe Blérald, *La Question nationale en Guadeloupe et en Martinique: essai sur l'histoire politique*, Paris: L'Harmattan, 1988, p. 177.

39   *Peau noire, masques blancs*, pp. 183, 187.

40   The OJAM manifesto is reprinted in full in Raphaël Confiant, *Aimé Césaire: une traversée paradoxale du siècle*, Paris: Stock, 1993, pp. 313–16.

41   Ibid., pp. 199-203.

42   Interview with Marcel Manville. The proceedings are published as *Mémorial international Frantz Fanon, 31 mars–3 avril 1982, Fort-de-France*, Paris and Dakar: Présence africaine, 1984.

43   Philippe Leyarie, 'Martinique: le fantôme de Frantz Fanon', *Le Matin de Paris*, 6 April 1982.

44   André Mandouze, 'Le Retour de Frantz Fanon', *Le Monde*, 7 April 1982, p. 8.

45   Blérald, *La Question nationale*, p. 143.

46   René Pierre, 'Martinique: Mémorial pour les damnés des DOM', *Libération*, 9 April 1982, pp. 14–16.

47   Marius Larcher, 'Le Livre de Frantz Fanon', *L'Information*, 22 May 1962.

48   France-Line Fanon, 'La Congruence', *Antilla*, 23, November–December 1991, p. 28.

49   Olivier Fanon, interviewed by F. Benadadji, *Algérie-actualité*, 24–30 December 1987, p. 35; interview with Olivier Fanon.

50   Peter Geismar, *Fanon*, New York: The Dial Press, 1971, p. 9.

51   Edouard Glissant, *Le Discours antillais*, Paris: Seuil, 1981, p. 36.

52   Conversation with Assia Djebar.

53   Interview with Patrick Chamoiseau. Cf. the comments made in his *Ecrire en pays dominé*, Paris: Gallimard, 1987. Chamoiseau's novel *L'Esclave vieil homme et le molosse*, Paris: Gallimard, 1987, is a powerful invocation of slavery and *marronage*.

54   Interview with Robert Berthellier; cf. his *L'Homme maghrébin dans la littérature psychiatrique*, Paris: L'Harmattan, 1994.

55   Interview with Jacques Postel; Jacques Postel, 'Frantz Fanon à cinquante ans', *L'Information psychiatique*, vol. LI, no. 10, December 1975, pp. 1049–50. This issue of *L'Information* reprints substantial extracts from Fanon's thesis and two of his major papers. Postel's article, co-authored with C. Razanajao, on 'La Vie et l'oeuvre psychiatrique de Frantz Fanon' is a good introduction to his clinical work.

56   Michel-Ange Burnier, 'Frantz Fanon, le colonisé', *Magazine littéraire*, January 1970, p. 39.

57   See *Libération*, 10 June 1999.

58   The expression a 'war without a name' appears to have been first used in the title of John Talbott's *The War Without a Name:*

*France in Algeria 1954-1962*, London: Faber and Faber 1981. The French phrase '*la guerre sans nom*' was popularized when it was used as the title for a documentary film about the experience of French conscripts made for GMT/Canal Plus by Patrick Rotman and Bernard Tavernier in 1990; the script is published as *La Guerre sans nom: les appelés d'Algérie 54–62*, Paris: Seuil, 1992. As the bibliography appended to Benjamin Stora's *Appelés en Algérie*, Paris: Gallimard, 1997, demonstrates, there is now an immense corpus of memoirs, diaries, novels and films about the conscripts' war. Accounts from the other side of the Mediterranean are much less common. For the French literary and cinematic image of the war, see Philip Dine, *Images of the Algerian War: French Film and Fiction 1954–1962*, Oxford: Clarendon Press, 1994.

59    This partial amnesia and this uneasy memory are by no means uniquely French phenomena. British readers would do well to ask themselves what they remember of the Malayan Emergency, Kenya or Cyprus. On the *harkis*, see Michel Roux, *Les Harkis, ou les oubliés de l'histoire*, Paris: Maspero, 1991; Mohand Hammoumon, 'Les Harkis, un trou de mémoire franco-algérien', *Esprit*, May 1990, and Martin Bright, 'The Outsiders', *Observer Magazine*, 31 October 1999, pp. 26–32; on the *pieds noirs*, see Jean-Jacques Jordi, *1962: l'Arrivée des pieds-noirs*, Paris: Autrement, 1995; on the events of October 1961, see Jean-Luc Einaudi, *La Bataille de Paris: 17 octobre 1961*, Paris: Seuil, 1991 and Anne Tristan, *Le Silence du fleuve: octobre 1961*, Bezons: Editions au nom de la mémoire, 1991.

60    *Le Monde*, 28 October 1996.

61    Claude Liauzu, 'Prétoires, mémoire, histoire: la guerre d'Algérie a eu lieu', *Les Temps modernes* 606, November–December 1999, p. 113.

62    *Le Monde*, 26 July 1959.

63    *Le Monde*, 4 June 1970, 6 June 1970.

64    Frantz Fanon, *Les Damnés de la terre*, Paris: Maspero, 1961, p. 141.

65    Aimé Césaire, 'La Révolte de Frantz Fanon', *Jeune Afrique*, 13–19 December 1961, p. 24.

66    Frantz Fanon, *Pour la Révolution africaine*, Paris: Maspero, 1964. References given here are to the 'Petite Collection Maspero' edition published in 1969.

67    Eqbal Ahmad, letter to *Times Literary Supplement*, 2 April 1993. Gellner's comments are made in his review of Edward Said's *Culture and Imperialism, Times Literary Supplement*, 19 February 1993. Born in 1933, Ahmad died in 1999; see the obituary by Said, *Guardian*, 14 May 1999.

68    Claude Liauzu, 'Intellectuels du Tiers Monde et intellectuels

français: les années algériennes des Editions Maspero', in J.-P. Rioux and J.-F. Sirinelli (eds), *La Guerre d'Algérie et les intellectuels français*', Brussels: Editions Complexe, 1991, p. 173.

69  *Publisher's Weekly*, 12 April 1965; William V. Shannon, 'Violence vs the American Dream', *New York Times*, 27 July 1967. Fanon's final book was translated by Constance Farrington as *The Wretched of the Earth*, New York: Grove Press, 1965.

70  Jean-Paul Sartre, Preface to *Les Damnés de la terre*, p. 10. Reprinted in *Situations V; Colonialisme et néo-colonialisme*, Paris: Gallimard, 1964.

71  For Maschino's story, see his *Le Refus*, Paris: Maspero, 1960. His *L'Engagement*, Paris: Maspero, 1961 is one of the best contemporary accounts of the motives of those who either deserted or refused to fight in Algeria.

72  Maurice Maschino, 'Présence de Frantz Fanon', *Le Petit Matin*, 12 December 1961, p. 1.

73  'Etude biologique du citrate de lithium dans les accés maniaques' (1955–7), unpublished paper written in collaboration with J. Sourdine; collection of Jacques Postel.

74  Paul Nizan, *Aden-Arabie*, Paris: Petite Collection Maspero, 1971, p. 55.

75  See my 'Paul Nizan: A Posthumous Life', *Studi Francesi* Anno XXX, fascicolo 1, January–April 1986.

76  Paul Nizan, *Les Chiens de garde*, Paris: Petite Collection Maspero, 1969,. p. 123.

77  Sartre, preface to *Aden-Arabie*, pp. 15, 51.

78  'Maurienne' (i.e. Jean-Louis Hurst), preface to *Le Déserteur*, Levallois-Peret: Editions Manya, 1991, p. 11. First published by Editions de Minuit in 1960, and promptly banned, *Le Déserteur*, together with Maschino's writings, is one of the best accounts of French opposition to the Algerian war.

79  I discuss the Fanon-Nizan composite in more detail in my '*Insoumis*: Nizan, Sartre, Fanon', in James Dolamore (ed.), *Making Connections: Essays in French Culture and Society in Honour of Philip Thody*, Bern: Peter Lang, 1999.

80  François Maspero, 'Quelqu'un "de la famille"', *Les Temps modernes* 531–3, October–December 1990, vol. 2, pp. 123, 1016.

81  Hervé Hamon and Patrick Rotman, *Génération I: Les Années de rêve*, Paris: Seuil, 1987, p. 218.

82  Juliette Minces, *L'Algérie de la révolution (1963–1964)*, Paris: L'Harmattan, 1988, p. 13. See also Monique Gadant, *Parcours d'une intellectuelle en Algérie: nationalisme at anti-colonialisme dans les sciences sociales*, Paris: L'Harmattan, 1995.

83  T. M. Maschino and Fadela M'Rabet, *L'Algérie des illusions: la révolution confisquée*, Paris: Robert Laffont, 1972.

84   Fadéla M'Rabet, *La Femme algérienne, suivi de Les Algériennes*, Paris: Maspero, 1979.

85   See Robert Malley, *The Call from Algeria: Third Worldism, Revolution and the Turn to Islam*, Berkeley, Los Angeles and London: University of California Press, 1996.

86   Pascal Bruckner, *Le Sanglot de l'homme blanc: Tiers-monde, culpabilité, haine de soi*, Paris, Seuil, 1983, p. 224.

87   André Glucksmann, 'Un Terrorisme du troisième type', *Libération*, 30 May–1 June 1982, p. 19.

88   Allan Bloom, 'Western Civ' in *Giants and Dwarves: Essays 1960–1990*, New York: Simon and Schuster, 1990, p. 31.

89   Jacques Marseille, 'Assez de clichés sur l'Afrique', *L'Evénement du jeudi*, 12–18 July 1990, pp. 32–3.

90   Gilbert Comte, 'Quand Sartre préface le livre d'un ennemi', *Le XXe siècle*, 23 March 1962; 'Un *Mein Kampf* de la décolonisation', *La Nation française*, 21 March 1962. Cf. the unsigned review that appeared in *Paris-Presse*, 9 December 1961: 'This indictment has to be read, painful as it may be. It is as profitable and interesting to read *Les Damnés de la terre* as it was to read *Mein Kampf.* Frantz Fanon's book does not merely shed light on the present; it also sheds light on the future to the extent that it gives expression to one of the temptations facing colonized Africa: the temptation to turn its back on the West and its values.'

91   Alain Finkielkraut, *La Défaite de la pensée*, Paris: Folio, 1989, pp. 98–9

92   Michel Wievorka, *La France raciste*, Paris: Seuil, collection 'Points', 1992, p. 331. This part of the large study of French racism undertaken by the Centre d'Analyse et d'Intervention Sociologiques was carried out by Angelina Peralva. She describes her experience in an interview with Stella Hughes published as 'Hate Couture', *Times Higher Education Supplement*, 2 June 1995, p. 17.

93   Benjamin Stora, *L'Algérie en 1995: La Guerre, l'histoire, la politique*, Paris: Editions Michalon, pp. 45–6, citing the editorial to *El-Mounquid* 4, April 1994.

94   Hannah Arendt, *On Violence*, New York, Harcourt, Brace and Company, 1970.

95   'A Frantz Fanon', *Partisans* 3, February 1962, p. 2.

96   Grove Press publicity material, Dossier *Partisans*/Editions Maspero, IMEC, Paris.

97   C.B. '"Wretched of the Earth" Take Over in Two Books', *Durham Morning Herald*, 27 February 1966. Cf. Donald Mintz, 'Find Something Different', *Washington Evening Star*, 23 April 1965; Perry London, 'Multi-faceted Treatise on Colonial Revolution', *Los Angeles Times*, 23 May 1965; anon. 'Speaking for

Africa's Masses', *Houston Chronicle*, 2 May 1965; Alfred L, Malabre Jr., 'A Disturbing Diatribe from the Third World', *Wall Street Journal*, 23 July 1965.

98  Nat Hentoff, 'Bursting into History', *The New Yorker* 15 January 1966, p. 115.

99  William V. Shannon, 'Negro Violence vs. the American Dream', *New York Times*, 27 July 1967.

100  Lawrence Lipton, 'Radio Free America', *LA Free Press*, 18 August 1967.

101  Stokely Carmichael, 'Black Power' in David Cooper (ed.), *The Dialectics of Liberation*, Harmondsworth: Penguin, 1968, p. 150. Cf. Stokely Carmichael and Charles V. Hamilton, *Black Power*, Harmondsworth: Penguin, 1969.

102  On the 'black power' readings of Fanon, see Geneviève Fabre and Namman Kousouss, 'Frantz Fanon et la révolte noire', *Le Monde diplomatique*, December 1971.

103  Yovery T. Mosevini, 'Fanon's Theory of Violence: Its Verification in Liberated Mozambique' in N.M. Shamuyanra (ed.), *Essays on the Liberation of Southern Africa*, Dar es Salaam: Tanzania Publishing house, 1975, pp. 1–24.

104  Edouard Saab, 'L'Omniprésence en Jordanie des organisations palestiniennes', *Le Monde*, 7 December 1968.

105  Ronald Segal, *The Black Diaspora*, London: Faber and Faber, 1995, p. 240.

106  Pierre Vallières, *Nègres blancs d'Amérique*, Montréal: Typo, 1994, p. 341 (first edn, 1968).

107  Gérald Godin, 'La Folie bilingue', *Parti-pris*, May 1966, pp. 56–8.

108  Frantz Fanon, *L'An V de la Rèvolution Algérienne*, Paris: Maspero, 1959, p. 76.

109  Peire Causset, 'Frantz Fanon, théoricien de la décolonisation', supplement to *La Lùgar* no. 6, June 1972; 'Libérer les régions', *Enbata*, 19 February 1970.

110  Yann-Cheun Veillard, '*Les Damnés de la terre*', *Ar Vro*, April 1963; *Peau noire, masques blancs*, p. 22.

111  Peter Worsely, 'A Voice from the Third World', *Peace News*, 18 October 1963, p.7.

112  Evelyne Pisier, 'Frantz Fanon, 1925–1961: *Les Damnés de la terre*, 1961' in F. Châtelet, O. Duhamel and E. Pisier (eds), *Dictionnaire des oeuvres politiques*, Paris: PUF, 1986, p. 277.

113  See Lewis R. Gordon, *Fanon and the Crisis of European Man*, New York and London: Routledge, 1995; Lewis R. Gordon, T. Denean Sharpley-Whiting and Renée T. White (eds), *Fanon: A Critical Reader*, Oxford: Blackwell, 1996; Ato Sekyi-Otu, *Fanon's Dialectic of Existence*, Cambridge MA and London: Harvard University Press, 1996; Deborah Wyricck, *Fanon For Beginners*,

New York and London: Readers and Writers, 1998; Anthony C. Alessandrini (ed), *Frantz Fanon: Critical Perspectives*, London and New York: Routledge, 1999.

114 Bill Ashcroft, Gareth Griffiths and Helen Tiffin, *The Empire Writes Back: Theory and Practice in Post-Colonial Literatures*, London and New York: Routledge, 1989, p. 2. The key anthologies are Ashcroft, Griffiths and Tiffin's *Post-colonial Studies Reader*, London: Routledge, 1995 and P. Williams and L. Chrisman (eds), *Colonial Discourse and Post-Colonial Theory*, New York: Columbia University Press, 1994. For a good critical overview, see Bart Moore-Gilbert, *Post-colonial Theory: Contexts, Practices, Politics*, London: Verso, 1997.

115 *Mirage; Enigmas of Race, Difference and Desire*, London: Institute of Contemporary Arts and Institute of International Visual Arts, 1995; Alan Read (ed.), *The Fact of Blackness: Frantz Fanon and Visual Representation*, London and Seattle: Institute of Contemporary Arts and Institute of International Visual Arts, and Bay Press, 1995.

116 Edward W. Said, *Culture and Imperialism*, London: Chatto & Windus, 1993, pp. 286–7.

117 Homi K. Bhabha, 'Interrogating Identity: Frantz Fanon and the Post-Colonial Prerogative' in *The Location of Culture*, London: Routledge, 1994, p. 41. The reference is to Benjamin's 'Theses on the Philosophy of History'. This argument was originally put forward in 'Foreword: Remembering Fanon: Self, Psyche and the Colonial Condition' in Fanon, *Black Skin, White Masks*, London: Pluto, 1986. Cf. the same author's 'What Does the Black Man Want?', *New Formations* 1, Spring 1987.

118 Ibid., p. 42.

119 Gordon, Sharpley-Whiting and White, p. 2.

120 *Peau noire, masques blancs*, p. 11.

121 Isaac Julien's *Frantz Fanon: Black Skin, White Mask* was first shown on BBC in 1995; a slightly longer version was released for cinematic distribution in 1997. The script is published in French as *Frantz Fanon, scénario du film de Isaac Julien*, Paris: Editions film k, 1998.

122 Cf. Henry Louis Gates. Jr., 'Critical Fanonism', *Critical Inquiry* 17, Spring 1991, pp. 457–70.

123 Françoise Vergès, 'Chains of Madness, Chains of Colonialism: Fanon and Freedom' in Read (ed.) *The Fact of Blackness*; 'To Cure and to Free: The Fanonian Project of Decolonized Psychiatry' in Gordon, Sharpley-Whiting and White, *Fanon: A Critical Reader*.

124 Gordon et al, *Fanon: A Critical Reader*, p. 5.

125 Mohammed Lebjouai, cited Jean Ziegler, 'Frantz Fanon', *Le*

*Nouvel Observateur*, 18 January 1971. This is a review of the French translation of Renate Zahar's *Kolonialismus und Entfremdung*, Frankfurt am Main: Europuäische Verlagsanstalt, 1970 (translated into English by W. F. Freuser as *Frantz Fanon: Colonialism and Alienation, Concerning Frantz Fanon's Political Theory*, New York: Monthly Review Press, 1974) and David Caute, *Fanon*, London: Fontana/Collins, 1970.

126 Gates, 'Critical Fanonism', p. 458n.

127 Peter Geismar, *Frantz Fanon*, New York: Dial Press, 1971. Geismar's biography is an attractive and engaging book, and it is by no means an inaccurate account of Fanon's life, but it is quite uncritical. It is also very difficult to use in that, in a bizarre attempt to avoid his own words being confused with those of his informants, the author gives no sources for his information and very few references.

128 *Black Skin, White Masks*, pp. 34, 112; cf. *Peau noire*, pp. 27, 90.

129 *Black Skin*, p. 200; *Peau noire*, p. 162.

130 Léopold Sédar Senghor, 'Poème liminaire', in *Hosties Noires, Oeuvre poétique*, Paris: Seuil 1990, p. 55. On the history and advertising of Banania, see Jan Nederveen Pieterse, *White on Black: Images of Africa and Blacks in Western Popular Culture*, New Haven and London: Yale University Press, 1995, pp. 159–63. Banania is still on sale in France, but its racist advertising material has been greatly toned down. Postcards of the original 'tirailleur' poster are sold in novelty card shops and afficionados of racist kitsch can buy expensive porcelain breakfast sets that reproduce it on a bright yellow ground.

131 *Peau noire*, p. 89.

132 Gordon, *Fanon and the Crisis*, p. 98.

133 *Black Skin*, p. 25; *Peau noire*, p. 15.

134 *Peau noire, p.* 73.

135 Ibid., p. 10; ibid., p. 9.

## 2 Native Son

1 Edouard Glissant, *Le Discours antillais*, Paris: Seuil, 1981, p. 11. Although Glissant is increasingly recognized as one of the major figures in Caribbean literature, relatively little of his extensive output has been translated into English. His novel *La Lézarde* (1958) has been translated by J. Michael Dash as *The Ripening*, London: Heinemann, 1985, and his play *Monsieur Toussaint* (1961) by Joseph Foster and Barbara Franklin as *Monsieur Toussaint*, Washington: Three Continents Press, 1981. A bilingual edition of his 1956 collection of poems, *Les Iles*, trans. Dominique O'Neill, is published by Gref,

Toronto, 1992. *Caribbean Discourse*, trans. J. Michael Dash, Charlottesville: University of Virginia Press, 1989, is an abridged version of *Le Discours antillais*. See also *Poetics of Relation*, trans. Betsy Wing, Ann Arbor: University of Michigan Press, 1998. The only full-length studies in English are J. Michael Dash, *Edouard Glissant*, Cambridge: Cambridge University Press, 1995, and Celia Britton's *Eduoard Glissant and Post Colonial Theory*, Charlottesville: University Press of Virginia, 1999.

2   One such map is reproduced in Mireille Rosello's valuable introduction to Aimé Césaire, *Notebook of a Return to My Native Land*, trans. Mireille Rosello with Annie Pritchard, Newcastle-Upon-Tyne: Bloodaxe Books, 1995, p. 14.

3   Michel Giraud, *Races et classes à la Martinique: les relations sociales entre enfants de différentes couleurs à l'école*, Paris: Editions Anthropos, 1979, pp. 242, 226.

4   Henri Charrière, *Papillon*, trans. Patrick O. Brian: London: Rupert Hart-Davis, 1970.

5   See Aldrich and Connelle, *France's Overseas Frontier*; Jean-Luc Mathieu, *Histoire des DOM-TOM*, Paris: Presses Universitaires de France, Collection 'Que sais-je?', 1993.

6   Irmine Romanette, *Sonson de la Martinique*, Paris: Société française d'éditions littéraires et techniques, 1932, p. 7.

7   Lilien Legone, 'Naissance de la France au grand large', *Le Monde*, 17–18 March 1996, p. 10.

8   See, for example, Robert Deville and Nicolas Georges, *Les Départements d'outre-mer: l'autre décolonisation*, Paris: Gallimard, Collection Découvertes, 1996.

9   Patrick Chamoiseau, *Texaco*, trans. Rose-Myriam Réjouis and Val Vinokurv, London: Granta Books, 1997.

10  See, for example, Juliette Minces, *La Génération suivante*, La Tour d'Aigue: L'Aube, 1997.

11  Maurice Lemoine, *Le Mal antillais: leurs ancêtres les Gaulois*, Paris: L'Harmattan, 1982, p. 57.

12  *Peau noire*, p. 73.

13  Simone de Beauvoir, *La Force des choses*, Paris: Livre de poche, 1971, vol II, p. 426.

14  Giraud, *Race et classes à la Martinique*, p. 276. In his delightful memoir about his schooling in Martinique, Patrick Chamoiseau (born in 1953) also describes learning to reel off the seasons: 'summer, fall, winter, spring' and of being shown 'strange images of snow', *School Days*, trans. Linda Coverdale, London: Granta Books, 1998, pp. 30, 26.

15  *Peau noire, masques blancs*, p. 131n.

16  Conversation with Marie-Hélène Léotin, who teaches history at the Lycée Frantz Fanon in La Trinité.

17    See Jacques Fredj, 'Situation de l'histoire en Martinique', *Les Temps modernes* 359, June 1976.

18    See, for instance, Lilian Chauleau, *Dans les Iles du vent: La Martinique, XVIIe–XIXe siècle*, Paris: L'Harmattan, 1993.

19    *Les Damnés de la terre*, p. 40.

20    Glissant, *Le Discours antillais*, pp. 155–6.

21    Chamoiseau, *Texaco*, pp. 3–6.

22    Raphaël Confiant, *Le Nègre et l'Amiral*, Paris: Livre de poche, 1993; *L'Allée de soupirs*, Paris: Livre de poche, 1996; Vincent Placoly, *L'Eau de mort guildive*, Paris: Denoël, 1973.

23    'Les Sang coule aux Antilles sous domination française', in *Pour la Révolution africaine*, originally in *El Moudjahid*, 58, 5 January 1960.

24    Patrick Chamoiseau and Raphaël Confiant, *Lettres créoles: tracées antillaises et continentales de la littérature 1655–1975*, Paris: Hatier, 1991, p. 17.

25    Marina Warner, *Managing Monsters: Six Myths of Our Time*, London: Vintage, 1994, p. 72.

26    Giraud, *Races et classes à la Martinique*, p. 36; Chalumeau, *Dans les Iles*, p. 73.

27    Robert Louis Stein, *The French Slave Trade in the Eighteenth Century: An Old Regime Business*, Madison: University of Wisconsin Press, 1979, p. 152. For more general accounts of the Atlantic slave trade, see Robin Blackburn, *The Making of New World Slavery: From the Baroque to the Modern 1492–1800*, London: Verso, 1997; Hugh Thomas, *The Slave Trade: The History of the Atlantic Slave Trade 1440–1870*, London: Picador, 1977.

28    Stein, *The French Slave Trade*, p. 71.

29    Edouard Glissant, 'Les Indes', in *Poèmes complètes*, Paris: Gallimard, 1994, p. 145. 'Les Indes' is a long historical poem, using both verse and prose. The introduction to the section on the slave trade begins: 'The slave trade. Something that can never be erased from the face of the sea. The traders in flesh stocked up on the west coast of Africa. For two hundred years, the profitable trade more or less openly supplied the Islands, North America and, on a similar scale, Central and South America. A massacre here (in the African storeroom) to compensate for a massacre over there. The monstrous mobilization, the oblique crossing, the song of Death', ibid., p. 139.

30    *Le Code noir,* with introduction and notes by Robert Chesnais, Paris: L'Esprit frappeur, 1998.

31    See Mark Kurlansky, *Cod: A Biography of the Fish that Changed the World*, London: Jonathan Cape, 1998.

32    Jean-Louis Saux, 'Célébrant l'abolition de l'esclavage, M. Chirac

vante "le modéle français d'intégration",' *Le Monde* 24 April 1998, p. 6.

33  *Peau noires, masques blancs*, p. 186.
34  Françoise Vergès, 'Colonizing Cititizenship', *Radical Philosophy* 95, May–June 1999, p. 6.
35  *Libération*, 25–26 April 1998, p. 15.
36  *Peau noire*, p. 186.
37  Philippe Haudrère and Françoise Vergès, *De L'Esclave au citoyen*, Paris: Gallimard, 1998, p. 142.
38  Cited, Tzvetan Todorov, *On Human Diversity: Nationalism, Racism and Exoticism in French Thought*, trans. Catherine Porter. Cambridge MA and London, Harvard University Press, 1993, p. 193.
39  France's Indian 'concessions' were finally handed back to India in 1954.
40  Edouard Glissant, 'Je crois à l'avenir des cultures métisées', *France-Observateur*, 4 December 1958, p. 17.
41  Eugène Revert, *Les Antilles*, Paris: Armand Colin, 1954, p. 176.
42  Interview with Joby Fanon.
43  Victor Curidon, *Mon pays, mon pays: Martinique! Martinique!*, Paris: Editions de Paris, 1937, p. 38.
44  André Breton, 'Eaux troubles' in *Martinique charmeuse de serpents*, Paris: Jean-Jacques Pauvert, 1972, pp. 78–9.
45  Michel Leiris, 'Martinique, Guadeloupe, Haiti', *Les Temps modernes* 52, February 1950, p. 1349.
46  Michel Leiris, *Contacts de civilisations en Martinique et en Guadeloupe*, Paris: Gallimard, 1987, pp. 39, 61 (original edition: UNESCO, 1955).
47  Jean-Claude Guillebaud, *Les Confettis de l'empire*, Paris: Seuil, 1976, p. 235.
48  Victor Sablé, *Mémoires d'un Foyalais: des îles d'Amérique aux bords de la Seine*, Paris; Maisonneuve et Larose, 1993, p. 33.
49  *Peau noire*, p. 37n.
50  Marie-Reine de Jaham, *Le Maître-Savane*, Paris: Pocket, 1995, p. 227.
51  *Les Damnés de la terre*, p. 40.
52  The 'short creole lexicon' appended to Raphaël Confiant's *Ravines du devant-jour*, Paris: Folio, 1995, p. 253, describes the *béké* thus: 'When he landed from Normandy, Poitou or Brittany, he exterminated the native Caribs with fire and the sword. A younger son with no inheritance or a scoundrel who had been sent to the colonies, he added an aristocratic '*de*' to his name; more often than not it was false.'
53  Nathalie Raulin, 'Il faut aussi payer pour le Crédit Martiniquais', *Libération*, 21 April 1997, p. 27.

54   Blackburn, *The Making of New World Slavery*, p. 22.

55   Giraud, *Races et classes à la Martinique*, p. 89ff.

56   Ibid., p. 174.

57   Annick Cojean, 'L'"Héritage" de l'esclavage aux Antilles', *Le Monde*, 24 April 1998, p. 11; Béatrice Bantman, 'Martinique, terre de castes', *Libération*, 26 April 1998, p. 3.

58   Giraud, *Races et classes*, pp. 172–3.

59   This section draws upon conversations and interviews with Edouard Fanon, Joby Fanon, and Marcel Manville. Unattributed quotations are from Joby Fanon, 'Pour Frantz, pour notre mère', *Sans Frontière*, February 1982, pp. 5–11 and 'Formons un homme neuf', *Antilla* 23, November–December 1991, pp. 22–7.

60   Marcel Manville, *Les Antilles sans fard*, Paris: L'Harmattan, 1992, p. 19.

61   The exception to the rule was the garment trade, which was controlled by the so-called 'Syrians', who actually came from the then French protectorate of Lebanon.

62   Joseph Zobel, *La Rue des cases-nègres*, Paris and Dakar: Présence africaine, 1984, p. 287.

63   Ibid., p. 262.

64   Ibid., p. 278.

65   René Ménil, 'Géneralités sur "l'ecrivain" de couleur antillais', *Légitime Défense* (1932), Paris: Jean-Michel Place, 1979 (facsimile reproduction), p. 7.

66   Giraud, *Races et classes à la Martinique*, p. 36.

67   A. Juvénal Linval, 'Note touchant la bourgeoisie de couleur française', *Légitime Défense*, p. 4.

68   Patrick Leigh Fermor, *The Traveller's Tree: A Journey through the Caribbean Islands*, Harmondsworth: Penguin, 1984 (first edn, 1950).

69   On the development of Fort-de-France see Solange Contour, *Fort-de-France au début du siècle*, Paris: L'Harmattan, 1994.

70   Life in St Pierre before 1902 is described in Michel Tauriac's richly documented historical novel *La Catastrophe*, Paris: La Table Ronde, 1982.

71   Cf. Sablé, *Mémoires d'un Foyalais*, p. 33: 'The *békés* took little part in social life. You would see them at the funerals of notables, when everyone shook hands.'

72   Ibid.

73   See J.-L. Danglades, 'Une Empreinte dans l'urbanisme de Fort-de-France', *Revue Le Rebelle* 3, September 1995, pp. 59–70.

74   Aimé Césaire, 'Cahier d'un retour au pays natal' in *La Poésie*, Paris: Seuil, 1994, p. 10.

75   *Peau noire, masques blancs*, p. 17.

76   Césaire, 'Cahier', pp. 9, 11.

77   Ibid., p. 13.

78   Revert, *Les Antilles*, p. 172.

79   Philippe de Baleine, *Les Danseuses de la France*, Paris: Plon, 1979, p. 25.

80   Maurice-Sabas Quitman, 'Le Paradis sur terre', *Légitime Défense*, Paris: Jean-Michel Place, 1979, p. 6.

81   Curidon, *Mon Pays*, p. 12.

82   Ibid.

83   Martinican punch is made by mixing white rum and sugar syrup; the addition of ice and a slice of lime gives a more sophisticated version. *Blaffe* is a spicy courtbouillon made with either white fish or shellfish.

84   Manville, *Les Antilles*, p. 245.

85   Irene Gendzier, *Frantz Fanon: A Critical Study*, London: Wildwood House, 1973, p. 11.

86   Richard D.E. Burton, *La Famille coloniale: La Martinique et la mère-patrie 1789–1992*, Paris: L'Harmattan, 1994, p. 93 and n.

87   *Peau noire*, p. 19.

88   Over fifty years later, Jamaica Kincaid found it necessary to adopt a very similar strategy in her description of Antigua. It begins: 'If you go to Antigua as a tourist, this is what you will see . . .' and then subverts the picture painted by the travel industry. See her *A Small Place*, London: Virago, 1988.

89   Irmine Romanette, *Sonson de la Martinique*, Paris: Société française d'éditions technique et littéraires, 1932, p. 235. The Cannebière and the place des Qinconces are in Marseille and Bordeaux respectively. The children in question must have been white: a *da* was a black nanny to white children. Marie-Reine de Jahan's novels give a good picture of the importance of the *da* in colonial Martinique.

90   Interview with Félix Fanon, cited in Hussein Abdilahi Bulhan, *Frantz Fanon and the Psychology of Oppression*, New York: Plenum Press, 1985, p. 30.

91   Fermor, *The Traveller's Tree*, p. 70.

92   *Peau noire*, p. 21, citing Michel Leiris, 'Martinique-Guadeloupe-Haiti.'

93   'Aux Antilles, naissance d'une nation?', *El Moudjahid* 16, 15 January 1958, reprinted *Pour la Révolution africaine*, p. 90.

94   *Peau noire*, p. 15.

95   Ibid., p. 12.

96   In the words of Chamoiseau's 'Monsieur le Directeur' (the headmaster): 'What do I hear – you're speaking Creole? And what do I see – shameless monkeyshines? Just where do you think you are? Speak properly and behave in a civilized manner', *Schooldays*, p. 45.

97   In 1998, France signalled that it intended to ratify the European

Charter on Regional Languages. Press coverage of the debate gave figures for the teaching of regional languages at that time. Eighty-five per cent of Corsican children received some teaching in their own language, as did 5 per cent of Breton children and 18 per cent of Basques. No figures at all were given for Creole. See Jean-Louis Andreani and Gaëlle Dupont, 'La France devrait ratifier la Charte européenne des langues régionales en 1999', *Le Monde*, 9 October 1998, p. 11. Parts of Brittany have bilingual French-Breton road signs, even though Breton is spoken only by a small minority; everyone in Martinique can speak Creole, but there are no bilingual road signs.

98　Chamoiseau and Confiant, *Lettres créoles*, p. 71.

99　Leiris, *Contacts de civilisations*, p. 109n.

100　Victor Sablé, *Les Antilles sans complexe: une expérience de décolonisation*, Paris: Maisonneuve et Larose, 1976, p. 16.

101　*Peau noire*, p. 155.

102　Ibid., p. 119.

103　Ibid., p. 120.

104　The original 'Tirailleurs sénégalais' were scouts located locally by Faidherbe during the conquest of Senegal in the 1850s. The term was subsequently applied to the black infantry regiments recruited from all France's colonies in sub-Saharan Africa.

105　*Peau noire*, p. 132n.

106　Ibid., p. 132n.

107　Ibid., p. 155.

108　Ibid., p. 90.

109　Frantz Fanon, 'Antillais et Africains', *Esprit*, February 1955, p. 26.

110　Antoine de Gaudemar, 'D'Ile en exil', *Libération*, 16 October 1997, p. III. Martinicans do tend to speak of 'le béké' in the singular.

111　Glissant, 'Je crois à l'avenir des cultures métisées', *France-Observateur*, 4 December 1958, p. 17.

112　Richard C. Onwuanide, *A Critique of Revolutionary Humanism: Frantz Fanon*, St Louis, Missouri: Warren H. Green Inc. 1983, p. 8. The story is unquestioningly repeated by Gordon, *Fanon and the Crisis of European Man*, p. 95. It appears to originate from a misreading of Geismar's admittedly ambiguous statement (p. 12) that Fanon 'attended a black lycée, with the *béké* children carefully segregated in another private religious school'.

113　*Peau noire*, p. 132n.

114　Aldrich and Connell, *France's Overseas Frontier*, p. 28.

115　The literature on Césaire is extensive. A good biography is provided by Roger Toumson and Simonne Henry-Valmore, *Aimé Césaire: Le Nègre inconsolé*, Fort-de-France: Vents des îles, Paris: Syros, 1993. For a very critical study by one of the theorists of 'creoleness', see Confiant, *Aimé Césaire*.

116  Césaire, *Cahier*, p. 19.
117  Ibid., p. 28.
118  Ibid., p. 18
119  Jacqueline Leiner, 'Entretien avec Aimé Césaire', *Tropiques*, vol 1, p. X. This is the preface to the facsimile edition, Paris: Editions J.-M. Place, 1978.
120  Manville, *Les Antilles*, p. 32.
121  Glissant, 'Je crois à l'avenir des cultures métisées', p. 17.
122  Aimé Césaire, 'Homage to Frantz Fanon', *Présence africaine 60*, 1972, pp. 131–4.
123  Aimé Césaire, 'Par tous mots Guerrier-Silex', *Le Progressiste*, 24 March 1982.
124  Fanon, 'Antillais et Africains', p. 26.

## 3 An Tan Robè

1  Claude Lévi-Strauss, *Tristes Tropiques*, trans. John and Doreen Weightman, London: Picador, 1989, p. 26; Mark Polizzotti, *Revolution of the Mind: The Life of André Breton*, London: Bloomsbury, 1995, p. 494.
2  The spa town of Vichy in the central department of the Allier *département* was the seat of Pétain's government. Legend has it that it was chosen because it had more hotel rooms than any other town in France. For the history of the Vichy regime, see Robert O. Paxton, *Vichy France: Old Guard and New Order, 1940–1944*, New York: Knopf, 1972.
3  Lévi-Strauss, *Tristes Tropiques*, p. 30.
4  Ibid., p. 39.
5  Ibid., p. 37.
6  Ibid., p. 32.
7  André Breton, 'Eaux troubles' (1942), in *Martinique, Charmeuse de serpents*, Paris: Jean-Jacques Pauvert Editeur, 1972, pp. 76–7.
8  André Breton, 'Le Brise-larmes', ibid., p. 37.
9  André Breton, 'Un grand poète noir', ibid., p. 95.
10  A complete facsimile edition has been published in two volumes by Editions Jean-Michel Place, Paris, 1978. A very good discussion of the journal, and generous selections from it, can be found in Michael Richardson (ed.), *Refusal of the Shadow: Surrealism and the Caribbean*, trans. Michael Richardson and Krzysztof Fijalkowski, London: Verso, 1996.
11  Aimé Césaire, 'Présentation', *Tropiques* 1, pp. 5–6.
12  René Menil's contributions to *Tropiques* have been republished, together with later essays, in his *Tracées: Identité, négritude, esthétiques aux Antilles*, Paris: Robert Laffont, 1981.

13    Breton, "Un grand poète noir', in *Martinique, Charmeuse de serpents,* op. cit., p. 98.

14    *Peau noire,* p. 31.

15    Suzanne Césaire, 'Malaise d'une civilisation', *Tropiques* 5, April 1942, pp. 47–8.

16    René Ménil, 'Situation de la poésie aux Antilles', *Tropiques* 11, May 1944, reprinted, *Tracées,* p. 122.

17    Leiris, 'Martinique, Guadeloupe, Haiti', p. 1345; *Peau noire,* p. 118.

18    Lévi-Strauss, *Tristes Tropiques,* pp. 37–8.

19    Ibid., p. 38.

20    Amiral Georges Robert, *La France aux Antilles 1939–1943,* Vadez (Liechtenstein): Calivras Anstalt, 1979, pp. 8–11 (first edn 1950).

21    Interview with Charles Cézette.

22    Cited, Jean Lacouture, *De Gaulle: The Rebel, 1890–1944,* trans. Patrick O'Brian, London: HarperCollins, 1993, p. 268.

23    Fanon, 'Antillais et Africains', *Pour La Révolution africaine,* p. 29. The Brazzaville Conference was held to discuss the future of 'the French peoples of the African continent', but, whilst it promised to let Africa 'evolve', the closing statement noted that France's civilizing mission ruled out the possibility of either autonomy or internal self-government. See Lacouture, *De Gaulle: The Rebel,* pp. 504–6.

24    Richard D. Burton, 'Nos Journées de juin: The Historical Significance of the Liberation of Martinique (June 1943)' in H. R. Kedward and Nancy Woods (eds), *The Liberation of France: Image and Event,* Oxford: Berg, 1995, p. 227.

25    Camille Chauvet, 'La Martinique au temps de l'Amiral Robert (1939–1940)', in *Historial antillais,* Fort-de-France: Société Dajani, 1985, vol 5, pp. 423–4. This is the fullest available account of Martinique during the war.

26    Robert, *La France,* pp. 36–7.

27    Ibid., p. 87; F.-A. Baptiste, 'Le Régime de Vichy à la Martinique (juin 1940 à juin 1943)', *Revue d'histoire de la deuxième guerre mondiale,* 111, July 1978, p. 6.

28    Lacouture, *De Gaulle: The Rebel,* pp. 273–9.

29    Fanon, 'Antillais et africains', p. 27; Robert, *La France,* p. 140.

30    Chauvet, 'La Martinique', p. 258.

31    Ibid., p. 435.

32    Robert, *La France,* p. 25.

33    'Décision nommant les membres du Conseil municipal de la Commune du Lamentin' (22 February 1942) and 'Décision nommant les conseillers municipaux de la Commune de Fort-de-France' (22 February 1941), reproduced in Marie-Hélène Leotin (ed.), *La Martinique pendant la Deuxième Guerre*

*Mondiale,* Fort-de-France: Archives départementales/ Centre
régional de documentation pédagogique des Antilles et de la
Guyane, 1993, pp. 33–4. This collection of primary documents is
an invaluable source of information on wartime Martinique.

34   See Raphaël Confiant, *Le Nègre et l'amiral,* Paris: Grasset, 1988;
Alice Delpech, *La Dissidence,* Paris: L'Harmattan, 1991; Tony
Delsham, *An Tan Robè,* Schoelcher: Editions MGG, 1994.

35   *La Petite Patrie,* 17 June 1940, cited Richard D. E. Burton, *La
Famille coloniale: La Martinique et la mère-patrie,* Paris:
L'Harmattan, 1994, pp. 152–3.

36   Ibid., p. 153.

37   Cited, ibid., p. 149.

38   For a full account, see Michael R. Marrus and Robert O. Paxton,
*Vichy France and the Jews,* New York: Schoken Books, 1983.

39   Documents reproduced, Léotin, pp. 41–2.

40   Baptiste, 'Le Régime de Vichy', pp. 16–22.

41   'Lettre du Lieutenant de Vaisseau Bayle, chef du service d'information, au directeur de la revue *Tropiques*', reprinted, facsimile
edition, p. xxxviii.

42   Breton, 'Eaux troubles', pp. 74–5.

43   'Antillais et Africains', p. 27.

44   Lévi-Strauss, *Tristes Tropiques,* p. 30.

45   Edouard Glissant, *Le Quatrième Siècle* (1964), Paris: Gallimard,
Collection L'Imaginaire, 1990, p. 266.

46   Raphaël Confiant, *Ravines du devant-jour,* Paris: Folio 1995,
p. 146.

47   Patrick Chamoiseau, *Texaco,* trans. Rose-Myriam Réjouis and Val
Vinokurv, London: Granta Books, 1997, p. 238.

48   Chauvet, 'La Martinique', p. 439–41.

49   The reference is to Sartre's 'Paris sous l'occupation' (1944),
reprinted in *Situations III,* Paris: Gallimard, 1949.

50   Edouard Glissant, *Le Discours antillais,* Paris: Seuil, 1981, p. 46.

51   Baptiste, 'Le Régime de Vichy', p. 24.

52   'Antillais et africains', pp. 27–8.

53   Marcel Manville, 'Témoignage d'un ami et d'un compagnon de
lutte', in Elo Dacy (ed.), *L'Actualité de Frantz Fanon: Actes du
Colloque de Brazzaville (12–16 décembre 1984),* Paris: Karthala,
1986, p. 15.

54   *Peau noire,* p. 157.

55   'Circulaire relatif aux vols d'embarcations', reproduced Léotin,
*La Martinique,* p. 90.

56   Chauvet, 'La Martinique', p. 460.

57   Letter of 12 April 1945 to his parents, reproduced *Mémorial
international,* p. 269.

58   *Peau noire,* p. 164.

59 Interview with Charles Cézette.

60 *Peau noire*, p. 98.

61 Interviews with Joby Fanon. Cf. his 'Pour Frantz, pour notre mère' and 'Formons un homme neuf'.

62 Robert, *La France*, p. 168.

63 'Communication à la population', 30 June 1943, reproduced Léotin, *La Martinique*, p. 102.

64 Cited Burton, *La Famille coloniale*, p. 156.

65 *Le Monde*, 15 March 1946, 4 October 1946, 6 February 1948.

66 Robert, *La France*, pp. 28–9.

67 Unless otherwise stated, all information on the 5ème. Bataillon de Marche is drawn from the archives of the Service Historique de l'Armée de Terre, Château de Vincennes. The dossiers in question are 11 P148, 11 P 147, 11 P 150, 11 P 262 and 12 P 260.

68 Manville, 'Témoignage d'un ami', p. 16.

69 Pierre Marie-Claire Mosole died in January 1982. Information from the address given at his funeral by Marcel Manville. I am profoundly grateful to Mme Odette Fresel for making a copy available to me. Marcel Manville himself died in December 1998.

70 Interviews with Marcel Manville and Joby Fanon.

71 Marcel Manville, *Les Antilles sans fard*, Paris: L'Harmattan, 1992, p. 38.

72 Ibid., p. 42.

73 Ibid.

74 Joseph Issoufou Conombo, *Souvenirs de guerre d'un Tirailleur sénégalais*, Paris: L'Harmattan, 1989, pp. 35f.

75 Gilles Manceron and Hassan Remaoun, *D'Une Rive à l'autre': la guerre d'Algérie de la mémoire à l'histoire*, Paris: Syros, 1993, p. 29.

76 On Mediterranean piracy, see Fernand Braudel, *The Mediterranean and the Mediterranean World in the Age of Philip II*, trans. Siân Reynolds, abridged by Richard Ollard, London: Book Club Associates, 1996, pp. 624–49.

77 John Ruedy, *Modern Algeria: The Origins and Development of a Nation*, Bloomington and Indianapolis: Indiana University Press, 1992, p. 89.

78 For an account of wartime Algiers, see Jacques Cantier, '1939–1945: une métropole coloniale en guerre' in Jean-Jacques Jordi and Guy Pervillé (eds), *Alger 1940–1962: une ville en guerre*, Paris: Autrement, 1999, pp. 16–61.

79 For a detailed account, see Michel Abitbol, *The Jews of North Africa during the Second World War*, trans. Catherine Tihanyi Zentelis, Detroit: Wayne University Press, 1989.

80 Ruedy, *Modern Algeria*, pp. 145–6.

81   See Ferhat Abbas, *Le Jeune Algérien*, Paris: Editions Garnier, 1981.

82   Emmanuel Roblès, *Les Hauteurs de la ville*, Algiers: Charlot, 1948.

83   Lacouture, *De Gaulle: The Rebel*, pp. 490–1.

84   The literature on Operation Anvil is slight when compared with the mass of documentation available on Overlord, and general histories of the Second World War devote little space to it. An invaluable overview is given by Franklin L. Gurley, 'Le Débarquement en Provence: le 15 août 1944', *Guerres mondiales et conflits contemporains*, 174, April 1994, pp. 23–45.

85   Interview with Marcel Manville.

86   *Peau noire*, p. 20.

87   *Les Damnés de la terre*, p. 234.

88   Albert Camus, 'Misère de la Kabylie' in *Actuelles III: Chroniques algériennes 1939–1958*, Paris: Gallimard, 1958, pp. 38, 45.

89   Saadia and Lakhdar, 'L'Aliénation colonialiste et la résistance de la famille algérienne', *Les Temps modernes* 182, June 1961, p. 1684.

90   Cantier, '1939–1945', p. 43.

91   J. Vernet, *Le Réarmement et la réorganisation de l'armée de terre française (1943–1946)*, Vincennes: SHAT, 1980, p. 17.

92   SHAT, Dossier 11 P 147.

93   Robert Merle, *Ben Bella*. trans. Camilla Sykes, London: Michael Joseph, 1967, pp. 61–2, 64.

94   For a detailed account, see Vernet, 'Le Réarmement'.

95   *Peau noire*, p. 20.

96   See Joseph Issoufou Conombo, *Souvenirs de guerre*.

97   The 'battle' was in fact a complex series of engagements involving huge numbers of troops on both sides, and it lasted until March 1945. The prize was valuable: access to the Rhine and then to Germany itself. The Michelin 1:200,000 map of 'La Bataille d'Alsace' produced in 1947 (and reprinted in facsimile in 1992) provides a general overview of the operations.

98   The full text of the citation is reproduced, *Le Progressiste*, 24 March 1982: 'Colonel Salan, Commanding Officer of the 6th Regiment of Colonial Infantry, certifies that Private Frantz Fanon has been mentioned in Brigade dispatches for his brilliant conduct during operations in the Doubs loop. Serving an 81m mortar in the Bois des Grappes on 25 November 1944, he was wounded while carrying munitions during an enemy mortar bombardment. This citation gives him the right to wear the Croix de Guerre with bronze star.'

99   Merle, *Ben Bella*, p. 67.

100  Reproduced *Mémorial International*, p. 269.

101  *Peau noire*, p. 127.

102  Manville, *Les Antilles*, p. 48.

103 Letter of 5 August 1945 to Mme. L.C., reproduced Jeannie Darsières, 'Un Révolutionnaire nommé Fanon: qui est-ce?', *Le Progressiste*, 24, March 1982, p. 3.
104 Manville, *Les Antilles*, p. 48.
105 Documents in the possession of Mme Odette Fresel, who has inherited her father's remarkable gift for hospitality.
106 Manville, *Les Antilles*, p. 53.
107 Interview with Edouard Fanon.
108 *Peau noire*, p. 31.
109 For an account of Césaire's political career, with extracts from his parliamentary speeches, see Ernest Moutoussamy, *Aimé Césaire: Député à l'Assemblée nationale, 1945–1993*, Paris: L'Harmattan, 1993.
110 'Antillais et Africains', pp. 28–9.
111 Ibid., p. 22.
112 Aimé Césaire, *Discours sur le colonialisme*, Paris and Dakar: Présence Africaine, 1995, p. 12. Fanon either cites or alludes to this passage in 'Fureur raciste en France', *El Moudjahid*, 42, 25 May 1959, reprinted *Pour la Révolution africaine*, p. 168; 'Unité et solidarité effective sont les conditions de la liberation africaine', *El Moudjahid* 58, 5 January 1960, reprinted ibid., p. 173; *Les Damnés de la terre*, p. 95. He also alluded to it in the lectures on psychiatry given in Tunis in 1959–1960.

## 4 Dr Frantz Fanon

1 *Peau noire*, p. 18.
2 *Doudou*, which can be either masculine or feminine, is still commonly used in Martinique as an affectionate (and slightly ironic) form of address. For the tourist trade, a *doudou* is a kitsch figurine of a Martinican man or woman in 'traditional dress'. The figurines are as tasteless and offensive as the posters of the 'Banania' soldier.
3 Gilbert Gratiant, 'Ti-Manmzell-la' in Léopold Sédar Senghor (ed.), *Anthologie de la nouvelle poésie nègre et malgache de langue française*, Paris: PUF, 1992, p. 38 (first edn. 1948).
4 See Buchi Emecheta, *Second-Class Citizen*, London: Alison and Busby, 1974.
5 *Peau noire*, pp. 15, 19.
6 *Peau noire*, p. 18.
7 Ibid., p. 16.
8 Ibid.
9 Ibid., p. 58.
10 Ibid., p. 59.
11 Ibid, p. 155.

12   Julie Lirus, *Identité antillaise. Contribution à la connaissance psychologique et anthropologique du Guadeloupéen et du Martiniquais*, Paris: Editions Caribéennes, 1979, p. 89.

13   *Peau noire*, p. 98.

14   Ibid., p. 28.

15   Ibid., p. 24.

16   Ibid., p. 90.

17   Cited, Alain Ruscio, *Le Credo de l'homme blanc*, Brussels: Editions complexe, 1995, p. 256.

18   Françoise Dolto, *Correspondence I: 1914–1938*, (ed.) Colette Percheminier, Paris: Hatier, 1991, pp, 44, 45, 53, 58–9, 64.

19   *Peau noire*, p. 16.

20   Ibid., p. 125n.

21   For the *boursier/héritier* distinction, see Pierre Bourdieu and Jean-Claude Passeron, *The Inheritors: French Students and their Relation to Culture*, trans. R. Nice, Chicago: University of Chicago Press, 1979 (first French edn 1964).

22   Jean-Pierre Rioux, *The Fourth Republic 1944–1958*, trans. Godfrey Rogers, Cambridge and Paris: Cambridge University Press and Editions de la Maison des Sciences de l'homme, 1987, pp. 114, 122.

23   Ibid., pp. 129–30.

24   Peter Geismar, *Frantz Fanon*, New York: Dial Press, 1971, p. 44.

25   Manville, *Les Antilles*, p. 242.

26   Ibid.

27   *Peau noire*, p. 29.

28   Ibid.

29   Ibid., p. 145.

30   Edouard Glissant, 'Un Nouveau Sens de l'humanité pour les pays du Sud', *Antilla* 23, November–December 1991, p. 38.

31   Joby Fanon, 'Formons un homme neuf', interview with Joby Fanon.

32   Manville, *Les Antilles*, p. 47.

33   Interview with Robert Berthellier.

34   *Peau noire*, pp. 14–15.

35   Geismar, *Frantz Fanon*, p. 46.

36   On the history of immigration to Lyon and on its Algerian community, see Azouz Begag, *Place du Pont, ou la médina de Lyon*, Paris: Autrement, 1997. For more general accounts of Algerian immigration, see Tayeb Belloula, *Les Algériens en France*, Algiers: Editions nationales algériennes, 1965; Benjamin Stora, *Ils Venaient d'Algérie: l'immigration algérienne en France 1912–1992*, Paris: Fayard, 1992. The great cinematic document on North African immigration is Yamina Benguigui's *Mémoires d'immigrés: l'héritage maghrébin*, originally made for the Canal+ television

channel in 1997 and then re-edited for cinematic distribution in the spring of 1998.

37  Cited, Begag, *Place du Pont*, p. 44.

38  *La Voix du peuple*, 9 January 1937, cited, ibid., p. 48.

39  Ibid., p. 41.

40  I examine aspects of this image in 'The Algerian with the Knife', *Parallax* 7, April–June 1998, pp. 159–68.

41  See Jean Damase's deeply unpleasant novels, *Les Nouveaux Barbares,* Paris: Fasquelle, 1935 and *Sidi de banlieue* Paris: Fasquelle, 1937.

42  'Le Syndrome nord-africain', in *Pour la Révolution africaine*, p. 9.

43  Letter of February 1947 to his mother.

44  Interview with Joby Fanon.

45  *Peau noire*, p. 184.

46  *Peau noire*, p. 136.

47  Interview with Nicole Guillet.

48  Charles Geronimi, 'Rencontre avec Fanon', unpublished typescript.

49  *Peau noire*, p. 36.

50  *Les Damnés de la terre*, p. 181.

51  Françoise Vergès, *Monsters and Revolutionaries: Colonial Family Romance and Métissage*, Durham NC: Duke University Press, 1999, p. 136.

52  'A Propos d'un plaidoyeur', *El Moudjahid* 12, 15 November 1975; *Pour La Révolution africaine*, p. 71.

53  See his 'Negro Spirituals', *Esprit*, May 1951.

54  *Peau noire*, p. 24.

55  Ibid., p. 150.

56  Chester Himes, *The Quality of Hurt: The Early Years. The Autobiography of Chester Himes*, New York: Paragon House, 1972, p. 342.

57  Letter of 2 November 1947 to his mother.

58  Simone de Beavoir, *La Force des choses*, Vol. II, p. 426.

59  *Peau noire*, p. 13.

60  *Peau noire*, p. 148. The reference is to Simone de Beauvoir, *L'Amérique au jour le jour*, Paris: Folio, 1997, p. 382.

61  Although there is no conclusive evidence that Fanon read the founding text of modern French feminism, there are similarities between his analysis and Beauvoir's. See Toril Moi, *Simone de Beauvoir: The Making of a Woman Intellectual*, Oxford: Blackwell, 1994, pp. 204–11. The similarity stems from their common use of the basic tenets of existentialism.

62  *Peau noire,*, pp. 69, 112–13. The anecdote about the performance of the play given in North Africa and the General who told Sartre that the play should be staged in Black Africa to demonstrate that

blacks in French countries were happier than those in the United States, is cited almost verbatim from Francis Jeanson's 'Sartre et le monde noir', *Présence africaine* 7, p. 197. *La Putain repectueuse* was first performed in October 1946. It has not been possible to find any details on the North African performance.

63  *Peau noire*, pp. 43–4, 180. The reference is to Emmanuel Mounier, *L'Eveil de l'Afrique noire* (1947), in *Oeuvres complètes Tome II: 1944–1950*, Paris: Seuil, 1962.

64  'Tam-tam de nuit', 'Tam-tam I' and 'Tam-tam II' in *Les Armes miraculeuses*, Paris: Gallimard, 1946.

65  Garry O'Connor, *French Theatre Today*, London: Pitman, 1975, p. 89.

66  Interview with Nicole Guillet.

67  Abdelmadjid Kaouah. ' Entretien exclusif avec Mme Josie Fanon', *Révolution africaine*, 11 December 1987, p. 33.

68  *Peau noire*, p. 134.

69  *Peau noir*, p. 129.

70  Carl Gustav Jung, 'The Association Method' in *Collected Works of C.G. Jung*, vol 2, Princeton: Princeton University Press, 1973.

71  *Peau noire*, p. 30.

72  Léopold Sédar Senghor, *Anthologie de la nouvelle poésie nègre et malgache de langue française*, Paris: PUF, 1949. The anthology appeared in a series commissioned by the historian Charles-André Julien to mark the centenary of the 1848 revolution.

73  *Peau noire*, p. 183.

74  Glissant's poems were republished in his 'Le Sang Rivé' collection, now in his *Poèmes complets* ; Breton's poem is included in *Signe ascendant*, Paris: Gallimard, Collection 'Poesie', 1968 (first edn 1949).

75  André Breton, 'Légitime défense' in *Point du jour*, Paris: Gallimard, 1970, p. 33.

76  René Ménil, 'Généralités sur "l'écrivain" de couleur antillais', *Légitime Défense* (1932), p. 9.

77  Léonard Sainville, 'Le Noir antillais devant la littérature', *Les Lettres françaises* 1 August 1952. In 1952 Sainville won the Prix Antillais for his novel *Dominique, esclave nègre* (Paris and Dakar, Paris: Présence africaine, 1978), which tells the story of a slave in the years leading up to abolition. His *Au Fond du bourg* (Paris: Maspero nd) describes a strike on a plantation in the north of 'Tropicanie' and is close to a form of socialist realism.

78  A facsimile edition was published by Editions Jean-Michel Place in 1978 as part of a programme to republish a series of important but unobtainable avant-garde journals. The greater part of *Légitime Défense* is available in English translation in Michael Richardson, *Refusal of the Shadow*.

79   Miles Davis and Quincey Troupe, *Miles: The Autobiography*, London: Picador, 1990, pp. 116–17.

80   'Trouble mental et trouble neurologique', p. 1082n. See Henri Ey, 'Le psychiatrie devant la surréalisme', in *Etudes psychiatriques*, Paris: PUF, 1948.

81   Interviews with Nicole Guillet and Mireille Fanon Mendès-France.

82   Interview with Olivier Fanon.

83   *Peau noire*, p. 51.

84   Ibid., p. 137.

85   Ibid., p. 8.

86   See David Macey, 'The Recall of the Real: Frantz Fanon and Psychoanalysis', *Constellations*, vol. 6, no. 1, 1991, and the next chapter below.

87   Interview with Jacques Postel.

88   Razanjao and Jacques Postel, 'La Vie et l'oeuvre psychiatrique de Frantz Fanon', *Information psychiatrique*, vol. L1, no. 10, December 1975, p. 1053, interview with Jacques Postel.

89   Ibid.

90   P. Noël and D. Thérond, 'La Formation des psychiatres de 1945 à 1975 à travers trente ans d'*Information psychiatrique*', *Information psychiatrique*, June 1996, p. 540.

91   Madeleine Humbert, letter of 20 July 1973 to Jacques Postel, cited Razanjao and Postel, p. 1054.

92   *Peau noire*, p. 167.

93   Ibid, p. 165.

94   Jacques Postel (ed.), *Dictionnaire de psychiatrie et de psychopathologie clinique*, Paris: Larousse, 1993, p. 481.

95   *Peau noire*, p. 168.

96   See David Macey, *Lacan in Contexts*, London: Verso, 1988, pp. 35–8.

97   Jacques Lacan, 'La Famille', in Henri Wallon (ed.), *Encyclopédie française*, vol. 8, and republished as *Les Complexes familiaux dans la formation de l'individu: essai d'analyse d'une fonction en psychanalyse*, Paris: Navarin, 1984.

98   *Peau noire*, p. 39.

99   This section is reprinted as 'Le Trouble mental et le trouble neurologique', *Information psychiatrique*, LC 10, 1975.

100  Cited, Geismar, *Frantz Fanon*, p. 11.

101  In Jacques Lacan, *Ecrits*, Paris: Seuil, 1966, pp. 151–93.

102  Lucien Bonnafé, Henri Ey, Sven Follin, Jacques Lacan and Julien Rouart, *Le Problème de la psychogénèse des névroses et des psychoses*, Paris: Desclée de Brouwer, 1950.

103  Elisabeth Roudinesco, *Jacques Lacan & Co. A History of Psychoanalysis in France 1925–1985*, trans. Geoffrey Mehlman, London: Free Association Books, 1990, p. 58.

104 Ibid., p. 320.

105 Ibid. p. 158.

106 Henri F. Ellenberger, *The Discovery of the Unconscious: The History and Evolution of Dynamic Psychiatry*, New York: Basic Books, 1970, pp. 290–1.

107 Fanon's account of Ey is based largely on a reading of Henri Ey and Julien Rouart, *Essai d'application des principes de Jackson à une conception dynamique de la neuro-psychiatrie* (1938). This, together with other papers from 1936–8, is reprinted as Henri Ey, *Des Idées de Jackson à un modéle organo-dynamique en psychiatrie*, Toulouse: Privat, 1975.

108 Fanon, 'Trouble mental', pp. 1087–8.

109 Paul Balvet, 'La Valeur humaine de la folie', *Esprit*, September 1947.

110 Ibid., p. 289.

111 'Antillais et africains', pp. 13–14.

112 Ibid., p. 15.

113 *Peau noire*, p. 25.

114 'Le Syndrôme nord-africain', p. 18.

115 Ibid., pp. 15–16.

116 E. Stern, 'La Médecine psychosomatique', *Psychè* 27–8, January–February 1949, p. 130.

117 Jacques Arveiller, 'Mon Maître Tosquelles', *Evolution psychiatrique*, vol. 60, no. 3, 1995, p. 665.

118 François Tosquelles, 'Fanon à Saint-Alban', *Information psychiatrique*, XI, no. 10, October 1975, pp. 1073–4.

119 François Tosquelles, 'Biographie d'un psychiste' in *Education et psychothèrapie institutionnelle*, Mantes-la-Ville: Hiatus Edition, 1984, p. 213. Written in the third person, this very brief 'biography' is in fact an autobiography.

120 'François Tosquelles par lui-même', *L'Ane* 13, November–December 1983, p. 5.

121 Ibid.

122 Tosquelles, 'Biographie', p. 214.

123 Ibid., p. 215.

124 Arveiller, 'Mon Maître Tosquelles', p. 667.

125 François Tosquelles, 'La Guerre d'Espagne', *Vie sociale et traitements* 172, August–September 1987, p. 38.

126 Roudinesco, *Jacques Lacan & Co*, p. 190.

127 Anne Grynberg, 'Les Camps français, des non-lieux de la mémoire', in Dimitri Nicolaidis (ed.), *Oublier nos crimes: l'amnésie nationale, une spécificité française?*, Paris: Autrement, 1994, p. 55. On the history of the Spanish refugees and their internment in French camps, see Geneviève Dreyfus-Armand and Emile Temime, *Les Camps sur la plage, un exil espagnol*, Paris: Autrement, 1995. For a full history of

France's concentration camps, see Anne Grynberg, *Les Camps de la honte: les internés juifs dans les camps français, 1939–1944*, Paris: La Découverte and Syros, 1991.

128 François Tosquelles, 'In Memoriam: sur G. Daumézon, quelques autres et moi', *Information psychiatrique* vol. 56, no. 5, June 1980, p. 576.

129 François Tosquelles, *L'Enseignement de la folie*, Toulouse: Privat, 1992, p. 116.

130 Grynberg, 'Les Camps français', p. 60.

131 Jean Aymé, 'Hommage à François Tosquelles', *Information psychiatrique*, 10, December 1994, p. 883.

132 François Tosquelles, 'Essai sur le sens du vécu en psychopathologie (le témoignage de Gérard de Nerval)', Faculté de Médecine de Paris, 1948.

133 *Information psychiatrique*, June 1953, p. 152.

134 François Tosquelles, 'L'Effervescence saint-albanaise', *Information psychiatrique*, October 1987, p. 960.

135 Paul Balvet, 'L'Ambre du musée', *Information psychiatrique*, October 1978, p. 862; Lucien Bonnafé, 'Rencontres autour de François Tosquelles', *Evolution psychiatrique*, vol. 60, no. 3, 1995, p. 661.

136 See David Macey. 'The Honour of Georges Canguilhem', *Economy & Society*, vol. 27, nos 2/3, May 1988.

137 See *Peau noire*, p. 116n. Canguilhem's thesis was first published in 1943 as *Essai sur quelques problèmes concernant le normal et le pathologique*. It is likely that Fanon knew it in the second edition published in 1950 by PUF. He found it 'very instructive' even though it deals exclusively with 'the biological problem'.

138 Aymé, 'Hommage à François Tosquelles,' p. 403; M. Lafont, 'L'Extermination douce dans les HP français', *Information psychiatrique* vol. 72, no. 8, October 1996.

139 C. Claveri, 'Aspects historiques de la psychothérapie institutionnelle', *Information psychiatrique*, vol. 63, no. 8, October 1987, p. 967.

140 The literature on institutional psychiatry is extensive. This brief account is drawn from Y. Teuilé's account, written in 1954 and reproduced in Tosquelles, *Education et psychothérapie institutionnelle*.

141 Félix Guattari, 'Students, the Mad and "Delinquents",' (1968) in *Molecular Revolution: Psychiatry and Politics*, trans. Rosemary Sheed, Harmondsworth: Penguin, 1984, p. 208.

142 Interview with Nicole Guillet.

143 Tosquelles, 'F. Fanon à Saint-Alban', p. 1074.

144 The term is used in French psychiatry to describe the moment

when an individual such as a psychotic moves from a violent idea to the corresponding act, such as murder.

145  Tosquelles, 'F. Fanon à Saint-Alban,' pp. 1076–7.
146  Interviews with Edouard Fanon and Joby Fanon.

## 5 'Black Skin, White Masks'

1  M'Hamed Ferid Ghazi, 'Doublement prolétaires', *Esprit*, February 1952, p. 220.
2  For the origins and early history of the journal, see Michel Winnock, *'Esprit': Des Intellectuels dans la cité 1930–1950,* Paris: Seuil, collection 'Points', 1996 (revised edn).
3  See Howard Davies, *Sartre and 'Les Temps modernes'*, Cambridge: Cambridge University Press, 1987.
4  Louis-Jean Calvet, *Roland Barthes: A Biography*, trans. Sarah Wykes, Cambridge: Polity Press, 1994, p. 103.
5  Interview with Jean-Marie Domenach.
6  For the history of *Présence africaine*, see V. Y. Mudimbe (ed.), *The Surreptitious Speech: Présence africaine and the Politics of Otherness 1947–1987*, Chicago: University of Chicago Press, 1992; Antoine de Gaudemar, 'Expressions d'Afrique', *Libération*, 4 December 1997.
7  *Peau noire*, p. 183.
8  An English translation – *Bantu Philosophy* – appeared in 1957. The book remains very controversial. See, for example, the discussion in Paulin J. Hountondji, *African Philosophy: Myth and Reality*, trans. Henri Evans with the collaboration of Jonathan Rée, introduction by Abiola Irele, London: Hutchinson, 1983.
9  Cited, *Peau noire*, p. 150.
10  Aimé Césaire, *Discours sur la colonialisme*, Paris and Dakar: Présence africaine, 1995, pp. 36–7.
11  *Peau noire*, p. 150. Although not identified as such by Fanon, 'Enough of this scandal' (*Assez de ce scandale*) is a quotation from *Cahier d'un retour au pays natal*, p. 50.
12  François Tosquelles, 'La Société vécue par les malades psychiques', *Esprit*, December 1952, pp. 897–904.
13  Maurice Nadeau, 'Romanciers d'Afrique du Nord', *Mercure de France*, 1075, March 1953.
14  *Esprit*, February 1952, p. 219.
15  Emmanuel Mounier, *L'Eveil de l'Afrique noire*, Paris: Seuil, 1947; André Gide, *Voyage au Congo*, Paris: Gallimard, 1927; *Le Retour du Tchad*, Paris: Gallimard, 1928.
16  See in particular André Mandouze, 'Impossibilités algériennes, ou le mythe des trois départements', *Esprit*, July 1947.

17 E. J. Rovan, 'La France devant l'Indochine', *Esprit*, November 1945; R. Boudry, 'Le Problème malgache', *Esprit*, February 1948; for a general account, see Winock, *Esprit*, pp. 335–49.

18 Francis Jeanson, *Le Problème moral et la pensée de Sartre*, Paris: Seuil, 1947.

19 Francis Jeanson, *Algéries: de retour en retour*, Paris: Seuil 1998, pp. 9–10.

20 Francis Jeanson, 'Cette Algérie, conquise et pacifiée . . .', *Esprit*, April and May 1947.

21 Ibid., pp. 633–4.

22 Francis Jeanson, 'Reconnaissance de Fanon', p. 213, published as an afterword to the 1965 Seuil edition of *Peau noire, masques blancs*. This edition also reprints Jeanson's original preface; neither text appears in subsequent editions, and neither has been translated.

23 *Peau noire*, p. 31.

24 Jeanson, 'Reconnaissance', pp. 213, 215.

25 Jeanson, 'Préface', p. 12.

26 The quotation is from *Peau noire*, p. 130.

27 Jeanson, 'Préface', pp. 21–2.

28 See the reviews in *Le Populaire*, 12 May 1952 (C. de Fréminville), *Livres et lectures*, June 1952 (A. de Parvillex), *Réforme*, 13 September 1952, *Parallèle 50*, 26 June 1952 (this also discusses Sainville's *Dominique*), *Foi et vie*, December 1952, *Revue de la pensée française*, September 1953 (Bernard Voyenne). Extracts from Jeanson's preface were published as 'Opprimés noirs, oppresseurs blancs', *République algérienne*, 11 April 1952. Copies of all these reviews are held in Editions du Seuil's press dossier on *Peau noire*.

29 Maxime Chastaing, 'Frantz Fanon: *Peau noires, masques blancs*', *Esprit*, October 1952, p. 559.

30 See, for example, Belinda Jack, *Francophone Literatures: An Introductory Survey*, Oxford: Oxford University Press, 1996.

31 *Guardian*, 1 June 1994.

32 Francis Jeanson, 'Albert Camus ou l'âme révoltée', *Les Temps modernes*, May 1952.

33 *Peau noire*, p. 14.

34 *Peau noire*, p. 13.

35 Ibid., p. 93.

36 See Claude Lévi-Strauss, *The Elementary Structures of Kinship* (1949), trans. James Harle Bell, John Richard von Sterner and Rodney Needham, London: Eyre and Spottiswoode, 1969 and particularly, *The Savage Mind*, London: Weidenfeld and Nicolson, 1972, pp. 16–36 (translator unidentified).

37 *Peau noire*, p. 130.

38    *Peau noire*, p. 181, citing *The Eighteenth Brumaire of Louis Bonaparte*: 'The social revolution of the nineteenth century can only create its poetry from the future, not from the past. It cannot begin its own work until it has sloughed off all its superstitious regard for the past. Earlier revolutions have needed world-historical reminiscences to deaden their awareness of their own content. In order to arrive at its own content the revolution of the nineteenth century must let the dead bury the dead. Previously the phrase transcended the content; here the content transcends the phrase.' In *Surveys from Exile* (ed.) David Fernbach, Harmondsworth: Penguin, 1973, p. 149.

39    Alexandre Kojève, *Introduction à la lecture de Hegel*, Paris: Gallimard, 1947; see also the twenty essays on Hegel included in Jean Hyppolite's *Figures de la pensée philosophique*, vol. 1 Paris: PUF, 1971.

40    *Peau noire*, p. 179n.

41    *Peau noire*, p. 112n.

42    Paul Balvet, 'La Valeur humaine de la folie', *Esprit*, September 1947, p. 299.

43    Martin Heidegger, *Being and Time*, trans. John Macquarrie and Edward Robinson, Oxford: Basil Blackwell, 1980, p. 72n.

44    Maurice Merleau-Ponty, *La Phénoménologie de la perception*, Paris: Gallimard, 1945, p. 466.

45    Ibid., p. 113.

46    *Peau noire*, p. 13.

47    Ibid., p. 187.

48    Ibid., p. 7.

49    George Lamming, 'The Negro Writer and his World', *Présence africaine*, nos 8–9–10, June–November 1956, p. 321.

50    Lamming, 'The Negro Writer', p. 321.

51    Sartre, *L'Etre et le néant*, p. 309.

52    *Peau noire*, p. 88.

53    Merleau-Ponty, *La Phénoménologie*, pp. 173–9.

54    Jean Lhermitte, *L'Image de notre corps*, Paris: Editions de la Nouvelle Revue Critique, 1939, p. 11. Lhermitte's other major works are *Les Fondements biologiques de la psychologie*, Paris: Gauthier-Villiers, 1925; *Le Sommeil*, Paris: Colin, 1930; *Les Méchanismes du cerveau*, Paris: Gallimard, 1938.

55    Ibid.

56    Ibid., pp. 22–3.

57    Merleau-Ponty, *La Phénoménologie*, pp. 114, 117.

58    Once again, Fanon departs from normal usage. The noun *chiquenaude* means a flick or snap of the finger; the verb *chiquenauder* is not included in standard dictionaries like the *Petit Robert*.

59    *Peau noire*, p. 90.

# Notes

60  Ibid.

61  Jean-Paul Sartre, *L'Etre et le néant*, Paris: Gallimard, Collection 'Tel', 1972, p. 307.

62  Ibid., p. 265.

63  *Peau noire*, p. 92.

64  Ibid.

65  Janet G. Vaillant, *Black, French and African: A Life of Léopold Sedar Senghor*, Cambridge MA and London: Harvard University Press, 1990, p. 71.

66  Sam Selvo, *The Lonely Londoners*, London: Longman, 1998, p. 87 (first edn 1956).

67  W. E. B. Du Bois, *The Souls of Black Folk* (1903), Harmondsworth: Penguin, 1996; bell hooks, *Wounds of Passion*, London: Women's Press, 1998, p. 54: 'The gaze of white folks disturbs me. It is always for me the would-be colonizing look.'

68  Aimé Césaire, *Une Tempête*, Paris: Seuil, 1969, p. 83.

69  *Peau noire*, pp. 34, 92.

70  Francis Affergan, *Anthropologie à la Martinique*, Paris: Presse de la Fondation Nationale des Sciences Politiques, 1983, p. 177.

71  Raphaël Confiant, *Ravines du devant-jour*, Paris: Folio, 1995, p. 253.

72  *Peau noire*, p. 71. The verb *amènier* is Fanon's coinage.

73  Jean-Paul Sartre, *Réflexions sur la question juive*, Paris: Gallimard, Collection 'Idées', 1969, pp. 83–4, 173.

74  Ibid., pp. 183–4.

75  *Peau noire*, p. 93.

76  'Mayotte Capécia', *Encyclopédie Antillaise. Littérature antillaise (prose) Fort-de-France, Désormeaux*, 1971, p. 135. See also Jack Corzani, *La Littérature des Antilles-Guyane Françaises. Tome IV: La Négritude*, Fort-de-France: Désormeaux, 1978, pp. 199–210.

77  Christiane P. Makward, *Mayotte Capécia, ou l'aliénation selon Fanon*, Paris: Karthala, 1999.

78  *I Am a Martinican Woman and The White Negress: Two Novelettes of the 1940s*, trans. Beatrice Sith Clark, Pueblo, Col.: Passaggiata Press, 1997.

79  Mayotte Capécia, *Je suis Martiniquaise*, Paris: Editions Corréa, 1948, p. 113.

80  Ibid., p. 9.

81  Donald Bogle, *Toms, Coons, Mulattoes, Mamaies and Bucks: An Interpretive History of Blacks in American Films*, New York: Continuum, 1997 (third edn), p. 68.

82  Capécia, *Je suis Martiniquaise*, p. 65; *Peau noire*, p. 41.

83  Capécia, *Je suis Martiniquaise*, p. 202.

84  Ibid., p. 131.

85  Ibid., p. 185.

86  Ibid., pp. 172, 185.
87  Mayotte Capécia, *La Négresse blanche*, Paris: Editions Corréa, 1950, p. 133.
88  Ibid., p. 44.
89  Ibid., p. 174.
90  Ibid., p. 11.
91  Robert Coiplet, review of *La Négresse blanche*, *Le Monde*, 22 April 1950, p. 7.
92  J. Caillens, 'Culture et civilisation noire à travers l'édition française', *Présence africaine*, 1947, pp. 844–5.
93  *Présence africaine*, January 1948, p. 886.
94  Corzani also criticizes (pp. 199–200) Capécia's 'regionalist pseudo-realism' and remarks that her novels are so full of 'local colour' that they resemble postcards.
95  Makward, *Mayotte Capécia*, pp. 158, 150. Makward's study reconstructs the production of the two 'Capécia' novels in extraordinary – and exhaustive – detail.
96  Richard D. E. Burton, *La Famille coloniale: La Martinique et la mère-patrie 1789–1992*, Paris: L'Harmattan, 1994, p. 134, citing Antoine Régis, *Les Ecrivains français et les Antilles. Des Premiers pères blancs aux surréalistes noirs*, Paris: Maisonneuve et Larose, 1978.
97  It might be added that Martinican society was – and is – a very masculinist society and that the Union des Femmes de la Martinique does not, for instance, have an easy existence. See *Femmes de la Martinique* 2, January 1997. A detailed and depressing account of the position of women in Guadeloupe will be found in France Alibar and Pierrette Lembeye-Boy, *Le Couteau seul. Sé Koutou sèl: la condition féminine aux Antilles*, two vols. Paris: Editions caribéennes/Agence de Coopération Culturelle et Technique, 1981, 1982. The cultural and social similarities are so great that its findings can easily be extrapolated from Guadeloupe to Martinique.
98  *Peau noire*, p. 164. In Isaac Julien's film, Fanon's brother Joby describes his marriage to a white woman in the same terms: he met a woman, fell in love with her and simply forgot that she was a *métropolitaine*.
99  Gwen Bergner, 'Who is that Masked Woman? or, The Role of Gender in Fanon's *Black Skin, White Masks*,' *Publications of the Modern Language Association of America*, vol. 110, no. 1, January 1995, pp. 85, 84.
100  See the photographs reproduced in Contour's *Fort de France au début du siècle*, pp. 92, 94.
101  Capécia, *Je suis Martiniquaise*, p. 131.
102  T. Denean Sharpley-Whiting, 'Anti-black Femininity and Mixed-

Race Identity: Engaging Fanon to Reread Capécia' in Gordon, Sharpley-Whiting and White, *Fanon: A Critical Reader*, Oxford: Blackwell, 1996, pp. 156–7.

103 Makward, *Mayotte Capécia*, p. 15.
104 Ibid., p. 17.
105 Ibid., p. 21.
106 *Peau noire*, p. 34.
107 Ibid., p. 38.
108 Ibid., p. 36.
109 Ibid.
110 Ibid., p. 43.
111 Patrick Chamoiseau and Raphaël Confiant, *Lettres créoles: tracées antillaises et continentales de la littérature 1635 à 1975*, Paris: Hatier, 1991, p. 114.
112 Amadou Abdoulaye Sadji, *Abdoulaye Sadji: Biographie 1910–1961: Sa vie et sa pensée à un tournant de l'histoire africaine*, Paris and Dakar: Présence africaine, 1997.
113 Abdoulaye Sadji, *Nini, mulâtresse du Sénégal*, Paris and Dakar: Présence africaine, 1988, p. 7. *Nini* was first published in book form in the collective *Trois Ecrivains noirs*, Paris and Dakar: Présence africaine, 1951.
114 Ibid., p. 95.
115 Ibid., pp. 177–8.
116 Ibid., p. 73.
117 *Peau noire*, p. 44.
118 Ibid., p. 46.
119 Sadji, *Nini*, p. 178.
120 *Peau noire*, pp. 35–6. The inaccuracy of the translation can be gauged by the fact that this sentence is rendered (p. 44) as 'Her resentment feeds on her artificiality.'
121 Ibid., p. 37.
122 Sartre, *L'Etre et le néant*, p. 376.
123 Sartre, *Réflexions sur la question juive*, p. 109.
124 Sartre, *L'Etre et le néant*, p. 551.
125 *Peau noire*, p. 48. The technical meaning of eretheism is an abnormal sensitivity or responsiveness in some part of the body and, by extension, an abnormal emotional sensitivity.
126 The literature on negritude is extensive. See, inter alia, Lilyan Kestelkoot, *Les Ecrivains noirs de langue française: Naissance d'une littérature*, Brussels: Editions de l'Institut de sociologie, Université libre de Bruxelles, 1971 (fourth edn); Jack Corzani, *La Littérature des Antilles-Guyane Française. Vol IV: La Négritude*, Fort-de-France, Désormeaux, 1978; René Depestre, *Bonjour et adieu à la négritude*, Paris: Seghers, 1980; René Ménil, *Tracées: Identité, négritude, esthétique aux Antilles*, Paris: Robert Laffont, 1981;

Alain Blérald, *Négritude et politique aux Antilles*, Paris: Editions caribéennes, 1981.

127   'Aux Antilles, naissance d'une nation?', *El Moudjahid* 16, 15 January 1958, *Pour la Révolution africaine*, pp. 93–4; *Peau noire*, p. 110.

128   Jacques Roumain, 'Sales Nègres', in *La Montagne ensorcelée*, Paris: Messidor, 1987, pp. 150, 155–6.

129   *Peau noire*, p. 124. Cf. 'Antillais et africains', p. 26: 'For the first time, we saw a lycée teacher . . . telling West Indian society that it is fine and good to be a *nègre*.'

130   See the brief article on Lascascade in *Encyclopédie antillaise. Vol. II: Littérature antillaise (prose)*, Fort-de-France: Desormeaux, 1971, p. 225.

131   Suzanne Lacascade, *Claire-Solange: âme africaine*, Paris: Editions Eugène Figuière, nd (1924), p. 37.

132   Ibid., pp. 66, 99.

133   Maryse Condé, 'Order, Disorder, Freedom and the West Indian Writer', *Post/Colonial Conditions, Migrations and Nomadisms: Yale French Studies* 93, 1993, vol. 2, p. 131.

134   Janet Vaillant, *Black, French, and African. A Life of Leopold Sédar Senghor*, Cambridge MA and London: Harvard University Press, 1990, pp. 93, 244. Although consecrated by Locke, the term was in use before 1925 and entered the vocabulary after race riots swept America in 1919. See David Levering Lewis's introduction to his *Portable Harlem Renaissance Reader*, New York: Penguin, 1995.

135   Léopold Sédar Senghor, 'Le Portrait', *Oeuvre poétique*, Paris: Seuil, 1990, pp. 219–20.

136   The standard biography is Janet Vaillant's *Black, French and African*. See also the introduction to Armand Guibert's anthology *Léopold Sedar Senghor*, Paris: Pierre Seghers, 1961, and Jean-Pierre Péroncel-Hugoz's profile, 'Senghor, poète d'abord', *Le Monde*, 11 October 1996, p. 13.

137   See the essays in his *On African Socialism*, trans. Mercer Cook, London and Dunmow: Pall Mall Press, 1964.

138   In *Peau noire*, he cites (pp. 15–16) Damas's poem 'Le Hocquet' to illustrate a Martinican mother's attempt to persuade her child to acquire good French manners and to speak 'The French of France, Frenchman's French, French French'. 'Le Hoquet' was first published in *Pigments* in 1937; now in Dama's *Pigments/Névralgies*, Paris and Dakar: Présence africaine, 1972.

139   Léon-Gontran Damas, 'Naissance et vie de la négritude' in Daniel Racine, *Léon-Gontras Damas L'Homme et l'oeuvre*, Paris and Dakar: Présence africaine, 1993, p. 189.

140   Fanon, *Sociologie d'une révolution*, Paris: Maspero, 1966, p. 29.

141  'Antillais et africains', p. 26.
142  Césaire, 'Cahier', pp. 50–1.
143  Ibid., p. 31.
144  *Peau noire*, p. 106.
145  Césaire, 'Cahier', p. 31. On Toussaint, see C. L. R. James, *The Black Jacobins: Toussaint L'Ouverture and the San Domingo Revolution*, London: Alison and Busby, 1980 (first edn, 1938); Ralph Korngold, *Citizen Toussaint*, London: Gollancz, 1945.
146  Césaire, 'Cahier', p. 42.
147  Ibid.
148  Léopold Sédar Senghor, 'Aux tirailleurs sénégalais morts pour la France', *Oeuvre poètique*, Paris: Seuil, collection 'Points', 1990, p. 63.
149  Léon-Gontran Damas, 'Et Caetera' in *Pigments/Névralgie*, pp. 79–80.
150  Cheik Anta Diop, *Nations nègres et cultures*, Paris and Dakar: Présence africaine, 1954 (Diop published numerous articles in *Présence africaine* before this date); Martin Bernal, *Black Athena: The Afroasiatic Roots of Classical Civilization*, London: Free Association Books, two vols, 1987, 1991. For critical studies of the 'Black Athena' hypothesis, see Mary R. Lefkowitz and Guy Maclean (eds), *Black Athena Revisited*, Chapel Hill and London: North Carolina University Press, 1996.
151  *Peau noire*, pp. 183–4. Senghor's cult of 'rhythm' is implicitly criticized by the ironic lines of Césaire's *Cahier* (p. 103): 'they simply love us so much!/Gaily obscene, doudou about jazz in their excess of boredom/ I can do the tracking, the lindy hop and the tap dance.'
152  Ibid., p. 187.
153  Léopold Sédar Senghor, *Liberté I. Négritude et humanisme*, Paris: Seuil, 1964, pp. 7, 37, 70.
154  Tzvetan Todorov. *On Human Diversity: Nationalism, Racism and Exoticism in French Thought*, trans. Catherine Porter, Cambridge MA: Harvard University Press, 1993, p. 31.
155  Guy Tirolien, 'Adieu "Adieu foulards"' in *Balles d'or*, Paris and Dakar: Présence africaine, 1961, pp. 29–30.
156  Ibid., p. 188.
157  Ibid., p. 108.
158  *Peau noire*, p. 108.
159  Cf. G. W. F. Hegel, *The Philosophy of History*, New York: Dover, 1956, p. 99: 'Africa . . . has no movement or development to exhibit . . . what we properly understand by Africa, is the Unhistorical, Undeveloped Spirit, still involved in the conditions of mere nature.'
160  *Peau noire*, pp. 7–8.

161  Ibid., p. 8.

162  Ibid., p. 123.

163  Cited Elisabeth Roudinesco, *Jacques Lacan & Co.*, *A History of psychoanalysis in France 1925–1985*, trans. Geoffrey Mehlman, London: Free Association Books, 1990, p. 234.

164  *Peau noire*, p. 67. The articles in question are Octave Mannoni, 'Le complexe de dépendance et la structure de la personnalité', *Psyché* 12, 13, 1947. Fanon may also have known his 'La Personnalité malgache. Ebauche d'une analyse des structures', *Revue de psychologie des peuples*, vol. 3, no. 3, July 1948, and 'Psychologie de la révolte malgache', *Esprit*, April 1950. *Psychologie de la colonisation* was published by Charles Baladier in 1950; references here are to the second edition, entitled *Prospéro et Caliban: Psychologie de la colonisation*, Paris: Editions Universitaires, 1984.

165  The history of the 1947 rebellion is still poorly documented. A brief account will be found in Chapter 5 of Anthony Clayton, *The Wars of French Decolonization*, London: Longman, 1994. For a much fuller account, see Jacques Tronchon, *L'Insurrection malgache de 1947. Essai d'interprétation historique*, Paris: Karthala, 1986. Tronchon is a Franciscan who has worked with the homeless in Tananarive since the 1970s. See his interview with Jean-Pierre Langellier, *Le Monde* 16–17 March 1997; Langellier's accompanying article on 'Les 100,000 morts de l'insurrection malgache' gives a useful summary of the events of 1947.

166  Cited, Tronchon, *L'Insurrection malgache*, pp. 127–8.

167  The relevant biographical note ends: 'The poet has spent almost a year in a prison in Tananarive, and the ordeal has matured his talent. For our part – and proclaiming this is not a partisan act – we cannot believe that this bard of nobility and love has caused innocent blood to be spilled' (p. 194).

168  *Peau noire*, pp. 67, 10.

169  Mannoni, 'Le complexe de dépendance', p. 1230.

170  Mannoni, *Prospéro et Caliban*, p. 51.

171  Ibid., p. 153.

172  Ibid., p. 88.

173  Mannoni, 'Le complex de dépendance', p. 1476.

174  Antoine Bouillon, *Madagascar: le colonisé et son 'âme'. Essai sur le discours psychologique colonial*, Paris: L'Harmattan, 1981, p. 203.

175  See his 'La Plainte du noir', *Esprit*, May 1951.

176  'Le complexe de dépendance', p. 1230.

177  Mannoni, *Prospéro et Caliban*, p. 191.

178  *Peau noire*, p. 86.

179  Ibid., pp. 69, 67.

180  The relevant passages read as follows: 'Almost all the symptoms

had arisen in this way as residues – "precipitates" they might be called – of emotional experiences. To these experiences, therefore, we later gave the name of "psychical traumas", while the particular nature of the symptoms was explained by their relation to the traumatic scenes which were their cause. They were, to use a technical term, "determine" by the scenes of whose recollection they represented residues, and it was no longer necessary to describe them as capricious or enigmatic products of the neurosis. One unexpected point, however, must be noticed. What left the symptom behind was not always a *single* experience. On the contrary, the result was usually brought about by the convergence of several traumas, and often by the repetition of a great number of similar ones. Thus it was necessary to reproduce the whole chain of pathogenic memories in chronological order, or rather in reversed order, the latest ones first and the earliest ones last; and it was quite impossible to jump over the later traumas in order to get back more quickly to the first, which was often the more potent one . . . It is true that [hysterical patients and other neurotics] have driven [the idea] out of consciousness and out of memory and have apparently saved themselves a large amount of unpleasure. *But the repressed wishful impulse continues to exist in the unconscious.* It is on the look-out for an opportunity of being activated, and when that happens it succeeds in sending into consciousness a disguised and unrecognizable *substitute* for what had been repressed, and to this there soon become attached the same feelings of unpleasure which it was hoped had been saved by the repression.' (Sigmund Freud, 'Five Lectures on Psycho-Analysis', *SE*, vol. XI, pp. 14, 27.)

181   *Peau noire*, p. 117.
182   Ibid., p. 123.
183   Ibid., p. 143.
184   Ibid., p. 146n. Fanon immediately adds, however, that there are 'men dressed as ladies, who wear jackets and skirts'. He is convinced, or tries to convince himself, that they have 'a normal sexual life'.
185   Ibid., n.
186   Ibid., pp. 127, 113.
187   Chester Himes, *If He Hollers Let Him Go*, London: Serpent's Tail, 1999, p. 33.
188   Ibid., p. 82.
189   Ibid., p. 222.
190   Ibid., p. 224.
191   *Peau noire*, pp. 123–4.
192   In the second edition, the title is revised as *Le Syndrôme d'abandon*, Paris: PUF, 1973. The change from 'neurosis' to the broader

'syndrome' may reflect the author's awareness that her original concept had not gained wide acceptance. This appears to be the significance of her personal communication to the author of one of the standard dictionaries of psychoanalysis; see the entry on 'Neurosis of abandonment' in Jean Laplanche and J.-B. Pontalis, *The Language of Psychoanalysis*, trans. Donald Nicholson-Smith, London: Hogarth Press, 1977, p. 270. References given here are to the second edition. Guex's book owes, as she acknowledges, a lot to Chapter 3 of her partner Charles Odier's *L'Angoisse et la pensée magique* ('La Névrose d'abandon'), 1948.

193  Guex, *Le Syndrôme d'abandon*, pp. 24–5.

194  Ibid., pp. 16, 17.

195  Ibid., p. 52.

196  The best, if somewhat impressionistic, source of information on Maran is the collective *Hommage à René Maran*, Paris: Présence africaine, 1965. See also Régis Antoine, *La Littérature franco-antillaise*, pp. 154–66.

197  René Maran, *Un Homme pareil aux autres*, Paris: Editions Arc-en-ciel, 1947, p. 226.

198  The second non-white Goncourt winner was the Moroccan Tahar Ben Jalloun with his *La Nuit sacrée* (1987).

199  Maran, *Un Homme pareil aux autres*, pp. 135, 136.

200  *Peau noire*, p. 52.

201  Maran, *Un Homme pareil aux autres*, p. 25.

202  Ibid., p. 83.

203  Ibid., p. 227, cited *Peau noire*, p. 60, Fanon's emphasis.

204  *Peau noire*, pp. 5, 188.

## 6 In Algeria's Capital of Madness

1  'Médicat des hôpitaux psychiatriques', *Information psychiatrique*, June 1953, pp. 150–2.

2  Pierre Bouvier, *Fanon*, Paris: Editions Universitaires, 1971, p. 37.

3  Fanon and François Tosquelles, 'Sur quelques cas traités par la méthode de Blini'; 'Indications de la thérapeutique de Blini dans le cadre des thérapeutiques institutionnelles'; 'Sur un essai de réadaptation chez une malade avec épilépsie morphéïque et troubles de caractère grave'; Fanon and Maurice Despinoy, 'A propos d'un cas de syndrôme de Cotard avec balancement psychosomatique'; Fanon, Maurice Despinoy and W. Zemmer, 'Notes sur les techniques de cure de sommeil avec conditionnement et contrôle électro-encéphelographique', all published in *Congrès des médicins aliénistes et neurologues de France et des pays de langue française, Pau 1953*.

4 Tosquelles and Fanon, 'Sur un essai de réadaptation', p. 363.
5 Undated letter (June 1953) to Maurice Despinoy, reproduced *Sans Frontière* (numéro spécial, hors série) February 1982, p. 46.
6 Ibid.
7 Interview with Edouard Fanon.
8 Cited, Joby Fanon, 'Formons un homme neuf', *Antilla* 23, November–December 1982, p. 24.
9 Philippe Lucas, *Sociologie de Frantz Fanon: Contribution à une anthropologie de la libération*, Algiers: SNED, 1971, p. 119.
10 'Le Syndrôme nord-africain', in *Pour la révolution africaine*, p. 21.
11 Boucif Mekhaled, *Chroniques d'un massacre: 8 mai 1945, Sétif, Guelma, Kherrata*, Paris: Syros, 1995, p. 118. Mekhaled's study of the events of May 1945 is based on the thesis he defended at the Sorbonne in June 1989; it was the first thesis on the Algerian war by an Algerian historian to be awarded a French doctorate.
12 Rachid Boudjedra, *Lettres algériennes*, Paris: Grasset, 1995, pp. 165–6.
13 Cited Mekhaled, *Chroniques*, p. 122.
14 Ibid., p. 131.
15 Ibid., p. 162.
16 *Sociologie d'une révolution*, p. 123.
17 Simone de Beauvoir, *La Force des choses*, Paris: Livre de Poche, 1969, Vol. I, pp. 50–1.
18 Edward Behr, *The Algerian Problem*, Harmondsworth: Penguin, 1961, p. 55.
19 *Les Echos de la Soummam*, 9, May 1985, cited, Mekhaled, *Chroniques*, p. 188.
20 Droz and Lever, *Histoire de la guerre d'Algérie*, p. 32.
21 Mekhaled, *Chroniques*, p. 182.
22 *Information psychiatrique*, November 1953, p. 266.
23 Charles Geronimi, 'Portrait de Fanon', unpublished typescript.
24 Interview with Jacques Postel.
25 M. Despinoy, F. Fanon and W. Zinner, 'Notes sur les techniques de cure de sommeil', pp. 617–20.
26 Cited C. Razanajao and Jacques Postel. 'La Vie et l'oeuvre psychiatrique de Frantz Fanon', *Information psychiatrique*, vol. L1, no. 10, December 1975, p. 1055; interview with Jacques Postel.
27 Cited, ibid.
28 Their status had recently been redefined by the law of 11 July 1953. At that time, there were almost three million *bouilleurs de cru* in France. It was estimated that in Brittany, the average male adult consumed between 54 and 70 litres of pure alcohol per year. Cf. Theodore Zeldin, *France 1848–1945: Taste and Corruption*, Oxford: Oxford University Press, 1980, pp. 413–14. *Bouilleurs de*

*cru* still exist, but they lost the privilege of being able to bequeath their right to distil in 1960.

29   Interview with Edouard Fanon.

30   See Michel Winnock, 'La Chute de Mendès France' in *Etudes sur la France de 1939 à nos jours*, Paris: Seuil, collection 'Points', 1985, pp. 267–82.

31   Michel Leiris, 'Martinique, Guadeloupe, Haiti', *Les Temps modernes*, 52, February 1950; *Contacts de civilisations en Martinique et en Guadeloupe*, Paris: Gallimard/UNESCO, 1951. On Leiris, see the biography by Aliette Armel, *Michel Leiris*, Paris: Fayard, 1997.

32   Alfred Métraux, *Le Vaudou haïtien*, Paris: Gallimard, 1958.

33   Alfred Métraux, *Itinéraire I 1935–1953: Carnets de notes et journaux de voyage*, Paris: Payot, 1978, p. 523. The relevant diary entry is dated Tuesday 15 September 1953.

34   Tosquelles and Fanon, 'Indications de la thérapeutique de Bini', p. 545.

35   H. Aubin, 'L'Assistance psychiatrique indigène aux colonies', *Congrès des Médecins aliénistes et neurologues de France et des pays de langue française: Alger 1938*, p. 158.

36   De de Leyritz, 'L'Assistance aux aliénés aux Antilles françaises', *Information psychiatrique*, January 1955, p. 57; Maurice Despinoy, 'Les Débuts de l'hôpital psychiatrique de la Martinique', *Information psychiatrique*, October 1955, p. 402.

37   R. L. Fayaud, 'Expérience d'un psychiatre en Martinique', *Information psychiatrique*, vol. 60, no. 4, April 1984, p. 405.

38   'L'Hôpital psychiatrique de Blida de 1961 à 1968', *Information psychiatrique*, vol. 45, no. 8, 1969, p. 823.

39   Pierre Mannoni, *Les Français d'Algérie: Vies, moeurs, mentalités. De la conquête des territoires du Sud à l'Indépendance*, Paris: L'Harmattan, 1993, p. 204.

40   Marie Cardinal, *Aux Pays des mes racines*, Paris: Livre de poche, 1982, pp. 146–9.

41   Marie Cardinal, *Les Pieds-noirs*, Paris: Belfond, 1988, p. 130; see also Georges Mutin, 'Ce "Chef d'oeuvre" de la France: la Mitidja' in Charles-Robert Ageron (ed.), *L'Algérie des Français*, Paris: Seuil, collection 'Points', 1993.

42   Cardinal, *Les Pieds-noirs*, p. 130.

43   Reproduced, *Photographes en Algérie au XIXe siècle*, Paris: Musée-Galerie de la SEITA, 1999, pp. 11, 30.

44   *Le Damnés de la terre*, p. 32.

45   Assia Djebar, *Les Enfants du nouveau monde*, Paris: 10/18, 1973, p. 13.

46   Jean Cohen, 'Colonialisme et racisme en Algérie', *Les Temps modernes*, November 1955, pp. 856–7.

47 Jean-Michel Bégué, *Un Siècle de psychiatrie française en Algérie (1830–1939)*, Mémoire pour le Certificat d'Etudes Spéciales de Psychiatrie, Université Pierre et Marie Curie, Faculté de Médecine Saint-Antoine, 1989 (unpublished), pp. 45, 61, 63.

48 Cited, Maurice Desruelles and Henri Bersot, 'Note sur l'histoire de l'assistance aux aliénés en Algérie depuis la conquête', *Congrès 1938*, p. 312.

49 Robert Berthelier, *L'Homme maghrébin dans la littérature psychiatrique*, Paris: L'Harmattan, 1994, pp. 71–2.

50 The use of 'front line' is a reminder that Porot was originally a military man.

51 Maurice Desruelles and Henri Bersot, 'L'Assistance aux aliénés en Algérie', *Annales médico-psychologiques* 1939, vol. 2. p. 591.

52 Bégué, *Un Siècle de psychiatrie française*, p. 64.

53 Interview with Olivier Fanon.

54 'Entretien exclusif avec Mme Josie Fanon', *Révolution africaine*, 11 December 1987.

55 Dr Aymé, 'Le Relévement de nos traitements', *Information psychiatrique*, February 1955; Monique Gadant, *Islam et nationalisme en Algérie d'après 'El Moudjahid', organe centrale du FLN de 1956 à 1962*, Paris: L'Harmattan, 1988, p. 101.

56 Charles Geronimi, 'Portrait de Frantz Fanon', unpublished typescript.

57 Cited ibid., Geronimi draws here on Azoulay's unpublished thesis 'Contribution à l'étude de la social-thérapie dans un service d'aliénés musulmans', University of Algiers, 1954.

58 Charles Geronimi, 'Rencontre avec Fanon'; interview with Charles Geronimi.

59 *Sociologie d'une révolution*, pp. 107, 122.

60 Monique Gadant, *Islam et nationalisme en Algérie*, p. 101.

61 *Sociologie d'une révolution*, pp. 121n, 114n.

62 Frantz Fanon, 'Lettre au ministre Résident', *Pour la Révolution africaine*, p. 50.

63 Patricia M. E. Lorcin, *Imperial Identities: Stereotyping, Prejudice and Race in Colonial Algeria*, London: I. B. Tauris, 1995, p. 120.

64 Ibid., p. 121.

65 Edward W. Said, *Orientalism*, London: Routledge and Kegan Paul, 1978.

66 The best discussion of the Kabyle question is Lorcin's *Imperial Identities*. I discuss her study in the review article 'A French Algeria', *Economy and Society*, vol. 25, no. 4, November 1996.

67 Paul Raynal, *L'Expédition d'Algers. Lettres d'un témoin* (1830), cited, Philippe Lucas and Jean-Claude Vatin, *L'Algérie des anthropologues*, Paris: Maspero, 1975. This anthology gives invaluable insights into racial stereotyping in colonial Algeria.

68    Bégué, *Un siècle de psychiatrie française*, p. 69.
69    Lucas and Vatin, *L'Algérie des anthropologues*, p. 26.
70    Lorcin, *Imperial Identities*, p. 123.
71    Dr Boigey, 'Etude psychologique sur l'Islam', *Annales médico-psychologiques*, October 1908, p. 5.
72    Ibid., p. 6.
73    Ibid., p. 7.
74    Ibid., p. 12.
75    See Sleim Ammar, 'Antoine et Maurice Porot à Tunis', *Psychopathologie médicale*, vol. 15, no. 10, 1983.
76    H. Reboul and E. Régis, 'L'Assistance des aliénés aux colonies', *Congrès 1912*, pp. 47–8, 208.
77    See Fanny Colonna, 'Islam in the French Sociology of Religion', trans. David Macey, *Economy and Society*, vol. 24, no. 2, May 1995.
78    *Constantine: son passé, son centenaire (1837–1937): Recueil des notices et mémoires de la Société Archéologique de Constantine, vol LXIV*, Constantine: Editions Braham, 1937.
79    Louis Bertrand, preface to *Le Sang des races*, Paris: Albin Michel, 1930. For literature's role in the creation of 'French Algeria', see Peter Dunwoodie, *Writing Algeria*, Oxford: Clarendon Press, 1998.
80    Albert Camus, *Noces, suivi de L'Eté*, Paris: Folio, 1980.
81    Antoine Porot, 'Notes de psychiatrie musulmane', *Annales médico-psychologiques*, May 1918, pp. 380, 381, 382–3.
82    Ibid., p. 378.
83    A. Porot and D. C. Arrii, 'L'Impulsivité criminelle chez l'indigène algérien: ses facteurs', *Annales médico-psychologiques*, December 1932, pp. 588–611.
84    Cf. Fanon, *Sociologie d'une révolution*, p. 134n: 'The "djinn" is a spirit. It haunts houses and fields. Popular belief credits it with an important role in all the phenomena of life: birth, circumcision, marriage, illness, death. In the case of illness itself, any medical ailment was interpreted as the action of an evil djinn.'
85    Porot and Arrii, 'L'Impulsivité criminelle', p. 596.
86    John Ruedy, *Modern Algeria, The Origins and Development of a Nation*, Bloomington and Indianopolis: Indiana University Press, 1992, pp. 95–6.
87    Lorcin, *Imperial Identities*, p. 54.
88    Xème Région militaire, Service psychologique, *Connaissance de l'Algérie*, Algiers: Société nationale des entreprises de presse, nd., p. 29. The copy in my possession bears the handwritten inscription: '23 May–29 November 1956.'
89    Lorci, *Imperial Identities*, p. 123.
90    Lucien Lévy-Bruhl, *Les Fonctions mentales dans les sociétés*

*inférieures*, Paris: Alcan, 1910; *La Mentalité primitive*, Paris: Alcan, 1922; *L'Ame primitive, 1927; Le surnaturel et la nature dans la mentalité primitive*, 1931; *La Mythologie primitive* and *L'Expérience mystique et les symboles chez les primitifs*, 1938.

91   Lucien Lévy-Bruhl, *Carnets*, Paris: PUF, 1949.

92   A. Porot and J. Sutter, *Le 'Primitivisme' des indigènes Nord-Africains. Ses incidences en pathologie mentale*, Marseille: Imprimerie marseillaise 1939, p. 18. This pamphlet is an off-print of an article that first appeared in *Le Sud médical et chirurgical* in April 1939.

93   Yves Pellicier, 'Intégration des données sociologiques à la psychiatrie clinique', *Congrés* LVII, Marseille 1964, p. 135.

94   Antoine Porot (ed.), *Manuel alphabétique de psychiatrie clinique et thérapeutique*, Paris: PUF, 1975 (third edn), pp. 348, 452, 515–16. After protests from Robert Berthelier, Jacques Postel and others, these articles were deleted from later editions.

95   'Le Syndrôme nord-africain', pp. 12, 14.

96   Ghania Hammadou, 'Fanon-Blida, Blida-Fanon', *Révolution africaine* 11, December 1987.

97   Geronimi, 'Portrait de Fanon'.

98   Irene Gendzier, *Frantz Fanon: A Critical Study*, London: Wildwood House, 1973, p. 76.

99   Françoise Vergès, 'Chains of Madness, Chains of Colonialism: Fanon and Freedom', in Alan Read (ed.), *The Fact of Blackness: Frantz Fanon and Visual Representation*, London: Institute of Contemporary Arts and Institute of International Visual Arts, 1996, p. 48.

100  See Michel Foucault, *Histoire de la folie à l'âge classique*, Paris: Gallimard, Collection 'Tel', 1972, pp. 483–4.

101  *Les Damnés de la terre*, p. 201.

102  Interview with Fanny Colonna.

103  F. Fanon and J. Azoulay, 'La socialthérapie dans un service d'hommes musulmans: difficultés méthodologiques', *Information psychiatrique*, 30è Année, no. 9, 1954, pp. 349–61; interview with Jacques Azoulay.

104  Interview with Alice Cherki. Cf. Cherki's 'Témoignage d'une militante algérienne', in *Mémorial international*.

105  Hammadou, 'Fanon-Blida', p. 14.

106  Fanon and Azoulay, 'La socialthérapie', p. 354.

107  Ibid., p. 355.

108  Hammadou, 'Fanon-Blida', p. 14.

109  'La socialtherapie', p. 356.

110  J. McCulloch, *Black Soul, White Artifact: Fanon's Clinical Psychology and Social Theory*, Cambridge: Cambridge University Press, 1983, p. 132.

111 Ibid., p. 360.

112 Ibid., p. 361.

113 Anonymous informant, cited Boualem Souibes, 'Frantz Fanon. Un enfant du pays', *Parcours maghrébins*, 12 September 1987, p. 87.

114 Joby Fanon, 'Formons un homme neuf', p. 24.

115 See J. Dequeker, F. Fanon, R. Lacaton, M. Micucci and F. Ramée, 'Aspects actuels de l'assistance mentale en Algérie', *Information psychiatrique*, 31ème Année, no. 11, 1955.

116 F. Fanon and C. Geronimi, 'Le TAT chez les femmes musulmanes: sociologie de la perception et de l'imagination', *Congrès des médecins aliénistes et neurologues de France et des pays de langue française*. LIVe Session: Bordeaux, 1956, p. 365.

117 Ibid., p. 366.

118 Ibid., p. 367. Cf. Pierre Bourdieu, *Algérie 60: structures économiques et structures temporelles*, Paris: Editions de minuit, 1977, pp. 28–8: '*Azka d azqa*, "tomorrow is the grave": the future is a void which it is pointless to try to grasp, a void that does not belong to us . . . "the future belongs to God".'

119 Fanon and Geronimi, 'Le TAT', pp. 367–8.

120 Ibid., p. 368.

121 Interview with Jacques Azoulay.

122 Lucas, *Sociologie de Frantz Fanon*, p. 88.

123 Frantz Fanon and François Sanchez, 'Attitude du musulman algérien devant la folie', *Revue pratique de la psychologie de la vie sociale et d'hygiène mentale*, no 1, 1956, pp. 24–7.

124 Ibid., p. 26.

125 Jacques Azoulay, François Sanchez and Frantz Fanon, 'Introduction aux troubles de la sexualité chez le Nord-Africain', unpublished typescript (11 pp.) in the collection of Olivier Fanon.

126 A 'taleb' is literally one who can write, or a student (of the Koran).

127 Women's use of magic to control the behaviour of men is also described by Marnia Lazreg in her *The Eloquence of Silence: Algerian Women in Question*, New York and London: Routledge, 1994, pp. 113–15. Whilst she does not discuss the use of 'tying' to make men impotent, her description does broadly tally with that given by Azoulay, Sanchez and Fanon.

128 The paradox is that, when he discusses magical practices and possession cults in *Les Damnés de la terre*, Fanon takes a much less sympathetic view and describes them as a flight from reality.

129 T. S. Kuhn, *The Structure of Scientific Revolutions*, Chicago: University of Chicago Press, 1962.

130 Fanon and J. Sourdoire, 'Etude biologique de l'action du citrate de lithium dans les accès maniaques', unpublished typescript (4 pp.) in the possession of Jacques Postel; J. Sourdoire, letter of 29 August 1975 to Jacques Postel.

131  Interview with Edouard Fanon.
132  Reproduced, Joby Fanon, 'Pour Frantz, pour notre mère'.


## 7 The Explosion

1  This enigmatic phrase obviously does not refer to Algeria; it may be a memory of a line from Sartre's play *Huis clos* (1944): 'One always dies too early – or too late', Sartre, *Huis clos, suivi de Les Mouches*, Paris: Folio, 1975, p. 89.

2  Robert Barrat, *Les Maquis de la liberté*, Algiers: Entreprise Algérienne de Presse; Paris: Editions Témoignage Chrétien, 1987, p. 102n.

3  Born in 1926 and the son of a very poor family, Bitat had long been involved in political and terrorist activities and had been sentenced to death *in absentia*.

4  Henri Alleg (ed.), *La Guerre d'Algérie*, Paris: Temps actuels, 1981, vol. I, pp. 430–1.

5  Commandant Si Azzedine, *On nous appelait fellaghas*, Paris: Stock, 1976, p. 50.

6  Yves Courrière, *La Guerre d'Algérie*, Paris: Robert Laffont, Collection 'Bouquins' 1991, vol. I, p. 499.

7  Djamila Amrane, *Les Femmes algériennes dans la guerre*, Paris: Plon, 1991, p. 229, citing reports published in the daily *Dépêche quotidienne d'Alger*. In the mountains of the Tebessa area in the east of the country there were twenty-six significant engagements over the same period, and army patrols were attacked on fifty-three separate occasions.

8  *L'Humanité*, 2 November 1954.

9  Mouloud Feraoun, *Journal 1955–1962*, Paris: Seuil, 1962, p. 13.

10  *Paris Match*, 4 November 1954.

11  Jacques Droz and Evelyne Lever, *Histoire de la guerre d'Algérie 1954–1962*, Paris: Seuil, collection 'Points', 1991, p. 345.

12  Charles-Robert Ageron, *La Décolonisation française*, Paris: Armand Colin, 1991, pp. 144–7.

13  On Tunisia, see Charles-André Julien, *Et La Tunisie devient indépendante . . . (1951–1957)*, Paris: Editions Jeune Afrique, 1985. The case of Morocco is less fully documented, but see the same author's *Le Maroc face aux impérialismes (1415–1956)*, Paris: Editions Jeune Afrique, 1978. For the military aspects, see Anthony Clayton, *The Wars of French Decolonization*, London and New York: Longman, 1994, pp. 88–107.

14  The phrase was apparently current long before 1954, but no one knows if it was coined by Algerian nationalists or colonialist provocateurs. Cf. Monique Gadant, *Islam et nationalisme en Algérie*

*d'après 'El Moudjahid', organe centrale du FLN de 1956 à 1962*, Paris: L'Harmattan, 1988, p. 142.

15    See Jean-Jacques Jordi, *1963: L'Arrivée des pieds-noirs*, Paris: Autrement, 1995.

16    Anthony Clayton, *The Wars of French Decolonization*, London: Longman, 1994, pp. 69–71. General V.N. Giap's own account of the battle is given in his classic *Guerre du peuple, armée du peuple*, Hanoi: Editions en langues étrangères, 1961. For a general account of the war in Indochina, see Jacques Dalloz, *La Guerre d'Indochine 1945–1954*, Paris: Seuil, 1987.

17    Alistair Horne, *A Savage War of Peace: Algeria 1954–1962*, London: Papermac, 1987, pp. 167, 168.

18    Ibid., p. 189.

19    François Mauriac, *Bloc-notes. Tome I 1952–1957*, Paris: Seuil, collection 'Points', 1993, p. 214.

20    Droz and Lever, *Histoire de la guerre d'Algérie*, p. 70.

21    Courrière, *La Guerre d'Algérie*, vol. I, pp. 385–6.

22    See Chapter Nine of Manville's *Les Antilles sans fard*.

23    Ghedefi Ben Ali, letter of 18 January 1955 to his lawyer Maître Douzon, reproduced in Patrick Kessel and Giovanni Pirelli (eds), *Le Peuple algérien et la guerre: lettres et témoignages 1954–1963*, Paris: Maspero, 1962, pp. 2–3.

24    Alleg, *La Guerre d'Algérie* vol. 1, p. 277.

25    Feraoun, *Journal*, p. 112.

26    *Le Monde*, 15 February 1999.

27    *Des Rappelés témoignent*, Clichy: Comité Résistance Spirituelle, 1957, p. 69.

28    Robert Bonnaud, 'La Paix des Nementchas', *Esprit*, April 1957, p. 591.

29    See Jacques Isnard's obituary of Louis Delarue, *Le Monde*, 4 April 1998.

30    The directive was eventually published in issue 200 of the *Revue Historique des Armées*, September 1995. The *Revue* did not, however, reproduce the much more compromising descriptions of the 'coercive methods' used to instil 'respect'; see *Le Monde* 25 October 1995.

31    Alleg, *La Guerre d'Algérie*, vol. I, p. 467.

32    Droz and Lever, *Histoire de la guerre d'Algérie*, p. 62.

33    *Le Monde*, 5 February 1999.

34    Assia Djebar, *Les Enfants du nouveau monde*, Paris: 10/18, 1973, p. 19.

35    Reproduced, Mohammed Harbi (ed.), *Les Archives de la Révolution algérienne*, Paris: Editions Jeune Afrique, 1981, pp. 102–3. The text is also reproduced by Courrière, vol. I, pp. 399–401 and Alleg, vol III, pp. 507–10.

36 Born in 1919, Boudiaf had worked in the inland revenue service and served in the army as a warrant officer. Captured in 1956, he remained in prison until 1962 and was then forced into exile when he came into conflict with Ben Bella. In January 1992, Mohamed Boudiaf became President of Algeria; he was assassinated in June of the same year. Didouche was one of the few founders of the FLN to come from a middle-class background; he was killed in action in January 1955.

37 Mohammed Harbi, *1954: La Guerre commence en Algérie*, Brussels: Editions complexe, 1984, p. 25.

38 Ali Haroun, *La 7e Wilaya: La Guerre du FLN en France, 1954–1962*, Paris: Seuil, 1986, p. 13.

39 Courrière, *La Guerre d'Algérie*, vol. I, p. 229.

40 For the official FLN account, see the 'Procès-verbal' reproduced in Courrière, *La Guerre d'Algérie*, vol. I, pp. 902–30.

41 Droz and Lever, *Histoire de la guerre d'Algérie*, pp. 62–3; Clayton, *The Wars*, p. 115.

42 Horne, *A Savage War*, pp. 152–3.

43 A useful chronological account of the development of Algerian nationalism is given in Mohammed Harbi, *Aux Origines du Front de Libération Nationale: La Scission du PPA/MTLD. Contribution à l'histoire du populisme révolutionnaire en Algérie*, Paris: Christian Bourgois, 1975.

44 E. J. Hobsbawm, *Primitive Rebels*, London: Weidenfeld and Nicolson, 1959.

45 The standard biography is Benjamin Stora's *Messali Hadj*, Paris: L'Harmattan, 1986.

46 The founding declaration of the PPA is reproduced in Patrick Eveno and Jean Planchais (eds), *La Guerre d'Algérie*, Paris: La Découverte and *Le Monde*, 1990, pp. 20–1.

47 Robert Merle, *Ben Bella*, trans. Camilla Sykes, London: Michael Joseph, 1967, pp. 77–85.

48 Born in 1917, Ben Bouliad was a miller who became a bus operator. Arrested in 1955, he succeeded in escaping but was killed by a booby trap in March 1956.

49 A former soldier and assistant secretary to a *commune mixte*, born in 1922, Krim took to the mountains in 1945 after having been wrongly accused of murder. In 1958, he became the Vice-President of the GPRA. After independence, he attempted to oppose Ben Bella and then retired from political life. In 1970, he was assassinated in mysterious circumstances in Frankfurt.

50 Ben M'Hidi was captured by paratroopers in February 1957 and was 'suicided' shortly afterwards.

51 Born in 1924 and the son of a Kabyle caid, Ait was one of the few FLN leaders to have a high level of education. See his *Mémoires*

*d'un combattant. L'Esprit d'indépendance 1942–1952*, Paris: Sylvie Messinger, 1983.

52  Khider was involved in the OS's attack on the Oran post office. Jailed in 1956, he was released in 1962. He was murdered in Madrid in 1967.

53  Reproduced, Courrière, *La Guerre d'Algérie*, vol. I, p. 909.

54  Jean Cohen, 'Colonialisme et racisme en Algérie', *Les Temps modernes*, November 1955, p. 584.

55  Benamar Meidenne, 'Le Voyage fanonien: de l'archipel au continent', *Algérie-Actualité*, 5–11 December 1991, p. 23; Claudine Chaulet, 'Relecture sociologique de Fanon', *Kalim* 4, 1982, p. 7; Ghania Mouffok, 'Fanon par ceux qui l'ont connu', *Algérie–Actualité*, 17–25 December 1992, p. 33.

56  Chaulet describes his background in the discussion that follows Aline Coutrot's paper on 'Les Scouts de France et la guerre d'Algérie', *Cahiers de l'Institut de l'Histoire du Présent*, 8 October 1988, special issue on *La Guerre d'Algérie et les chrétiens*.

57  Founded in 1939 and more or less tolerated by the colonial authorities, the Fédération des scouts musulmans algériens was quickly infiltrated by the PPA and became one of the nurseries of Algerian nationalism. Scouts played a conspicuous role in the demonstrations in Sétif and elsewhere in 1945. The importance of the scout movement does not appear to have been the object of serious study, but see the brief comments made in Mekhaled, *Chroniques d'un massacre*, pp. 53–7.

58  Cited, Courrière, *La Guerre d'Algérie*, vol. I, p. 609.

59  Jean-Jacques Jordi, 'L'Inconscience ou le péril' in Jean-Jacques Jordi and Guy Pervillé, *Alger 1940–1962: une ville en guerre*, Paris: Autrement, 1999, p. 98. On the *bidonvilles* that developed in the suburbs of Paris – and particularly Nanterre – see Abdelmalek Sayad, with Eliane Dupuy, *Une Nanterre algérien, terre de bidonvilles*, Paris: Autrement, 1995. The Nanterre *bidonville* was finally demolished at the beginning of the 1970s.

60  Cohen, 'Colonialisme et racisme', p. 580.

61  Ibid., p. 585.

62  Francis Jeanson, 'Cette Algérie, conquise et pacifiée', *Esprit*, April, May 1950, p. 620.

63  See André Mandouze, 'Plage, montagne et université', *Esprit* April, 1952.

64  André Mandouze, 'Impossibilités algériennces, ou le mythe des trois départements', *Esprit* 7, July 1947, p. 13. A *pinson* is a chaffinch and a *raton* a young rat. Both were commonplace racist epithets. *Ratonnade* ('rat-hunt') became the expression used to describe the lynchings and attacks on Algerians carried out by civilians in response to FLN acts of terrorism. Mandouze's comments

on the use of *tu* recall Fanon's remarks in *Peau noire*. The standard justification for this demeaning usage was that Arabic makes no distinction equivalent to that between *tu* and *vous*; whilst that may be true, Algerians were well aware of what the French distinction meant.

65  André Mandouze, *Mémoires d'outre siècle: Tome I. D'Une Résistance à l'autre*, Paris: Editions Viviane Hamy, 1998, p. 104.
66  *Consciences algériennes*, p. 216.
67  Ibid., p. 223.
68  Cited ibid., p. 223.
69  'Considérations éthno-psychiatriques', *Consciences maghrébines*, 5, Summer 1955. My thanks are due to Charles Geronimi for supplying me with a photocopy.
70  Marcel Manville, *Les Antilles sans fard*, Paris: L'Harmattan, 1992, p. 242.
71  Interview with André Mandouze.
72  Alice Cherki, 'Témoignage d'une militante algérienne', *Mémorial international*, p. 182; interview with Alice Cherki. Cherki's former husband Charles Geronimi insists that the talk was on 'fear' and maliciously notes that, having trained as a psychoanalyst, Cherki 'really ought to know the difference between fear and anxiety'.
73  Colette and Francis Jeanson, *L'Algérie hors la loi*, Paris: Seuil, 1955, p. 170.
74  Courrière, *La Guerre d'Algérie*, vol. I, p. 610.
75  *La Révolution algérienne par les texts; documents présentés par André Mandouze,* Paris: Maspero, 1961.
76  Azzedine, *On Nous Appelait Fellaghas*, pp. 18–23.
77  Charles Geronimi, 'Rencontre avec Fanon', unpublished typescript; interview with Charles Geronimi.
78  Courrière, *La Guerre d'Algérie*, vol. 1, p. 654.
79  Claudine Chaulet, 'Relecture sociologique de Fanon'; Ghania Mouffok, 'Fanon par ceux qui l'ont connu', *Algérie-actualité* 17–25 December 1982, p. 33; Benamar Medienne, 'Le Voyage fanonien: de l'archipel au continent', *Algérie-actualité*, 5–11 1991, p. 23.
80  Medienne, 'Le Voyage', p. 23.
81  Alleg, *La Guerre d'Algérie*, vol. II, p. 144.
82  *Sociologie d'une révolution*, pp. 124–5.
83  Horne, *A Savage War*, p. 131.
84  Slimane Chikh, *L'Algérie en armes, ou le temps des certitudes*, Paris: Economica, 1981, p. 221, citing *El Moudjahid*, 1 November 1958.
85  Horne, *A Savage War*, pp. 120–1.
86  Louis Arti, *El Halia, le sable d'El Halia,*, Chambéry: Editions Comp'act, 1996, p. 28.

87    Cited, Horne, *A Savage War*, p. 121.

88    An FLN document dated June 1955 and reproduced, Harbi, *Les Archives*, p. 105, explains that the ban on smoking and drinking was both a declaration of faith in the Revolution and a way of striking a blow against 'the imperialist economy' (the sale of tobacco was a state monopoly): 'Boycotting tobacco and alcohol is a way of showing the world that the Algerian people is mature, that it is capable of obeying an order and that it knows where it is going.'

89    Chikh, p. 232–3; cf. Pierre Bourdieu, 'The Sense of Honour in Kabyle Society', trans. P. Sherrard, in J. G. Peristiany (ed.), *Honour and Shame: The Values of Mediterranean Society*, London: Weidenfeld and Nicolson, 1965.

90    Horne, *A Savage War*, pp. 105–6, 107.

91    Ibid., p. 118.

92    Feraoun, *Journal*, pp. 252–3. Feraoun tells the same story in his letter of 30 November 1957 to Albert Camus, in Feraoun, *Lettres à ses amis*, Paris: Seuil, 1969, p. 206.

93    See his rather disappointing autobiography, *Le Feu du sang: auto-biographie politique et charnelle*, Paris: Grasset, 1977. The book on the West Indies was Daniel Guérin, *Les Antilles décolonisées*, Paris: Présence africaine, 1977.

94    Letter of 27 February 1956, reproduced Daniel Guérin, *Ci-gît le colonialisme*, p. 329.

95    Letter of 1 March 1956, ibid.

96    'Lettre à un Français', *Pour la Révolution africaine*.

97    Mandouze, *Mémoires*, p. 246.

98    Philippe Bourdrel, *La Dernière Chance de l'Algérie française. Du Gouvernement socialiste au retour de De Gaulle*, Paris: Albin Michel, 1996, p. 21.

99    Courrière, *La Guerre d'Algérie* I, p. 564.

100   Mandouze, *Mémoires*, pp. 246–7; interviews with André Mandouze and Charles Geronimi.

101   Jean-Marie Domenach, 'Négocier en Algérie', *Esprit*, February 1956, p. 321.

102   Ortiz died in 1995. See the obituary published in *Le Monde*, 18 February 1995, p. 13.

103   Although it is a somewhat plodding exercise in hagiography, the best source of information is Khalfa Mammeri's *Abane Ramdane: héros de la guerre d'Algérie*, Paris: L'Harmattan, 1988.

104   Michel Fabre, *The World of Richard Wright*, Jackson: University of Mississippi Press, 1985, p. 212.

105   'Le Premier Congrès Mondial des Ecrivains et Artistes Noirs s'est ouvert en Sorbonne', *Le Figaro*, 20 September 1956.

106   The proceedings are published in *Présence africaine* (nouvelle

série), nos 7–8–9, June–November 1956. A facsimile edition was published in November 1997. Fanon's contribution was republished in 1964 in *Pour la Révolution africaine*. References given here are to the original journal publication.

107 Richard Wright, 'Tradition and industrialization. The Plight of the Tragic Elite in Africa', *Présence africaine*, June–November 1956, pp. 347–8.

108 The bibliographical notes appended to the published conference proceedings were singularly, and perhaps deliberately, uninformative: 'Fanon, Frantz. Born 20 July 1925. Qualifications; *Médecin des hôpitaux psychiatriques.* Publications: *Peau noire, masques blancs* (Editions du Seuil, 1952).'

109 Letter of 6 January 1953 to Richard Wright, reproduced, David Ray and Robert M. Farnsworth (eds), *Richard Wright: Impressions and Perspectives*, Ann Arbor, University of Michigan Press, 1973, p. 150. The original is in the Richard Wright Archive, University of Yale. See also Michel Fabre, 'Frantz Fanon et Richard Wright', in Dacy (ed.), *L'Actualité de Frantz Fanon.*

110 James Baldwin, 'Princes and Paupers', in *Nobody Know My Name: More Notes of a Native Son*, Harmondsworth: Penguin, 1991, p. 25. Baldwin's report on the Congress was first published in the January 1957 issue of *Encounter*.

111 'Après le Congrès', *Présence africaine* 11, December 1956, pp. 3, 4.

112 'Antillais et Africains', p. 23.

113 'Après le Congrès', p. 383.

114 For the suggestion that Richard Wright went to the US Embassy to voice concern about the 'leftist tendencies' of *Présence africaine's* executive committee, see the account of the Congress given in James Campbell, *Paris Interzone: Richard Wright and Others on the Left Bank 1946–1960*, London: Secker and Warburg, 1994, pp. 212–17.

115 See his *Anthologie de la nouvelle poésie algérienne*, Paris: Librairie Saint-Germain-des-près, 1971, and the posthumously published autobiographical novel *Ebauche du père; pour en finir avec l'enfance*, Paris: Gallimard 1989. Sénac was murdered in Algiers in 1973.

116 *Présence africaine*, June–November 1956, pp. 380–1.

117 Jacques Rabemananjara, 'L'Europe et nous', *Présence africaine*, June–November 1956, p. 22.

118 Basil Davidson, *In the Eye of the Storm: Angola's People*, Harmondsworth: Penguin, 1975, p. 158.

119 Horace Mann Bond, 'Reflections, Comparative, on West African Nationalist Movement', *Présence africaine*, June–November 1956, p. 134.

120 The literal meaning of *fidai* (masc. sing; the feminine is *fidaia; fidayine* and *fidayate* are the respective plural forms) is 'one who is willing to give his life for an ideal'.

121 Reproduced, Patrick Kessel and Giovanni Pirelli, *Le Peuple algérien et la guerre: Lettres et témoignages 1954–1962*, Paris: Maspero, 1962, pp. 46-7.

122 Droz and Lever, *Histoire de la guerre d'Algérie p.* 128.

123 Jacqueline Delange, 'Ethnologie du 1er congrès des intellectuels noirs', *Les Temps modernes*, April 1957, p. 1609.

124 Léopold Sédar Senghor, 'L'Esprit de la civilisation, ou les lois de la culture négro-africaine', *Présence africaine*, June-November 1956, pp. 51–65; Amadou Hampaté Bâ, 'Culture peuhle', ibid., pp. 85–97; the people known in English as the Fulah are referred to in French as the 'Peuhl', which derives from the Wolof.

125 'Débats', *Présence africaine*, 8, 9, 10, June–November 1956, p. 67. On Wright's attitude to negritude, see Fabre, *The World of Richard Wright*.

126 'Racisme et culture', p. 122.

127 Ibid., p. 126.

128 Ibid., p. 124. *Djemma* refers both to the traditional 'village assemblies' of Kabylia and to the paved stone squares on which they met.

129 Ibid., p. 124.

130 Cited by Tzvetan Todorov in his introduction to Alexis de Tocqueville, *De La Colonie en Algérie*, Brussels, Editions Complexe, 1988, p. 30.

131 *Des Rappelés témoignent*, Clichy Comité Resistance spirituelle, 1957, p. 68.

132 'Racisme et culture', p. 129; cf. *Peau noire*, p. 69.

133 'Racisme et culture', p. 123.

134 Ibid., pp. 125, 128.

135 Ibid., p. 131.

136 The press coverage is discussed in Jacques Howlett's 'Le 1er Congrès des écrivains et artistes noirs et la presse internationale', *Présence africaine*, 20, July 1958.

137 *L'Humanité*, 21 September 1956; *Le Monde*, 22 September 1956.

138 Jacqueline Delange, 'Ethnologie du 1er Congrès', p. 1615; Fanon, 'Racisme et culture', p. 130.

139 Fabre, *The World of Richard Wright*, p. 208.

140 Courrière, *La Guerre d'Algérie*, vol. I, p. 741.

141 Ibid., p. 747.

142 Cited, Jordi, 'L'Inconscience ou le péril', p. 140.

143 Manville, *Les Antilles sans fard*, pp. 158–9.

144 Geismar, *Frantz Fanon*, pp. 76–7. Regrettably, it is not possible to date this incident with any precision.

145  Cherki, 'Témoignage', pp. 182–3.
146  *Les Damnés de la terre*, p. 191.
147  Ibid., pp. 206–7. Fanon explains in a footnote that Rivet was a village where, in 1956, forty Algerian men had been dragged from their beds and shot by a French militia.
148  Ibid., p. 70.
149  Ibid., pp. 203–4.
150  Ibid., pp. 201–2.
151  Bernard Sigg, *Le Silence et la honte*, Paris: Messidor/Editions sociales, 1989, p. 124.
152  Mameri, *Abane Ramdane*, p. 224, citing an FLN leaflet distributed after the rue de Thèbes bombing.
153  Courrière, *La Guerre d'Algérie*, vol. 1, p. 734.
154  Mandouze, *Mémoires*, p. 246.
155  Ibid., p. 252; interview with André Mandouze.
156  Cited, Andrée Dore-Audibert, *Des Françaises d'Algérie dans la guerre d'Algérie*, Paris: Karthala, 1995, p. 200.
157  'Evocation de Frantz Fanon', *Alger républicain*, 7 January 1992.
158  Reproduced, *Information psychiatrique*, May 1957, p. 292.

## 8 Exile

1  Peter Geismar, *Frantz Fanon*, New York: Dial Press, 1971, p. 99.
2  Marcel Manville, *Les Antilles sans fard*, Paris: L'Harmattan, 1992, p. 244; interview with Marcel Manville.
3  Daniel Guérin, *Ci-gît le colonialisme*, The Hague and Paris: Mouton, 1983, p. 97.
4  Jeanson, 'Reconnaissance de Fanon', pp. 213–14.
5  Ibid., p. 215.
6  'Sa pensée était gênante à tous les égards' (interview with Mejid Daboussi Ammar), *Sans Frontiére*, February 1982.
7  *Le Monde*, 11 October 1956; cf. Eugéne Mannoni, '"Luttes à mort" entre Algériens en France', *Le Monde*, 12 October 1956.
8  *La Gangrène*, Paris: Minuit, 1959, pp. 14, 46.
9  Alexis Berchadsky, *'La Question' d'Henri Alleg: un livre-événement dans la France en guerre d'Algérie*, Paris: Larousse, 1994, p. 69.
10  'Cela s'est fait de façon tout à fait naturelle' (Entretien avec Francis Jeanson, par Denise Barrat), *Actualité de l'émigration*, 28 September 1987, p. 60.
11  A good account of the Jeanson network emerges from the transcripts of the trial in which its members were found guilty of betrayal of national security: Marcel Pejeu (ed.), *Le Procès du réseau Jeanson*, Paris: Maspero 1961; see also Francis Jeanson,

*Notre Guerre*, Paris: Minuit, 1960 and Hervé Hamon and Patrick Rotman, *Les Porteurs de valises: la résistance française à la guerre d'Algérie*, Paris: Seuil, collection 'Points', 1982.

12  Ali Haroun, *La 7ème Wilaya: la guerre du FLN en France 1954–1962*, Paris: Seuil, 1986, pp. 3078, 309.

13  Simone de Beauvoir, *La Force des choses*, Paris: Livre de poche, 1971, vol. I, p. 231; vol. 2, p. 58. On Beauvoir's opposition to the Algerian war, see Julien Murphy, 'Beauvoir and the Algerian War: Toward a Post-colonial Ethics' in Margaret A. Simon (ed.), *Feminist Interpretations of Simone de Beauvoir*, University Park, PA: Pennsylvania State University Press, 1995, pp. 263–97.

14  *Les Damnés de la terre*, p. 232.

15  Alistair Horne, *A Savage War of Peace: Algeria 1954–1962*, London: Papermac, 1987, pp. 159–60. Ben Bella's account of the incident is given in Robert Merle, *Ben Bella*, trans. Camilla Sykes, London: Michael Joseph, 1967, pp. 106–21.

16  *Sociologie d'une révolution*, p. 39.

17  Horne, *A Savage War*, pp. 160–1.

18  'Frantz Fanon, notre frère', *El Moudjahid*, 21 December 1961. It is difficult to reconcile the date given by *El Moudjahid* with Manville's 'month in Paris', and it is probable that his memory was faulty on this point.

19  Haroun, *La 7ème Wilaya*, pp. 28–9.

20  Interview with Assia Djebar.

21  Edward Behr, *The Algerian Problem*, Harmondsworth: Penguin. 1961, p. 119

22  Horne, *A Savage War*, p. 192.

23  Behr, *The Algerian Problem*, p. 112.

24  Djilali Sari, *Huit jours de la bataille d'Alger (28 janvier–4 février 1957)*, Algiers: Entreprise nationale du livre, 1987, p. 42.

25  See the photo-reportage 'Alger attend', *L'Express*, 8 February 1957, pp. 10–11.

26  Courrière, *La Guerre d'Algérie*, vol. I, p. 794.

27  Ibid., citing the 4 March issue of *Résistance algérienne*.

28  Jean-Jacques Jordi, avec la collaboration de Jean-Louis Planche, '1860–1930: une certaine idée de la construction de la France', in Jean-Jacques Jordi and Jean-Louis Planche, *Alger 1860-1939: le modèle ambigu du triomphe colonial*, Paris: Autrement, 1999, p. 26.

29  Cited, Gilles Manceron and Hassan Remaoun, *D'Une Rive à l'autre: la guerre d'Algérie de la mémoire à l'histoire*, Paris: Syros, 1993, p. 178.

30  Horne, *A Savage War*, p. 195.

31  Ibid., pp. 208–10.

32  Commandant Azzedine, *On nous appelait fallaghas*, Paris: Stock, 1976, pp. 317–18.

33　See Martin Thomas, 'Policing Algeria's Borders, 1956–1960: Arms supplies, Frontier Defences and the Sakiet Affair', *War & Society*, vol. 13, no. 1, May 1995.

34　'A Propos d'un cas de spasme de torsion', *La Tunisie médicale*, vol. XXXVI, no. 9, 1958, pp. 506–23; 'Premiers Essais de méprobamate injectable dans les états hypochondriaques', *La Tunisie médicale*, vol. XXXVI, no. 10, 1958, pp. 175–91.

35　S. Ammar, 'Antoine et Maurice Porot à Tunis', *Psychologie médicale*, vol. 15, no. 10, 1983, p. 1717.

36　Geismar, *Frantz Fanon*, p. 132. Fanon did not write about his experiences at the Manouba, and Geismar provides the only reliable account of his work there.

37　Interview with Charles Geronimi.

38　Salah Habib, 'Fusion et confusion des identités', *Passerelles* 11, Winter 1995–96, p. 57. Cf. *Les Damnés de la terre*, pp. 122–3.

39　Beauvoir, *La Force des choses*, vol. II, p. 427.

40　Albert Memmi, 'La Vie impossible de Frantz Fanon', *Esprit*, September 1971, p. 261.

41　Geismar, *Frantz Fanon*, pp. 133–4.

42　Ibid., p. 140; interview with Charles Geronimi.

43　'L'Hospitalisation de jour en psychiatrie: valeur et limites', *Tunisie médicale*, vol. XXXVII, no. 10, 1959, pp, 689-732; reprinted *Information psychiatrique*, vol. LIX, no. 10, pp. 1117–30.

44　'Témoignage de Charles Geronimi' in *Sociologie d'une révolution*, p. 167.

45　'L'Hospitalisation', p. 1122.

46　Ibid., p. 1117.

47　Interview with Charles Geronimi.

48　Interview reproduced, Danièle Djamila Ammanne-Minne, *Les Femmes dans la guerre d'Algérie: entretiens*, Paris: Karthala, 1994, p. 52.

49　Cited, Andrée Dore-Audibert, *Des Françaises d'Algérie dans la guerre d'Algérie*, Paris: Karthala, 1995, p. 201. I assume 'A.C.' to be Alice Cherki.

50　*Les Damnés de la terre*, p. 216.

51　Ibid., pp. 196–8.

52　Ibid., pp. 211–12.

53　Ibid., pp. 198–200.

54　'L'Hospitalisation', p. 1118.

55　Ibid., pp. 1118–19.

56　Ibid., p. 1120.

57　The only other evidence for this is the fleeting mention in *Peau noire* (p. 163) of 'the very even light that wells up from Van Gogh's red'.

58　Amal Kaddour, 'Farés époque Fanon', *El Moudjahid*, 16 December 1987.

59  'L'Hospitalisation', p. 1123.

60  Ibid., p. 1120.

61  'A Propos d'un cas de spasme de torsion', p. 522.

62  In the UK, it is the active substance in Equagesic, marketed in tablet form by Wyeth Laboratories.

63  'Premiers Essais du méprobamate injectable', p. 191.

64  Frantz Fanon, 'Rencontre de la société et de la psychiatrie (Notes de cours, Tunis, 1959–60', Oran: CRIDSSH, 1984.

65  Chester Himes, *My Life of Absurdity: The Later Years. The Autobiography of Chester Himes*, New York: Paragon House, 1976, p. 126.

66  The most useful account of *El Moudjahid* is that given in Monique Gadant's *Islam et nationalisme en Algérie*.

67  Horne, *A Savage War*, p. 245.

68  Ibid. p. 202; Courrière, *La Guerre d'Algérie*, vol. I, p. 852.

69  Djamal Amrani, *Le Témoin*, Paris: Editions de Minuit, 1960, p. 57. Amrani was Boumendjel's brother-in-law. He too was arrested, together with his brother. Although he was not himself a member of the FLN and had no history of political activism, he confessed under torture to having collected funds for the FLN and passing them on to Ali Boumendjel, whom he named as one of that organization's leaders.

70  *Vérité-liberté*, 11 July 1961, cited Alleg, *La Guerre d'Algérie*, vol. II, p. 510.

71  Ibid., p. 511.

72  Guy Claisse, 'La Radio à Tunis 1960–1962' in Michèle de Bussierre, Cécile Méadel and Caroline Ulman-Mauriat (eds), *Radios et télévision au temps des 'événements d'Algérie' 1954–1962*, Paris and Montréal: L'Harmattan, 1999, pp. 98–100.

73  John Ruedy, *Modern Algeria. The Origin and Development of a Nation*, Bloomington and Indianapolis: Indiana University Press, 1992, p. 126.

74  Jacques C. Duchemin, *Histoire du FLN*, Paris: La Table ronde, 1962. The photographs reproduced by Duchemin are not of particularly good quality. They are war souvenirs taken from prisoners and corpses, or found on the battlefield.

75  *Sociologie d'une révolution*, pp. 64–5.

76  Charles-Robert Ageron, 'Un Aspect de la guerre d'Algérie: la propagande du FLN et des Etats arabes', in Charles-Robert Ageron (ed.), *La Guerre d'Algérie et les Algériens 1954–1962*, Paris: Armand Colin/Institut d'histoire du temps présent, 1997, pp. 245–62. See also Benjamin Stora, 'Comment le FLN écoutait la radio', in Bussierre, Méadel and Ulmann-Mauriat, *Radios et télévision*, pp. 109–13.

77  Ageron, 'Un Aspect', pp. 246–9.

78   *Sociologie d'une révolution*, pp. 68–9.
79   Ibid., p. 69.
80   Ibid., pp. 72–3, 75.
81   François Mauriac, *Bloc-notes, Tome II, 1958–1960*, Paris: Seuil, 1993, p. 14.
82   Redha Malek, interviewed in Algiers in July 1988, reprinted Patrick Eveno and Jean Planchais, *La Guerre d'Algérie*, Paris: La Récouverte/*Le Monde*, 1990, p. 183.
83   Mouloud Feraoun, *Journal*, Paris: Seuil, 1962, p. 187.
84   Behr, *The Algerian Problem*, p. 224.
85   Charles-Henri Favrod, 'Les Hommes, les indigènes', *Gazette de Lausanne*, 27 January 1962.
86   'Nota biografica' in *I Dannati della terra*, Turin, 1962. This, together with conversations with Pirelli, became the basis for the introduction to Renate Zahar's *Kolonialismus und Entfremdung*, Frankfurt am Main: Europäische Verlagsanstalt, 1962; translated by W.F. Feuser, *Frantz Fanon: Colonialism and Alienation*, New York: Monthly Review Press, 1974.
87   Geismar, *Frantz Fanon*, p. 127.
88   'Aux Antilles, naissance d'une nation?', *El Moudjahid* 16, 15 January 1958, and 'Le Sang coule aux Antilles sous domination française', *El Moudjahid* 58, 5 January 1960.
89   Malek Redha, cited Eveno and Planchais, *La Guerre d'Algérie*, p. 183.
90   'Fureur raciste en France', *El Moudjahid* 42, 25 May 1959; *Pour La Révolution*, pp. 166–7. See *Le Monde*, 13 May 1959, p. 16 and 19 May 1959, p. 12.
91   Francis Jeanson, 'Lettre à Jean-Paul Sartre', *Les Temps modernes*, 169–70, April–May 1960, p. 1537.
92   'Les Intellectuels et les démocrates français devant la Révolution algérienne', *El Moudjahid*, 1, 15 and 30 December 1957, reprinted *Pour la Révolution africaine*.
93   'Un Article d'*El Moudjahid*: Le FLN attaque la gauche française', *France-Observateur*, 26 December 1957, pp. 3–4. Extracts from the final section, which included the appeal to the left, appeared in the same journal on 2 January 1958, pp. 4–5, as 'Un Nouvel Article d'*El Moudjahid*'.
94   Gilles Martinet, 'Réponse au FLN', *France-Observateur*, 2 January 1958, p. 4. Martinet subsequently reviewed *Les Damnés de la terre* in the same magazine, but appears not to have made the connection.
95   Mohammed Harbi, 'Avec ceux de la Wilaya IV', *Sans Frontière*, February 1982.
96   Mammeri, *Abane Ramdane*, p. 276.
97   Amrouche's main publications are *Cendres*, Paris: L'Harmattan,

1983 (first published Tunis, 1934), *Etoile secrète*, Paris: L'Harmattan, 1983 (first published Tunis, 1937) and *Chants berbères de Kabylie*, Paris: L'Harmattan, 1983 (first published Tunis, 1939). On Amrouche, see the exhibition catalogue *Jean Amrouche: L'Eternel Jugurtha (1906–1962)*, Marseille: Archives de la Ville de Marseille, 1985.

98    Cited in Tasaadit Yacine's long introduction to *Un Algérien s'adresse aux Français*, p. lxv.

99    Kateb Yacine, 'C'est vivre', *Jeune Afrique*, 5–11 November, 1962, p. 28.

100    'Pour un dialogue entre Algériens et Français', in Jean El-Mouhoub Amrouche, *Un Algérien d'adresse aux Français, ou l'histoire d'Algérie par les textes (1943–1961)*, Paris: L'Harmattan/Awal, 1994, p. 66 (first published in *France-Observateur*, 16 January 1958).

101    Ibid., p. 70.

102    Jean-Luc Einaudi, 'Paris au temps de la guerre d'Algérie', *Passerelles* 11, Winter 1995–96.

103    For a detailed discussion, see Danièle Joly, *The French Communist Party and the Algerian War*, London: Macmillan, 1991.

104    Maurice Thorez, 'La France du Front populaire et sa mission dans le monde', in *Oeuvres choisies en trois volumes: Tôme 1: 1924–1937*, Paris: Editions sociales, 1967, pp. 435–56.

105    Cited Joly, *The French Communist Party*, p. 75.

106    René Lespès, *Pour Comprendre l'Algérie*, Algiers: Gouvernement Général, 1937, p. 195.

107    Yvon Evenou-Norves, 'La Province d'Algérie', *Mercure de France*, April 1922, cited Peter Dunwoodie, *Writing French Algeria*, Oxford: Clarendon Press, 1998, p. 135.

108    Cited ibid., p. 80.

109    See, for example, Madeleine Riffaud's reports in *L'Humanité* and *La Vie ouvrière*. These, together with her coverage of the liberation of Paris in 1944 and of Vietnam, are reprinted as *De Votre Envoyée Spéciale*, Paris: Editeurs français réunis, 1964.

110    Hamon and Rotman, *Les Porteurs de valises*, p. 279.

111    Philippe Labro, *Des Feux mal éteints*, Paris: Folio, 1993, p. 38. First published in 1967, Labro's novel accurately captures the mixture of fear and boredom experienced by so many conscripts in Algeria.

112    See Alain Monchablon, 'Syndicalisme étudiant et génération algérienne' in Rioux and Sirinelli, *La Guerre d'Algérie et les intellectuels français*. For a more detailed account, see Jean-Yves Sabot, *Le Syndicalisme étudiant et la guerre d'Algérie*, Paris: L'Harmattan, 1995.

113    Edgar Morin, *Autocritique*, Paris: Seuil, collection 'Points', 1970, pp. 187–93.

114    *Le Monde*, 24 January 1956.

115    Beauvoir, *La Force des choses*, vol. I, pp. 227, 228.

116    Ibid., p. 234.

117    Jean-Paul Sartre, 'Le Colonialisme est un système', *Situations V: Colonialisme et néo-colonialisme*, Paris: Gallimard, 1964; originally published in *Les Temps modernes* 123, March–April 1956.

118    Aimé Césaire, 'La Mort des colonies', *Les Temps modernes*, 123, March–April 1956, pp. 1366-70.

119    'Quelques raisons de la révolte algérienne', in *Un Algérien s'ad-dresse aux Français*, pp. 26, 29–30.

120    The most significant articles were Robert Bonnaud, 'La Paix des Nemenchetas', *Esprit*, April 1957; Georges M. Mattei, 'Jours kabyles', *Les Temps modernes*, July–August, 1957; Jacques Pucheu, 'Un An dans les Aurès', *Les Temps modernes*, September 1957.

121    Jean-Jacques Servan-Schreiber, *Lieutenant en Algérie*, Paris: Seuil, 1957. This account of 'pacification' was first published in instalments in *L'Express* in March–April 1957.

122    Ibid., p. 73.

123    Pierre Vidal-Naquet, 'Une Fidélité têtue: la résistance française à la guerre d'Algérie', in *Face à la raison d'Etat: un historien dans la guerre d'Algérie*, Paris: La Découverte, 1989 (first published in *Vingtième siècle, revue d'histoire*, 10, 1986.

124    On the origins of Editions de Minuit, see the account given by its founder in Vercors, *La Bataille du silence: souvenirs de Minuit*, Paris: Presses de la cité, 1967.

125    Pierre Vidal-Naquet, *Mémoires II: Le Trouble et la lumière, 1955–1998*, Paris: Seuil/La Découverte, 1998, p. 32.

126    See Pierre-Vidal Naquet, *Mémoires I: La Brisure et l'attente, 1930–1955*, Paris: Seuil/La Découverte, 1995.

127    Pierre Vidal-Naquet, *Les Assassins de la mémoire*, Paris: La Découverte, 1987.

128    Henri Alleg, *La Question*, Paris: Editions du Minuit, 1961, p. 35 (first edition 1958).

129    The letter from Lieutenant-Colonel Mayer, which provides the official explanation, is reproduced in Pierre-Vidal Naquet, *L'Affaire Audin (1957–1978)*, Paris: Editions de Minuit, 1989. This is a vastly expanded version of the pamphlet of the same title published in 1957. See also Vidal-Naquet's *La Torture dans la République*, Paris: Maspero, 1983. French censorship meant that this book could not be published in France in 1963. It first appeared as *Torture: Cancer of Democracy*, Harmondsworth: Penguin, 1963. It is dedicated to the memory of the author's parents.

130    For his account of his years in prison, see his *Prisonniers de guerre*, Paris: Editions de Minuit, 1961.

131  The fullest account of the Alleg Affair is Alexis Berchadsky's invaluable '*La Question*' *d'Henri Alleg: un livre-événement dans la France en guerre d'Algérie*, Paris: Larousse, 1994.

132  Patrick Kessel, 'En l'Absence d'Audin', *France-Observateur*, 5 December 1957, p. 3.

133  *Sociologie d'une révolution*, p. 127.

134  'L'Algérie face aux tortionnaires français', *El Moudjahid*, 10, September 1957; *Pour la Révolution*, pp.66–7. Fanon is referring to Mattéi's 'Jours kabyles' and Louis Martin-Chauffier, *Contre la torture*, Paris: Seuil, 1957.

135  Mattéi, 'Jours kabyles', p. 159.

136  Alleg, *La Question*, p. 91.

137  'L'Algérie face aux tortionnaires', p. 67.

138  'A Propos d'un plaidoyer', *El Moudjahid* 12, 15 November 1957, *Pour la Révolution africaine*, pp. 69–71. Fanon is referring to Georges Arnaud and Jacques Vergès, *Pour Djamila Bouhired*, Paris: Editions du Seuil, 1957.

139  Cited Alleg, *La Guerre d'Algérie*, vol. II, p. 524. Bouhired was not executed; President Coty commuted her sentence to twenty years' hard labour to be served in France. She survived the war and married Saadi Yacef.

140  Cited, Pierre Vidal-Naquet, 'Une Fidélité têtue: la résistance française à la guerre d'Algérie' in *Face à la raison d'état: un historien dans la guerre d'Algérie*, Paris: La Découverte, p. 59.

141  Horne, *A Savage War*, pp. 221–2.

142  *Résistance algérienne*, June 1957, cited Zahir Ihaddaden, 'La Propagande du FLN pendant la guerre de libération nationale' in Charles-Robert Ageron (ed.), *La Guerre d'Algérie et les Algériens 1954–1962*, Paris: Armand Colin, 1997, p. 192.

143  Ibid., p. 193.

144  *Le Monde*, 2–3 June 1957.

145  *Le Monde*, 5 June 1957.

146  A very similar account is given in *Sociologie d'une révolution*.

147  Mohammed Harbi; *Le FLN: Mirage et réalité. Des origines à la prise de pouvoir*, Algiers: NAQO/ENAL, 1993, p. 421.

148  Manceron and Remaoun, *D'Une Rive à l'autre*, p. 153; Ihaddaden, 'La Propagande, p. 192.

149  Claude Bourdet, 'Melouza, crime et faute', *France-Observateur*, 6 June 1957, p. 4.

150  Courrière, *La Guerre d'Algérie*, vol. II, p. 46.

151  *Les Damnés de la terre*, p. 39.

152  See Courrière, *La Guerre d'Algérie*, vol. II, pp. 162f; Horne, *A Savage War*, pp. 228–30; Mameri, *Abane Ramdane*, pp. 291–303. Boussouf retired from politics after independence and went into business. He died in December 1980.

153  Harbi, *Le FLN, mirage et réalité*, p. 195.
154  Mohammed Harbi, 'Avex ceux de la Wilaya IV', *Sans Frontière*, February 1982, p. 23.
155  Beauvoir, *La Force des choses*, vol. II, p. 430.
156  Courrière, *La Guerre d'Algérie*, vol. II, p. 163.
157  Manceron and Remaoun, *D'Une Rive à l'autre*, p. 227.

## 9 'We Algerians'

1  Inexplicably, the passport, which is in the possession of Olivier Fanon, is inscribed with two different dates of issue. The first page is inscribed 'Given at Tunis, the tenth day of September 1958'; the third page reads 'Issued at Tunis, 10 August 1958'.
2  Interview with Olivier Fanon.
3  Henri Alleg, *La Guerre d'Algérie*, vol. II, Paris: Temps actuels, 1981, pp. 94–9.
4  Rehda Malek, *L'Algérie à Evian: histoire des négotiations secrètes 1956–1962*, Paris: Seuil, 1995, p. 73.
5  Jacques Droz and Evelyne Lever, *Histoire de la guerre d'Algérie*, Paris: Seuil, collection 'Points', 1991, p. 213.
6  Mohammed Harbi, *Le FLN: Mirage et réalité. Des origines à la prise de pouvoir*, Algeria NAQD/ENAL, 1993, pp. 230–1.
7  'Le Sang maghrébin ne coulera pas en vain', *El Moudjahid*, 18, 15 February 1958, *Pour la Révolution africaine*, pp. 95–9.
8  'La Farce qui change de camp', *El Moudjahid*, 21, 1 April 1958; *Pour la Révolution africaine*, p. 101.
9  Droz and Lever, *Histoire de la guerre d'Algérie*, pp. 166–8.
10  Ibid., pp. 171. Trinquier took over the command from Bigeard after the Battle of Algiers.
11  There is an immense literature on 13 May 1958. This brief account draws mainly on Droz and Lever's *Histoire de la guerre d'Algérie*. A good short account is given in René Rémond, *Le Retour de de Gaulle*, Brussels: Editions complexe, 1987. For the contemporary press coverage of the events, see André Debatty, *Le 13 mai et la presse*, Paris: Armand Colin, 1960 and the materials reproduced in *Le 13 mai 1958*, Paris: La Documentation française, 1985.
12  Droz and Lever, *Histoire de la guerre d'Algérie*, p. 173.
13  The fullest account is Rehda Malek's *L'Algérie à Evian*.
14  Jean Lacouture, *De Gaulle: The Ruler 1945–1970*, trans. Alan Sheridan, London: HarperCollins, 1993, p. 187.
15  Ibid., p. 189.
16  Droz and Lever, *Histoire de la guerre d'Algérie*, p. 211.
17  *Le Monde*, 28 May 1957.

18  See the full account given in chapter five of Ali Haroun's *La 7éme Wilaya*.

19  See Blanche Finger and William Karel, *Opération 'Vent printanier'. 16–17 juillet 1942: la rafle du Vel d'Hiv*, Paris: La Découverte, 1992.

20  'La Leçon de Cotonou', *El Moudjahid*, 28, 22 August 1958; *Pour la Révolution africaine*, p. 130.

21  'Appel aux Africains', *El Moudjahid*, 29, 17 September 1958; *Pour la Révolution africaine*, p. 135.

22  Droz et Lever, *Histoire de la guerre d'Algérie*, p. 198.

23  Ibid., pp. 200–1.

24  Basil Davidson, *Which Way Africa? The Search for a New Society*, Harmondsworth: Penguin, 1971, pp. 64–6.

25  See Claude E. Welch, Jr., *Dream of Unity: Pan-Africanism and Political Unification in West Africa*, Ithaca: Cornell University Press, 1966.

26  *The Times*, 24 November 1958.

27  *The Times*, 9 December 1958.

28  André Blanchet, 'La Conférence d'Accra prend l'allure d'une manifestation contre la France', *Le Monde*, 11 December 1958.

29  'La Leçon de Cotonou', *El Moudjahid*, 28, 22 August 1958; 'Appel aux Africains', *El Moudjahid*, 29, 17 September 1958; *Pour la Révolution africaine*, pp. 130, 135.

30  *The Times*, 12 December 1958.

31  Basil Davidson, *Black Star: A View of the Life and Times of Kwame Nkrumah*, London: Allen Lane, 1973, p. 169.

32  *The Times*, 10 December 1958.

33  *Le Monde*, 12 December 1958.

34  In his *Autobiography of Kwame Nkrumah*, London: Panaf Books, 1973, p. 92, Nkrumah defines positive action as 'the adoption of all legitimate and constitutional means by which we could attack the forces of imperialism in the country. The weapons were legitimate political agitation, newspaper and educational campaigns and, as a last resort, the constitutional application of strikes, boycotts and non-cooperation based on the principle of absolute non-violence, as used by Gandhi in India.' 'What I mean by Positive Action' was the title of a pamphlet he published in 1951.

35  *The Times*, 10 December 1958; cf. *Le Monde*, 11 December 1958.

36  'L'Algérie à Accra' and 'Accra: L'Afrique affirme son unité et définit sa stratégie', *El Moudjahid*, 34, 24 December 1958; *Pour la Révolution africaine*.

37  'La Guerre d'Algérie et la libération des hommes', *El Moudjahid*, 31, 1 November 1958; *Pour la Révolution*, p. 148.

38  *Pour la Révolution*, pp. 157–8.

39  Basil Davidson, *In the Eye of the Storm*, pp. 199–200; Mario de

Andrade, 'Fanon et l'Afrique combattante', in *Mémorial international*, pp. 253–4.

40 See Wunyabari O Maloba, *Mau Mau and Kenya: An Analysis of a Peasant Revolt*, Bloomington and Indianapolis: Indiana University Press, 1993; Greet Kershaw, *Mau Mau From Below*, Oxford: James Currey, Nairobi: EAEP and Athens: Ohio University Press, 1997.

41 Simone de Beauvoir, *La Force des choses*, vol. 2, Paris: Livre de Poche, 1971, p. 423.

42 Jean Daniel, '*Les Damnés de la terre* par Frantz Fanon', *L'Express*, 30 November 1961, p. 36.

43 Romain Rainero, 'L'Italie entre amitié française et solidarité algérienne' in Jean-Pierre Rioux (ed.), *La Guerre d'Algérie et les Français*, Paris: Fayard, 1990, p. 395.

44 Beauvoir, *La Forces des choses*, vol. II, p. 430.

45 The main proceedings were published in *Présence africaine*, 24–25, February–May 1959; a facsimile edition was produced in 1997. Other contributions appeared in *Présence africaine*, 27–28, August–November 1959.

46 *Le Monde*, 27 March 1959.

47 Alioune Diop, 'Le Sens de ce congrès', *Présence africaine*, 24–25, February–May 1959, p. 41.

48 Ibid., p. 44.

49 These included Claude Lévi-Strauss's *Race et histoire*, Paris: UNESCO, 1952.

50 J. Price-Mars, 'La Paléontologie, la préhistoire et l'archéologie au point de vue des origines de la race humaine et du role joué par l'Afrique dans la génèse de l'humanité', *Présence africaine*, 24–25, February–May 1959, p. 59.

51 Cheikh Anta Diop, 'L'Unité culturelle africaine', *Présence africaine*, 24–25, February–May 1959, pp. 60–5.

52 Amadou Hampaté Bâ, 'Sur l'animisme (à travers les mythes de l'Afrique noir)', ibid., pp. 152.

53 William T. Fontaine, 'Vers une philosophie de la littérature noire américaine', ibid., pp. 153–65.

54 Robert L. Carter, 'La Cour suprême des Etats-Unis et le problème de la discrimination raciale depuis 1940', ibid., pp. 166–84.

55 Benetta Jules-Rosette, *Black Paris: The African Writers' Landscape*, Urbana and Chicago: University of Illinois press, 1998, p. 64.

56 *Présence africaine*, 24–25, February–May 1959, pp. 389–90.

57 Fanon, 'Antillais et Africains'.

58 'Fondement réciproque de la culture nationale et des luttes de libération', *Présence africaine* 24–25, February–May 1959, p. 87.

59 Ibid., p. 83.

60 *Les Damnés de la terre*, p. 162.

61  Ibid., p. 175.

62  Ibid.

63  Ibid.

64  Ibid., p. 162.

65  Ibid., pp. 175–6.

66  Bernard Mouralis, *Littérature et développement*, Paris: Agence de Coopération culturelle et Technique/ Editions silex, 1984, p. 429; Jacques Rabemananjara, 'Quarantième Anniversaire de la revue *Présence africaine*', *Présence africaine* 144, 4e trimestre 1987. See also the pamphlet, *Premiers Jalons pour une politique de la culture*, Paris: Présence africaine, 1968.

67  *Les Damnés de la terre*, pp. 83–4.

68  Ibid., p. 84.

69  The term is derived from *Le Parnasse contemporain*, which was the generic title of three anthologies of poetry published between 1866 and 1876. Parnassianism celebrated an impersonal lyricism typified by Théophile Gautier's 'art for art's sake'.

70  *Les Damnés de la terre*, p. 164.

71  'Fondement réciproque', p. 85.

72  See, for example, Christopher L. Miller, *Theories of Africans: Francophone Literature and Anthropology in Africa*, Chicago: University of Chicago Press, 1990, p. 48.

73  'Fondement réciproque', p. 85.

74  Ibid., p. 86.

75  Ibid., p. 85.

76  Ghani Merad, *La Littérature algérienne d'expression française: approches socio-culturelles*, Paris: Pierre Jean Oswald, 1976, p. 67.

77  Jean El -Mouhoub Amrouche, 'La France comme mythe et comme réalité', in *Un Algérien s'adresse aux Français*, pp. 56–7, originally published in *Le Monde*, 11 January 1958. Fanon makes the same point: 'Rediscovering one's people means turning oneself into a *bicot*, making oneself as native as possible, as unrecognizable as possible, cutting off the wings one had grown', *Les Damnés de la terre*, p. 165.

78  Aït Djafer, 'Complainte des mendiants arabes de la Casbah et de la petite Yasmina, tuée par son pére', *Les Temps modernes* 98, January 1954, p. 1227.

79  Jean Sénac, 'Honte honte honte' in *Oeuvres poètiques*, Arles: Actes Sud, 1991, pp. 257–8, first published in *Matinale de mon peuple*, Rodez: Subervie, 1961.

80  There are now many studies of this literature. See, *inter alia*, *Europe* 567–8, July–August 1976 (*Littérature algérienne*), Merad's *Le Littérature algérienne* (1976) and Charles Bonn, *Le roman algérien de langue française*, Montréal and Paris: Presse de l'Université de Montréal and l'Harmattan.

81 See Peter Dunwoodie, *Writing French Algeria*, Oxford: Clarendon Press, 1998.

82 Maurice Nadeau, 'Romanciers d'Afrique du Nord', *Mercure de France*, March 1953.

83 Kateb Yacine, *Nedjma*, Paris: Seuil, collection 'Points', 1981, p. 175.

84 Mohammed Dib, *La Grande Maison*, Paris: Seuil, 1952; *L'Incendie*, Paris: Seuil 1954; *Le Métier à tisser*, Paris: Seuil, 1957.

85 Dib, *La Grande Maison*, pp. 19–22.

86 See Denise Brahimi, 'Littérature algérienne et conscience nationale: avant l'Indépendance', *Notre Librairie*, 85, October–December 1986.

87 Dib, *L'Incendie*, Paris: Seuil, collection 'Points', 1989, pp. 131–2.

88 Ibid., p. 82.

89 Mohammed Dib, 'Le Compagnon', in *Au Café*, Arles: Actes-Sud, 1996, p. 97.

90 Mohammed Dib, interviewed in 1958 and 1964 and cited, Monique Gadant, 'Vingt ans de littérature algérienne', *Les Temps modernes*, July–August 1982, p. 355.

91 'Lendemains d'un plébiscite en Afrique', *El Moudjahid*, 30, 10 October 1958; *Pour la Révolution*, p. 142.

92 Miller, *Theories of Africans*, p. 52.

93 *Les Damnés de la terre*, p. 174; Miller, *Theories of Africans*, p. 61.

94 *Les Damnés de la terre*, p. 173.

95 Miller, *Theories of Africans*, pp. 58–9.

96 *Les Damnés de la terre*, p. 159.

97 Cited, Courrière, *La Guerre d'Algérie* vol. I, p. 926.

98 Cited, Gadant, *Islam et nationalisme*, p. 51.

99 Ibid., p. 201.

100 Cited, ibid, p. 50.

101 See Jean Déjeux, 'Romans algériens et guerre de libération', *L'Esprit créateur*, vol. XXVI, no. 1, Spring 1986; Monique Gadant, 'Vingt ans de littérature algérienne', *Les Temps modernes*, July–August 1982, pp. 422–23.

102 Cited, Jean Sénac, *Anthologie de la nouvelle poésie algérienne*, p. 18; originally published in the collection *Chacun son métier*, Algiers: SNED, 1966.

103 Assia Djebar, *La Soif*, Paris: René Julliard, 1957; *Les Impatients*, Paris: René Julliard, 1958.

104 Djebar, *La Soif*, p. 14.

105 'La Nouvelle Algérienne', *France-Observateur*, 24 May 1962, p. 24 (interview by Sylvie Marion).

106 Interview with Assia Djebar.

107 Her major achievement to date is the trilogy made up of *L'Amour, la fantasia*, Paris: Jean-Claude Lattés, 1985, *Ombre sultane*, Paris:

Jean-Claude Lattés, 1987 and *Vaste est la prison*, Paris: Albin Michel 1995. On Djebar, see Monique Gadant, 'La Permission de dire "Je"', *Peuples méditerranéens* no. 48–49, July–December 1989, pp. 93–105; Joëlle Vitiello, 'Ecriture féminine et lieux interdits', *Notre Librairie* 117, April-June 1994, pp. 80–6.

109    Mostefa Lacheraf, 'L'Avenir de la culture algérienne' (interview by M. Brumagne), *Les Temps modernes*, October 1963, pp. 733–4.

109    Fanon, 'Fondement réciproque', p. 88.

110    Ibid., p. 82.

111    Cited, Droz and Lever, *Histoire de la guerre d'Algérie*, p. 28n.

112    Ahmed Mahsas, *Le Mouvement révolutionnaire en Algérie de la Première Guerre Mondiale à 1954: essai sur la formation du mouvement national*, Paris: L'Harmattan, 1979, pp. 20, 23.

113    Charles-Robert Ageron: 'Présentation: pour une histoire critique de l'Algérie de 1830 à 1972' in Ageron (ed.), *L'Algérie des Français*, p. 7.

114    Benedict Anderson, *Imagined Communities: Reflections on the Origin and Spread of Nationalism*, London: Verso, 1991 (revised edn).

115    'Fondement réciproque', p. 88.

116    Ibid.

117    *Sociologie d'une révolution*, p. 141.

118    Gadant, *Islam et nationalisme*, p. 57.

119    Interview by Bennetta Jules-Rosette, cited in her *Black Paris*, p. 144.

120    See Amilcar Cabral, *Revolution in Guinea: An African People's Struggle*, London: Stage 1, 1969; Basil Davidson, *The Liberation of Guiné: Aspects of an African Revolution*, Penguin: Harmondsworth, 1969; Patrick Chabal, *Amilcar Cabral: Revolutionary Leadership and People's War*, Cambridge: Cambridge University Press, 1983. Cabral was assassinated in January 1973.

121    Mario de Andrade, 'Fanon et L'Afrique combattante', in *Memorial International*, pp. 253–5.

122    Cited Basil Davidson, *In the Eye of the Storm: Angola's People*, Harmondsworth: Penguin, 1975, p. 186.

123    Mohammed Harbi, 'Avec ceux de la Wilaya IV', *Sans Frontière*, February 1982.

124    Arslan Humbaraci, *Algeria: A Revolution That Failed: A Political History since 1954*, London: Pall Mall Press, 1966, p. 161.

125    Davidson, *In the Eye of the Storm*, p. 202; cf. William Minter, *Portuguese Africa and the West*, Harmondsworth: Penguin, 1972, pp. 58–60.

126    Ibid. See also Lawrence W. Henderson, *Angola: Five Centuries of Conflict*, Ithaca: Cornell University Press, 1979.

# Notes

127  Davidson, *In the Eye of the Storm*, pp. 190–1.

128  Andrade, 'Fanon et l'Afrique combattante', p. 261.

129  Amar Belkhodja, 'Frantz Fanon', *El Moudjahid*, 1 July 1992.

130  There are a number of versions of this story. According to Geismar (*Frantz Fanon*, p. 43), Fanon's car hit a mine. It has also been said that he was shot. The account given by Boukari is so detailed that it appears to be the correct one.

131  Interview with Assia Djebar.

132  This is not as improbable as it may sound: the FLN delegation in Bonn operated out of the Tunisian Embassy there.

133  *The Times*, 6 July 1959; *Le Monde*, 7, 8, 9 and 10 July 1959.

134  Beauvoir, *La Force des choses*, vol. 2, p. 425.

135  Maurice Maschino, *L'Engagement*, Paris: Maspero, 1961, p. 97; Renate Zahar, *L'Oeuvre de Frantz Fanon*, Paris: Maspero, 1970, p. 11.

136  Peter Geismar, *Frantz Fanon: A Critical Study*, London: Wildwood House, 1973, p. 143; Irene Gendzier, *Frantz Fanon*, New York: Dial Press, 1971, p. 195.

137  Jean-Francis Held, 'Les Deux Doigts de la "Main-Rouge"', *France-Observateur*, 15 October 1959, p. 15.

138  'La Main Rouge revendique ses exploits', *France-Observateur*, 3 December 1959, p. 4.

139  Courrière, *La Guerre d'Algérie*, vol. I, pp. 584, 181.

140  Cited, Harbi, *Le FLN*, p. 245.

141  Ibid., p. 246.

142  Mostefa Lacheraf, '"Il doit tout à l'Algérie"', *Le Matin*, 24 December 1992, p. 2.

143  Droz and Lever, *Histoire de la guerre d'Algéri*e, p. 101n. Lacheraf's main articles are collected as *L'Algérie: nation et société*, Paris: Maspero, 1965.

144  François Maspero, 'Homage to Frantz Fanon', *Présence africaine*, vol. XL, 1962, p. 148.

145  Ibid., p. 172.

146  This is the edition used here.

147  Ferhat Abbas, *Autopsie d'une guerre: l'aurore*, Paris: Garnier, 1980, pp. 316–17.

148  François Maspero's novel *Le Figuier*, Paris: Seuil, 1988, provides a fascinating 'fictionalized' account of his publishing activities and of his 'La Joie de lire' bookshop.

149  Sartre, 'Préface' to *Les Damnés de la terre*, p. 15.

150  'Fondement réciproque', p. 88.

151  Sartre, 'Préface' to *Les Damnés de la terre*, p. 20.

152  Pierre Vidal-Naquet, *Face à la raison d'état: un historien dans la guerre d'Algérie*, Paris: La Découverte, 1989, p. 24.

153  Ibid., p. 26.

154 Pierre Vidal-Naquet, *Mémoires* II. *Le Trouble et la lumière 1955–1998*, Paris: Seuil/La Découverte, 1998, p. 118.

155 Vidal-Naquet, *Face à la raison d'état*, p. 25.

156 *Sociologie d'une révolution*, pp. 139–40.

157 *Sociologie d'une révolution*, p. 141.

158 Ibid, pp. 141, 146–7.

159 Ibid., p. 138.

160 Ibid., pp. 46–7.

161 Ibid., p. 39.

162 Ibid., pp. 246–7. The files studied by Amrane were originally created after independence to allow FLN fighters and activists to be provided with certificates proving that they were genuine patriots. As at the end of the Second World War in France, when numerous 'eleventh-hour resisters' suddenly appeared with grandiose claims to a glorious past, a lot of previously unknown *moudjahidine* began to crawl out of the woodwork in Algeria in the summer of 1962. Possession of an authentic *attestation de militantisme* was a distinct advantage when it came to looking for a job or a house.

163 *Sociologie d'une révolution*, p. 83.

164 Ibid., p. 41.

165 Ibid.

166 Courrière, *La Guerre d'Algérie*, vol. I, p. 769; Alleg, *La Guerre d'Algérie*, vol. II, p. 297; Miguel, *La Guerre d'Algérie*, p. 261.

167 Saadi Yacef, *La Bataille d'Alger*, vol. 1, Algiers: ENAL, 1984, p. 395.

168 Interview cited Danièle-Djamila Amrane-Minne, *Les Femmes dans la guerre d'Algérie*, Paris: Karthala, 1994, p. 50.

169 Interview, cited Djamila Amrane, *Les Femmes algériennes dans la guerre*, p. 132.

170 *Sociologie d'une révolution*, p. 43n.

171 Saadi Yacef, *Souvenirs de la bataille d'Alger*, Paris: Julliard, 1962, p. 23.

172 *Sociologie d'une révolution*, p. 83.

173 Reproduced, Courrière, *La Guerre d'Algérie*, vol. I, p. 922.

174 Interview cited, Amrane-Minne, *Les Femmes algériennes dans la guerre d'Algérie*, p. 145.

175 Hervé Hamon and Patrick Rotman, *Les Porteurs de valises: résistance française à la guerre d'Algérie*, Paris: Seuil, collection 'Points', 1987, pp. 338–89.

176 Cited, Martin Evans, *The Memory of Resistance: French Opposition to the Algerian War*, Oxford: Berg, 1997, p. 157.

177 Ibid., p. 146.

178 Cited, Amrane-Minne, *Les Femmes algériennes dans la guerre*, p. 250.

179 *Sociologie d'une révolution*, pp. 16–17. Fanon immediately has to qualify his own sweeping statement by adding a footnote pointing

out that it does not apply to rural areas, where women were often unveiled; nor, he adds, does it apply to Kabylia, where women did not wear the veil.

180 Rachida Titah, *La Galerie des absentes: la femme algérienne dans l'imaginaire masculin*, La Tour d'Aigue: Editions de l'aube, 1996, pp. 34–5.

181 Camus, *Le Premier Homme*, p. 257.

182 *Sociologie d'une révolution*, pp. 42–3.

183 Ibid., p. 31.

184 See the very critical discussion of Fanon on Algerian women in Marnia Lazreg, *The Eloquence of Silence: Algerian Women in Question*, New York and London: Routledge, 1994, pp. 125–33.

185 Xème Région militaire, Service psychologique, *Connaissance de l'Algérie*, Algiers: SNEP nd., p. 47.

186 *Sociologie d'une révolution*, p. 103.

187 Ibid., p. 25.

188 See the discussion in Titah. For a useful discussion of orientalist painting, see Linda Nochlin, 'The Imaginary Orient' in her *The Politics of Vision: Essays on Nineteenth-Century Art and Society*, London: Thames and Hudson, 1991, pp. 33–59. Many of the relevant paintings are reproduced in the exhibition catalogue *The Orientalists: Delacroix to Matisse. European Painters in North Africa and the Near East*, Mary Anne Stevens (ed.), London: Royal Academy of Arts in association with Weidenfeld and Nicolson, 1984.

189 A number of these photographs are reproduced in the exhibition catalogue *Photographes en Algérie au XIXe siècle*. For the postcards, see Rebecca J. DeRoo, 'Colonial Collecting: Women and Algerian *Cartes postales*', *Parallax* 7, April–June 1998.

190 *Sociologie d'une révolution*, pp. 28–9.

191 Daniel Guérin, *Ci-gît le colonialisme*, The Hague and Paris: Mouton, 1983, p. 136.

192 Claude Liauze, 'Intellectuels du Tiers Monde', p. 172.

193 Reproduced, Guérin, *Ci-gît le colonialisme*, pp. 330–1.

194 Pierre Stibbe, review of *L'An V*, *France-Observateur*, 24 December 1959, p. 18.

195 Maurice Maschino, '*L'An V de la révolution algérienne* de Frantz Fanon', *Les Temps modernes*, 167–68, February–March 1960, p. 1425.

196 Cited Martin Evans, *The Memory of Resistance, French opposition to the Algerian War*, Oxford: Berg, 1997, p. 88.

197 Cited, ibid., p. 135.

## 10 The Year of Africa

.1   Anthony Clayton, *The Wars of French Decolonization*, London: Longman, 1994, pp. 160–1; Alleg, *La Guerre d'Algérie*, Paris: Temps actuels, 1981, vol. 3, pp. 126–7.

2   Rehda Malek, *L'Algérie à Evian: histoire des négotiations secrètes 1956–1962*, Paris: Seuil, 1995, p. 73.

3   Kwame Nkrumah, letter of 21 August 1967 to his literary executrix June Milne, in June Milne (ed.), *Kwame Nkrumah: The Conakry Years. His Life and Letters*, London and Atlantic Highlands, NJ: Panaf, 1990, p. 174.

4   Interview with Charles Geronimi, who was introduced to the drink by Fanon.

5   Milne, op.cit. Nkrumah also described Fanon as having 'a beautiful wife and two or three (sic) children'.

6   Thomas Kanza, *Conflict in the Congo: The Rise and Fall of Lumumba*, Harmondsworth: Penguin, 1972, p. 50.

7   Fanon, 'Cette Afrique à venir', *Pour la Révolution*, p. 185.

8   'Aux Antilles, naissance d'une nation?', *El Moudjahid*, 16, 15 January 1958; *Pour la Révolution africaine*, p. 90.

9   'Lendemains d'un plébiscite en Afrique', *El Moudjahid*, 30, 18 October 1958; *Pour la Révolution africaine*, p. 142.

10   'Le Sang coule aux Antilles sous domination française', *El Moudjahid* 58, 5 January 1960; *Pour la Révolution africaine*, pp. 169–71.

11   Marie-Hélène Léotin, *Martinique: 50 ans de départementalisation 1946–1996*, Fort-de-France: APAL Production, 1997, p. 37.

12   Patrick Chamoiseau, *Texaco*, trans. Rose-Myriam Réjouis and Val Vinokurv, London: Granta Books, 1997, p. 313.

13   *Le Monde*, 30 and 31 December 1959.

14   See the accounts given by Georges Crabot, 'Chômage, racisme et centralisation excessive sont à l'origine du malaise à la Martinique', *Le Monde*, 29 December 1959 and Léotin, *Martinique*, pp. 37–9.

15   *Le Monde*, 24 December 1959.

16   'Homage à Frantz Fanon', *Présence africaine* 40, 1962, p. 138.

17   Ibid., p. 139.

18   Raphaël Confiant, *Aimé Césaire: une traversée paradoxale du siècle*, Paris: Stock, 1973, pp. 190, 193. See also the fictionalized account given in his *L'Allée des soupirs*, Paris: Livre de poche, 1994.

19   Leotin, *Martinique*, p. 38.

20   *Le Monde*, 16 January 1960.

21   Jean-Marie Domenach, 'Les Antilles, avant qu'il ne soit trop tard', *Esprit*, April 1962, pp. 513–14.

22   Yvon Leborgne, 'Le Climat social', ibid., p. 540.

23    Edouard Glissant, 'Culture et colonisation: l'équilibre antillais', ibid., p. 591.

24    Ibid., p. 595.

25    Simone de Beauvoir, *La Force des choses,* vol. 2, p. 429.

26    For Memmi's dismissal of the suggestion that he had been 'inspired' by Fanon, see his 'Note sur Frantz Fanon et la notion de carence' (1965) in his *L'Homme dominé,* Paris: Petite Bibliothèque Payot, 1973, pp. 87–92.

27    Albert Memmi, *Portrait du colonisé, précédé de Portrait du colonisateur,* Paris: Gallimard 1985, p. 106.

28    Ibid., p. 93.

29    Ibid., p. 137.

30    Ibid., p. 138.

31    Ibid., pp. 162–3.

32    Albert Memmi, 'La Vie impossible de Frantz Fanon', *Esprit,* September 1971, pp. 253–4.

33    Ibid., pp. 254–8.

34    Françoise Vergès, 'Creole Skin, Black Masks: Fanon and Disavowal', *Critical Inquiry,* 23, Spring 1997, p. 579.

35    Sigmund Freud, 'Family Romances', in *The Standard Edition of the Complete Psychological Works of Sigmund Freud,* James Strachey (ed.), London: The Hogarth Press and the Institute of Psychoanalysis, 1953–74, 24 vols, vol. IX, pp. 235–41.

36    François Vergès, *Monsters and Revolutionaries: Colonial Family Romance and Métissage,* Durham: NC: Duke University Press, 1999.

37    Vergès, 'Creole Skin', p. 579.

38     See in particular Sigmund Freud, 'Some Psychical Consequences of the Anatomical Distinction between the Sexes', *Standard Edition,* vol. XIX, pp. 241–58 and 'Fetishism', *Standard Edition,* vol. XXI, pp. 147–57.

39    Vergès, 'Creole Skin', p. 593. The appeal to Fanon of Algerian 'virility' has become one of the themes of post-colonial readings of Fanon; as will be argued below, they tend to rely upon an excessive 'queering' of some very banal statements and circumstances.

40    Aimé Césaire, 'Et les Chiens se taisaient', in *Les Armes miraculeuses,* Paris: Gallimard, Collection 'Poésie', 1970, pp. 73–4, 104; *Les Damnés de la terre,* p. 64.

41    Ibid., p. 64.

42    'Un Example toujours vivant', *El Moudjahid,* 21 December 1961.

43    'Cette Afrique à venir', p. 186.

44    *Le Monde,* 26 January 1960, 27 January 1960.

45    Jean Lacouture, *De Gaulle: The Ruler 1945–1970,* trans. Alan Sheridan, London: HarperCollins, 1993, p. 248–9.

46    Ibid., pp. 253–4.

47   For a detailed, if very journalistic, contemporary account, see Merry and Serge Bromberger, Georgette Elgey and J.-F. Chauvel, *Barricades et colonels: 24 janvier 1960*, Paris: Librairie Arthème Fayard, 1960.

48   Alleg, *La Guerre d'Algérie*, vol. II, p. 181.

49   *Le Monde*, 13 April 1960.

50   *Le Monde*, 14 April 1960.

51   Beauvoir, *La Force des choses*, vol. II, p. 428.

52   Even today, the women who sunbathe 'topless' on Martinique's beaches are tourists and not locals.

53   *Le Monde*, 12 April 1960.

54   *Le Monde*, 14 April 1960.

55   Peter Worsely, 'Revolutionary Theories', *Monthly Review*, May 1960, pp. 30–1. Inexplicably, Worsely refers to the conference he attended in Accra in 1960 as 'The All-Africa People's Congress', which actually took place in 1958.

56   *Le Monde*, 14, 17, 19 and 20 June 1960.

57   Jean Daniel, *La Blessure, suivi de Le Temps qui vient*, Paris: Grasset, 1992, pp. 65–6.

58   Jean Daniel, 'Fanon, un "Pied-Noir" et le gaullisme', *L'Express*, 14 December 1961, p. 17.

59   *Le Monde*, 27 August 1960, 28 August 1960.

60   Cited, Kanza, *Conflict in the Congo*, p. 277.

61   'La Mort de Lumumba: pouvions-nous faire autrement?', *Afrique action*, 19, 10 February 1961; *Pour la Révolution africaine*, p.195.

62   'Cette Afrique à venir', p. 178.

63   *The Times*, 30 March 1960.

64   Russell Warren Howe, *Black Africa: Africa South of the Sahara from Pre-History to Independence, Parts 3 and 4*, Croydon: New African Library, 1967, pp. 259–60.

65   *Le Monde*, 2 November 1960, 3 November 1960.

66   This account is based upon Engelbert Mueng, *Histoire du Cameroun*, Paris: Présence africaine, 1963, pp. 839–41.

67   'Cette Afrique à venir', p. 179.

68   Mueng, p. 441.

69   The original is in the possession of Olivier Fanon.

70   'Cette Afrique à venir', p. 177.

71   Ibid., p. 179.

72   Ibid., p. 180.

73   Terry Goldie, 'Saint Fanon and "Homosexual Territory"', in Anthony C. Alessandrini, *Frantz Fanon: Critical Perspectives*, London and New York: Routledge, 1999, p. 78.

74   Edward Behr, *The Algerian Problem*, Harmondsworth: Penguin, 1961, p. 204.

75   Jacques Frémeaux, 'La Guerre d'Algérie et le Sahara' in Charles-

Robert Ageron (ed.), *La Guerre d'Algérie et les Algériens 1954–1962*, pp. 93–109.

76 'The Stooges of Imperialism', *Mission in Ghana Information Service*, vol. 1, no. 6, 14 December 1960. Collection of Olivier Fanon.

77 Cited Annie Cohen-Solal, *Sartre 1905–1980*, Paris: Folio, 1989, p. 720.

78 Geismar, *Frantz Fanon*, p. 178.

79 Clinical data from *ABPI Data Sheet Compendium*.

## 11 The Wretched of the Earth

1 Jean-Paul Sartre, '"Vous êtes formidables"', *Les Temps modernes*, 135, May 1957, reprinted *Situations V: colonialisme et néo-colonialisme*, Paris: Gallimard, 1964, pp. 57–67; 'Une Victoire', *L'Express* 6 March 1958, reprinted, ibid., pp. 72–88.

2 In a clandestine press conference given in April 1960, Françis Jeanson spoke of 'three thousand deserters'; see Hervé Hamon and Patrick Rotman, *Les Porteurs de valises: la résistance française à la guerre d'Algérie*, Paris: Seuil, collection 'Points', 1982, p. 392.

3 'Jeunesse et guerre d'Algérie' (entretien avec K. S. Karol), *Vérité-Liberté*, 3, July–August 1960, extracts reproduced, Michel Contat and Michel Rybalka, *Les Ecrits de Sartre*, Paris: Gallimard, 1970, p. 356.

4 Dionys Mascolo died in August 1997. See the obituaries by Nicolas Weill and Jean-Luc Douin, *Le Monde*, 22 August 1997, and Douglas Johnson, *Guardian*, 26 August 1997.

5 Annie Cohen-Solal, *Sartre 1905–1980*, Paris: Folio, 1989, p. 697.

6 Vidal-Naquet, *Mémoires II*, p. 139.

7 The full text and the list of signatories are reproduced in *Les Porteurs de valises*, pp. 393–86 and in Jean-François Sirinelli, *Intellectuels et passions françaises: manifestes et pétitions au XXè siècle*, Paris: Fayard, 1990, pp. 211–13.

8 Marcel Péju, *Le Procès du réseau Jeanson*, p. 98.

9 Hamon and Rotman, *Les Porteurs de valises*, p. 380.

10 *Les Damnés de la terre*, p. 108.

11 See the documents reproduced as '*OAS parle*', Paris: Julliard, 1964.

12 *Le Figaro*, 21 September 1960, cited Cohen-Solal, *Sartre*, p. 705.

13 Cited ibid.

14 Ibid., p. 711.

15 There is some confusion over dates here. According to Cohen-Solal (p. 717), this meeting took place in the summer of 1960. Fanon's leukaemia had not yet declared itself then. Fanon spoke of

the murder of Patrice Lumumba, which occurred on 17 January 1961; the most likely date for the meeting is therefore the spring or early summer of 1961.

16    Simone de Beauvoir, *La Force des choses*, Paris: Livre de poche, 1971, vol. II, p. 413.

17    Cohen-Solal, *Sartre*, p. 717, citing her interview with Claude Lanzmann.

18    *El Moudjahid*, p. 648.

19    Cited Cohen-Solal, *Sartre*, p. 720.

20    François Maspero, 'Quelqu'un "de la famille"', *Les temps modernes*, 531–3, October–December 1990, p. 1018.

21    *Les Damnés de la terre*, pp. 231, 235.

22    Ibid., p. 223.

23    Ibid., p. 66.

24    Ibid., p. 75.

25    'Homage à Frantz Fanon', *Présence africaine*, vol. XL, 1962, p. 140.

26    Behr, *The Algerian Problem*, p. 178.

27    Ibid., pp. 178–9.

28    Sean Lacouture, *De Gaulle: The Ruler 1945–1970*, trans. Alan Sheridan, London: HarperCollins, 1993, p. 274.

29    Beauvoir, *La Force des choses*, Vol. II, p. 243.

30    Ibid., p. 425.

31    Alistair Horne, *A Savage War of Peace: Algeria 1954–1962*, London: Papermac, 1987, p. 475.

32    Beauvoir, *La Force des choses*, vol. II, p. 429.

33    They were echoed by Minister for Culture André Malraux, who took the view that it was 'better to let Sartre shout "Vive le FLN on the place de la Concorde" than to make the mistake of arresting him', Cohen-Solal, *Sartre*, pp. 709–10.

34    Beauvoir, *La Force des choses*, vol. II, p. 432.

35    Daniel Racine, *Léon-Gontras Damas: L'homme et l'oeuvre*, Paris: Présence africaine, 1993, p. 40.

36    As reported by Assia Djebar; cf. her *Le Blanc d'Algérie*, p. 124.

37    Edouard Glissant, 'Un Nouveau Sens de l'humanité pour les pays du Sud', *Antilla* 23, November–December 1991, p. 39.

38    Beauvoir, *La Force des choses*, vol. II, p. 432.

39    Benny Lévy, citing an undated conversation with Sartre in Jean-Paul Sartre and Benny Lévy, *Hope Now: The 1980 Interviews*, trans. Adrian van den Hoven, with an Introduction by Ronald Aronson, Chicago and London: University of Chicago Press, 1996, p. 94.

40    Sartre, *L'Etre et le néant*, p. 691.

41    Ronald Hayman, *Writing Against: A Biography of Sartre*, London: Weidenfeld and Nicolson, 1986, p. 220.

# Notes

42   Jean-Paul Sartre, *Notebooks for an Ethics,* trans. David Pellauer, Chicago and London: University of Chicago Press, 1992, p. 142.

43   Jean-Paul Sartre, *Critique de la raison dialectique*, Paris: Gallimard, 1960, p. 686.

44   Sartre, 'Préface', *Les Damnés de la terre*, pp. 10, 11.

45   Ibid., p. 20.

46   Ibid., p. 11.

47   Ibid., p. 13.

48   Aristide R. Zolberg, 'Frantz Fanon – A Gospel for the Damned', *Encounter*, vol. 27, no. 5, October 1966, p. 98; cf. Paul Nursey-Bray, 'Marxism and Existentialism in the thought of Frantz Fanon', *Political Studies*, vol. 20, no. 2, 1972, pp. 158–9.

49   *Les Damnés de la terre*, p.83.

50   Georges Sorel, *Reflections on Violence*, trans. T. E. Hulme, introduction by Edward A. Shils, London: Collier Books, 1970, p. 92.

51   *Peau noire, masques blancs*, p. 78.

52   Jean-Mairie Domenach, '*Les Damnés de la terre*. Sur une préface de Sartre', *Esprit*, March 1962, pp. 454–63; '*Les Damnés de la terre*', *Esprit*, April 1962, pp. 634–45.

53   Domenach, 'Sur une préface de Sartre', p. 455; '*Les Damnés de la terre*', p. 636.

54   Sean Daniel, *La Blessure, suivi de le Temps qui vient*, Paris: Grasset, 1992, p. 59.

55   Ibid., pp. 60, 67.

56   Ibid., p. 67.

57   Ibid., p. 60.

58   Sartre, 'Préface', p. 19.

59   Reproduced *Jeune Afrique*, 25 June 1967.

60   *El Moudjahid*, 6 June 1967, 7 June 1967.

61   Josie Fanon, 'A Propos de Frantz Fanon, Sartre, le racisme et les Arabes', *El Moudjahid*, 10 June 1967, p. 6.

62   Ibid., citing, *Les Damnés de la terre*, p. 239.

63   Sartre and Levy, *Hope Now*, p. 94.

64   See David Macey, *The Lives of Michel Foucault*, London: Hutchinson, 1993, pp. 298–300; Christophe Bourseiller, *Les Maoïstes: la folle histoire des gardes rouges français*, Paris: Plon, 1996.

65   *Les Damnés de la terre*, p. 241.

66   Ibid., pp. 50–1.

67   Ibid., p. 75.

68   Césaire, *Discours sur le colonialisme*, p. 12.

69   *Les Damnés de la terre*, p. 31–2.

70   Jean-Jacques Jordi, avec la collaboration de Jean-Louis Planche, '1860-1930: une certaine idée de la construction de France', in

Jean-Jacques Jordi and Jean-Louis Planche, *Alger 1869–1939: le modèle ambigu du triomphe colonial*, Paris: Autrement, 1999, pp. 37–40.

71  André Frémont, *Algérie-El Djazaïr: les carnets de guerre et de terrain d'un géographe*, Paris: Maspero, 1982, pp. 62–3.

72  *Les Damnés de la terre*, p. 34.

73  Camus refused to support the FLN and the struggle for independence, not least because he could not condone a terrorism that might affect those close to him. Hence the famous statement that whilst he loved justice, he loved his mother still more.

74  *Les Damnés de la terre*, p. 40.

75  Ibid., p. 190.

76  Ibid., p. 40.

77  Ibid. p. 44.

78  Ibid., p. 43.

79  Ibid., pp. 44, 45.

80  Michel Wievorka, *La France raciste*, Paris: Seuil, 1992, p. 331.

81  Dominique Dhombres, 'La Violence, tabou des sociétés démocratiques', *Le Monde*, 3 November 1999, pp. 1, 27.

82  *Les Damnés de la terre*, p. 55.

83  Hannah Arendt, *On Violence*, p. 65. Arendt regards Fanon as having inspired the rhetoric of violence (and sometimes the real violence) associated with the student revolts and the 'Black Power' movements of the late 1960s. Astonishingly, she never mentions Algeria at all.

84  'A quoi rêvent les enfants d'Algérie?', *Les Temps modernes* 164, October 1959, pp. 720–4.

85  *Les Damnés de la terre*, p. 29.

86  Ibid., p. 30.

87  Alleg, *La Guerre d'Algérie*, vol. I, pp. 62–8.

88  *Les Damnés de la terre*, p. 87.

89  Saadia and Lakhdar, 'L'Aliénation colonialiste et la résistance de la famille algérienne', *Les Temps modernes*, 182, June 1961, p. 1689.

90  Frémont, *Algérie-El Djazaïr*, p. 173.

91  Cited Alleg, *La Guerre d'Algérie*, vol. I, pp. 63–4.

92  Ibid., p. 62.

93  Mohammed Dib, *La Danse du roi*, Paris: Seuil, 1968, p. 80.

94  Sartre, *Critique de la raison dialectique*, p. 672.

95  Ibid., p. 675.

96  *Les Damnés de la terre*, p. 241.

97  Sartre, *Critique de la raison dialectique*, p. 64.

98  Ibid., p. 63.

99  *Les Damnés de la terre*, p. 63.

100  Sartre, *Critique de la raison dialectique*, p. 672.

101  See Paul A. Beckett, 'Algeria versus Fanon: The Theory of

# Notes

Revolutionary Decolonization and the African Experience',
*Western Political Quarterly*, vol. 26, no. 1, March 1973, pp. 5–27;
Robert Blackey, 'Fanon and Cabral: A Contrast in Theories of
Revolution for Africa', *Journal of Modern African Studies*, vol.
12, no. 2, 1974, pp. 191–201; A. C. Bourgui and J. C. Williams,
'La Pensée politique de Frantz Fanon', *Présence africaine*, 88, 4e
trimestre 1973, pp. 139–62; Pietro Clemente, *Frantz Fanon tra
esistenzialismo e rivoluzione*, Bari: Laterza, 1971; Nguyen Nghe,
'Frantz Fanon et les problèmes de l'indépendance', *La Pensée* 107,
January–February 1963, pp. 23–36; Marie B. Perinbam, 'Fanon
and the Revolutionary Peasantry – The Algerian Case', *Journal of
Modern African Studies*, vol. 11, no. 3, 1973, pp. 427–45; Willie
Thompson, 'Frantz Fanon', *Marxism Today*, August 1968,
pp. 245–51; Jack Woddis, *New Theories of Revolution*, New York:
International Publishers, 1972.

102   Gendzier, *Frantz Fanon*, p. 203.
103   *Les Damnés de la terre*, citing Frederick Engels, *Anti-Dühring*,
      Peking: Foreign Languages Press, 1976, pp. 211–12.
104   *Peau noire, masques blancs*, p. 13, citing the eleventh 'Thesis on
      Feuerbach'.
105   Ibid., pp. 181–2.
106   Aimé Césaire, *Lettre à Maurice Thorez/Discourse à la Maison du
      Sport*, Fort-de-France: Parti Progressiste Martiniquais, nd., p. 13.
      Césaire resigned from the PCF after the revelations of
      Khrushchev's secret speech about Stalin's crimes. He also
      remarked (p. 17) that he wanted Marxism and communism to
      serve black peoples, rather than to see black peoples serving
      Marxism and communism.
107   *Les Damnés de la terre*, p. 32.
108   'England has to fulfil a double mission in India: one destructive,
      the other regenerating – the annihilation of the old Asiatic society,
      and the laying of the material foundations of Western society in
      Asia'. In 'The Future Results of the British Rule in India', in
      *Surveys from Exile* David Fernbach (ed.), Harmondsworth:
      Penguin, 1973, p. 320.
109   Cited Robert Malley, *The Call from Algeria: Third Worldism,
      Revolution and the Turn to Islam*, Berkeley, Los Angeles and
      London: University of California Press, 1966, p. 25.
110   *Les Damnés de la terre*, p. 84.
111   Nghe, 'Frantz Fanon et les problèmes de l'indépendance', pp. 29,
      31, 32.
112   *Les Damnés de la terre*, p. 32.
113   Cohen, 'Colonialisme et racisme en Algérie', p. 582.
114   *Les Damnés de la terre*, p. 32.
115   Jack Woddis, *New Theories of Revolution*, p. 62.

116   Pierre Bourdieu, *Algérie 60*, p. 80.
117   Pierre Bourdieu, *Sociologie de l'Algérie*, Paris: PUF, Collection 'Que suis-je?', 1958, p. 124.
118   Mohammed Harbi, *Le FLN: Mirage et réalité. Des origines à la prise de pouvoir*, Algiers: NAQD/ENAL, 1993, p. 245.
119   *Les Damnés de la terre*. p. 84.
120   Francis Jeanson, 'Cette Algérie, conquise et pacifée', *Esprit*, April, May 1950, p. 847.
121   Benjamin Stora, *Ils venaient d'Algérie: L'immigration algérienne en France 1912–1992*, Paris: Fayard, 1992, p. 143.
122   Jeanson, 'Cette Algérie', p. 845.
123   *Les Damnés de la terre*, p. 91.
124   Ibid., p. 96.
125   Ibid., p. 97.
126   *Les Damnés de la terre*, p. 107.
127   Ibid., p. 108.
128   Ibid.
129   Ibid. p. 70.
130   Sartre, *Critique de la raison dialectique*, p. 672.
131   Reproduced, Courrière, *La Guerre d'Algérie*, vol. I, p. 906.
132   An Algerian author has suggested that Sartre's long analysis of the role of the oath (pp. 439–59), which refers mainly to the Oath of the Jeu de Paume, also contains a coded reference to the FLN's anthem *Kassaman* ('We have sworn to die so that Algeria may live'). See Slimane Chikh, *L'Algérie en armes, ou le temps des certitudes*, Paris: Economica, 1988, p. 227. Whilst the suggestion is very intriguing, it would be very difficult to either prove it or disprove it.
133   Fanon's knowledge of the Mau Mau was probably limited to what he had heard about it at conferences. For an account of Mau Mau oaths, see Chapter 3 of Josiah Mwangi Kariuki, *Mau Mau Detainee. An Account by a Kenyan African of his Experience in Detention Camps 1953–1960*, London and Nairobi: Oxford University Press, 1963. For a more general account, see Wunyahari O Maloba, *Mau Mau and Kenya: An Analysis of a Peasant Revolt*, Bloomington and Indianapolis: Indiana University Press, 1993.
134   *Les Damnés de la terre*, p. 64.
135   The expression derives from the Portuguese for 'buyer' and originally applied to the Chinese agents of foreign businesses based in concessions. It subsequently came to mean an agent of a foreign power.
136   Mao Tse Tung, 'The Chinese Revolution and the Chinese Communist Party', in *Selected Works of Mao Tse Tung, Vol. 2*, Peking: Foreign Languages Press, 1967, pp. 320–1.

137    Ruedy, *Modern Algeria*, p. 124.
138    *Les Damnés de la terre*, p. 113.
139    See Aristide R. Zolberg, *One-Party Government in the Ivory Coast*, Princeton: Princeton University Press, 1964.
140    *Les Damnés de la terre*, p. 124.
141    Ibid., p. 114.
142    Ibid.
143    Ibid., p. 150.
144    Ibid., p. 140.
145    Ibid., p. 141.
146    Beauvoir, *La Force des choses*, vol. II, p. 443.
147    Gendzier, *Frantz Fanon*, p. 232.
148    Homage to Frantz Fanon, p. 135.
149    Beauvoir, *La Force des choses*, vol. II, p. 444.
150    *Peau noire, masques blancs*, 89–90.
151    Letter to *New Statesman*, 30 January 1970, p. 150.
152    *Le Monde*, 23–4 February 1969.
153    See Edwin M. Yoder Jr, *Joe Alsop's Cold War: A Study of Journalism, Influence and Intrigue*, Chapel Hill and London: University of North Carolina Press, 1995; Frances Stonor Saunders, *Who Paid the Piper? The CIA and the Cultural Cold War*, London: Granta, 1999.
154    'Une Mise au point de M. Yazid à propos de la mort de Frantz Fanon', *Le Monde*, 2–3 March 1969, p. 7.
155    François Maspero, *Tribune socialiste*, 16 December 1961; *L'Humanité*, 11 December 1961.
156    *Aux Ecoutes*, 29 December 1961.

# Bibliography

## A: Works by Frantz Fanon

'Altérations mentales, modifications caractérielles, troubles psychiques et déficit intellectuel dans l'hérédo-dégénération spino-cérébelleuse. Un Cas de maladie de Friedrich avec délire de persécution.' Unpublished thesis defended at Faculté mixte de médecine et de pharmacie, Lyon, 29 November 1951. Extract published as 'Le Trouble mental et le trouble neurologique', *Information psychiatrique* vol. LIX, no. 10, 1975.

'Le Syndrôme Nord-Africain', *Esprit*, February 1952; reprinted, *Pour la Révolution africaine*.

*Peau noire, masques blancs*, Paris: Editions du Seuil, 1952. Trans. Charles Lam Markmann, *Black Skin, White* Masks, London: MacGibbon & Kee, 1968. Reprinted, London: Pluto Press, 1986 with an introduction by Homi K. Bhabha.

'A Propos d'un cas de syndrôme de Cotard avec balancement psychosomatique', in collaboration with Maurice Despinoy, *Annales médico-psychologiques* 2, June 1953.

'Sur quelques cas traités par la méthode de Bini', in collaboration with François Tosquelles, *Congrès des médecins aliénistes et neurologues de France et des pays de langue française*, Pau, 1953.

'Indications de la thérapeutique de Blini dans le cadre des thérapeutiques institutionnelles', in collaboration with François Tosquelles, ibid.

'Sur un essai de réadaptation chez une malade avec épilépsie morphéïque et troubles de caractère graves', in collaboration with François Tosquelles, ibid.

# Bibliography

'Note sur les techniques de cure de sommeil avec conditionnement et contrôle électro-encéphelographique', in collaboration with Maurice Despinoy and W. Zenner, ibid.

'La Socialthérapie dans un service d'hommes musulmans: difficultés méthodologiques', in collaboration with Jacques Azoulay, *Information psychiatrique*, vol. XXX, no. 9, 1954. Reprinted *Information psychiatrique*, vol. LIX no. 10, 1975.

'Introduction aux troubles de la sexualité chez les Nords-Africains', in collaboration with Jacques Azoulay and François Sanchez. Unpublished.

'Antillais et Africains', *Esprit*, February 1955. Reprinted, *Pour la Révolution africaine*.

'Aspects actuels de l'assistance mentale en Afrique du nord', in collaboration with J. Dequeker, R. Lacaton, M. Micucci and F. Ramée, *Information psychiatrique*, vol. XXXI, no. 11, 1955. Reprinted *Information psychiatrique*, vol. LIX, no. 10, 1975.

'Conduites d'aveu en Afrique du nord', in collaboration with R. Lacaton, *Congrès des médecins aliénistes et neurologues de France et des pays de langue française*, Nice, 1955.

'Attitude du musulman maghrébin devant la folie', in collaboration with François Sanchez, *Revue pratique de psychologie de la vie sociale et d'hygiène sociale* I, 1956.

'Le TAT chez la femme musulmane: sociologie de la perception et de l'imagination' in collaboration with Charles Geronimi, *Congrès des médecins aliénistes et neurologues de France et des pays de langue française*, Bordeaux 1956.

'Lettre à un français' (1956), first published in *Pour la Révolution africaine*.

'Lettre au Ministre-résident' (1956), first published in *Pour la Révolution africaine*.

'Racisme et culture', *Présence africaine*, 8–10, June–November 1956. Reprinted *Pour la Révolution africaine*.

'Le Phénomène de l'agitation en milieu psychiatrique: considérations générales, signification psychopathologique', in collaboration with S. Assehah, *Maroc médical* vol. XXXVI, no. 380, 1957.

'Etude biologique du citrate de lithium dans les accès maniaques', in collaboration with J. Sourdine. Unpublished.

'Conférence de presse, 4 mai, Tunis', *Le Monde*, 5 June 1957.

'Déceptions et illusions du colonialisme français', *El Moudjahid* 10, September 1957. Reprinted *Pour la Révolution africaine*.

'L'Algérie face aux tortionnaires français', *El Moudjahid* 10, September 1957. Reprinted *Pour la Révolution africaine*.

'A propos d'un plaidoyeur', *El Moudjahid* 12, November 1957. Reprinted *Pour la Révolution africaine*.

'Les Intellectuels et les démocrates français devant la révolution algérienne',

*El Moudjahid* 15, December 1957. Reprinted *Pour la Révolution africaine*

'Aux Antilles, naissance d'une nation?', *El Moudjahid* 16, January 1958. Reprinted *Pour la Révolution africaine*.

'La Sang maghrébin ne coulera pas en vain', *El Moudjahid* 18, February 1958. Reprinted *Pour la Révolution africaine*.

'La Farce qui change de camp', *El Moudjahid* 22, April 1958. Reprinted *Pour la Révolution africaine*

'Décolonisation et indépendance', *El Moudjahid* 22, April 1958. Reprinted *Pour la révolution africaine*.

'Une Crise continuée', *El Moudjahid* 23, May 1958. Reprinted *Pour la Révolution africaine*.

'Lettre à la jeunesse africaine', *El Moudhahid* 24, May 1958. Reprinted *Pour la Révolution africaine*.

'Vérités premières à propos du problème colonial', *El Moudjahid* 26, July 1958. Reprinted *Pour la Révolution africaine*

'La Leçon de Cotonou', *El Moudjahid* 28, August 1958. Reprinted *Pour la Révolution africaine*.

'Appel aux Africains', *El Moudjahid* 29, August 1958. Reprinted *Pour la Révolution africaine*

'A Propos d'un spasme de torsion', in collaboration with Lucien Lévy, *La Tunisie médicale*, vol. XXXVI, no. 9, 1958.

'Lendemains d'un plébiscite en Afrique', *El Moudjahid* 30, October 1958. Reprinted *Pour la Révolution africaine*.

'La Guerre d'Algérie et la libération des hommes', *El Moudjahid* 31, November 1958. Reprinted *Pour la Révolution africaine*.

'Accra: l'Afrique affirme son unité et définit sa stratégie', *El Moudjahid* 34, December 1958. Reprinted *Pour la Révolution africaine*.

'Fondements réciproques de la culture nationale et des luttes de libération', *Présence africaine* 24–25, February–May 1959. Reprinted in *Les Damnés de la terre*.

*L'An V de la Révolution africaine*, Paris: Maspero, 1959. Reprinted as *Sociologie d'une révolution* (*L'An V de la Révolution algérienne*), Paris: Maspero, 1966. Trans. Haakon Chevalier, *Studies in a Dying Colonialism*, Harmondsworth: Penguin, 1970.

'Les Tentatives désespérées de M. Debré, *El Moudjahid* 37, February 1959. Reprinted *Pour la Révolution africaine*.

'Fureur raciste en France', *El Moudjahid* 42, May 1959. Reprinted *Pour la Révolution africaine*.

'Premiers essais de méprobamate injectable dans les états hypochondriaques', in collaboration with Lucien Lévy , *La Tunisie médicale*, vol. XXXVII, no. 10, 1959.

'L'Hospitalisation de jour en psychiatrie: valeur et limites', *La Tunisie médicale*, vol. XXXVII, 10, 1959. Reprinted *Information psychiatrique*, vol. LIX, no. 10, 1975.

# Bibliography

'Unité et solidarité effectives sont les conditions de la libération africaine', *El Moudjahid* 58, January 1960. Reprinted *Pour la Révolution africaine*.

'Le Sang coule aux Antilles sous domination française', *El Moudjahid* 58, January 1960. Reprinted *Pour la Révolution africaine*.

'Intervention à la Conférence pour la paix et la sécurité en Afrique', *El Moudjahid* 63, April 1960.

'Intervention en qualité du représentant de l'Algérie à la Conférence Afro-asiatique de Conakry', *El Moudjahid* 63, April 1960.

'Cette Afrique à venir' (Autumn 1960), first published in *Pour la Révolution africaine*.

'The Stooges of Imperialism', *Mission in Ghana. Information Service*, vol. 1, no. 6, 14 December 1960.

'La Mort de Lumumba: pouvions-nous faire autrement?', *Afrique Action* 19, 20 February 1961. Reprinted *Pour la Révolution africaine*.

*Les Damnés de la terre*, Paris: Maspero, 1961, Préface de Jean-Paul Sartre. Trans. Constance Farrington, *The Wretched of the Earth*, New York: Grove Press 1965.

*Pour la Révolution africaine*, Paris: Maspero, 1964. Trans. Haakon Chevalier, *For the African Revolution*, Harmondsworth: Penguin, 1970.

'Rencontre de la sociétie et de la psychiatrie' (Notes de cours, Tunis, 1959–60), *Etudes et recherches sur la psychologie en Algérie*, Oran: CRIDSSH, 1984.


## B: Other Works Consulted


'A Frantz Fanon', *Partisans* 3, February 1962.

'A Quoi rêvent les enfants algériens?' *Les Temps modernes* 164, October 1959.

Abbas, Ferhat, *Autopsie d'une guerre: l'aurore*, Paris: Garnier, 1980.

—— *Le Jeune Algérien*, Paris: Garnier, 1981.

—— *L'Indépendance confisquée*, Paris: Flammarion, 1984.

Abitbol, Michel, *The Jews of North Africa during the Second World War*, trans. Catherine Tihanyi Zentelis, Detroit: Wayne University Press, 1989.

Achille, Louis T., 'Negro Spirituals', *Esprit*, May 1951.

Adams, Paul L., 'The Social Psychiatry of Frantz Fanon', *American Journal of Psychiatry*, vol. 127, no. 6, December 1970.

Affergan, Francis, 'Etude sur quelques rapports psycho-sociaux en Martinique', *L'Homme et la société*, 39–40, 1972.

—— *Anthropologie à la Martinique*, Paris: Presse de la Fondation Nationale des Sciences Politiques, 1983.

Ageron, Charles-Robert, *Histoire de l'Algérie contemporaine (1830–1964)*, Paris: Presses Universitaires de France, 1964.

—— *Histoire de l'Algérie contemporaine. Vol 2. De l'insurrection de 1871 au déclenchement de la guerre de libération (1954)*, Paris: Presses Universitaires de France, 1979.

—— (ed.), *L'Algérie des Français*, Paris: Seuil, collection 'Points', 1993.

Aït Ahmed, Hocine, *Mémoires d'un combattant: l'esprit d'indépendance 1942–1952*, Paris: Sylvie Messinger, 1983.

Akeb, Fatiba, 'L'Homme des ruptures', *Algérie-actualité*, 17–25 November 1987.

Aldrich, Robert and Connell, John, *France's Overseas Frontier: Départements and Térritoires d'Outre-Mer*, Cambridge: Cambridge University Press, 1992.

Alessandrini, Anthony C. (ed.), *Frantz Fanon: Critical Perspectives*, London and New York: Routledge, 1999.

'Alger attend', *L'Express*, 8 February 1957.

Alibar, France and Lembeye-Boy, Pierrette, *Le Couteau seul: Sé koutou seul. La Condition féminine aux Antilles*, Paris: Editions caribbéennes/Agence de Coopération Culturelle et Technique, 1981, 1982, two vols.

Alleg, Henri, *La Question*, Paris: Minuit, 1961.

—— *Prisonniers de guerre*, Paris: Minuit, 1961.

—— (ed.), *La Guerre d'Algérie*, Paris: Temps actuels, 1981, three vols.

Alloula, Malek, 'L'Oeuvre de Fanon aujourd'hui', *Algérie-actualité*, 5–11 December 1981.

Alpha, Jenny, review of Mayotte Capécia, *Je suis Martiniquaise*, *Présence africaine*, January 1948.

Amghal, Mohammed, '*El Thagafa*, "Fanon et la pensée occidentale" de Mohammed El Mili', *El Moudjahid*, 2 June 1971.

Amin, Samir, *The Maghreb in the Modern World: Algeria, Tunisia, Morocco*, trans. Michael Perl, Harmondsworth: Penguin, 1970.

Ammar, Sleim, 'Antoine et Maurice Porot à Tunis', *Psychopathologie médicale*, vol. 15, no. 10, 1983.

Amrane, Djamila, *Les Femmes algériennes dans la guerre*, Paris: Plon, 1991.

Amrane-Minne, Danièle-Djamila, *Les Femmes dans la guerre d'Algérie: entretiens*, Paris: Karthala, 1994.

Amrani, Djamal, *Le Témoin*, Paris: Minuit, 1960.

Amrouche, Jean, *Cendres*, Paris: L'Harmattan, 1983.

—— *Etoile secrète*, Paris: L'Harmattan, 1993.

—— *Chants berbères de la Kabylie*, Paris: L'Harmattan, 1993.

—— *Un Algérien s'adresse aux français, ou l'histoire d'Algérie expliquée par les textes (1943–1961)*, Paris: L'Harmattan/AWAL, 1994.

Anderson, Benedict, *Imagined Communities: Reflections of the Origins and Spread of Nationalism*, London: Verso, 1991, revised edn.

Andrade, Mario de, 'Fanon et l'Afrique combattante', in *Mémorial international*, 1994.

Andreani, Jean-Louis and Dupont, Gaëlle, 'La France devrait ratifier la charte européenne des langues régionales en 1999', *Le Monde*, 9 October 1998.

Antoine, Régis, *La Littérature franco-antillaise: Haiti, Guadeloupe et Martinique*, Paris: Karthala, 1992.

'Après le Congrès', *Présence africaine* 11, December 1956.

Arendt, Hannah, *On Violence*, New York: Harcourt, Brace and Company, 1970.

Armel, Aliette, *Michel Leiris*, Paris: Fayard, 1997.

Arnaud, Georges and Vergès, Jacques, *Pour Djamila Bouhired*, Paris: Minuit, 1957.

Arnold, James A., *Modernism and Negritude: The Poetry and Poetics of Aimé Césaire*, Cambridge MA: Harvard University Press, 1981.

Arti, Louis, *El Halia: le sable d'El Halia*, Chambéry: Editions Compact, 1996.

Arveiller, Jacques, 'Mon Maître Tosquelles', *Evolution psychiatrique*, vol. 60, no. 3, 1995.

Ashcroft, Bill, Griffiths, Gareth and Tiffin, Helen, *The Empire Writes Back: Theory and Practice in Post-Colonial Literatures*, New York and London: Routledge, 1989.

—— *The Post-Colonial Studies Reader*, New York and London: Routledge, 1995.

Aubin, H., 'L'Assistance psychologique indigène aux colonies', *Congrès des médecins aliénistes et neurologues de France et des pays de langue française*, Alger 1938.

Aymé, Jean, 'Hommage à François Tosquelles', *Information psychiatrique* 10, December 1994.

Aymé, Dr, 'Le Relèvement de nos traitements', *Information psychiatrique*, February 1955.

Azzedine, Commandant, *On nous appelait fellaghas*, Paris: Stock, 1976.

Baldwin, James, *Nobody Knows My Name: More Notes of a Native Son*, Harmondsworth: Penguin, 1991.

Baleine, Philippe de, *Les Danseuses de la France*, Paris: Plon, 1989.

Balvet, Paul, 'La Valeur humaine de la folie', *Esprit*, September 1947.

—— 'L'Ambre du musée', *Information psychiatrique*, October 1978.

Bantman, Béatrice, 'Martinique, terre des castes', *Libération* 26, April 1998.

Baptiste, F. A., 'Le Régime de Vichy à la Martinique (juin 1940 à juin 1943), *Revue d'histoire de la Deuxième Guerre mondiale* 111, July 1978.

Barrat, Denise, 'Regard en arrière vers l'avenir', *Actualité de l'émigration* 114, 23–30 December 1987.

Barrat, Robert, *Les Maquis de la liberté*, Algiers and Paris: Entreprise Algérienne de Presse and Editions Témoignage chrétien.

Beauvoir, Simone de, *La Force des choses*, Paris: Livre de poche, 1971, two vols.

—— *L'Amérique au jour le jour*, Paris: Folio, 1997.

Beckett, Paul A., 'Algeria versus Fanon: The Theory of Revolutionary Decolonization and the African Experience', *Western Political Quarterly*, vol. 26, no. 1, March 1973.

Begag, Azouz, *Place du pont, ou la médina de Lyon*, Paris: Autrement, 1997.

Bégué, Jean-Michel, *Un Siècle de psychiatrie française en Algérie (1830–1939)*, *Mémoire pour le Certificat d'Etudes Speciales en Psychiatrie*, Université Pierre et Marie Curie, Faculté de Médecine Saint-Antoine, 1989. Unpublished.

Behr, Edward, *The Algerian Problem*, Harmondsworth: Penguin, 1961.

Belkhodja, Mohammed Tahar, 'Frantz Fanon ou l'exigence de la démocratie révolutionnaire', *Actualité de l'émigration* 115, 10 December 1987–6 January 1988.

Belloula, Tayeb, *Les Algériens en France*, Algiers: Editions Nationales Algériennes, 1965.

Berchadsky, Alexis, *'La Question' d'Henri Alleg: un livre-événement dans la France en guerre d'Algérie*, Paris: Larousse, 1994.

Bergner, Gwen, 'Who is that Masked Woman? Or, The Role of Gender in Fanon's *Black Skin, White Masks*', *Publications of the Modern Languages Association of America*, vol. 110, no. 1, January 1995.

Bernal, Martin, *Black Athena: The Afroasiatic Roots of Classical Civilization*, London: Free Association Books, 1989, 1991, two vols.

Berthellier, Robert, 'Psychiatrie et psychiatres devant le musulman algérien', *Information psychiatrique*, vol. 110, no. 1, January 1969.

—— *L'Homme maghrébin dans la littérature psychiatrique*, Paris: L'Harmattan, 1994.

Bertrand, Louis, *Le Sang des races*, Paris: Albin Michel, 1930.

Bhabha, Homi K., 'What Does the Black Man Want?', *New Formations* 1, Spring 1987.

—— *The Location of Culture*, London: Routledge, 1994.

Biondi, Jean-Pierre and Morin, Gilles, *Les Anticolonialistes (1881–1962)*, Paris: Robert Laffont, 1992.

Blackburn, Robin, *The Making of New World Slavery: From the Baroque to the Modern*, London: Verso, 1997.

Blackey, Robert, 'Fanon and Cabral: A Contrast in Theories of Revolution for Africa', *Journal of Modern African Studies*, vol. 12, no. 2, 1974.

Blanchet, André, 'La Conférence d'Accra prend l'allure d'une manifestation contre la France', *Le Monde*, 11 December 1958.

Blérald, Alain-Philippe, *La Question nationale en Guadeloupe et en Martinique: Essai sur l'histoire politique*, Paris: L'Harmattan, 1988.

Bloom, Allan, 'Western Civ', in *Giants and Dwarves: Essays 1960–1990*, New York: Simon and Schuster, 1990.

Bogle, Donald, *Toms, Coons, Mulattoes, Mammies and Bucks: An Interpretive History of Blacks in American Films*, New York: Continuum, 1997, third edn.

Boigey, Dr, 'Etudes psychologiques sur l'Islam', *Annales médico-psychologiques*, October 1908.

Bondy, François, 'The Black Rousseau', *New York Review of Books*, 31 March 1966.

Bonnafé, Lucien, 'Rencontres autour de François Tosquelles', *Evolution psychiatrique*, vol. 60, no. 3, 1995.

—— Ey, Henri, Lacan, Jacques and Rouart, Julien, *Le Problème de la psychogénèse des névroses et des psychoses*, Paris: Desclée de Brouwer, 1950.

Bonnaud, Robert, 'La Paix des Nemenchetas', *Esprit*, April 1957.

Bouillon, Antoine, *Madagascar: le colonisé et son âme. Essais sur le discours psychologique colonial*, Paris: L'Harmattan, 1981.

Boujedra, Rachid, *Lettres algériennes*, Paris: Grasset, 1995.

Bourdet, Claude, 'Melouza, crime et faute', *France-Observateur*, 6 June 1947.

Bourdieu, Pierre, *Sociologie de l'Algérie*, Paris: Presses Universitaires de France, Collection 'Que sais-je?', 1958.

—— 'The Sentiment of Honour in Kabyle Society', trans. P. Sherrard, in J. G. Peristiany (ed.), *Honour and Shame: The Values of Mediterranean Society*, London: Weidenfeld & Nicolson, 1965.

—— *Algérie 60: Structures économiques et structures temporelles*, Paris: Minuit, 1977.

—— and Passeron, Jean-Claude, *The Inheritors: French Students and their Relation to Culture*, trans. R. Nice, Chicago: University of Chicago Press, 1979.

Bourgui, A. C. and Williams, J. C., 'La Pensée politique de Frantz Fanon', *Présence africaine* 88, 4ème trimestre 1973.

Bourseiller, Christophe, *Les Maoïstes: la folle histoire des gardes rouges français*, Paris: Plon, 1996.

Bouvier, Pierre, *Fanon*, Paris: Editions universitaires, 1971.

Brahimi, Denise, 'Littérature algérienne et conscience nationale: avant l'indépendance', *Notre librairie* 85, October–December 1986.

Braudel, Fernand, *The Mediterranean and the Mediterranean World in the Age of Philip II*, trans. Siân Reynolds, abridged by Richard Ollard, London: Book Club Associates, 1996.

Breton, André, *Signe ascendant*, Paris: Gallimard, collection 'Poésie', 1968.

—— *Point du jour*, Paris: Gallimard, 1970.

—— *Martinique, charmeuse de serpents*, Paris: Jean-Jacques Pauvert, 1972.

Bright, Martin, 'The Outsiders', *Observer Magazine*, 31 October 1999.

Britton, Celia, *Edouard Glissant and Post-colonial Theory*, Charlottesville: University Press of Virginia, 1999.

Bromberger, Serge, *Les Rebelles algériens*, Paris: Plon, 1958.

—— and Bromberger, Merry, Elgey, Georgette and Chauvel, J.-F., *Barricades et colonels: 24 janvier 1960*, Paris: Librairie Arthème Fayard, 1960.

Bruckner, Pascal, *Le Sanglot de l'homme blanc: Tiers monde, culpabilité, haine de soi*, Paris: Seuil, 1983.

Bulhan, Hussein Abdilahi, 'Frantz Fanon: The Revolutionary Psychiatrist', *Race and Class*, vol. XXI, no. 3, 1980.

—— *Frantz Fanon and the Psychology of Oppression*, New York: Plenum Press, 1985.

Burnier, Michel-Ange, 'Frantz Fanon, le colonisé', *Magazine Littéraire*, June 1970.

Burton, Richard D. E., 'Towards 1992: Political-Cultural Assimilation and Opposition in Contemporary Martinique', *French Cultural Studies*, 3, 1992.

—— *La Famille coloniale: La Martinique et la mère-patrie 1789–1992*, Paris: L'Harmattan, 1994.

—— '"*Nos Journées de juin*": The Historical Significance of the Liberation of Martinique (June 1943)', in H. R. Kedwood and Nancy Woods (eds), *The Liberation of France: Image and Event*, Oxford: Berg, 1995.

Bussière, Michèle, Méadel, Cécile and Ulmann-Mauriat, Caroline (eds), *Radios et télévision au temps des 'événements' d'Algérie 1954–1962*, Paris and Montréal: L'Harmattan, 1999.

Cabral, Amilcar, *Revolution in Guinea: An African People's Struggle*, London: Stage 1, 1969.

Caillens, J., 'Culture et civilisation nègre à travers l'édition française', *Présence africaine*, 1948.

Calvet, Jean-Louis, *Roland Barthes: A Biography*, trans. Sarah Wykes, Cambridge: Polity Press.

Campbell, James, *Paris Interzone: Richard Wright and Others on the Left Bank 1946–1960*, London: Secker and Warburg, 1994.

Camus, Albert, 'Misère de la Kabylie', in *Actuelles III: Chroniques algériennes 1939–1958*, Paris: Gallimard, 1958.

—— *Le Premier Homme*, Paris: Gallimard, 1994.

Capécia, Mayotte, *Je suis Martiniquaise*, Paris: Editions Corréa, 1948.

—— *La Négresse blanche*, Paris: Editions Corréa, 1950.

Cardinal, Marie, *Aux Pays de mes racines*, Paris: Livre de poche, 1982.

—— *Les Pieds noirs*, Paris: Belfond, 1988.

Carmichael, Stokely and Hamilton, Charles V., *Black Power*, Harmondsworth: Penguin, 1969.

Causset, Pierre, 'Frantz Fanon, théoricien de la décolonisation', supplément à *La Lugar* 6, June 1972.

# Bibliography

Caute, David, *Fanon*, London: Fontana/Collins, 1970.

'C. B.', '"Wretched of the Earth" Take Over in Two Books', *Durham Morning Herald*, 29 February 1966.

Césaire, Aimé, 'La Révolte de Frantz Fanon', *Jeune-Afrique*, 13–19 December 1961.

—— 'Homage à Frantz Fanon', *Présence africaine*, 60, 1962.

—— *Une Tempête*, Paris: Seuil, 1969.

—— *Les Armes miraculeuses*, Paris: Gallimard, Collection 'Poésies', 1970.

—— 'Par tous mots Guerrier Silex', *Le Progressiste*, 26 March 1982.

—— *La Poésie*, Paris: Seuil, 1994.

—— *Discours sur le colonialisme*, Paris: Présence africaine, 1995.

—— *Lettre à Maurice Thorez/Discours à la Maison du sport*, Fort-de-France: Parti Progressiste Martiniquais, nd.

—— *Notebook of a Return to My Native Land*, trans. Mireille Rosello with Annie Pritchard , Newcastle upon Tyne: Bloodaxe Books, 1995.

Chabal, Patrick, *Amilcar Cabral: Revolutionary Leadership and People's War*, Cambridge: Cambridge University Press, 1983.

Chaleau, Liliane, *Dans les Iles du vent: La Martinique XVII-XIXè siècles*, Paris: L'Harmattan, 1993.

Chamoiseau, Patrick, *Texaco*, trans. Rose-Myriam Réjouis and Val Vinokurv , London: Granta Books, 1997.

—— *Schooldays*, trans. Linda Coverdale, London: Granta Books, 1998.

—— *Ecrire en pays dominé*, Paris: Gallimard, 1997.

—— *L'Esclave vieil homme et le molosse*, Paris: Gallimard, 1997.

—— and Confiant, Raphaël, *Lettres créoles: tracées antillaises et continentales de la littérature 1635 à 1975*, Paris: Hatier, 1991.

Charrière, Henri, *Papillon*, trans. Patrick O'Brian, London: Rupert Hart-Davis, 1970.

Chastaing, Maxime, 'Frantz Fanon: *Peau noire, masques blancs*', *Esprit*, October 1952.

Châtelet, F., Duhamel O. and Pisier E., *Dictionnaire des oeuvres politiques*, Paris: PUF, 1986.

Chaulet, Claudine, 'Relecture sociologique de Fanon', *Kalim* 4, 1982.

Chauvet, Camille, 'La Martinique au temps de l'Amiral Robert (1939–1943)', in *Historial Antillais*, Fort-de-France: Société Dajani, 1985, vol. 5.

Chérif, Mohammed, 'La Science au service de la révolution', *Jeune Afrique* 4, September 1966.

Cherki, Alice, 'Témoignage d'une militante algérienne', in *Mémorial international*, 1984.

Cheurfi, A., 'Une Pensée en action', *El Moudjahid*, 9 December 1987.

—— 'Un Engagement multiforme', *El Moudjahid*, 13 December 1987.

Chikh, Slimane, *L'Algérie en armes, ou le temps des certitudes*, Paris: Economica, 1981.

Claveri, C. 'Aspects historiques de la psychothérapie institutionnelle', *Information psychiatrique*, vol. 63, no. 8, October 1987.

Clayton, Anthony, *The Wars of French Decolonization*, London: Longman, 1994.

Clemente, Pietro, *Frantz Fanon tra esistenzialismo e rivoluzione*, Bari: Laterza, 1971.

*Code noir* (ed.), Robert Chesnais, Paris: L'Esprit frappeur, 1998.

Cohen, Jean, 'Colonialisme et racisme en Algérie', *Les Temps modernes*, November 1955.

Cohen-Solal, Annie, *Sartre 1905–1980*, Paris: Folio, 1989.

Coiplet, Robert, Review of Mayotte Capécia, *La Négresse blanche*, *Le Monde*, 24 April 1948.

Cojean, Annick, 'Alfred Marie-Jeanne, habile et étrange "Nègre-marron" de la Martinique', *Le Monde*, 5–6 April 1998.

—— '"L'Héritage" de l'esclavage aux Antilles', *Le Monde*, 24 April 1998.

Colonna, Fanny (ed.), *Aurès/Algérie: les fruits verts d'une révolution*, Paris: Autrement, 1994.

—— 'Islam in the French Sociology of Religion', trans. David Macey, *Economy & Society*, vol. 24, no. 2, May 1995.

Comte, Gilbert, 'Un *Mein Kampf* de la décolonisation', *La Nation française*, 9 December 1961.

—— 'Quand Sartre préface le livre d'un ennemi', *XXè siécle*, 23 March 1962.

Conan, Eric, 'Martinique, ce département dont le patron est indépendantiste', *L'Express*, 4 March 1999.

Confiant, Raphaël, *Aimé Césaire: une traversée paradoxale du siècle*, Paris: Stock, 1973.

—— 'Fanon en son pays', *Sans Frontière*, February 1982.

—— *Le Nègre et l'amiral*, Paris: Livre de poche, 1993.

—— *L'Allée des soupirs*, Paris: Livre de poche, 1994.

—— *Ravines du devant-jour*, Paris: Folio, 1995.

Cononbo, Joseph Issoufou, *Souvenirs de guerre d'un Tirailleur sénégalais*, Paris: L'Harmattan, 1989.

Constant, Fred, *La Retraite aux flambeaux: société et politique en Martinique*, Paris: Editions caribbéennes, 1988.

*Constantine: son passé, son centénaire (1837–1937). Recueil des notices et mémoires de la Sociéte Archéologique de Constantine. Vol LXIV*, Constantine: Editions Braham, 1937.

Contat, Michel and Rybalka, Michel, *Les Ecrits de Sartre*, Paris: Gallimard, 1970.

Contour, Solange, *Fort-de-France au début du siècle*, Paris: L'Harmattan, 1994.

Cooper, David (ed.), *The Dialectics of Liberation*, Harmondsworth: Penguin, 1968.

Courrière, Yves, *La Guerre d'Algérie*, Paris: Robert Laffont, collection 'Bouquins', 1991, two vols.

# Bibliography

Coutrot, Aline, 'Les Scouts de France et la guerre d'Algérie', *Cahiers de l'Institut de l'Histoire du Présent* 8, October 1988.

Crabot, Georges, 'Chômage, racisme et centralisation excessive sont à l'origine du malaise à la Martinique', *Le Monde*, 29 December 1959.

Curidon, Victor, *Mon Pays, mon pays. Martinique! Martinique!*, Paris: Editions de Paris, 1937.

Dacy, Elio (ed.), *L'Actualité de Frantz Fanon: Actes du Congrès de Brazzaville*, Paris: Karthala, 1986.

Dalloz, Jacques, *La Guerre d'Indochine 1945–1954*, Paris: Seuil, 1987.

Damas, Léon-Gontran, *Pigments/Névralgie*, Paris: Présence africaine, 1972.

Damase, Jean, *Les nouveaux Barbares*, Paris: Fasquelle, 1935.

—— *Sidi de banlieue*, Paris: Fasquelle, 1937.

Danglades, J.-L., 'Une Empreinte dans l'urbanisme de Fort-de-France', *Revue le Rebelle* 3, September 1995.

Daniel, Jean, '*Les Damnés de la terre* de Frantz Fanon', *L'Express*, 30 November 1961.

—— 'Fanon, un "pied-noir" et le gaullisme', *L'Express*, 14 December 1961.

—— *La Blessure, suivi de le Temps qui vient*, Paris: Grasset, 1992.

Darsières, Camille, 'Discrètement mais éfficacement, depuis longtemps, le PPM a oeuvré à faire connaître Frantz Fanon', *Le Progressiste*, 24 March 1982.

Darsières, Jeannie, 'Un Révolutionnaire nommé Fanon: qui est-ce?', *Le Progressiste*, 24 March 1982.

Dash, Michael J., *Edouard Glissant*, Cambridge: Cambridge University Press, 1995.

Davezies, Robert, *Le Front*, Paris: Seuil and Club du livre chrétien, 1959.

Davids, M. Fakhry, 'Frantz Fanon: The Struggle for Inner Freedom', *Free Associations*, vol. VI, pt 2, no. 35, 1996.

Davidson, Basil, *The Liberation of Guiné: Aspects of an African Revolution*, Harmondsworth: Penguin, 1969.

—— *Which Way Africa? The Search for a New Society*, Harmondsworth: Penguin, 1971.

—— *Black Star: A View of the Life and Times of Kwame Nkrumah*, London: Allen Lane, 1973.

—— *In the Eye of the Storm: Angola's People*, Harmondsworth: Penguin, 1975.

Davis, Miles and Troupe, Quentin, *Miles: The Autobiography*, London: Picador, 1990.

'De Fort-de-France à Ain Sultane', *Révolution africaine*, 11 December 1987.

Debatty, André, *Le 13 mai et la presse*, Paris: Armand Colin, 1960.

Déjeux, Jean, 'Romans algériens et guerre de libération', *L'Esprit créateur*, vol. XXVI, no. 1, Spring 1986.

Delange, Jacqueline, 'Ethnologie du 1er Congrès des intellectuels noirs', *Les Temps modernes*, April 1957.

Delpech, Alice, *La Dissidence*, Paris: L'Harmattan, 1991.

Delsham, Tony, *An Tan Robè*, Schoelcher, Editions MGG, 1994.

Depestre, René, *Bonjour et adieu à la négritude*, Paris: Seghers, 1980.

DeRoo, Rebecca J., 'Colonial Collecting: Women and Algerian *Cartes postales*', *Parallax* 7, April–June 1998.

*Des Rappelés témoignent*, Clichy: Comité Résistance Spirituelle, 1957.

Despinoy, Maurice, 'Les Débuts de l'hôpital psychiatrique de la Martinique', *Information psychiatrique*, October 1955.

Desruelles, Maurice and Bersot, Henri, 'Note sur l'histoire de l'assistance aux aliénés en Algérie depuis la conquête', *Congrès des médecines aliénistes et neurologues de France et des pays de langue français*, 1938.

—— 'L'Assistance aux aliénés en Algérie', *Annales médico-psychologiques*, 1939.

Deville, Robert and Georges, Nicolas, *Les Départements d'Outre-mer: l'autre décolonisation*, Paris: Gallimard, Collection 'Découvertes', 1996.

Dhombre, Dominique, 'La Violence, tabou des sociétés démocratiques', *Le Monde*, 3 November 1999.

Dib, Mohammed, *La Grande Maison*, Paris: Seuil, 1952.

—— *L'Incendie*, Paris: Seuil, 1954.

—— *Le Métier à tisser*, Paris: Seuil, 1957.

—— *La Danse du roi*, Paris: Seuil, 1968.

—— *Au Café*, Arles: Actes-Sud, 1996.

Dieng, Amady Ali, '*Les Damnés de la terre* et les problèmes d'Afrique noire', *Présence africaine* 62, 1967.

Dine, Philip, *Images of the Algerian War: French Film and Fiction 1954–1962* , Oxford: Clarendon Press, 1994.

Diop, Cheik Anta, *Nations nègres et cultures*, Paris: Présence africaine, 1979, third edn.

Djafer, Aït, 'Complainte des mendiants arabes de la Casbah et de la petite Yasmina, tuée par son père', *Les Temps modernes* 98, January 1954.

Djebar, Assia, *La Soif*, René Julliard, 1957.

—— *Les Impatients*, Paris: René Julliard, 1958.

—— *Les Enfants du nouveau monde*, Paris: 10/18, 1973.

—— *L'Amour, la fantasia*, Paris: Jean-Claude Lattès, 1975.

—— *Ombre sultane*, Paris: Jean-Claude Lattès, 1982.

—— *Vaste est la prison*, Paris: Albin Michel, 1995.

—— *Le Blanc d'Algérie*, Paris: Albin Michel, 1995.

—— *Femmes d'Alger dans leur appartement*, Paris: des femmes, 1995.

Djeghloul, Abdelkader, 'Mémoire active', *Actualité de l'émigration*, 23–30 December 1987.

Dolto, Françoise, *Correspondance I: 1914-1938*, (ed.) Colette Percheminier, Paris: Hatier, 1991.

Domenach, Jean-Marie, 'Négocier en Algérie', *Esprit*, February 1956.

# Bibliography

Domenach, Jean-Marie, '*Les Damnés de la terre*'. I: sur une préface de Sartre', *Esprit*, March 1962.

—— 'Les Antilles avant qu'il soit trop tard', *Esprit*, April 1962.

—— '*Les Damnés de la terre*', *Esprit*, April 1962.

Dore-Audibert, Andrée, *Des Françaises d'Algérie dans la guerre d'Algérie*, Paris: Karthala, 1995.

Dreyfus-Armand and Temine, Emile, *Les Camps sur la plage, un éxil espagnol*, Paris: Autrement, 1995.

Droz, Bernard and Lever, Evelyne, *Histoire de la guerre d'Algérie 1954–1962*, Paris: Seuil, Collection 'Points', 1991, revised edn.

Duchemin, Jacques C., *Histoire du FLN*, Paris: La Table ronde, 1962.

Dunwoodie, Peter, *Writing French Algeria*, Oxford: Clarendon Press, 1998.

Einaudi, Jean-Luc, *La Bataille de Paris: 17 Octobre 1961*, Paris: Seuil, 1991.

—— 'Paris au temps de la guerre d'Algérie', *Passerelles* 11, Winter 1995–6.

Ellenberger, Henri F., *The Discovery of the Unconscious: The History and Development of Dynamic Psychiatry*, New York: Basic Books, 1970.

Emecheta, Buchi, *Second-Class Citizen*, London: Alison & Busby, 1974.

*Encyclopédie antillaise: Littérature antillaise (prose)*, Fort-de-France: Désormeaux, 1971.

Etienne, Bruno, *L'Algérie: cultures et révolution*: Paris: Seuil, 1977.

Evans, Martin, *The Memory of Resistance: French Opposition to the Algerian War*, Oxford: Berg, 1977.

Eveno, Patrick and Planchais, Jean, *La Guerre d'Algérie*, Paris: La Découverte/*Le Monde*, 1990.

'Evocation de Frantz Fanon', *Alger républicain*, 7 January 1992.

'Exemple toujours vivant', *El Moudjahid*, 21 December 1961.

Ey, Henri, *Des Idées de Jackson à un modèle organo-dynamique en psychiatrie*, Toulouse: Privat, 1975.

Fabre, Geneviève and Koussouss, Mammon, 'Frantz Fanon et la révolte noire,' *Le Monde diplomatique*, December 1971.

Fabre, Michel, 'Fanon et Richard Wright', in Dacy (ed.), *L'Actualité de Frantz Fanon*.

—— *The World of Richard Wright*, Jackson: University Press of Mississippi, 1985.

Fairchild, Halford F., 'Frantz Fanon's *Wretched of the Earth* in Contemporary Perspective', *Journal of Black Studies* vol. 25, no. 2, December 1994.

Fanon, France-Line, 'La Conséquence', *Antilla* 23, November–December 1991.

Fanon, Joby. 'Pour Frantz, pour notre mère', *Sans Frontière*, February 1982.

—— 'Formons un homme neuf', *Antilla* 23, November–December 1982.

Fanon, Josie, 'A Propos de Frantz Fanon, Sartre, le racisme et les Arabes', *El Moudjahid,* 10 June 1967.

Favrod, Charles-Henri, 'Les Hommes, les indigènes', *Gazette de Lausanne,* 27 January 1962.

Fayaud, R.-L., 'Expérience d'un psychiatre en Martinique', *Information psychiatrique,* vol. 60, no. 4, April 1984.

Feraoun, Mouloud, *Journal 1955–1962,* Paris: Seuil, 1962.

—— *Lettres à ses amis,* Paris: Seuil, 1969.

Fermor, Patrick Leigh, *The Traveller's Tree: A Journal through the Caribbean Islands,* Harmondsworth: Penguin, 1984.

Feuchtwang, Stephan, 'Fanon's Politics of Culture: The Colonial Situation and its Extension', *Economy & Society,* vol. 14, no. 4, November 1985.

—— 'Fanonian Spaces', *New Formations* 1, Spring 1987.

Finger, Blanche and Kael, William, *Operation 'Vent printanier', 16–17 juillet 1942: la rafle du Vel d'Hiv,* Paris: La Découverte, 1992.

Finkielkraut, Alain, *La Défaite de la pensée,* Paris: Folio, 1989.

Foucault, Michel, *Histoire de la folie à l'âge classique,* Paris: Gallimard, Collection 'Tel', 1972.

'François Tosquelles par lui-même', *L'Ane* 13, November–December 1983.

Francos, Ania and Séréni, J.-P., *Un Algérien nommé Boumédienne,* Paris: Stock 1976.

'Frantz Fanon, *Peau noire masques blancs*', *Parallèle 50,* June 1952.

'Frantz Fanon, *Peau noire, masques blancs*', *Réforme,* 13 September 1952.

'Frantz Fanon, *Peau noire, masques blancs*', *Foi et vie,* December 1952.

'Frantz Fanon et la révolution algérienne', *El Moudjahid,* 20 March 1971.

'Frantz Fanon, notre frère', *El Moudjahid,* 21 December 1971.

*Frantz Fanon, scénario du film de Isaac Julien,* Paris: Films K editions, 1998.

Fredj, Jacques, 'Situation de l'histoire en Martinique', *Les Temps modernes* 359, June 1976.

Fréminville, C. de, 'Frantz Fanon, *Peau noire, masques blancs*', *Le Populaire,* 12 May 1952.

Frémont, André, *Algérie-El Djazaïr: les carnets de guerre et de terrain d'un géographe,* Paris: Maspero, 1982.

Freud, Sigmund, 'Family Romances', *The Standard Edition of the Psychological Works of Sigmund Freud,* London: Hogarth Press and the Institute of Psychoanalsis, 1953–74, 24 vols, vol. IX.

—— 'Five Lectures on Psychoanalysis', *Standard Edition* , vol. XI.

—— 'Some Psychical Consequences of the Anatomical Distinction between the Sexes', *Standard Edition,* vol. XIX.

—— 'Fetishism', *Standard Edition,* vol. XXI

Gadant, Monique, 'Vingt ans de littérature algérienne', *Les Temps modernes,* July–August 1982.

Gadant, Monique, *Islam et nationalisme en Algérie d'après 'El Moudjahid', organe centrale du FLN de 1956 à 1962*, Paris: L'Harmattan, 1988.

—— 'La Permission de dire "je"', *Peuples méditerranéens* 48–49, July–December 1989.

—— *Parcours d'une intellectuelle en Algérie. Nationalisme et anticolonialisme dans les sciences sociales*, Paris: L'Harmattan, 1995.

Gates, Henry Louis Jr., 'Critical Fanonism', *Critical Inquiry* 17, Spring 1991.

Gaudemar, Antoine de 'De l'île en exile', *Libération*, 16 October 1977.

—— 'Expressions d'Afrique', *Libération*, 4 December 1997.

Geismar, Peter, *Frantz Fanon*, New York: Dial Press, 1971.

Gendzier, Irene, *Frantz Fanon: A Critical Study*, London: Wildwood House, 1973.

Geronimi, Charles, 'Rencontre avec Fanon', unpublished typescript.

Ghazi, M'Hmad Ferid, 'Doublement prolétaires', *Esprit*, February 1952.

Giap, Général V.N., *Guerre du peuple, armée du peuple*, Hanoi: Editions en langues étrangères, 1961.

Gide, André, *Voyage au Congo*, Paris: Gallimard, 1927.

—— *Retour du Tchad*, Paris: Gallimard, 1928.

Girardet, Raoul, *L'Idée coloniale en France de 1871 à 1962*, Paris: La Table ronde, 1972.

Giraud, Michel, *Races et classes à la Martinique: les relations sociales entre enfants de différentes couleurs à l'école*, Paris: Editions Anthropos, 1979.

Glissant, Edouard, 'Je crois à l'avenir des cultures métisées', *France-Observateur*, 4 December 1958.

—— 'Culture et colonisation: l'équilibre antillais', *Esprit*, April 1962.

—— *Le Discours antillais*, Paris: Seuil, 1981.

—— *Monsieur Toussaint*, trans. Joseph Foster and Barbara Franklin, Washington: Three Continents Press, 1981.

—— *The Ripening*, trans. Michael J. Dash, London: Heinemann, 1985.

—— *Caribbean Discourse*, trans. Michael J. Dash, Charlottesville: University of Virginia Press, 1989.

—— *Le Quatrième siècle*, Paris: Gallimard, Collection 'L'Imaginaire', 1990.

—— 'Un nouveau Sens de l'humanité pour les pays du Sud', *Antilla* 23, November–December 1991.

—— *Les Iles*, trans. Dominique O'Neill, Toronto: Gref, 1992, bilingual edn.

—— *Poèmes complets*, Paris: Gallimard, 1994.

—— *Poetics of Relation*, trans. Betsy Wing, Ann Arbor: University of Michigan Press, 1998.

Glucksmann, André, 'Un Terrorisme du troisième type', *Libération*, 30 May–1 June 1982.

Goldie, Terry, 'Saint Fanon and "Homosexual Territory"' in Alessandrini (ed.), *Frantz Fanon: Critical Perspectives*.

Gordon, Gérald, 'La Folie bilingue', *Parti-pris*, May 1966.

Gordon, Lewis R., *Fanon and the Crisis of European Man: An Essay on Philosophy and the Human Sciences*, New York and London: Routledge, 1995.

—— Sharpley-Whiting, T. Denean and White, Renée T., *Fanon: A Critical Reader*, Oxford: Blackwell, 1996.

Grohs, G. K., 'Frantz Fanon and the Algerian Revolution', *Journal of Modern African Studies*, vol. 6, no. 4, 1968.

Grynberg, Anne, *Les Camps de la honte: les internés juifs dans les camps français*, Paris: La Découverte and Syros, 1991.

Guattari, Félix, *Molecular Revolution: Psychiatry and Politics*, trans. Rosemary Sheed, Harmondsworth: Penguin, 1984.

Guérin, Daniel, *Les Antilles décolonisées*, Paris: Présence africaine, 1956.

—— *Le Feu du sang: autobiographie politique et charnelle*, Paris: Grasset, 1977.

—— *Quand l'Algérie s'insurgeait: 1954–1962. Un Anticolonialiste témoigne*, Claix: La Pensée sauvage, 1979.

—— *Ci-gît le colonialisme*, The Hague and Paris: Mouton, 1983.

Guex, Germaine, *Le Syndrôme d'abandon*, Paris: PUF, 1973.

Guibert, Armand, *Léopold Sedar Senghor*, Paris: Pierre Seghers, 1961.

Guilhaume, Jean-François, *Les Mythes fondateurs de l'Algérie française*, Paris: L'Harmattan, 1992.

Guillebaud, Jean-Claude, *Les Confettis de l'Empire*, Paris: Seuil, 1976.

Gurley, Franklin L., 'Les Débarquements de Provence: le 15 août 1944', *Guerres mondiales et conflits contemporains* 174, April 1994.

Habib, Salah, 'Fusion et confusion des identités', *Passerelles* 11, Winter 1995–6.

Hammadou, Ghania, 'Fanon-Blida, Blida-Fanon', *Révolution africaine* 11, December 1987.

Hammoumon, Mohand, 'Les Harkis, un trou de mémoire franco-algérienne', *Esprit*, May 1990.

Hamon, Hervé and Rotman, Patrick, *Les Porteurs de valises: la résistance française à la guerre d'Algérie*, Paris: Seuil, collection 'Points', 1982, expanded edn.

—— *Génération. I: Les Années de rêve*, Paris: Seuil, 1987.

Hanse, Emmanuel, *Frantz Fanon: Social and Political Thought*, Columbus: Ohio State University Press, 1977.

Harbi, Mohammed, *Aux Origines du Front de Libération Nationale: la scission du PPA/MTLD. Contribution à l'histoire du populisme révolutionnaire en Algérie*, Paris: Christian Bourgois, 1975.

—— (ed.), *Les Archives de la révolution algérienne*, Paris: Editions Jeune Afrique, 1981.

—— 'Avec ceux de la Wilaya IV', *Sans Frontière*, February 1982.

Harbi, Mohammed, *1954: La Guerre commence en Algérie*, Brussels: Editions Compexe, 1984.

—— *Le FLN: Mirage et réalité. Des origines à la prise de pouvoir*, Algiers: NAQD/ENAL, 1993, revised edn.

Haroun, Ali, *La 7ème Wilaya: la guerre du FLN en France 1954–1962*, Paris: Seuil, 1986.

Haudrère, Philippe and Vergès, Françoise, *De L'Esclave au citoyen*, Paris: Gallimard, 1998.

Hayman, Ronald, *Writing Against: A Biography of Sartre*, London: Weidenfeld & Nicolson, 1986.

Hegel, G. W. F., *The Philosophy of History*, New York: Dover, 1956.

Heidegger, Martin, *Being and Time*, trans. John MacQuarrie and Edward Robinson, Oxford: Basil Blackwell, 1908.

Held, Jean-François, 'Les Deux Doigts de la Main Rouge', *France-Observateur*, 15 October 1959.

Henissart, Paul, *Wolves in the City: The Death of French Algeria*, London: Paladin, 1973.

Hermassi, Abdelbaki, 'L'Idéologie fanonienne', *Jeune Afrique*, 4 September 1966.

Himes, Chester, *The Quality of Hurt: The Early Years. The Autobiography of Chester Himes*, New York: Paragon House, 1972.

—— *My Life of Absurdity: The Later Years. The Autobiography of Chester Himes*, New York: Paragon House, 1976.

—— *If He Hollers Let Him Go*, London: Serpent's Tail, 1999.

Hobsbawm, Eric J., *Primitive Rebels*, London: Weidenfeld & Nicolson, 1959.

—— 'Postmodernism in the Forest', in *On History*, London: Weidenfeld & Nicolson, 1997.

Hoechstetter, Irène, 'L'Homme de la décolonisation', *Réforme*, December 1961.

'Homage to Frantz Fanon', *Présence africaine* 69, 1962.

'Hommage à Frantz Fanon', *El Moudjahid*, 27 September 1992.

*Hommage à René Maran*, Paris and Dakar: Présence africaine, 1965.

'Hôpital psychiatrique de Blida de 1961 à 1968', *Information psychiatrique*, vol. 45, no. 8, 1969.

Horne, Alistair, *A Savage War of Peace: Algeria 1954–1962*, London: Papermac 1987, revised edn.

Hountondji, Paulin J., *African Philosophy: Myth and Reality*, trans. Henri Evans with the collaboration of Jonathan Rée, introduction by Abiole Irele, London: Hutchinson, 1983.

Howe, Russell Warren, *Black Africa: Africa South of the Sahara from Pre-history to Independence, Parts 3 and 4*, Croydon: New African Library, 1967.

Howlett, Jacques, 'Le 1er Congrès des écrivains et artistes noirs et la presse internationale', *Présence africaine* 20, July 1958.

Humbaraci, Arslan, *Algeria: A Revolution that Failed: A Political History since 1954*, London: Pall Mall Press, 1966.

Ignasse, Gérard and Wallon, Emmanuel (eds), *Demain l'Algérie*, Paris: Syros, 1995.

Isaacs, Harold R., 'Portrait of a Revolutionary', *Commentary*, July 1965.

Jack, Belinda, *Francophone Literatures: An Introductory Survey*, Oxford: Oxford University Press, 1996.

Jackson, Henry F., *The FLN in Algeria: Party Development in a Revolutionary Society*, Westport: Greenwood Press, 1977.

Jaham, Marie-Jeanne de, *La Grande Bekée*, Paris: Robert Laffont, 1989.

—— *Le Maître-savane*, Paris: Pocket, 1995.

James, C. L. R., *The Black Jacobins: Toussaint L'Ouverture and the San Domingo Revolution*, London: Alison and Busby, 1988.

Jardel, J.-P., 'Identité et idéologie aux Antilles françaises. Négrisme, négritude et antillanité', *Recherches sociologiques*, vol. XV, nos. 2–3, 1984.

*Jean Amrouche: l'éternel Jugurtha (1906–1962)*, Marseille: Archives de la Ville de Marseille, 1985.

Jeanson, Colette and Jeanson, Francis, *L'Algérie hors la loi*, Paris: Seuil, 1955.

Jeanson, Francis, *Le Problème moral et la pensée de Sartre*, Paris: Seuil, 1947.

—— 'Cette Algérie, conquise et pacifiée', *Esprit*, April, May 1950.

—— 'Sartre et le monde noir', *Présence africaine* 7.

—— 'Albert Camus ou l'âme révoltée', *Les Temps modernes*, May 1952.

—— *Notre Guerre*, Paris: Minuit, 1960.

—— 'Lettre à Jean-Paul Sartre', *Les Temps modernes* 169–70, April–May 1960.

—— 'Reconnaissance à Fanon' in *Peau noire, masques blancs*, Paris: Seuil, 1965.

—— *La Révolution algérienne*, Milan: Feltrinelli, 1962.

—— *Algéries: de retour en retour*, Paris: Seuil, 1998.

Jinadu, Adele L., *Fanon: In Search of the African Revolution*, Enugu, Nigeria: Fourth Dimension Publishers, 1980.

Joachim, Paulin, 'Les Damnés de la terre ne veulent pas la mort de l'Europe', *Communauté franco-eurafrique*, February 1962.

Joanne, Adolphe, *Géographie de l'Algérie*, Paris: Hachette, 1885.

Joly, Danièle, *The French Communist Party and the Algerian War*, London: Macmillan, 1991.

Jordi, Jean-Jacques, *1962: L'Arrivée des pieds-noirs*, Paris: Autrement, 1995.

—— and Pervillé, Guy (eds), *Alger 1940–1962: une ville en guerres*, Paris: Autrement, 1999.

—— and Planche, Jean-Louis (eds), *Alger 1860–1939: le modèle ambigu du triomphe colonial*, Paris: Autrement, 1999.

'Journée d'hommage à Frantz Fanon: 25 septembre 1982, Université d'Alger', *Kalim* 4, 1982.

Julien, Charles-André, *Le Maroc face aux impérialismes (1415–1956)*, Paris: Editions Jeune Afrique, 1978.

—— *Et La Tunisie devient indépendante, 1951–1957*, Paris: Editions Jeune Afrique, 1985.

Kaddour, Amal, 'Farés époque Fanon', *El Moudjahid*, 16 December 1987.

Kader, F., 'Le Visionnaire d'un monde nouveau', *El Moudjahid*, 14 October 1982.

Kahler, Miles, *Decolonization in Britain and France: The Domestic Consequences of International Relations*, Princeton: Princeton University Press, 1984.

Kahn, Jean-François, 'Les Conjurés voulaient défiler jeudi à Alger', *Paris-presse*, 3 July 1962.

Kanza, Thomas, *Conflict in the Congo*, Harmondsworth: Penguin, 1972.

Kariuki, Josiah Mwangi, *Mau Mau Detainee: An Account by a Kenyan African of his Experience in Detention Camps, 1953–1960*, London and Nairobi, Oxford University Press, 1963.

*Kateb Yacine: l'oeuvre en mouvement*, Thionville: Ville de Thionville, 1996.

Kershaw, Greet, *Mau Mau from Below*, Oxford, Nairobi and Athens: James Currey, EAEP and Ohio University Press, 1997.

Kessel, Patrick, 'En l'Absence d'Audin', *France-Observateur*, 5 December 1957.

—— and Pirelli, Giovanni, *Le Peuple algérien et la guerre: lettres et témoignages 1954–1962*, Paris: Maspero, 1962.

Kestelkoot, Lilyan, *Les Ecrivains noirs de langue française. Naissance d'une littérature*, Brussels: Editions de l'Institut de sociologie, Université libre de Bruxelles, 1971.

Kincaid, Jamaica, *A Small Place*, London: Vintage, 1997.

Korngold, Ralph, *Citizen Toussaint*, London: Gollancz, 1945.

Kuhn, T. S., *The Structure of Scientific Revolutions*, Chicago: University of Chicago Press, 1962.

Kurlansky, Mark, *Cod: A Biography of the Fish that Changed the World*, London: Jonathan Cape, 1998.

Labro, Philippe, *Des Feux mal éteints*, Paris: Folio, 1993.

Lacan, Jacques, *Ecrits*, Paris: Seuil, 1966.

—— *Les Complexes familiaux dans la formation de l'individu: essai d'analyse d'une fonction en psychanalyse*, Paris: Navarin, 1984.

Lacascade, Suzanne, *Claire-Solange: âme africaine*, Paris: Eugène Figuière, nd. (1924).

Lacheraf, Mostefa, 'L'Avenir de la culture algérienne', *Les Temps modernes*, October 1963.

Lacheraf, Mostefa, *L'Algérie: nation et société*, Paris: Maspero, 1969.

—— '"Il doit tout à l'Algérie"', *Le Matin*, 24 December 1992.

Lacouture, Jean, 'Témoignages et réquisitoires sur l'affaire algérienne', *Le Monde*, 1 July 1960.

—— *De Gaulle: The Rebel 1890–1944* , trans. Patrick O'Brian, London: HarperCollins, 1993.

—— *De Gaulle: The Ruler 1945–1970*, trans. Alan Sheridan, London: HarperCollins, 1993.

Lafont, M., 'L'Extermination douce dans les HP français', *Information psychiatrique*, vol. 72, no. 8, October 1996.

*La Gangrène,* Paris: Minuit, 1959.

'La Main rouge revendique ses exploits', *France-Observateur*, 3 December 1959.

Lamming, George, 'The Negro Writer and his World', *Présence africaine* 8–10, June–November 1956.

Langellier, Jean-Pierre, 'Les 100,000 morts de l'insurrection malgache', *Le Monde*, 16–17 March 1997.

'La Nouvelle Algérienne', *France-Observateur*, 24 May 1962.

Laplanche, Jean and Pontalis, J.-B., *The Language of Psychoanalysis*, trans. Donald Nicholson-Smith, London: Hogarth Press and the Institute of Psychoanalysis, 1973.

Larcher, Marius, 'Le Livre de Frantz Fanon', *L'Information*, 23 May 1962.

Lazreg, Marnia, *The Eloquence of Silence: Algerian Women in Question*, New York and London: Routledge, 1994.

Leborgne, Yvon, 'Le Climat social', *Esprit*, April 1962.

Lefkowitz, Mary R. and Maclean, Guy (eds), *Black Athena Revisited*, Chapel Hill and London: University of North Carolina Press, 1996.

*Légitime Défense*, Paris: Editions Jean-Michel Place, 1979, facsimile edition.

Legune, Liliane, 'Naissance de la France au grand large', *Le Monde*, 17–18 March 1996.

Leiris, Michel, 'Martinique, Guadeloupe, Haiti', *Les Temps modernes* 52, February 1950.

—— *Contacts de civilisations en Martinique et Guadeloupe*, Paris: Gallimard, 1987.

Lemoine, Maurice, *Le Mal antillais: leurs ancêtres les Gaulois*, Paris: L'Harmattan, 1982.

Léotin, Marie-Hélène (ed.), *La Martinique pendant la deuxième guerre mondiale*, Fort-de-France: Archives départementales and Centre régional de documentation pédagogique des Antilles et de la Guyane, 1993.

—— *Martinique: 50 ans de départementalisation*, Fort-de-France: APAL Production, 1997.

Lepine, Edouard de, 'Fanon et Césaire', *Le Progressiste*, 24 March 1992.

Lespès, René, *Pour comprendre l'Algérie*, Algiers: Gouvernement Général, 1937.

*Le 13 mai 1958*, Paris: La Documentation française.

'Lettre de Ain-Kerma', *El Moudjahid*, 11–12 December 1987.

Lévi-Bruhl, Lucien, *Les Fonctions mentales dans les sociétés inférieures*, Paris: Alcan, 1910.

—— *La Mentalité primitive*, Paris: Alcan, 1922.

—— *l'Ame primitive*, Paris: Alcan, 1927.

—— *Le Surnaturel et la nature dans la mentalité primitive*, Paris: Alcan, 1931.

—— *La Mythologie primitive*, Paris: Alcan, 1938.

—— *L'Expérience mystique et les symboles chez les primitifs*, Paris: Alcan, 1938.

—— *Carnets*, Paris: PUF, 1949.

Lévi-Strauss, Claude, *The Elementary Structures of Kinship*, trans. James Harle Bell, John Richard van Sterne and Rodney Needham, London: Eyre and Spottiswoode, 1969.

—— *The Savage Mind*, London: Weidenfeld & Nicolson, 1972.

—— *Tristes Tropiques*, trans. John and Doreen Weightman, London: Picador, 1989.

Lewis, David Levering (ed.), *The Portable Harlem Renaissance Reader*, New York: Penguin, 1995.

Leyarie, Philippe, 'Martinique: le fantôme de Frantz Fanon', *Le Matin de Paris*, 6 April 1982.

Leyritz, Dr de, 'L'Assistance aux aliénés aux Antilles françaises', *Information psychiatrique*, January 1955.

Lhermitte, Jean, *Les Fondements biologiques de la psychologie*, Paris: Gauthier-Villiers, 1925.

—— *Le Sommeil*, Paris: Armand Colin, 1930.

—— *Les Mécanismes du cerveau*, Paris: Gallimard, 1938.

—— *L'Image de notre corps*, Paris: Editions de la nouvelle revue critique, 1939.

Liauzu, Claude, 'Intellectuels du Tiers Monde et intellectuels français: les années algériennes des Editions Maspero', in Rioux and Sirinelli (eds), *La Guerre d'Algérie et les intellectuels français*.

—— 'Prétoires, mémoires, histoire: la guerre d'Algérie a eu lieu', *Les Temps modernes*, 606, November–December 1999.

'Libérer les régions', *Embata*, 19 February 1970.

Liebman, Marcel, 'Les Juifs devant le problème algérien', *Les Temps modernes*, 180bis, April 1961.

Linval, Juvénal A., 'Note touchant la bourgeoisie de couleur', *Légitime défense*, 1932.

Lipton, Lawrence, 'Radio Free America', *LA Free Press*, 18 August 1967.

Lirus, Julie, *L'Identité antillaise. Contribution à la connaissance psychologique et anthropologique du Guadeloupéen et du Martiniquais,* Paris: Editions caribbéennes, 1997.

London, Perry, 'Multi-faceted Treatise on Colonial Revolution', *Los Angeles Times,* 23 May 1965.

Lorcin, Patricia, M. E., *Imperial Identities: Stereotypying, Prejudice and Race in Colonial Algeria,* London: I. B. Tauris, 1995.

Lucas, Philippe, *Sociologie de Frantz Fanon: contribution à une anthropologie de la libération,* Algiers; SNED, 1971.

—— and Vatin, Jean-Claude, *L'Algérie des anthropologues,* Paris: Maspero, 1975.

Lyotard, Jean-François, *La Guerre des Algériens: Ecrits 1956–1963,* Paris: Editions Galilée, 1989.

Macey, David, 'Paul Nizan: A Posthumous Life', *Studi Francesi,* Anno XXX, fascicolo 1, January–April 1986.

—— *Lacan in contexts,* London: Verso, 1988.

—— *The Lives of Michel Foucault,* London: Hutchinson, 1993.

—— 'A French Algeria', *Economy & Society,* vol. 27, nos 2–3, May 1998.

—— 'Frantz Fanon 1925–1961', *History of Psychiatry* 7, 1996.

—— 'Fort-de-France', *Granta* 59, Autumn 1997.

—— 'The Algerian with the Knife', *Parallax* 7, April–June 1998.

—— 'The Honour of Georges Canguilhem', *Economy & Society,* vol. 27, nos 2–3, May 1998.

—— 'The Recall of the Real: Frantz Fanon and Psychoanalysis', *Constellations,* vol. 6, no. 1, May 1999.

—— 'Fanon, Phenomenology, Race', *Radical Philosophy* 95, May–June 1999.

—— '*Insoumis*: Nizan, Sartre, Fanon', in James Dolamore (ed.), *Making Connections: Essays in French Culture and Society in Honour of Philip Thody,* Bern: Peter Lang, 1999.

Mahsas, Ahmed, *Le Mouvement révolutionnaire en Algérie de la Première Guerre Mondiale à 1954: essai sur la formation du mouvement national,* Paris: L'Harmattan, 1979.

Makward, Christiane P., *Mayotte Capécia, ou l'aliénation selon Fanon,* Paris: Karthala, 1999.

Malabre, Alfred L. Jr., 'A Disturbing Diatribe from the Third World', *Wall Street Journal,* 23 July 1965.

Malek, Rehda, *L'Algérie à Evian: histoire des négotiations secrètes 1956–1962,* Paris: Seuil, 1995.

Malley, Robert, *The Call from Algeria: Third Worldism, Revolution and the Turn to Islam,* Berkeley, Los Angeles and London: University of California Press, 1996.

Maloba, Wunyebari O., *Mau Mau and Kenya: An Analysis of a Peasant Revolt,* Bloomington and Indianapolis: Indiana University Press, 1993.

Malsa, Garcia, 'La Chose la plus essentielle', *Antilla* 23, November–December 1991.

Mameri, Khalfa, *Abane Ramdane, héros de la guerre d'Algérie*, Paris: L'Harmattan, 1998.

Manceron, Gilles and Remanoun, Hassan, *D'Une Rive à l'autre: la guerre d'Algérie de la mémoire à l'histoire*, Paris: Syros, 1993.

Mandouze, André, 'Impossibilités algériennes, ou le mythe des trois départements', *Esprit*, July 1947.

—— 'Plage, montagne et université', *Esprit*, April 1952.

—— (ed.), *La Révolution algérienne par les textes*, Paris: Maspero, 1961.

—— 'Fanon, le responsable', *Sans Frontière*, February 1982.

—— 'Le Retour de Fanon', *Le Monde*, 7 April 1982.

—— *Mémoires d'outre-siècle. Tome I: D'Une Résistance à l'autre*, Paris: Viviane Hamy, 1998.

Mannon, André, 'L'Etrange Conseil du psychiatre FLN: Haïssez-vous les uns les autres', *Paris-Presse*, 20 January 1962.

Mannoni, Eugène, '"Luttes à mort" entre Algériens en France', *Le Monde*, 12 October 1956.

Mannoni, Octave, 'Le Complexe de dépendance et la structure de la personnalité', *Psyché* 12, 13, 1947.

—— 'La Personnalité malgache: ébauche d'une analyse des structures', *Revue de la psychologie des peuples*, vol. 13, no. 3, July 1948.

—— 'Psychologie de la révolte malgache', *Esprit*, April 1950.

—— 'La Plainte du noir', *Esprit*, May 1951.

—— *Prospéro et Caliban: Psychologie de la colonisation*, Paris: Editions universitaires, 1984.

Mannoni, Pierre, *Les Français d'Algérie: vies, moeurs, mentalités. Des Térritoires du Sud à l'Indépendance*, Paris: L'Harmattan, 1993.

Manville, Marcel, 'Hommage à Frantz Fanon', *Sans Frontière*, February 1982.

—— 'Témoignage d'un ami et d'un compagnon de lutte', in Dacy (ed.), *L'Actualité de Frantz Fanon*.

—— 'La Voie royale', *Antilla* 23, November–December 1991.

—— *Les Antilles sans fard*, Paris: L'Harmattan, 1992.

Mao Tse Tung, *Selected Works of Mao Tse Tung, Vol. 2*, Peking: Foreign Languages Publishing House, 1967.

Maran, René, *Un Homme pareil aux autres*, Paris: Editions Arc-en-ciel, 1947.

Marrus, Michael and Paxton, Robert O., *Vichy France and the Jews*, New York: Schoken Books, 1983.

Marseille, Jacques, 'Assez de clichés sur l'Afrique', *L'Evénement du jeudi*, 12–18 July 1990.

Martinet, Gilles, 'Réponse au FLN', *France-Observateur*, 2 January 1958.

Marton, Imre, 'A Propos des thèses de Fanon. I: Le Rôle de la violence dans la lutte de libération nationale', *Action* 7, 2ème trimestre 1965.

—— 'A Propos des thèses de Fanon. II: Le Rôle des classes sociales après l'indépendance', *Action* 8–9, 3ème–4ème trimestres 1965.

Marx, Karl, *Surveys from Exile* David Fernbach (ed.), Harmondsworth: Penguin, 1973.

Maschino, Maurice, '*L'An V de la Révolution algérienne* de Frantz Fanon', *Les Temps modernes*, February–March 1960.

—— *Le Refus*, Paris: Maspero, 1960.

—— *L'Engagement*, Paris: Maspero, 1961.

—— 'Présence de Frantz Fanon', *Le Petit matin*, 12 December 1961.

—— and M'Rabet, Fadéla, *L'Algérie des illusions: la révolution confisquée*, Paris: Robert Laffont, 1972.

Maspero, François, 'Entre les chiens et les hommes', *Vérité-liberté*, 14 December 1961.

—— 'Pour étouffer un homme libre', *Tribune socialiste*, 16 December 1961.

—— *Le Figuier*, Paris: Seuil, 1988.

—— 'Quelqu'un "de la famille"', *Les Temps modernes* 531–3, October–December 1990.

Mathieu, Jean-Luc, *Histoire des DOM-TOM*, Paris: PUF, Collection 'Que sais-je?', 1993.

Mattei, Georges M., 'Jours kabyles', *Les Temps modernes*, July–August 1957.

Mauriac, François, *Bloc-notes. Tôme I: 1952–1957*, Paris: Seuil, Collection 'Points', 1993.

—— *Bloc-notes. Tôme II: 1958–1960*, Paris: Seuil, Collection 'Points', 1993.

Maurienne, *Le Déserteur*, Levallois-Peret: Editions Manya, 1991.

Mbom, Clément, *Frantz Fanon aujourd'hui et demain; refléxions sur le tiers monde*, Paris: Nathan, 1985.

McCulloch, J., *Black Soul, White Artifact: Fanon's Clinical Psychology and Social Theory*, Cambridge: Cambridge University Press, 1983.

Medienne, Benamar, 'Le Voyage fanonien: de l'archipel au continent', *Algérie-actualité*, 5–11 December 1991.

Mekhaled, Boucif, *Chroniques d'un massacre: 8 mai 1945, Sétif, Guelma, Kherrata*, Paris: Syros, 1995.

Memmi, Albert, 'La Vie impossible de Frantz Fanon', *Esprit*, September 1971.

—— *L'Homme dominé*, Paris: Payot, 1968.

—— *Portrait du colonisé, précédé de Portrait du colonisateur*, Paris: Gallimard, 1985.

*Mémorial International Frantz Fanon: 31 mars–3 avril 1992*, Paris and Dakar: Présence africaine, 1994.

Ménil, René, 'Généralités sur l'écrivain de couleur antillais', *Légitime Défense*.

—— *Tracées: identité négritude, esthétique aux Antilles*, Paris: Robert Laffont, 1981.

Merad, Ghani, *La Littérature algérienne d'expression française: approches socio-culturelles*, Paris: Editions Pierre Oswald, 1976.

Merle, Robert, *Ben Bella*, trans. Camilla Sykes, London: Michael Joseph, 1967.

Merleau-Ponty, Maurice, *Phénoménologie de la perception*, Paris: Gallimard, 1945.

Métraux, Alfred, *La Vaudou haïtien*, Paris: Gallimard, 1958.

—— *Itinéraire I. 1935–1953. Carnets de notes et journaux de voyages*, Paris: Payot, 1978.

M'Hamsadji, Kaddour, 'Sociologie de Frantz Fanon de Philippe Lucas', *El Moudjahid*, 14 January 1972.

Miller, Christopher L., *Theories of Africans: Francophone Literature and Anthropology in Africa*, Chicago: University of Chicago Press, 1990.

Milne, June (ed.), *Kwame Nkrumah: The Conakry Years. His Life and Letters*, London and Atlantic Highlands NJ: Panaf, 1990.

Minces, Juliette, *L'Algérie de la révolution (1963–1964)*, Paris: L'Harmattan, 1988.

—— *La Génération suivante*, La Tour d'Aigue: L'Aube, 1997.

Minter, William, *Portuguese Africa and the West*, Harmondsworth: Penguin, 1972.

Mintz, Donald, 'Find Something Different', *Washington Evening Star*, 23 April 1965.

Miquel, Pierre, *La Guerre d'Algérie*, Paris: Fayard, 1993.

*Mirage: Enigmas of Race, Difference and Desire*, London: Institute of Contemporary Arts and Institute of International Visual Arts, 1995.

'Mise au point de M. Yazid à propos de la mort de Frantz Fanon', *Le Monde*, 2–3 March 1969.

Moeckil, Gustave, 'Testament d'un colonisé', *Journal de Genève*, 21 April 1962.

Moi, Toril, *Simone de Beauvoir: The Making of an Intellectual Woman*, Oxford: Basil Blackwell, 1994.

Moore-Gilbert, Bart, *Post-Colonial Theory: Contexts, Practices, Politics*, London: Verso, 1997.

Morin, Edgar, *Autocritique*, Paris: Seuil, Collection 'Points', 1970.

Mosevini, Yovery T., 'Fanon's Theory of Violence: Its Verification in Liberated Mozambique', in N. M. Shamuyarra (ed.), *Essays on the Liberation of Southern Africa*: Dar es Salaam: Tanzania Publishing House, 1975.

Mouffok, Ghania, 'Fanon par ceux qui l'ont connu', *Algérie-actualité* 17–25 December 1992.

Mounier, Emmanuel, *L'Eveil de l'Afrique noire*, in *Oeuvres complètes II: 1944–1950*, Paris: Seuil, 1962.

Mouralis, Bernard, *Littérature et développement*, Paris: Agence de Coopération Culturelle et Technique/Editions Silex, 1984.

Moutoussamy, Ernest, *Aimé Césaire, Député à l'Assemblée nationale 1945–1993*, Paris: L'Harmattan, 1993.

M'Rabet, Fadéla, *La Femme algérienne, suivi de Les Algériennes*, Paris: Maspero, 1979, nouvelle édition.

Mudimbe, V. Y. (ed.), *The Surreptitious Speech: 'Présence africaine' and the Politics of Otherness 1947–1987*, Chicago: University of Chicago Press, 1992.

Mueng, Engelbert, *Histoire du Congo*, Paris: Présence africaine, 1963.

Nadeau, Maurice, 'Romanciers d'Afrique du Nord', *Mercure de France*, March 1953.

Nghe, Nguyen, 'Frantz Fanon et les problèmes de l'indépendance', *La Pensée*, 107, January–February 1963.

Nicolaidis, Dimitri, *Oublier nos crimes: l'Amnésie nationale, une spécificité française?* Paris: Autrement, 1994.

Nicolas, Armand, 'La Révolution anti-esclavagiste de mai 1848 à la Martinique', *Action* 13, May 1967.

Nizan, Paul, *Aden-Arabie*, Paris: Maspero, 1969.

—— *Les Chiens de garde*, Paris: Maspero, 1971.

Nkrumah, Kwame, *The Autobiography of Kwame Nkrumah*, London: Panaf Books, 1973.

Nochlin, Linda, *The Politics of Vision: Essays on Nineteenth-Century Art and Society*, London: Thames & Hudson, 1991.

Noël, Paul and Théraond, D., 'La Formation des psychiatres de 1945 à 1975 à travers trente ans d'*Information psychiatrique*', *Information psychiatrique*, June 1996.

Nursey-Bray, Paul, 'Marxism and Existentialism in the Thought of Frantz Fanon', *Political Studies*, vol. 20, no. 2, 1972.

'*OAS parle*', Paris: Juilliard, 1964.

O'Brien, Conor Cruise, 'The Neurosis of Colonalism', *The Nation*, 21 June 1965.

Ochetto, Valerio, 'Prospettive della rivoluzione algerina', *Leggere-Roma*, September 1962.

O'Connor, Garry, *French Theatre Today*, London: Pitman, 1975.

Odier, Charles, *L'Angoisse et la pensée magique*, Paris, 1948.

Onwuanide, Richard C., *A Critique of Revolutionary Humanism: Frantz Fanon*, St Louis, Missouri: Warren H. Green Inc., 1983.

Oukselt, Djoher, 'Voix d'un homme – voix des hommes – voix d'un peuple', *Passerelles* 11, Winter 1995–6.

Pablo, Michel, '*Les Damnés de la terre* de Frantz Fanon', *Quatrième Internationale*, April 1962.

Parvillex, A. de, 'Frantz Fanon, *Peau noire, masques blancs*', *Livres et lectures*, June 1952.

Pascalis, Gérald, 'Le Professeur Maurice Porot à Alger', *Psychologie médicale* , vol. 15, no. 10, 1983.

Paxton, Robert O., *Vichy France: Old Guard and New Order*, New York: Knopf, 1972.

Peju, Marcel (ed.), *Le Procès du réseau Jeanson*, Paris: Maspero, 1961.

# Bibliography

Pélage, David, 'Rencontre International Frantz Fanon (Alger, 10–15 décembre 1987)', *Présence africaine* 145, 1er trimestre 1988.

Pellicier, Yves, 'Intégration des données sociologiques à la psychiatrie clinique', *Congrès des médecins aliénistes et neurologues de France et des pays de langue française vol. LVII*, Marseille 1964.

Perinbam, Marie B., 'Fanon and the Revolutionary Peasantry – the Algerian Case', *Journal of Modern African Studies*, vol. 11, no. 3, 1973.

Péroncel-Hegoz, Jean-Pierre, 'Senghor, poète d'abord', *Le Monde*, 11 October 1996.

*Photographes en Algérie au XIXème siècle*, Paris: Musée-Galerie de la SEITA, 1999.

Pierre, René, 'Martinique: Mémorial pour les damnés des DOM', *Libération*, 9 April 1982.

Pieterse, Jan Nederveen, *White on Black: Images of Africans and Blacks in Western Popular Culture*, New Haven and London: Yale University Press, 1995.

Placoly, Vincent, *L'Eau de mort guildive*, Paris: Denoël, 1973.

Polizzotti, Mark, *Revolution of the Mind: The Life of André Breton*, London: Bloomsbury, 1995.

Porot, Antoine, 'Notes de psychiatrie musulmane', *Annales médico-psychologiques*, May 1918.

—— (ed.), *Manuel alphabétique de psychiatrie clinique et thérapeutique*, Paris: PUF, 1975, third edn..

—— and Arrii, D. C., 'L'Impulsivité criminelle chez l'indigène algérien: ses facteurs', *Annales medico-psychologiques*, December 1932.

—— and Sutter, D., *Le 'Primitivisme' des indigènes Nord-Africains. Ses incidences en pathologie mentale*, Marseilles: Imprimérie marseillaise, 1939.

'Porte-voix des damnés de la terre: un mémorial à Paris le 9 mai', *El Moudjahid*, 4 May 1982.

*Post/Colonial Conditions: Migrations and Nomadisms: Yale French Studies* 93, 1993, two vols.

Postel, Jacques, 'Frantz Fanon à cinquante ans', *Information psychiatrique*, vol. LI, no. 10, December 1975.

—— (ed.), *Dictionnaire critique de la psychiatrie et de la psychopathologie clinique*, Paris: Larousse, 1993.

*Pour Frantz Fanon: Rencontre Internationale d'Alger, Centre des Arts Rihad El Fath*, 10 au 15 décembre 1982.

'Premier Congrès des écrivains et artistes noirs s'est ouvert en Sorbonne', *Le Figaro*, 20 September 1956.

Pucheu, Jacques, 'Un An dans les Aurés', *Les Temps modernes*, September 1957.

Quandt, William B., *Revolution and Political Leadership in Algeria 1954–1968*, Cambridge MA and London: MIT Press, 1969.

Quitman, Maurice-Sabas, 'Le Paradis sur terre', *Légitime Défense*, 1932.

Rabemananjara, Jacques, 'Quarantième anniversaire de la revue *Présence africaine*', *Présence africaine* 124, 4ème trimestre, 1987.

Racine, Daniel, *Léon-Gontras Damas: l'homme et l'oeuvre*, Paris: Présence africaine, 1993.

Ramazò, Elie, 'Fanon retrouvé', *Afrique-Asie*, 19 July 1992.

Raulin, Nathalie, 'Il faut payer aussi pour le Crédit martiniquais', *Libération*, 21 April 1997.

Ray, David and Farnsworth, Robert M., *Richard Wright: Impressions and Perspectives*, Ann Arbor: University of Michigan Press, 1973.

Razanjao, C., and Postel, Jacques, 'La Vie et l'oeuvre psychiatrique de Frantz Fanon', *Information psychiatrique* vol. LI, no. 10, December 1975.

Read, Alan (ed.), *The Fact of Blackness: Frantz Fanon and Visual Representation*, London and Seattle: Institute of Contemporary Arts and Institute of International Visual Arts, Bay Press, 1995.

Reboul, H. and Régis, E., 'L'Assistance aux aliénés aux colonies', *Congrès des médecins aliénistes et neurologues de France et des pays de langue française*, 1912.

'Reconnaissance à Frantz Fanon', *Partisans* 23, June–July 1965.

'Relire Fanon', *Algérie-actualité*, 30 September 1982.

Rémond, René, *Le Retour de de Gaulle*, Brussels: Editions complexe, 1987.

Revert, Eugène, *Les Antilles*, Paris: Armand Colin, 1954.

Richardson, Michael (ed.), *Refusal of the Shadow: Surrealism and the Caribbean*, London: Verso, 1996.

Riffaud, Madeleine, *De Votre Envoyée spéciale*, Paris: Editeurs français réunis, 1964.

Rioux, Jean-Pierre, *The Fourth Republic 1944–1958*, trans. Godfrey Rogers, Cambridge and Paris: Cambridge University Press and Editions de la Maison des Sciences de l'Homme, 1989.

—— (ed.), *La Guerre d'Algérie et les Français*, Paris: Fayard, 1990.

—— and Sirinelli, Jean-François (eds.), *La Guerre d'Algérie et les intellectuels français*, Brussels: Editions complexe, 1991.

Rivière, Michel, 'Un Acte d'accusation du colonialisme', *Le Drapeau rouge*, 31 March 1962.

Robert, Admiral Georges, *La France aux Antilles 1939–1943*, Vadez, Liechtenstein: Calivsas Anstalt, 1979.

Robinson, Cedric, 'The Appropriation of Frantz Fanon', *Race and Class*, vol. 35, no. 1, July–September 1993.

Roblès, Emmanuel, *Les Hauteurs de la ville*, Algiers: Charlot, 1948.

Romanette, Irmine, *Sonson de la Martinique*, Paris: Société française d'éditions techniques et littéraires, 1932.

Rosello, Mireille, *Littérature et identité créole aux Antilles*, Paris: Karthala, 1992.

Rosette, Benetta-Jules, *Black Paris: The African Writer's Landscape*, Urbana and Chicago: University of Illinois Press, 1998.

Rotman, Patrick and Tavernier, Bernard, *La Guerre sans nom: les appelés en Algérie 1954–1962*, Paris: Seuil, 1992.

Roudinesco, Elisabeth, *Jacques Lacan & Co., A History of Psychoanalysis in France 1925–1985*, trans. Geoffrey Mehlman, London: Free Association Books, 1990.

Rougement, Denis de, 'Sartre contre l'Europe', *Arts*, 17–23 January 1962.

Roumain, Jacques, *La Montagne ensorcelée*, Paris: Messidor, 1987.

Rousso, Henry, *The Vichy Syndrome: History and Memory in France since 1944*, trans. Arthur Goldhammer, Cambridge MA and London: Harvard University Press, 1992.

Roux, Michel, *Les Harkis ou les oubliés de l'histoire*, Paris: Maspero, 1991.

Roy, Jules, *La Guerre d'Algérie*, Paris: Christian Bourgois, 1994.

Ruedy, John, *Modern Algeria: The Origins and Development of a Nation*, Bloomington and Indianapolis: Indiana University Press, 1992.

Ruscio, Alain, *Le Credo de l'homme blanc: regards coloniaux français, XIX–XXème siècles*, Brussels: Editions complexe, 1995.

'Sa Pensée était génante à tous les égards', *Sans Frontière*, February 1982.

Saab, Edouard, 'L'Omniprésence en Jordanie des organisations paléstiniennes', *Le Monde*, 7 December 1968.

Saadia and Lakhdar, 'L'Aliénation colonialiste et la résistance de la famille algérienne', *Les Temps modernes* 182, June 1961.

Sablé, Victor, *Les Antilles sans complexe: une expérience de décolonisation*, Paris: Maisonneuve et Larose, 1976.

—— *Mémoires d'un Foyalais: des Iles d'Amérique aux bords de la Seine*, Paris: Maisonneuve et Larose, 1993.

Sabot, Jean-Yves, *Le Syndicalisme étudiant et la guerre d'Algérie*, Paris: L'Harmattan, 1995.

Sadji, Abdoulaye, *Nini, mulâtresse du Sénégal*, Paris: Présence africaine, 1988.

Sadji, Amadou Abdoulaye, *Abdoulaye Sadji: Biographie 1910–1961. Sa Vie et sa présence à un tournant de l'histoire de l'Afrique*, Paris and Dakar: Présence africaine, 1997.

Said, Edward W., *Orientalism*, London: Routledge and Kegan Paul, 1978.

—— 'Representing the Colonized: Anthropology's Interlocutors', *Critical Inquiry* 15, Winter 1989.

—— *Culture and Imperialism*, London: Chatto and Windus, 1993.

Sanville, Léonard, 'Le Noir antillais devant la littérature', *Les Lettres françaises*, 1 August 1952.

—— *Dominique, esclave nègre*, Paris and Dakar: Présence africaine, 1973.

—— *Au Fond du bourg*, Paris: Maspero, nd.

Sari, Djilali, *Huit Jours de la bataille d'Alger (28 janvier–4 février 1957)*, Algiers: Entreprise Nationale du Livre, 1987.

Sartre, Jean-Paul, 'Paris sous l'occupation', in *Situations III* , Paris: Gallimard, 1949.

—— *Critique de la raison dialectique*, Paris: Gallimard, 1960.

Sartre, Jean-Paul, *Situations V: Colonialisme et néo-colonialisme*, Paris: Gallimard, 1964.

—— *Refléxions sur la question juive*, Paris: Gallimard, Collection 'Idées', 1969.

—— *L'Etre et le néant*, Paris: Gallimard, Collection 'Tel', 1972.

—— *Huis clos, suivi de Les Mouches*, Paris: Folio, 1975.

—— *Notebooks for an Ethics*, trans. David Pellauer, Chicago and London: University of Chicago Press, 1992.

—— and Lévy, Benny, *Hope Now: The 1980 Interviews*, trans. Aidan van den Hoven, introduction by Ronald Aranson, Chicago and London: University of Chicago Press.

Saux, Jean-Louis, 'Célébrant l'abolition de l'esclavage, M. Chirac vante "le modèle français d'intégration"', *Le Monde*, 24 April 1998.

Sayad, Abdelmalek, avec la collaboration de Eliane Dupuy, *Un Nanterre algérien, terre des bidonvilles*, Paris: Autrement, 1995.

Schmidt, Nelly, *Victor Schoelcher et l'abolition de l'esclavage*, Paris: Fayard, 1994.

Segal, Ronald, *The Black Diaspora*, London: Faber and Faber, 1995.

Sekyi-Otu, Ato, *Fanon's Dialectic of Experience*, Cambridge MA and London: Harvard University Press, 1996.

Selvon, Sam, *The Lonely Londoners* , London: Longman, 1998.

Sénac, Jean (ed.), *Anthologie de la nouvelle poésie algérienne*, Paris: Librairie St Germain des prés, 1971.

—— *Ebauche du père, pour en finir avec l'enfance*, Paris: Gallimard, 1989.

—— *Oeuvres poètiques*, Arles: Actes-sud, 1991.

Senghor, Léopold Sedar, *Liberté I. Négritude et humanisme*, Paris: Seuil, 1964.

—— *On African Socialism*, trans. Mercer Cook, London and Dunmow: Pall Mall Press, 1964.

—— (ed.), *Anthologie de la nouvelle poésie nègre et malgache de language française*, Paris: PUF, 1992.

—— *Oeuvre poètique*, Paris: Seuil, 1990

Servan-Schreiber, Jean-Jacques, *Lieutenant en Algérie*, Paris: Seuil, 1957.

Shannon, William B., 'Negro Violence vs the American Dream', *New York Times*, 27 July 1967.

Sigg, Bernard, *Le Silence et la honte: névroses de la guerre d'Algérie*, Paris: Messidor/Editions sociales, 1989.

Simon, Pierre-Henri, *Contre la torture*, Paris: Seuil, 1957.

Simons, Margaret A. (ed.), *Feminist Interpretations of Simone de Beauvoir*, University Park, PA: Pennsylvania University Press, 1995.

# Bibliography

Sirinelli, Jean-François, *Intellectuels et passions françaises: manifestes et pétitions au XXème siècle*, Paris: Fayard, 1990.

Sitbon, Guy, 'Les Officiers de l'ALN ne cherchent pas à prendre le pouvoir, mais à la constituer étroitement au nom du peuple', *Le Monde*, 3 May 1962.

Sivan, Emmanuel, *Communisme et nationalisme en Algérie: 1920–1964*, Paris: Presse de la Fondation Nationale des Sciences Politiques, 1976.

Slama, Alain-Gérard, *La Guerre d'Algérie: histoire d'une déchirure*, Paris: Gallimard, 1996.

Sorel, Georges, *Reflections on Violence*, trans. T. E. Hulme, introduction by Edward A. Shils, London: Collier Books, 1970.

Souibes, Boualem, 'Frantz Fanon: un enfant du pays', *Parcours maghrébins* 12, September 1987.

'Speaking for Africa's Masses', *Houston Chronicle*, 2 May 1965.

Stein, Robert Louis, *The French Slave Trade in the Eighteenth Century: An Old Regime Business*, Madison: University of Wisconsin Press, 1979.

Sterne, E., 'La Médecine psychosomatique', *Psyché* 27–8, January–February 1949.

Stevens, Mary Anne, *The Orientalists: Delacroix to Matisse. European Painters in North Africa and the Middle East*, London: Royal Academy of Arts in association with Weidenfeld & Nicolson, 1984.

Stibbe, Pierre, '*L'An V de la révolution algérienne* de Frantz Fanon', *France-Observateur*, 24 December 1959.

—— 'Frantz Fanon, théoricien de la décolonisation intégrale', *Cahiers de la république*, January–February 1962.

Stora, Benjamin, *Dictionnaire des militants nationalistes algériens: ENA, PPA, MTLD, 1926–1954*, Paris: L'Harmattan, 1985.

—— *Les Sources du nationalisme algérien: parcours idéologiques, origines des acteurs*, Paris: L'Harmattan, 1989.

—— *La Gangrène et l'oubli: la mémoire de la guerre d'Algérie*, Paris: La Découverte, 1991.

—— *Histoire de l'Algérie coloniale 1830–1954*, Paris: La Découverte, 1991.

—— *Ils venaient d'Algérie: l'immigration algérienne en France 1912–1992*, Paris: Fayard, 1992.

—— *Histoire de la guerre d'Algérie (1954–1962)*, Paris: La Découverte, 1993.

—— *Histoire de l'Algérie depuis l'indépendance*, Paris: La Découverte, 1994.

—— *L'Algérie en 1995: la guerre, l'histoire, la politique*, Paris: Editions Michalon, 1995.

—— *Appelés en Algérie*, Paris: Gallimard, 1997.

Suvelor, Roland, 'Faut-il célébrer Frantz Fanon?', *Le Progressiste*, 24 March 1992.

617

Talbott, John, *The War Without a Name: France in Algeria 1954–1962*, London: Faber and Faber, 1981.

Tauriac, Michel, *Le Catastrophe*, Paris: La Table ronde, 1982.

Thomas, Hugh, *The Slave Trade: The History of the Atlantic Slave Trade 1440–1870*, London: Picador, 1977.

Thomas, Martin, 'Policing Algeria's Borders 1956–1960: Arms Supplies, Frontier Defences and the Sakhiet Affair', *War & Society*, vol. 13, no. 1, May 1995.

Thompson, Willie, 'Frantz Fanon', *Marxism Today*, August 1968.

Thorez, Maurice, *Oeuvres choisies en trois tomes: tome I. 1924–1937*, Paris: Editions sociales, 1967.

Tirolien, Guy, *Balles d'or*, Paris and Dakar: Présence africaine, 1961.

Titah, Rachida, *La Galerie des absentes: la femme algérienne dans l'imaginaire masculin*, La Tour d'Aigue: L'aub, 1996.

Tlemcani, Rachid, *State and Revolution in Algeria*, Boulder, Col. and London: Westview Press and Zed Books.

Tocqueville, Alexis de, *De la Colonie en Algérie*, Brussels: Editions complexe, 1988.

Todorov, Tzvetan, *On Human Diversity: Nationalism, Racism and Exoticism in French Thought*, trans. Catherine Porter, Cambridge MA and London: Harvard University Press, 1993.

Tosquelles, François, 'La Société vécue par les malades psychiques', *Esprit*, December 1952.

—— 'Fanon à Saint-Alban', *Information psychiatrique*, vol. LI, no. 19, 1975.

—— 'La Mémoire: sur G. Daumézon, quelques autres et moi', *Information psychiatrique*, vol. 56, no. 5, June 1980.

—— *Education et psychothérapie institutionnelle*, Mantes-la-Ville: Hiatus Editions, 1984.

—— 'La Guerre d'Espagne', *Vie sociale et traitements* 112, August–September 1987.

—— 'L'Effervescence saint-albanaise', *Information psychiatrique*, October 1987.

—— *L'Enseignement de la folie*, Toulouse: Privat, 1992.

Toumson, Roger and Henry-Valmore, Simonne, *Aimé Césaire: le nègre inconsolé*, Fort-de-France and Paris: Vent des Iles and Syros, 1993.

Traoré, Bakory, 'On *Les Damnés de la terre*', *Présence africaine*, vol. XVII, no. 45, 1963.

Tristan, Anne, *Le Silence du fleuve: octobre 1961*, Bezons: Editions au nom de la mémoire, 1991.

Tronchon, Jacques, *L'Insurrection malgache de 1947: essai d'interprétation historique*, Paris: Karthala, 1986.

*Tropiques*, Paris: Editions J. M. Place, 1978. Facsimile reproduction, two vols.

'Un Article d'*El Moudjahid*: le FLN attaque la gauche française', *France-Observateur*, 26 December 1957.

Vaillant, Janet G., *Black, French and African: A Life of Léopold Sedar Senghor*, Cambridge MA and London: Harvard University Press, 1990.

Vallières, Pierre, *Nègres blancs d'amérique*, Montréal: Typo, 1994.

Veillard, Yann-Cheun, '*Les Damnés de la terre*', *Ar Vro*, April 1963.

Vergès, Françoise, 'To Cure and to Free: The Fanonian Project of "Decolonized Psychiatry"', in Gordon, Sharpely-Whiting and White, *Fanon: A Critical Reader*.

—— 'Chains of Madness, Chains of Colonialism: Fanon and Freedom', in Read (ed.), *The Fact of Blackness*.

—— 'Creole Skin, Black Masks: Fanon and Disavowal', *Critical Inquiry* 23, Spring 1997.

—— 'Colonizing Citizenship', *Radical Philosophy* 95, May–June 1999.

—— *Monsters and Revolutionaries: Colonial Family Romance and Métissage*, Durham NC.: Duke University Press, 1999.

Vernet. J., *Le Réarmement et la réorganisation de l'armée de terre française (1943–1946)*, Vincennnes: SHAT, 1980.

Vidal-Naquet, Pierre, *La Torture dans la République*, Paris: Maspero, 1983.

—— *Les Assassins de la mémoire*, Paris: La Découverte, 1987.

—— *L'Affaire Audin (1957–1978)*, Paris: Minuit, 1989.

—— *Face à la raison d'état: un historien dans la guerre d'Algérie*, Paris: La Découverte, 1989.

—— *Mémoires I. La Brissure et l'attente 1930–1955*, Paris: Seuil/La Découverte, 1995.

—— *Mémoires II. Le Trouble et la lumière 1955–1998*, Paris: Seuil/La Découverte, 1998.

Vinay, Nicolas, '*Les Damnés de la terre*', *La Voie communiste* 26, January–February 1962.

'Vingt ans aprés, Fanon vu par une Antillaise, un jeune Français et un immigré algérien', *Sans Frontière*, February 1982.

Voyenne, Bernard, 'Frantz Fanon, *Peau noire, masques blancs*', *Revue de la pensée française*, September 1953.

Warner, Marina, *Managing Monsters: Six Myths of Our Time*, London: Vintage, 1994.

Welch, Claude E. Jr., *Dream of Unity: Pan-Africanism and Political Unification in West Africa*, Ithaca: Cornell University Press, 1966.

Wievorka, Michel, *La France raciste*, Paris: Seuil, 1992.

Williams, P. and Chrisman L. (eds.), *Colonial Discourse and Post-Colonial Theory*, New York: Columbia University Press, 1994.

Williams, Philip M., *Wars, Plots and Scandals in Post-War France*, Cambridge: Cambridge University Press, 1970.

Winnock, Michel, *La République se meurt 1956–1958*, Paris: Gallimard 1985.

—— *'Esprit'. Des Intellectuels dans la cité 1930–1950*, Paris: Seuil, Collection 'Points', 1996, revised edn.

Woddis, Jack, *New Theories of Revolution: A Commentary on the Views of Frantz Fanon, Régis Debray and Herbert Marcuse*, New York: International Publishers, 1972.

Worsely, Peter, 'Revolutionary Theories', *Monthly Review*, May 1960.

—— 'A Voice from the Third World', *Peace News*, 18 October 1963.

—— 'The Coming Inheritor', *Guardian*, 22 October 1965.

Wright, D., 'Fanon and Africa: A Retrospect', *Journal of Modern African Studies,* vol. XXIV, no. 4, December 1986.

Wyricck, Deborah, *Fanon for Beginners*, New York and London: Readers and Writers, 1998.

Xème Région militaire, section psychologique, *Connaissance de l'Algérie*, Algiers: Société nationale des entreprises de presse, nd.

Yacef, Saadi, *Souvenirs de la bataille d'Alger*, Paris: Julliard, 1962.

—— *La Bataille d'Alger. I: L'Embrassement*, Algiers: ENAL, 1984.

Yacine, Kateb, *Le Cercle de répresailles*, Paris: Seuil, 1959.

—— *Nedjma*, Paris: Seuil, Collection 'Points', 1981.

—— *Le Polygone étoilé*, Paris: Seuil, Collection 'Points', 1994.

—— *Le Poète comme boxeur. Entretiens 1958–1989*, Paris: Seuil, 1994.

Yazid, M'Hamed, 'Fanon le militant', *Sans Frontière*, February 1982.

Yoder, Edwin M. Jr., *Joe Alsop's War: A Study of Journalism, Influence and Intrigue*, Chapel Hill and London: University of North Carolina Press, 1995.

Zahar, Renate, *Frantz Fanon and Alienation: Concerning Frantz Fanon's Political Theory*, trans. W.F. Freuser, New York: Monthly Review Press, 1974.

Zeldin, Theodore, *France 1848–1945: Taste and Corruption*, Oxford: Oxford University Press, 1980.

Ziegler, Jean, 'Frantz Fanon', *Le Nouvel Observateur*, 19 January 1971.

—— 'Antilles: Résurrection de Frantz Fanon', *Afrique-Asie*, 4 June 1984.

Zobel, Joseph, *Rue cases-nègres*, Paris and Dakar: Présence africaine, 1984.

Zolberg, Aristide R., *One-Party Government in the Ivory Coast*, Princeton: Princeton University Press, 1964.

—— 'Frantz Fanon: A Gospel for the Damned', *Encounter*, vol. 27, no. 5, October 1966.

# Index

# Index

# Index